ALTERNATIVE CRIMINOLOGIES

Alternative Criminologies celebrates a kaleidoscopic process of permanent critique and a diversity of social and scientific knowledges. It examines complex and global crime issues in light of the many alternative scientific, artistic, empathetic, campaigning and otherwise imaginative criminologies that attempt to understand and/or fundamentally change why crime and justice take the forms they do.

From cutting edge topics such as crimes against humanity, the criminology of mobility, terrorism, cybercrime, corporate crime and green criminology; to gendered perspectives on violence against women, sexualities and feminist and queer criminologies; to key issues in penology such as mass incarceration, the death penalty, desistance from crime, risk and the political economy of punishment; *Alternative Criminologies* demonstrates the breadth, the variety and the vibrancy of contemporary perspectives on crime, criminalization and punishment.

Bringing together 34 leading experts from around the world, this international collection unites fresh and insightful theoretical positions with innovative empirical research and marks an important juncture for criminologies and their imagined futures. *Alternative Criminologies* is essential reading for students of crime and criminal justice.

Pat Carlen is Visiting Professor at the Open University, UK and has published over 20 books on criminal and social justice. Co-founder (with Chris Tchaikovsky) of the UK campaigning group Women in Prison and Editor-in-Chief of the *British Journal of Criminology* 2006–2013, she has been a recipient of: the American Society of Criminology's Sellin-Glueck Prize for Outstanding International Contributions to Criminology, the British Society of Criminology's Award for Outstanding Achievement and an honorary Doctorate of Laws from Lincoln University.

Leandro Ayres França works as a professor, researcher, writer and translator. He is Professor of Criminology, Criminal Law and Criminal Procedure at Faculdade Estácio Rio Grande do Sul; Coordinator of Estácio's Criminology Graduation Program; Doctor and Master in Criminal Sciences from Pontifícia Universidade Católica do Rio Grande do Sul's (PUCRS) Criminal Sciences Graduation Program. He is coordinator of the Contemporaneous Criminologies Study Group, member of the research group Modern Trends in the Criminal System and host of the radio progr   afé e Fúria.

ALTERNATIVE CRIMINOLOGIES

Edited by Pat Carlen and
Leandro Ayres França

Routledge
Taylor & Francis Group

LONDON AND NEW YORK

First published 2018
by Routledge
2 Park Square, Milton Park, Abingdon, Oxon OX14 4RN

and by Routledge
711 Third Avenue, New York, NY 10017

Routledge is an imprint of the Taylor & Francis Group, an informa business

British Library Cataloguing in Publication Data
A catalogue record for this book is available from the British Library

Library of Congress Cataloging in Publication Data
Names: Carlen, Pat, editor. | França, Leandro Ayres, editor.
Title: Alternative criminologies / edited by Pat Carlen and
Leandro Ayres França.
Description: Abingdon, Oxon ; New York, NY : Routledge, 2018. |
Includes bibliographical references and index.
Identifiers: LCCN 2017013028 | ISBN 9781138067424 (hardback) |
ISBN 9781138067431 (pbk.) | ISBN 9781315158662 (ebook)
Subjects: LCSH: Criminology. | Criminal justice, Administration of.
Classification: LCC HV6025 .A624 2018 | DDC 364–dc23
LC record available at https://lccn.loc.gov/2017013028

ISBN: 978-1-138-06742-4 (hbk)
ISBN: 978-1-138-06743-1 (pbk)
ISBN: 978-1-315-15866-2 (ebk)

Typeset in Bembo
by Out of House Publishing

A project of the research group Modern Trends in the Criminal System – Brazil, coordinated by
Prof. Dr Paulo César Busato. Originally published in Portuguese by Café e Fúria (www.cafeefuria.com),
Canal Ciências Criminais (www.canalcienciascriminais.com.br) and Modern Trends in the Criminal System
research group (www.sistemacriminal.org).

CONTENTS

FIGURES

TABLES

CONTRIBUTORS

EDITORS

Pat Carlen has published 20 books and over 100 articles on criminal and social justice. Co-founder (with Chris Tchaikovsky) of the UK campaigning group Women in Prison and Editor-in-Chief of the *British Journal of Criminology* 2006–2013, she has been a recipient of: the American Society of Criminology's Sellin-Glueck Prize for Outstanding International Contributions to Criminology, the British Society of Criminology's Award for Outstanding Achievement, and an honorary Doctorate of Laws from Lincoln University. Best known among her books are *Magistrates' Justice* and *Women's Imprisonment*. A short biographical chapter is to be found in *Fifty Key Thinkers in Criminology* (Routledge 2010). A collection of her selected works entitled *A Criminological Imagination: Essays on Punishment, Justice, Discourse* was published in Ashgate's Pioneers in Contemporary Criminology Series in 2010.

Leandro Ayres França works as professor, researcher, writer and translator. He is Professor of Criminology, Criminal Law and Criminal Procedure at Faculdade Estácio Rio Grande do Sul; Coordinator of Estácio's Criminology Graduation Program; Master in Criminal Sciences from Pontifícia Universidade Católica do Rio Grande do Sul's (PUCRS) Criminal Sciences Graduation Program; and Coordinator of the Contemporaneous Criminologies Study Group. Member of the research group Modern Trends in the Criminal System. Host of the radio program Café e Fúria, broadcasted by minima.fm. He is also author/editor of the books: *Ensaio de uma Vida Bandida* (2007), *Inimigo ou a Inconveniência de Existir* (2012), *Vestígios da Copa* (co-authored with Alysson Ramos Artuso, Gisele Eberspächer, Henrique Valle, Leonardo Carbonieri Campoy, Maira da Silveira Marques and Uriel Moeller, 2014), *As Marcas do Cárcere* (co-authored with Alfredo Steffen Neto and Alysson Ramos Artuso, 2016).

CONTRIBUTORS

Mary Bosworth is Professor of Criminology and Fellow of St Cross College, University of Oxford and Professor of Criminology at Monash University, Australia. She is Assistant

Director of the Centre for Criminology and Director of Border Criminologies, an interdisciplinary research group focusing on the intersections between criminal justice and border control. She also conducts research into the ways in which prisons and immigration detention centres uphold notions of race, gender and citizenship and how those who are confined negotiate their daily lives. Her research is international and comparative and has included work conducted in Paris, Britain, the USA and Australia. Currently heading a five-year project on 'Subjectivity, Identity and Penal Power: Incarceration in a Global Age' funded by a Starting Grant from the European Research Council as well as a Leverhulme International Network on External Border Control. Currently UK Editor-in-Chief of *Theoretical Criminology*, a co-editor of *Routledge Studies in Criminal Justice, Borders and Citizenship* and a member of the editorial boards of *Race & Justice*, the *International Journal of Migration and Border Studies* and *Clarendon Studies in Criminology* at Oxford University Press.

David Brown, Emeritus Professor at the University of New South Wales, Australia, taught Criminal Law, Advanced Criminal Law, Criminal Justice, Crime Prevention, Community Corrections and Penology courses at the University of NSW in Sydney from 1974 to 2008. He is a co-author of the major and innovative *Criminal Laws* (1990 2nd edn 1996, 3rd edn 2001, 4th edn 2006, 5th edn 2011, 6th edn 2015) which has become the leading student text in criminal law in universities in NSW. He is very widely published across the broad areas of criminal law, criminal justice, criminology and penology, both in Australia and internationally. He has co-authored or co-edited 14 books, including *Justice Reinvestment: Winding Back Imprisonment* (2016), *Penal Culture and Hyperincarceration: The Revival of the Prison* (2013), *The New Punitiveness* (2005); *Prisoners as Citizens* (2002); *Rethinking Law and Order* (1998); *Death in the Hands of the State* (1988); *The Judgments of Lionel Murphy* (1986); and *The Prison Struggle* (1982); has published 39 chapters in books, and over 140 articles in journals and in conference proceedings; and is a regular media commentator on criminal justice issues.

Eamonn Carrabine is a Professor in the Department of Sociology at the University of Essex. His books include *Crime in Modern Britain* (co-authored, 2002); *Power, Discourse and Resistance: A Genealogy of the Strangeways Prison Riot* (2004); *Crime, Culture and the Media* (2008); and *Crime and Social Theory* (2017). He has published widely on media criminology, the sociology of punishment and cultural theory. The textbook he co-authors with colleagues from the University of Essex, *Criminology: A Sociological Introduction*, is now in its third edition. He currently holds a Leverhulme Trust Major Research Fellowship to research his project 'The Iconography of Punishment: From Renaissance to Modernity', which will be published as a book. Since 2015 he has been co-editing the journal *Crime, Media, Culture* with Michele Brown (University of Tennessee) and they have recently edited the *Routledge International Handbook of Visual Criminology* (2017). With Avi Brisman (Eastern Kentucky University) and Nigel South (University of Essex) he has also co-edited the *Routledge Companion to Criminological Theory and Concepts* (2017).

Kerry Carrington is a Professor in and Head of the School of Justice in the Faculty of Law at Queensland University of Technology, Australia. An internationally leading scholar in criminology with expertise across a number of fields including youth justice, rural crime, gender and violence, she is the author of *Feminism and Global Justice* (2015), *Offending Youth* (2009), *Policing the Rural Crisis* (2006), several earlier books and around 100 other publications. She is the co-Chief Editor of the *International Journal for Crime, Justice and Social Democracy*. In 2014 she was the recipient of the Lifetime Achievement award of the Division of Critical Criminology of the American Society of Criminology, and in 2013 recipient of the Distinguished Scholar Award of the Division of Women and Crime of the American Society of Criminology. In 2016 she became a Fellow of the Academy of Social Sciences Australia.

Neil Chakraborti is a Professor of Criminology, Head of Department and Director of the Centre for Hate Studies at the Department of Criminology, Leicester University. He is an Adjunct Professor at the University of Ontario Institute of Technology, sits on the editorial boards of the *British Journal of Criminology* and *Palgrave Communications* and is an Advisory Board member of *Tell MAMA*, a monitoring body which records anti-Muslim attacks in the UK. Neil has researched extensively within the field of hate crime, victimization and diversity, and has led a range of studies commissioned by Amnesty International UK, the Economic and Social Research Council, the Equality and Human Rights Commission, Leicester City Council, Suffolk County Council and numerous policing areas including West Midlands Police, Warwickshire Police, Greater Manchester Police, Leicestershire Police, Northamptonshire Police and Hertfordshire's Office for Police and Crime Commissioner. He has amassed more than 40 peer-reviewed publications, and his books include *Hate Crime: Impacts, Causes and Responses* (Sage, 2015 (2nd edn); 2009 (1st edn), with Jon Garland); *Responding to Hate Crime: The Case for Connecting Policy and Research* (Policy Press, 2014, with Jon Garland); *Islamophobia, Victimisation and the Veil* (Palgrave, 2014, with Irene Zempi); *Hate Crime: Concepts, Policy, Future Directions* (Routledge, 2010); and *Rural Racism* (Routledge, 2004, with Jon Garland).

Elliott Currie is Professor of Criminology, Law and Society at the University of California, Irvine, USA, and Adjunct Professor in the Faculty of Law, School of Justice, Queensland University of Technology, Australia. He is the author of many works on crime, delinquency, drug abuse, and social policy, including *Confronting Crime: An American Challenge*, *Dope and Trouble: Portraits of Delinquent Youth*, *Reckoning: Drugs, the Cities, and the American Future*, *The Road to Whatever: Middle Class Culture and the Crisis of Adolescence*, and *The Roots of Danger: Violent Crime in Global Perspective*. His book *Crime and Punishment in America*, revised and expanded in 2013, was a finalist for the Pulitzer Prize in General Nonfiction in 1999. He is a co-author of *Whitewashing Race: The Myth of a Colorblind Society*, winner of the 2004 Book Award from the Benjamin L. Hooks Institute for Social Change and a finalist for the C. Wright Mills Award of the Society for the Study of Social Problems. He is a graduate of Roosevelt University in Chicago, and received his PhD in sociology from the University of California, Berkeley.

Jeff Ferrell is currently Professor of Sociology at Texas Christian University, USA, and Visiting Professor of Criminology at the University of Kent, UK. He is the author of the books *Crimes of Style*, *Tearing Down the Streets*, *Empire of Scrounge*, and, with Keith Hayward and Jock Young, *Cultural Criminology: An Invitation*, winner of the 2009 Distinguished Book Award from the American Society of Criminology's Division of International Criminology. He is the co-editor of the books *Cultural Criminology*, *Ethnography at the Edge*, *Making Trouble*, *Cultural Criminology Unleashed*, and *Cultural Criminology: Theories of Crime*. Jeff Ferrell is the founding and current editor of the New York University Press book series

Alternative Criminology, and one of the founding editors of the journal *Crime, Media, Culture: An International Journal*, winner of the Association of Learned and Professional Society Publishers' 2006 Charlesworth Award for Best New Journal. In 1998 he received the Critical Criminologist of the Year Award from the Division of Critical Criminology of the American Society of Criminology.

Katja Franko is Professor at the Institute of Criminology and Sociology of Law, University of Oslo, Norway. She has published widely in globalization, migration control, borders, security and surveillance of everyday life. She is author of *The Borders of Punishment: Migration, Citizenship, and Social Exclusion* (co-edited with M. Bosworth; Oxford University Press, 2013), *Globalization and Crime* (SAGE, 2007/2013), *Cosmopolitan Justice and Its Discontents* (co-edited with C. Baillet, Routledge, 2011), *Technologies of Insecurity* (co-edited with H. M. Lomell and H. O. Gundhus; Routledge-Cavendish, 2009) and *Sentencing in the Age of Information: From Faust to Macintosh* (Routledge-Cavendish, 2005).

David Garland is the Arthur T. Vanderbilt Professor of Law and Professor of Sociology at New York University. Born and raised in Scotland, he is a graduate of the University of Edinburgh and taught there from 1979 to 1997. Garland is the author of *Punishment and Modern Society* (1990), *The Culture of Control* (2001) and *Peculiar Institution: America's Death Penalty in an Age of Abolition* (2010) and the editor of *Mass Imprisonment: Social Causes and Consequences* (2001). His most recent book is *The Welfare State: A Very Short Introduction*, published by Oxford University Press in 2016.

Alessandro De Giorgi is Associate Professor at the Department of Justice Studies, San Jose State University. He received his PhD in Criminology from Keele University (United Kingdom) in 2005. Before joining the Department of Justice Studies, he was a Research Fellow in Criminology at the University of Bologna (Italy), and a Visiting Scholar at the University of Bern (Switzerland), the University of Saarland (Germany), and the Center for the Study of Law and Society, University of California, Berkeley. His teaching and research interests include critical theories of punishment and social control, urban ethnography, and radical political economy. He is the author of *Rethinking the Political Economy of Punishment: Perspectives on Post-Fordism and Penal Politics* (Ashgate, 2006) and the editor of *Beyond Mass Incarceration: Crisis and Critique in North American Penal Systems* (2016), a special issue of the journal *Social Justice*. His current project is an ethnographic study of the socioeconomic dimensions of concentrated incarceration and prisoner reentry in Oakland, California.

Hannah Graham is a Lecturer in Criminology in the Scottish Centre for Crime and Justice Research (SCCJR) at the University of Stirling, Scotland. She is a Co-Editor of the *European Journal of Probation* and the author of three books published internationally by Routledge: *Rehabilitation Work: Supporting Desistance and Recovery* (Graham, 2016), *Innovative Justice* (Graham & White, 2015), and *Working with Offenders: A Guide to Concepts and Practices* (White & Graham, 2010). In 2015–2016, Hannah was an academic co-lead with Prof. Gill McIvor undertaking the Scottish component of an EU-funded international comparative research project on the uses of electronic monitoring as an alternative to imprisonment in EU member states. From 2011–2014, Hannah lectured in Criminology and Sociology at the University of Tasmania, Australia.

Penny Green is Professor of Law and Globalisation at Queen Mary University of London. She has published extensively on state crime theory (including her monograph with Tony Ward, *State Crime: Governments, Violence and Corruption*), state violence, Turkish criminal justice and politics, 'natural' disasters, transnational crime, mass forced evictions/displacement and resistance to state violence. She has conducted fieldwork in the UK, Turkey, Kurdistan, Palestine/Israel, Tunisia and Myanmar and is Founder and Director of the award-winning International State Crime Initiative (ISCI) – a multi-disciplinary international initiative to collate, analyse and disseminate research-based knowledge about criminal state practices and resistance to them. Most recent projects include a comparative study of civil society resistance to state crime in Turkey, Tunisia, Colombia, PNG, Kenya and Myanmar; Myanmar's genocide against its Muslim ethnic Rohingya; and forced evictions in Palestine/Israel. Currently Distinguished Visiting Fellow at the University of NSW and Ulster University; Adjunct Professor at Birzeit University; Trustee of the Howard League for Penal Reform and Secretary of the Democratic Progress Institute's Board of Trustees; member of the ESRC Peer Review College; Co-editor in Chief of the international journal *State Crime*; and Editor of the Pluto Press State Crime monograph series.

Steve Hall is Professor of Criminology at the Teesside Centre for Realist Criminology, Teesside University, UK. He is the author of *Theorising Crime and Deviance: A New Perspective* (Sage, 2001), and co-author of *Violent Night: Urban Leisure and Contemporary Culture* (Berg, 2006), *Criminal Identities and Consumer Culture: Crime, Exclusion and the New Culture of Narcissism* (Willan, 2008), *Rethinking Social Exclusion: The End of the Social?* (Sage, 2013), *Riots and Political Protest: Notes from the Post-Political Present* (Routledge, 2015), *Revitalizing Criminological Theory: Towards a New Ultra-Realism* and *Rise of the Right: English Nationalism and the Transformation of Working-Class Politics* (Policy Press, 2016).

Stevie-Jade Hardy is a Lecturer in Hate Studies at the Centre for Hate Studies, which is based in the Department of Criminology at University of Leicester and has published widely on hate crime perpetration and victimisation, and has considerable experience of conducting small- and large-scale research projects. As part of these studies she has engaged with more than 6,000 members of diverse and 'hard to reach' communities and has heard from more than 2,000 hate crime victims, and has an established track record as a trainer in the field of hate studies. Over the past three years she has delivered evidence-based training on diversity and hate-related themes to more than 600 practitioners and policy-makers across England and Wales. In particular she has been commissioned by police forces, the Crown Prosecution Service (CPS), local authorities, NHS Partnership Trusts, schools and charities to deliver bespoke training packages which enable practitioners to be more effective at engaging with diversity, supporting victims and tackling hate. She is also a member of various national and regional advisory boards, including the CPS Homophobic and Transphobic Hate Crime Scrutiny Panel and the National Police Chiefs' Council Deaf and Disability Forum.

Keith Hayward is Professor of Criminology at the Faculty of Law, University of Copenhagen, Denmark and Adjunct Professor in the Faculty of Law, School of Justice, Queensland University of Technology, Australia. He has published widely in the areas of criminological theory, spatial and social theory, visual and popular culture, and terrorism and fanaticism. As one of the leading figures in the field of cultural criminology, Dr Hayward is particularly interested in the various ways in which cultural dynamics intertwine with the practices of crime and crime control within contemporary society; as a consequence, he has written on everything from the role of documentary filmmaking in criminology to the existential allure of 'Jihadi cool'. He is the author, co-author, or editor of eleven books, the most recent being *Cultural Criminology* (2017), a four-volume edited collection for Routledge's Critical Concepts in Criminology series.

Roger Hood is Professor Emeritus of Criminology at Oxford University and Emeritus Fellow of All Souls College. From 1973 to 2003 he was Director of the Oxford Centre for Criminological Research (now Centre for Criminology). His research has embraced the death penalty; race and sentencing; the parole system; and penal history. He was consultant to the United Nations, leading to publication of *The Death Penalty: A Worldwide Perspective* in 1989 (5th edn with Carolyn Hoyle, 2015). Since retirement he has held visiting professorships at the University of Virginia, Hong Kong University and the City University of Hong Kong. He edited (with Surya Deva) *Confronting Capital Punishment in Asia* (2013); carried out research for the Death Penalty Project on the mandatory death penalty in Trinidad and Malaysia; published articles on capital punishment and lectured on the subject in many countries, including China, India, Pakistan, Uganda, Vietnam and Singapore. He was elected FBA in 1992, appointed CBE (1995), Honorary QC (2000) and Hon Ll.D by Birmingham (2008) and Edinburgh Napier (2011) Universities, received the Sellin-Glueck Award of the American Society of Criminology (1986), the Cesare Beccaria Medal of the International Society of Social Defence (2011) and the ESC European Criminology Award (2012).

Carolyn Hoyle is Professor of Criminology and Director of the Centre for Criminology at the University of Oxford, and Fellow of Green Templeton College. She teaches and researches on the death penalty in all jurisdictions around the world, and has published (along with Professor Roger Hood) the 4th and 5th editions of *The Death Penalty: A Worldwide Perspective* (Oxford University Press, 2008; 2015), and various other articles and chapters on capital punishment, including for the United Nations. She is currently working with National Law University, Delhi and the Death Penalty Project, London, on a study of public opinion on the death penalty in India. Her research into applications to the Criminal Cases Review Commission concerning alleged miscarriages of justice has been ongoing since 2010 and her book (with Dr Mai Sato) will be published by Oxford University Press (*Last Resorts: Decisions and Discretion at the Criminal Cases Review Commission*) in 2017. This year, she has also published work for the *Criminal Law Review* on the 'Wrongful Conviction of Refugees and Asylum Seekers', and for the *Howard Journal of Crime and Justice* on 'The Impact of Being Wrongly Accused of Abuse in Occupations of Trust'.

Susanne Karstedt is Professor in the School of Criminology and Criminal Justice at Griffith University since 2015. She previously held Chairs in Criminology at the University of Leeds and Keele University, UK and positions at the Universities of Bielefeld and Hamburg, Germany. She has researched mass atrocities and state crime, extremely violent societies, and transitional justice. Her historical work on these themes covers post-war Germany. Recent work includes contemporary transitional justice processes and their impact in complex conflicts, the position of victims, and the role of emotions. She is presently working on using the evidence-base of criminology for prevention and intervention in mass atrocities. Her work has been recognised by several awards, including the International Award of the Law and Society Association, 2016, and the Thorsten Sellin and Eleanor and Sheldon Glueck Award of the American Society of Criminology, 2007. Publications include: 'Extremely Violent Societies', Focus, *International Journal of Conflict and Violence* (2016); 'After Justice', Symposium, *Journal of International Criminal Justice* (2015, with C. Brants); 'State Crime: The European Experience' (*The Routledge Handbook of European Criminology*, 2014); 'Atrocity Crimes and Transitional Justice', Special Issue of the *European Journal of Criminology* (2012, with S. Parmentier); and *Legal Institutions and Collective Memories* (Hart, 2009).

Michael Levi has degrees from Oxford, Cambridge, Southampton and Cardiff Universities and has been Professor of Criminology at Cardiff University since 1991. He has been conducting international research on the control of white-collar and organised crime, corruption and money laundering/financing of terrorism since 1972, and has published widely on these subjects as well as editing major journals, most recently the *Journal of Cybersecurity* (Oxford University Press). He is an Associate Fellow of RUSI and a Senior Fellow at RAND Europe, and is on several UK and European advisory groups dealing with corruption, organised crime and cybercrimes. In 2013 he was given the Distinguished Scholar Award by the International Association for the Study of Organised Crime, and in 2014 he was awarded the Sellin-Glueck prize for international and comparative criminology by the American Society of Criminology. He has recently completed work on the detection of insider cyber threats; led an evaluation of the criminalisation of organised crime membership and special investigative measures in the EU; and researched the extent and impact of bank de-risking and anti-money laundering evaluations. He is currently researching pathways to fraud and the detection and prevention of online mass marketing fraud.

Clara Moura Masiero is a PhD student in Public Law from the University of Rio dos Sinos (UNISINOS/Brasil), CAPES/PROEX scholar, researching social movements, discrimination, hate crimes and criminal policy. She has a Master's degree in Criminal Sciences from the University Pontifícia Universidade Católica do Rio Grande do Sul (PUCRS/Brasil), where she worked on the homophobia criminalization theme. She was visiting researcher at the Criminology Institute (IAIC) of University of Málaga (UMA/Spain) in 2017. She is Professor in Criminal Law and Criminology at the Law Faculty of the University Paulista (UNIP/Brasil) and at Campos Salles Faculties (FICS/Brasil). She has written on the LGBT movement, homophobia, social struggle, criminal policy and critical theory.

Fergus McNeill is Professor of Criminology and Social Work at the University of Glasgow where he works in the Scottish Centre for Crime and Justice Research and in Sociology. His research explores – and seeks to challenge and change – institutions, cultures and practices of punishment and rehabilitation. For example, between 2017 and 2020, he is leading 'Distant Voices: Coming Home', an ESRC/AHRC-funded project (with Jo Collinson Scott, Oliver Escobar and Alison Urie) that combines creative practice (principally song-writing and sharing), research and public-political dialogue to explore punishment and re/integration. Books include: *Offender Supervision: New Directions in Theory, Research and Practice* (with Peter Raynor and Chris Trotter); *Offender Supervision in Europe* (with Kristel Beyens); *Reducing Reoffending: Social Work and Community Justice in Scotland* (with Bill Whyte); *Understanding Penal Practice* (with Ioan Durnescu); and *Youth Offending and Youth Justice* (with Monica Barry). His most recent collections include *Community Punishment: European Perspectives* (co-edited with Gwen Robinson), published by Routledge in 2015; *Probation: 12 Essential Questions* (co-edited with Ioan Durnescu and Rene Butter), published by Palgrave in 2016; and *Beyond the Risk Paradigm in Criminal Justice* (co-edited with Chris Trotter and Gill McIvor), published by Palgrave in 2016.

Gabe Mythen is Professor of Criminology at Liverpool University. Over the last decade he has been researching the impacts of risk on everyday life, including in personal and collective security, crime, politics, welfare, work, the environment and food safety. His research has focused on the multiple dimensions of what we recognize and understand as 'risk'. He has published in a range of social science journals including the *British Journal of Criminology*, *Sociological Review*, *Current Sociology*, *Security Dialogue* and *Environmental Politics*. His monograph, *Ulrich Beck: A Critical Introduction to the Risk Society*, provides the first book-length exposition and critique of the risk society thesis. In 2014 he published *Understanding the Risk Society: Crime, Security and Welfare* (Palgrave Macmillan).

Pat O'Malley is Distinguished Honorary Professor at the Australian National University, and previously was Professorial Research Fellow in Law at the University of Sydney and Canada Research Chair in Criminology and Criminal Justice in Ottawa. His research has focused largely on risk as a governmental technology especially in relation to criminal justice. Linked with this he has been involved in the development of 'governmentality' as an analytical approach to understanding governance in diverse fields including drug policy, insurance and fire prevention. Beginning in 2008, his research interests began shifting to the importance of money sanctions in shaping contemporary justice, and the ways these facilitated the development of 'simulated justice'. This is typified by the use of remote sensors and computerisation to create a large-scale assemblage of surveillance and crime control that operates primarily in the virtual environment. Most recently, with Gavin Smith, his research has begun to examine how the internet facilitates resistance to such justice and, more widely, how such developments involve the emergence of resistant 'popular' criminologies that draw on internet resources, big data and mass experience.

Jo Phoenix is Professor of Criminology at the Open University. She is interested in sex, sexualities and their regulation, child sexual exploitation, prostitution and prostitution policy and youth crime, youth justice and youth policy. She has written *Making Sense of Prostitution* (Palgrave, 2001), *Illegal and Illicit: Sex, Regulation and Social Control* (co-authored with Sarah Oerton, Willan, 2005), and *Out of Place* (Howard League for Penal Reform, 2012), and edited *Sex Work Today: Prostitution Policy Reform in England and Wales* (Policy Press, 2010). Her latest research monograph is *Youth Justice 2.0* which will be published by Palgrave in 2017. Jo has also published many book chapters and journal articles covering a wide range of topics from the politics of youth justice practitioners' professional education to the politics of prostitution policy reform, from the policing of girls' sexuality to, more recently, the experiences of young people and youth policies in the countries of the Arab Spring 'democratic revolutions'.

Sharon Pickering, Professor of Criminology and Head of the School of Social Sciences at Monash University, has written in the areas of refugees and trafficking with a focus on gender and human rights. Recently an Australian Research Council Future Fellow on Border Policing, she is also Series Editor with Katja Franko Aas (Oslo University) and Mary Bosworth (Oxford University) of *Routledge Studies in Criminal Justice, Borders and Citizenship*, and Founder and Director of the Border Crossing Observatory. She has authored 14 books and over 60 articles and book chapters, leads a series of Australian Research Council projects focusing on security and migration, deportation, and police and community responses to prejudice-motivated crimes. She won the Australian Human Rights Award 2012 for print and online media on human rights and asylum. Her co-authored book with Leanne Weber *Globalisation and Borders: Death at the Global Frontier* won the Christine M. Alder book prize in 2013 and she won the *British Journal of Criminology* Radzinowicz Memorial Prize for 'Hotpants at the border' with Julie Ham. With Leanne Weber she established the Australian Border Deaths Database.

José Carlos Portella Junior has a Master's in Law from the the University Center Curitiba (UNICURITIBA) and is Professor of Law and co-ordinator of the research group on International Criminal Law at UNICURITIBA Brazil.

Giane Silvestre is Post-Doctoral Researcher at The Center for the Study of Violence from University of São Paulo (NEV-USP). She received her PhD in Sociology at Federal University of São Carlos, Brazil and her Master's in Sociology from the same University. Her doctoral research focused on state crime control in São Paulo, analyzing different institutions and agents of crime control – police officers, public prosecutor, judges – and the relationships among them. During her PhD, she was Visiting Scholar at The Center for the Study of Law and Society (CSLS) from University of California, Berkeley. Her Master's dissertation focused on mass incarceration and the growth of the prison population in the State of São Paulo, Brazil and was published as a book entitled *Visiting Days: A Sociology of Prison and Punishment* (published only in Portuguese). Since 2009 she has been a member of the 'Center for the Study of Violence and Management of Conflict' and Researcher Fellow of the São Paulo Research Foundation (FAPESP). She has published on incarceration, crime control, police violence and racial profiling in Brazil, mainly in the State of São Paulo.

Jonathan Simon joined the Berkeley Law faculty in 2003. His scholarship concerns the role of crime and criminal justice in governing contemporary societies. His past work includes two award-winning monographs *Poor Discipline: Parole and the Social Control of the Underclass* (University of Chicago, 1993, winner of the American Sociological Association's sociology of law book prize, 1994), and *Governing through Crime: How the War on Crime Transformed American Democracy and Created a Culture of Fear* (Oxford University Press, 2007, winner of the American Society of Criminology, Hindelang Award 2010). His most recent books are *The Sage Handbook of Punishment and Society* (Sage, 2013) (edited with Richard Sparks) and *Mass Incarceration on Trial: A Remarkable Court Decision and the Future of Prisons in America* (New Press, 2014). He has served as the editor-in-chief of the journal, *Punishment and Society*, and is a reviewer for numerous law and society and criminology journals. He blogs at prawfsblawg and governingthroughcrime.

Loïc Wacquant is Professor of Sociology at the University of California, Berkeley, and Researcher at the Centre de sociologie européenne, Paris. A MacArthur Prize Fellow and recipient of the Lewis Coser Award of the American Sociological Association, his research spans urban relegation, ethnoracial domination, the penal state, incarnation, and social theory and the politics of reason. His books are translated in some 20 languages and include the trilogy *Urban Outcasts* (2008), *Punishing the Poor* (2009) and *Deadly Symbiosis* (in press), as well as *The Two Faces of the Ghetto* (2017). He holds the 2016–17 Pitt Professorship in American History and Institution at Cambridge University. For more information, see loicwacquant.net.

Reece Walters joined the Queensland University of Technology School of Justice in 2011 and took up the position of Assistant Dean, Research for the Faculty of Law in early 2012. Prior to this he worked at the Open University in England, University of Stirling in Scotland, Victoria University of Wellington in New Zealand and LaTrobe University in Melbourne. He has undertaken various roles in research and managerial leadership, advocacy and strategic development. Professor Walters' research in eco-crime and environmental justice, state violence and corporate crime has produced six books and over 100 publications. Professor Walters has a number of qualifications including a BA Law, MA Criminological Studies (*LTU*), PGCE Environmental Law and Management (*Wales*), Dip.Crim, (*Melb*), PhD (*Well*).

Nicole Westmarland is Professor of Criminology at Durham University where she is Director of the Durham Centre for Research into Violence and Abuse. She has conducted around 30 studies in the field of domestic and sexual violence and has published widely in this area. Her most recent book is *Violence Against Women: Criminological Perspectives on Men's Violences* (Routledge, 2015). Her recent academic advisor and consultancy positions have included Special Advisor to the House of Commons and House of Lords Joint Committee on Human Rights for their Inquiry into Violence against Women and Girls (2014–15) and the Association of Chief Police Officers (2012–15). Previously, she has held the position of Special Advisor to government's Victims of Violence and Abuse Prevention Project and chaired one of its Expert Groups. Nicole held the voluntary position of Chair of Rape Crisis (England and Wales) for five years and continues to be involved as a trustee of her local Rape Crisis Centre.

Simon Winlow is Professor of Criminology at the Teesside Centre for Realist Criminology, Teesside University, UK. He is the author of *Badfellas: Crime, Tradition and New Masculinities* (Berg, 2001), and co-author of *Bouncers: Violence and Governance in the Night-Time Economy* (Oxford University Press, 2003), *Violent Night: Urban Leisure and Contemporary Culture* (Berg, 2006), *Criminal Identities and Consumer Culture: Crime, Exclusion and the New Culture of Narcissism* (Willan, 2008), *Rethinking Social Exclusion: The End of the Social?* (Sage, 2013), *Riots and Political Protest: Notes from the Post-Political Present* (Routledge, 2015), *Revitalizing Criminological Theory: Towards a New Ultra-Realism* and *Rise of the Right: English Nationalism and the Transformation of Working-Class Politics* (Policy Press, 2016). He is the Vice President of the British Society of Criminology.

PREFACE

A book is formed by the arguments of which it is made; they are what actually matter. Therefore, a book does not deserve to be ruled or reduced in a single first act. Moreover, as Foucault (1961/1972: 10) has remarked, a preface runs the risk of being a declaration of tyranny. It risks attempting to establish the monarchy of the author – or editors. But still, this is a preface – but not really. It is a preface because it reserves for itself an initial space in the book. But it ceases to be so because it does not intend to present or explain the book's contents. My purpose here is simply to answer the recurring question that people ask me and Pat: where did the book come from?

About five years ago, the research group Modern Trends in the Criminal System[1] (*Modernas Tendências do Sistema Criminal*), which meets monthly in Curitiba (Brazil), decided to develop a postgraduate course project in criminal sciences. When we began to structure the criminology disciplines, we were faced with a problem: the lack of an accessible and up-to-date bibliography which could be a reference for studies. Few criminology books are available to the Brazilian academic public. Although there is a production of good quality articles, most English language articles and books have not yet been translated into Portuguese, and neither have criminology books and papers written in other languages. The lack of interest of the academy and the publishing market for criminological works in general was also notable: the few previously translated works are now out of print, and recent translations have only resulted from the preferences and efforts of individual researchers. The anachronism of most available material was also a problem. In short, the Brazilian academy seemed to have become stuck in the 1970s 'critical criminology' of Ian Taylor, Paul Walton and Jock Young (1975).

In order to solve the problems of the accessibility and topicality of our project, we had an initial plan to compile an edited collection of materials that were already available and could cover as many contemporary topics of interest as possible. The book was envisaged as a reference book showcasing the best of contemporary criminology. Then, another idea came up: what if, instead of contacting authors asking for authorization to republish their works, we invited them to write something new about their respective researches, in an expositive style and aimed at the public of Brazilian academics and professionals in criminology and criminal justice? The proposal was accepted by the research group.

That was when I turned to Pat Carlen. Counting on her experience as an editor and her friendship, I invited her to coordinate the collection and the response came quickly: yes, let's do it. First, we listed the theories, themes, topics and authors that we thought we would like to include; and then we were very lucky insofar as the majority of people we approached not only accepted our invitation but also presented us with excellent essays. The final line-up is here. Originally the book was planned only for Brazilian readers, but the quality of the contributing authors and originality of the chapters offered made it clear that an English version should be published too. So, here's the book. It is presented neither as a new brand of criminology nor as a brand new criminology. Rather it is offered as a resource which may allow readers to appreciate the multiple realities which have been, are, or might be, lumped together and called criminology and criminal justice. It is for everyone who is (or might be) interested in imagining, appreciating and challenging the multiple and alternative ways of understanding and transforming criminological knowledge and social justice.

Leandro Ayres França
Porto Alegre/London, 2017

Note

1 The research group Modern Trends in the Criminal System, established in 2008 and coordinated by Professor Dr Paulo César Busato, gathers professors, researchers and students linked to a range of educational institutions in Brazil, and promotes regular meetings, in which diverse trends of punitive social control are studied. The Group also produces a scientific journal, entitled *Justiça e Sistema Criminal*, which is published semi-annually (for more information see www.sistemacriminal.org).

References

Foucault, Michel. (1961/1972) *Folie et Déraison: Histoire de la folie à l'âge classique*, Paris: Gallimard.
Taylor, I., Walton, P. and Young, J. (1975) *Critical Criminology*, London: Routledge and Kegan Paul.

ACKNOWLEDGEMENTS

The Editors would like to thank all the members of the research group Modern Trends in the Criminal System (Modernas Tendências do Sistema Criminal) which meets monthly in Curitiba, Brazil and is coordinated by Professor Dr Paulo César Busato. It is to them that we are indebted for the idea of this collection of modern criminology essays. We are also grateful to the contributing authors who made editing the book so enjoyable; and to everyone at Routledge, especially Hannah Catterall and Tom Sutton, and also Emma Harder and Rebecca Storr, who eased our way at every stage of production.

PART I

Theoretical perspectives

1

ALTERNATIVE CRIMINOLOGIES

An introduction

Pat Carlen

Crime, as Durkheim (1896/1955) said, is normal. But the critical alternative criminologies which lend their collective name to this book are all about Others: those who make the rules and because they are rich and powerful have many alternatives; those who break the rules and, because they are poor and powerless, have few alternatives; and all of the academic, professional and everyday criminological observers – those whose rules are so frequently alternatives to others' rules and for whom there is no truth of the matter, no matters of fact and no binding rules for knowing – only continually changing tropes of science, art, law, morality and politics – and ever-changing emotional as well as intellectual, moral and artistic responses to all kinds of rule-breaking and law-breaking. Love it? Loathe it? Love it *and* loathe it? Whatever and/or however: crime is everywhere – in novels, scientific articles, books, rap lyrics, cartoons, films, conferences, online exchanges, financial deals, gossip and private fantasies. It is to be found in the highest echelons of governments, political parties, churches, universities, mass media, business, armed services, professions, families – everywhere. But it is not its ubiquity that makes crime so important. Crime is of such crucial importance because it is also one of the Others of people's notions of justice, morality, order, security. By deconstructing crime and criminal justice it is possible to find out who has the power to make, break and enforce both the Rule of Law and the economic, social, cultural and political rules, roles and relationships conditioning the Rule of Law. Yet, at the same time, analytic deconstructions of crime and justice suggest that crime is a precarious, if not an imaginary, Other. For, history, geography, anthropology, sociology, philosophy and jurisprudence teach that the meanings of crime and justice vary by time, place, culture and social position (see Runciman 1966; Rawls 1972). Additionally, deconstruction of political and everyday discourse suggests that people can act on several seemingly opposed meanings of crime, justice, morality and order simultaneously – and then, later, give totally different, but logically coherent and/or legally acceptable, accounts of what happened, why it happened and what it meant (see Carlen 2008, 2010: xiv). The alternatives are endless, the combinations kaleidoscopic.

Alternative Criminologies examines the simultaneously alternative dimensions of crime and the professional and non-professional, visual, artistic and emotional criminologies that alternately, or simultaneously, attempt to portray, explain, understand or fundamentally change why crime and justice take the forms they do. This first chapter, however, is not intended as an introduction to the other chapters. Each ensuing chapter has its specific focus and style; each is a possible alternative (or not) to other alternatives. Moreover, in introducing the book's eponymous theme, this chapter is not itself as Other-wise as, ideally, it should be; and this is primarily because it focuses exclusively upon criminology in the anglophone countries; and says little about criminology in any of the others. Readers, therefore, are forewarned that the alternative perspectives described in this chapter may have to be made emotionally, culturally and/or politically relevant by being constantly re-read and rewritten other-wise. (See, for instance, Cain 2000 on the oriental and the occident, Liu 2009 on Asian Criminology and Carrington, Hogg and Sozzo 2016 on Southern Criminology.) In fact, reading and writing critical alternative criminologies otherwise is an essential precondition for taking them seriously, regardless of geopolitical location. None the less, however often alternative criminologies are re-read and re-written, three fundamental questions of definition remain: what are alternative criminologies alternatives *to?* Does not the very term 'alternative criminologies' involve a rampant relativism unless it is further and more closely defined? How can anyone choose between alternatives? Many dictators have produced alternative criminologies which have neither respected human rights nor reduced political, economic or cultural oppressions. Indeed, post-revolutionary governments have again and again produced alternative criminologies characterised by savage punishments and the grossest violations of human rights. Agreed. That is why this chapter distinguishes between conservative alternative criminologies and critical alternative criminologies.

In this essay, conservative alternative criminologies are typified as either preserving the status quo, deliberately or by default, or as changing it in such ways that exploitation of the poor and powerless by the rich and powerful is less likely to be diminished and more likely to be increased. Examples of conservative alternative criminology are to be found in criminological projects which focus on attempting to reduce crime and prison populations without critically examining the social structures and forms of law which produce both. By contrast, critical alternative criminologies aim to deconstruct the meanings of crime and criminal justice so as to expose the relationships between social structural inequalities, criminal injustices, laws and human identities. In so doing, however, critical alternative criminologies do not restrict critique to literary deconstruction. Instead, in the imagining of critical alternative criminologies, it is assumed that deconstruction of present modes of criminal justice may be achieved by a variety of modes of knowing: analytically via critique; artistically via the dramatic or visual arts and/or musical forms; mathematically via statistical calculation; historically via cultural memories and records; and empathetically via the emotions. How those varied forms of understanding are then used, will of course, be in part determined by local ongoing economic, political and cultural conditions and processes, in part by international relations and in part by presently unpredictable global events. And, of course, it should go without saying, that the term 'critical alternative criminologies' ultimately names a process of permanent critique, a series of transitional states of new knowledge and ideology rather than sets of closed theories. For at the moment of recognition of a critical alternative criminology the critical alternative becomes subject to alternative critique itself. At such time it may be analysed by others as being neither critical nor alternative! By the same logic, apparently conservative alternative criminology projects may, in changing political conditions, have socially progressive effects. Thus, the brand names and brand-name criminology claims (including the name 'critical alternative criminologies') employed in this chapter are expected to have only a nominalist and discursive saliency, they are not proffered as having any essential empirical reality or guaranteed progressive policy pay-off.

The rest of the chapter is divided into three sections, each focusing on a different dimension of critical alternative criminologies. First, the many critical alternative perspectives on crime and justice that have been developed since Ian Taylor, Paul Walton and Jock Young (1973 and 1975) developed their Marxist critiques in the UK in the 1970s are identified. Second, there is a focus on some of the critical alternative modes of knowing about crime – critical modes which both engage in deconstructive and reconstructive critique and, most importantly, are themselves open to continuous critique. (Ironically, continuous critique is, theoretically and supposedly, already a feature of the legal systems of democratic countries. In practice, continuous critique of democratic legal systems is most readily – and in some cases, exclusively – available to those who can afford to pay a large number of lawyers to scrutinise and 'deconstruct' the state's case against them and then fund phenomenally expensive court delays in order for successive legal quibbles to be dealt with; for a recent and dramatic example, see Davies (2014) on the way in which Rupert Murdoch's newspapers in the UK were able to pay for very costly and effective defences against the many criminal charges brought against their staff in 2013 and 2014.) In the chapter's third and concluding section, the possible political significance of critical alternative criminologies today is briefly discussed.

Critical alternative criminologies with and without Marx 1973–2015

Today's critical alternative criminologies have a history. As, therefore, it is a fundamental tenet of this chapter that new knowledge is, in part, reconstructed out of the deconstructed and re-theorised particles of the old, let us begin with *The New Criminology* published by Ian Taylor, Paul Walton and Jock Young in 1973. When that book made its début in the mid-1970s (at a time when criminology in the UK was sometimes studied under the more wide-ranging title 'sociology of deviance') it made a massive impression; not because it was the first book to attempt a Marxist analysis of crime and justice (Bonger 1916; Chambliss and Seidman 1971; Quinney 1977; Rusche and Kirschheimer 1939 amongst many others, had already done that) but because it was aspirational in its scope and humane in its vision. When, two years later, *The New Criminology* was followed by *Critical Criminology* (Taylor, Walton and Young 1975) it quickly became apparent that the parameters of criminology in the UK (and maybe elsewhere) were never going to be the same again. From then on, anglophone criminology, which had, with a few exceptions, morphed into a punishment versus welfare debate about the best way to respond to crime, was reinvigorated with that very exciting notion of critique that had been apparent in Emile Durkheim's (1896/1955) foundational radical insight that 'crime is normal'. Other European books published around that time, and which helped buttress the burgeoning of diverse UK criminologies committed to constant critique, included Habermas's *Knowledge and Human Interests* (1972), Donzelot's *The Policing of Families* (1979), Foucault's *Discipline and Punish* (1977), Mathiesen's *The Politics of Abolition* (1974), Melossi and Paverini's *The Prison and the Factory* (1981) and a variety of non-criminological works by Marxist philosophers such as Louis Althusser (1971), psychoanalytic writers like Jacques Lacan (1975), linguistic philosophers such as Ferdinand Saussure (1974) and Jacques Derrida (1967/ 1976); and feminist writers such as Julia Kristeva (1980).

Renewal of the Marxist critique of crime and justice gave new impetus to the study of white collar crime (e.g. Levi 1987/2014) while the constant stream of critical and qualitative case studies already coming to the UK from the United States (e.g. Becker 1963; Skolnick 1965; Matza 1969) imbued a new generation of UK criminologists with the courage to engage in qualitative case studies and the development of new theoretical perspectives. The later 1970s and 1980s qualitative studies were oriented less towards previous criminological writings and more theoretically informed by a variety of social science, literary and philosophical perspectives. Yet the emphasis on the relationships between crime, economy and politics was never abandoned. Now, during the first decades of the 21st century, a continuing emphasis on the relationships between politics, economy, culture and crime has been manifest in radical criminological works in the UK, Australia, the United States and elsewhere. These latest critical alternative ways of writing about, and deconstructing, crime and justice issues have variously highlighted the following: neo-liberal governance (Simon 2007); the globalisation of crime (Findlay 1999; Aas 2012); penal populism (Pratt 2006; Freiberg and Gelb 2008); risk (Hudson 2003; O'Malley 2010); consumerism (Hall, Winlow and Ancrum 2008; O'Malley 2009); eco-crime (Walters 2010); acquiescence and repressive surveillance (Mathiesen 2004, 2012); social exclusion (De Giorgi 2006; Winlow and Hall 2013); precarity and vertigo (Young 2007); orientalism and occidentalism (Cain 2000; Young 2007); acquiescence in various types of oppressions (Cohen 2000; Mathiesen 2004); and cultural change (Garland 2001; Wacquant 2004/2009; Matravers, 2005; Simon 2007; Comfort 2008; O'Malley 2009; Winlow and Hall 2013). Theoretical criminologies have increasingly drawn upon works not directly concerned with crime but whose focus is more upon: political economy (Esping-Andersen 1990); philosophy (e.g. Taylor 2004; Butler 2004; Chomsky 2006; Sassen 2014); politics (e.g. Fraser 1997); history (Thompson 1963); sociology (e.g. Bourdieu 1990; Sennett 2006); feminism (e.g. Butler 1990; May 2015); and even epidemiology (see Wilkinson and Pickett 2009) together with many, many more – as will be seen in the other chapters of this book.

Innovations in criminological perspectives since *The New Criminology* have been generated by substantive, as well as by theoretical and conceptual issues. Once criminology held up a critical mirror to its looking-glass self, Others soon came crowding in to ask why the criminal subject of criminology was always, traditionally, a male, working class and/or black individual lawbreaker? What about: Women? Corporate crime? Middle class crime? Racism? War crime? Political crime? State crime? Green crime? State regulation of sexuality? Violence against women? Crime victims? Hate crime? Child abuse? Elder abuse? People trafficking? Modern forms of slavery? Why are only a minority of lawbreakers ever criminalised? Why do women commit less crime than men? What are the roles of the criminal law, police, courts, prisons, official statistics, media and political creeds and political parties in shaping popular and professional conceptions of what is crime and who are the criminals? Who is included and who is excluded from the economic and social life of the modern city and how does cultural and social zoning shape popular conceptions of crime and criminals? How have innovations in science and technology – such as the internal combustion engine, the silicon chip and the worldwide web – given birth to new crime opportunities, new criminals and new questions of the relationships between global and local justice? What are the relationships between social justice and criminal justice? Why not abolish prisons? What kind of police do we need? How are conceptions of right, wrong, security and crime shaped by time, place, culture, inequalities of power and wealth, gender, ethnicity, age, emotions? Are most criminologies ethnocentric? (Enter here comparative criminology, e.g. Cain 1989; Downes 1993; Whitman 2003; Newburn and Sparks 2004; Carrington and others 2013; Pratt and Erikson 2013.) Why, and under what conditions do people stop committing crime? (Enter desistance theory: Maruna 2001.) And do academic criminologists speak only to each other, rather than to the publics they should serve? (Enter public criminology: Loader and Sparks 2010; *British Journal of Criminology Review Symposium* 2011.)

All of the foregoing are alternative questions. They are alternatives both to each other and to the amalgam of literal and taken-for-granted conceptions of crime which forever essentialise stereotypes of lawbreakers as being the (mainly poorer) persons in the criminal justice system who are there solely because they have committed a very serious crime and/or pose a serious threat to society. The post-1980s critical alternative theorists insisted that criminology should not only develop more critical and more radical theories of crime and justice in relation to the poor and dispossessed but that it should also focus more sharply on the other Others – those who, for a variety of reasons, are absences in conservative criminology texts and research projects – the very serious and very dangerous lawbreakers who pose a global threat and who are seldom criminalised and seldom poor! (War criminals, corporate criminals, political criminals, for example.) Additionally, and most recently, the criminology spotlight has also been extended to people excluded from human and citizen rights as a result of wars, migration, sexual orientations, physical or mental difference and/or poverty. These latter, though they have usually committed no crime, are also being characterised as being *not like us: as being Other* – and *their* existence poses (or is portrayed or seen as posing) a vertiginous threat to the economic and psychological security of those who are still enjoying (though maybe only precariously) the unequal distribution of wealth in late modern capitalist economies (Young 2007). And all the time, class, gender, racist, legal and geographical barriers and boundaries are excluding new categories of Others from sharing in the global wealth of nations. Those who break through the geographical barriers are increasingly subject to new penalties and exclusions (see Pickering 2005; Sandberg and Pedersen 2009). The work of critical alternative criminologies has, however, not been confined to posing new substantive questions. With equal vigour, critical alternative criminologies have also searched, and continue to search, for alternative ways of knowing (see, for an early example, Burton and Carlen 1979/2013; for more recent examples see Gilligan and Pratt 2004; Jacobsen and Walklate 2016).

Alternative criminologies as constant critique and new ways of knowing

The term 'critical criminology' no longer refers solely to Marxist perspectives on crime (see Carrington and Hogg 2002; Anthony and Cunneen 2008). Nowadays it is used to denote any theoretical position which, in saying 'No' to old ways of knowing and taken-for-granted hierarchies of knowledge, also challenges the taken-for-granted social or political arrangements which give rise to inequalities of wealth, knowledge and power with their accompanying exploitative criminal justice systems. (But see also Walton and Young 2009 for a review of some of the theoretical innovations in criminology in the 25 years following *The New Criminology*.) Varied as critical alternative criminological perspectives are, what they all have in common is that, unlike official or what has been called 'administrative criminology' (Young 1988) they refuse to accept uncritically the definitions of crime and justice as realised by the official administration of criminal justice by governments, the courts, the police and the prisons. At this point, therefore, it is worth discussing further the definition and continuing practice of 'administrative criminology' as, although it will be argued below that neat distinctions between administrative and critical criminologies are not always instructive or useful, administrative criminologies are still recognisably in the ascendant in many countries and in repressive political regimes still work ideological wonders to justify the status quo and silently silence all forms of critique (see Mathiesen 2004; Young 2011).

Jock Young coined the term administrative criminology in the 1980s (Young 1988) to refer to policy-making criminology which seeks knowledge about lawbreaking in order to reduce crime. Because administrative criminology as originally defined was seen to be necessarily concerned only with activities that have already been defined as criminal by law and that have the main aim of producing policing and penal policies which reduce lawbreaking via detection, deterrence and punishment, there has been a tendency for theorists to see administrative criminology as always and necessarily being the opposite of critical criminology. Today, however, in the era of multidisciplinary and alternative criminologies, such stark oppositions are less easy to justify. In the UK, for instance, two sets of official statistics are produced annually with the intent of monitoring possible racist and sexist biases in the administration of the criminal justice system (Ministry of Justice 2013, 2014); and much critical work has been undertaken by official crime agencies in relation to violence against women, rape, policing, victims and other crime issues. And even if the crimes of poorer and less powerful people are punished more frequently than those of the rich and powerful, it has to be remembered that poorer people also suffer more than richer people do when they are victims of crime. Nor, moreover, is it fanciful to assume that, if critical alternative criminologists working in universities labour in the hope that their work will produce new conceptions of crime and justice, they might also hope that it will eventually have some influence on policy – and specifically on the development of structurally embedded measures to help protect the weak against the strong, the poor against the rich and the less powerful from the more powerful. Many of today's officially recognised crime issues (for example, the neglect of crime victims by the police and courts; and gender, racist and class biases in the administration of criminal justice) were first brought to prominence by university-based academics, then further researched by government agencies and, then (in some cases after further debate, lobbying and campaigning) ameliorated (though not, alas, resolved) by changes in law and administrative procedures and practice. A concern with both the actual and the fictitious divide between policy-oriented research which is not necessarily critical and critical research that has little chance of having an effect on policy is one of the driving concerns of those who have recently been debating the importance (or not) of developing a more 'public criminology' (Loader and Sparks 2010; *British Journal of Criminology Review Symposium* 2011).

Formally, criminological research might be described as being a more or less critical alternative to administrative or official criminologies according to the extent to which it calls into question legal definitions and existing theoretical, common-sense or taken-for-granted conceptions of crime and justice. In practice, however, when different theories are critically read by different people in different times and places, it is likely that many will be seen to have both conservative and radical elements. For example, two of the most popular of recent criminological perspectives – desistance theory and restorative justice – might be seen as having both conservative and radical dimensions and effects. Desistance theory (Maruna 2001), for instance, in some of its manifestations seems to be little more than the flip side of the old 'causes of crime' theories which asked why do poorer people commit crime. Yet, in some of its administrative applications, desistence theory research has been influential in lobbying for a better deal in terms of employment, housing and other welfare opportunities for ex-prisoners (see McNeill forthcoming). Restorative justice likewise can be criticised for failing to ask who restores what to whom? (Carlen 2000), the implication being that, again, it is the poor who are expected to make amends to the rich, rather than the other way round. Yet, in 2009 John Braithwaite, the founding theorist of restorative justice perspectives, radically and convincingly argued that the logic of restorative justice could very usefully be applied to the development of a scale of effective punishments appropriate to the very serious crimes of lawbreaking bankers (Braithwaite 2009). The point is, that as the conditions for change constantly change, the political salience of competing theories changes, too. Once that is recognised (together with acknowledgement of the multidimensional nature of crime and criminal justice issues) the utility of the current academic practice of analysing crime theories in terms of their conservative or radical potential becomes ever more questionable. Certainly, one of the uses of the analytic critique of social theories is that it can alert putative adherents of a specific theoretical perspective to the dangers inherent in some of the either conservative or radical ideological assumptions on which the theory is built. But it is an abuse of social criticism to insist that a theory built upon conservative social assumptions must necessarily have retrogressive policy effects. In changing cultural and political circumstances theoretical perspectives may be read and acted upon very differently at different times, and also have quite the opposite effects to what could have been predicted by a literal analysis of their foundational assumptions. Hence the need for constantly changing perspectives on, and alternative readings of, the meanings of crime and justice – and of the theories that attempt to read and translate them into public policies. Giving criminological perspectives or theories brand names is a useful heuristic device to distinguish the specific crime dimensions, objects of knowledge or ways of knowing with which they are concerned, but their social effectivity is determined by their historical conditions of existence in conjunction with the penal politics and struggles of their own time and those of succeeding generations.

It is likely that all criminological theories (academic or otherwise) are written and read from a range (and often a mix) of epistemological, anti-epistemological, cultural, political and emotional standpoints. Indeed, the 'otherness' of criminology has always been such that some of its best-known practitioners have argued that criminology does not exist at all as an academic discipline (see Cohen 1988) and is merely a ragbag of concepts and perspectives purloined from older disciplines. For, even before Maureen Cain (1989) argued for a 'transgressive criminology' imbued by concepts and philosophical positions crossing criminology's traditional constitutive discipline boundaries – jurisprudence, law, mathematics, sociology, anthropology and psychology – western criminology had regularly been enriched by perspectives taken from modernist and postmodernist writings (Lyotard 1979); as well as from history (Thompson 1963; Hobsbawm 1965, 1969); feminism (Kristeva 1980); cultural and multi-cultural studies (Hall and others 1978); politics (Arendt 1970); and urban geography (Harvey 1973). In the last 15 years, also, there has been an increasing emphasis upon the roles of imagination (Young 2011; Jacobsen and Walklate 2016); emotions (Karstedt, Loader and Strang 2011; Clarke, Broussine and Watts 2015); aesthetics (Carrabine 2012; Jacobsen 2014); narrative (Presser and Sandberg 2015); cinema (Rafter and Brown 2011); carnival (Presdee 2000); geography (Piacentini 2004; Pallot and Piacentini 2012); queer perspectives (Ball 2016) in the creation of tantalising visions of new forms of human organisation and conceptions of justice. But if any single impulse can be singled out as providing most impetus to the recent diversity of critical alternative criminologies, it is, in my opinion, a renewal of the cultural turn in criminology (Ferrell and others 2004; Ferrell, Hayward and Young 2008). This cultural renaissance in criminological perspectives endowed critical alternative criminologies with all the glittering prizes of the imagination, creativity and critique which are so vital to the scientific artistry of criminology, founded, as it is, not only on the darker side of law and order but also on the brighter side of human endeavour and visions of justice. My own critical alternative preference is for an 'imaginative criminology' which is also multi-cultural.

> The promise of imaginative criminology is that by deconstructing the minutiae of already-known criminal justice issues, it can sort through the debris of old ways of thinking about criminal justice and in recognition that new knowledge always arises from the deconstruction and creative reconstruction of pre-existing and existing modes of knowing, imaginative criminology is not essentially exclusionary of any modes of knowing. When one perspective fails to shed light on what is happening, other perspectives are tried, and if none of them works, the question is changed and maybe, too, the modes of knowing and recognition. Perhaps a metaphor sheds light on what has previously been so puzzling; perhaps there is a sudden awareness of a glaring absence in the text or that the logic of people's explanations is absurd insofar as it is formally contradictory or substantively incredible; or sometimes it is a line from a play, a theme from a novel, some well-worn folk cliché or the lyric of a pop song that is inspirational. And, occasionally, it is a throwaway line by a colleague or a new understanding of someone else's arguments. And so the process of deconstruction, reconstruction and deconstruction continues, taking people to places they never expected to be… An imaginative criminologist should also be able to imagine how elements of the imaginary of today's criminal justice might, if imagined differently, give birth to new and more democratic conceptions and practices of a just criminal justice.
>
> *(Carlen 2016: 21)*

There are always multiple, ever-coalescing and ever-atomising alternatives. However, the search for alternative ways of theorising the relationships between social and criminal justice in the present, and then imagining how they could be different in the future, calls less and less for ever newer and newer 'brand-name' criminologies (Carlen 1998) and more and more urgently for new forms of democratic governance committed to justice (both social and legal) as fairness, and to the building of state forms in which such an ameliorative distributive justice might be achieved. What role might critical alternative criminologists play in such an endeavour? Should academics ever jump out of the ivory tower into the maelstrom of penal politics and political action? Are they ever justified in not doing so?

The significance of alternative criminologies today

> The radical imagination waits to be unleashed through social movements in which injustice is put on the run and civic literacy, economic justice, and collective struggle once again become the precondition for agency, hope and the struggle over democracy.
>
> *(Giroux 2013)*

During the first 15 years of the 21st century, politics, economy and culture have continued to dominate criminological debate, albeit in new theorisations which have produced competing perspectives on the relationships between states, politics, criminal justice policies and ideologies. Critiques of policing, criminal justice practice and imprisonment have taken new forms. Developments in technology and changes in public fears, social mores and sensibilities have produced alternative criminological issues and theorisations. Impassioned arguments continue to be waged – and especially about the regulation of drugs, controls against geographical mobility, ever-changing ordinances about permitted and prohibited forms of sexuality and the use of the death penalty. All of these issues are addressed in this book. Other wide-ranging overviews of some of the major issues as seen by UK and American criminologists can also be found in two recent collections of articles: *What Is Criminology?* edited by Mary Bosworth and Carolyn Hoyle (2011) and *New Directions in Criminological Theory* edited by Steve Hall and Simon Winlow (2012). In one of the most original UK criminology books of recent years, *Rethinking Social Exclusion*, Winlow and Hall (2013) invoke the works of Slavoj Žižek (2009), Gaston Bachelard (1940), Jacques Lacan (1975) and Alain Badiou (2001) to craft a trenchant argument that the market ethic of neo-liberalism has destroyed the social. Interestingly, it seems that as criminology comes of age, there is less and less emphasis upon different 'brands' of competing criminologies. Instead, and paradoxically, in the tolerance of, and insistence upon, alternative ways of knowing, there is increasingly recognition by critical alternative criminologies that the fundamental unifying objective of criminological work is not the competitive theorising of criminal justice but the democratic achievement of social justice.

Academic, campaigning and everyday criminologists in the UK, USA and Australia have persistently been involved in legal and/or political battles against injustice and corruption in relation to the police (Carrington 1998; Scraton 2009), prisons (Davis 2005), the press (Davies 2014), as well as in relation to many other criminal justice areas when local issues have arisen. Indeed, some of the most incisive and informative books on criminal justice written towards the end of the 20th century and in the first decades of the 21st century have been written by criminal justice campaigners or campaigning academics (see, for examples: Bianchi and Swaaningen 1986; Campbell 1993; Hannah-Moffat 2001; Ramsbotham 2003; Currie 2004; Green and Ward 2004; Beckett and Sasson 2000/2004; Phoenix and Oerton 2005; Wilson 2005; Stern 2006; Sim 2009; Sudbury 2005; Richie 2012; Cunneen and others 2013; Moore and others 2014). This is not surprising; it is in the ongoing struggle for justice that critical alternative criminologies are born. For – and to go back to the question that provoked the public criminology debate – is there any point of even imagining *critical* alternative criminologies if, when developed, they remain locked in the lecture and conference rooms of the academy, or closed within the pages of academic books such as this one? If, after shunning some of the conservative assumptions of administrative criminology, critical alternative criminologists merely chatter to each other in academic journals and within their universities, they will also disenfranchise themselves from having input into any social or criminal justice policies whatever.

What, therefore, can be the relationship of academic critical alternative criminologists to political policy-making and political campaigning? That is often seen as the question central to the debate about public criminology. However, for academic criminologists, an even more crucially focused question concerns whether researchers can maintain academic credibility while, at the same time, espousing radical interpretations of data and redefinitions of issues – activities which may leave them open to accusations of bias. This is an ethical question which individual criminologists will decide for themselves. But it seems to me,

> that to maintain academic integrity researchers always have to conduct their research according to transparent and professionally approved research protocols. But, that once the research has been completed, they have to develop arguments which go beyond the methodological validity (or not) of their research findings or the logic (or not) of their theoretical perspectives, and those arguments will depend upon the choices they make according to their own religious, political or ethical values. Furthermore, to have any success with those arguments, they will need to make them not only as academic criminologists, but also within campaigning groups or political parties, or with the help of sympathetic officials, or within segments of the criminology profession committed to the same policies and values. Thus, when criminologists enter the realm of penal politics, they leave in part their professional terrain and enter penal politics as academics in the service of some group with a particular political interest. They draw on their professional expertise, but only in the service of a politics which they support. The different protagonists in penal politics act within collectives, but they are usually not acting within a collective of academic criminologists. The force of critique and new knowledge depends upon the power of the discourses, the collectives and the historical conjunctures within which they are expressed. Accordingly, although it is important for a democratic penal politics that when critical alternative criminologists do critique they adhere to professionally recognised rules for research, it is equally important that when they enter penal politics they do so explicitly as adherents of critical and democratic ideologies of justice.
>
> *(Carlen 2012: 27)*

In the 18th and 19th centuries, Goethe, Humboldt and Darwin (amongst others) insisted that art and science must be united via imagination (Wulf 2015). Social science has long recognised the importance of imaginative speculation and the denial of discipline boundaries. Yet imagination is not enough. Alternatives to injustice are not achieved outwith struggle. And in every struggle there are alternatives. The task of critical alternative criminologies – whether their genesis be in law, literature, music, drama, culture, politics, sociology, mathematics … whatever! – or in modes of knowing as yet undreamed of – may well be to take seriously all new forms of theorising about crime while being forever Other wise in the pursuit of social justice.

References

Aas, K. (2012) '"The Earth Is One but the World Is Not": Criminological Theory and Its Geopolitical Divisions'. *Theoretical Criminology* 16(1): 5–20.

Althusser, L. (1971) *Lenin and Philosophy and Other Essays*. London: New Left Books.

Anthony, T. & C. Cunneen (eds.) (2008) *The Critical Criminology Companion*. Sydney: Hawkins Press.

Arendt, H. (1970) *On Violence*. New York: Harcourt, Brace.

Bachelard, G. (1940) *The Philosophy of No* (Trans. G. C. Waterson). London: Orion Press.

Badiou, A. (2001) *Ethics: An Essay on the Understanding of Evil*. London Verso.

Ball, M. (2016) *Criminology and Queer Theory: Strange Bedfellows?* London: Palgrave Macmillan.

Becker, H. (1963) *Outsiders*. New York: Viking.

Beckett, K. & T. Sasson (2000/2004) *The Politics of Injustice: Crime and Punishment in America*. London: Sage.

Bianchi, H. & R. Swaaningen (eds.) (1986) *Abolitionism*. Amsterdam: Free University Press.

Bonger, W. (1916) *Criminality and Economic Conditions*. Boston: Little, Brown & Co.

Bosworth, M. & C. Hoyle (eds.) (2011) *What Is Criminology?* Oxford: Oxford University Press.

Bourdieu, P. (1990) *In Other Words: Essays towards a Reflexive Sociology*. Cambridge: Polity Press.

Braithwaite, J. (2009) 'Restorative Justice for Banks through Negative Licensing'. *British Journal of Criminology* 49(4): 439–450.

British Journal of Criminology (2011) 'A Symposium of Reviews of "Public Criminology" by Ian Loader and Richard Sparks'. Reviews by Nils Christie, Elliott Currie, Helena Kennedy, Rod Morgan, Gloria Laycock, Joe Sim, Jacqueline Tombs and Reece Walters. *BJC* 51(4): 707–738.

Burton, F. & P. Carlen (1979/2013) *Official Discourse: On Discourse Analysis, Government Publications, Ideology and the State*. London Routledge.

Butler, J. (1990) *Gender Trouble: Feminism and the Subversion of Identity*. London: Routledge.

Butler, J. (2004) *Precarious Life: The Powers of Mourning and Violence*. New York: Verso Books.

Cain, M. (ed.) (1989) *Growing up Good*. London: Sage.

Cain, M. (2000) 'Orientalism, Occidentalism and the Sociology of Crime'. *British Journal of Criminology* 40(2): 239–260.

Campbell, B. (1993) *Goliath: Britain's Dangerous Places*. London: Methuen.

Carlen, P. (1998) 'Criminology Ltd: The Search for a Paradigm' in P. Walton & J. Young (eds.) *The New Criminology Revisited*. Basingstoke: Macmillan, pp. 64–67.

Carlen, P. (2000) 'Youth Justice? Arguments for Holism and Democracy in Responses to Crime' in P. Green & A. Rutherford (eds.) *Criminal Policy in Transition*. Oxford: Hart Publishing, pp. 63–78.

Carlen, P. (2008) *Imaginary Penalities*. Cullompton: Willan.

Carlen, P. (2010) *A Criminological Imagination*. Farnham: Ashgate.

Carlen, P. (2012) 'Criminological Critique: Doing Crime, Doing Politics' in S. Hall & S. Winlow (eds.) *New Directions in Criminological Theory*. London: Routledge.

Carlen, P. (2016) 'Doing Imaginative Criminology' in M. H. Jacobsen & S. Walklate (eds.) *Liquid Criminology: Doing Imaginative Criminological Research*. London: Routledge.

Carrabine, E. (2012) 'Just Images: Aesthetics, Ethics and Visual Criminology'. *British Journal of Criminology* 52(3): 463–489.

Carrington, K. (1998) *Who Killed Leigh Leigh? A Story of Shame and Mateship in an Australian Town*. Sydney, New South Wales: Random House.

Carrington, K. & R. Hogg (eds.) (2002) *Critical Criminology: Issues, Debates, Challenges*. Cullompton: Willan.

Carrington, K., M. Ball, E. O'Brien & J. Tauri (eds.) (2013) *Crime, Justice and Social Democracy: International Perspectives*. Basingstoke: Palgrave Macmillan.

Carrington, K., R. Hogg & M. Sozzo (2016) 'Southern Criminology'. *British Journal of Criminology* 56(1): 1–20.

Chambliss, W. J. & R. B. Seidman (1971) *Law, Order and Power*. Boston: Addison-Wesley Pub. Co.

Chomsky, N. (2006) *Failed States: The Abuse of Power and the Assault on Democracy*. London: Hamish Hamilton.

Clarke, C., M. Broussine & L. Watts (eds.) (2015) *Researching with Feeling: The Emotional Aspects of Social and Organisational Research*. London: Routledge.

Cohen, S. (ed.) (1988) *Against Criminology*. New Jersey: Transaction Books.

Cohen, S. (2000) *States of Denial: Knowing about Atrocities and Suffering*. Cambridge: Polity.

Comfort, M. (2008) *Doing Time Together: Love and Family in the Shadow of the Prison*. Chicago: University of Chicago Press.

Cunneen, C., E. Baldry, D. Brown & others (2013) *Penal Culture and Hyperincarceration: The Revival of the Prison*. Farnham: Ashgate.

Currie, E. (2004) *The Road to Whatever: Middle-Class Culture and the Crisis of Adolescence*. New York: Henry Holt.

Davies, N. (2014) *Hack Attack: How the Truth Caught up with Rupert Murdoch*. London: Chatto & Windus.

Davis, A. (2005) *Abolition Democracy: Beyond Prisons, Torture, and. Empire; Interviews with Angela Davis.* New York: Seven Stories Press.

De Giorgi, A. (2006) *Rethinking the Political Economy of Punishment: Perspectives on Post-Fordism, and Penal Politics.* Aldershot: Ashgate.

Derrida, J. (1967/1976) *Of Grammatology.* London: Johns Hopkins University Press.

Donzelot, J. (1979) *The Policing of Families.* London: Hutchison.

Downes, D. (1993) *Contrasts in Tolerance: Post-War Penal Policy in The Netherlands and England and Wales.* Oxford Socio-Legal Studies. Oxford: Oxford University Press.

Durkheim, E. (1896/1955) *The Rules of Sociological Method.* New York: Free Press.

Esping-Andersen, G. (1990) *The Three Worlds of Welfare Capitalism.* Cambridge: Polity Press.

Ferrell, J., K. Hayward, W. Morrison & M. Presdee (eds.) (2004) *Cultural Criminology Unleashed.* London: Glasshouse Press.

Ferrell, J., K. Hayward & J. Young (2008) *Cultural Criminology.* London: Sage.

Findlay, M. (1999) *The Globalisation of Crime: Understanding Transitional Relationships in Context.* Cambridge University Press: Cambridge.

Foucault, M. (1977) *Discipline and Punish.* London: Penguin Books.

Fraser, N. (1997) *Justice Interruptus: Critical Reflections on the Post Socialist Condition.* New York: Routledge.

Freiberg, A. & K. Gelb (eds.) (2008) *Penal Populism, Sentencing Councils and Sentencing Policy.* Cullompton: Willan.

Garland, D. (2001) *The Culture of Control: Crime and Social Order in Contemporary Society.* Oxford: Oxford University Press.

Gilligan, G. & J. Pratt (2004) *Crime, Truth and Justice: Official Inquiry, Discourse, Knowledge.* Cullompton: Willan.

Giroux, H. (2013) 'The Politics of Disimagination and the Pathologies of Power'. www.truthdig.com/report/item/the_politics_of_disimagination_and_the_pathologies.

Green, P. & T. Ward (2004) *State Crime: Government, Violence and Corruption.* London: Pluto Press.

Habermas, J. (1972) *Knowledge and Human Interests.* London: Heinemann.

Hall, S. & S. Winlow (eds.) (2012) *New Directions in Criminological Theory.* London: Routledge.

Hall, S., C. Critcher, T. Jefferson, J. Clarke & B. Roberts (1978) *Policing the Crisis: Mugging, the State and Law and Order.* London: Macmillan.

Hall, S., S. Winlow & C. Ancrum (2008) *Criminal Identities and Consumer Culture.* Cullompton: Willan.

Hannah-Moffat, K. (2001) *Punishment in Disguise: Penal Governance and Federal Imprisonment of Women in Canada.* Toronto: University of Toronto Press.

Harvey, D. (1973) *Social Justice and the City.* Oxford: Basil Blackwell.

Hobsbawm, E. (1965) *Primitive Rebels: Studies in Archaic Forms of Social Movement in the 19th and 20th Centuries.* London: Norton.

Hobsbawm, E. (1969) *Bandits.* London: Weidenfeld and Nicolson.

Hudson, B. (2003) *Justice in the Risk Society.* London: Sage.

Jacobsen, M. H. (ed.) (2014) *The Poetics of Crime: Understanding and Researching Crime and Deviance through Creative Sources.* Farnham: Ashgate.

Jacobsen, M. H. & S. Walklate (eds.) (2016) *Liquid Criminology.* London: Routledge.

Karstedt, S., I. Loader & H. Strang (eds.) (2011) *Emotions, Crime and Justice.* Oxford: Oxford University Press.

Kristeva, J. (1980) *Desire in Language: A Semiotic Approach to Literature and Art.* New York: Columbia University Press.

Lacan, J. (1975) *The Language of the Self.* New York: Delta.

Levi, M. (1987/2014) *Regulating Fraud.* London: Macmillan.

Liu, J. (2009) 'Asian Criminology: Challenges, Opportunities, and Directions'. *Asian Journal of Criminology* 4(1): 1–9.

Loader, I. & R. Sparks (2010) *Public Criminology?* London: Routledge.

Lyotard, J.-F. (1979) *The Postmodern Condition: A Report on Knowledge.* Manchester: Manchester University Press.

Maruna, S. (2001) *Making Good: How Ex-Convicts Reform and Rebuild Their Lives.* Washington, DC: American Psychological Association.

Mathiesen, T. (1974) *The Politics of Abolition*. New York: Wiley.

Mathiesen, T. (2004) *Silently Silenced: Essays on the Creation of Acquiescence in Modern Society*. Hampshire: Waterside Press.

Mathiesen, T. (2012) *Towards a Surveillant Society: The Rise of Surveillance Systems in Europe*. Hampshire: Waterside Press.

Matravers, M. (ed.) (2005) *Managing Modernity: Politics and the Culture of Control*. London: Routledge.

Matza, D. (1969) *Becoming Deviant*. Englewood Cliffs, NJ: Prentice Hall.

May, V. (2015) *Pursuing Intersectionality: Unsettling Dominant Imaginaries*. New York: Routledge.

McNeill, F. (forthcoming) 'Desistance and Criminal Justice in Scotland' in H. Croall, G. Mooney & M. Munro (eds.) *Crime, Justice and Society in Scotland*. London: Routledge.

Melossi, D. & M. Pavarini (1977. Eng. trans. 1981) *The Prison and the Factory: Origins of the Penitentiary System*. London: Macmillan.

Ministry of Justice (2013) *Race and the Criminal Justice System*. London: Ministry of Justice.

Ministry of Justice (2014) *Women and the Criminal Justice System 2013*. London: Ministry of Justice.

Moore, J., B. Rolston, D. Scott & M. Tomlinson (eds.) (2014) *Beyond Criminal Justice*. Weston-super-Mare: European Group for the Study of Deviance and Social Control.

Newburn, T. & R. Sparks (eds.) (2004) *Criminal Justice and Political Cultures: National and International Dimensions of Crime Control*. Cullompton: Willan.

O'Malley, P. (2009) *The Currency of Justice: Fines and Damages in Consumer Societies*. Oxford: Routledge.

O'Malley, P. (2010) *Crime and Risk*. London: Sage.

Pallot, J. & L. Piacentini (2012) *Gender, Geography and Punishment: The Experience of Women in Carceral Russia*. Oxford: Oxford University Press.

Phoenix, J. & S. Oerton (2005) *Illicit and Illegal: Sex, Regulation and Social Control*. Cullompton: Willan.

Piacentini, L. (2004) *Surviving Russian Prisons: Punishment, Economy and Politics in Transition*. Cullompton: Willan.

Pickering, S. (2005) *Refugees and State Crime*. Sydney: Federation Press.

Pratt, J. (2006) *Penal Populism: Key Ideas in Criminology*. London: Routledge.

Pratt, J. & A. Erikson (2013) *Contrasts in Punishment: An Explanation of Anglophone Excess and Nordic Exceptionalism*. London: Routledge.

Presdee, M. (2000) *Cultural Criminology and the Carnival of Crime*. London: Routledge.

Presser, L. & S. Sandberg (2015) *Narrative Criminology: Understanding Stories of Crime*. New York: New York University Press.

Quinney, R. (1977) *Class, State and Crime*. New York: Longman.

Rafter, N. & M. Brown (2011) *Criminology Goes to the Movies: Crime Theory and Popular Culture*. New York: New York University Press.

Ramsbotham, D. (2003) *Prison-Gate: The Shocking State of Britain's Prisons and the Need for Visionary Change*. London: The Free Press.

Rawls, J. (1972) *Theory of Justice*. London: Oxford University Press.

Richie, B. (2012) *Arrested Justice: Black Women, Violence and America's Prison Nation*. New York: New York University Press.

Runciman, W. (1966) *Relative Deprivation and Social Justice*. London: Routledge and Kegan Paul.

Rusche, G. & O. Kirschheimer (1939) *Punishment and Social Structure*. New York: Russell and Russell.

Sandberg, S. & W. Pedersen (2009) *Street Capital: Black Cannabis Dealers in a White Welfare State*. Bristol: Policy Press.

Sassen, S. (2014) *Expulsions: Brutality and Complexity in the Global Economy*. Boston: Harvard.

Saussure, F. (1974) *Course in General Linguistics*. London: Fontana.

Scraton, P. (2009) *Hillsborough: The Truth*. Edinburgh: Mainstream Publishing.

Sennett, R. (2006) *The Culture of the New Capitalism*. Connecticut: Yale University Press.

Sim, J. (2009) *Punishment and Prisons: Power and the Carceral State*. London: Sage.

Simon, J. (2007) *Governing through Crime: How the War on Crime Transformed American Democracy and Created a Culture of Fear*. New York: Oxford University Press.

Skolnick, J. (1965) *Justice without Trial*. New York: Wiley.

Stern, V. (2006) *Creating Criminals: Prisons and People in a Market Society*. London: Zed Books.

Sudbury, J. (ed.) (2005) *Global Lockdown: Race, Gender and the Prison Industrial Complex*. New York: Routledge.

Taylor, C. (2004) *Modern Social Imaginaries*. Durham and London: Duke University Press.

Taylor, I., P. Walton & J. Young (1973) *The New Criminology*. London: Routledge and Kegan Paul.

Taylor, I., P. Walton & J. Young (1975) *Critical Criminology*. London: Routledge and Kegan Paul.

Thompson, E. P. (1963) *The Making of the English Working Class*. London: Pelican.

Wacquant, L. (2004. Eng. edn 2009) *Punishing the Poor: The Neoliberal Government of Social Insecurity*. Durham and London: Duke University Press.

Walters, R. (2010) *Eco Crime and Genetically Modified Food*. London: Routledge.

Walton, P. & J. Young (eds.) (2009) *The New Criminology Revisited*. Basingstoke: Macmillan.

Whitman, J. (2003) *Harsh Justice: Criminal Punishment and the Widening Divide between America and Europe*. New York: Oxford University Press.

Wilkinson, R. & K. Pickett (2009) *The Spirit Level: Why Equality Is Better for Everyone*. London: Penguin.

Wilson, D. (2005) *Death at the Hands of the State*. London: Howard League for Penal Reform.

Winlow, S. & S. Hall (2013) *Rethinking Social Exclusion*. London: Sage.

Wulf, A. (2015) *The Invention of Nature: How Alexander Von Humboldt Revolutionized Our World*. London: Hodder and Stoughton.

Young, J. (1988) 'Radical Criminology in Britain: The Emergence of a Competing Paradigm'. *British Journal of Criminology* 28(2): 159–183.

Young, J. (2007) *The Vertigo of Late Modernity*. London: Sage.

Young, J. (2011) *The Criminological Imagination*. Cambridge: Polity Press.

Žižek, S. (2009) *Violence*. London: Profile Books.

2

CULTURAL CRIMINOLOGY CONTINUED

Jeff Ferrell and Keith Hayward

Cultural criminology is concerned with the convergence of cultural, criminal and crime control processes; as such, it situates criminality and its control in the context of cultural dynamics and the contested production of meaning. In this way cultural criminology seeks to understand the everyday realities of a profoundly unequal and unjust world, and to highlight the ways in which power is exercised and resisted amidst the interplay of rule-making, rule-breaking and representation. The subject matter of cultural criminology, then, crosses a range of contemporary issues: the mediated construction and commodification of crime, violence and punishment; the symbolic practices of those engaged in illicit subcultural or post-subcultural activities; the existential anxieties and situated emotions that animate crime, transgression and victimization; the social controls and cultural meanings that circulate within and between spatial arrangements; the interplay of state control and cultural resistance; the criminogenic cultures spawned by market economies; and a host of other instances in which situated and symbolic meaning is at stake. To accomplish such analysis, cultural criminology embraces interdisciplinary perspectives and alternative methods that regularly move it beyond the boundaries of conventional criminology, drawing from media studies, anthropology, youth studies, cultural studies, cultural geography, sociology, philosophy and other disciplines, and utilizing new forms of ethnography, textual analysis and visual production. In all of this, cultural criminology seeks to challenge the accepted frameworks of criminological analysis, and to reorient criminology to contemporary social, cultural and economic conditions.

In this way cultural criminology has from the first embraced an open, invitational orientation toward criminological analysis, and has been less interested in definitional certainty than in dynamic, emergent critique. The question, then, is not so much what cultural criminology is, as how cultural criminology *continues* – how, that is, cultural criminology has drawn on existing perspectives within and beyond criminology, and continued to reinvent and resituate them with the intent of developing a criminology conversant with the contemporary world and its crises.[1]

Emergence of cultural criminology

When cultural criminology first emerged as a distinct criminological perspective in the mid-1990s (Ferrell and Sanders, 1995; Ferrell, 1999), it did so by synthesizing and revitalizing two lines of criminological thought, one North American, the other British (see Hayward, 2016). The North American tradition included labelling theory, with its understandings of crime and deviance as social constructions, and more particularly its insights into the ways that power is exercised through the assignment of meaning to human action. Equally important was the sort of subcultural analysis developed by Albert Cohen and others, which found in the collective actions of marginalized groups not simple disobedience or self-destruction, but rather the creation of alternative meanings and interpretations in response to assorted injustices. In this North American tradition were also the sort of 'naturalistic' approaches to criminal and deviant behaviour advocated by David Matza, and the vivid experiential ethnographies that Howard Becker, Ned Polsky and others employed to illuminate the insights of interactionist and labelling approaches.

The line of British criminological thought that led to cultural criminology echoed these North American perspectives, but situated them in larger frameworks of social change, structural inequality and cultural representation. British scholars who were engaged with new forms of cultural studies and critical criminology began to re-conceptualize social class as lived experience – as a shifting cluster of attitudes, orientations and cultural practices – and so to understand that social class and social inequality were often policed, enforced and reinforced by differential controls on leisure activities and cultural endeavours. They likewise began to analyse the ways in which mediated moral panics emerged in response to, but also as deflections from, deep structural changes in the social order. As in the North American tradition, subcultural practices and subcultural styles also came under consideration, but with an emphasis on how such practices and styles can function as forms of cultural resistance while also inviting scrutiny and surveillance.

These North American and British lines of criminological analysis were in some ways already intertwined – with for example British 'new criminologists' of the 1960s and 1970s inspired by and engaged with the subversive epistemic potential of labelling theory and the cultural depth of naturalistic ethnography – but cultural criminology now sought to craft a new and distinct sort of criminology from these two intellectual threads. As it emerged in the mid-1990s, this new cultural criminology emphasized the decisiveness of meaning in matters of crime and justice, arguing that both crime and its control took shape through contested processes of interpretation and representation. Likewise, it highlighted the ways in which the politics of crime and criminal justice operate in the realm of cultural dynamics, and the ways in which power and control increasingly rest on the deployment of symbolism, stigma and emotion. In all of this, cultural criminology argued for a methodology of attentiveness and cultural awareness – that is, for ways of exploring crime and justice that were attuned to the nuances of language and the image, and to the interactional dynamics of subcultural and spatial situations.

This effort to meld British and North American traditions into a distinct cultural criminology in the 1990s was not undertaken simply for the sake of intellectual innovation, though. Instead it was undertaken in two specific contexts, and for two specific purposes. The first of these contexts was the ascendancy of positivist perspectives and methodologies in criminology, and the parallel development of the pseudo-discipline of 'criminal justice'. Especially in North America, the growth and governmental support of criminal justice programmes had developed in concert with the sorts of quantitative methods and administrative criminologies that could buttress such programmes. From the view of cultural criminology such approaches forfeited the critical distance necessary for viable criminological analysis of both crime and criminal justice. Equally, these interrelated approaches evacuated meaning from the subject matter of criminology, reducing people and situations to data sets and statistical summaries, and in this way erasing from criminological discourse the very dimensions that cultural criminologists saw as essential to understanding and analysis. As a result, cultural criminology emerged not simply as an alternative to such approaches, but as a perspective designed to confront and overcome them. To revitalize and reinvent British and North American traditions of cultural analysis and sociological critique was to recover what criminal justice and its administrative criminologies had long since usurped.

More broadly, cultural criminologists sought to import these North American and British traditions into a new historical context. As cultural criminologists have carefully demonstrated, the perspectives on which they draw – labelling theory, subcultural theory, critical criminology, the British 'new criminology', cultural studies, etc. – did not emerge in an intellectual or historical vacuum. Rather, just as Marx, Durkheim and Weber once undertook to theorize the emergence of modernity, these theorists attempted to theorize the profound social upheavals that occurred post-World War II in Europe, the United States and elsewhere, and to link these upheavals to changes in the nature of crime and social control. Conflicts over civil rights and social inclusion, emergent youth subcultures, a proliferating consumer culture, new styles of deviance and transgression, and with them new forms of social and legal control – all of these constituted both the context and broader subject matter of the alternative criminological perspectives that emerged in the 1960s and 1970s. These perspectives of course remain of great value, as do those of Weber, Marx and the theorists of previous times. But as cultural criminologists realized, the world in which such perspectives emerged had shifted once again, and with this shift had come the need to reinvent these perspectives, to resituate them in the distinctive dynamics of the contemporary social order. This, then, was cultural criminology's second context and purpose: to craft a criminology of the present moment – a criminology of and for late modernity.

Late modernity and its discontents

Late modernity offers a global panorama of ambiguity and confusion, and with this a spiralling sense of uncertainty for many of its inhabitants. For more and more people, the old anchors of geographic or occupational stability have been cut loose, to be replaced only by multiplying marginalities: ongoing migration within and across nations, unpredictable episodes of temporary work and serial reinventions of the self. Raw material for these serial reinventions comes from another of late modernity's features: the endless, instantaneous, globalized flow of images, information and advertised identities via mobile phones and computer screens, all of this providing both a free-flowing panoply of possibility and the sense that no possible choice is ever the right one. This hyper-pluralism of identities and cultural orientations in turn feeds hyper-individualism – the sense that one's place in the world is defined not by long-standing community membership but by the successful construction of oneself through appropriate consumption and mediated attainment. The fluid, globalized world of late modernity in this way also confounds the local and the universal, the distinction between place and no place, such that its dislocations come to be both geographic and existential. If the socio-logical imagination allows us to find social forces in personal experience, then these are late modernity's personal residues: rampant existential and ontological uncertainty, a precarious sense of personal identity, and with this, often desperate longings for certainty and definition. To the extent that each historical period can be characterized by a particular trajectory, then the trajectory of late modernity – those decades since the criminological insights of the 1960s and 1970s – seems not so much up or down as sideways and adrift.

Amidst this late modern flux cultural criminologists have identified three constellations of actions, attitudes and images that seem particularly salient for an understanding of contem-porary crime and crime control. The first of these clusters around emotion, expressivity and uncertainty. Here tensions and contradictions abound. Meaning and self-expression are sought in a world whose hyper-pluralism and cultural fluidity regularly overwhelm the self, and where new forms of surveillance and control make the concept of individual autonomy all but meaningless. Excitement, immediacy and the consumption of experience are sold as markers of a life well lived, but like most consumer products offer more in the packaging than in the payoff. For the affluent a sense of vertigo haunts their constructions of certainty and assured security, and with it a fear of falling from whatever heights remain; for those on the margins, the experience of drifting – between jobs, between cities, between relationships – creates a life of ongoing interstitiality (Young, 2007; Ferrell, 2012a). As a result anger, panic and humiliation circulate through the social system; pleasure and excitement remain mostly just out of reach; and identities take shape in the shadows, or sometimes in synthetic forms once unimaginable. As regards crime and transgression, this mix of emotion and uncertainty means that new forms of criminality emerge – are in fact sought by some for their promise of emotional validation or crafted identity – and that existing criminological models of risk, motivation and causality may no longer hold.

A second constellation of actions and attitudes is provided by the managers of late moder-nity, who employ the methods of this late modern world – imagery, deception, manipulated meaning – and at the same time attempt to lay over the top of its endless fluctuations a grid of certainty and control. For them the risky uncertainty of late modernity is something to be calculated and controlled, its emergent crimes a problem to be predicted and thereby pre-vented (Hayward, 2007). As a result, late modernity also comes to feature new forms of social and cultural exclusion, and new patterns of social and spatial control, as pervasive as they are insidious. Many of these new forms are revanchist in nature, meant to reclaim that which is now hopelessly confounded; others are instituted so as to police the increasing and incessant inequality spawned by late modern economies. Often these new exclusions and controls are interwoven with the cultural creation of 'the other' – a readily identifiable outsider who can be made the focus of public scrutiny and the scapegoat for late modernity's vicissitudes. Of interest to cultural criminologists for its sweep and scope – stretching from the localized use of 'anti-homeless spikes' to the global war on terror – this constellation of controls is notable for another reason as well: if unintentionally, it sets up still further social and cultural tensions, and further iterations of the dialectic between social control and expressive transgression (Presdee, 2000; Hayward, 2002).

This tension between excitement and manipulation is also evident in a third constellation that we can refer to as the contemporary 'mediascape' (Appadurai, 1996). As today's fast-moving, omnipresent and increasingly interactive media shapes relations between space, time and identity, it also 'frames' how crime and its control come to be understood in society. For cultural criminologists, this mediascape constitutes an endless 'hall of mirrors' (Ferrell et al., 2015) where the on-the-ground realities of crime and crime control, and the images of these realities, continually reflect onto each other. Consequently, cultural criminologists understand that it no longer makes sense to study 'real world' crime and its mediated representation separately. Instead, in a hyper-connected society where mass-mediated images of crime and deviance proliferate, and where crime and control intertwine with entertainment and popular culture, forms of criminological analysis are required that can make sense of the blurred line between the real and the virtual. And, as always with cultural criminology, this focus is political as well as theoretical: in late modernity, with power increasingly exercised through mediated representation and symbolic production, battles over image, style and mediated meaning become essential in the contest over crime and crime control, deviance and normality, and the emerging shape of social justice.

A cultural criminology of and for late modernity

Embracing the sociological and criminological imagination (Mills, 1959; Young, 2011), cultural criminologists understand that human agency and historical circumstance inevitably intertwine; within the broad sweep of social structure and social change, emerging patterns of power and control seep into everyday life, there to be augmented or resisted in the sensuality of lived experience. Consequently, cultural criminologists do not posit that contemporary forms of crime and justice simply 'reflect' late modern tendencies. Instead, the crimes and controls of late modernity engage with its larger dynamics, amplifying them in some moments, altering and undermining them in others. We now take a closer look at the three themes outlined above by way of a general introduction to cultural criminology and some of its approaches to late modernity, its crimes and its controls.

The immediacy of illicit identity and transgression

The flux of the late modern world suggests that the crimes of this era will themselves often need to be understood in terms of immediacy, ephemerality and uncertainty; just as identities associated with occupation or spatial location have been destabilized, so too have those spawned within the interplay of crime and transgression. In this sense older models of criminality and criminal causation, often founded in assumptions of linear sequencing, positivist predictability and stable criminal identity, may well require reimagining. In this reimagining, the meaning of crime often emerges in moments and situations, and then morphs amidst the endless reproduction of its image; essentialist assumptions about biological nature or social determination disappear into fluid states of being and becoming; and the sense of a criminal subculture as a bounded collectivity of meaning, or of everyday policing as a shared manual of practices, gives way to more fluid and rhizomatic understandings of crime, its participants and its control.

A foundational perspective in this regard has been offered by Jack Katz (1988), with his understanding of crime's foreground and the emotional seductions that there emerge. In Katz's view, criminology has long been constituted back to front – built, that is, on an underlying assumption that structural factors can predict the nature of crime and criminality. Constituted in this way, criminology has inquired mostly into the background factors that lead to crime and criminality – differential association, strain, loosened social controls, social class and social inequality – while largely ignoring situations of crime and crime control as emergent phenomena in their own right. Yet as Katz argues, when we go inside the immediacy of crime (Ferrell, 1997) – inside moments of interpersonal violence, intellectual property theft or street policing – we find something that is in many ways *unpredictable* via existing criminological theories: an ephemeral, unstable mix of emotions that emerge within the situated social dynamics of the moment. These fleeting emotions, flashing between those sharing in the situation, in turn act as momentary seductions, pulling participants past what background theories can predict or what participants themselves might imagine. Here notions of linear, structural causality are lost to the immediacy of the moment, and criminal identity is seen to be more an emergent, situated phenomenon (Garot, 2010) than a fixed state of self-conceptualization. As other cultural criminologists have pointed out (Ferrell, 1992; Young, 2003; Hayward, 2004), and as the sociological imagination reminds us, background or structural factors are, of course, always present amidst this foreground of crime – but now understood in dialectical tension with its emergent meanings and emotions, rather than as predictors or causes of it. And as cultural criminologists have also noted, this phenomenon of crime as a moment of fragile emotional intensity seems likely to proliferate in a late modern world of destabilized affect and identity.

Destabilized identity underlies a second cultural criminological approach to self-conception and transgression as well. The deskilling of work, and with it the disassociation of the worker from the work process, is a longstanding feature of capitalist economies (Braverman, 1974); now, with the late modern proliferation of temporary work and emotionally managed service economies, the alienation of workers from the situations and processes of their own labour is redoubled. For more and more people, work offers neither the Fordist promise of occupational stability nor the potential for crafting skill and identity. Likewise, the ongoing bureaucratization of social life under late modernity continues to add bars to the iron cage that Weber (1978) first identified, and so to reduce human identity to organizational categories and constellations of big data. This same trajectory can be seen in the proliferation of risk-management controls on everyday life; by their logic, situations of risk or uncertainty are to be contained – or, ideally, to be expunged from a world of enforced safety, big data and carefully managed identities. Taken as a whole, these dimensions of late modern life coalesce into a profound loss of personal identity, a sense of seeping containment and for many a 'vast collectivity of boredom' (Ferrell, 2004a: 287, 2010).

Into this void of meaning and emotion flows the experience of edgework. As conceptualized by Stephen Lyng (1990, 2005) and others (Ferrell et al., 2001; Lyng and Ferrell, 2016), edgework at its simplest denotes acts of voluntary and often illicit risk-taking – activities such as street racing, sky diving, BASE jumping and graffiti writing. But beyond this, edgework is conceptualized as a distinct response to the accumulating degradations of late modernity. Voluntary engagement in high-risk activities reverses the logic of contemporary risk management, instead embracing risk for its sensual pleasures and transgressive possibilities. Through the risks of edgework participants in turn regain some sense of identity, one developed from vivid emotions and radical self-determination; in moments of extreme risk to self and survival, emotions and self-perception escape their late modern containment within service economies and bureaucratic categories. Significantly, though, edgework is not only grounded in risk; it is as much so grounded in skill. Ongoing participation in extreme risk requires the sorts of long-practised, specialized skills necessary to survive it; such skills in turn allow for the pursuit of ever riskier activities over time. In this sense edgework not only spirals its participants towards the outer edges of human possibility; it also shapes the very sorts of self-made skills and skill-based identities that have been erased from many occupations within late modern economies.

As this edgework model has been increasingly employed in cultural criminological research over the past quarter-century, still other links to crime, crime control and identity have surfaced. Much of the early cultural criminological research into *criminal* edgework was oriented around physically dangerous, street-level activities that often embodied prototypically masculine dynamics – street robbery (de Haan and Vos, 2003), graffiti (Ferrell, 1996), fire setting (Presdee, 2005), organized brawling (Jackson-Jacobs, 2004), etc. Subsequent research, however, has expanded this research so as to account for a wider range of gender dynamics, gender identities and gendered emotions in edgework, and to explore forms of edgework distinctive to women and their lives under late modernity. Here research ranges from the edgework activities of female street hustlers (Miller, 1991) and poor, drug-using women in abusive intimate relationships (Rajah, 2007) to the gendered emotional strategies of mountain rescue teams (Lois, 2005) and the mix of risk and skill that shapes anorexic practices (Gailey, 2009) and female body-building (Worthen and Baker, 2016). Subsequent ethnographic research has also revealed a particularly intractable dilemma for those agents of control who mistake edgework for senseless self-destruction, or who seek to prevent it by policing its ongoing occurrence. Given edgework's essential role in filling the vacuums of identity and emotion created by late modern social conditions, its participants are loath to abandon it, even under policing pressure. Perhaps more to the point, this pressure creates yet another layer of risk, and with it the impetus for the development of further skills – and thus becomes for edgeworkers less a legal deterrent than a further inducement (Ferrell, 1996; Garrett, 2014).[2]

Cultural criminology's focus on the situated ephemerality of crime's seductions, and the immediacies of risk and skill that animate edgework, have in turn led to a reimagining of methodology. Cultural criminology has long been associated with long-term ethnographic inquiry, and more broadly with an ethnographic sensibility attuned to meaning, symbolism and shared emotion (Ferrell and Hamm, 1998). More recently, however, cultural criminologists have also developed the notion of 'instant ethnography' (Ferrell et al., 2015) – that is, ethnographic exploration of the immediate, ephemeral social and cultural dynamics that emerge within moments of crime and crime control. In the same way that existing theories of deterministic criminal causality must be recalibrated to a late modern world of flux and uncertainty, the thinking goes, so must models of ethnographic research that have traditionally emphasized sustained research into stable groups and static situations. As in the realm of theory, the intent is not to abandon such research traditions, but rather to augment their value by realigning them with the uncertainty of contemporary conditions. In these ways a cultural criminology of and for late modernity denotes not only an updating of criminology's subject matter, but a reinvention of criminology as a field of inquiry and understanding.

The pervasiveness of power, control and resistance

As a critical perspective on crime and justice, cultural criminology concerns itself not only with emerging forms of crime and transgression in late modernity, but with evolving patterns of late modern power, control and surveillance. Invoking once again the dialectics of the sociological and criminological imagination, cultural criminologists interrogate the smallest of everyday moments for the secrets of social control that they harbour, while also investigating the largest of global conflicts by way of the ideologies, emotions and socio-cultural dynamics that animate them.

A large body of cultural criminological work explores forms of low-order, everyday criminality like loitering, graffiti writing, shoplifting, busking and scavenging, while also documenting the legal responses and public controversies that surround such criminality (Ferrell, 1996, 2001, 2006; Presdee, 2009; Ilan, 2011). Critics of cultural criminology have at times argued that this focus ignores the larger political economy of crime, and fails to address more serious forms of criminality (see e.g. O'Brien, 2005; Tierney, 2010: 357–358). Cultural criminologists respond to this now rather clichéd critique in two ways. First, developing the insights of labelling theory, they argue that the 'importance' or 'seriousness' of any form of criminality is largely determined by the legal response to it, and by the ability of those in power to encase it in particular cultural meanings and public interpretations. As cultural criminological research shows, campaigns of aggressive enforcement or political outrage often transform inconsequential transgressions into first-order offences, both in the eyes of the law and in the mind of the public. Equally, power and control flow in the other direction; activities that might otherwise be considered dangerously consequential can be hidden behind ideological constructs that define them as legal, harmless or necessary (Jenkins, 1999; Ferrell, 2004b). For cultural criminologists, then, the cultural construction of crime remains always at issue – and in consequence, the criminality of the everyday merits as much critical attention as does the criminality of the exceptional (see e.g. Redmon, 2015; Ilan, 2015).

Second, cultural criminologists emphasize a particular understanding of late modern power in their explorations of everyday criminality and control. In a late modern world awash in mediated communication, surveillance technology and identity politics, they suggest, power is less likely to operate as a blunt instrument of physical violence than it is to circulate insidiously, encoded in spatial arrangements, hidden behind ideologies of risk management and public safety, and deployed via mythologies of daily comfort and convenience (Raymen, 2016). In this sense social control is most potent, and most dangerously problematic, precisely to the extent that it comes to be hidden away in the little domains of everyday life – in the credit card and the corporate database, the sidewalk and the shop window, the closed circuit television (CCTV) camera and the school counsellor (Ferrell et al., 2015: 87–123). Here lies the hegemonic, or at least the late modern tendency towards hegemonic control: forms of social and legal control, unnoticed and meant to be unnoticed, that operate in ways that come to seem natural if not inevitable (Hayward, 2012). And yet, as cultural criminologists have also documented, the denizens of everyday life sometimes *do* notice, and do resist – and when they do, their seemingly 'small' battles over a park wall or an urban advert therefore also invoke larger issues of power, control and social justice (Ferrell, 1996, 2001).

This analytic approach requires close attention to the micro-circuitry of surveillance and control; it also necessitates locating this micro-circuitry within the larger trajectories of late modernity. Over the past few decades, for example, global cities have developed increasingly aggressive approaches to the everyday policing of the homeless and other dislocated populations; encased in ideologies of public safety and public civility, and buttressed by the conservative pseudo-criminology of the 'broken windows' model, these approaches range from the installation of anti-homeless sprinkler systems and the ongoing police dispersal of public gatherings to the privatization of public space and the criminalization of those feeding homeless and migrant populations. Yet, importantly, these strategies constitute something more than simple mean-spiritedness; they are strategies for policing the crisis (Hall et al., 2013) of late modernity. Late modern cities rely on the economic engine of 'consumption-driven urban development', where the city is reconstructed as an image of itself and sold to the privileged as a constellation of lifestyle preferences, designer properties and retail experiences. In such environments, homeless and migrant populations come to be defined, and policed, as issues of image, as threats to the city's carefully crafted aesthetic, to be excluded lest they intrude on the city's consumerist economy. Moreover, the vast economic inequalities of late modernity, and the predations of its retail and service industries, produce profound precariousness for more and more people, who are left to drift between occupation, abode and country (Ferrell, 2018). The injustice is in the irony: the rampant inequality of late modern political economies engenders the very sort of drifting dislocation on which much contemporary law-making and everyday policing focus (Ferrell, 2012a).

In recent years cultural criminologists have also developed a keen interest in the many harms caused by the state – harms that extend beyond the everyday and into the realm of global conflict – from genocide to state terrorism, imperialism to militarized policing. Within cultural criminology there is now a considerable body of work on both state crime (e.g. Morrison, 2006, 2010; Hamm, 2007; Cunneen, 2010; Klein, 2011; Burrows, 2013; Linnemann et al., 2014; Wall and Linnemann, 2014a) and on various agents of state control (e.g. Kraska, 1998; Morrison, 2004; Ferrell, 2004b; Wender, 2004, 2008; Root et al., 2013; Aiello, 2014; Wall and Linnemann, 2014b; Linnemann, 2017). In undertaking this work, cultural criminologists have in turn developed a theoretical position that differs from previous criminological work in the area of state crime and state control. Instead of limiting their analysis to international humanitarian law, the perspective of 'social harm' or the socio-historical contingencies that constitute state power, cultural criminology looks to draw together the macro-influence of structure (in the form of governance and ideology) with more mid-level theories of subculture and 'learnt transgression' – a combination that also allows for an analysis of how state crimes and mass killings can be 'neutralized' by both the state and by the collective forces involved in human rights violations (e.g. Hamm, 2007; Linnemann et al., 2014).

As always, though, no cultural criminological analysis would be complete without the third element on which cultural criminology was founded: a micro-level understanding of the experiential and phenomenological dynamics that compel one actor to engage in transgressive violence and another in the same socio-cultural setting to desist. Here, cultural criminology draws on the small, subterranean literature in sociology and military history that powerfully illuminates the sensations and emotions associated with war and combat (see Cottee and Hayward, 2011 and Cottee, 2011, for useful cultural criminological introductions). Consider, for example, the following quote from Sebastian Junger's (2010) brilliant micro-sociological study of combat, in which he attempts to explain the allure of firefights for US infantrymen serving in Afghanistan:

> War is a lot of things and it's useless to pretend that exciting isn't one of them. It's insanely exciting. The machinery of war and the sound it makes and the urgency of its use and the consequences of almost everything about it are the most exciting things anyone engaged in war will ever know. Soldiers discuss that fact with each other and eventually with their chaplains and their shrinks and maybe even their spouses, but the public will never hear about it. It's just not something that many people want acknowledged. War is supposed to feel bad because undeniably bad things happen in it, but for a nineteen-year-old at the working end of a .50 cal during a firefight that everyone

comes out of okay, war is life multiplied by some number that no one has ever heard of. In some ways twenty minutes of combat is more life than you could scrape together in a lifetime of doing something else.

(Junger, 2010: 144–145)

Here once again is the sensual immediacy and emotional seduction of violent transgression – not on the city streets or in the bedroom, but flowering amidst the vagaries of geo-political conflict.

This multi-level approach is equally useful for understanding the actions of those who seek to confront or destabilize the state, whether via counter-insurgency operations or terrorist campaigns. For cultural criminologists the goal, as the terrorist scholar Martha Crenshaw famously put it, is to create approaches that synthesize structural factors with an analysis of group dynamics, ideological influences, individual incentives and personal motivations (Gunning, 2009: 166). Such approaches must also be interdisciplinary – because this really is the only way to ensure a truly comprehensive understanding of how macro-, meso- and micro-dynamics intertwine. So, for example, when we look at the econometric data on the structural poverty that produces Palestinian support for Hamas's Izz ad-Din al-Qassam military brigades, we must also apply visual methods to analyse how martyr posters and billboards on the streets of Gaza reproduce and cultivate a bizarre culture of street-level celebrity that aggrandizes suicide bombing and other forms of *istishhad*. Likewise, while we must pose broad geo-political questions – such as whether Iraq and other Middle Eastern countries would have been the subject of so many US-backed interventions if their primary export were not oil but avocados (Stokes, 2009) – we must not end our analyses of state crime there. Instead, we must embark on further anthropologically and situationally attuned forms of research into local and micro-level dynamics, such as the particular techniques employed by occupying forces when patrolling unfamiliar neighbourhoods and gathering intelligence, or, for that matter, the pre-existing religious/sectarian schisms that may constitute the on-the-ground spatial reality of those neighbourhoods in the first place (Kilcullen, 2009).[3] Such a multi-dimensional approach to the study of terrorism closely mirrors cultural criminology's broader approach to the study of criminality – one that conceptualizes certain transgressive behaviours as attempts to resolve internal psychic/individual conflicts spawned by the wider environmental or structural conditions associated with late modernity (Young, 2003; Hayward, 2004: chapter 5).

Today's world of international conflict is fast changing and complex, wracked by such problems as the unfettered development of private military power (Balko, 2014) and the dangerous revival of interest in orthodox religious doctrines that run against late modernity's plurality of perspectives and experiences. As such, it becomes all the more important to develop a criminology capable of understanding the social havoc that such developments cause. In doing so, cultural criminologists argue, we must always remain vigilant when critiquing the processes by which war crimes are defined and constructed, and state power is attained and enforced. But equally we must guard against the tendency to focus only on the existing power structures and socio-historical contingencies that constitute state power, lest our analyses become blunt or one-dimensional. On the contrary, the cultural criminological approach to studying power is avowedly multi-dimensional: an ongoing process of intellectual cross-fertilization in which each dimension incorporates something of the other, informs the other's development and so becomes more than any one could be singly.

As Jock Young (2007) has noted, many of the contemporary world's crimes and social controls can be understood as fundamentalist responses to late modernity's hyper-pluralism and ontological uncertainty. The spatial policing of homeless populations, the bombing of abortion clinics and the terrorism of jihadi militants are decidedly different phenomena – yet each targets an essentialized other. Just as contemporary policing attempts to map and manage the inevitable dislocations and risks of late modernity, violent fundamentalists of all stripes undertake to put the exploding plurality of the late modern world back in the box of cultural certainty. From the unnoticed indignities enforced on the homeless drifter and the undocumented migrant, to the most high-profile of terrorist attacks or Middle Eastern military engagements, the cultural contours of contemporary power and control are always in play. And in this way, the question is not whether cultural criminology will focus on the details of everyday existence, or instead document the broad sweep of economic and political power; the question is how to discover one in the other, how to find and follow the avenues by which structures shape social relations and how this in turn affects the way we see and make sense of the world (Ferrell, 2012b).

The spiralling energy of image and representation

A ubiquitous feature of late modern life is the contemporary 'mediascape', that constellation of media that manufactures information and disseminates images via an expanding array of digital technologies. In this ever-evolving sphere an extraordinary inversion has occurred. Today, as a result of the pervasiveness of digital media, images of crime and its control are becoming almost as 'real' as crime and criminal justice itself – if by 'real' we denote those dimensions of late modern life that produce consequences; shape popular attitudes and public policies; manufacture the effects of crime and criminal justice; generate fear, avoidance and pleasure; and affect the lives of those who are involved or ignored. This is a late modern world where, as cultural criminologists have commented, 'the screen scripts the street and the street scripts the screen' (Hayward and Young, 2004: 259), where the line between the real and the virtual (de Jong and Schuilenburg, 2006), the factual and the fictional, becomes ever more blurred, if not entirely lost. In this world perpetrators and witnesses post images of crime and violence to YouTube and Instagram; politicians formulate criminal justice policy to ensure that it will 'play in the media'; attorneys take acting lessons and repackage evidence so as to sway juries steeped in television crime dramas; and advertisers and marketers utilize images of crime and transgression to sell everything from energy drinks to family cars (Muzzatti, 2010; Ferrell et al., 2015).

Some would argue that this is nothing new – that for over a century, the 'story of crime' has been promulgated and interpreted through various forms of media – and that criminology's long interest in the crime–media relationship has produced important theoretical and methodological orientations towards crime's popular representation. For cultural criminologists, though, the extant scholarship on the crime–media nexus, although useful, offers only a relatively formulaic and dated reading of crime's current relationship with media. Clearly, established approaches such as 'content analysis', 'effects research' and 'media production observation' have a place within cultural criminology, given cultural criminology's concern for understanding mediated representations of crime, their effects within individual and collective behaviour and their connections to power, domination and injustice. Yet none of these approaches are sufficient for untangling the complex, non-linear relationships that now exist between crime and the media in a late modern world saturated with global satellite television, independent news blogs, cell phone cameras, social networks and duelling websites. What is required now are new modes of analysis that utilize aspects of existing approaches while moving beyond now outdated dualisms: too much or too little media content regarding crime, effects or no effects of violent imagery, media coverage of crime that is democratic or elitist. Consequently, cultural criminologists seek to intellectually reorient and radically repoliticize the study of crime and the media by exploring the circulating fluidities of meaning through which the crime–media dynamic 'socializes and directs our thinking and actions in a range of hierarchical, complex, nuanced, insidious, gratifying, pleasurable and largely imperceptible ways' (Carter and Weaver, 2003: 167).

For cultural criminologists, then, established media approaches that constitute the criminological canon demand radical reinvention, not simple regurgitation (see Hall, 2012). As a start, cultural criminology's more holistic approach to tracing the flow of meaning in a world suffused with images of crime and violence emphasizes, in place of cause-and-effect linearity, the looping and spiralling dynamics of crime and media – that is, the way in which various images of crime and justice play off and reproduce one another, while at the same time seeping out into the courtroom and the street (Ferrell et al., 2015). In addition, cultural criminologists highlight the *affective processes* of crime's representation, showing how visceral crime images affect us not just in terms of policy or criminal justice practice, but bodily and sensually (Young, 2004, 2010). And overall, cultural criminologists move beyond older notions of 'the media' to explore the multiplicity of representational forms entangled with crime and justice, from the reconstitution of reality in rap music (de Jong and Schuilenburg, 2006) to representations of crime and power in comic books (Phillips and Strobl, 2013).

Amidst this wide-ranging work on crime, media and representation, cultural criminologists are in turn increasingly interested in the 'will to representation' (Yar, 2012). This notion asserts that those interested in studying the relationship between crime and the media must now move beyond the idea of the public as a passive internalizer of mass communication, and recognize instead that large numbers of 'ordinary people' are now primary producers of self-generated mediated representations. Thanks to social networking, handheld cameras, 'webcams', blogs, vlogs and other new media forms, today's subject 'no longer interprets or attends to representations produced elsewhere, but becomes her- or himself the source of those representations' (Yar, 2012: 248). Thus we are confronted with the spectacle of individuals and groups staging, performing, recording, sharing and publishing their acts of deviance – everything from schoolyard bullying to moments of rioting, even terrorism. In itself, this is not entirely new, but what is interesting is the notion that this intersection of user-generated content with the desire of individuals to mediate themselves through self-representation might *itself be a motivating factor for offending behaviour.*

This kind of 'will to communicate' or 'will-to-representation' may be seen in itself as a new kind of causal inducement to law- and rule-breaking behaviour. It may be that, in the new media age, the terms of criminological questioning need to be sometimes reversed: instead of asking whether 'media' instigates crime or fear of crime, we must ask how the very possibility of mediating oneself to an audience through self-representation might be bound up with the genesis of criminal behaviour (Yar, 2012: 246).

The will-to-representation, then, becomes crucial for understanding a late modern world where individuals 'desire to be seen, and esteemed or celebrated, by others for their criminal activities' (Yar, 2012: 252). Consequently, we now increasingly witness the criminogenic phenomenon of deviant and criminal acts being engineered or instigated specifically to be recorded and later shared via social networks and other Internet platforms. Spree killers like Seung-Hui Cho (VirginiaTech shooting, 2007) and Elliot Rodger (University of California, Santa Barbara shooting, 2014), for example, record ex-ante video confessions or post lengthy online 'manifestos' explaining their motivation. Rodger, who had a history of posting videos about himself online and was acutely aware of the importance of managing his mediated self-image after his suicide, even went as far as to create a series of bizarrely compelling video blogs in which he filmed himself sitting in his car or by the side of the road, calmly discussing his hatred of ethnic minorities and interracial couples, his frustration at not being able to find a girlfriend, and his virginity. While these videos bear witness to Elliot Rodger's abject narcissism, they also illustrate something else – a knowing awareness of his non-degradable digital 'presence', his *eternal mediated being*. In other words, they testify to his will-to-represent, both before and after his own physical death.

High-profile, media-savvy mass shooters are clear illustrations of the will-to-representation, but there are countless other cases where violent crimes are not just being committed but rather *enacted* for the camera. In the world of the Black US street gang, for example, the term 'driller' – a name given to gangbangers who stir up trouble on Facebook, Twitter and Instagram – is now more common than old school gang labels like 'OG' (Original Gangster). The use of the Internet as a means to start 'beef', enhance 'rep' and 'call out' other cliques is now so common that a video of a gang member 'drilling' a cross-town rival uploaded to YouTube or Instagram in the morning can result in a related shooting later that same day (Austen, 2013). But in a global world suffused by the tension between late modern hyper-pluralism and fundamentalist essentialism, perhaps the most interesting form of the will-to-representation is found among today's Islamic terrorists and insurgents. It is indeed an irony, given the anti-Western, anti-modern sentiments associated with radical Islamist politics, that supporters of the medieval Caliphate have become so adept at using new modes of digital communication to disseminate their deplorable message. Whether it is the staggered release of barbaric but carefully choreographed beheading videos, or the more subtle propaganda of blog and vlog posts uploaded by European Muslims documenting their lives in Syria as a way of enticing others to join them, it is clear that today's jihad in the Levant and elsewhere relies heavily on the very mediated spectacle and will-to-representation that it otherwise condemns.

To think critically about 'crime and the media' – to move past simple measures of media content or media effects, and on to a holistic sense of loops and spirals, of fluidity and saturation – is not only to understand the dynamics of crime and transgression in late modernity, but to open new avenues of intellectual inquiry appropriate to these confounded circumstances. In this context cultural criminology endeavours to develop new criminological models and criminological critiques that can converse with late modern culture at large, and that can account for the complex cultural interplay of crime, crime control and representation. 'Instant' and 'liquid' ethnographic approaches can attune researchers to the swirling, looping dynamics of the contemporary mediascape, and to the affective immediacy of its impact. Forms of visual ethnography and visual criminology can likewise trace the image-driven contours of the contemporary society, and can capture a late modern world where crime and crime control are increasingly inseparable from the politics of representation (Brown and Carrabine, 2017; Ferrell et al., 2015; Hayward and Presdee, 2010).

To be continued ...

Synthesizing long-standing North American and British criminological traditions, integrating into this synthesis newer perspectives from a host of affiliated fields, cultural criminology has from the first attempted to construct a 'loose canon' (Ferrell, 2010) for critical inquiry into the intersections of crime, crime control, representation and meaning. While retaining its roots in critical and cultural analysis, cultural criminology is in this way meant to remain open and invitational, an animated alternative to the reductionist orthodoxies of positivist criminology. It is also meant to be supple – meant, that is, to move with the emerging dynamics of crime and crime control in late modernity. To date, this orientation has produced inquiry into immediacy and emotion, into contemporary forms of social and cultural control and into the spiralling dynamics of crime and representation. These inquiries are themselves now part of the cultural criminological canon, but they are not the closure of it. Instead, as new intersections of crime and culture emerge from the inequities of late modernity, cultural criminology remains to be continued.

Notes

1   For general introductions to cultural criminology, see Ferrell, Hayward and Young (2015) and Hayward and Young (2012).
2   It is important to stress that cultural criminology's interest in the emotions and subjectivities associated with crime and transgression is not limited solely to edgy or risk-laden activities – far from it. Cultural criminologists have expended considerable effort outlining an alternative, diverse range of emotions that are the very antithesis of risk and thrill. Mike Presdee (2004: 45), for example, cared little for risk or excitement, and largely dealt instead with emotions such as 'loss', 'humiliation', 'resentment' and the concerns associated with 'the hidden injuries of class', the 'sheer sense of survival' and 'the personal intricacies of everyday life'. On one occasion he even devoted an entire paper to the subject of 'loneliness' (Presdee, 2006). Likewise, Jonathan Wender (2004), a former beat-cop-turned-cultural criminologist, drew on his field experience to document how domestic violence is rendered bureaucratic and emotionally neutral by the strictures of police procedure. Indeed, whether it is David Brotherton's (Brotherton and Barrios, 2011) accounts of the perfunctory, emotionless justice meted out to Central American deportees by the NYC court system, Kevin Steinmetz's (2015) research on the boredom and frustration experienced by computer hackers or Carl Root's (Root et al., 2013) personal examination of the feelings of shame experienced after being a victim of unjustified police violence, cultural criminologists have shown time and again their analytic interest in a range of late modern emotions.
3   When developing a cultural criminology of war or terrorism it is essential that one does not automatically collapse religion into politics. Instead, religion must be recognized as a powerful shaping force in and of itself. Cultural criminology is uniquely attuned to capture the potent appeal and allure of religious or 'theistic violence' and the promise of transcendental bliss and heroic validation it offers (see Cottee, 2014).

References

Aiello, M. F. (2014). 'Policing the masculine frontier: Cultural criminological analysis of the gendered performance of policing', *Crime, Media, Culture*, 10(1): 59–79.
Appadurai, A. (1996). *Modernity at Large*, Minneapolis: University of Minnesota Press.
Austen, B. (2013). 'Public enemies: Social media is fueling gang wars in Chicago', 17 September. Available at www.wired.com/2013/09/gangs-of-social-media/all/.

Balko, R. (2014). *Rise of the Warrior Cop*, New York: Public Affairs.

Braverman, Harry. (1974). *Labor and Monopoly Capital*, New York: Monthly Review.

Brotherton, David and Barrios, Luis. (2011). *Banished to the Homeland: Dominican Deportees and Their Stories of Exile*, New York: Columbia University Press.

Brown, Michelle and Carrabine, Eamonn, eds. (2017). *The Routledge International Handbook of Visual Criminology*, London: Routledge.

Burrows, Dan. (2013). 'Framing the Iraq War', PhD thesis, University of Kent.

Carter, C. and Weaver, C. (2003). *Violence and the Media*, Buckingham: Open University Press.

Cottee, Simon. (2011). 'Fear, boredom and joy: Sebastian Junger's piercing phenomenology of war', *Studies in Conflict and Terrorism*, 34: 439–459.

Cottee, Simon. (2014). 'We need to talk about Mohammad: Criminology, theistic violence and the murder of Theo van Gogh', *British Journal of Criminology*, 54(6): 981–1001.

Cottee, Simon and Hayward, Keith J. (2011). 'Terrorist (e)motives: The existential attractions of terrorism', *Studies in Conflict and Terrorism*, 34(12): 963–986.

Cunneen, Chris. (2010). 'Framing the crimes of colonialism', in Keith Hayward and Mike Presdee (eds) *Framing Crime*, London: Routledge.

de Haan, W. and Vos, J. (2003). 'A crying shame: The over-rationalized conception of man in the rational choice perspective', *Theoretical Criminology*, 7(1): 29–54.

de Jong, Alex and Schuilenburg, Marc. (2006). *Mediaopolis*, Rotterdam: 010 Publishers.

Ferrell, Jeff. (1992). 'Making sense of crime', *Social Justice*, 19(2): 110–123.

Ferrell, Jeff. (1996). *Crimes of Style*, Boston: Northeastern University Press.

Ferrell, Jeff. (1997). 'Criminological verstehen: Inside the immediacy of crime', *Justice Quarterly*, 14(1): 3–23.

Ferrell, Jeff. (1999). 'Cultural criminology', *Annual Review of Sociology*, 25: 395–418.

Ferrell, Jeff. (2001). *Tearing Down the Streets*, New York: Palgrave.

Ferrell, Jeff. (2004a). 'Boredom, crime and criminology', *Theoretical Criminology*, 8(3): 287–302. Translated/reprinted (2010) in *Revista Brasileira de Ciencias Criminais*, 81/82(Spring).

Ferrell, Jeff. (2004b). 'Speed kills', in Jeff Ferrell, Keith Hayward, Wayne Morrison and Mike Presdee (eds) *Cultural Criminology Unleashed*, London: GlassHouse.

Ferrell, Jeff. (2006). *Empire of Scrounge*, New York: New York University Press.

Ferrell, Jeff. (2010). 'Cultural criminology: The loose can[n]on', in Eugene McLaughlin and Tim Newburn (eds) *The SAGE Handbook of Criminological Theory*, London: Sage.

Ferrell, Jeff. (2012a). 'Outline of a criminology of drift', in Steve Hall and Simon Winlow (eds) *New Directions in Criminological Theory*, London: Routledge/Willan.

Ferrell, Jeff. (2012b). 'Cultural criminology: Crime, meaning, and power'/'Criminologia Cultural: Crime, Significado e Poder', *Revista Brasileira de Ciencias Criminais*, 99(November–December): 173–185.

Ferrell, Jeff. (2018). *Drift: Illicit Mobility and Uncertain Knowledge*, Berkeley, CA: University of California Press.

Ferrell, Jeff and Hamm, Mark S. eds. (1998). *Ethnography at the Edge*, Boston: Northeastern.

Ferrell, Jeff and Sanders, Clinton eds. (1995). *Cultural Criminology*, Boston: Northeastern University Press.

Ferrell, Jeff, Hayward, Keith and Young, Jock. (2015). *Cultural Criminology: An Invitation*, 2nd edn, London: Sage.

Ferrell, Jeff, Milovanovic, Dragan and Lyng, Stephen. (2001). 'Edgework, media practices, and the elongation of meaning', *Theoretical Criminology*, 5(2): 177–202.

Gailey, Jeannine. (2009). 'Starving is the most fun a girl can have', *Critical Criminology*, 17: 93–108.

Garot, Robert. (2010). *Who You Claim*, New York: New York University Press.

Garrett, Bradley L. (2014) *Explore Everything: Place-Hacking the City*, London: Verso.

Gunning, J. (2009). 'Social movement theory and the study of terrorism', in R. Jackson, M. Breen-Smyth and J. Gunning (eds) *Critical Terrorism Studies*, Abingdon: Routledge.

Hall, Steve. (2012). *Theorizing Crime and Deviance*, London: Sage.

Hall, Stuart, Critcher, Chas, Jefferson, Tony, Clarke, John and Roberts, Brian. (2013). *Policing the Crisis, 35th Anniversary Edition*, London: Palgrave Macmillan.

Hamm, Mark. (2007). 'High crimes and misdemeanours: George W. Bush and the sins of Abu Ghraib', *Crime, Media, Culture*, 3(3): 259–284.

Hayward, Keith J. (2002). 'The vilification and pleasures of youthful transgression', in J. Muncie, G. Hughes and E. McLaughlin (eds) *Youth Justice*, London: Open University Press.

Hayward, Keith J. (2004). *City Limits: Crime, Consumer Culture and the Urban Experience*, London: GlassHouse.

Hayward, Keith J. (2007). 'Situational crime prevention and its discontents: Rational choice theory versus the "culture of now"', *Social Policy and Administration*, 41(3): 232–250.

Hayward, Keith J. (2012). 'Five spaces of cultural criminology', *British Journal of Criminology*, 52(3): 441–462.

Hayward, Keith J. (2016). 'Cultural criminology: Script rewrites', *Theoretical Criminology*, 20(3): 297–321.

Hayward, Keith J. and Presdee, Mike. (2010). *Framing Crime: Cultural Criminology and the Image*, London: GlassHouse.

Hayward, Keith J. and Young, Jock. (2004). 'Cultural criminology: Some notes on the script', *Theoretical Criminology*, 8(4): 259–273.

Hayward, Keith J. and Young, Jock. (2012). 'Cultural criminology', in M. Maguire, R. Morgan and R. Reiner (eds) *The Oxford Handbook of Criminology*, Oxford: Oxford University Press.

Ilan, Jonathan. (2011). 'Reclaiming respectability? The cross-cultural dynamics of crime, community and governance in inner-city Dublin', *Urban Studies*, 48: 1137–1155.

Ilan, Jonathan. (2015). *Understanding Street Culture*, Basingstoke: Palgrave-Macmillan.

Jackson-Jacobs, C. (2004). 'Taking a beating: The narrative gratifications of fighting as an underdog', in Jeff Ferrell, Keith Hayward, Wayne Morrison and Mike Presdee (eds) *Cultural Criminology Unleashed*, London: Cavendish.

Jenkins, Phillip. (1999). 'Fighting terrorism as if women mattered', in Jeff Ferrell and Neil Websdale (eds) *Making Trouble*, New York: Aldine.

Junger, Sebastian. (2010). *War*, London: Fourth Estate.

Katz, Jack. (1988). *Seductions of Crime*, New York: Basic Books.

Kilcullen, David. (2009). *The Accidental Guerrilla*, London: Hurst.

Klein, Joshua. (2011). 'Toward a cultural criminology of war', *Social Justice*, 38(3): 86–103.

Kraska, Peter. (1998). 'Enjoying militarism: Political/personal dilemmas in studying U.S. police paramilitary units', in Jeff Ferrell and Mark Hamm (eds) *Ethnography at the Edge*, Boston, MA: Northeastern University Press.

Linnemann, Travis. (2017). 'Proof of death: Police power and the visual economies of seizure, accumulation and trophy', *Theoretical Criminology*, 21(1): 57–77.

Linnemann, Travis, Wall, Tyler and Green, Edward. (2014). 'The walking dead and the killing state: Zombification and the normalization of police violence', *Theoretical Criminology*, 18(4): 506–527.

Lois, Jennifer. (2005). 'Gender and emotion management in the stages of edgework', in Stephen Lyng (ed.) *Edgework: The Sociology of Risk-Taking*, New York: Routledge.

Lyng, Stephen. (1990). 'Edgework', *American Journal of Sociology*, 95(4): 851–886.

Lyng, Stephen, ed. (2005). *Edgework*, New York: Routledge.

Lyng, Stephen and Ferrell, Jeff. (2016). 'In conversation: Stephen Lyng and Jeff Ferrell', *Kinfolk Magazine*.

Miller, Eleanor. (1991). 'Assessing the risk of inattention to class, race/ethnicity and gender', *American Journal of Sociology*, 96: 1530–1534.

Mills, C. Wright. (1959). *The Sociological Imagination*, Oxford: Oxford University Press.

Morrison, Wayne. (2004). 'Reflections with memories: Everyday photography capturing genocide', *Theoretical Criminology*, 8(3): 341–358.

Morrison, Wayne. (2006). *Criminology, Civilization and the New World Order*, London: GlassHouse.

Morrison, Wayne. (2010). 'A reflected gaze of humanity: Cultural criminology and images of genocide', in Keith Hayward and Mike Presdee (eds) *Framing Crime: Cultural Criminology and the Image*, London: Routledge.

Muzzatti, Steven. (2010). '"Drive it like you stole it": A cultural criminology of car commercials', in Keith Hayward and Mike Presdee (eds) *Framing Crime: Cultural Criminology and the Image*, London: GlassHouse.

O'Brien, Martin. (2005). 'What is cultural about cultural criminology?', *British Journal of Criminology*, 45(5): 599–612.

Phillips, Nicola and Strobl, Staci. (2013). *Comic Book Crime: Truth, Justice, and the American Way*, New York: NYU Press.

Presdee, Mike. (2000). *Cultural Criminology and the Carnival of Crime*, London: Routledge.

Presdee, Mike. (2004). 'The story of crime: Biography and the excavation of transgression', in Jeff Ferrell, Keith Hayward, Wayne Morrison and Mike Presdee (eds) *Cultural Criminology Unleashed*, London: Cavendish.

Presdee, M. (2005). 'Burning issues: Fire, carnival and crime', in Moira Peelo and Keith Soothill (eds) *Questioning Crime and Criminology*, Cullompton: Willan.

Presdee, Mike. (2006). *Only the lonely: Crime and the collective loneliness of contemporary society*. Paper presented at the 58th Annual Meeting of the American Society of Criminology, Los Angeles, 1–4 November.

Presdee, Mike. (2009). 'Volume crime and everyday life', in Chris Hale, Keith Hayward, Azrini Wahidin and Emma Wincup (eds) *Criminology*, Oxford: Oxford University Press.

Rajah, Valli. (2007). 'Resistance as edgework in violent intimate relationships of drug-involved women', *British Journal of Criminology*, 47: 196–213.

Raymen, Thomas. (2016). 'Designing-in crime by designing-out the social? Situational crime prevention and the intensification of harmful subjectivities', *British Journal of Criminology*, 56(3): 497–514.

Redmon, David. (2015). *Beads, Bodies, and Trash*, London: Routledge.

Root, Carl, Ferrell, Jeff and Palacious, Wilson. (2013). 'Brutal serendipity: Criminological verstehen and victimization', *Critical Criminology*, 21(2): 141–155.

Steinmetz, Kevin. (2015). 'Craft(y)ness: An ethnographic study of hacking', *British Journal of Criminology*, 55(1): 125–145.

Stokes, Doug. (2009). 'Ideas and avocados', *International Relations*, 23(1): 85–92.

Tierney, J. (2010). *Criminology*, Harlow: Pearson.

Wall, Tyler and Linnemann, Travis. (2014a). 'Accumulating atrocities: Capital, state killing and the cultural life of the dead', in Dawn Roethe and Dave Kauzlarich (eds) *Towards a Victimology of State Crime*, New York: Routledge.

Wall, Tyler and Linnemann, Travis. (2014b). 'Staring down the state: Police power, visual economies, and the "War on Cameras"', *Crime, Media, Culture*, 10(2): 133–149.

Weber, Max. (1978). *Economy and Society*, Berkeley, CA: University of California Press.

Wender, Jonathan. (2004). 'Phenomenology, cultural criminology and the return to astonishment', in Jeff Ferrell, Keith Hayward, Wayne Morrison and Mike Presdee (eds) *Cultural Criminology Unleashed*, London: Cavendish.

Wender, Jonathan. (2008). *Policing and the Politics of Everyday Life*, Champaign: University of Illinois Press.

Worthen, Meredith G. F. and S. Abby Baker. (2016). 'Pushing up on the glass ceiling of female muscularity: Women's bodybuilding as edgework', *Deviant Behavior*, 37(5): 471–495.

Yar, Majid. (2012). 'Crime, media and the will-to-representation', *Crime, Media, Culture*, 8(3): 245–260.

Young, Alison. (2004). *Judging the Image*, London: Routledge.

Young, Alison. (2010). 'The scene of the crime: Is there such a thing as just looking?', in Keith Hayward and Mike Presdee (eds) *Framing Crime: Cultural Criminology and the Image*, London: GlassHouse.

Young, Jock. (2003). 'Merton with energy, Katz with structure', *Theoretical Criminology*, 7(3): 389–414.

Young, Jock. (2007). *The Vertigo of Late Modernity*, London: Sage.

Young, Jock. (2011). *The Criminological Imagination*, Cambridge: Polity.

3

CRIMINOLOGIES OF THE MARKET

Elliott Currie

The central message of 'criminologies of the market' is that the fundamental principles of market capitalism contain powerful pressures toward crime. Societies that prioritize the pursuit of private gain to the eclipse of other values and aspirations are likely to be societies that generate an unusual amount of crime—not only 'ordinary' crime in the streets and in the home, but 'white collar' crimes as well. Crime, then, is one among many costs of the dominance of market values and institutions—part of the 'dark side' of a system that is often promoted as a beneficent and progressive engine of prosperity.

A focus on the deep and pervasive damage that unmitigated market forces can impose on communities, institutions, and individuals can help to explain the distribution of crime among societies and within them, as well as the trajectories of crime over time. It is a lens through which we can understand the persistence and sometimes growth of crime in the midst of unprecedented levels of affluence and technological capacity, and can make sense of what I have sometimes called the 'violence divide'—the radically unequal distribution of violent crime around the world (Currie 2015). It sheds light on why many societies today, including a majority of the most affluent industrial countries, have achieved relatively low levels of serious violence—and why others remain wracked by it, often in the face of enormous investments in punitive social control. The market's impact is not the only explanation for these differences, or for the specific patterns of crime in any given society: but it is a crucial part. By the same token, focusing on the market's destructive effects gives us an essential framework for social action and social policy—a framework that can both illuminate the limits of conventional approaches to crime control and point to more effective strategies for the future.

The issues raised by criminologies of the market are, accordingly, ones that carry special significance and urgency today. Around the world, a particularly extreme variety of market capitalism—what I have elsewhere called 'capitalism with the lid off' (Currie 2016)—has become increasingly dominant ideologically and increasingly ubiquitous in its impact. It has reshaped social and economic relationships and transformed established institutions both in the advanced societies and in the developing world. In the process, it is arguably undermining the essential conditions that have helped some societies achieve high levels of public safety, while exacerbating conditions in others—especially parts of the global South (Carrington, Hogg, and Sozzo 2016) and the United States—where violent crime has long been rampant. To an important degree, the future of crime around the world—as much else—will depend on our ability to understand and, ultimately, to challenge the adverse impact of a predatory global social order on community, culture, and personality.

Origins

There is not really a formal school of 'market' criminology, but rather a history of work from many different sources that, taken together, offers a fairly consistent set of key themes illuminating the connections between what I and others have called 'market society' and crime (see Currie 1997; Taylor 1999). It is a tradition that goes back a long way. A revulsion against the impact of nascent capitalism on traditional communal values is a running theme in literature and social criticism from the 16th century onward. It is eloquently conveyed in the Irish poet Oliver Goldsmith's famously plaintive lines from his poem 'The Deserted Village' (1770/1996):

> Ill fares the land, to hastening ills a prey,
> where wealth accumulates, and men decay.

Goldsmith was lamenting the destruction of traditional communal values in the face of the takeover of village lands by great wealth, and more generally the destructive impact of what he called the 'rage for gain,' which had permanently broken the social order of rural England and forced masses of people off the land and into lives of idleness, poverty, prostitution, and crime.

The devastating effects of a new social order grounded in the 'rage for gain' were more extensively described in the 1840s by Friedrich Engels in his remarkable *The Condition of the Working Class in England in 1844* (1845/1973), which stands as a foundational document in the evolution of theories of crime and market society. It is sometimes argued that Marx and Engels had little to say about crime, but that is belied by this extraordinary early example of compelling empirical social observation linked to an emerging theory of the dynamics of capitalist society. Engels' work was what might now be called a 'multi-method' research project, making use of a wealth of official reports and investigations along with assiduous field research conducted in the slums of Manchester, London, and other English cities. Its aim is to reveal the actual consequences of industrial capitalism on human lives—in the country where capitalism was most advanced and most celebrated.

And to Engels those consequences are both appalling and predictable. The overarching picture is one of a pervasive struggle for survival in what has become a chaotic and fundamentally uncaring social order:

> The social war, the war of all against all, is here openly declared … people regard each other only as useful objects, each exploits the other, and the end of it all is, that the stronger treads the weaker under foot, and that the powerful few, the capitalists, seize everything for themselves, while to the weak many, the poor, scarcely a bare existence remains.
>
> *(Engels 1845/1973, p. 64)*

Throughout the 'great towns' of England, he sees

> Everywhere barbarous indifference, hard egotism on one hand, and nameless misery on the other: everywhere social warfare, every man's house in a state of siege, everywhere reciprocal plundering under protection of the law, and all so shameless, so openly avowed, that one shrinks before the consequences of our social state as they manifest themselves here undisguised, and can only wonder that the whole crazy fabric still holds together.
>
> *(p. 64)*

For Engels, then, capitalism's booming heartland is not only a brutal, unequal, and depriving society: it is also a society suffused from top to bottom with a 'hard egotism' in which no one, least of all the powerful, *cares* much if at all that it is brutal and unequal. He charts in excruciating detail the dire consequences of the deprivation that capitalism inflicts on the poor: it is a poverty that kills. Writing well before anything resembling a 'safety net' had been established in industrial capitalist countries, Engels describes conditions in cities like London and Manchester that are truly horrific. But the consequences for the working class go beyond physical squalor and poverty. Equally significant, for Engels, is the *moral and psychological* degradation that this system inflicts on the poor. They are 'cast out and ignored by the class in power, morally as well as physically and mentally' (p. 153). The condition of the working class under capitalism is not only about deprivation: even more crucially, it is about exclusion and dehumanization. His language in describing that dehumanization is harsh, unsparing, and sometimes a little shocking: 'Like the dullest of the brutes,' he writes, members of the new urban–industrial proletariat are 'treated to but one form of education, the whip:' and 'there is, therefore, no cause for surprise if the workers, treated as brutes, actually become such' (p. 153).

If people are treated as less than fully human for long enough, they become in a very real sense less than fully human in their attitudes and behavior. That deep critique of the moral consequences of capitalist industrialization is central to the Marxian view of crime, and for Engels the links between that broader process of dehumanization and crime are complex and mutually reinforcing.

On the simplest level, poverty as extreme as what he witnessed in the squalid cities of industrial England can make some kinds of crime a practical necessity—often one of the only means of survival given the virtually complete absence of public or private social supports to blunt its impact:

> Want leaves the working man the choice between starving slowly, killing himself speedily, or taking what he needs where he finds it—in plain English, stealing. And there is no cause for surprise that most of them prefer stealing to starvation and suicide...
>
> *(p. 154)*

But the impact of 'want' is not only to make stealing a matter of potential survival, but also to weaken or destroy the social bonds that might otherwise keep the poor from solving the problem of 'want' through crime. Poverty at this level creates a deep alienation from society—an alienation exacerbated by the rise of money to the pinnacle of importance in capitalist society.

'Money,' Engels says, 'is the God of this world' (p. 154): not having any is the source of disconnection as well as deprivation:

> His whole position and environment involves the strongest temptation to immorality. He is poor, life offers him no charm, almost every enjoyment is denied him, the penalties of the law have no further terrors for him: why should he restrain his desires, why leave to the rich the enjoyment of his birthright, why not seize a part of it for himself? What inducement has the proletarian *not* to steal?
>
> *(p. 154, emphasis added)*

But even worse than poverty in terms of its effect on the moral state of the proletariat, according to Engels, is the fundamental *insecurity* of life under capitalism—insecurity for almost everyone, but most of all for the workers. Today, when 'free market' values have become far more thoroughly entrenched around the world, we tend to take for granted the idea that people will be vulnerable to violent and sudden shifts in jobs and living arrangements—and indeed to embrace that insecurity as part of the price we pay for having a 'dynamic' economy. But at the time Engels began writing, this idea of life as a sort of constant ongoing shuffle, a systematic chaos, a kind of game in which people's circumstances can change radically overnight, was a new and unwelcome idea for almost everyone except the people at the top who benefitted from it.

The rise of capitalism brought the destruction of traditional, mainly agrarian, ways of life that, if nothing else, often offered a degree of stability from year to year. Indeed, *without* destroying that way of life that tied people to the land, capitalism as we know it would never have gotten off the ground, because it needs workers to be 'freed' from these more stable local lives to migrate to the cities and the factories. Without that process there would be no proletariat, and thus no capitalism. But the result was to introduce a new level of routine uncertainty into the lives of working people. And that uncertainty, Engels argues, has very destructive effects on their personality—on their moral character. 'Far more demoralizing than his poverty in its influence upon the English working man,' Engels (p. 155) writes,

> is the insecurity of his position, the necessity of living upon wages from hand to mouth … The proletarian, who has nothing but his two hands, who consumes today what he earned yesterday, who is subject to every possible chance and has not the slightest guarantee for being able to earn the barest necessities of life, whom every crisis, every whim of his employer may deprive of bread, this proletarian is placed in the most revolting, inhuman position conceivable for a human being.
>
> The slave is assured of a bare livelihood by the self-interest of his master. The serf has at least a scrap of land on which to live. Each has at worst a guarantee for life itself. But the proletarian must depend upon himself alone, and is yet prevented from so applying his abilities as to be able to rely upon them.

So something new and very disturbing has happened. Capitalism has created a new class of people who do not *have* anything—or more precisely, they have only one thing—their capacity to work, their 'own two hands.' But at the same time they have no control over whether they actually work or not. Someone else—the employer—does. Thus they have no guarantee that they will even be able to keep themselves or their families minimally afloat from one day to the next. And in Engels' view this 'inhuman' condition has devastating human effects. Among other things, it destroys working people's motivation to plan for the future. They become radically 'present-oriented,' as a later language would describe it, because no matter how hard they may try to plan and persevere in life, they are constantly swimming upstream against a current much more powerful than they are:

> Everything that the proletarian can do to improve his position is but a drop in the ocean compared with the floods of varying chances to which he is exposed, over which he has not the slightest control. He is the *passive subject* of all possible combinations of circumstances, and thus must count himself fortunate when he has saved his life even for a short time; and his character and way of living are naturally shaped by these conditions.
>
> *(p. 154, emphasis added)*

There are a variety of possible responses to being tossed around by the 'floods of varying chances,' of which crime is only one. Some become full of rage at the system and the people who profit from it: they 'feel the inhumanity of their position' and 'refuse to be degraded to the level of brutes' (p. 157). They fight back. But others 'either bow humbly before the fate that overtakes them,' or they '*lose their moral hold* upon themselves as they have already lost the economic hold, live along from day to day, drink and fall into licentiousness; and in both cases they are brutes' (p. 157, emphasis added). Engels notes wryly that the bourgeoisie, the ruling class, is unsurprisingly 'horrified' by this behavior—but their revulsion is hypocritical, because it is they who have set in motion 'the causes which give rise to it' (p. 157).

'That they drink heavily,' says Engels (pp. 155–6), 'is to be expected,' for 'To accumulate lasting property for himself is impossible … What better thing can he do then when he gets high wages than live well upon them?' And when they are not drinking themselves into oblivion the workers are having careless sex:

> Next to intemperance in the enjoyment of intoxicating liquors, one of the principal faults of English working men is sexual license. But this too follows with relentless logic, with inevitable necessity, out of the position of a class left to itself, with no means of making fitting use of its freedom. The bourgeoisie has left the working class only these two pleasures, while imposing upon it a multitude of labors and hardships, and the consequence is that the working men in order to get *something* from life concentrate their whole energy upon these two enjoyments, carry them to excess, surrender to them in the most unbridled manner. When people are placed under conditions which appeal to the brute only, what remains to them but to rebel, or to succumb to utter brutality?
>
> *(pp. 166–7)*

In these passages, Engels expresses what appears on the surface as a strait-laced moralism about the behavior of working people—an attitude that appears in some of Marx's writings as well. They are not by any means *romanticizing* poverty or idealizing the proletariat as it is: they are appalled by what has become of them—or at least many of them. One of the reasons for their deep revulsion against capitalism is precisely that it forces this level of 'demoralization' on working people—that it not only deprives but degrades, profoundly inhibiting the full realization of human potential. The language can seem quaint today: but that insistence on the demoralizing character of capitalism is a key part of their indictment of it.

Engels sums up this attitude concisely in the *Condition of the Working Class in England in 1844*: 'The failings of the workers in general may be traced to … the general inability to sacrifice the pleasure of the moment to a remoter advantage' (p. 167). So far he could be a middle-class preacher railing against the moral decline of the working masses. But then he goes on to link that decline to its predictable structural sources:

> A class about whose education no one troubles himself, which is a play-ball to a thousand chances, knows no security in life—what incentives has such a class to providence, to 'respectability' … A class which bears all the disadvantages of the social order without enjoying its advantages, one to which the social system appears in purely hostile aspects—who can demand that such a class respect this social order? Verily, that is asking much!
>
> *(p. 167)*

It would be stretching things to say that Engels provided anything like a systematic theory of the relationship of capitalism to crime. But what he did offer was a consistent view that is distinctive from other perspectives at that time, even critical ones, and whose key themes remain central to more recent 'criminologies of the market.' Engels' view is holistic: it points to multiple, mutually reinforcing ways in which the brutal conditions of 19th-century capitalism create a corresponding 'brutality' or demoralization in many of the people subjected to them. On one level, capitalist society fosters material conditions that make some forms of crime utterly predictable techniques of survival, especially for the poorest of the poor. But, against the common idea that the early Marxian thinkers were simple economic determinists, Engels simultaneously emphasizes the inner transformations—the changes in consciousness—produced by a social order rooted in unfeeling individualism and dependent for its very existence on the exploitation of some people by others. The material deprivations that capitalism inevitably produces at the bottom are understood by its victims, at least dimly, as unjustly inflicted: the sense of being 'ripped off' for the benefit of others weakens or destroys the natural bonds of social solidarity that would otherwise restrain the deprived from simply taking what they need.

Beyond that, capitalism also works against the capacity of institutions to instill and enforce moral behavior. Both extreme poverty and the brutalizing character of work under industrial capitalism—its overwhelming monotony and its heedless exploitation of the labor of women and children—weaken the family as an agency of moral education. At the same time, the fundamental insecurity of livelihood that is for Engels the hallmark of industrial capitalism undercuts the link between prudent and moral behavior in the present and the expectation of a good life in the future—generating a careless and present-dominated orientation to the world in which nearly anything is possible. It is easy to see here elements of several theories that emerged much later as staples of academic criminology—including what would now be called 'strain,' 'control,' 'social disorganization,' and 'social learning' theories. But in Engels' work all of these elements are parts of a unified whole. They are not treated as competing theoretical explanations to be 'tested' against each other, but as complementary windows onto the accumulated effects of an entire social order—one that has been newly thrust on what is a new kind of person belonging to a new kind of social group. Crime is only one of many consequences—many 'costs,' to use language that capitalism itself inspired—of that social order: but it cannot be adequately understood outside of it.

A second key theme follows from this one: that crime is not an incidental or transient cost of capitalism, but a fundamental one. This distinguishes Engels' analysis from other critical perspectives linking crime to social ills like poverty, inequality, and joblessness. In Engels' view these are enduring and essential aspects of capitalism as a system. That does not necessarily mean that combatting crime must mean overturning the entire social order, but does imply that there are strong limits to what more piecemeal tactics can accomplish.

These themes were expanded and elaborated by the Dutch scholar and political activist Willem Adrian Bonger in the early 20th century, especially in his massive work *Criminality and Economic Conditions* (Bonger 1916/1967), arguably the first systematic analysis of crime grounded in a broadly Marxian framework. Like Engels, Bonger places the idea of 'demoralization' at the heart of his analysis, and argues that the demoralization exhibited by the ordinary criminal is both a consequence and a mirror of the larger demoralization that is the essence of modern capitalism. And also like Engels, Bonger's analysis is explicitly holistic. He is critical of earlier writers on the linkages between crime and economic conditions because they tended to look at one or another piece of the problem—economic fluctuations, for example, or poverty—rather than analyzing the impact on crime of what he called the 'present economic system'—that is, late 19th/early 20th-century capitalism—as a whole.

For Bonger, what is most distinctive about that system as a unique 'mode of production' is that economic activity is singularly devoted to the pursuit of profit. There have always been 'markets' in which people exchanged goods for their own use, but with the advent of modern capitalism, something more happens: for the first time in history, the entire socioeconomic order becomes oriented toward personal profit, and other social ends recede into the background. That momentous shift is intrinsically criminogenic, for several closely related reasons. Most importantly, the emergence of a society in which the exchange of goods and labor for profit has eclipsed other social ends means that human relations in general become characterized by a spirit of what Bonger (again following Engels) calls 'egoism.' Capitalism 'weakens the social instincts in man' and encourages the egoistic and individualistic potentials that are present in everyone to the point where they dominate social life. The society as a whole becomes suffused with the calculating orientations of the market, and the result is a general weakening of the social sentiments and bonds that could inhibit crime; 'a society based upon exchange isolates the individuals by weakening the bond that unites them' (1916/1967, p. 402).

But how that pervasive egoism manifests itself depends very much on where it appears in the class structure. For capitalism is not only a system of production for profit suffused by a particular value orientation but also a system whose essence is the division of society into those who own and control the means of production—and hence are in a position to make a profit—and those who own nothing but their ability to sell their labor power in the market. Bonger argues that at the top, among the bourgeoisie, egoism appears in a willingness to treat others as ends in the service of personal gain and to abandon any feelings of reciprocity toward other classes (among other things, that makes members of the bourgeoisie particularly prone to what we would now call white-collar crimes). But the bourgeoisie's material advantages—more stable families, access to better education, housing, and health care—mean that they are less likely to commit ordinary crimes or to wind up in prison.

For the proletariat, however, things are much different. Like Engels, Bonger suggests several related ways in which the essential conditions of the working class nurture capitalism's inherent tendency toward 'demoralization.' The fundamental reality of being compelled to survive by selling their labor power in a constantly shifting and precarious market creates a pervasive, existential economic insecurity. 'This, then, is what freedom of labor means,' Bonger wrote: 'a freedom that the slave never knows, freedom to die of hunger' (1916/1967, p. 271). And Bonger too links that fundamental insecurity with a tendency toward fatalism, short-term thinking, and an inability to plan. But the problem is not just the uncertainty of having work at all, but also the mindless and 'stupefying' character of work itself under capitalism. As Engels had argued more than half a century before, 'immoderate labor brutalizes a man,' 'coarsening' (Bonger 1916/1967, p. 420) the sensibilities, and making the abuse of alcohol more appealing.

Bonger devotes considerable attention to capitalism's impact on working-class families, noting that even beyond the effects of economic insecurity, poverty, and brutalizing work, the organization of labor under modern capitalism undermines families' capacity for socialization and nurturance. The massive recruitment of women into the industrial workforce, coupled with the absence of other community institutions—including good schools that might provide an alternative source of moral education—meant that working-class children, if they were not pressed into work themselves, were often left on their own, exposed to the demoralizing influence of the streets. Meanwhile, the crowding together of people of all ages and sexes in cramped housing conditions meant that children were exposed to adult sexuality to a degree that undermined their moral sense: and a toxic mix of poverty, inadequate wages for women, and general demoralization also caused prostitution to flourish.

But if capitalism tended, in multiple ways, to demoralize the proletariat, things were even worse for what Bonger called the 'lower' proletariat. Where people's well-being is dependent on their ability to sell their labor power, those who for one reason or another could not do so, or could do so only intermittently, would feel all of the adverse effects of poverty, insecurity, poor housing, and alcohol—only more so. The lower proletariat also lacked the saving grace of self-respect that the more stable working class often enjoyed. Those who work can, at least, see themselves as useful to society. Those who cannot come to define themselves—and to be defined by others—as essentially useless, which could only add to the pressures toward demoralization and criminality. Bonger emphasizes that the differences between the proletariat and the 'lower' proletariat are mainly a matter of degree—but the degree is important. The deeper level of insecurity and poverty and the absence of self-respect destroys solidarity and ultimately 'kills the social sentiments in man'—for 'he who is abandoned by all can no longer have any feeling for those who have left him to his fate' (1916/1967, p. 436).

As with Engels, Bonger's multilayered analysis foreshadows elements of several contemporary theoretical perspectives in criminology that are often seen as opposed—notably anomie, social disorganization, and control theory, and also theories of societal reaction, differential association and social learning. But for Bonger, these are not competing explanations but integral parts of a holistic understanding of the impact of an entire social order—the 'civilization' of modern capitalism—on crime. The lines between 'micro' and 'macro,' 'structure' and 'culture' are thoroughly blurred.

And while that understanding of capitalism's impact is generally bleak and profoundly critical, it also has a brighter side. Since the demoralization of the proletariat is not the result of fate or of innate differences (the Lombrosian biological perspective comes in for harsh and sustained criticism in Bonger's work), but rather a predictable consequence of the 'present economic system,' it was not inevitable and could change when that system changed. Indeed, Bonger believed not only that the condition of the proletariat could change for the better, but that it was *already* changing, and was far better than it had been when Engels wrote. And that general improvement would be accompanied by declining crime—not because of any inherent progressive quality of capitalism itself, but because workers had increasingly begun to understand the systemic sources of their common condition and to successfully organize to improve it. The more the proletariat developed an awareness that they were all subject to the same adverse forces and formed a collective willingness to challenge them, the more the egoistic tendencies elicited by the profit system would be replaced by solidaristic ones. The growing influence of working-class political action—and of socialist politics in particular—would not only force a general improvement of material conditions, but also would elevate the level of civilization among working people and 'awaken' a feeling of solidarity. Bonger suggests that under socialism, once the common ownership of the means of production has eliminated the causes of material and intellectual poverty, crime would diminish markedly, and might very nearly disappear. Socialism 'will not only remove the causes which now make men egoistic, but will awaken, on the contrary, a strong feeling of altruism … in such a society there can be no question of crime properly so called' (1916/1967, p. 671).

The tradition represented by Engels and Bonger, it is fair to say, had little direct influence on the development of formal academic criminology in the early to mid-20th century. It is important to note, however, that some key themes surfaced in more 'mainstream' work, most notably in Robert Merton's (1957) seminal paper on 'Social Structure and Anomie,' arguably the single most influential work of criminological thinking in the mid-20th century. Consider Bonger's discussion of the criminogenic impact of what he described as a growing 'covetousness' that had put its 'stamp of absolute supremacy on the whole of life':

> Large-scale investment capital has taken hold of the retail trade, employing every possible (and impossible) means to draw the attention of the people to its never-ending stream of goods. The big towns now have a social atmosphere of covetous desire forced up to the very top; Buy, buy more!—is shouted into the ears of the masses—there is plenty of everything! But many are not able to buy that which they desire so much—and with this we come to the criminological aspect of the matter.
>
> *(Bonger 1936, p. 94)*

Contemporary developments

Criminological thinking explicitly focused on the critique of market capitalism remerges most strongly with the explosion of New Left social-science scholarship, particularly in the United Kingdom, beginning in the 1960s—a response, in part, to the stubborn persistence and often increase of crime in the midst of post-World War II prosperity and the growth of the welfare state, and the inability of conventional criminologies to adequately comprehend those developments. Much established criminology, from this perspective, was 'correctional,' serving mainly as a handmaiden of the forces of social control in tamping down the consequences of a flawed and partial welfare state. Much of what passed for criminology of the left, on the other hand, veered into a kind of relativism that denied the significance of ordinary crime in general and downplayed its destructive impact, especially on the poor and marginal. Against both tendencies, some writers called for new criminologies that, as Ian Taylor, Paul Walton, and Jock Young put it in the early 1970s, would aim toward a 'political economy of criminal action' (1973/2013, p. 294). Like Bonger and Engels, these scholars regarded crime as a social cost of capitalist development—a cost that had not disappeared with the blunting of capitalism's sharpest edges in the 20th century. They sought to reconnect with, and revitalize, the classical Marxian understanding of the destructive impact of market capitalism on social and personal life, especially on the well-being, values, and traditions of working people in the postwar industrial societies, and to develop progressive strategies of intervention against it.

Central to this thinking was, again, the understanding that contemporary capitalism affected crime in a multitude of ways—material, cultural, communal, psychological—and therefore that an adequate criminology had to 'deal with the society as a totality' (Taylor, Walton, and Young 1973/2013, p. 294). This meant understanding the ways in which modern capitalism had changed as well as the ways in which it had not. John Lea and Jock Young's seminal book *What Is to Be Done about Law and Order?* (1993) zeroed in on the problem of 'relative deprivation' as a key framework for grasping the pressures toward crime in postwar industrial capitalist society—in effect modernizing Engels' 19th-century analysis. 'Absolute' poverty was no longer as virulent or as widespread as it had been in capitalism's past: but many people still suffered exclusion from 'the glittering prizes of capitalist society—be they material wealth or individual status and prestige—and marginalization from legitimate channels for redressing the balance' (1993, p. ix). Alongside that 'endemic' relative deprivation were more subtle communal and cultural consequences that might be superficially masked by the shallow affluence of the postwar economic boom—notably 'the development of the consumer culture and at the same time the relentless breaking down of older community values, which to some extent shielded traditional working class communities from relative deprivation' (p. ix). Like relative deprivation itself, these effects were not to be understood as 'deviations' from an otherwise stable and healthy social and economic order: they were reflections of 'the core dynamics of capitalism' (p. ix).

Like Bonger, Lea and Young argue that though these effects strike hardest at working people and the marginalized, they 'can be felt at all levels of the social structure' and are 'a major spur to white-collar crime.' And they are psychological as well as social-structural, profoundly shaping the way individuals perceive the world around them and relate to others. Like Engels and Bonger, Lea and Young single out the 'pure egoism' that is engendered at all levels by 'the structure of capitalist market society,' from business elites to 'the young inner-city mugger,' and that is now 'unmediated by traditions of class solidarity' (p. xi). The toxic spread of 'egoistic' values is facilitated by the corrosive effects of heedless capitalist development on the economic and social structure of working-class communities: 'The fragmentation of communities through economic decay and increased long-term unemployment reduces the level of collective social control over potential offenders at the same time as levels of egoism and relative deprivation may increase.' Families and schools simultaneously weaken as bulwarks against demoralization and the spread of predatory individualism (p. xiii).

Importantly, Lea and Young argue that crime is by no means an automatic response to this complex of conditions. Like Engels, and especially Bonger, they see political action as a potential alternative to crime. Crime becomes the default response to adverse conditions in the absence of a more constructive political alternative: 'discontent where there is no political solution leads to crime' (1993, p. 88).

On the other side of the Atlantic, I began to develop a similar perspective around the same time, initially as a way of shedding light on the distinctive pattern of crime and incarceration in the contemporary United States—which, in the 1980s as today, stood out sharply among other advanced industrial countries in both its level of serious violence and its rates of incarceration (Currie 1985). I argued that the United States differed from other industrial societies in several ways that helped explain its status as an 'outlier,' including greater extremes of inequality, deeper and more widespread poverty, greater erosion of family and community ties through disruptive economic development, and fewer supports for individuals and families in the face of economic insecurity and deprivation. Other advanced countries had faced similar underlying strains, but in most of them, the effects had been buffered, to varying degrees, by 'countervailing mechanisms of social obligation and support' (1985, p. 225). The American version of capitalism, by contrast, had been 'marked by the relatively unbuffered play of market forces,' and had accordingly been 'exceptionally disruptive of the institutions necessary for the healthy development of character and community' (p. 225).

In a later discussion, I tried to look more deeply into the impact of 'market society' on crime, and to apply the analysis on a wider global scale. I began by distinguishing the idea of 'market *society*' from the narrower concept of a 'market economy.' I defined market society as

> The spread of a civilization in which the pursuit of personal economic gain becomes increasingly the dominant organizing principle of social life—a social formation in which market principles, instead of being confined to some parts of the economy and appropriately buffered and restrained by other social institutions and norms, come to suffuse the whole social fabric—and to undercut and overwhelm other principles that have historically sustained individuals, families, and communities.
>
> *(Currie 1997, pp. 151–2)*

Virtually all societies have a market sector of the economy, but there are great differences—even within societies that are formally capitalist—in the degree to which market behavior and values 'suffuse' the society as a whole in this sense, and I argued that these differences help to explain variations in levels of serious crimes of violence in the contemporary world. 'Market society' is, of course, an ideal type: but some societies, both developed and less developed, fit the description better than others.

Like others in this tradition, I saw the links between market society and crime as being multiple and mutually reinforcing, and operating on several levels at once—economic, communal, cultural, and psychological. I specified seven of these links, which I called: (1) the progressive destruction of livelihood; (2) the growth of extremes of economic inequality and material deprivation; (3) the withdrawal of public services and supports (especially for families and children); (4) the erosion of informal and communal networks of mutual support, supervision, and care; (5) the spread of a materialistic, neglectful, and 'hard' culture; (6) the unregulated marketing of the technology of violence; and, not least, (7) the weakening of social and political alternatives. I argued that these worked together in varying combinations across different 'postindustrial' societies, leading to specific patterns that were often quite complex and historically specific. For example, the relative strength of informal communal institutions, such as extended families and stable local communities, might help to explain why levels of serious violence—at least 'street' violence—could be remarkably low in some relatively poor developed countries, like Spain or Greece. The striking absence of controls on the marketing of firearms in the United States helped explain why American rates of homicide were not only predictably higher, but *far* higher, than in other advanced societies where guns were more tightly regulated. Likewise, the distinctive history of racial inequality in the United States compounded the adverse effects of the country's extreme version of market society, and helped to explain both its unusually high levels of violence and the striking concentration of both violence and incarceration among racial minorities.

Varieties of evidence

How does this perspective hold up in the light of research and historical experience? My own feeling is that its core argument has held up very well—and indeed has yet to be successfully challenged empirically. The evidence—from several different sources—confirms that societies that have done more to rein in the excesses of the 'market' have been far more successful in reducing violence than those in which social and economic life remains dominated by market forces. And that reality has important implications for how we think about the future of crime and about strategies to combat it.

Some of the most important evidence can be gleaned from comparative analysis of the distribution of violent crime across countries with different levels of intervention into the 'market.' Here the assessment of violence, particularly homicide, in the United States is especially significant. The dramatic differences between the United States and more 'social democratic' countries in homicide rates (Currie 2015; Hall and McLean 2009), and firearm homicide rates in particular (Grinshteyn and Hemenway 2016), are not in dispute. The disparities are most striking when the effects of the marginalization of many youth are joined with the unregulated market in firearms: deaths from firearm violence among young men aged 15 to 24 are more than 50 times as high in the United States as the average of 22 other high-income countries (Grinshteyn and Hemenway 2016). Indeed, this 'exceptional' level of violence is all the more remarkable given the country's similarly exceptional rate of incarceration—which suggests that America's propensity to breed violence is even more extreme than the already outsized homicide rates would indicate (for a discussion of this issue, see Currie 2003). Globally, the brutal stratification of violence between the world's 'haves' and 'have-nots'—the 'winners' and 'losers' in the world capitalist economy—is the sharpest defining feature of violent crime in our time. The worst levels of homicide by far are in lower- to middle-income countries that suffer the most disruptive impacts of an increasingly 'lidless' capitalism while receiving some of the fewest and most unevenly shared benefits. From the perspective of a 'criminology of the market,' it is no accident that the homicide rate in Honduras is more than 80 times the rate in Sweden, or that South Africa's rate is over 100 times that of Japan (Currie 2015; UNODC 2017).

Along with the broad evidence of contemporary global experience, there have been a small number of quantitative studies linking levels of crime with the degree to which market relations have been tamed by social policy. In the late 1990s, for example, Steven Messner and Richard Rosenfeld (1997) explored the effects of what they call 'political restraint of the market' on rates of homicide. Their analysis builds on the concept of 'decommodification,' developed by the Swedish sociologist Gosta Esping-Anderson (1990)—meaning the development of social policies that serve to insulate people from the raw impact of market forces in the economy. Messner and Rosenfeld (1997, p. 1394) concluded that 'the higher the level of political protection from the vicissitudes of the market, the lower the national homicide rate.' The beneficial effect of decommodification on homicide rates persisted even when a variety of other potentially relevant variables were controlled, including inequality, economic development, and the ratio of men to women in the society. Another cross-national study by Jukka Savolainen (2000) similarly found that strong efforts at decommodification, in the form of generous spending on social protection, were associated with lower rates of homicide: and a more recent review of cross-national homicide research stretching back to the 1970s, by Amy Nivette (2011), confirms the link.

One study—by Olena Antonaccio and Charles Tittle (2007)—attempted to directly test some of the central tenets of Willem Bonger's argument by examining how what they call the 'degree of capitalism' in a society affects its crime rate. Looking at homicide rates in 100 countries around the turn of the 21st century, they created an index of the 'degree of capitalism' composed of four factors: (1) Social Security taxes as a percentage of government revenues; (2) the percentage of national expenditure on health that is private (presumably reflecting a low commitment to public provision of health care); (3) a measure of union density, which might reflect labor's ability to restrain the effects of unmitigated capitalism; and (4) the Gini Index of inequality, on the presumption that less restrained capitalist economies generate greater inequality. Antonacci and Tittle found that societies with a higher degree of capitalism—that is, relatively pure capitalist systems, a concept fundamentally similar to that of 'market society'—are associated with higher homicide rates.

From another angle, some research has explored the impact on crime of rapid shifts toward greater deregulation and 'marketization' in particular regions or countries. Once again, the pattern is clear: particularly in the early stages of what is often celebrated as the liberation of market forces from undue governmental restraint, societies that move closer to the model of the market society suffer higher crime rates (typically along with other indicators of social adversity, like rising infant mortality and declining life expectancy).

Rates of homicide and other serious crimes of violence rose sharply, along with other social pathologies, in Russia and other states of the former Soviet Union after the market-oriented economic reforms at the end of the 1980s (Karstedt 2003; Pridemore 2005; Slade and Light 2015; Lysova and Shchitov 2015; Stickley, Leinsalu, and Razvodovsky 2008), which brought rising joblessness and poverty and stripped away longstanding social supports. A similar, if somewhat less extreme, pattern is evident in several countries of East-Central Europe (Stamatel 2008). In many (but not all) of these countries, crime rates reached a peak in the mid-1990s and fell back thereafter, but typically remained higher than before the era of 'reform' (those effects, moreover, have probably been masked in some countries, including Russia, by continuing official manipulation of statistics on violent crime (see Lysova and Shchitov 2015).

Similar patterns appear to hold for China as well, where a rapid shift away from a more collective social model in the name of market reforms resulted in widespread joblessness, the destruction of once-stable rural communities, and a massive migration to the cities (Liu and Messner 2004). Rises in violent crime also wracked much of Latin America and the Caribbean under the impact of intensified market penetration and the adoption of neoliberal 'structural adjustment' policies in the 1980s and 1990s that brought rising poverty and mass joblessness as well as reductions in public social services (Ayres 1998). Though violence has receded from its peaks in many of these countries, including Brazil, it has continued to increase in others—giving countries like Honduras and El Salvador the highest rates of homicide in the world: and even where the highest rates of the 1990s have fallen, they still tower above those of most of the rest of the world. Though there has been a significant 'crime drop' in many countries around the world, it has been highly uneven—missing some countries, especially in Latin America and the Caribbean, altogether (Currie 2015; LaFree, Curtis, and McDowall 2015; UNODC 2017).

These findings are buttressed by what is now a long tradition of research that has consistently confirmed the linkages between high levels of violent crime and some of the essential facets of 'market society'—most notably deep economic inequality and weak public spending for social protection. The link between economic inequality and violence has been affirmed both cross-nationally and within specific countries for decades (for reviews, see Currie 1985, 2015; Nivette 2011; Ouimet 2012; Pratt and Cullen 2005; Wilkinson and Pickett 2010). The exact nature of that relationship is complex, and there is some debate over whether economic inequality or poverty is the most important contributor to high rates of homicide (see Pridemore 2008; Pridemore and Trent 2010). But this may be a distinction without a difference, since, in the real world, a wide spread of economic inequality typically goes along with extreme poverty at the bottom of the scale. The United States, which leads the rest of the advanced industrial world in homicide, also leads it in both its extremes of inequality and its depth of poverty: in the developing world, the most extreme levels of violence are invariably found in countries where both extreme poverty and unusually high levels of economic inequality are rampant. In a study of the correlates of homicide in a large sample of 165 countries, Marc Ouimet (2012) found that both economic inequality generally and a measure he calls 'excess infant mortality'—a level of infant death higher than would be expected given a country's level of economic development—were associated with unusually high levels of homicide in countries ranging from the United States to a number of countries in Latin America and the Caribbean, Africa, and the former Soviet bloc.

Some of the most illuminating empirical confirmations of the strength of the links between market capitalism and crime have come from ethnographic studies of communities hit hard by the destabilizing—and demoralizing—influence of global consumer capitalism. In the United Kingdom, for example, Steve Hall, Simon Winlow, and Craig Ancrum (2008) have provided an in-depth look at the lives of young people in several housing estates in the north-east of England where stable working-class jobs have largely disappeared and where a strident consumer culture that equates successful identity with the display of consumer commodities has come to suffuse local life and displace earlier traditions of mutuality and solidarity. In extensive interviews, Hall, Winlow, and Ancrum reveal the emergence of a local culture in which routine crime in the service of consumer acquisition is widely understood as a means of escaping what would otherwise be lives not only of material deprivation but of impoverished identities as well—a way to avoid being seen, and seeing oneself, as a 'nobody' in a community of nobodies. 'Every street criminal we spoke to,' they write,

> Appeared to believe wholeheartedly that the good life should be understood in terms of the acquisition and conspicuous display of commodities and services that signified cultural achievement in the most shallow of terms. To be wealthy was to be happy. To be happy was to indulge, to buy, to squander, to be released from the normal restrictions of everyday life on estates like these.
>
> *(2008, p. 48)*

Linking with a tradition that extends back to Bonger, Hall, Winlow, and Ancrum argue that the effect of consumer values is heightened by the erosion of more traditional working-class values of reciprocity and solidarity. Those values were rooted in reasonably solid livelihoods and expectations; as those have been lost under the onslaught of neoliberal social policy, a competitive culture of 'winners and losers' has increasingly taken their place. Writing at the start of the

20th century, Bonger anticipated that growing working-class organization would lead to lower crime: but the eclipse of stable working-class communities has undone that prediction.

Looking to the future

A variety of evidence, then, supports the argument that 'market societies' are especially fertile breeding grounds for crime and that concerted efforts to reduce the scope of the market's impact on individuals and communities can reduce it. Indeed, it can be argued that the reduction of violence has been one of the great achievements of those societies that we may broadly call 'social democratic'—along with the reduction of poverty, preventable illness, infant mortality, and early death. Regardless of whether they *set out* to reduce violence, that is one happy by-product of larger social interventions designed to reduce inequality, deprivation, and economic insecurity, and—not least—to counter the *cultural* imperatives and distortions of what Willem Bonger would have called an 'egoistic' society by institutionalizing values of solidarity and social support.

That evidence also points to implications for social action and social policy. Without attempting to draw a blueprint here, let me suggest some of them.

The first, and most important, implication is that the kind of societies we build really do matter. There has been no lack of voices—including some from within academic criminology—telling us that crime has little to do with social structure—with the larger social, economic, and cultural context that in all other ways shapes people's lives. But the enormous variation in serious crime across different societies tells us otherwise. And this suggests that, difficult as they are, it is the big social changes that matter most. No one credibly argues that the reason countries like Denmark or Sweden have lower rates of violence than the United States or Guatemala, for example, is that they have discovered vastly more effective policing strategies or better models of therapeutic intervention for violent offenders. The primary reasons for these stark differences—which translate into huge differences in the quality of life—are structural. Accordingly, the best and most enduring anti-crime strategies will continue to be those that are less about crime itself than about ensuring lives of dignity, security, and purpose for everyone. Strategies to reduce extremes of inequality, poverty, and economic insecurity, in particular, are critically important if we hope to reduce violence in the long term. Particularly critical in this respect are more effective strategies to achieve genuine full employment in work that provides sustenance, stability, and meaning—a terrain on which even the most successful societies continue to struggle.

This does not by any means suggest that incremental improvements on a variety of levels—from democratic policing to individual intervention with offenders—may not be useful. But it does mean that the most helpful and effective incremental approaches will be those that are linked to a larger strategy for social change—a larger vision that involves challenging the 'egoistic' and predatory character of social life in market societies. Market theories, for example, would suggest that efforts at 'rehabilitation' that simply try to adjust offenders into constricted and demeaning lives at the bottom of an insecure and depriving market society are unlikely to be effective in the long run, even on their own narrow terms. But we can also build on the understanding of the ways in which market societies breed a criminogenic 'egoism' to fashion intervention strategies that are both more promising and more progressive—'transformative' interventions designed to help people involved in predatory crime to understand the sources of their common condition, to regard others as potential comrades instead of targets, and to work toward transforming mere visceral discontent and alienation into collective political action (Currie 2013). There is much important work to be done to develop these kinds of strategic intervention, put them into practice in the real world, and subject them to rigorous evaluation—while remaining committed to the work of broader social change.

And it is important to stress the urgency of that work. The social institutions that have historically underpinned the reduction in violence throughout a good part of the 20th century are under unprecedented attack—buffeted by the relentless encroachment of the global market economy itself and by a startlingly successful ideological, political, and cultural assault on the principles of social protection of the vulnerable and restraint of the market. It is not hard to envision a downward spiral—toward what we could call the 'Americanization' of crime in the advanced industrial world, which would likely be met by an expansion of the apparatus of repression and control of populations increasingly demoralized by the multiple adverse forces of an increasingly dominant, and increasingly heedless, global market society. The flip side of the market's tendency to generate high levels of crime is the 'shadow' growth of that apparatus of mass repression—which is why the coexistence in the United States of the world's highest incarceration rate with the developed world's highest levels of serious violent crime is not surprising, and why the rapid growth of mass incarceration in countries like Brazil and El Salvador is not surprising either. By continuing to insist that violence is indeed a predictable cost of the thrust toward the 'marketization' of global society, criminologists can play an important role in helping to avoid that scenario.

References

Antonaccio, Olena, and Charles R. Tittle. 2007. 'A Cross-National Test of Bonger's Theory of Criminality and Economic Conditions.' *Criminology* 45: 925–58.

Ayres, Robert L. 1998. *Crime and Violence as Development Issues in Latin America and the Caribbean.* Washington, DC: World Bank.

Bonger, Willem Adrian. 1916/1967. *Criminality and Economic Conditions.* New York: Agathon Press.

Bonger, Willem Adrian. 1936. *An Introduction to Criminology.* London: Methuen and Co.

Carrington, Kerry, Russell Hogg, and Maximo Sozzo. 2016. 'Southern Criminology.' *British Journal of Criminology* 56(1): 1–20.

Currie, Elliott. 1985. *Confronting Crime: An American Challenge.* New York: Pantheon Books.

Currie, Elliott. 1997. 'Market, Crime, and Community: Toward a Mid-Range Theory of Post-Industrial Violence.' *Theoretical Criminology* 1: 147–72.

Currie, Elliott. 2003. 'Of Punishment and Crime Rates: Some Theoretical and Methodological Consequences of Mass Incarceration.' In *Punishment and Social Control,* enlarged 2nd edn, edited by Thomas G. Blomberg and Stanley Cohen. New York: Aldine De Gruyter.

Currie, Elliott. 2013. 'Consciousness, Solidarity and Hope as Prevention and Rehabilitation.' *International Journal of Crime, Justice, and Social Democracy* 2(2): 3–11.

Currie, Elliott. 2015. *The Roots of Danger: Violent Crime in Global Perspective,* revised edn. New York: Oxford University Press.

Currie, Elliott. 2016. 'The Futures of Criminology.' Plenary Address, British Society of Criminology, Plymouth, June.

Engels, Friedrich. 1845/1973. *The Condition of the Working Class in England in 1844.* Moscow: Progress Publishers.

Esping-Anderson, Gosta. 1990. *The Three Worlds of Welfare Capitalism.* Princeton, NJ: Princeton University Press.

Goldsmith, Oliver. 1770/1996. 'The Deserted Village.' In *The Cry for Justice: An Anthology of the Great Social Protest Literature of All Time,* edited by Upton Sinclair. New York: Barricade Books.

Grinshteyn, Erin, and David Hemenway. 2016. 'Violent Death Rates: The US Compared with Other High-Income OECD Countries, 2010.' *American Journal of Medicine* 129: 266–73.

Hall, Steve, and Craig McLean. 2009. 'A Tale of Two Capitalisms: Preliminary Spatial and Historical Comparisons of Homicide Rates in Western Europe and the USA.' *Theoretical Criminology* 13: 313–39.

Hall, Steve, Simon Winlow, and Craig Ancrum. 2008. *Criminal Identities and Consumer Culture.* Cullompton: Willan.

Karstedt, Suzanne. 2003. 'Legacies of a Culture of Inequality: The Janus Face of Crime in Post-Communist Societies.' *Crime, Law, and Social Change* 40: 295–320.

LaFree, Gary, Karise Curtis, and David McDowall. 2015. 'How Effective Are Our Better Angels? Assessing Country-Level Declines in Homicide since 1950.' *European Journal of Criminology* 12(4): 482–504.

Lea, John, and Jock Young. 1993. *What Is to Be Done about Law and Order?*, 2nd edn. London: Pluto Press.

Liu, Jianhong, and Steven F. Messner. 2004. 'Modernization and Crime Trends in China's Reform Era.' In *Crime and Social Control in a Changing China*, edited by Jianhong Liu, Lening Zhang, and Steven Messner. Westport, CT: Greenwood Press.

Lysova, Alexandra, and Nikolay Shchitov. 2015. 'What Is Russia's Real Homicide Rate? Statistical Reconstruction and the "Decivilizing" Process.' *Theoretical Criminology* 19(2): 257–77.

Merton, Robert K. 1957. 'Social Structure and Anomie.' In *Social Theory and Social Structure*, revised and enlarged edn. New York: Free Press.

Messner, Steven F., and Richard Rosenfeld. 1997. 'Political Restraint of the Market and Levels of Criminal Homicide: A Cross-National Application of Institutional Anomie Theory.' *Social Forces* 75: 1393–426.

Nivette, Amy. 2011. 'Cross-National Predictors of Crime: A Meta-Analysis.' *Homicide Studies* 15(2): 103–31.

Ouimet, Marc. 2012. 'A World of Homicides: The Effect of Economic Development, Income Inequality, and Excess Infant Mortality on the Homicide Rate for 165 Countries in 2010.' *Homicide Studies* 13(1): 238–58.

Pratt, Travis C., and Francis T. Cullen. 2005. 'Assessing Macro-Level Predictors and Theories of Crime: A Meta-Analysis.' In *Crime and Justice: A Review of Research*, Vol. 32, edited by Michael Tonry. Chicago, IL: University of Chicago Press.

Pridemore, William Alex. 2005. 'Social Structure and Homicide in Post-Soviet Russia.' *Social Science Research* 34: 732–56.

Pridemore, William Alex. 2008. 'A Methodological Addition to the Cross-National Empirical Literature on Social Structure and Homicide: A First Test of the Poverty-Homicide Thesis.' *Criminology* 46: 133–54.

Pridemore, William Alex, and Carol L. S. Trent. 2010. 'Do the Invariant Findings of Land, McCall, and Cohen Generalize to Cross-National Studies of Social Structure and Homicide?' *Homicide Studies* 14: 296–335.

Savolainen, Jukka. 2000. 'Inequality, Welfare State, and Homicide: Further Support for Institutional Anomie Theory.' *Criminology* 38: 1021–42.

Slade, Gavin, and Matthew Light. 2015. 'Crime and Criminal Justice after Communism: Why Study the Post-Soviet Region?' *Theoretical Criminology* 19(2): 147–58.

Stamatel, Janet P. 2008. 'Using Mortality Data to Refine Our Understanding of Homicide Patterns in Select Postcommunist Countries.' *Homicide Studies* 12: 117–35.

Stickley, Andrew, Mall Leinsalu, and Yury E. Razvodovsky. 2008. 'Homicide in Post-Soviet Belarus: Urban–Rural Trends.' *European Journal of Public Health* 19: 117–20.

Taylor, Ian. 1999. *Crime in Context: A Critical Criminology of Market Societies.* Cambridge: Polity Press.

Taylor, Ian, Paul Walton, and Jock Young. 2013. *The New Criminology*, 40th Anniversary edn. London and New York: Routledge.

UNODC (United Nations Office of Drugs and Crime). 2017. *Intentional Homicide: Counts and Rates per 100,000 Population*, www.unodc.org/data (accessed February 2017).

Wilkinson, Richard, and Kate Pickett. 2010. *The Spirit Level: Why Greater Equality Makes Societies Stronger.* New York: Bloomsbury Press.

4

PUNISHMENT AND POLITICAL ECONOMY

Alessandro De Giorgi

Since its origins in the first decades of the 19th century, and for most of the 20th century, 'criminology' has been the study of *crime* rather than the study of *punishment*: punishments, criminal policies, and strategies of social control were not the objects of criminological analysis, but rather 'tools' to govern the criminal question. The main objective of criminology, particularly in its positivist currents, was the scientific production of effective strategies for the government of deviance and criminality (Pasquino, 1980).

Between the late 1960s and the early 1970s, however, these epistemological boundaries were challenged by the emergence of radical perspectives on punishment and social control. The main target of this new critical approach was exactly the positivist paradigm that had dominated the field of criminological research since its very birth. The rejection of what David Matza famously defined as the 'correctional perspective' (1969: 15–40) concerned in the first place the theoretical and methodological tenets of positivist criminology – its presumed scientific neutrality, its assumption that social problems had objective causes that social scientists could discover through adequate methodologies, and its ambition to unveil objective truths about criminal behavior. Most importantly, the emerging 'new criminology' (Taylor et al., 1973) would question the political implications of the positivist approach – in particular, its emphasis on the elaboration of strategies that could effectively address the causes of deviance, correct criminals, and ideally eradicate crime itself.

The political context of the 1960s, with its radical critique of all 'repressive' institutions (family, university, asylum, prison), and the irruption of Marxism into the academic field, laid a fertile ground for the emergence of critical perspectives on social and penal control.[1] The forms of punishment, rather than the causes of crime, became the focus of the new criminological agenda. In particular the prison, the technology of punishment peculiar to modernity, became the object of critical inquiry. Several studies began to investigate the historical trajectory through which imprisonment had come to replace earlier forms of punishment and the reasons for its persistence in contemporary societies. Looking beyond the rhetorical legitimation of the prison – the defense of society from crime in the name of 'public safety' – critical scholars began to reveal its latent functions.

A first direction of analysis focused on the role of penal systems in the history of capitalist societies. The new 'revisionist' histories of punishment that appeared between the late 1960s and the early 1980s deconstructed mainstream penal historiography, criticizing in particular its teleological bias – that is to say, its tendency to represent the history of punishment as an ongoing process of reform and as a linear advancement toward more humane sanctions. Against this 'reformist historiography' (Ignatieff, 1983: 76), characterized by a narrative of progress that obscured the role played by penal technologies in the consolidation of class power, revisionist historians attempted to re-politicize the history of punishment, reconstructing it from the point of view of the privileged targets of social control: the working classes, the poor, the dispossessed (Platt, 1969; Foucault, 1977; Ignatieff, 1978; Melossi and Pavarini, 1981).

A second body of research emerged toward the end of the 1970s and focused on the transformations of penality in contemporary late-capitalist social formations (Quinney, 1980). In this context, changes in penal practices – and specifically variations in the severity of punishment, as measured by rates of imprisonment – were analyzed against the background of the transformation of class relations in advanced capitalist societies (Spitzer, 1975; Quinney, 1980; Adamson, 1984). Thus, while revisionist historians of punishment unveiled the historical connections between the invention of the penitentiary and the birth of a capitalist system of production based on the extensive exploitation of wage labor, neo-Marxist critics of contemporary penal politics examined the persistence of that same connection in late-capitalist societies, analyzing the relationship between current penal forms and capitalist labor markets (for a review of this literature, see Chiricos and DeLone, 1992; Melossi, 1998; De Giorgi, 2006: 19–39).

Taken together, these two perspectives contend that penal politics plays a very different role than 'defending society' from crime: both the historical emergence of specific penal practices and their persistence in contemporary societies, are structurally linked to the dominant relations of production and to the hegemonic forms of work organization. In a society divided into classes, criminal law cannot reflect any 'general interest':

> The would-be theories of criminal law that derive the principles of penal policy from the interests of society as a whole are conscious or unconscious distortions of reality. Society as a whole does not exist, except in the fantasy of the jurists. In reality we are faced only with classes, with contradictory, conflicting interests. Every historically given system of penal policy bears the imprint of the class interests of that class which instigated it.
>
> *(Pashukanis, 1978: 174)*

Whether in the context of a structural critique of bourgeois legal ideologies (as in the work of Evgeny Pashukanis just quoted), of a cultural analysis of the role of moral panics in 'policing the crisis' of late-capitalist societies (Hall et al., 1978), or of a deconstruction of penal discourses as 'ideological state apparatuses' (Althusser, 1971), the ground had been set for a materialist critique of punishment as a tool of class control.

The foundations of the political economy of punishment

The sociological foundations of what would later become the political economy of punishment had already been laid down in the late 1930s by Georg Rusche and Otto Kirchheimer in the early pages of their classic *Punishment and Social Structure*:

Every system of production tends to discover punishments which correspond to its productive relationships. It is thus necessary to investigate the origin and fate of penal systems, the use or avoidance of specific punishments, and the intensity of penal practices as they are determined by social forces, above all by economic and then fiscal forces.

(1939 [2003]: 5)²

Rusche and Kirchheimer argued that a sociological understanding of the historical and contemporary transformations of penal systems should be informed by a structural analysis of the connections between penal technologies and transformations of the economy – in particular, the transition of modern societies from a pre-capitalist to a capitalist mode of production.

The birth of what Michel Foucault would later define as 'disciplinary' practices and institutions of confinement in place of the torturous 'spectacles of suffering' staged in the main squares of European cities until the 18th century (see Spierenburg, 1984), should thus be interpreted as a constitutive part of the broader shift toward a new system of production based on the 'complete separation between the workers and the ownership of the conditions for the realization of their labor' (Marx, 1867 [1976]: 874). Against the background of a new emerging class structure shaped by the relation between capital and wage labor, the political economy of proto-capitalist societies started to conceive the human body as a resource to be exploited in the process of production, rather than wasted in the symbolic rituals of corporal punishment:

In fact the two processes – the accumulation of men and the accumulation of capital – cannot be separated; it would not have been possible to solve the problem of the accumulation of men without the growth of an apparatus of production capable of both sustaining them and using them; conversely, the techniques that made the cumulative multiplicity of men useful accelerated the accumulation of capital.

(Foucault, 1977: 221)

Modern penal institutions played a decisive role in the consolidation of a process of capitalist production based on the factory and grounded in the commodification of human labor (Marx, 1867 [1976]: 896–926). At the outset of the bourgeois revolution, the 'great confinement' of beggars, criminals, prostitutes, and the 'idle poor' in workhouses, poorhouses, and houses of correction throughout Europe (Foucault, 1965: 38–64) contributed to transform the 'free and rightless proletariat' (Marx, 1867 [1976]: 896) created by the crisis of the feudal economy into a docile, obedient, and disciplined labor force ready to be incorporated into the emerging sites of capitalist production. The historical emergence, consolidation, and ongoing transformation of modern penal practices would thus reflect capital's need to carve a docile and laborious workforce out of the unruly, undisciplined, and sometimes riotous 'dangerous classes' constantly generated by capital itself as a by-product of its movement of 'accumulation by dispossession' (Harvey, 2003: 137–82).

According to this materialist framework, the specific configurations of the relationship between penal technologies and economic structures would be shaped by the logic of *less eligibility*. This concept, first developed in England in the early 19th century, had provided the main rationale for the English Poor Laws of 1834. In its early formulation, the principle held that:

The first and most essential of all conditions, a principle which we find universally admitted, even by those whose practice is at variance with it, is, that his [the relief recipient's] situation on the whole shall not be made really or apparently so eligible [i.e. desirable] as the situation of the independent laborer of the lowest class.

(Quoted in Piven and Cloward, 1993: 35)

According to this logic, public assistance should never raise the living conditions of the destitute above the standards of life available to the poorest among the working poor; otherwise, public relief would become 'more eligible' (more desirable) than waged work. Georg Rusche's intuition was to apply the principle of less eligibility to the analysis of penal change: since the aim of any penal system is to deter the most marginalized classes of society from committing 'crimes of desperation' (Rusche, 1933 [1978]: 4) – thus violating the capitalist injunction to rely only on their work to survive – it follows that the conditions of life generally available in the lowest regions of the class structure will invariably set the standards of living for those who are caught in the net of the penal system. In Rusche's words:

> Although experience shows the rich to occasionally break the law too, the fact remains that a substantial majority of those who fill the prisons come from the lower strata of the proletariat. Therefore, if it is not to contradict its goals, the penal system must be such that the most criminally predisposed groups will prefer a minimal existence in freedom, even under the most miserable conditions, to a life under the pressure of the penal system.
>
> *(1930 [1980]: 42)*

In Rusche's view, however, the rationality of penal practices is not limited to the negative logic of deterrence. Indeed, the function of less eligibility is not only to deter the most disadvantaged classes from resorting to crime (or public assistance) to survive, but also – and even more importantly – to force the poor to 'prefer' any available working conditions to the sanctions attached to criminal behavior and refusal to work. By setting the standards of living for those punished below 'the situation of the lowest socially significant proletarian class' (Rusche, 1933 [1978]: 4), the principle of less eligibility ensures that the most marginalized fractions of the working class will accept any level of exploitation in the capitalist labor market, as this will be in most cases preferable to being punished for refusing to work at the given conditions. In a capitalist economy, this means that the situation of the marginal proletarian class will shape criminal policies, and therefore the conditions of those who are punished:

> One can also formulate this proposition as follows: all efforts to reform the punishment of criminals are inevitably limited by the situation of the lowest socially significant proletarian class which society wants to deter from criminal acts. All reform efforts, however humanitarian and well meaning, which go beyond this restriction, are condemned to utopianism.
>
> *(Rusche, 1933 [1978]: 4)*

What Rusche is criticizing here is the representation of the history of punishment as a sequence of humanitarian reforms toward civility. This progressive description of penal transformation is unrealistic, Rusche argues, because the principle of less eligibility – to which any penal system must ultimately conform – sets a structural limit to any reform effort or 'civilization process'. The pace and direction of penal change are dictated by the overall situation of the working class, and in a capitalist economy that situation is determined in the first place by the labor market. The dynamics of the market will establish the 'fair price' of labor as of any other commodity: an increase in the supply of workers that are 'superfluous to capital's average requirements for its own valorization' (Marx, 1867 [1976]: 782), will lessen the value of human labor, worsening the conditions of the working class. The consequence, according to the principle of less eligibility, is that any increase in the size of the 'surplus population' will prompt harsher penal policies:

> Unemployed masses, who tend to commit crimes of desperation because of hunger and deprivation, will only be stopped from doing so through cruel penalties. The most effective penal policy seems to be severe corporal punishment, if not ruthless extermination … In a society in which workers are scarce, penal sanctions have a completely different function. They do not have to stop hungry people from satisfying elementary needs. If everybody who wants to work can find work, if the lowest social class consists of unskilled workers and not of wretched unemployed workers, then punishment is required to make the unwilling work, and to teach other criminals that they have to content themselves with the income of a honest worker.
>
> *(Rusche, 1933 [1978]: 4)*

Consequently, the emergence or the demise of different penal practices cannot be ascribed to the ideas of the reformers: penal change is ultimately determined by the conditions of labor and, more specifically, of the labor market. This implies that no penal reform is irreversible, and that humane punishments will be quickly replaced by penal cruelty whenever new socioeconomic conditions will prompt this shift; and penal institutions will turn again into 'places of pure torture, suitable to deter even the most wretched' (Rusche, 1933 [1978]: 6).[3]

Rusche and Kirchheimer reinterpret the whole history of punishment institutions, from the late Middle Ages to the 1930s, according to this basic principle. Thus, when in the 16th century Europe was affected by a huge demographic crisis (in part as a consequence of the Thirty Years War), the labor force became scarce and wages started to grow. These circumstances prompted several European states to revise their policies toward the poor: those who were able-bodied had to be put to work. The imposition of work would deal with two crucial issues at once: on the one hand, the social problems created by the visible presence of beggars, and on the other hand, the decline of capitalist profits caused by rising wages. Inspired by this new philosophy of poverty, the first institutions for the confinement of the poor spread throughout Europe: the Bridewell in England, the Hôpital General in France, the Zuchtaus and the Spinnhaus in the Netherlands. Confinement emerged as an alternative to corporal punishments for the control of the marginal classes: its utility went beyond the segregation of socially undesirable populations (poor, beggars, prostitutes, or criminals) from the rest of society, to include the possibility to transform – through discipline – the unruly criminal into a productive worker.

The future transformations of the penitentiary would also be influenced by changes in the labor markets. According to Rusche and Kirchheimer, labor market dynamics explain the emergence of the Philadelphian model (based on solitary confinement), its later crisis, and the ultimate prevalence of the Auburn model (based on work in common during daytime and solitary confinement at night) in the USA – a country whose capitalist economy was suffering an acute shortage of labor in a period of rapid industrial development.

In Europe, by contrast, the significant size of the 'industrial reserve army of labor' through-out much of the 19th century led to an increase in penal severity and prompted the demise of the idea of a productive prison in favor of a purely punitive model of solitary confinement (Rusche and Kirchheimer, 1939 [2003]: 133–7). Toward the end of the 19th century, when the rise of an organized working class and changes in the labor market led to an improvement of the living standards of the poor, penal policies changed again: social policies were imple-mented in order to deal with a working class in turmoil, and a new climate of penal tolerance spread throughout European prisons.

At the end of their historical analysis, Rusche and Kirchheimer hypothesized a further shift toward the replacement of incarceration by monetary sanctions. This section, less convinc-ing than the first part of the book, is the result of Kirchheimer's later reworking of Rusche's original manuscript.[4]

The prison and the factory: punishment as class control

After its publication in 1939, *Punishment and Social Structure* was almost ignored for a long time, both by penal historians and criminologists. Its politico-economic critique of punish-ment virtually disappeared from the purview of criminological theory until a second edition of the book appeared in 1969, prompting a revival of Rusche and Kirchheimer's structural perspective within the emerging field of critical criminology. Both the initial oblivion and the subsequent interest in the political economy of punishment have a historical explana-tion: the first edition of Rusche and Kirchheimer's work appeared in a period characterized by a strong adversity to Marxism in the USA and to the social sciences in Europe. The emer-gence of totalitarian regimes, the Second World War, and later the postwar reconstruction with its technocratic approach to social problems (including crime), all conjured against the success of *Punishment and Social Structure* and its materialist perspective. It was only in the transformed cultural atmosphere of the 1960s and 1970s that the structural critique elabo-rated by Rusche and Kirchheimer could be rediscovered. Although not always inspired by the neo-Marxist framework, the revisionist histories of punishment that appeared between the late 1960s and the early 1980s signaled the broad influence (whether acknowledged or not) of *Punishment and Social Structure* (Platt, 1969; Foucault, 1977; Ignatieff, 1978; Melossi and Pavarini, 1981).[5]

Elsewhere I have analyzed the relationship between Marxist theory and the emergence of radical histories of punishment (De Giorgi, 2006: 9–19). Here I will concentrate specifically on Melossi and Pavarini's *The Prison and the Factory*, since this is the most systematic attempt to develop a politico-economic critique of the history of the prison. This work situates the birth of the penitentiary in the specific phase of capitalist development that Marx describes as 'primitive accumulation' (Marx, 1867 [1976]: 873–940). In its early stages, capitalism had to create the conditions for its own development, and this required first of all the creation of a capitalist labor force. In order to establish a new system of production based on wage labor, capital had first to separate the producers from the means of production, unraveling the economic structure of feudal society; then, it had to transform the dispossessed populations generated by that dissolution into a unified and disciplined working class.

Capitalism liberated labor from feudal exploitation only to subject it to a purely economic form of subordination. Thus, the 'liberation' of work took the form of an expropriation of producers, replacing one kind of enslavement with another:

Hence, the historical movement which changes the producers into wage-workers, appears, on the one hand, as their emancipation from serfdom and from the fetters of the guilds, and this side alone exists for our bourgeois historians. But, on the other hand, these new freedmen became sellers of themselves only after they had been robbed of all their own means of production, and of the guarantees of existence afforded by the old feudal arrangements.

(Marx, 1867 [1976]: 875)

The consolidation of the factory system gave birth to the process Marx defined as 'real subsumption of labor under capital' (1867 [1976]: 1034–8). In the wake of capitalism's struggle to establish itself as a new mode of production, the various typologies of pre-capitalist work are subsumed under the general form of abstract wage labor. Independent producers are transformed into a social labor force, and the 'collective worker' replaces the individual worker:

[W]ith the development of the real subsumption of labor under capital, or the specifically capitalist mode of production, the real lever of the overall labor process is not the individual worker. Instead, labor-power socially combined and the various competing labor powers, which together form the entire production machine, participate in very different ways in the immediate process of making commodities, or, more accurately in this context, creating the product.

(Marx, 1867 [1976]: 1039–40)

Penal institutions played a crucial role in the historical process of subsumption of labor under capital. The penitentiary emerged as an institution ancillary to the factory, as a penal technology whose power effects were consistent with the requirements of an emerging industrial system of production. The unfolding of a disciplinary penal regime connects the internal dynamics of the prison (both in its material and ideological forms) to the transformations taking place in the sphere of production. The logic of penal discipline characterizes all the institutions of confinement that emerged since the end of the 17th century:

Over and above their specific functions, one overall aim united them: control over a rising proletariat. The bourgeois state assigns to all of them a directing role in the various moments of the formation, production and reproduction of the factory proletariat: for society they are essential instruments of social control, the aim of which is to secure for capital a workforce which by virtue of its moral attitude, physical health, intellectual capacity, orderliness, obedience, etc. will readily adapt to the whole regime of factory life and produce the maximum amount of surplus labor.

(Melossi and Pavarini, 1981: 42)

A new class of individuals is shaped by the penitentiary institution. The mission of the prison is to inculcate new habits into the minds and bodies of the expropriated masses, turning these unruly subjects into a disciplined labor force that, having interiorized an entirely new concept of time and space, will be ready to obey, execute orders, and comply with the rhythms of production dictated by the capitalist division of labor (Thompson, 1967). Thus, the penal institution transforms the poor into a criminal, the criminal into a prisoner, and, finally, the prisoner into a proletarian.

Outside the prison, in the factory, the disciplined body of the individual proletarian will be associated with other bodies, and the capitalist organization of labor will turn this 'collective worker' into a source of surplus-value:

> This discipline is the basic condition for the extraction of surplus-value, and is the only real lesson that bourgeois society has to propose to the proletariat. If legal ideology rules outside production, within it reign servitude and inequality. But the place of production is the factory. Thus, the institutional function of the workhouses and later of the prisons was to teach the proletariat factory discipline.
>
> *(Melossi and Pavarini, 1981: 195)*

Unlike Rusche and Kirchheimer, who had focused exclusively on the instrumental role of penal institutions in the material reproduction of a capitalist labor force, Melossi and Pavarini insist on the crucial contribution provided by disciplinary penal technologies to the *ideological* reproduction of capitalist relations of production. The prison is surely a repressive institution because it imposes on its confined populations a regime of deprivation and complete subordination to authority. But it is also an ideological tool because it represents the unconditional acceptance of that subordination as the only way to break free – one day – from this condition. Thus, the prison creates, on the one hand, the condition of 'prisoner', and it imposes, on the other, the prisoner's subjection to a regime of labor, obedience, and discipline (elements that constitute that very condition) as the only path to freedom. In this way, the suffering generated by the prison is ideologically represented as the consequence of the prisoner's own refusal to submit to the discipline of work.

The ideological normalization of the prison is also reinforced by the contractual logic of imprisonment as a punishment whose severity is measured by time:

> Deprivation of freedom, for a period stipulated in the court sentence, is the specific form in which modern, that is to say bourgeois-capitalist, criminal law embodies the principle of equivalent recompense. This form is unconsciously yet deeply linked with the conception of man in the abstract and abstract human labor measurable in time.
>
> *(Pashukanis, 1978: 180–1)*

The capitalistic principle of the exchange of equivalents provides ideological legitimacy to the sanction of imprisonment through the same mystification that makes a work contract 'fair': in both cases, exploitation, violence and subordination disappear from the smooth logic of the contractual reason. The legal fiction of punishment as retribution conceals the disciplinary dimension of the prison in the same way as the economic fiction of the work contract as an exchange of equivalents conceals the exploitative dimension of wage labor.

The limits of the 'old' political economy of punishment

In an excoriating review of the 1939 edition of *Punishment and Social Structure* published in the March–April 1940 issue of the *Journal of Criminal Law and Criminology*, American legal theorist Jerome Hall came to the following conclusions about the significance of Rusche and Kirchheimer's work:

[D]espite the importance of the thesis, abundant descriptive data, and many acute observations, the study falls far short of being an important contribution to our present
knowledge. For it becomes rather quickly apparent that the authors' 'social situation',
and 'historical-sociological analysis of penal methods' simmer down to 'economic' influence – and 'economic' becomes sometimes the conditions of the labor market, occasionally methods of production, often the bias of dominant economic classes, usually
the bourgeoisie. As a consequence it is impossible to determine just what their thesis
is. The most persistent current of their debate suggests, but never explicitly, Marxist
determinism.

(1940: 971–2)

Jerome Hall was not alone in accusing *Punishment and Social Structure* of economic determinism; indeed other early reviewers agreed, although sometimes in a less acrimonious tone, that
this was the book's main theoretical flaw. For example, in a review published in *The Economic
Journal*, renowned British sociologist T.H. Marshall argued that 'the authors try to press their
point too far and to make everything fit in too neatly', adding in particular that as soon as
their analysis focused on the 19th century (and on the emergence of modern prisons), 'the
simple correlation between penal methods and economic systems breaks down' (Marshall,
1940: 126–7). A few months later, David Riesman Jr added his voice to the choir, stating that
Rusche and Kirchheimer's analysis neglected the role of politics, religion, and culture in penal
transformation, and concluding that 'social scientists have a right to demand an analysis of the
plurality of factors, and an attempt to assign a proper weight to each' (1940: 1299). Finally,
Chicago sociologist Ernest W. Burgess reiterated in his own review of the book that 'the
authors overemphasize the relation of crime to economic conditions and ignore or minimize
cultural and psychogenic factors' (1940: 986).

   Despite having attracted the early attention of such prestigious scholars, *Punishment and
Social Structure* would almost disappear from the criminological landscape for almost 30 years.
Once the book reemerged from oblivion, the charge of economic reductionism and/or determinism would again haunt Rusche and Kirchheimer's work, along with the materialist critique of punishment built on it. Thus, in one of the founding texts in the field of punishment
and society, David Garland concluded his chapter on the political economy of punishment
suggesting that:

> *Punishment and Social Structure* seriously overestimates the effective role of economic
> forces in shaping penal practice. It grossly understates the importance of ideological and
> political forces and has little to say about the internal dynamics of penal administration
> and their role in determining policy. It gives no account of the symbols and social mes-
> sages conveyed by penal measures to the law–abiding public and hence no sense of the
> ways in which these symbolic concerns help shape the fabric of penal institutions.
>
> *(Garland, 1990: 108–9)*

   It is not surprising that these critiques became particularly strong during the 1980s and
1990s, when, as Dario Melossi writes in his introduction to the third edition of Rusche
and Kirchheimer's book, 'Marxism was symbolically burnt at the stake, while honoring the
totem pole of "cultural insight"' (2003: ix). What is slightly more surprising, however, is that

the distancing of critical sociologies of punishment from the structural approach took place despite the fact that in those years advanced capitalist societies were witnessing the most significant process of structural transformation since the Industrial Revolution. In fact, those decades witnessed the crisis of the Fordist-industrial paradigm, the demise of the Keynesian welfare state, the globalization of production and consumption, the consolidation of a neoliberal model of socioeconomic (de)regulation,[6] and – particularly in the USA – the unfolding of a punitive turn that would lead to a radical reconfiguration of the penal landscape. However, with the notable exception of Stuart Hall et al.'s (1978) analysis of the role of penal discourses in the reproduction of class (and racial) hegemony in late capitalism (see also Laclau and Mouffe, 1985), the 'cultural turn' in the sociology of punishment coincided with (and to some extent encouraged) a rejection of the Marxist political economy at a time when this was most needed in order to elaborate a grounded critique of penal change.[7]

This is not to suggest that the traditional politico-economic analysis, with its reductive focus on the relationship between unemployment and imprisonment (Jankovic, 1977; Greenberg, 1980; Wallace, 1980; Galster and Scaturo, 1985; Inverarity and McCarthy, 1988), had been able to elaborate a persuasive structural critique of contemporary punishment; nor to argue that an exclusive emphasis on punishment as an instrument of class control would provide an exhaustive explanation of the transformations of penal politics in contemporary societies. Indeed, from the standpoint of what I would define as a 'post-reductionist' political economy of punishment, the challenge is to envision a non-orthodox critique of penal strategies that is able to overcome the false alternative between 'structure' and 'culture' while addressing the important theoretical concerns raised by other critical perspectives in the field of punishment and society.

In this respect, I would suggest that at least three main themes addressed by recent narratives of penal change (particularly in the USA) deserve the attention of neo-Marxist criminologists:

(1) the already mentioned issue of the *symbolic dimension* of punishment, which points to the materialist framework's excessive focus on the instrumental side of penal practices;
(2) the issue of the broader *governmental effects* generated by penal strategies, which points to the neo-Marxist paradigm's narrow focus on socioeconomic marginality as the exclusive target of penal technologies;
(3) the issue of the specific *politico-institutional* contexts that define the background against which specific forms of penality unfold, which points to the tendency of the political economy of punishment to favor 'global' accounts of penal transformation over comparative analysis.

In some cases, these theoretical concerns have emerged from works directly or indirectly engaged with the neo-Marxist perspective (Cavadino and Dignan, 2006; Lacey, 2008; Wacquant, 2009), while in others they emerged from critical analyses of penality the background of which is rather distant from the materialist paradigm (Simon, 2007; Barker, 2009). I suggest that we engage with each of these themes, since they shed light on relevant dimensions of the penal question that have been left underexplored by the 'old' political economy of punishment.

The first theme points to one of the most persistent critiques addressed to neo-Marxist criminology: its apparent lack of interest for the cultural, expressive, and discursive dimensions of penality. While this critique is clearly well grounded, it is worth noting here that the emphasis on the symbolic dimensions of punishment has often come at the cost of deemphasizing (if not ignoring) the historically determined structural dimensions of penality, almost in a kind of zero-sum logic where 'more culture' seems to imply 'less structure' (see for example Garland, 1990, 2001). Recently, the issue of the culture/structure schism has resurfaced in Loïc Wacquant's (2009) analysis of neoliberal penality and of the emergence of an American 'penal state'. This work aims explicitly at bridging the gap between instrumental and symbolic dimensions of punishment. In the very first pages of his *Punishing the Poor*, in fact, Wacquant states that his work 'does not belong to the genre … of the "political economy of imprisonment" inaugurated by the classic work of Georg Rusche and Otto Kirchheimer, *Punishment and Social Structure*', since its ambition is:

> [t]o hold together the material and symbolic dimensions of the contemporary restruc-
> turing of the economy of punishment that this tradition of research has precisely been
> unable to wed, owing to its congenital incapacity to recognize the specific efficacy and
> the materiality of symbolic power.
>
> *(2009: xvii)*

Wacquant argues that the unfolding of the American penal experiment over the last three decades should not be interpreted – as the *leitmotiv* of the 'old' political economy of punishment would suggest – as a simple reflection of the transition from a Fordist-industrial model of production based on stable labor markets, extensive networks of social protection, and inclusive welfare policies, to a post-Fordist economic system based on deregulated labor markets, flexible working conditions, and weak social protections. Indeed, an exclusive focus on the instrumental dimension of the 'new punitiveness' would prevent a deeper understanding of the significance of the American penal state as a broader political project.

According to Wacquant, the emerging penal state would pursue three distinct strategies with both instrumental and symbolic outcomes. At the instrumental level, the American penal experiment would entail a massive warehousing of the surplus populations generated by the restructuring of the Fordist-industrial economy. In turn, by increasing the cost of any attempt to escape from the lowest regions of the labor market (according to the well-known principle of *less eligibility*) this new 'great confinement' would contribute to impart a new discipline of labor on the marginal sectors of the post-industrial workforce. Finally, at the symbolic level, the new penal discourse would appease the growing insecurities experienced by the middle class, by staging a ritual reassertion of the state's power to neutralize the unworthy and dangerous classes.

In other words, the tentacles of the penal state would extend deeply into the fabric of American society, reshaping – both at the instrumental and symbolic level – its public sphere, its political institutions and its cultural orientations. Distancing himself from the reductionist tendency of the political economy of punishment, Wacquant suggests that the punitive turn leads not only to the consolidation of a repressive machine whose operations are functional to the reproduction of current capitalist relations, but also to the configuration of 'new categories and discourses, novel administrative bodies and government policies, fresh social types and associated forms of knowledge' (2009: 295).

Wacquant's attempt to assign proper weight to the discursive and symbolic effects of penal politics provides important insights toward a post-reductionist revision of the materialist critique of punishment. Yet, the image that emerges most often from the pages of *Punishing the Poor* is that of a penal state involved in a struggle to regulate (by repressive means) the most precarious sectors of the post-industrial labor force, while less emphasis is given to its symbolic reach across other regions of American society. Thus, despite Wacquant's insistence on the necessity to 'escape the narrowly materialist vision of the political economy of punishment' (2009: xviii), his approach risks reproducing the much contested material/symbolic divide. Not unlike other materialist critiques of penality, indeed, Wacquant's work seems to come to the conclusion that the neoliberal penal state reveals its *instrumental* side against the new poor, while projecting its purely *symbolic* hold on the rest of society – specifically, on the middle classes it struggles to reassure by allowing them to witness the punitive excess unleashed against the new dangerous classes. In other words, *Punishing the Poor* might be less distant from the traditional politico-economic critique of punishment than its author acknowledges, since once again the symbolic and discursive dimensions of penal politics appear mostly as ideological 'outgrowths' of a penal state whose main role is to punitively regulate the poor in order to force them into the post-Fordist labor market. Finally, we are left with our unsolved dilemma: how can the symbolic and instrumental dimensions of punishment be reconnected under a comprehensive structural critique of penal change? How do penal discourses and practices consolidate themselves as powerful technologies for governing not just social marginality, but late-capitalist/neoliberal societies at large?

This question points to the issue of the broader governmental effects generated by penal discourses and practices in contemporary societies. In its basic formulation, this theme draws on the Foucauldian insight that penal practices, as historically determined technologies of power, are always inscribed within broader rationalities of government. Thus, according to Foucault's genealogy, the emergence of modern penality (with the transition from the 'spectacle of suffering' to the consolidation of disciplinary technologies) would mirror a broader shift from a *destructive* sovereign power that struggles to neutralize its enemies to a *productive* governmental rationality engaged in the efficient regulation of whole populations (Foucault, 2009: 117). It is worth emphasizing the connection, often overlooked, between Foucault's theorization of the power to punish and the neo-Marxist analysis of capitalist reproduction, particularly in light of the French philosopher's own emphasis on the role played by the emergence of a capitalist 'political economy' in the unfolding of modern governmental rationalities (Foucault, 2009: 106–7). What matters the most here, however, is Foucault's insistence that penal strategies (and governmental technologies in general) should not be seen simply as repressive tools for the control of the poor, but rather as elements of broader rationalities for the governing of entire social formations.

Following this perspective, in his work Jonathan Simon (2007) situates the critique of the American penal experiment within a theoretical framework that is rather distant from the one advanced by Rusche and Kirchheimer. The level privileged by Simon is that of a socio-legal and political analysis of the governmental rationalities that emerged as a consequence of the increasing centrality of the penal question in the USA. In the last 30 years, the ongoing proliferation of discourses, practices, and knowledge on crime and punishment would have resulted in a distinct governmental rationality that Simon calls 'governing through crime':

> When we govern through crime, we make crime and the forms of knowledge historically associated with it … available outside their limited original subject domains as powerful tools with which to interpret and frame all forms of social action as a problem for governance.
>
> *(2007: 17)*

Simon offers a rigorous genealogy of this new governmental rationality, whose origins can be situated in the 'legitimation crisis' affecting the liberal-welfarist forms of governance that had been hegemonic in the USA for most of the 20th century. Simon reconstructs the concatenation of 'discursive events' that provided the symbolic background for the unfolding of the American punitive turn – from Goldwater's incendiary 1964 electoral campaign, to the wars on crime and drugs launched by Nixon, Reagan, and Bush Sr, to the war on terror declared by George W. Bush in the aftermath of 9/11. All these transformations have converged toward a new paradigm of social governance based on the prevention and neutralization of criminal risks as a constitutive element of governmental action at all levels of American society.

This Foucauldian perspective eschews a 'top–down' concept of penal power common to much neo-Marxist criminology, and describes the punitive turn from the point of view of both its politico-institutional consequences and the diffusion of lifestyles, cultures of work, and patterns of consumption revolving around the crime–punishment nexus. Simon deconstructs, on the one hand, the peculiar governmental technologies that emerged around this punitive shift, and on the other, the discursive chains that allowed these rationalities to resonate with punitive and neo-authoritarian declinations of fear and insecurity in a neoliberal society. If analyzed under this particular lens, the punitive turn appears as a broad social dynamic whose power effects are constantly reproduced through the daily interactions between citizens (not only the poor) and a power to punish that is part of a broader strategy for regulating the social.

However, I would suggest, this reconfiguration of governmental technologies is not disconnected from the deep structural inequalities affecting the social and urban landscape of American society. The molecular diffusion of the power effects associated with this new model of 'governing through crime' does not mean that such effects spread evenly. Although we can agree with Simon that we should focus on 'both the criminal justice system that is concentrated on poor communities and the private sector of middle-class securitized environments as class-specific modes of governing through crime that interact with each other' (Simon, 2007: 7), we also need to emphasize that these rationalities of government do not generate similar (or even comparable) effects at different latitudes of the American socioeconomic hierarchy. The neo-Foucauldian argument that 'crime does not govern only those on one end of structures of inequality' (Simon, 2007: 18) needs to be qualified by the Marxist insight that penal strategies contribute to the overall reproduction of those very structures of socioeconomic inequality, in directions that resonate with current dynamics of capitalist accumulation.

Furthermore, the actual configuration of this symbiotic relationship between penal technologies and socioeconomic processes cannot be taken for granted, nor can it be presumed to unfold along the same coordinates across all late-capitalist societies. This question sheds light on the third theme I would like to discuss here: the specific politico-institutional arrangements through which the relations between punishment and social structure are mediated. Such issue also points to what recently John Sutton has identified as a serious theoretical flaw in the political economy of punishment: its tendency to assume 'that all capitalist economies are the same and that business cycles are wholly exogenous to other kinds of social processes' (Sutton, 2004: 171).

The issue of the lack of comparative institutional analysis in neo-Marxist accounts of penal change has been recently raised in particular by theoretical perspectives directly engaged with (if not internal to) the politico-economic framework (Sutton, 2004; Cavadino and Dignan, 2006; Lacey, 2008). In *The Prisoners' Dilemma*, for example, Nicola Lacey clearly situates her analysis in the materialist field, broadly accepting the politico-economic argument that current penal trends must be linked to the socioeconomic transformations affecting late-capitalist societies. However, rather than assuming a global spread of the neoliberal ideology sustained by a uniform shift toward penal severity, Lacey offers a detailed comparative analysis of the different 'varieties of capitalism' existing in the Western world (Hall and Soskice, 2001), and suggests that their specific features must be given proper weight in the analysis of punishment and social structure:

> My analysis builds on structural theories inspired by Marxism, but it argues that political-economic forces at the macro level are mediated not only by cultural filters, but also by economic, political, and social institutions ... It is this institutional stabilization of and mediation of cultural and structural forces, and the impact which this has on the perceived interests of relevant groups of social actors, which produce the significant and persistent variation across systems at similar stages of capitalist development.
>
> *(Lacey, 2008: 57)*

According to Lacey, the American shift toward a punitive governance of social marginality has not spread to all advanced capitalist democracies, and the specific configurations of the punitive turn (where it has indeed taken place) cannot be automatically derived from the emergence of a post-industrial, neoliberal economy. Instead, different capitalist social formations show diverging trends. If some neoliberal market economies such as the USA (and to a much more limited extent, the UK) have witnessed a significant transition from social to penal means for governing the poor, this has not been the case in the social-democratic or corporatist economies of continental Europe, where in the last few decades welfare protections have not been drastically reduced and indicators of penal severity have remained relatively stable. In this sense, social-democratic and corporatist economies would seem to be better positioned than their neoliberal counterparts to resist the punitive turn (despite their own problems of rising unemployment and growing social inequality), thanks to their politico-economic and institutional structures based on stable labor markets, long-term public investments in the workforce, coalition-oriented electoral politics, and greater insulation of the judiciary from the ebbs and flows of public opinion (see also Cavadino and Dignan, 2006: 3–39). Conversely, in neoliberal economic formations – characterized by flexible labor markets, low levels of investment in public services, two-party political systems, a single-issue orientation in political debate, and a hegemonic orientation favoring individual competitiveness over social equality – the most disruptive consequences of the crisis of the industrial economy (namely, the production of a large surplus of labor) would unfold in a politico-institutional context that facilitates the shift toward a more punitive model of social regulation. Lacey suggests that in order to be able to explain *both* the punitive shift of neoliberal societies *and* the relative penal moderation of other late-capitalist social formations, the materialist approach needs to be grounded in a comparative analysis of the institutional, political, and cultural arrangements which, in each variety of capitalism, mediate (and sometimes mitigate) the effect of economic forces on penal politics.

Taken together, the three themes discussed – the symbolic dimension of penality, the governmental effects of penal politics and the different politico-institutional contexts in which penal practices unfold – can assist neo-Marxist criminology in its effort to overcome some of the old conundrums of materialist criminology. Indeed, as far as they are not seen as *alternatives* to structural explanations of penal change, these themes are not incompatible with a politico-economic critique of penality. Instead, as I will argue more extensively in the final section of this chapter, they can help us envision a conceptual roadmap for the construction of a post-reductionist, culturally informed political economy of punishment.

New directions in the political economy of punishment

In the 1933 article which outlined the thesis to be later developed in *Punishment and Social Structure*, Georg Rusche had already been careful to emphasize the complexity of the relationship between economic structure and penal forms:

> The dependency of crime and crime control on economic and historical conditions does not, however, provide a total explanation. These forces do not alone determine the object of our investigation and by themselves are limited and incomplete in several ways.
> *(1933 [1978]: 3)*

This early warning against oversimplified interpretations of the economy/punishment nexus would not inoculate the political economy of punishment against the dangers of economic determinism. It must also be said that the reductionist drift would indeed become particularly evident in the neo-Marxist criminological literature of the 1970s and 1980s, whose attempts to apply Rusche and Kirchheimer's paradigm to late-capitalist societies focused on narrow statistical analyses of the relationship between changes in the labor market and variations in imprisonment rates (for a review see Chiricos and DeLone, 1992; Melossi, 1998; De Giorgi, 2006: 19–39). This literature was for the most part able to provide empirical support to the hypothesis of a positive and direct correlation between unemployment and incarceration and to show how, in accordance with Rusche and Kirchheimer's insights, penal severity tended to increase in times of economic crisis and rising unemployment. However, the narrowly quantitative approach to socioeconomic change privileged by most of these analyses (perhaps in an attempt to give 'scientific validation' to the materialist approach through the use of ever more complex statistical models), has prevented a deeper understanding of the *extra-economic* and *extra-penal* factors that contribute to the structuring of this relationship (for notable exceptions see Box, 1987; Melossi, 1993, 2000).

The reductionist tendency of the political economy of punishment has resulted in an unnecessary oversimplification of Rusche and Kirchheimer's perspective, which in turn has deprived the materialist framework of the theoretical tools it needs in order to elaborate a comprehensive critique of the capitalist restructuring that has unfolded in Western societies since the early 1970s. This broad process of socioeconomic transformation has certainly involved (particularly in the early stage of the transition) a massive expulsion of the labor force from the industrial sectors of the economy, as shown by the vertical growth of unemployment rates between the late 1970s and the early 1980s. More importantly, however, it has resulted in a deep restructuring of the specific *regime of capitalist accumulation* that had been hegemonic in Europe and (to a lesser extent) in the USA between the 1930s and the 1960s.

The concept of 'regime of accumulation' has been elaborated by neo-Marxist political economists belonging to the so-called 'regulation school' (see Aglietta, 1979; Jessop, 1990). This perspective reconstructs the historical trajectory of capitalist development in light of the contradictory tendency of capitalism to generate crises and instabilities, on the one hand, and to consolidate new institutions, new norms, and new cultural orientations in response to those crises, on the other hand.[8] According to this perspective (Jessop, 2002: 56–8), each different regime of capitalist accumulation can be described according to four main elements: (1) a distinctive type of *labor process*, which identifies the dominant form of production and the corresponding composition of the workforce (e.g. mass production, the industrial working class); (2) a specific strategy of *macroeconomic growth*, which identifies the leading sectors of an economic formation (e.g. industrial production, manufacturing); (3) a particular system of *economic regulation*, which describes the prevailing regulatory framework (e.g. collective bargaining, market regulation, monetary policies); and (4) a coherent mode of *societalization*, which identifies the hegemonic forms of cultural, institutional, and social organization (e.g. cultures of welfare, fiscal policies, patterns of consumption, etc.).

According to this perspective, the Fordist-Keynesian regime of capitalist accumulation was based on a system of mass-industrial production centered on the assembly line, stable labor markets regulated by comprehensive industrial policies, high levels of labor unionization favored by an extended system of collective bargaining, significant public interventions in the economy, cultural orientations favoring mass consumption, and a tacit social pact between labor and capital (often mediated by an interventionist state) according to which high wages and generous social protections would reward high levels of labor productivity and work discipline. Bob Jessop summarizes the internal consistency between the economic, institutional, and cultural dimensions of this specific regime of accumulation as follows:

> If the Keynesian welfare national state helped secure the conditions for Fordist economic expansion, Fordist economic expansion helped secure the conditions for the Keynesian welfare national state. Welfare rights based on national citizenship helped to generalize norms of mass consumption and thereby contributed to full employment levels of demand; and they were sustained in turn by an institutionalized compromise involving Fordist unions and Fordist firms.
>
> *(2002: 79)*

The gradual demise in Western economies of this model of capitalist development during the 1970s was prompted by several crisis-generating features of the Fordist-Keynesian paradigm, such as the steady decline in capitalist profits produced by the radicalization of class struggles, the fiscal crisis of the welfare state precipitated by increasing demands for social provisions (coupled, particularly in the USA, with the rise of anti-tax movements), the inflationary tendencies generated by high wages and high welfare expenditures, the saturation of domestic markets for durable goods, and the loss of competitive advantage suffered by Western economies in the wake of economic globalization.

In liberal societies such as the USA, whose economic history has traditionally leaned toward a *laissez-faire* model of capitalist development based on deregulated markets, minimal public interventions in the economy, and a system of social protections resembling a 'charitable state' (Wacquant, 2009: 48), the dismantling of the Fordist-Keynesian regime has unfolded in a neoliberal variant characterized by extreme labor market flexibility, a vertical decline in labor unionization, a drastic curtailment of welfare provisions, and soaring levels of socioeconomic inequality (Sennett, 1998; Shipler, 2004; Katz and Stern, 2006). In this respect, the crisis of the Fordist-Keynesian paradigm and the concurring process of capitalist restructuring have involved much more than the expulsion of a significant fraction of the industrial labor force from the system of production – the only aspect captured by a narrow focus on unemployment and imprisonment. Indeed, the transition to a post–Fordist/post–Keynesian regime of accumulation has taken the form of a broad capitalist offensive against the work-force, in a successful attempt to break the Fordist-Keynesian compromise and to reestablish suitable conditions for profitable capitalist accumulation in a global economy: a stricter work discipline, higher levels of labor flexibility, more insecure working conditions, lower social protections, and an increased competition *for* work among the poor. This process of capitalist restructuring resulted in a significant shift in the balance of power from labor to capital. As Melossi puts it, 'sometimes in the mid-1970s the "social system" started squeezing the work-ing class for the juice of production, not with only one hand, but with two hands at the same time' (2003: xxv).

It is in the context of this broader realignment of social power throughout the structure of late-capitalist societies that a materialist analysis of contemporary penal change must situate its critique. And such a critique must be able to take into account not only the measurable dynamics of the labor market, but also the political, institutional, and cultural transformations that have contributed to redefine existing structures of socioeconomic inequality in the wake of a new emerging regime of capitalist accumulation.

In order to illustrate some of the theoretical implications of this 'qualitative shift', I will return once again to Rusche's original formulation of the concept of *less eligibility* as the logic governing the relation between punishment and social structure:

> All efforts to reform the punishment of criminals are inevitably limited by the *situation* of the lowest socially significant proletarian class which society wants to deter for crimi-nal acts. All reform efforts, however humanitarian and well-meaning, which go beyond this restriction, are condemned to utopianism.
>
> *(Rusche, 1933 [1978]: 4, emphasis added)*

Here I would argue that Rusche's concept of the '*situation* of the lowest socially significant pro-letarian class' lends itself to a much broader conceptualization than the narrowly economistic approach privileged by most of the literature on unemployment and imprisonment: one that encourages a productive integration between the traditional materialist critique of punish-ment and some of the theoretical issues raised by the recent sociologies of the punitive turn.

Indeed, if the relative power of the workforce in a capitalist economy is ultimately determined by the economic value of its labor,[9] the overall *situation* of that workforce – its contingent position inside existing hierarchies of social worthiness, or its 'social value' – is not simply the product of narrow economic dynamics. Rather, it results from the ongoing interaction between structural processes of economic transformation (modes of production, patterns of economic growth, labor market dynamics), governmental technologies of social regulation (varieties of welfare/workfare, strategies of public intervention in the economy, politico-institutional arrangements, modes of economic regulation/deregulation, patterns of wealth redistribution/concentration), and discursive/symbolic dynamics of cultural reproduc-tion (racialized and gendered taxonomies of social worth, mainstream narratives about social deservingness and undeservingness). In other words, the overall 'situation' of marginalized social classes is determined by their place in the economic structure as much as by their position in the 'moral economy' of capitalist social formations (Sayer, 2001). It should be noted here that this ongoing process of redefinition of the economic and social worth of labor represents a constant feature in the history of capitalism, and that the trajectory of this 'repositioning' of the labor force in the social structure tends to follow a clear pattern: the overall 'situation' of the marginal classes tends to improve when a stable dynamic of capital-ist valorization guarantees extended periods of economic growth and social stability, while it tends to deteriorate when the crisis of a specific mode of development prompts capitalist social formations to revolutionize the system of production and spark a new regime of accu-mulation (Marx, 1867 [1976]: 896–904).

Following this perspective, a post-reductionist political economy of the punitive turn in the USA should analyze the changing 'situation' of the marginal classes in America against the background of the economic *and* extra-economic processes that have redefined the position of the poor within the material *and* moral economy of American society. Over the last three decades, structural processes of capitalist transformation (deindustrialization, downsizing, out-sourcing, etc.) have significantly reduced the economic value of wage labor and consolidated a tendency toward rising work insecurity, declining wages, longer working hours, and an overall increase in the socially acceptable levels of 'exploitability' of the American labor force (Schor, 1992; Sennett, 1998; Ehrenreich, 2001). At the same time, however, a broad reconfiguration of governmental strategies of social regulation – such as the transition from welfare to workfare, the growing politico-institutional emphasis on individual responsibility, and the emergence of neoliberal forms of governance that encourage the 'secession of the successful' in fields like taxation, housing, education, etc. (Reich, 1991) – has eroded the Fordist-Keynesian compro-mise, deepening social fractures along lines of race and class. Finally, in the field of cultural signification, the powerful neoconservative hold on public debates on socioeconomic inequal-ity – reinforced by the cyclical emergence of racialized moral panics about the underclass, wel-fare dependency, street crime and drugs, illegal immigration, etc. – has helped to consolidate hegemonic representations of the poor as undeserving and potentially dangerous (Handler and Hasenfeld, 1991; Gans, 1995; Quadagno, 1995).

In the field of penal politics, the broadened materialist framework sketched above would allow the political economy of punishment to overcome its traditional emphasis on the instrumental side of penality, and to analyze the emergence of the American 'penal state' from the point of view of its impact on each of the different levels at which this broad reconfiguration of the American social structure (and of the 'situation' of its marginalized populations) has taken place since the 1970s. In this direction, a post-reductionist critique of the punitive turn should of course emphasize the structural dimension of recent penal practices, illustrating their instrumental role in 'imposing the discipline of desocialized wage work … by raising the cost of strategies of escape or resistance that drive young men from the lower class into the illegal sectors of the street economy' (Wacquant, 2009: xvii). But it should also analyze the widespread governmental effects of penal technologies – particularly in conjunction with other tools of socioeconomic regulation, such as fiscal and social policies – and illustrate their tendency to reproduce and reinforce existing structures of socioeconomic inequality. Most importantly, however, it should elaborate a culturally sensitive materialist critique of the symbolic implications of contemporary penal forms, and analyze how hegemonic representations of deservingness and undeservingness reson-ate with (and provide cultural legitimacy to) an emerging post-Fordist model of capital-ist production whose regime of accumulation is grounded in the material and symbolic devaluation of the poor and their labor.

Finally, the epistemological shift proposed here would enable neo-Marxist criminology to approach penal politics no longer as an outgrowth of capitalist relations of production (a 'superstructure' of the capitalist economy, in the language of orthodox Marxism), but rather as a set of material and symbolic practices that contribute to the overall reproduction of capitalist social formations and of their specific regimes of accumulation.

Acknowledgment

This chapter was originally published in: Simon, J. and Sparks, R. (eds) (2012) *The SAGE Handbook of Punishment and Society*. London: SAGE.

Notes

1   Several directions of research contributed in this period to the consolidation of 'critical' or 'radical' perspectives in criminology (radical feminism, critical race theory, postcolonial studies, etc.), not all of which can be ascribed to Marxism. The focus of this chapter, however, is the political economy of punishment, an approach that owes much to Marxist theory. For a broad reconstruction of different currents of thought in critical criminology, see Van Swaaningen (1997), Lynch et al. (2006) and DeKeseredy (2010).

2   It is worth noting here that a few years before the publication of *Punishment and Social Structure*, Georg Rusche had already exposed some of his ideas in two articles. The first article, originally published in 1930 in the German newspaper *Frankfurter Zeitung*, analyzed prison conditions in the USA during the Depression era (Rusche, 1930 [1980]). The second article, conceived as a research project for the Institute for Social Research in Frankfurt, was published in 1933 in the Institute's journal *Zeitschrift für Sozialforschung*, and outlined the main concepts of the materialist critique of punishment (Rusche, 1933 [1978]).

3   For an analysis of the return of corporal punishment in the USA during the last quarter of the 20th century, see Cusac (2009).

4   For a broad reconstruction of the complex history of *Punishment and Social Structure*, detailing both Rusche's biographic vicissitudes and the problematic reworking of the original manuscript by Otto Kirchheimer, see Melossi (1978, 1980).

5   In the first pages of *Discipline and Punish*, Michel Foucault acknowledges that 'Rusche and Kirchheimer's great work, *Punishment and Social Structure* provides a number of essential reference points', adding that 'we can surely accept the general proposition that, in our societies, the systems of punishment are to be situated in a certain "political economy" of the body' (1977: 24–5).

6   Following David Harvey's recent work, here I use the term neoliberalism to identify a political project developed by Western power elites, particularly in the USA and in the UK between the late 1970s and the early 2000s, in order 'to reestablish the conditions for capital accumulation and to restore the power of economic elites' (Harvey, 2005: 19) after the social turbulence of the 1960s and early 1970s. As a politico-economic system, neoliberalism emphasizes individual freedom over social responsibility, competition over cooperation, market forces over state intervention, capital mobility over financial regulation, and corporate interests over the rights of organized labor.

7   This statement might seem to overlook the contributions of those authors – most notably David Garland (1985, 1990; but see also Howe, 1994) – who during the 1980s and 1990s have engaged in a critical conversation with the political economy of punishment. The point I would like to make here, however, is that most of these works focused on stigmatizing the inability of the neo-Marxist perspective to grasp the symbolic and cultural dimensions of punishment, rather than on promoting any significant advancement in this approach.

8   Bob Jessop and Ngai-Ling Sum have summarized the distinctive approach of the regulation school as follows: 'The regulation approach is a variant of evolutionary and institutional economics that analyzes the economy in its broadest sense as including both economic *and extra-economic* factors. It interprets the economy as an ensemble of socially embedded, socially regularized and strategically

selective institutions, organizations, social forces and actions organized around (or at least involved in) capitalist reproduction' (2001: 91, original emphasis).

9   Which in turn depends on the pressure exercised on the labor market by the unemployed population that fills the ranks of the Marxian industrial reserve army of labor: 'The industrial reserve army, during the periods of stagnation and average prosperity, weighs down the active army of workers; during the periods of over-production and feverish activity, it puts a curb on their pretensions' (Marx, 1867 [1976]: 792).

References

Adamson, C. (1984) 'Towards a Marxian penology: captive criminal populations as economic threats and resources', *Social Problems*, 41(4): 435–58.

Aglietta, M. (1979) *A Theory of Capitalist Regulation*. London: New Left Books.

Althusser, L. (1971) *Lenin and Philosophy and Other Essays*. New York: Monthly Review Press.

Barker, V. (2009) *The Politics of Imprisonment: How the Democratic Process Shapes the Way America Punishes Offenders*. New York: Oxford University Press.

Box, S. (1987) *Recession, Crime and Punishment*. London: Rowman & Littlefield.

Burgess, E.W. (1940) 'Book review: Punishment and Social Structure, by G. Rusche and O. Kirchheimer', *The Yale Law Journal*, 49(5): 986.

Cavadino, M. and Dignan, J. (2006) *Penal Systems: A Comparative Approach*. London: SAGE.

Chiricos, T. and DeLone, M. (1992) 'Labor surplus and punishment: a review and assessment of theory and evidence', *Social Problems*, 39(4): 421–46.

Cusac, A. (2009) *Cruel and Unusual: The Culture of Punishment in America*. New Haven, CT: Yale University Press.

De Giorgi, A. (2006) *Re-Thinking the Political Economy of Punishment: Perspectives on Post-Fordism and Penal Politics*. Aldershot: Ashgate.

DeKeseredy, W. (2010) *Contemporary Critical Criminology*. London: Routledge.

Ehrenreich, B. (2001) *Nickel and Dimed: On (Not) Getting By in America*. New York: Holt.

Foucault, M. (1965) *Madness and Civilization*. New York: Pantheon.

Foucault, M. (1977) *Discipline and Punish: The Birth of the Prison*. London: Penguin.

Foucault, M. (1991) 'Governmentality', in G. Burchell, C. Gordon and P. Miller (eds), *The Foucault Effect: Studies in Governmentality*. Chicago: University of Chicago Press, pp. 7–104.

Foucault, M. (2009) *Security, Territory, Population: Lectures at the Collège de France, 1977–1978*. New York: Picador.

Galster, G. and Scaturo, L. (1985) 'The US criminal justice system: unemployment and the severity of punishment', *Journal of Research in Crime and Delinquency*, 22(2): 163–89.

Gans, H.J. (1995) *The War against the Poor*. New York: Basic Books.

Garland, D. (1985) *Punishment and Welfare: A History of Penal Strategies*. Aldershot: Gower.

Garland, D. (1990) *Punishment and Modern Society: A Study in Social Theory*. Chicago: University of Chicago Press.

Garland, D. (2001) *The Culture of Control: Crime and Social Order in Contemporary Society*. Oxford: Oxford University Press.

Greenberg, D. (1980) 'Penal sanctions in Poland: a test of alternative models', *Social Problems*, 28(2): 194–204.

Hall, J. (1940) 'Book review: Punishment and Social Structure, by G. Rusche and O. Kirchheimer', *Journal of Criminal Law and Criminology*, 30(6): 971–3.

Hall, P.A. and Soskice, D. (eds) (2001) *Varieties of Capitalism*. Oxford: Oxford University Press.

Hall, S., Critcher, C., Jefferson, T., Clarke, J. and Roberts, B. (1978) *Policing the Crisis: Mugging, the State, and Law and Order*. London: Palgrave.

Handler, J.F. and Hasenfeld, Y. (1991) *The Moral Construction of Poverty: Welfare Reform in America*. London: SAGE.

Harvey, D. (2003) *The New Imperialism*. Oxford: Oxford University Press.

Harvey, D. (2005) *A Brief History of Neoliberalism*. Oxford: Oxford University Press.

Howe, A. (1994) *Punish and Critique*. London: Routledge.

Ignatieff, M. (1978) *A Just Measure of Pain: The Penitentiary in the Industrial Revolution, 1750–1850*. New York: Pantheon.

Ignatieff, M. (1983) 'State, civil society and total institutions: a critique of recent social histories of punishment', in S. Cohen and A. Scull (eds), *Social Control and the State*. Oxford: Martin Robertson, pp. 75–106.

Inverarity, J. and McCarthy, D. (1988) 'Punishment and Social Structure revisited: unemployment and imprisonment in the United States, 1948–1984', *The Sociological Quarterly*, 29(2): 263–79.

Jankovic, I. (1977) 'Labor market and imprisonment', *Crime and Social Justice*, 8: 17–31.

Jessop, B. (1990) 'Regulation theories in retrospect and prospect', *Economy & Society*, 19(2): 153–216.

Jessop, B. (2002) *The Future of the Capitalist State*. Cambridge: Polity Press.

Jessop, B. and Sum, N. (2001) 'Pre-disciplinary and post-disciplinary perspectives in political economy', *New Political Economy*, 6(1): 89–101.

Katz, M.B. and Stern, M.J. (2006) *One Nation Divisible: What America Was and What It Is Becoming*. New York: Russell Sage Foundation.

Lacey, N. (2008) *The Prisoners' Dilemma: Political Economy and Punishment in Contemporary Democracies*. Cambridge: Cambridge University Press.

Laclau, E. and Mouffe, C. (1985) *Hegemony and Socialist Strategy: Towards a Radical Democratic Politics*. London: Verso.

Lynch, M.J., Michalowski, R.J. and Byron Groves, W. (2006) *Primer in Radical Criminology: Critical Perspectives on Crime, Power & Identity*. Monsey, NY: Criminal Justice Press.

Marshall, T.H. (1940) 'Book review: Punishment and Social Structure, by G. Rusche and O. Kirchheimer', *The Economic Journal*, 50(197): 126–7.

Marx, K. (1867 [1976]) *Capital: Volume I*. Harmondsworth: Penguin.

Matza, D. (1969) *Becoming Deviant*. Englewood Cliffs, NJ: Prentice Hall.

Melossi, D. (1978) 'Georg Rusche and Otto Kirchheimer: Punishment and Social Structure', *Social Justice*, 9: 73–85.

Melossi, D. (1980) 'Georg Rusche: a biographical essay', *Crime and Social Justice*, 14: 51–63.

Melossi, D. (1993) 'Gazette of morality and social whip: punishment, hegemony, and the case of the U.S., 1970–1992', *Social & Legal Studies*, 2: 259–79.

Melossi, D. (ed.) (1998) *The Sociology of Punishment*. Aldershot: Dartmouth.

Melossi, D. (2000) 'Changing representations of the criminal', *British Journal of Criminology*, 40: 296–320.

Melossi, D. (2003) 'Introduction to the Transaction edition. The simple "heuristic maxim" of an "unusual human being"', in G. Rusche and O. Kirchheimer (eds), *Punishment and Social Structure*. New Brunswick, NJ: Transaction Publishers, pp. ix–xlv.

Melossi, D. and Pavarini, M. (1981) *The Prison and the Factory: Origins of the Penitentiary System*. London: Macmillan.

Pashukanis, E.B. (1978) *Law and Marxism: A General Theory*. London: Ink Links.

Pasquino, P. (1980) 'Criminology: the birth of a special savoir', *Ideology & Consciousness*, 7: 17–33.

Piven, F. and Cloward, R. (1993) *Regulating the Poor: The Functions of Public Welfare*. New York: Vintage.

Platt, A. (1969) *The Child Savers: The Invention of Delinquency*. Chicago: University of Chicago Press.

Quadagno, J. (1995) *The Color of Welfare*. New York: Oxford University Press.

Quinney, R. (1980) *Class, State and Crime*. New York: Longman.

Reich, R. (1991) 'The secession of the successful', *New York Times Magazine*, 20 January. www-personal. umich.edu/~gmarkus/secession.html (accessed 18 March 2012).

Riesman, D. Jr (1940) 'Book review: Punishment and Social Structure, by G. Rusche and O. Kirchheimer', *Columbia Law Review*, 40(7): 1297–301.

Rusche, G. (1930 [1980]) 'Prison revolts or social policy: lessons from America', *Social Justice*, 13: 41–4.

Rusche, G. (1933 [1978]) 'Labor market and penal sanction: thoughts on the sociology of punishment', *Social Justice*, 10: 2–8.

Rusche, G. and Kirchheimer, O. (1939 [2003]) *Punishment and Social Structure*. New Brunswick, NJ: Transaction.

Sayer, A. (2001) 'For a critical cultural political economy', *Antipode*, 33(4): 687–708.

Schor, J. (1992) *The Overworked American*. New York: Basic Books.

Sennett, R. (1998) *The Corrosion of Character: The Personal Consequences of Work in the New Capitalism*. New York: Norton.

Shipler, D.K. (2004) *The Working Poor: Invisible in America*. New York: Vintage.

Simon, J. (2007) *Governing through Crime: How the War on Crime Transformed American Democracy and Created a Culture of Fear*. New York: Oxford University Press.

Spierenburg, P. (1984) *The Spectacle of Suffering*. Cambridge: Cambridge University Press.

Spitzer, S. (1975) 'Toward a Marxist theory of deviance', *Social Problems*, 22(5): 638–51.

Sutton, J. (2004) 'The political economy of imprisonment in affluent western democracies, 1960–1990', *American Sociological Review*, 69: 170–9.

Taylor, I., Walton, P. and Young, J. (1973) *The New Criminology: For a Social Theory of Deviance*. London: Routledge.

Thompson, E.P. (1967) 'Time, work-discipline and industrial capitalism', *Past & Present*, 38(1): 56–97.

Van Swaaningen, R. (1997) *Critical Criminology: Visions from Europe*. London: SAGE.

Wacquant, L. (2009) *Punishing the Poor: The Neoliberal Government of Social Insecurity*. Durham, NC: Duke University Press.

Wallace, D. (1980) 'The political economy of incarceration trends in late US capitalism: 1971–1977', *The Insurgent Sociologist*, 11(1): 59–66.

5

GOVERNING THROUGH CRIME

Jonathan Simon and Giane Silvestre

Introduction

The title claim in Jonathan Simon's book, *Governing through crime* may be polemical, however, it has at its core a key insight into a central feature of contemporary American law and society; one that may be played out in other societies too. Since the late 1960s, Americans have been building new civil and political structures around the problem of violent crime, creating in effect a new order, in which the values the country was founded on, such as freedom and equality, have—in the name of repressing seemingly endless waves of violent crime—been revised, in ways that would have been unimaginable in the 1960s. After more than four decades, governing through crime has fundamentally altered American democracy, forging profound changes in the institutions of democracy: legislative; executive; and judicial.

This new order is a kind of 'organized barbarism' that many Americans have come to tolerate as a necessary response to unacceptable risks of violence in everyday life. It produces a culture of fear around crime in a variety of contexts. But this fear is irrational in its scope and in the primary place it has assumed in American consciousness. Only in recent years, after more than 20 years of historically low crime levels is this new order coming into question politically. Even so, real reform will be difficult. Crime became so central to the exercise of authority in the United States, from the president of the United States down to the classroom teacher or the parent, that it will now take a concerted effort by citizens themselves to dislodge it. They will have to find ways to disrupt the flow of information, discourse, and debate tied to crime, while coming to new ways of understanding and making decisions about those accused of a crime. In the meantime, in those societies which have developed rapidly in the last two decades, from Brazil to South Africa, to India and China, rising politicization of violent crime and related fears are fueling a similar cycle of governing through crime.

Governing through crime generates three specific and important corollaries. First, crime has now become a significant strategic issue. Across all kinds of institutional settings, people are seen as acting legitimately when they act to prevent crimes or other troubling behaviors. Most notably, political 'executives,' especially governors, have sought to expand their roles on issues ranging from the death penalty to restoring voting rights for felons. Second, people have begun to use the idea of crime to legitimize interventions that have other motivations; a number of social problems have been re-conceptualized as criminal problems. Finally, the technologies, discourses, and metaphors around crime and criminal justice have become more visible in all kinds of institutions, where they have tended to expand the scope of governance.

The consequences of crime gaining such status have been enormous. First, the reorienting of fiscal and administrative resources toward the criminal justice system, at both the federal and state levels, has resulted in a shift from the 'welfare state' to a 'penal state'; resulting in a more authoritarian political executive, a more passive legislature, and a more defensive judiciary. In this sense, governing through crime is making America less democratic and more racially polarized; it is exhausting our social capital and repressing our capacity for innovation. Governing through crime does not and cannot make us more secure; indeed, it fuels a culture of fear and control that inevitably lowers the threshold of fear, even as it places greater and greater burdens on ordinary Americans. In short, we now govern through crime in ways that have altered American democracy and reconstituted American citizens.

In the second decade of the twenty-first century, the unprecedented number of Americans confined in prisons, jails, detention centers, and in detention spaces within schools by the end of the twentieth century has experienced only a slight downturn of uncertain duration. The racial skewing of this incarceration boom reversed key aspects of the civil rights revolution. For the first time since the abolition of slavery, a definable group of Americans (a shocking percentage of them descendants of those freed slaves) now lives in a state of non-freedom—either because of a single life sentence, repeated incarceration, or the long-term consequences of criminal conviction. Governing this population through the criminal justice system has not provided the guarantees of security that might inspire greater investment in inner cities, but instead has further stigmatized communities already beset by intractable poverty—not to mention that the middle class has also been transformed in many ways by fear of crime.

The durability of mass incarceration rests in part on its linkage with the crime victim's perspective that has come to define, at least in part, the mission of representative government. Many are now concerned that this erodes the basic structures of American democracy itself (Garland 2001a; Gottschalk 2010), and that the emotionalism of the victim's perspective, when allowed to influence policy, may undermine the significance of broader issues.

This configuration of power has been further embedded and transformed by the astounding terrorist attack of September 11, 2001. The USA's now infamous overreaction to the attacks (Guantanamo, Iraq, torture prisons) can be seen as retroactively justifying the culture of fear that had already been established. At the same time the 'war on terror' represents a major reconfiguration of the security state away from drugs and domestic crime and toward immigration and global jihad. As the recent rise of Donald Trump demonstrates, the reframing of the threat from violent crime toward terror is likely to delay a much-needed rethinking of our commitment to governing through crime, and escalate America's behavior in the world arena.

While the USA may have reached a point of transformation in the cycle of governing through crime (Simon 2014), in other nations, especially newly developed economies like South Africa and Brazil, it may only be beginning. It is critical that scholars, lawyers, and policy makers study the American case and the damage this mode of governing can do to even the most durable democratic constitution in the world.

Thinking about crime and government

A new relationship between crime and governance has emerged in the United States since the 1960s. The emergence of the modern democratic state coincided with the emergence of crime as a 'social problem' and the emergence of criminology as a science of criminal behavior and an expert adjunct of state power in the nineteenth century. For much of this time crime was considered best regulated by modern techniques of social governance developed in response to the major economic and social features of modern industrial poverty rather than through punitive criminal justice (Garland 2001a; Horn 2003). In the USA roughly from 1960 to the present, crime has become a model problem for government rather than a derivative topic to be solved with the solutions of more fundamental social and economic problems.

Of course, there is something self-evident about calling criminal law a form of government. Those convicted and incarcerated are subjected to the most exacting domination allowed in contemporary democracies. The unprecedented growth of those governed as prisoners and former prisoners is indeed a defining feature of the age of mass incarceration. To these we must add the families of the incarcerated who are also subjected to being governed as criminals (Comfort 2008; Silvestre 2012, 2016). Yet beyond those directly threatened by the carceral state there are innumerable ways in which crime regulates the self-governing activity of people who are not targets of criminal justice repression, but only eager consumers of public and private governmental tools to protect themselves from crime (Garland 2001a). We must begin to map the relationship between both faces of governing through crime—the penal state and the security state. A crucial starting point would be to criticize the growing gap between the way our political leaders talk about crime and the vision of government they otherwise promote. Neither side of the political spectrum claims to extol the kind of penal state and gated civil society created over the past several decades, yet even now when reforms are being discussed, both liberals and conservatives consider a 'zero-risk' crime environment an expectation and a right (even though that objective is routinely failed for poor communities).

Considering crime as a governing institution in this wider sense requires us to correct three common misconceptions about the war on crime: that it is primarily about the poor and minorities; that it is primarily about repressing active criminals; and that it is primarily about the exercising of state power. Crime governs not only those on one end of the structure of inequality, but actively reshapes how power is exercised throughout hierarchies of class, race, ethnicity, and gender. If this period saw the formation of a distinctive way of punishing the poor (Wacquant 2009), it also saw the organization of middle class life worlds undergo an unprecedented securitization (Low 2003).

The most visible and commonly discussed features of governing through crime involve practices of punishing, repressing, and confining people. But much of the process involves equipping and guiding law enforcement in the socially valorized pursuit of security and justice. Police and prison focus on people who are, by socialization or social construction, highly recalcitrant to these efforts at governance. Here we are no longer talking primarily about the work of imposing discipline or punishment upon a resentful, resistant criminal. Many middle class subjects of crime governance are instead managed by fear of crime and the increasing validity of victim ideal includes mostly those highly motivated to conform.

The American 'war on crime' and its consequences

According to Garland (2001a), the political response to crime in the United States (as well as the United Kingdom) transformed with the emergence of mass incarceration and the politicization of crime. Essentially, contemporary criminal justice practice and discourse as well as the political order have been reshaped by fear of crime. The post-1980s penal policies combining pragmatic risk management of presumably dangerous populations with populist punitive policy belong to, indeed anchor, a new political order.

As Garland (2001a) showed, the 'crime complex'—or set of principles that embody a mentality—determines not only crime policy and practice, but influences the broader tone and direction of government, especially when it comes to other policies for managing the poor. The crime complex is a response to new realities experienced in 'high-crime societies' (Garland 2001a). The large post-war birth populations and growing affluence in both the USA and the UK created a fragmentation of work and family life and led to economic, geographic, and demographic changes that by the 1960s had increased society-wide levels of anxiety about crime.

Crime did increase rapidly in American cities during the 1960s, as it is increasing in the cities of many newly industrialized nations today. But just as importantly, the political meaning of the experience of crime increased just as rapidly as the media, politicians, and local institutions used crime as a tool in long-running struggles over race discrimination, government responsibility for economic planning, and for aiding the urban poor. Those forms of crime knowledge helped undermine the political support for the modest social democratic welfare structures created during New Deal[1] and Great Society periods of the 1930s–1940s, and 1960s. Crime became a major basis for discrediting liberal more than other important issues at that time. In their place came an enormous expansion of the carceral state, first police, and then prisons. Crime became a privileged focus for legislation with the federal government enacting major crime bills every few years between 1968 and 1994 (Moore 2015) and countless state measures in the same period.

The rise of the prosecutor politician

The war on crime has reshaped key aspects of the American state beginning with the executive branch. Presidents and governors have moved from their post-New Deal role as maestros of a complex ensemble of regulatory and service agencies to be judged by the social results of their performance, to a set of lonely crime fighters measured only in how much they seem to share the community's outrage at crime.

The political executive as law enforcer is surely not a new story. The American prosecutor has long been a unique and important officeholder with deep but limited powers and a special claim to represent the local community as a whole. In the last decades of the twentieth century, the war on crime reshaped the ideal of the prosecutor into an important model for political authority while giving actual prosecutors enormous jurisdiction over the welfare of communities with little democratic accountability.

The USA is unique in giving the power of prosecution over to a locally elected executive official. This has given prosecutors an important advantage in competing for higher office from the very start of the Republic. The New Deal further built up the political status of the prosecutor as both a tool of activist government, and a reaction to the organized criminality and corruption that many opponents of the New Deal saw as intrinsically tied up with the growth of activist government. Later as the New Deal style of governance entered a crisis in the 1960s, the prosecutor as crime fighter emerged as offering a new model of political leadership. This prosecutorial shift of executive leadership can be traced through a rise in his power and through changes in political rhetoric. For example, in recent campaigns for executive offices (that of mayor, governor and president), candidates must show that they identify with the experience of criminal victimization, typically by supporting the death penalty or other severe punishment, although this varies state by state. In this expansion of the prosecutor's role, executive power has become tightly bound up with crime and the political technologies available to confront it.

A peculiar institution

Some institutional features, too, make the American prosecutor a powerful model for governing.[2] Since the early nineteenth century and still the pattern today, the American prosecutor (i.e., the district attorney) has been elected,[3] a fact that has traditionally been seen as compromising the autonomy necessary for professional prosecutors to exercise their discretion. Though a prosecutor may be brought down over a particularly unpopular decision, elections go a long way toward establishing the autonomy and legitimacy of the prosecutor, who is not even subordinate to the mayor or governor. Furthermore, whereas criminal justice policies in most societies are set at the national or provincial level, nearly every county or municipality in the United States has its own set of policies based on which charges the prosecutor chooses to bring or not bring—illustrating his extraordinary level of discretion.

The unique role of the American prosecutor is one of a combination of factors that has long given American justice a distinctive character. The growth of extreme sentences with no possibility of parole deepens the significance of charges brought by a prosecutor. By charging a suspect with any of the many forms of enhancements, such as using a gun during the primary offense or having a previous serious or violent conviction, the prosecutor today can effectively eliminate a person from the community for a generation.

Legislative changes have given prosecutors a larger role in choosing the fate of juvenile offenders too. At the height of the juvenile justice movement in the 1970s, only judges could waive a juvenile's right to be dealt with in juvenile court with its then-dominant rehabilitative narrative and much more limited prison sentence. Today, virtually all states allow prosecutors to place juveniles who are charged with serious or violent crimes in adult court.

The emergence of the prosecutor as a more important locus of governing power has taken place broadly across the United States during the war on crime. Because of the local nature of prosecution, the national picture remains extraordinarily variegated. In many American communities, particularly those angered by publicized instances of violent crime, some prosecutors have responded directly to the potent fear of crime and passion for punishment they can arouse.

It is clear that the war on crime has helped shaped a rationale for prosecutorial misconduct in the very metaphor of war and its premise of extraordinary circumstances. Viewing themselves as frontline war operatives, prosecutors may assume a mandate to go to the very limits of the law to address forces they view as evil.

The local prosecutor may be the purest expression of the American crime governance, and an important path to power, but its political logic is today expressed in two higher executive offices that were not originally so tethered to crime as a problem of prosecution as a normative ideal: the attorney general (both state and federal) and governors.

The attorney general and the war on crime

Most of those who have studied the war on crime for its effects on American politics and government have focused, understandably, on the US president. It is tempting to view the US president as a kind of 'commander in chief' in the war on crime, but recent history suggests that even tough-on-crime presidents have often found their crime policies overshadowed by economic conditions and international relations. In a dynamic that began in the early days of the New Deal, the attorney general has moved from being a relative outsider to one of the most politicized cabinet offices within the entire executive branch, with criminal prosecution functions stationed front and center. That growth of the attorney general's role from a minor to major player in a federal power can be traced to three historical moments: 'reconstruction, 1865–1875; the New Deal, 1932–1952; and the war on crime, 1965 to the present' (Simon 2007: 46).

As the Department of Justice has expanded in size and has been altered by its crime-oriented functions, it has also risen in political importance. Most historians consider the attorney general's office to have been of only minor importance until a crisis of judicial review during the 1930s helped place law at the center of executive authority, and drove the function of attorney general from being a bridge between the president and the Supreme Court to one of being the president's chief strategist in getting his policies validated by that Court.

The attorney general, as we see, combines the functions of a post-New Deal administrator of a large, influential agency with the actual powers of a prosecutor. In this regard, the federal and, in many cases, state attorney general is one of the few high-profile political officeholders who can directly prosecute crime.

The death penalty and governors

To governors whose leadership role had been subordinate to the federal government since the New Deal, the rebirth of public interest in executing murderers offered a unique way back to relevance. Federal agencies might clean air, renew downtowns, or build university dormitories; they could even wage a war on crime. The one thing the federal government could not do from 1972 until the late 1990s was seek and carry out the death penalty. Residual liberal opposition to the resumption of the death penalty kept the federal government out of the issue until the first broad federal death penalty in a generation was adopted in the mid-1990s.

Although generally denied the prosecutor's unique ability to seek the death penalty in a particular case, governors found in the death penalty multiple benefits to their standing as representatives of victims and as opponents of murder—a kind of emblematic crime widely seen as expressing the threat hinted at by all crime. Those governors involved in reestablishing the death penalty after *Furman v. Georgia*[4] have been able to participate in a unique act of political creation, the formation of a political will to the power to kill in a way that galvanized a community.

In those states with the greatest popular support for the death penalty, the move was nearly immediate and generally represented a moment of unity between liberals and conservatives as well as Republicans and Democrats. In those states with substantial opposition to the death penalty independently of *Furman*, restoration came after bitter battles pitting conservatives against liberals.

In conclusion, prosecutors have long represented a distinct American innovation in executive government. Almost everywhere in the world, prosecution is exercised by local representatives appointed by a nation—or at least state-wide executive. Only in the United States (and other countries that have adopted the model) do local elected officials exercise deep if jurisdictionally limited powers and a special claim to represent the local community as a whole. In the last decades of the twentieth century, the war on crime further reshaped the American prosecutor into an important model for political authority, giving governors the tacit political support to govern like a prosecutor.

Fearing crime and making law

The ascension of crime to a privileged status as a social problem in the USA has significantly influenced the rise of a distinct style of lawmaking in which the crime victims emerge as an idealized political subject. Both state and congressional legislatures have produced a notable flow of laws concerning the power to punish criminals since the late 1960s, most of which have increased the authority to punish and have invested more public funds in criminal justice, especially the vast and expensive prison system. This process illustrates clearly how institutions govern through crime.

As mentioned previously, at the center of this new lawmaking rationality is the crime victim. Throughout our history, historic forms of legislation, like the Reconstruction statutes that followed the federal victory in the civil war of the 1860s, which protected freed slaves and attempted to reform local institutions, or the New Deal statutes enacted in the 1930s in response to the Great Depression, which granted a host of new protections and benefits to industrial workers (while leaving agricultural workers out), have framed the citizen in an idealized form of a real social type (freedmen, workers, crime victims). The threat of crime has become a unifying theme in US politics: it simultaneously minimizes the real differences between social groups (say in exposure to crime risk) and authorizes government to take consequential steps against some communities in the name of all. As a result, during decades of increasing partisan divide, a significant proportion of lawmaking by contemporary American representative institutions has concerned crime.[5] The vulnerabilities and needs of victims define conditions for government intervention. Interestingly, it is not all victims, but primarily white, middle class victims, whose exposure has driven that flow of crime legislation.

Crime legislation, which covering a wide range of topics and measures, has a distinctive imagined location: safe and 'respectable' residential areas—typically located in the suburbs (although today a new 'safe city' model of affluent neighborhood is emerging with much the same crime centeredness)—a recognized sub-population against which crime, poverty, and typically minority demographics are pushing. Victims of violent crime have formed the public face of the justification for the war on crime, even as that war has targeted mainly crimes that are not violent (like drug offenses). This is crucial because the decline in the war on drugs as a source of imprisonment since the turn of the century has not seen an end to the broader potency of violent crime fears which are being increasingly refocused on foreign terrorists and immigrants. The basic opposition (often unstated) that crime legislation sets up between potential victims and potential criminals (ignoring that frequently they are the same people), allows for an incredibly diverse set of concerns to be organized within the category of crime problem from youth gangs, to radicalized religious militants, to a wide range of sexual illegalities like possession of child pornography.

A history of the idealized citizen subject

In the birth of the Republic, Thomas Jefferson put forth one of the most well-known ideals of the citizen subject—the small landowning settler. Jefferson was instrumental in articulating this ideal in order to lift the ordinary citizen out of the role of serf, slave, or tenant farmer. Not surprisingly, he had opponents who favored keeping power and wealth in the hands of the government. But his election to the presidency in 1800 helped him realize his vision—for the time being. The question of how much land ownership, and thereby power, the small farmer or ordinary citizen should have was essential to many long-running, foundational struggles for the country, including states' rights, the changing legality of 'squatting' on government land, and eventually matters involving the Civil War and the Homestead Act of 1862.

Land legislation in the nineteenth century reflected a master strategy for fostering democracy and for governing. These laws recognize a certain kind of citizen subject as the dominant interlocutor of government: the white male farmer who, with family or employees, works a relatively small piece of land. Land legislation also created new consumers and experts about the land and its resources. Landowners engaged in active cultivation and development of the land produced this new knowledge and formed a powerful consumer base. Even though any serious notion of a nation of farmers was fading into nostalgia by the end of the nineteenth century, the circuitry created around this idealized political subject remained (and continues even to this day) as an appreciable influence on legislation.

In the course of the Reconstruction Era (1864–1880), Congress passed a series of sweeping measures to address the post-Civil War political and legal ambiguities left by the uncertain status of former slaves, and that of the real property of former slave owners and Confederates. These laws established broad government enterprises designed to sustain newly recognized legal subjects—former slaves—and also marked the start of a new way of making federal law. Legislation highlighted a whole range of idealized political subjects—most importantly freed slaves, but also federal officers, federal employees working under hostile conditions in the South, and pro-Union citizens of the former Confederacy. The laws also recognized important new negative subjects requiring attention, especially the former rebels and slaveholders and formations like the Ku Klux Klan, which threatened freedom.

Interestingly, the Civil Rights movement of the 1950s and its legislative triumphs in the mid-1960s echoed the legal trends of the Reconstruction and renewed the spirit of legislation associated with it. Like the laws of the first Reconstruction, the Civil Rights Act of 1964 and the Voting Rights Act of 1965 created new federal agencies, empowered federal courts to hear civil suits by citizens against state and local government agencies, and produced over time a host of internal responses by state and private organizations to enhance compliance. In its broadest form, the civil rights movement merges into the realm of human rights and the burgeoning bodies of national and international laws being produced around it.

After the Reconstruction era, New Deal legislation (1930s) also brought about one of the great constitutional transformations in American history and recognized a new set of idealized subjects. In its first phase, best known for the National Recovery Act and the Agricultural Adjustment Act, the main subjects were producers in industrial capitalism and its agricultural equivalents. The New Deal now focused on unionized industrial workers, just as Reconstruction focused on freedmen. New possibilities for governance opened up, reflected in new waves of 'consumer' legislation and a range of idealized or demonized consumer subjects.

The rise of the crime victim

Enacted in 1968,[6] the 'Safe Streets Act' was a conglomerate of numerous measures addressing a wide variety of crime and law enforcement-related topics, covering four major themes: Title I authorized more than $400 million in federal funds for planning and innovation in law enforcement, corrections, and courts. The act created a new federal agency to distribute funds through a system of competitive grants to those state and local agencies ready to improve criminal justice at the federal level. Title II established a new rule of evidence for federal courts regarding the admission of confessions in criminal cases. It allowed judges more leeway to deem such statements 'voluntary.' The new standard, if read literally, had the effect of mandating that federal courts ignore several new criteria that the US Supreme Court had established in addition to the voluntariness test. Title III authorized both federal and local police to engage in wiretapping and other forms of electronic eavesdropping with and without a court order under certain circumstances. Title IV set up a federal licensing structure for gun dealers, requiring them to keep information on the purchases of weapons, banning pistol sales by mail order, and banning sales altogether to a range of presumably dangerous subjects, such as dishonorably discharged veterans, felons, and the insane.

At the same time, the apparent rise in violent street crime—primarily armed and unarmed robbery—was concentrated in the big cities that were the traditional anchors of the Democratic Party and the social democratic 'New Deal' style of government. This kind of one-on-one crime linked the term 'violence' to the riots and antiwar protests that had become common for the first time in a century during the mid-1960s, with the extreme opposition to the Vietnam War among younger citizens. Riots and protests were associated with urban blacks and college students, two 'subjects' supported in the New Deal and Great Society eras.

The menace of crime in city streets directly threatened the political coalition and methods of the New Deal at two of its most crucial sectors: the urban working and middle classes, and the organized interests represented by those downtown streets, such as municipal unions, banks, insurance companies with large real estate holdings, large public institutions including the corporations that sustain them, and, by 1968, the civil rights community as a representative of black America. Delivering more effective security to citizens as potential crime victims was imperative to prevent fear of crime from undermining both these newly established social categories. Competition in addressing the crime fears of white citizens became as critical to the party realignment of this period as any other issue.

Law enforcement agencies also emerge as a subject in the Safe Streets Act, perhaps even more strongly than victims. The largest portion of the federal revenues directed to the states under the Act was intended to directly benefit these agencies. These laws reflect the twin principles underlying the federal crime legislation model: the system is the problem and the victim is the key. Nothing has moved legislatures more than the idea that public safety has been sacrificed to the convenience or indifference of the judiciary and the correctional bureaucracy.

Reform has taken the form of 'zero-tolerance rules' that transfer effective discretion to law enforcement and prosecutors, allowing them to decide when to invoke the decision-making process.

Although the Safe Streets Act did little to directly increase criminal penalties or expand the prison system, the representational system it modeled has led to both. Any vote to expand punishment essentially becomes a vote for law enforcement and victims—the paradigmatic act of lawmaking in our time. Among other things, this act changed the rules of evidence and authorized new federal funding for law enforcement, corrections, and courts. It created a harsh but lasting representational legacy, one that implies that to be 'for the people,' legislators must be for victims and law enforcement and thus never for (or capable of being portrayed as being for) criminals or prisoners as individuals or as a class.

Judgment and distrust in the war on crime

As a reflection of government, criminal law would seem to place high value on adjudication. The criminal trial remains the popular paradigm of justice. But during the war on crime, these same adjudicatory values have been delegitimized as unacceptably weak in combating crime. The American courts have been affected by the framing of street crime as a fundamental political problem to be solved by government, including courts, and the resulting 'war on crime,' as discussed.

At the beginning of the twentieth century, the idea of courts producing a distinctively modern form of governance appropriate to the ills of industrialized societies found its most charismatic and expansive vision in the figure of the juvenile court judge, a local figure working among the cities' poor and immigrant classes who had nearly dictatorial power over adolescents and their families and discretion to pursue the public interest by saving the child from a life of crime.

In the period between 1960 and 1980, courts, especially federal courts, played a significant role in reforming US prisons (especially the plantation style prisons of the deep South). Beginning in the 1980s, however, the role of courts generally as appropriate movers of social policy has been under effective attack and in particular their role in reforming state prisons. The federal courts in particular reduced their intervention into public institutions and embraced a very different model of authority, one based on deference to prison expertise and populist punitive sentiment. Only recently has the US Supreme Court suggested limits to this deference in *Brown v. Plata* (2011), upholding a lower court order for massive population reductions in California prisons (Simon 2014).

Courts have also been diminished in their role as punishers. Juvenile courts have found themselves under attack as too weak a deterrent against violent youth crime, and have been stripped of much of their control over minors accused of serious crimes. Changes in the sentencing of adults convicted of crime in federal and many state courts have also seen a decline in the authority of judges. In this sense, the war on crime, and the changing mentalities and logics of government it has encouraged, has been harder on judges than on any other category of governmental actors.

The resulting jurisprudence is increasingly convoluted, result-oriented, and defensive. This is manifest in the way American courts have come to respond to issues of criminal justice, including punishment, capital punishment, and juvenile justice. From the mid-1970s, courts have favored the government's power to punish through a broad body of law (Bilionis 2005). Much of this work has been accomplished through 'valorization' of police, victims, and prosecutors.

Race, the war on crime, and mass imprisonment

Since the 1980s, America has created a distinctive penal form called by some experts 'mass imprisonment' (Garland 2001b). However, mass does not mean racially uniform. The term is meant to point to three distinctive features of imprisonment in the United States: its scale, its categorical application, and its increasingly warehouse-like or even waste management-like qualities (Feeley and Simon 1992).

In the nineteenth and twentieth centuries, prisons operated in accordance with a number of competing—and effective—principles. Among them were essentially coercive monasteries where penitence was produced through solitary confinement; locked factories, mills, and mines, and where criminals were subjected to the discipline of silence and group labor under the ever-present threat of the whip; and correctional institutions, where prisoners were forced into group therapy and received college educations. Building prisons served to remove troublesome individuals from the community, while supporting investment in construction contracts, through the production of a docile labor force, with the help of new forms of psychiatric and psychological expertise.

The distinctive new form and function of the prison today is a space of pure custody, a human warehouse or even a kind of social waste management facility, where adults and some juveniles are concentrated for purposes of protecting the wider community. The 'waste management prison' promises to promote security in the community simply by creating a space physically separated from the community in which to hold people whose propensity for crime makes them appear to be an intolerable risk for society.

An examination of the history of American prisons and how they functioned provides a context for the current 'waste management' vision. The Eastern State Penitentiary in Philadelphia, Pennsylvania is the most famous example in the world of the solitary confinement penitentiary. Its individual cells, designed for the prisoners to live and work in full time, aimed at achieving total isolation of prisoners from other prisoners and allowing for total administrative control over what came in and out of the cells. Staff responded with a variety of strategies aimed at coercing cooperation, including pressure on the body (although seeking to avoid the visible and intense contact of whipping). There is also compelling contemporary evidence that solitary confinement went too far in breaking down inmates' subjectivity, leaving them incapable of constructing a new reliable self. Its persistence is due to the fact that the Pennsylvania solitary system fit well with the political order that was taking shape in the early Republic.

The Pennsylvania model helped to constitute a political order outside prison walls in two quite distinct ways. First, the prison would become the center of a vast, informal web of stories about the horrors of life for those locked up. Second, the confinement of the 'morally corrupt,' like that of the physically ill in the hospital, was seen to similarly cut off 'infection,' enable objective observation, and concentrate efficient therapeutic procedures (Foucault 1977). This model of prison was called big-house prison and was operated through the middle of the twentieth century, when the social peace of the prison could collapse, leading to violence among inmates and between inmates and guards. Violence in the prison in turn produced more scandal.

The large supply of big-house prisons meant that the physical structures would remain dominant, but the new model of classification reshaped routines and individualized treatment carried out by a staff of treatment professionals. Though policies of rehabilitation had continuities with the reform policies of the big-house prison and the penitence of the solitary confinement prison, it promoted a very different grid upon inmates and their conduct and implemented a very different set of interventions. Labor had been central to earlier reform hopes, but even after the end of the Great Depression and the subsequent rise in unemployment, labor never regained its place in the prison. Instead, education and therapy were the major forms of treatment and the building blocks of a new control regime that took shape, now dubbed 'correctional institutions.'

In those states in which the New Deal mentality was most successfully articulated, the state's claim to reform criminals through punishment was greatly expanded. The penitentiary and the big-house prison promised to reform prisoners by giving them the opportunity to repent spiritually or by submitting them to discipline and a life bereft of comforts. But neither the early republic nor the patronage state staked its legitimacy on reform. In both cases, the individual prisoner was thought to have the major responsibility for reforming. The correctional institution, by contrast, very much staked its legitimacy (and through it the state's) on an ambitious aspiration to transform recalcitrant subjects who had typically 'failed' in the softer sectors of society—such as the school system and social welfare agencies. The routines of the prison would not simply expose sinners to their consciences or scrub rogues clean of their bad habits, but reach inside with scientific techniques to address deep individual pathologies. Moreover, the correctional institution promised to accomplish this in relative transparency, using social science not only as a technology of rehabilitation but as a way of evaluating its own success.

By the 1960s, however, prisoners and college students were evidence to many of the failure of the New Deal state. Model subjects of a form of government staked on the ability to reap major social gains from extensive investment in the subjectivity of ordinary people, had become increasingly agitated and seemed to be turning on the New Deal state that privileged them. Not surprisingly, they became symbols of a perceived threat to 'law and order' around which the first new political coalition since the New Deal would take shape.

Thus, we see today the 'waste management prison' no longer works in its broad efforts at shaping the personalities and personal relations of inmates, but relies instead on specific behavioral objectives to be enforced over any degree of resistance, even total segregation of the most threatening prisoners. Solitary confinement also became an important disciplinary tool in the correctional institution, where it served to separate out those deemed 'unreformable' security threats. It is only in the prison that solitary confinement is deployed merely to achieve internal security. This prison lacks an internal regime—whether based on penitence, labor, or therapy—and increasingly relies on mechanical controls on movement and violent repression of resistance.

Despite its superficial resemblance to the penitentiary, today's prison uses its architectural and technological capacities not to transform the individual but to contain his toxic behavioral properties at reasonable fiscal, political, and legal costs. Some crime rates have increased and the fear of crime has risen. Mass imprisonment has thereby become a stable solution in the harsh political logic of governing through crime.

Though governments have found considerable political advantage through investing in prisons, and analogous techniques of exclusion and exile are spreading, it is possible that a security-conscious populace will question this arrangement. There is increasing public discussion of the effects of prisons that send back into society inmates who not only are not rehabilitated but who have been made more dangerous or rendered dysfunctional by imprisonment.

Ultimately, massive prison buildup poses a risk of delegitimizing the current political order. Just as the correctional institutions, welfare systems, and universities ultimately weakened the New Deal political order that invested so heavily in them, the post-New Deal order finds itself mass-producing subjects, namely prisoners that it can neither govern adequately nor eliminate permanently. This vulnerability is likely to emerge in the coming decade as the fiscal costs of an aging prison population and the economic losses of a heavily criminalized underclass both grow.

Governing social institutions through crime

The transformation of US political and legal institutions around the problem of crime has also moved into civil institutions such as the family, schools, and workplace.

The family

In the last two generations, the role of crime in the governance of the family has virtually flipped. At one time, truly violent conduct by parents over children, or adult men over women and girls in the family, was largely immune from the force of criminal law out of deference to patriarchal authority by many legal decision makers—legislators, judges, prosecutors, and police officers. Today, the problem of crime, starting with violence but including many other kinds of acts, has extended the institutional and metaphoric force of the criminal law into families with a scope and intensity at least as great, if not greater, than that of the marketplace. Also, contemporary American adults, especially parents, find themselves under a moral and sometimes legal mandate to manage crime risks in their domestic domain. Not surprisingly, Americans have become major consumers of security technologies, expertise, and services.

More than a quarter-century after the first efforts to win funding for shelters and obtain recognition for domestic violence victims, the criminal justice system in most states now reflects a new consensus that domestic violence of any kind is a crime, and one best deterred by quick sanctions against the violator.

On the other hand, the emergence of domestic violence as a contemporary crime issue is in large part a result of the work of second-wave feminist activists and their allies in law and the social sciences, and also may represent one of the triumphs of that generation of feminism. Since mandatory policies went into operation in the 1990s, a new wave of feminist criticism of this trend has developed that focuses on three issues: how effectively the hardening of the criminal justice response to domestic violence protects women from repeat violence; how the recasting of the domestic violence victim as a crime victim advances the equality of women more generally; and whether the idea of masculine domination as criminal violence increases cultural support for that domination. The complexity of these issues goes beyond this discussion, but it is interesting to consider them within the more general context of governing through crime.

Briefly, the question of whether increasing criminalization is actually reducing violence for women remains a prime one for advocates for victims of domestic violence (Mills 2003). Also, recent empirical research has called into question the specific deterrent effects of arrest on batterers. This evidence suggests that arrest may be counterproductive precisely in those communities of poverty and high unemployment where many of the most vulnerable victims are also situated. The domestic violence victim has been embraced by the state and the political establishment, but on terms that erase the role of gender inequality and distinctive sources of this victimization. Specifically, the problem of domestic violence is framed almost exclusively as one that needs to be addressed through mandatory arrest policies, increased prosecutorial attention, and enhanced penalties. As a result, little attention is paid to the underlying issues that trap women suffering from domestic violence, such as the lack of employment and child-care options. Treating the complex domestic violence issue simplistically has created blinders to broader issues and yields counterproductive results. This issue also uniquely illustrates the constraints of basing crime policy on victim logic.

Once a space deemed too private for the intrusion of criminal justice, the family has now become criss-crossed by tension resulting from crime, domestic violence, child abuse, school misconduct, among other problems. The family is also where we most directly experience the arts of governance, both as subjects and, for those of us who become parents, rulers of a most uncertain and frail sort. Perhaps no other set of relationships more powerfully anchors the constellation of meanings and practices we call governing through crime. In a very real sense, our ability to roll back the penal state and mass imprisonment may depend most on our ability to talk ourselves down from the way we prioritize the avoidance of crime risk in shaping our family life.

Safe schools

For a generation after the US Supreme Court's landmark school desegregation in *Brown v. Board of Education* (1954), public education in the USA was transformed around the problem of desegregation. Since the 1980s crime in and around schools has replaced racial equality as the dominant political problem that must be confronted and documented by a reinforcing spiral of political will and the production of new knowledge about school crime. Ironically, the idea of crime as a political problem in schools may have had recent origins in the desegregation era and the often violent conflicts that arose around efforts to dismantle racially bifurcated public school systems. Although the stamp of desegregation remains on many public school systems today, by the late 1970s, it had largely run its course, defeated by private action and judicial retreat. In the same period, crime became an increasing influence on school governance.

Some factors have accelerated the criminalization of schools in the last decades: a historical memory of high tides of youthful violence during the 1960s and again in the 1980s; the association of youth culture with drugs and drug trafficking, a linkage that began in the 1960s, and during the 1980s was framed as a major source of threat to the safety and educational mission of schools; and a growing right-wing movement against public schools has found it extremely useful to frame the public schools as being rife with crime.

The media have picked up on all these themes. Few issues are as likely to keep parents awake for the late local news broadcast as the latest breaking story on crime in schools. For many middle class Americans whose children will virtually never encounter guns or even knife fights at school, the real and imagined pictures of violence-plagued public schools in inner-city communities have created a neural pathway to a fearful concept of public school. The result has been policies in suburban schools that parallel, generally in softer forms, the fortress tactics employed at frontline inner-city schools. In 1994, the federal Safe Schools Act allocated federal money to encourage local schools to invest in security regimes and technologies. Police officers, known typically as 'school resource officers,' are now an on-campus feature of public schools across the nation. Many fear that in combination with harsh juvenile justice policies, these changes have fed what has been called 'the school to prison pipeline' (Wald and Losen 2003).

Significantly, schools have long been considered the most important gateway to citizenship in the modern state. Today in the United States, it is crime that dominates this symbolic passageway. And behind this surface, the pathways of knowledge and power within the school are increasingly being shaped by crime as the model problem, and tools of criminal justice as the dominant technologies. Through the introduction of police, probation officers, prosecutors, and a host of private security professionals into the schools, new forms of expertise now openly compete with pedagogic knowledge and authority for shaping routines and rituals of schools. At the macro level of school systems, many of these inner-city schools themselves have become larger versions of punishing rooms, identified by students and parents as places of disorder and risk.

As in the earlier era of reforming schools for racial equality, the federal government has played a crucial role in making crime a national problem for schools, and crime prevention a national agenda for school reform, using incentives and sanctions to spread it across state and local systems. In this sense, both desegregation and the war on crime, through court cases and legislation, have played a significant role in constructing a national problem and national solutions to making schools work. For racial equality, the signal year was 1965, when the Elementary and Secondary Education Act invested billions of federal dollars in poor schools provided they complied with desegregation orders. For safe schools, the pivotal legislation was the Safe Schools Act of 1994, a complex of laws ensuring security in schools. This Act operates far beyond the simple application of money to a local problem; rather, it requires changes in the way knowledge flows and decisions are made within schools:

> This move to nationalize the security response has had impressive results. According to one survey, more than 90 percent of schools have zero tolerance policies in place for weapons possession. More than 80 percent have recently revised their disciplinary codes to make them more punitive. Nearly 75 percent have been declared 'drug-free' zones, 66 percent, 'gun free' zones.
>
> *(Simon 2007: 216)*

Overall, crime has become an axis around which to recast much of the form and substance of schools, resulting in an enormous channeling of attention to schools through the lens of crime. In this context, students are reframed as a population of potential victims and perpetrators. At its core, the implicit fallacy dominating many school policy debates today consists of a gross conflation of virtually all the vulnerabilities of children and youth into variations on the theme of crime. This may work to raise the salience of education on the public agenda, but at the cost to students of an education embedded with themes of 'accountability,' 'zero tolerance,' and 'norm shaping.' The merging of school and penal system has also resulted in speeding the collapse of the progressive ideal of education and tilting the administration of schools toward a highly authoritarian and mechanistic model.

The workplace

Crime has always been part of the messy struggle for control of the workplace. American history includes numerous examples of how the instruments and metaphors of criminal law play into the cauldron of conflicts of the workplace. Slavery, most famously, was directly governed with the possibility of death for acts of rebellion against the master. Masters were formally entitled to exercise penal violence in the enforcement of their right to demand the labor of the slave. As the formally free contract became the dominant standard, dismissal replaced physical violence as the ultimate sanction.

After the industrial revolution, regimes of labor rose to dominance in the nineteenth century against a background of labor relations that looked far more like monarchies or slavery. In such settings, the power to govern work meant the power to define disobedience as crime and respond with sanctions, often physical. Discipline wielded by managers had an undeniably penal element that included flogging, confinement, and loss of pay. On the other side, employee resistance to modern labor systems and the capitalist factory was often defined by law as a form of property crime.

From the late 1930s through the beginning of the 1980s in the United States, the heyday of collective bargaining during the rise of labor unions corresponded to a time when the role of criminal law as instrument and metaphor was minimized in the governance of work. During this period, strikes were mostly considered a legitimate mode of civil conflict, meaning labor could take its grievances with management into open refusal to work without fear of being fired and pauperized, or even criminalized by the state.

Collective bargaining also ushered in an era of due process in disciplining and dismissing employees. Administrative courts produced a body of arbitration decisions on 'just cause' for dismissal that, instead of dismissal, highly favored rehabilitation and reintegration of the 'deviant' worker. But by the turn of the twenty-first century, the decline of collective bargaining and the general loss of bargaining power by American workers in the face of global competition for low-cost labor had undermined this practice and brought a return of crime as a central axis of regulation and resistance in the workplace.

Today the problem of crime security has been a key locus for workplace conflict. The workplace has been transformed by employers' needs to screen prospective and current employees not just for fraud and drugs, but also for violent behavior. From management's point of view, we can see multiple streams of influence, from concerns about crime itself inside the workplace to the metaphors of punishment. Globally, the general dominance of neoliberalism has enshrined the 'at-will' employment doctrine granting employers freedom to dismiss employees for unsatisfactory performance of almost any kind. From the perspective of the collective bargaining environment, where dismissal was openly seen as a severe punishment appropriate in response only to extreme or repetitive misconduct, the return of dismissal as a ready tool of management reflects a significant escalation in the punitiveness in labor relations. The at-will employment environment combined with the pervasive search for criminal behavior in the workforce creates a similar relationship of support between the penal law of the state and the disciplinary goals of management. Also, the decline of collective bargaining and the general loss of bargaining power by American workers in the face of global competition for low-cost labor have allowed for the return of crime as a central axis of regulation and resistance in the workplace.

Conclusion

To a remarkable degree in the post–World War II era, the idea of war has been accepted as a metaphor for transformations in how we govern. The war metaphor gains purchase from the proximity to danger and the demands for power and knowledge that such proximity brings. The subjects chosen are almost always those that can, in a single semantic leap, strike into the deepest horrors associated with wars, chaos, mass violence, and sudden and irreversible loss. Metaphors of governance of this magnitude tap into the fear of power so monstrous that inspired the generation that framed the American Constitution.

Since the September 11, 2001 attack, terrorism and a war on terrorism have entered American public discourse with a rapidity that seems remarkable even by the standards of hot-button issues like cancer and crime. This event brought many elements together to show how the war on crime since the late 1960s altered the way political authority has been exercised, including the transformation of American private life. The war on terrorism that has unfolded since 9/11 has been shaped in ways that skew toward security and the 'culture of control' (Garland 2001a). The current American 'war on terror' illustrates perfectly how a metaphoric war can reshape government.

Also, after 9/11, the response of our major political institutions to the attacks was conditioned by political rationalities previously produced by the war on crime. We have become more vulnerable to those who would use terrorism as an excuse to impose new strategies of governance. The high risks of relying on an essentially penal strategy to achieve global forms of security are already becoming visible in Iraq and elsewhere.

Indeed, the nationwide war on crime as panoply of political technologies and mentalities within the country's borders has profoundly shaped the strategic context of its worldwide war on terror. Many of the deformations in American institutions produced by the war on crime, developments that have made our society less democratic, are being publicly reconstituted as responses to the threat of terror. For example, the label 'enemy combatant' (Cole 2003) may exempt the case from the normal due process rights of the individual. This echoes the familiar assertion of primacy for the executive in representing the public's security interests in the 'war on crime' which, as previously noted, has led to a shift in power to the prosecutor over such processes as pretrial detention, juvenile court jurisdiction, and the length of prison sentences. Essentially, the claims of executive autonomy made in the war on terror track closely with the power assumed by prosecutors in the criminal justice system and by chief executives asserting prosecutorial prerogatives.

Interestingly, the war on crime—in the form of a sustained effort to incarcerate racialized classes of 'dangerous lawbreakers'—has produced only marginal drops in crime rates, and no real gains in the sense of security in society. Still, it remains deeply embedded in the current structure of American politics and policy making, with only incremental signs of reform. The impact of a similar global military enterprise in security through mass incarceration is not promising.

Of course, the human cost of the war on crime has been extreme. The percentage of minorities in American prisons and jails has increased, many of them through the accumulation of nonviolent offenses. This concentration has done substantial damage to American society. It has replaced discredited racist narratives of exclusion with new and seemingly ethical narratives of crime or terrorism. We must carefully monitor the people arrested, punished, or deported in any war on terrorism to make sure the government is targeting people who act like terrorists and not people who just look, talk, or pray like someone's idea of terrorists.

In a broader sense, the 'war on crime' has also created vulnerabilities in the various populations in different ways. There is the obvious massive concentration of black and Latino young men and, increasingly, women in the criminal justice system, and the attendant impact on their communities, dependants, families, and neighbors. It also includes a white middle class increasingly taxed by the weight of a private security apparatus that requires gated private police communities, long commutes to safe suburbs in high-polluting, gas-guzzling SUVs, and the high cost of keeping one's children in a state of organized supervision until the parents get home from work.

In opposition to the country's founding tenets and to the interests of the human being, the impulse to power that characterizes established governments has manifested in a complex, entrenched, and uncontrolled pattern in the United States, of governing through crime. This pattern affects the individual, the family, the school, the workplace, and government from its highest to most local levels. It has distorted democracy itself and turned the criminal justice complex into a monster that furthers the racist agendas of the nation's most shameful period. It has extended its fearsome reach beyond its own borders into the wider world. It is up to the academic and the average citizen to begin to see and name the phenomenon: governing through crime.

With prison populations having dropped a small amount in the last few years after decades of growth, and growing calls for further cuts and efforts to reduce the racial disparities of both incarceration and policing, the opportunity to challenge the pervasive influence of crime fear on the institutions of democracy and civil society has begun to emerge. A number of conjunctural features seem to encourage this challenge including historically low levels of crime, mounting evidence of inhumane treatment in our prisons, and the sheer fiscal cost of such an extended carceral state. However, change will not be easy and a significant correction of the past four decades of crime fear-based legal and political adaptations will require a concerted political effort. The warehouse prison, solitary confinement, and racial profiling by the police may be relatively easy to discredit and delegitimize. Much harder to shift will be the powerful presumptions that operate today in our legal system in favor of trusting power and authority to law enforcement and prosecutors while treating those who have been criminalized as inherently and unchangeably dangerous.

Notes

1 The political response to the mass poverty experienced in the collapse of the US economy in the Great Depression of the 1930s.
2 Simon (2007) analyzes in detail three examples of the prosecutorial ascendance in American politics. First, he looks to the attorney general, a figure whose growing stature within the executive branch from the 1930s on presages and perhaps explains the prosecutorial presidency. Second, he calls attention to the role of the death penalty in reenergizing the role of the nation's governors, which in turn has led many governors to become champions of the death penalty. Finally, Simon draws a parallel between these two trends by examining the rise of governor as the predominant pathway to presidency since the end of the 1970s.

3   With some exceptions, the American prosecutor is a local actor with a specific territorial jurisdiction, typically equivalent to the county or municipality. American prosecutors answer to a very specific electorate, a public they generally share with a variety of local law enforcement agencies, judges, and defense attorneys. This means that rather than Texas law or Florida law, one really has to talk about Houston and Dallas law, Miami and Jacksonville law (Simon 2007).

4   *Furman v. Georgia* was a 1972 United States Supreme Court decision that ruled on the requirement for a degree of consistency in the application of the death penalty. The case effectively led to a temporary moratorium on capital punishment throughout the United States by setting a new federal standard.

5   Interestingly, even today as the focus turns toward shrinking the carceral state, there are promising indicators of inter-party cooperation on reform statutes not found on any other issue (indeed most of the fighting seems to be within the ranks of the Republican Party which embraced tough on crime as its core value earlier and more enthusiastically than the Democratic Party).

6   https://transition.fcc.gov/Bureaus/OSEC/library/legislative_histories/1615.pdf.

References

Bilionis, Louis. 2005. Conservative reformation, popularization, and the lessons of reading criminal justice as constitutional law. 52 *UCLA Law Review* 979: 986.

Cole, David. 2003. *Enemy aliens: Double standards and constitutional freedoms in the war on terrorism.* New York: New Press.

Comfort, Megan. 2008. *Doing time together: Love and family in the shadow of the prison.* Chicago, IL: University of Chicago.

Feeley, Malcolm, and Simon, Jonathan. 1992. The new penology: Notes on the emerging strategy of corrections and its implications. *Criminology* 30(4): 449–474.

Foucault, Michel. 1977. *Discipline and punish: The birth of the prison.* New York: Vintage.

Garland, David. 2001a. *The culture of control: Crime and social order in contemporary society.* Chicago, IL: University of Chicago Press.

Garland, David. 2001b. *Mass imprisonment: Social causes and consequences.* London: Sage.

Gottschalk, Marie. 2010. Cell blocks & red ink: Mass incarceration, the great recession & penal reform. *Daedalus* 139(3): 62–73.

Horn, David G. 2003. *The criminal body: Lombroso and the anatomy of deviance.* Hove: Psychology Press.

Low, Setha. 2003. *Behind the gates: Life, security and the pursuit of happiness in fortress America.* London. Routledge.

Mills, Linda. 2003. *Insult to injury: Rethinking our responses to intimate abuse.* Princeton, NJ: Princeton University Press.

Moore, Nina M. 2015. *The political roots of racial tracking in American criminal justice.* New York: Cambridge University Press.

Silvestre, Giane. 2012. *Dias de visita: uma sociologia da punição e das prisões.* São Paulo: Alameda Editor.

Silvestre, Giane. 2016. Local consequences of the prison policies in state of São Paulo, Brazil: A case study of the town of Itirapina. *Crime, Law and Social Change* 65(3): 269–285.

Simon, Jonathan. 2007. *Governing through crime: How the war on crime transformed American democracy and created a culture of fear.* New York: Oxford University Press.

Simon, Jonathan. 2014. *Mass incarceration on trial: A remarkable court decision and the future of prisons in America.* New York: The New Press.

Wacquant, Loïc. 2009. *Punishing the poor: The neoliberal government of social insecurity.* Durham, NC: Duke University Press.

Wald, Johanna, and Losen, Daniel J. 2003. Defining and redirecting a school-to-jail pipeline. *New Directions for Youth Development* 99(Fall): 9–15.

6

CRIMINOLOGY AND CONSUMERISM

Simon Winlow and Steve Hall

Introduction

For too long criminologists have either ignored consumerism or misunderstood the role it plays in the constitution and reproduction of our current way of life. Few in criminology have acknowledged that consumerism is now integral to our global political economy, and even fewer have offered critical accounts of the vital functional and ideological roles consumerism has played throughout the history of capitalism. There is, of course, a valuable literature that covers most aspects of consumerism and consumer culture, but the illuminating concepts and analyses associated with this literature have yet to be integrated into our discipline. Here we argue that criminologists must now make a concerted attempt to push critical accounts of consumerism towards the centre of our discipline.

Consumerism

For those readers in the liberal democracies of Europe and North America, it should be perfectly clear why some sociologists have for decades talked about the rise of 'consumer culture' and the development of our present 'consumer society' (see, for example, Baudrillard, 1998; Bauman, 2007; see also Smart, 2010 for an overview). Consumerism is everywhere. It permeates the global North, especially in those nations that have fully embraced the principles of neoliberalism. It has forced change upon many modern institutions (Beck and Beck-Gernsheim, 1995, 2001) and transformed our cultures and our expectations of collective life (Baudrillard, 1998; Bauman, 2003, 2007). Perhaps more importantly, consumerism has infiltrated our dreams (Hall et al., 2008). It shapes our desires, our fantasies and our aspirations. As it has overpowered all alternative sources of meaning and value, it has furnished us with the symbols we use to gauge our own value and social significance (Winlow and Hall, 2006, 2009a). It mediates human relationships and informs the ways we perceive and interact with others (Baudrillard, 1998; see also Miles et al., 1998). It orders new hierarchies and new mechanisms of exclusion (see, for example, Hayward and Yar, 2006; Miles, 2014), and it reproduces and intensifies the competitive individualism that is such a socially disruptive yet economically dynamic feature of postmodern liberal societies (Winlow and Hall, 2012, 2013). Its symbols of 'conspicuous consumption' (Veblen, 2009) are used to display status and foment the envy of others (Hall et al., 2008), yet, paradoxically, they can also be used to communicate belonging and a desire for integration and acceptance (Winlow and Hall, 2009a; Miles et al., 1998). Consumerism's semiotic system is complex and changing. If our discipline is to construct new and enlightened models of socially contextualised motivation that are in keeping with the times, criminologists must try to understand consumerism's impact on our individual drives, desires and social motivations – why and how we act and interact as social beings.

Understanding the development of contemporary consumerism should encourage us to think again about our history and the forces that have transformed our economies, our cultures and our shared social life. We must also understand that these comprehensive changes to everyday social experience play a role in the gradual transformation of human subjectivity (Hall, 2012a, 2012b). This is not simply a matter of identifying the epidemic effects of consumer culture, such as mental ill-health, depression and anxiety (Sloan, 1996), and their various knock-on effects, which include obesity, body dysmorphia, anorexia, bulimia, self-harm, suicide and so on (Schrecker and Bambra, 2015). Whilst of course avoiding crude mechanistic determinism, we must look beneath these outcomes to the underlying processual context, particularly the dominance of instrumentalism, cynicism and narcissistic competition in our cultural lives. We should connect these processes to politics and economics, but we should also be brave enough to contemplate the suggestion that, after thirty years of socially destructive neoliberalism, a period in which we have been told repeatedly to value individual freedom and wealth above all things, our most basic dispositions and orientation to the world have changed (Hall, 2012a). To understand the role of consumerism in these changes we need to return to a critique of ideology. It is simply inadequate to keep repeating interpretivism's domain assumption – born in the past to attack crude positivist causality – which tells us that we interpret and negotiate meaning before we settle on various interpretations and act in the world. Consumer culture is constantly active in those complex webs of meaning and interpretation and the broader macro-processes of mass mediation – infiltrating, persuading, humiliating, affirming, eroding, reconstructing. We need to *rethink* consumerism from a criminological perspective, identify precisely its relationship to politics, economics, society and culture, and locate it firmly in a conjuncture in which the certainties of modernity are rapidly receding into the past. One vital aspect of this rethinking involves identifying and discarding obsolete ideas and theoretical frameworks from criminology's past (see Hall and Winlow, 2015) which clutter the field and prevent inquisitive researchers from coming to terms with the reality of contemporary consumerism.

Our starting point, however, should be to recognise that the democratisation of conspicuous consumption in the West has played a dynamic role in the reproduction of the capitalist system, with all of its stark inequalities and injustices (Hall et al., 2008). Consumerism feeds on such inequalities as it offers what now seems like the sole potential means of compensation and escape. However, the escape it offers is a centripetal *escape inwards* that keeps us invested in neoliberalism's political and economic project (Hall et al., 2008). It encourages us to forget what we have lost and imagine instead a ceaseless procession of technological innovation and novel indulgences that will lead us into a bright future, improve our lives and deliver to us enduring happiness. But, as it places individuals in competition with one another for symbols of social status, consumerism has eroded modern forms of civil society (see Baudrillard, 2007; Stiegler, 2009), and it has played a significant role in the dissipation of modernity's collectivist and universalist political projects (Badiou, 2007). As the future looks bright up above, it also looks more unstable and fragile down below.

Consumerism and desire

The pleasures of active consumerism are not all that they seem. As some scholars have noted (see, for example, Bauman, 2007), the pleasures of consumerism tend to be quite fleeting. Consumerism is not simply about now and then buying a few material goods that we want but do not need. It also involves the ritualised act of discarding consumer items that have lost their allure, only to begin the process all over again as new products come on to the market (see Appadurai, 2011). Consumerism holds out the prospect of satisfaction through ownership, but, quickly, we find ourselves assailed by new desires. New trinkets are placed before us, and the 'social' dialogue that accompanies them inspires us to return yet again to the market in the hope that these trinkets will assuage the anxieties that gnaw away at us from within. But somehow consumerism never quite manages to deliver. Dissatisfaction becomes permanent and active.

As Baudrillard (1998) notes, consumerism encourages us to believe that we are affluent, content and happy despite there being no rational foundation for such a belief. In fact, as we in the West move further and further away from the old world of industrial modernity – with its restrictive institutions and its powerful collective systems of belief – contentment and happiness appear to be diminishing. The liberalisation of our culture and economy has not produced new freedoms, and it has certainly not created a new world of contentment. Anxiety and insecurity abound, and these negative emotions are not restricted to the poor. They exist throughout the social structure (James, 2010).

Rarely these days do we reach a point at which we move away from the consumer sphere in the belief that it has lost its appeal and no longer has anything to offer us. The market's ideological support systems serve its fundamental growth-fetish by working tirelessly to incorporate older populations into the sphere of consumerism (Barber, 2007), just as they do with younger populations (Postman, 1996; see also Hayward, 2012; Smith, 2013). We now learn to consume at a very young age. We are bombarded with advertising messages and quickly become attuned to the power of brands, at home, in the street and even in institutions of early education (Beder, 2009). Advertisers now target children (Bakan, 2005; Barber, 2007) with incisive marketing campaigns that encourage anxiety and symbolic competition as a form of surrogate socialisation (see Hall et al., 2008). Consumerism does not relinquish its grip when the individual reaches retirement age. Everyone must consume, and everything that can be commodified – including health, education and all other needs once ministered in the public realm – must be commodified. All that is holy must continue to be profaned, even when it becomes difficult to remember what might have been holy in the first place.

Consumption is not simply the epiphenomenon of production. Consumer desires demand advancements in production, which in turn convince us that increased consumption is possible, justifying and unleashing further desires. If we were ever to reach a point at which we were no longer desirous of consumerism's products and services, capitalism would plunge into crisis. After the 9/11 terrorist attacks, George Bush Jr encouraged Americans to go shopping in order to get the economy moving again. 'Head down to Disneyworld in Florida', he said, bequeathing us one of his trademark quirky metaphors. Consume and enjoy your freedoms, he affirmed, and in so doing display to our cultural and geopolitical enemies our deep commitment to the American way of life. Americans did not get where they are today by not consuming. As consumerism is ideologically and practically normalised in such no-nonsense terms each individual is encouraged to understand herself in relation to its variegated sign-value system. As markets approach their limits they must be rejuvenated. New products need to be identified, and old products need to be recycled so that they can be resold to younger buyers who have yet to encounter their symbolic value. Capitalism is a self-revolutionising economic system. It changes only so that it may continue.

However, advanced knowledge of capitalism's systemic logic, no matter how detailed and sophisticated, does not tell us why consumers continue to consume beyond need. How is consumer desire constituted? This is the point where the damage caused by the relative marginalisation of psychoanalysis across the social sciences in favour of less sophisticated frameworks such as symbolic interactionism and post-structuralism – which celebrate autonomous resilience, creativity and resistance even when they are in their historically most beleaguered and parlous condition – comes into stark relief. Lacanian psychoanalysts have long known that desire signifies a lack (Lacan, 2007), an absence, and as such is contingent, fragile and ephemeral. As soon as we take ownership of the longed-for thing we are destined to lose our desire for it. Desire, therefore, is dependent upon the absence of the desired object. Consumer markets are reliant upon this basic principle. Taking ownership of a car, a house or a gadget we have longed for does not satisfy us, because desire is immediately reconstituted. We immediately begin to focus on another thing, or another experience, and desire begins again. Satisfaction, properly understood, threatens consumerism.

Furthermore, our desires are never fully our own. It is wrong to assume that they are simply a product of our imagination. Our desires are socially mediated. We desire what the other desires. Would we desire a Chanel handbag if others do not? Would we desire such an item in the absence of marketing campaigns, media coverage and the general cultural acceptance of branded 'style'? The advertising industry's general understanding of these processes has enabled it to reformulate desire and thus expand consumer markets in increasingly sophisticated ways by identifying, creating or exacerbating social anxieties, and stimulating the deep sense of lack that lies at the core of the human subject (Hall et al., 2008). Even today's social movements, conceptually provisioned by social science's conservative and liberal theoretical frameworks, promote themselves by feeding on the desire for what the neoliberal market has made absent – community, authority, security, autonomy, politics, resistance and so on. Once we have been made anxious about our social standing by having doubts cast on our imagined personal attributes it becomes that much easier to sell us a commodity that promises to mollify our anxieties and boost our esteem.

The process of stimulation and mollification, unlike its effect on the individual psycho-emotional constitution and social environment, is quite pragmatic and banal. Any material item made available for sale is accompanied to market by a range of symbolic lures. Increasingly, it is this symbolism that provokes desire and encourages the consumer to part with his money. As we hinted earlier, we should not make the mistake of assuming that consumerism and consumption are the same thing. Consumption, when it occurs within reasonable limits, is of course a basic need. Consumerism is quite different. Consumerism exceeds the functional materiality of the object. For example, it seems that many of us in the affluent West no longer simply buy a coat in order to keep warm during winter. There are other considerations. We choose a coat from a store that, in all likelihood, contains a great many coats. Our choice may be influenced by what appear as practical matters. We may go for the cheapest coat, or a coat that has been significantly reduced in price. We may also choose a coat because of its designer label, or we may simply like the style of the coat we have chosen above those others on offer. We may choose a coat because it is similar to coats worn by friends. We may disregard a coat for that very same reason. We may buy the coat because we have seen a celebrity wear a similar coat, or because that style of the coat is, at present, considered fashionable. None of these matters are clear cut. However, to imagine that we each possess a specific sense of taste entirely of our own creation is to accept uncritically the doctrine of the fully autonomous sovereign individual.

Consumerism, as Baudrillard (1998; see also Stiegler, 2009) noted, has replaced traditional systems of individuation to become a mode of rootless, free-floating competitive differentiation. Its purpose is not the satisfaction of needs or desires. In a western culture dominated by advertising, we are compelled to discard collective identities and pursue individuality, but all we have to construct a sense of uniqueness are the symbols presented to us by consumerism's panoramic sign-value system. Our 'individuality' is always anxious, incomplete and, ultimately, a myth that reflects our growing distance from reality and our complete submersion in a com-modified hyper-reality that has displaced all collective forms and mutual interests. We have stepped outside of history. Adorno and Horkheimer (1997) were similarly unimpressed by the promises of consumer individualism. Like Baudrillard, they presented such individualism as a functional myth, constructed and constantly reaffirmed by various facets of late capitalism's ideological machine. For them, the pursuit of individuality led only to an unfulfilling pseudo-individuality that rested upon the disavowal of the uniformity that structured consumer practice. The diner can choose from the menu, but our choice is limited to the options placed before us. Choice, where it existed at all, was restricted, and subject to highly advanced processes of manipulation (Ewen, 1998). We should not underestimate the skill and incisiveness of the advertising industry or its ability to create within us a desire for consumerism's objects (Lears, 1995; Ewen, 2001), and we should not simply ignore consumerism's social dimension, and the various pressures imposed upon us to emotionally attach ourselves to consumerism's object-symbols.

The way we are constantly persuaded to buy and display object-symbols is complex and paradoxical. Contradictory pressure is exerted simultaneously on all of us to both fit in with social groups and set ourselves apart from them (Miles et al., 1998; Winlow and Hall, 2009a), which energises a dynamic matrix fuelled by the constant adoption and dismissal of identities. It is comforting to imagine ourselves as autonomous, discerning consumers able to see the dominant ideology for what it is, and position ourselves in opposition to it. However, as we dress to reflect our unique choice of style, we also hope to triumph over others carrying out the same task. As we donate our energy and our money to consumer capitalism we simultaneously and constantly disrupt the social collective in favour of an unstable milieu of competitive individualism.

Of course, in most cases we buy our clothes from global corporations that have branches throughout the world. Quite often, these stores stock almost exactly the same items. We shop in Gap, Primark or Top Shop stores that are replicated across the country and other parts of the world, yet we still manage to retain the conceit that we are creative consumers shopping in ways that reflect our unique tastes. The conceit of the sovereign individual blinds us to the homogeneity beneath the surface of consumer culture, and draws our attention away from the process of capital accumulation with its myriad social, environmental and geopolitical problems. However, if we redirect our attention away from this spectacular procession of object-symbols and towards our experience of culture, we can begin to glimpse the underlying structures and processes in which our tastes are formed.

Consume now!

How can we contextualise consumerism's cultural triumph in both popular and intellectual life? Our narrative must begin in post-war Europe. The eventual cessation of hostilities after six long years of war produced across much of the continent a common desire to avoid further social and political upheaval. The establishment of social democratic governance across much of Europe fomented a sense of hope among the working class that the obscene hierarchies of the pre-war period were gone for good (Hennessy, 2007; Judt, 2010). The Keynesian economic model was adopted by politicians in France, West Germany, Britain, Scandinavia and the Benelux countries. Sizeable welfare states were constructed, and most mainstream politicians were committed to the principle of full employment (Judt, 2010). The capitalist class largely accepted the new state of affairs. Full employment, rising wages and comprehensive welfare systems ensured a degree of political and social stability, which counteracted the threat of leftist militancy and rebellion. Capitalism paid a significant price to ensure its survival (see Minsky, 2008). Taxes on wealth and income rose, and returns on investments fell.

In time, productivity began to rise, which prompted labour unions to become more strident in their demands. The lifestyles of the working class improved significantly. Most working-class families were not rich by any stretch of the imagination, but, in comparison to the realities of life for working-class families before the war, their lot had improved. The British working class had overcome many of the huge material pressures and insecurities they had faced from the beginning of the capitalist project. Education and healthcare were now free at the point of provision. Work was, for the most part, quite plentiful, and wage levels ensured that, once immediate costs had been met, a little disposable income remained that could be used for leisure pursuits and creature comforts (see Hennessy, 2007; Judt, 2010). This is not the 'origin' of consumerism, but it is the era in which consumerism permeated western societies to become a mass phenomenon.

The growth of consumer culture during the post-war period is indicative of a number of fundamental changes in political economy, but before we address these changes we must first of all explain in a little more detail the importance of capitalism's growth fetish. Capital is not simply money. It is money in search of investment. Capital must remain in constant motion, moving from investment to investment, securing profit and growing as it does so. If capital stands still or withdraws from the fray, it returns to its initial form and becomes once again mere money, and in most cases mere money tends to depreciate in value. Without profit-seeking investment the entire capitalist system is threatened. Capitalists must believe that investment in pursuit of profit is a risk worth taking. Without this investment factories lie still and financial markets crash.

During the relatively golden years of post-war social democracy, capitalists tended to accept a lower rate of return on their investments than they do today. Now the expectations of capitalist investors have grown. In a globalising economy the nation-state's ability to mediate the relationship between labour and capital has been diminished, and capital has, to all intents and purposes, withdrawn from the negotiating table. These days capitalists, unbound from their nation-states of origin, are unwilling to accept reduced profits in return for social and political order and neoliberal states have neither the desire nor the ability to impose their will on highly mobile capital.

However, in countries such as Britain during the post-war years there existed a political consensus that capital must be controlled and used to benefit the population. Capitalism's innate drive to secure maximum profit was attenuated by the politics of opposition and a robust state willing to intervene in the economy to maintain demand and truncate excessive inequality. Living standards for many improved significantly, inequality decreased, crime declined to record lows, and new markets keen to take advantage of the surplus income of the masses began to develop. The first wave of the consumer boom promised to make the lives of consumers easier. Washing machines, vacuum cleaners and gas cookers sold well. They possessed an obvious use-value. Consumers bought these items because they possessed an appealing and demonstrable function. Washing machines, and later spin dryers, made the task of dealing with the family's laundry that much easier. Vacuum cleaners were remarkably easy to use and a huge advance upon what had gone before. The initial love affair was with technology.

As markets grew rapidly early forms of consumer competition began to establish themselves in popular culture – in neighbourhoods and in family and friendship networks. Consumer market sectors relying exclusively on technological innovation quickly reach a saturation point. In time, everyone open to the idea of buying a vacuum cleaner already had one. At that point a change occurs in the mode of innovation. Technological innovation can no longer be relied upon as a constant, so each manufacturer then turns to the advertising industry in the hope of encouraging customers to choose their products over others. However, when a market such as this is quite advanced, manufacturers are forced to fight for business among a diminishing pool of potential customers. In a saturated market demanding more reliability and durability manufacturers can no longer wait to sell to those seeking to replace defective products. At this point the market must convince those who already own vacuum cleaners to decide that the vacuum cleaner they own is no longer good enough. Either its technology is outdated, and better machines are now available, or the *symbolic value* of the machine has depreciated, to the extent that one must purchase again to regain or improve one's social status in relation to others. By utilising sign-value and elevating its significance in the minds of consumers, the market was able to overcome the limitations of materiality. In time, the actual function of an electric kettle became, for many consumers, less important in purchasing decisions than the sign-value attached to the kettle itself. Even relatively uninteresting household items are signified and become part of the constellation of consumer culture. Consumerism is not just about fashionable markets in clothes and music; it infiltrates every aspect of common culture.

The gradual diminishment of use-value and the massive growth in the importance of sign-value enabled the market to keep expanding. Baudrillard (1998) was particularly taken with the unending stream of gadgets that began to flood the market from the 1960s onwards. His analysis occasionally overshot the runway – for instance, two-speed windscreen wipers are actually useful in variable weather conditions – but his general point that many products were bought primarily to titillate and distract hit the mark. The consumer became increasingly convinced that he had left behind the discomforts of reality to occupy a sphere of affluence, happiness and perpetual novelty. To the consumer, the commodification and increasingly formulaic character of cultural artefacts and the concomitant loss of cultural autonomy and authenticity (Adorno and Horkheimer, 1997), a process that continues today, became relatively less important than the entry into a realm of material comfort and imaginary social status.

This new Imaginary provoked cultural change in working-class communities (Hoggart, 1969). Many working-class lives were now liberated from the back-breaking toil and perennial economic insecurity that had beset previous generations. Working hours fell and incomes rose. Working conditions improved. Leisure time expanded, as did the range of commercialised cultural activities available for workers and their families. Amidst this cultural sea-change of displacement and renewal consumer items became progressively more important in processes of identity-building. Consumerism's symbolism worked its way into what had hitherto been organic aspects of culture – family, class, community, nation, religion. Slowly, the importance of these signs grew and more traditional aspects of common culture receded into history.

But how has consumerism achieved this position of cultural dominance during a neoliberal period in which livelihoods have become more precarious and the incomes of most of the population have either remained static or fallen? It is embedded within our cultures so completely that we often fail to notice its influence. Of course its means of dissemination are now technologically advanced and its seductive techniques have been developed to a fine art. Western nations are flooded with cheap goods manufactured abroad. But this does not obviate the basic financial fact that, strictly speaking, the majority of individuals still cannot afford the goods that would temporarily assuage their symbolically charged desires. So how have these individuals managed to maintain their commitment to consumerism?

The answer is quite straightforward. Debt. A vast ocean of debt, renamed 'credit' to avoid the traditional shameful connotations. Psychologically, the embrace of debt has been justified by a reworking of the Super-Ego. Whereas the traditional Super-Ego's harsh judgements made us feel guilty for desiring too much, the new 'Super-Ego injunction to enjoy' (Žižek, 2009) makes us feel guilty if we miss a single opportunity to indulge ourselves. 'Reward yourself' it says, 'you've earned it'. In this encouraging cultural climate consumer and household debts have grown enormously during the neoliberal epoch even as incomes have fallen in real terms, and as job insecurity has established itself as a norm throughout the post-industrial West (Horsley, 2015). As wages stagnated while productivity and profits continued to grow, a huge amount of capital was generated, which must find profitable investment opportunities. Rather than paying western workers more, capital has paid them less, invested in manufacturing centres abroad where profits were even higher and compelled these workers to take on debts and pay interest in order to sustain the illusion that they have a recognised place in mainstream society. In basic financial terms, capital has claimed larger profits by suppressing wages. It has then loaned the surplus capital back to workers as money so they can continue to purchase the consumer items that are judged to be of such crucial cultural importance (see Wolff, 2013). Thus a new investment mechanism has been created, yet another source of huge profits that accrue from developing markets in consumer debt (Horsley, 2015). These debts can be packaged, insured and traded in derivatives markets, creating yet another source of profits. In the neoliberal era the entirety of the global economy is structured in relation to debt.

We are now encouraged to take on debts while young. Then we must spend much of our lives attempting to pay them off. We are encouraged to look forward to an old age free from debt, which distracts us from a reality in which a growing proportion of the western population structure their existence in relation to their debt obligations. Consumer debt, it seems, plays a significant role in subjugating and depoliticising western populations, and encouraging them to abandon all hope of systemic change (Lazzarato, 2015). Debt – especially mortgage debt – bonds us to the current economic system and ensures that we submit to the established means of servicing debt. We work to pay down our debt, and we increasingly see the removal of consumer debt as a significant life goal (Lazzarato, 2015). We often spend our lives in jobs we hate in order to pay back what we owe (Horsley, 2015). We are encouraged to buy now, on credit, and then spend years paying back this money. For many, the psychological burden of debt is enormous: as the allure of luxury consumption quickly fades, only the debt remains.

However, this descent into the vortex of consumer debt could not have occurred without underlying changes in political economy. In the 1970s Britain's industrial economy ran into trouble. The reasons for this are complex, but we should note in particular the growth of global competition, the rise in oil prices and the insistent demands of organised labour for better wages and conditions. Capital had, since the close of the war in 1945, accepted a lower rate of return on investments. They had traded off higher profits for the relative social stability provided by the post-war social democratic consensus. However, as profits fell further during the 1970s while labour unions remained belligerent and taxes remained high, capital rebelled against the established consensus and agitated for new economic freedoms. These gradual, behind-the-scenes changes resulted in the transformation of the Conservative Party and the rise of Margaret Thatcher, a singularly divisive figure willing to take on the hard work of forging a new politics based upon entrepreneurialism, competition and individual reward (see Sandbrook, 2013; Bloom, 2015). She actively sought to break the power of the unions (Milne, 2014), and in this task she achieved a staggering degree of success. She began to deconstruct the protective barriers that restricted profitability. She embraced the rhetoric of the free market, and allowed cheap foreign products to flood into Britain. Almost immediately, Britain's industrial economy was thrown into crisis. Unemployment rose to historic heights (Milne, 2014). Thatcher did little to protect Britain's industrial base because, to her, mass unemployment, poverty and social distress were 'a price worth paying' in order to liberate capital from the shackles placed upon it by the social democratic state (see Vinen, 2010). In order to boost economic growth and shrink the size of the British state she privatised many of the country's most prized assets and looked to the city of London to boost the country's flagging Gross Domestic Product.

Her politics were revolutionary in many respects. Many believed her tenure in office would be an aberration, and that the post-war consensus would reassert itself upon her departure. Instead, she established a new consensus that encouraged all the politicians that followed her to commit to tax cuts and market liberalisation as a means of generating growth. Britain was abruptly thrown into a post-industrial economy dominated by an expansive and diverse service sector. Blair attempted to compete for hi-tech manufacturing jobs, but by this time the British economy was at a marked disadvantage in comparison to countries such as Germany and Japan, whose manufacturing infrastructure had been refurbished and modernised by US investment after the war. However, a liberated financial sector busied itself creating new investment opportunities for global capital, and a downgraded and highly unstable service sector mopped up the rest. Britain had moved from being a producer nation, defined by its entrenched class system and its extractive and manufacturing industries, to a consumer nation, defined by rising inequality, reduced welfare provision and precarious labour markets (Winlow and Hall, 2006). The new jobs produced by the service sector were no compensation for the loss of stable and reasonably well-paid industrial jobs. Britain had gone from being the 'workshop of the world' (Samuel, 1977) to an insubstantial retail park, a journey from the corporeal reality of manufacturing to the theme-park hyper-reality of consumerism (see Winlow and Hall, 2013).

Neoliberalism worked up an unstoppable head of steam. The 1990s are often represented as the decade in which neoliberalism solidified its reputation for growth and prosperity, but the economic reality of those times is more complicated (Stiglitz, 2004). It is true that the city of London boomed during those years, but the industrial economy in Britain withered still further. Inequality continued to rise and labour markets became yet more unstable. The growth of the city and the increased profitability of the financial sector encouraged the new investment class to become more confident and assertive in its representations to government. The rest of the country was, apparently, being pulled along on their coattails, an encumbrance creating too much drag on the sleek new machine. This new elite pushed for reductions in regulation and tax breaks, and, because the financial sector was vital to the national economy, the politicians of the main political parties were receptive. Politics, by this stage, had lost much of its traditional substance. The key characteristics of neoliberal ideology, economics and governance were accepted as a *fait accompli* (see Winlow and Hall, 2013).

The industrial nations of the old world were, with only one or two exceptions, now consumer nations that imported goods from the developing world. The developing world was developing rapidly because it was producing most of the basic volume goods for western markets. The United States of America underwent similar changes to Britain. At the end of the war it was by far the world's most productive nation. Such economic strength allowed it to offer the old-world European nations loans to rebuild after the war. This was not an act of largesse. It was clear that the United States would benefit economically as Europe redeveloped. Of course, as the USA was the global industrial superpower, a significant amount of the money advanced to the European states would flow back to the USA as these nations and their corporate sectors purchased American goods and services. The factories of the USA would be kept busy as European economies improved and as demand increased. However, as the century progressed the USA stepped down from its role as an industrial superpower. Deindustrialisation during the 1980s and 1990s was as disruptive there as it was in Britain, if not more so (see Currie, 2008). Although the economy retained proportionately more manufacturing than the UK, key American politicians had no desire for the USA to compete head-on with a new generation of productive economies. Instead they transformed the country's economy into a gigantic financial vacuum cleaner for global investment capital.

Germany and Japan remained hugely productive economies, and, as time passed, they were joined by China, India and one or two others. The economies of these countries produced significant surpluses. China, for example, tends to produce the consumer items that Americans buy, but it must reinvest its surplus in ways that sustain its markets – to enable those who buy its products to continue to buy its products. So, to generalise, China reinvests its surplus in western consumer economies. This inward investment, circulated through the credit system, supplies the West's army of consumers with the money they need to keep buying products manufactured in China and the other industrialising, surplus-generating nations. Money from the globe's key surplus economies flows into Wall Street to the tune of around $5 billion per day (Varoufakis, 2015), and, generally speaking, this money tends to flow back to these surplus economies as Americans purchase their products.

We now live in an era of low interest rates (Picketty, 2014). Western governments must keep interest rates low in order to lubricate consumer markets. The availability of cheap debt has played a crucial role in the development of the neoliberal project. As we have already noted, wages stagnated as profits rose. However, the availability of cheap debt to chase cheap consumer goods created a perception of incremental progress that curtailed any suggestion of renewed political militancy. Cheap debt enabled workers to continue with consumer lifestyles even though their incomes had not improved a great deal. In Britain and the United States the growth of home ownership bound the individual to the neoliberal economic project in a way that merely renting a home does not. It militates against political radicalism, and it tends to create the impression that one's lot in life is improving. Such an iconic asset as a house occasions us to imagine that we are richer than we are while the low-interest mortgage fades unnoticed into the background.

Criminology and consumerism

Misunderstanding and misrepresenting consumerism

Consumerism, we should note, is now so ubiquitous that it can often escape the attention of critical social analysts. In criminology, many of those who have addressed consumerism do so only in the most basic way. For example, some criminologists have used the term 'consumerism' to communicate only the basic need for goods (see Newburn et al., 2015). Some who place themselves on the criminological left have mistaken theoretical critiques of consumerism for some sort of condescension felt towards those who consume (see Cooper, 2012). Others approach it uncritically as the great gift capitalism has bestowed upon its populations (see Matthews, 2014), or even identify it as the new wellspring of political resistance (Hall, 1981). These positions overlook the key issues at stake and systematically ignore consumerism's most troubling characteristics.

While the material and environmental aspects of consumer culture should be of great interest to criminologists, especially those involved in the rapidly developing sphere of green criminology, deeper psychosocial accounts of consumer culture require analyses of ideology and symbolism (Baudrillard, 1998; Frank, 1998; Hall et al., 2008). However, for over four decades many on the political left in Britain have embraced consumerism and focused on its supposedly liberating qualities. Many leftist social scientists (see, for example, Featherstone, 1995; Hall and Jefferson, 2006) have argued that consumerism equips us with a new range of signifiers that allow individuals to transcend an inherently repressive social order that sought to control the population and reproduce its diverse historical injustices. Consumer culture, they argued, allows the individual to take a far more active and creative role in the construction of self-identity. For these critics, the old order was breaking apart. The rebellious young consumer could no longer be pinned down by the traditional mechanisms of control and repression. The consumer choices of these young people reflected their desire to break free from convention and forge a new path of their own creation. Above all, consumerism appeared to facilitate a 'rebellion into style', to bring choice and stylistic diversity to a dour and rather homogenous post-war cultural vista. It allowed younger generations to separate themselves from the restrictions of the parent culture and identify their own sources of value, which tended to be connected to fashion, music and other aspects of popular culture (see Hebdige, 1979; Hall and Jefferson, 2006). Consumer symbols could be reworked into new meanings on which forms of subcultural togetherness could be founded. Thus cultural in-groups could use consumerism and their own unique sense of style to set themselves apart as 'new communities', and to reaffirm their separateness by constructing their own norms and values, which were believed by some to resist modernity's expansive 'social control apparatus' (Cohen, 1979: 340).

Consumerism and the 'cultural turn' in criminology

Of course, the intellectuals who constructed these perspectives were perfectly aware that consumer products were intimately connected to processes of capital accumulation, and that corporately manufactured goods carried with them a range of signifiers constructed in relation to profit maximisation. They were also cognisant of the fact that these signifiers bonded the individual to the reproduction of capitalism. However, these new leftists were convinced that all the while the consumer symbols that represented capital accumulation and systemic reproduction were being reworked and subverted by creative youth. For instance, most of the subcultural analysis that came out of the Birmingham Centre for Cultural Studies focused on this process. Hall and Jefferson (2006) argued that the huge amount of importance placed on commodified clothes and music by youth subcultures did not indicate the triumph of modern capitalism. From the 1970s onwards cultural theory performed complex and at times rather obscurantist intellectual gymnastics to convince the reader that the members of various subcultures had invented a collective symbolic method of subverting capitalism, even though the majority spent most of their disposable income on mass-produced consumer items and showed only passing interest in substantive alternative politics. The youthful consumer was positioned as a romantic hero, a modern day David who could not be controlled by the ponderous capitalist Goliath. This 'cultural turn' was in essence an intellectual and political wrong-turn that is only just recently beginning to be seen for what it is – a colossal mistake (Smith, 2014; Hall and Winlow, 2015; Horsley, 2015; Raymen and Smith, 2016). Wildly overreacting to the failures of post-WWII state socialism and social democracy, the cultural turn founded itself negatively on the outright denial of the unavoidable fact that capitalism cannot be resisted at the point of consumption. Subsequently, it dismissed mass media and advertising's ability to develop niche markets and integrate ostensibly 'oppositional' cultural trends. As time passed the cultural turn showed its colours by openly revealing its fear of what might happen if fundamental changes were made to capitalism's economy and attendant ideological project.

The cultural turn made a high art out of the refusal to engage with reality. Its unwavering optimism still survives. Indeed, it continues to be canonised in the textbooks and remains very much in vogue among social scientific accounts of youth culture, music and fashion (see, for example, Beal, 1995; Martin, 2009; Haenfler, 2012). Those working in this tradition cannot or simply do not want to detect the fundamental lack that pervades contemporary consumer culture and captures so much of its subjects' energy. They tend to ignore the crass theme-park fakery of our shopping malls, the incessant privatisation of public space and the flood of advertising messages that debase our culture, foment hostile and envious social relations and solidify the position of money as the primary source of value. They cannot see consumerism's co-option of leisure (Raymen and Smith, 2016), the stupefying and infantilising populism of most mainstream media and the general dumbing down, fragmentation and depoliticisation of a once vibrant and threatening working-class culture. They ignore the rather obvious fact that many of the perceived benefits of ownership are calibrated against the inability of others to own. Instead, they see legions of young people dipping nimbly in and out consumerism's semiotic system, inverting corporate messages and constructing their own norms and values that are inherently noble and opposed to all that is wrong with western consumer society. We might speculate that this basic narrative continues to exist at the forefront of youth sociology at least partly because it celebrates the underdog and positions young people as inherently rebellious and politically engaged. Constructing and canonising a celebratory account of young people battling against a repressive social order also obviates the need to engage with the more challenging and far less optimistic theoretical accounts of consumer culture offered by European neo-Marxists and post-Marxists in France and Germany (see especially Adorno and Horkheimer, 1997; Adorno, 2001; Baudrillard, 2007; Althusser, 2008; Stiegler, 2009).

The cultural turn was imported into many aspects of critical criminology, but it found its true expression in cultural criminology. Despite the evolution of this sub-discipline and the growing interest of a small number of cultural criminologists in consumerism, ideology and political economy (see, for example, Hayward and Yar, 2006; Hayward, 2012), we should note that in general cultural criminology has not yet escaped the cultural turn to confront it on its own terms (see Ferrell, 1996; Presdee, 2000). To generalise, cultural criminology tends to assume that the stereotypically marginalised and under-educated 'criminal' is engaged in a fight against capital, cultural homogeneity and a broad system of oppressive social control. The criminal fights against the governance system that refused to give him a chance and criminalised his values on behalf of capitalist reproduction. With his crimes the criminal kicks back symbolically and materially at a system that has been stamping on his class for generations.

This position romanticises the working-class deviant and imbues him with characteristics difficult to find in the prisons, police stations and problem estates of the neoliberal era. Does the marginalised criminal truly or even vaguely understand the abstract system of capitalism and its social order, and is he so disgusted by his experiences of this capitalist reality that he structures his identity and social activity in opposition to it, even at the risk of significant punishment? Alternative research and theorisation suggest not (Ayres and Treadwell, 2012; Smith, 2014; Horsley, 2014; Hall and Winlow, 2015). Do not most acquisitive criminals, both in prisons and out on the street, tell us that their primary conscious motivation for committing crime is to acquire cash? Do they not blame their ignominious or traumatic experiences on anything but capitalism, and do they not display a clear desire to live a life defined by consumer indulgence? Too often liberal social scientists busy themselves scanning the barren landscape of contemporary neo-capitalism in search of cultural formations that might be construed as 'oppositional' (see Hall and Winlow, 2007), and in so doing ignore the reality that is right before their eyes.

The painful reality is that the vast majority of the population are not particularly radical, and nor are they ethically opposed to the continuation of liberal capitalism. They are not disgusted by the commodification of culture, they are not particularly angry at the growing vacuity of parliamentary-democratic politics and they are not morally opposed to neoliberalism's brutal reallocation of money upwards. The silent majority tend to accept the basic constituents of our present reality, and if they are angry or dissatisfied with anything, it tends to be their own failure to achieve success within the capitalism system, and not the grotesque excesses of the capitalist system itself. The same tends to be true of people involved in criminal markets (Winlow, 2001; Winlow and Hall, 2009b). Might it not be reasonable to suggest that most acquisitive crimes and even some violent crimes (Winlow, 2001; Winlow and Hall, 2009b; Hall and Wilson, 2014) are bound up with the logic of capitalism and the anxieties, drives and desires it inspires? Should we really continue with accounts of crime as resistance when reality indicates quite clearly that the desire to seek gratification in consumer capitalism's sign-value system is a well-established characteristic in most criminal cultures across the West? At the fundamental level of what we now call 'values', criminals are really very much like the rest of us. It is at the level of norms, or rather, the normative ways in which 'values' are enacted, that criminals tend to be a little different.

We must now accept that the legions of people who head out to the high street, the shopping mall or the retail park each weekend are not using their consumer practice to oppose the inequities of capitalism's social order. We must discard the comforts of romanticism and celebratory accounts of culture if our knowledge and understanding of contemporary culture is to progress. We must summon up the courage to appraise a truly disturbing reality. It is a reality in which we will see significant ecological change within our lifetime (Heinberg, 2011). We are already seeing the first signs of resource wars and mass migration caused by ecological change, the failure of nation-states and ongoing national and geopolitical conflict (Hiscock, 2012; Klare, 2012; Pearce, 2013). Democratic politics, it appears, has lost the capacity to regulate the market (see Winlow et al., 2015), and, in most western societies, the gap between rich and poor grows wider with every passing year (see Picketty, 2014). Why should we assume that young people are inherently rebellious and carry with them the will to transform the injustices of the world? A minority may be politically active and keen to effect real change, but a great many more care nothing for politics and are happily distracted by the shallow pleasures of consumer culture. Cynicism has grown to become one of the defining features of our post-crash cultural life. Some people may be angry at the injustices of the contemporary capitalism, but, for the moment at least, they can find no alternative to truly believe in. It is in this climate of *substantive political absence* that many western sociologists and criminologists see consumer culture as a site of political potential (see Winlow et al., 2015).

The challenge to criminology

We can see quite clearly the inadequacies of the cultural turn. But why should a renewed critique of consumerism in its politico-economic context be of interest to criminologists? Surely everyone is influenced by consumer culture, so theories based on a critique of consumer culture cannot explain why a minority commit crime. Of course this is the standard riposte that does have some critical potency when levelled against early criminological positions such as strain, differential association and subcultural theory. However, most criminological theories are hampered by various forms of naturalism, sometimes overt and other times disavowed (see Hall, 2012a) – the malady of infinite aspiration, affinity to the in-group's values, susceptibility to labelling, resistance to authority and so on. Tied down by these various assumptions, criminological theory in general has ignored consumerism's incursion and disruption of the basic processes that configure the individual's construction of identity.

We have explored this in fine detail elsewhere (see, for example, Hall et al., 2008), but the basic premise is that consumer culture has encouraged the growth of problematic forms of narcissism that rest not simply on advancing the interests of the self, but advancing one's interests in relation to the downfall of others. Earlier we laid out in basic detail how the neoliberal mode of political economy has cast western populations into a condition of precariousness. This general condition fosters anxiety in each individual regarding their position in the social order. In its natural form anxiety is latent whilst its manifest form – fear – is objectively contingent; put simply, latent low-level anxiety can erupt into fear when a threatening object appears. However, there is nothing natural about anxiety's permanent incitement in the form of *objectless anxiety*, where it cannot make the transition into fear because the real object of fear – the unstable and insecure capitalist system – is ideologically disavowed. There is nothing timeless and natural about a social system that casts its members into a permanent condition of objectless anxiety about their membership (Hall, 2012a). Capitalism was the first system in history to systematically dissolve the social for the purpose of generating permanent objectless anxiety and harnessing the ensuing human energy to the economy (Winlow and Hall, 2013). Life in the developing capitalist project cast individuals into a socio-symbolic competition ordered by the symbolic values carried by consumer objects. After generations of living in such a precarious and competitive environment, the fleeting pleasures that accompany the ownership of designer items become valuable only in relation to the inability of others to own. The committed consumer utilises consumer symbolism to incite envy in others, and, of course, this performs a vital socioeconomic function. The great pleasure of owning a Mercedes-Benz motor car comes not in driving the car but in being seen to drive the car. Others must know that we have achieved this great feat of consumer success and elevated the self above the quotidian social world, thus inspiring envious others to do the same. Thus a majority of individuals enter the vortex of long hours at work, lifelong debt repayment and the endless consumption of symbolic objects, every day donating most of their energy to capitalism's grid.

Consumerism exacerbates and plays upon the constitutive lack that lies at the heart of the human subject. It has intruded into the internal life of the subject and creates a cultural climate of anxiety and competition. We become orientated towards hedonism and excess, and seek to separate ourselves from our communities by raising ourselves above them. Consumerism encourages the immediate gratification of desires and places us in a vortex of unfulfilling work, debt repayment and objectless anxiety. Unless the individual has the financial means to cope with the systematic refusal of roles and the subsequent downward mobility, the only escape is upwards through the system. In such a perfect trap the temptation to discard traditional commitments to politics, civility and the common good is placed before all of us, no matter where we are located in the socioeconomic structure. Of course some relatively poor people commit minor acquisitive crimes to secure basic material goods, but even amongst the poor the lure of designer labels as the accepted means of avoiding humiliation is immensely powerful (Hall et al., 2008).

Initial research suggests that the crucial factor influencing those who make the decision to commit acquisitive or violent crime as a way out of the vortex is the degree of cynicism and nihilism that has been instilled in the individual by complex permutations of ideology, socialisation and humiliating personal experiences (Winlow and Hall, 2006, 2009b; Ellis, 2015). Of course the crime–consumer connection is woefully under-researched. Theories of the crime–consumer nexus are ignored by right-wing criminologists, and either ignored or met with various degrees of suspicion and hostility by a sub-dominant liberal-left paradigm that seems to almost wilfully misunderstand the basic position. In a discipline still fixated on mechanistic positivism or dated social constructionism and social reaction theory it features very rarely in journals and remains as a brief aside in most criminology textbooks. Criminology's enduring reluctance to construct new and convincing socially embedded accounts of criminal motivation in advanced capitalist consumer economies tells us a lot about the discipline's underlying politics and values. We have discussed that in detail elsewhere (see Hall, 2012a; Hall and Winlow, 2015; Winlow and Hall, 2013; Winlow et al., 2015). It is heartening to note that recently a new ripple of interest has appeared, which might eventually grow into a new wave, but all that remains to be said here is that a vast and complex vista beckons the explorations of new generations of criminologists.

References

Adorno, T. (2001) *The Culture Industry*, London: Verso

Adorno, T. and Horkheimer, M. (1997) *The Dialectic of Enlightenment*, London: Verso

Althusser, L. (2008) *On Ideology*, London: Verso

Appadurai, A. (2011) *The Social Life of Things*, Cambridge: Cambridge University Press

Ayres, T. and Treadwell, J. (2012) 'Bars, Drugs and Football Thugs: Alcohol, Cocaine Use and Violence in the Night Time Economy among English Football Firms', *Criminology and Criminal Justice*, 12, 1: 83–100

Badiou, A. (2007) *The Century*, Oxford: Polity

Bakan, J. (2005) *The Corporation*, London: Constable

Barber, B. (2007) *Consumed*, New York: Norton

Baudrillard, J. (1998) *The Consumer Society*, London: Sage

Baudrillard, J. (2007) *In the Shadow of the Silent Majorities*, Los Angeles: Semiotext(e)

Bauman, Z. (2003) *Liquid Love*, Oxford: Polity

Bauman, Z. (2007) *Consuming Life*, Oxford: Polity

Beal, B. (1995) 'Disqualifying the Official: An Exploration of Social Resistance through the Subculture of Skateboarding', *Sociology of Sport Journal*, 12: 252–267

Beck, U. and Beck-Gernsheim, E. (1995) *The Normal Chaos of Love*, Oxford: Polity

Beck, U. and Beck-Gernsheim, E. (2001) *Individualization*, London: Sage

Beder, S. (2009) *This Little Kiddy Went to Market: The Corporate Capture of Childhood*, London: Pluto

Bloom, C. (2015) *Thatcher's Secret War*, London: The History Press

Cohen, S. (1979) 'The Punitive City: Notes on the Dispersal of Social Control', *Crime, Law and Social Change*, 3, 4: 339–363

Cooper, C. (2012) 'Understanding the English "Riots" of 2011: "Mindless Criminality" or Youth "Mekin Histri" in Austerity Britain?', *Youth and Policy*, 109, 6

Currie, E. (2008) *The Roots of Danger*, New York: Prentice Hall

Ellis, A. (2015) *Men, Masculinities and Violence*, London: Routledge

Ewen, S. (1998) *PR! A Social History of Spin*, London: Basic Books

Ewen, S. (2001) *Captains of Consciousness: Advertising and the Social Roots of the Consumer Culture*, London: Basic Books

Featherstone, M. (1995) *Undoing Culture*, London: Sage

Ferrell, J. (1996) *Crimes of Style*, Boston, MA: Northwestern University Press

Frank, T. (1998) *The Conquest of Cool*, Chicago: University of Chicago Press

Haenfler, R. (2012) *Goths, Gamers and Grrrls*, Oxford: Oxford University Press

Hall, Steve. (2012a) *Theorizing Crime and Deviance: A New Perspective*, London: Sage

Hall, Steve. (2012b) 'The Solicitation of the Trap: On Transcendence and Transcendental Materialism in Advanced Consumer-Capitalism', *Human Studies*, 35, 3: 365–381

Hall, Steve and Wilson, D. (2014) 'New Foundations: Pseudo-Pacification and Special Liberty as Potential Cornerstones for a Multi-Level Theory of Homicide and Serial Murder', *European Journal of Criminology*, 11, 5: 635–655.

Hall, Steve and Winlow, S. (2007) 'Cultural Criminology and Primitive Accumulation: A Formal Introduction for Two Strangers Who Should Really Become More Intimate', *Crime, Media, Culture*, 3, 1: 82–90

Hall, Steve and Winlow, S. (2015) *Revitalizing Criminological Theory: Towards a New Ultra-Realism*, London: Routledge

Hall, Steve, Winlow, S. and Ancrum, C. (2008) *Criminal Identities and Consumer Culture: Crime, Exclusion and the New Culture of Narcissism*, Cullompton: Willan

Hall, Stuart (1981) 'Notes on Deconstructing "the Popular"', in R. Samuel (eds) *People's History and Socialist Theory*, London: Routledge

Hall, Stuart and Jefferson, T. (eds) (2006) *Resistance through Rituals*, London: Routledge

Hayward, K. (2012) 'Pantomime Justice: A Cultural Criminological Analysis of "Life Stage Dissolution"', *Crime, Media, Culture*, 8, 2: 213–229

Hayward, K. and Yar, M. (2006) 'The Chav Phenomenon: Consumption, Media and the Construction of a New Underclass', *Crime, Media, Culture*, 2, 1: 9–28

Hebdige, D. (1979) *Subculture: The Meaning of Style*, London: Routledge

Heinberg, R. (2011) *The End of Growth*, London: Clairview Books

Hennessy, P. (2007) *Having It So Good: Britain in the Fifties*, London: Allen Lane

Hiscock, G. (2012) *Earth Wars*, London: John Wiley and Sons

Hoggart, R. (1969) *The Uses of Literacy*, London: Penguin

Horsley, M. (2014) 'The "Death of Deviance" and the Stagnation of 20th Century Criminology', in M. Dellwing, J. Kotarba and N. Pino (eds) *The Death and Resurrection of Deviance*, London: Palgrave Macmillan

Horsley, M. (2015) *The Dark Side of Prosperity*, Farnham: Ashgate

James, O. (2010) *Britain on the Couch*, London: Vermillion

Judt, T. (2010) *Postwar*, London: Vintage

Klare, M. (2012) *The Race for What's Left*, New York: Picador

Lacan, J. (2007) *Ecrits*, New York: Norton

Lazaratto, M. (2015) *The Making of the Indebted Man: Essay on the Neoliberal Condition*, Los Angeles: Semiotext(e)

Lears, J. (1995) *Fables of Abundance: A Cultural History of Advertising in America*, London: Basic Books

Martin, G. (2009) 'Subculture, Style, Chavs and Consumer Capitalism: Towards a Critical Cultural Criminology of Youth', *Crime, Media, Culture*, 5, 2: 123–145

Matthews, R. (2014) *Realist Criminology*, London: Palgrave Macmillan

Miles, S. (2014) 'Young People, "Flawed Protestors" and the Commodification of Resistance', *Critical Arts*, 28, 1: 76–87

Miles, S., Cliff, D. and Burr, V. (1998) '"Fitting In and Sticking Out": Consumption, Consumer Meanings and the Construction of Young People's Identities', *Journal of Youth Studies*, 1, 1: 81–96

Milne, S. (2014) *The Enemy Within*, London: Verso

Minsky, H. (2008) *John Maynard Keynes*, London: McGraw Hill

Newburn, T., Cooper, K., Deacon, R. and Diski, R. (2015) 'Shopping for Free? Looting, Consumerism and the 2011 Riots', *British Journal of Criminology*, 55, 5: 987–1004

Pearce, F. (2013) *The Landgrabbers*, London: Eden Project Books

Picketty, T. (2014) *Capital in the Twenty-First Century*, Cambridge, MA: Harvard University Press

Postman, N. (1996) *The Disappearance of Childhood*, London: Vintage

Presdee, M. (2000) *Cultural Criminology and the Carnival of Crime*, London: Routledge

Raymen, T. and Smith, O. (2016) 'What's Deviance Got to Do with It? Black Friday Sales, Violence and Hyper-Conformity', *British Journal of Criminology*, 56, 2: 389–405

Samuel, R. (1977) 'Workshop of the World: Steam Power and Hand Technology in Mid-Victorian Britain', *History Workshop Journal*, 3, 1: 6–72

Sandbrook, D. (2013) *Seasons in the Sun: The Battle for Britain, 1974–1979*, London: Penguin

Schrecker, T. and Bambra, C. (2015) *How Politics Makes Us Sick: Neoliberal Epidemics*, London: Palgrave Macmillan

Sloan, T. (1996) *Damaged Life: The Crisis of the Modern Psyche*, London: Routledge

Smart, B. (2010) *Consumer Society*, London: Sage

Smith, O. (2013) 'Holding Back the Beers: Maintaining "Youth" Identity within the British Night-Time Leisure Economy', *Journal of Youth Studies*, 16, 8: 1069–1083

Smith, O. (2014) *Contemporary Adulthood and the Night-Time Leisure Economy*, London: Palgrave Macmillan

Stiegler, B. (2009) *Acting Out*, Stanford: Stanford University Press

Stiglitz, J. (2004) *The Roaring Nineties*, London: Penguin

Varoufakis, Y. (2015) *The Global Minotaur: America, Europe and the Future of the Global Economy*, London: Zed Books

Veblen, T. (2009) *Theory of the Leisure Class*, Oxford: Oxford University Press

Vinen, R. (2010) *Thatcher's Britain*, London: Pocket Books

Winlow, S. (2001) *Badfellas: Crime, Tradition and New Masculinities*, Oxford: Berg

Winlow, S. and Hall, S. (2006) *Violent Night: Urban Leisure and Contemporary Culture*, Oxford: Berg

Winlow, S. and Hall, S. (2009a) 'Living for the Weekend: Youth Identities in Northeast England', *Ethnography*, 10, 1: 91–113

Winlow, S. and Hall, S. (2009b) 'Retaliate First: Memory, Humiliation and Male Violence', *Crime, Media, Culture*, 5, 3: 285–304.

Winlow, S. and Hall, S. (2012) 'What Is an "Ethics Committee"? Academic Governance in an Epoch of Belief and Incredulity', *British Journal of Criminology*, 52, 2: 400–416

Winlow, S. and Hall, S. (2013) *Rethinking Social Exclusion: The Death of the Social?*, London: Sage

Winlow, S., Hall, S., Treadwell, J. and Briggs, D. (2015) *Riots and Political Present: Notes from the Post-Political Present*, London: Routledge

Wolff, R. (2013) *Capitalism Hits the Fan*, London: Interlink

Žižek, S. (2009) *The Ticklish Subject*, London: Verso

7

FEMINIST CRIMINOLOGIES

Kerry Carrington

In 1968 Frances Heidensohn (1968: 171) described the study of gender, women and deviance 'as lonely uncharted seas of human behaviour' and in 2012 'as one of the most robust, resilient and important features of modern criminology' (Heidensohn, 2012: 132). Today there are journals dedicated to publishing feminist scholarship in criminology including *Feminist Criminology, Violence Against Women*, the *Australian Feminist Law Journal, Gender and Violence* and *Women and Criminal Justice*. A number of handbooks, such as *Routledge International Handbook of Crime and Gender Studies* (Renzetti, Miller and Gover, 2013) and *The Oxford Handbook of Gender, Sex and Crime* (Gartner and McCarthy, 2014), have also appeared in print. This is a solid indication of the success, depth and breadth of research on gender, crime and criminal justice – a success 'unimaginable fifty years ago' (Gartner and McCarthy, 2014: 15). Not all this work is feminist however. Feminist research focuses on how offending, victimisation and social and institutional responses to crime are 'fundamentally gendered' (Renzetti, 2013: 13) – at the level of social organisation, social action and subjective agency. This chapter takes stock of key developments in feminist criminologies over the last fifty to sixty years. Importantly there was and still is no single identifiable feminist approach to theorising or researching gender and crime (Gelsthorpe, 1990: 90).

This chapter provides a summary of five distinctive approaches undertaken by feminist researchers on topics related to crime, justice and criminology. While the five perspectives overviewed emerged in approximate historical succession, many overlapped and still overlap. The five categorisations are simply a way of organising large, diverse and complex bodies of scholarship into a coherent conceptual schema. It does not attempt an exhaustive overview, and so selects themes and texts representative of the various perspectives, theories and directions of what is now a large body of international scholarship. It begins with an overview of the contribution of the woman centred radical feminism of the 1970s which called for the insertion of the woman question into the discipline of criminology. Next the chapter examines a body of transgressive feminist scholarship influenced by French feminism that called for the outright rejection of criminology as a masculinist knowledge. A third body of feminist scholarship took inspiration from postmodernism and post-colonialism criticising feminist criminology's universalisation of women. They argued this theory was incapable of representing the diversity of women's experiences of crime, violence and criminal justice. Next, drawing on both post-structuralism and post-colonialism, intersectionalism has exerted considerable influence over contemporary directions in feminist criminology. This approach does not necessarily privilege gender, conceiving it only as one of several inter-locking structures that position women differentially in relation to the operation of law and criminal justice, albeit an important one.

Alongside these bodies of three distinctive approaches to feminist scholarship in criminology emerged powerful feminist critiques of the treatment of victims by the law and the criminal justice system. These critiques stemmed largely from feminist grass roots struggles with the state for support for women experiencing sexual and domestic violence at the hands of men. This political project provided the impetus for the emergence of feminist victimology, largely outside of the discipline of criminology. This section charts the relative success of feminist activists and feminist scholars in putting violence against women firmly on the public and academic agenda.

The upsurge in global circuits of knowledge and power is transforming the direction and focus of feminist criminologies now and into the future. This last approach calls for the transnationalisation of feminist criminology, and argues that the privileging of theories and concepts imported from the northern metropoles are no longer appropriate for analysing the impact of law and criminal justice – at least in the global South. It draws on southern criminology as a corrective tool for analysing the diverse impacts of gendered violence across the globe. The chapter concludes with some observations about alliances and tensions between feminist and alternative criminologies.

Liberal feminism and criminology

Key conceptual shifts in feminist criminology have tended to mirror the shifts in feminist theory more broadly, from liberal, socialist, post-colonial and postmodern feminist thought. The initial critiques of criminology emerged out of the feminist radicalism of the late 1960s and 1970s. This was also a time during which the 'intellectual, institutional and political assumptions of modern criminology were challenged' (Garland and Sparks, 2000: 13). Carol Smart's iconic text *Women, Crime and Criminology* (1976) is often referred to as the starting point of the feminist challenge to criminology. This first wave of feminist scholarship engaged in critique as its main enterprise, taking issue with two main aspects of criminology: first, its omission of women, and second, its misogynist representation of female offenders (Adler, 1975; Simon, 1975; Bertrand, 1969; Heidensohn, 1968; Klein, 1973; Smart, 1976). Women, they argued, should not be left out of criminological research just because they comprised a small proportion of the criminal population. To remedy the problem these pioneering feminist scholars argued for the inclusion of women in the research agendas of criminology (Naffine, 1987: 2–5; Rafter, 2000: xxv).

While this new research aided our understanding of patterns of female crime and deviance, it also had notable limitations. Just adding women was no solution to the male-centric bias of positivist criminology, a discipline that for most of a century had generalized theories of crime from observations of mostly male prisoners and offenders (Allen, 1989). The core epistemological assumptions and methodologies of criminology's inherent phallocentrism remained intact (Allen, 1989; Cain, 1990; Young, 1992; Green, 1993; Heidensohn and Rafter, 1995; Naffine, 1997). While the contribution of initial feminist critiques of criminology is undeniable, this body of scholarship did not adequately challenge the underlying epistemological assumptions of criminology's theories, categories or methods (Cousins, 1980: 111). Instead feminists undertook a plethora of empirical studies comparing the treatment of men with women by the court system, the juvenile justice system and the prison system (see Naffine, 1997: 35–37). The problem succinctly identified by Alison Young (1992: 291) is that 'much of feminist criminology' existed 'as a criticism of something else'. What was needed 'were new theoretical approaches' (Renzetti, 2013: 9) that could explain how men's and women's experiences of crime and victimisation and criminalisation were 'fundamentally gendered' (Renzetti, 2013: 13).

While the feminist project of critique now appears limited, the late Christine Alder, widely regarded as a founder and advocate of feminist criminology, reminds us that this was a time when academic criminology was dominated by men 'not only in the corridors but in the pages of academic journals' (Alder, 1996: 19). As such the initial incursions of feminist critique were a necessary precondition to the development of more sophisticated feminist criminologies (Alder, 1996: 22).

Standpoint feminism and transgressive feminist criminologies

By the late 1980s and early 1990s it became clear that the feminist project had to broaden to include a critique of criminology's state-based definitions of crime that excluded socially invisible harms to women (such as domestic violence, rape in marriage and acquaintance rape). It also had to detach itself from the positivist research methods of criminology that had persistently failed to render visible the largely privatised harms endured by women at the hands of mostly men (Renzetti, 1999; Stanko, 1990; Graycar and Morgan, 1990). This called for nothing less than an epistemological revolution, sparking a decade of raging debate in feminist theory and philosophy (Tanesini, 1999: 3). The main sides of the debate were divided between standpoint feminisms, transgressive feminisms and postmodern/post-structuralist feminisms.

Despite the debate, there were nevertheless common understandings which broadly characterised most feminist approaches to studying crime, law and criminal justice during this period. First, feminist research questions the neat separation of objectivity from subjectivity, arguing that all research contains some subjective dimensions, embedded in the research design and choice of research question. Feminist research questions legal and criminological research that claims to be objective, value free and completely devoid of interpretation. They argue that such 'methods cannot convey an in depth understanding of, or feeling for those being researched and that they often ignore sex or gender differences or look at them without considering mediating variables' (Gelsthorpe, 1990: 90).

Second, for many feminist scholars questions about process and power are especially important in the doing of research, even more so in criminology where the power imbalances between victims/offenders, institutions and individuals are so fraught. This led feminist researchers to disentangle the exercise of power from the act of doing research by adopting reflexive methodologies. Reflexivity about the role of the researcher, the impact of subjectivity, the exercise of power and the muddiness of the research process, often concealed in official criminological research publications, is made more transparent in feminist research (Davies, 2000: 83).

Third, a great deal of feminist research assumes that knowledge is sexualised, that the history of the human sciences is a masculine discipline and that feminist ways of knowing and doing research have been historically subjugated, repressed and disqualified (Grosz, 1989; Harding, 1987; Gunew, 1990). Given this historical condition of the episteme, it is understandable that the initial priority of feminist criminology was to make visible and intelligible the formerly invisible voices and experiences of women as victims and offenders. The choice of topic then tended to follow logically as the study of women as gendered subjects for these reasons:

> The method of feminist standpoint criminology involves 'asking the woman question' – that is asking how patterns of crime, penal policies, crime prevention and community safety strategies, ideologies of law and order, or indeed criminological theories affect women … Feminist critical criminology exemplifies the traditional commitment of critical theory to acknowledging standpoints and having political/practical as well as theoretical objectives.
>
> *(Hudson, 2000: 185)*

For some (but by no means all) this led to the adoption of feminist standpoint methodologies as an antidote to the phallocentricism of the human sciences. Standpoint feminism attempted to construct feminist ways of knowing based largely on experience, leading to a preference for qualitative research and a total rejection of 'masculinist ways of knowing' (Stanley and Wise, 1983; Grosz, 1989). This is where consensus ends and debates emerged about the virtues and limitations of feminist standpoint methodologies among feminist criminologists (Cain, 1986; Smart, 1989; Carrington, 2002). Some feminist scholars questioned the automatic focus on the 'woman question', discovering the virtues of researching the masculinity of crime and criminalisation. As gender is fluid – that is, a practice that is dynamic – by focusing on the woman question, feminist standpoint theory unhelpfully fixes gender and turns it into a universal sexed dichotomy. However that is what happened for a period of around a decade in feminist criminology in the 1990s. Others questioned the automatic preference for qualitative methods. They argued that method is largely a practical matter, and what matters most is how the results of empirical research are interpreted regardless of whether it is qualitative or quantitative.

From the 1990s feminist scholars called for transgressive knowledge about women, gender and crime to be generated from outside what they saw as the hopelessly phallocentric discipline of criminology (Cain, 1990; Young, 1996; Heidensohn and Rafter, 1995). Following broader developments in feminist theory, and in particular the influence of French feminism (i.e. Grosz, 1989), this feminist agenda promoted a radical scepticism about phallocentric modes of inquiry engendered in disciplines such as history, science, sociology and criminology. This body of feminist analysis questioned the key concepts, methods of inquiry and claims to neutrality. This theoretically informed body of feminist scholarship rejected the positivist research methods which had dominated mainstream criminology, and encouraged the outright rejection of criminology's core disciplinary assumptions (cf. Allen, 1989; Cain, 1990; MacKinnon, 1987; Smart, 1990; Young, 1992; Naffine, 1997). During this period, criminology and feminism were widely regarded as oxymorons – irreconcilable contradictory enterprises (Britton, 2000: 58). Criminology was so oblivious to the fundamental gendered differences in criminal offending, for a time it became regarded as completely beyond redemption (Allen, 1989: 20–21; Cain, 1990: 11; Gelsthorpe and Morris, 1990: 4).

While these transgressive critiques of criminology were powerful they were not without their own conceptual weaknesses. In order to make the argument about the inherent phallocentricism of criminology, this radical feminist scholarship tended to fall into the trap of universalising women as the Other (Rice, 1990; Naffine, 1997). By solely focusing on gender as the primary source of female oppression, feminists inspired by the task of transgression frequently failed to take into account the historical, cultural and material diversity of women's offending and victimisation (Gelsthorpe, 1989: 152). They presumed that commonalities shared among the female sex made it possible to analyse women as a singular unitary subject of history (i.e. Allen, 1990: 88), despite their astonishing historical, cultural, socio-economic, ethnic and racial diversity. The diversity of women's experiences of criminalisation and victimisation could not be adequately represented by merely adopting a singular feminist standpoint. This kind of feminist criminology was accused of being theoretically isolationist, reformist and obsessed with 'middle class concerns' (Green, 1993: 112). Essentialist forms of analysis arising from transgressive approaches became the subject of strident internal feminist critique and renewal (Rice, 1990; Carrington, 1995; Naffine, 1997; Smart, 1990).

As women are differentiated in relation to the operation of the legal process, feminist standpoint methodologies which assume a commonality (or fixed essence) among women, and a universal subjectivity among men, run the risk of constructing fictive unities among cohorts of legal subjects whose statuses before the law are quite diverse (Carrington, 1995). For instance girls who are drawn into the orbit of criminal justice institutions tend to have little in common with the overwhelming majority of girls who never come into contact with youth justice (Carrington, 1993; Carrington Pereira, 2009). Most girls and women are insulated from its direct power effects. Those who are not so well protected tend to come from housing commission, Aboriginal and other poor neighbourhoods as studies of female offending have repeatedly shown (Carlen, 1983; Carrington, 1993; Daly, 1994; Maher, 1997). Consequently, there is no single universal essential female subject of law to be 'uncovered' through feminist standpoint methodologies.

Instead theories that elevated an essential feminist standpoint ironically led to a narrowing of the feminist gaze to gendered power relations and structures, such as patriarchy. Like much of criminology they confined their analysis to domestic issues within local criminal justice agencies. The placeless and timeless unified female subject of history, politics and culture posited in these essentialist feminist theories is a fictional one that either overlooks, excludes or marginalises women of colour, race and non-Anglo origin. When women as a category becomes a universal construct abstracted from the specificity and variability of women's real and ethnically diverse experiences across time, class, space, history, religion, economics, culture and geo-politics, women outside the normalised feminist constructions become colonised (Mohanty, 1984: 335). Given the persuasiveness of this critique, 'Feminism had to abandon its early frame-work and to start to look for other ways to think which did not subjugate other subjectivities' (Smart, 1990: 83).

Post-feminisms and feminist criminologies

Feminist approaches influenced by post-structuralism, post-colonialism and postmodernism were more circumspect about the epistemological knowledge claims of the social sciences – that truth can be impartial, ahistorical or universal. These approaches theorised knowledge as partial and contingent, opting instead for a non-universalist conception of knowledge which accepts multiplicity and fallibility as defining characteristics of the episteme (Carrington, 1995). Their critique of feminist standpoint methodology called for a different kind of feminist intellectual engagement to the one that totalised conceptions of law and criminal justice, attributing to them a false unity of purpose (Rice, 1990). Unlike standpoint feminism, deconstructionist approaches to feminist theory are sceptical of universal knowledge claims and consequently of the concept of a single feminist standpoint (Carrington, 1995). This kind of feminism no longer insisted on any singular relation between gender, deviance, law and crime and instead sought to locate its analysis more concretely in the field of power relations. Their aim was not to construct a more correct feminist version of the truth, but to deconstruct and analyse the power relations underpinning truth claims (Smart, 1990: 82). Nor did this kind of feminism restrict its focus to the Women Question. Their objects of deconstruction varied widely but concentrated on the images and representations of otherness, femininity, sexuality, masculinity, madness, deviance and other statuses deployed in the criminal justice and legal systems (Young, 1996). This approach spawned an array of innovative studies on the discursive effects of language in the law's positioning of women as the other (Mason and Stubbs, 2010; Threadgold, 1993); its discrediting of the rape victim (A.Young, 1998); the sexualised representations of deviance and victimisation in popular culture (Alexander, 2003) and ways of doing gender by doing crime (Miller, 2014: 31–33). Deconstructionist socio-legal feminist studies were especially effective in exposing how the mono-logic reasoning of law privileged masculinity (Naffine, 1991: 20–21) while simultaneously othering femininity (Kirkby, 1995: xviii).

One criticism of this approach has been the tendency to elevate 'the symbolic power of the law as an agent of change' and to use individual cases as the basis for reasoning upwards to the predicament of all women (Laster, 1996: 196). My research on the rape and murder of Leigh Leigh could be criticised for taking this naive approach (Carrington, 1998). Feminist demands for law reform around rape, domestic violence and marriage laws construct a set of priorities for feminist action – a set of priorities that Kathy Laster (1996: 196) argues may be irrelevant to the majority of women. It has also led to what she referred to as 'the feminisation of social control', the entry of women in traditional male domains such as policing, security and the judiciary, losing sight of the critical and radical aspirations of transgressive feminist criminologies. Deconstruction is not, as Stan Cohen (1998: 118) reminds us, an end itself as it does not necessarily undermine the power of dominant discourses, such as law. Hence the inclusion of feminist perspectives on the bench or in legal policy is not necessarily a panacea for the injustices faced by women, and women of colour, difference and disadvantage in particular.

The main challenge to what is sometimes called hegemonic feminist theory has come from scholars of colour (Mohanty, 1984, 2003; Rice, 1990; Sandoval, 1991). Although there is a large body of work on the struggles of women in developing countries and their roles and status in individual cultures, Mohanty (2003) argues that third world women are often described in terms of their 'problems', their 'oppression' or their 'achievements' in relation to an imagined free white liberal democracy. Western feminists, she argues, often define the 'third world woman' in terms of a viable oppositional alliance, with a common political struggle against sexist, racist and imperialist structures. However, third world women have very different post-colonial histories with regards to their inheritance of slavery, enforced migration, exploitative labour, colonialism and genocide (Mohanty, 2003: 5–7). According to Mohanty (2003) third world women's writings on feminism have located oppression as simultaneous to the experience of social and political marginality, and the grounding of feminist politics in histories of racism and imperialism. Additionally, they insist on the complex inter-relationships between feminist, anti-racist, anti-colonialist and nationalist struggles. Homogenised 'third world women' are represented as far more impoverished and inferior than their Western female counterparts who, in contrast, are represented as 'educated, modern, as having control over their own bodies and sexualities and the freedom to make their own decisions' (Mohanty, 1984: 337).

Sandoval (1991) argued the feminist theory needed a 'differential consciousness' which incorporated elements of post-colonialism and postmodernism to overcome the 'symbolic containers' of hegemonic white feminism. Only then could feminist theory be realigned and the subject woman deconstructed – no longer a timeless, placeless, universal category of history, politics, society and culture. In the junctures, intersections and spaces of difference a praxis emerges based on an oppositional and differential consciousness (Sandoval, 1991: 19). No longer is there a conception of a single feminism but multiple feminisms. No longer is there a concept of a universal woman of history but diverse women of colour, race, class, ethnicity, culture and religion. This is a feminism without borders (Mohanty, 2003) – an imaginary community of women that share some alliances based on gender but respect differences. These theoretical shifts in feminism, derivative of post-colonialism and postmodern feminisms, were the precursor to the rise of intersectionalism.

Intersectionalism and contemporary feminist criminology

In light of the post-colonial, post-structuralist and postmodernist critiques of feminism, it became obvious that a theory based singularly on gender was insufficient to explain the abundance of women of colour, rural women, Indigenous women and women from impoverished backgrounds susceptible to policing, criminalisation and imprisonment (i.e. studies of Pat Carlen, 1983; Kerry Carrington, 1993; Kathy Daly, 1994; Jodi Miller, 2004; Lisa Maher, 1997; and Lorraine Gelsthorpe, 1989). A feminist theory of gender was also insufficient to explain the marginalisation of black female victims of domestic violence (Crenshaw, 1991). African American women victimised by domestic violence face multiple forms of marginalisation within a criminal justice system capable of imprisoning blacks but far less competent in assisting them as victims of violence (Crenshaw, 1991). Much the same can be said of the experiences of female Aboriginal victims of family violence in Australian criminal justice systems (Hogg and Carrington, 2006). Only by incorporating the tapestry of interconnections encompassing social position, race, ethnicity, location and gender can the chronic over-representation of particular groups of women (as victims and offenders) in the criminal justice systems begin to be understood. Intersectionality 'views identity categories as analytically and empirically inseparable and refuses to organise oppressions hierarchically' (Creek and Dunn, 2014: 40). Intersectionality theorises gender as only one factor in the axis of power. Other significant factors in the social ordering of power operating in systems of criminal justice include race, colonisation and class (Burgess-Proctor, 2006: 37). This theoretical approach neither essentialises women nor pays too little regard to the politics of gender (Hautzinger, 2010: 244).

The methods and theories of intersectionality have been used to analyse how a complex web of inequalities intersect to position women differently in relation to the operation of criminal justice and law. This is especially the case with Indigenous women and girls in countries like Canada and Australia who are massively over-represented before the courts and in our prisons and figure disproportionately as victims of crime as well (Chesney-Lind and Sheldon, 2004; Carrington, 1993; Hogg and Carrington, 2006). Recent and important additions to this debate have come from feminist criminologists, such as Hillary Potter (2015),

Rosemary Barberet, (2014) and Claire Renzetti (2013), who are applying intersectionality as a contemporary theoretical framework.

Intersectionality is not without its critics. Henne and Troshynski (2013) point to the problematic nature of simply deploying intersectionality in a domestic politic, of emptying it of its post-colonial and geo-political importance, and of unintentionally reproducing representations of crime and violence that silence the subaltern voices and posit a Western feminist superiority. They argue that intersectionality has become a corrective tool to capture multiple and overlapping relations of inequality (Henne and Troshynski, 2013: 462). Because criminology has a history of being susceptible to post-colonialist universalist knowledges, they conclude:

> Intersectionality, however, is not a universalist concept, but rather a corrective concept
> …. If we are to pursue a transnational intersectionality within criminology, it needs to attend to, not negate, previous iterations of globalization that have informed the complexities of difference and subordination manifest in not only our research sites, but also our worldviews and methodologies.
>
> *(Henne and Troshynski, 2013: 468)*

Feminism and victimology

Academic interest in the victim has grown exponentially over recent decades among a diverse range of scholars in feminism, criminology, victimology, sociology, law and public policy (Zedner, 2003; Garland and Sparks, 2000; J. Young, 1998; Booth and Carrington, 2007). An assemblage of quite distinct feminist intellectual work focusing on women as victims began to emerge in the 1970s with the rise of radical feminism and demands to make violence a public not a private matter (Carmody and Carrington, 2000). Significant and influential works include Dobash and Dobash's (1979) study of family violence; Russell's (1975) exposé of rape, including rape in marriage, and Brownmiller's (1975) provocative analysis of rape to name only a few. These were followed by Stanko's (1990) work on everyday violence and Walklate's major and ongoing contributions to the field of victimology (2007a, 2007b; McGarry and Walklate, 2015). The main advance of feminist research of this kind is that it challenged the hidden and privatised nature of violence against women (Gelsthorpe and Morris, 1990: 3). Their studies were inspired by a great deal of feminist activism around the definition of rape, child abuse and wife battering and the mis-treatment of women prisoners and female delinquents (Carmody and Carrington, 2000).

Feminists working in victim support services in the UK, USA, Australia, New Zealand and other parts of the world have played a key historical role in elevating the needs of women and children as victims and lobbying for legislative reform to address their needs (Booth and Carrington, 2007). These movements emerged from an array of interest groups including: the refuge movement; women's support organisations; the women's electoral lobby; Indigenous, Aboriginal and community legal services; and sexual assault centres. The victims championed by these diverse interest groups were mainly women and children survivors of sexual assault and domestic violence who rarely rate a mention in law and order political agendas (Hogg and Brown, 1998).

The intellectual and political projects of feminists working with victims and feminists researching victims converged in what has become called victimology. They studied sexual assault (Breckenridge and Carmody, 1992), domestic violence (Scutt, 1983), violence during pregnancy (Taft, 2000); violence against Aboriginal women (Atkinson, 1990); violence against women in rural settings (Hogg and Carrington, 2006); and violence against Filipino migrant women (Cunneen and Stubbs, 2004). Feminists extended their analyses to the treatment of women as victims of the criminal justice system and the law as well (Threadgold, 1993; Naffine, 1991; Carrington, 1998; A. Young, 1998). Their research sought to demonstrate how women were doubly victimised by their subsequent treatment by the police, prison, legal and judicial authorities. This led feminist scholars to argue that at best the criminal justice system inadequately addressed the needs of victims, or at worst re-victimised the victim (Carmody and Carrington, 2000). These were such important insights into the workings of criminal justice that feminism can rightly claim that it played a leading role in the emergence of victimology.

Lamenting the growing concern for victims among feminist criminologists, Penny Green argued that 'Feminist criminology has become, to a large extent, victimology … and accordingly ripe for incorporation by an increasingly punitive state' (Green, 1993: 112). These comments were symptomatic of the lingering tension between feminist and alternative critical criminologies over the role of the victim to which I return in the conclusion.

Southern criminology and globalising the feminist criminological gaze

Southern criminology is an intellectual, political and empirical project concerned with how issues of vital criminological research and policy significance abound in the global South, with important implications for global security and justice. Yet much of criminology historically – as a theoretical, political and empirical project – overlooks the distinctive contributions of the global South (Carrington, Hogg and Sozzo, 2016). The global North is used here as a metaphor for the 'western' world and the global South as a metaphor for the countries and continents (not all from the global South) outside that 'western' world. Like social sciences more generally (Connell, 2007), the hierarchal production of criminological knowledge privileges theories, assumptions and methods based largely on empirical specificities of the global North. The purpose of southern criminology is not to dismiss the conceptual and empirical advances that criminology has produced over the last century, nor to cast negative aspersions on northern criminology, but to de-colonise and democratise the toolbox of available criminological concepts, theories and methods (see Carrington, Hogg and Sozzo, 2016).

Like much of criminology, feminist criminologists have tended to confine their critical gaze mostly to localised domestic issues that occur in the large metropolitan cities of the global North (Renzetti, 2013; Carrington, 2015; Barberet, 2014). There are and were good reasons for this given the need to render visible the victimisation of women and ineptitude of criminal justice responses to male violence against women (Naffine, 1997; Gelsthorpe, 1989). This should be applauded. But a theory based singularly on gender still is and always was insufficient to explain how women of colour, rural women, Indigenous women and women from impoverished backgrounds are uniquely susceptible to victimisation, criminalisation and imprisonment (Carlen, 1983; Potter, 2015). Many of these women are situated outside the metropole. It is this dynamic that southern criminology addresses.

My recent book *Feminism and Global Justice* (2015) uses southern criminology to produce a transnational perspective on the impact and nature of gendered violence. It draws on case studies that illustrate how the form of gendered violence varies considerably across the globe, shaped by social structures of super-capitalism and patriarchy and justified ideologically through localised expressions of religion, custom, culture and politics. It contrasts violence against women in Asia, the Middle East and Latin America, as well as violence between men on the mining frontiers in the global South and the warring drug cartels of South America. The book's theoretical lens combines southern theory and intersectionality with a range of critical concepts drawn from the social sciences to argue that the anomic spaces of global capitalism incubate multiple contexts for the production of various forms of gendered violence and male on male violence especially (Carrington, 2015: 101–102). It also uses southern theory and intersectionality in addition to a range of feminist concepts to interrogate how religion and custom are used to justify gendered inequities and atrocities adversely affecting the well-being and life chances of millions of girls and women in the global South. Chief among these atrocities include: genital mutilation; female infanticide; honour crimes and killings; dowry deaths and domestic violence; female child marriage authorised by religion and custom; forced labour, migration or trafficking of women into domestic or sexual service; the resurgence of Zina – the criminalisation of consensual adult sex outside marriage under Sharia law; the return of gruesome punishments such as lashing, stoning, de-limbing for breaches of Sharia law; and the torture, imprisonment and assassination of women who protest against these cultural, political and religious gendered inequities in the global South (Carrington, 2015: 32–67).

If feminist criminology wishes to enhance its global relevance it needs to widen its research agendas to include the different gendered patterns of crime and violence that occur across the globe (Renzetti, 2013: 96; Carrington, 2015: 77–97). The globalising of feminist criminology rejects the assumption that feminism is or ever was simply a western movement. Feminism in the global South has flourished relatively independently from the feminist movements in the anglophone world (Thayer, 2010: 36). Also there is a lot that western feminists and movements can learn from the struggles for justice in the global South. One example is the development of women-only police stations established for the first time in Brazil in 1985. Women-only police stations have since spread across Latin America, including Argentina, Bolivia, Brazil, Ecuador, Nicaragua, Peru and Uruguay. Evaluations by the United Nations have found they enhance women's willingness to report, increase the likelihood of conviction and enlarge access to a range of other services and social support (UN Women, 2011: 1). As an effective, though imperfect, method of combatting violence against women (Hautzinger, 2010), women-only police stations are now being introduced in other parts of the world, including India, the Philippines, Sierra Leone, South Africa and Uganda.

Alternative criminologies and the future of feminist criminology

In Chapter 1 of this volume Pat Carlen makes the point that, 'the term "critical alternative criminologies" ultimately names a process of permanent critique, a series of transitional states of new knowledge and ideology rather than sets of closed theories' (p. 4). The uneasy relationship between critical and feminist criminologies is symptomatic of the process of immanent critique, revision and renewal. While critical and feminist critiques of criminology grew out of a similar constellation of radical critiques of knowledge, power and the state (Cohen, 1998: 103), they took diametrically opposite views on some matters. The main tensions between feminist and other critical approaches to criminology arose from structuralist forms of analyses that privileged conceptual categories such as sex or class. Both theoretical frameworks succumbed to homogenising critiques based on false universalisms.

Feminist research required politicians, policy-makers and criminologists to completely rethink the invisibility of the victim in the criminal justice system (Sumner, 1990: xii). By contrast, the victim was almost entirely absent from the radical frameworks of much of the alternative criminology, at least in the 1970s, because they were regarded as the concern of conservatives in criminology and politics, not radicals (Smart, 1976: 180). Ultimately feminist concerns about the victims of domestic violence and sexual assault were taken seriously within left realist criminology. Jock Young (1998: 301), a key exponent, once wrote: 'The importance of feminist work in the recent development of radical criminology cannot be overestimated.'

Nevertheless a major conceptual problem continues to plague feminist research on victims. The key challenge for feminist criminologists going forward is how to continue the legacy of making women and children visible as victims of gendered crime, without constructing universal victim or survivor dichotomies (Carmody and Carrington, 2000). Walklate's (2011) work on resilience continues a tradition of challenging the gender-neutral construction of victims of crime, without lapsing into essentialisms, while theorising the social and individual factors that may enhance their resilience. Hence it is possible to re-theorise gender and victimisation in a way that does not regard all men as perpetrators and all women as victims.

Another problem continues to plague feminist criminologies – the binary construction of men as violent and women as passive. One of the central achievements of feminist criminology over the last fifty years has been to direct critical attention to the fact that men's violence far outweighs that for which women are responsible. However the gap is closing – and closing fast. The most recent global prison census found that women's imprisonment is increasing faster than men's and that over the last fifteen years it has increased by 50% (Walmsley, 2015: 2). The available historical trend data for Australia, UK, Canada and the USA also shows that statistics for violence-related crime has grown significantly for women and girls, and at a rate faster than that for men and boys (Carrington, 2015: 135–140). What is still largely missing from feminist criminology is a sophisticated theory of female violence that considers the global context, the politics, the power relations, the gender dynamics and the intersectionality of specific instances of female violence. This vacuum has left a discursive space for feminist backlash ideologues to ironically blame the historical legacy of feminism for the rising rates of female offenders and female violence (Carrington, 2015: 161). A central challenge for future feminist research, then, is how to more convincingly explain the historical shifts in gendered patterns of violence, rather than simply deny, rationalise or erase them. This requires overturning the assumption deeply embedded in feminist criminology that violence is essentially masculine, though much more research is needed to understand why (Carrington, 2015).

The twin influences of labelling theory and sub-cultural theory collided with neo-Marxism to form the basis for alternative critical criminology (Cohen, 1998: 100; also see Carlen, this volume). The legacy of this large body of scholarship as summarised in this edited volume attests to its importance. As class was regarded as the critical concept to understanding the punitive impact of the criminalisation process, initially critical criminology showed little interest in rethinking the gendered nature of criminological theories, practices and concepts (Heidensohn, 2000: 78). The opposite legacy is the case for feminist criminologies that conceived power unidimensionally as gender based, overlooking the diversity of women who were imprisoned and criminalised. Both theoretical perspectives were limited by crude structuralist interpretations of a much more complex social world. Intersectionality has to a great extent remedied the reductionist tendencies of both alternative criminologies and feminist criminologies going into the future.

Whilst feminist criminology has come a long way, it still needs to internationalise and cast its gaze outside the boundaries of the nation state (Barberet, 2014: 16), to examine global inequities and 'gendered experiences of colonisation' (Renzetti, 2013: 96) and 'to widen its research agendas to include the distinctively different gendered patterns of crime and violence that occur across the globe' (Carrington, 2015: 2). This chapter has explained how southern criminology can correct the biases inherent in metropolitan criminology (embedded in all its variations – feminist, alternative and mainstream) to de-colonise and democratise knowledge production and open a wider theoretical tool box. Dozens of scholars and activists have constructively contributed to the revision of alternative and feminist criminologies over the last fifty years, as the chapters in this volume illustrate. No doubt dozens more will continue to critique, revise and renew feminist criminologies well into the future, hopefully with a view to transnationalising and democratising criminological knowledge into the future.

References

Adler, F. (1975) *Sisters in Crime*, McGraw-Hill: New York.

Alder, C. (1996) 'Feminist Criminology in Australia', in N. Rafter and F. Heidensohn (eds), *International Feminist Perspectives in Criminology: Engendering a Discipline*, Open University Press: Buckingham.

Alexander, A. (2003) 'Sex, Crime and the "Liberated" Woman in the Virgin Bride and Buffy the Vampire Slayer', *Australian Feminist Law Journal*, 18: 77–91.

Allen, J. (1989) 'Men, Crime and Criminology: Recasting the Questions', *International Journal of the Sociology of Law*, 17: 19–39.

Allen, J. (1990) *Sex & Secrets: Crimes Involving Australian Women since 1880*, Melbourne: Oxford University Press.

Atkinson, J. (1990) 'Violence in Aboriginal Australia: Colonisation and Its Impacts on Gender', *Refractory Girl*, 36: 21–24.

Barberet, R. (2014) *Women, Crime and Criminal Justice*, Routledge: London & New York.

Bertrand, M. (1969) 'Self-Image and Delinquency: A Contribution to the Study of Female Criminality and Women's Image', *Acta Criminologica*, 2: 71–144.

Booth, T. and Carrington, K. (2007) 'Victim Policies: The Anlgo-Speaking Axis', in S. Walklate (ed.), *A Handbook on Victims and Victimology*, Willan: Devon.

Breckenridge, J. and Carmody, M. (eds) (1992) *Crimes of Violence: Australian Responses to Rape and Child Sexual Assault*, Allen & Unwin: Sydney.

Britton, D. (2000) 'Feminism in Criminology: Engendering the Outlaw', *The Annals of the American Academy of Political and Social Science*, 571: 57–76.

Brownmiller, S. (1975) *Against Our Will: Men, Women and Rape*, Penguin Books: London.

Burgess-Proctor, A. (2006) 'Intersections of Race, Class, Gender and Crime', *Feminist Criminology*, 1(1): 27–47.

Cain, M. (1986) 'Realism, Feminism, Methodology, and Law', *International Journal of the Sociology of Law*, 14: 255–267.

Cain, M. (1990) 'Towards Transgression: New Directions in Feminist Criminology', *International Journal of the Sociology of Law*, 18(1): 1–18.

Carlen, P. (1983) *Women's Imprisonment: A Study in Social Control*, Routledge and Kegan Paul: London.

Carmody, M. and Carrington, K. (2000) 'Preventing Sexual Violence?', *Australian and New Zealand Journal of Criminology*, 33: 341–361.

Carrington, K. (1993) *Offending Girls: Sex, Youth and Justice*, Allen & Unwin: Sydney.

Carrington, K. (1995) 'Postmodernism and Feminist Criminologies: Disconnecting Discourses', *International Journal of the Sociology of Law*, 22: 261–277.

Carrington, K. (1998) *Who Killed Leigh Leigh?* Random House: Sydney & New York.

Carrington, K. (2002) 'Feminism and Critical Criminology: Confronting Geneologies', in K. Carrington and R. Hogg (eds), *Critical Criminology: Issues, Debates and Challenges*, Willan Publishing: Cullompton, 114–142.

Carrington, K. (2015) *Feminism and Global Justice*, Routledge: London.

Carrington, K. and Pereira, M. (2009) *Offending Youth: Sex, Crime and Justice*, Sydney: Federation Press.

Carrington, K., Hogg, R. and Sozzo, M. (2016) 'Southern Criminology', *British Journal of Criminology*, 56(1): 1–20.

Chesney-Lind, M. and Sheldon, R. (2004) *Girls, Delinquency and Juvenile Justice*, 3rd edn, Wadsworth: Belmont.

Cohen, S. (1998) 'Intellectual Scepticism and Political Commitment: The Case of Radical Criminology', in P. Walton and J. Young (eds), *The New Criminology Revisited*, Macmillan: London; St Martins: New York.

Connell, R. (2007) *Southern Theory: The Global Dynamics of Knowledge in Social Science*, Allen & Unwin: Sydney.

Cousins, M. (1980) 'Men's Rea: A Note on Sexual Difference, Criminology and the Law', in P. Carlen and M. Collison (eds), *Radical Issues in Criminology*, Barnes & Noble Books: New York.

Creek, S. J. and Dunn, J. L. (2014) 'Intersectionality and the Study of Sex, Gender and Crime', in R. Gartner and B. McCarthy (eds), *The Oxford Handbook of Sex, Gender and Crime*, Oxford University Press: Oxford & New York.

Crenshaw, K. (1991) 'Mapping the Margins: Intersectionality, Identity Politics and Violence against Women of Color', *Stanford Law Review*, 43: 1241–1299.

Cunneen, C. and Stubbs, J. (2004) 'Cultural Criminology and Engagement with Race, Gender and Post-Colonial Identities', in J. Ferrell, K. Hayward, W. Morrison and M. Presdee (eds), *Cultural Criminology Unleashed*, Glasshouse Press: London, 97–108.

Daly, K. (1994) *Gender, Crime and Punishment*, Yale University Press: New Haven.

Davies, P. (2000) 'Doing Interviews with Female Offenders', in V. Jupp, P. Davies and P. Francis (eds), *Doing Criminological Research*, Sage: London, 82–95.

Dobash, R. and Dobash, R. (1979) *Violence against Wives*, Open Books: Cambridge.

Garland, D. and Sparks, R. (2000) 'Criminology, Social Theory and the Challenges of Our Times', in D. Garland and R. Sparks (eds), *Criminology and Social Theory*, Oxford University Press: Oxford.

Gartner, R. and McCarthy, B. (eds) (2014) *The Oxford Handbook of Gender, Sex and Crime*, Oxford University Press: Oxford & New York.

Gelsthorpe, L. (1989) *Sexism and the Female Offender*, Gower: Aldershot.

Gelsthorpe, L. (1990) 'Feminist Methodologies in Criminology: A New Approach or Old Wine in New Bottles', in L. Gelsthorpe and A. Morris (eds), *Feminist Perspectives in Criminology*, Open University Press: Buckingham.

Gelsthorpe, L. and Morris, A. (1990) 'Introduction: Transforming and Transgressing Criminology', in L. Gelsthorpe and A. Morris (eds), *Feminist Perspectives in Criminology*, Open University Press: Buckingham.

Graycar, R. and Morgan, J. (1990) *The Hidden Gender of Law*, Federation Press: Leichhardt.

Green, P. (1993) 'Review of Feminist Perspectives in Criminology', *British Journal of Criminology*, 33: 112–113.

Grosz, L. (1989) 'The In(ter)vention of Feminist Knowledges', in *Crossing Boundaries: Feminisms and the Critique of Knowledges*, Allen & Unwin: Sydney.

Gunew, S. (ed.) (1990) *Feminist Knowledge: Critique and Construct*, Routledge: London.

Harding, S. (ed.) (1987) *Feminism & Methodology*, Open University Press: Milton Keynes.

Hautzinger, S. (2010) 'Criminalising Male Violence in Brazil's Women's Police Stations: From Flawed Essentialism to Imagined Communities', *Journal of Gender Studies*, 11(3): 243–251.

Heidensohn, F. (1968) 'The Deviance of Women: A Critique and an Enquiry', *British Journal of Sociology*, 19: 160–175.

Heidensohn, F. (2000) 'Feminist Criminology, Britain', in N. H. Rafter (ed.), *Encyclopedia of Women and Crime*, ORYX Press: Arizona.

Heidensohn, F. (2012) 'The Future of Feminist Criminology', *Crime, Media and Culture*, 8: 123–134.

Heidensohn, F. and Hahn Rafter, N. (eds) (1995) *International Feminist Perspectives in Criminology*, Open University Press: Buckingham.

Henne, K. and Troshynski, E. (2013) 'Mapping the Margins of Intersectionality: Criminological Possibilities in a Transnational World', *Theoretical Criminology*, 17(4): 455–473.

Hogg, R. and Brown, D. (1998) *Rethinking Law & Order*, Pluto: Sydney.

Hogg, R. and Carrington, K. (2006) *Policing the Rural Crisis*, Federation Press: Sydney.

Hudson, A. (2000) 'Critical Reflection as Research Methodology', in V. Jupp, P. Davies and P. Francis (eds), *Doing Criminological Research*, Sage: London.

Kirkby, D. (ed.) (1995) *Sex, Power & Justice*, Oxford University Press: Melbourne.

Klein, D. (1973) 'The Etiology of Female Crime: A Review of the Literature', *Issues in Criminology*, 8(2): 3–30.

Laster, K. (1996) 'Feminist Criminology: Coping with Success', *Current Issues in Criminal Justice*, 8(2): 192–200.

McGarry, R. and Walklate, S. (2015) *Victims: Trauma, Testimony and Justice*, Routledge: London.

MacKinnon, C. (1987) *Feminism Unmodified: Discourses on Life and Law*, Harvard University Press: London.

Maher, L. (1997) *Sex(ed) Work: Gender, Race and Resistance in a Brooklyn Drug Market*, Clarendon: Oxford.

Mason, G. and Stubbs, J. (2010) *Feminist Approaches to Criminological Research*, Sydney Law School Legal Studies Research Paper No. 10/36.

Miller, J. (2004) 'The Girls in the Gang: What We've Learned from Two Decades of Research', in M. Chesney-Lind and L. Pasko (eds), *Girls, Women and Crime: Selected Readings*, Sage: California, 97–114.

Miller, J. (2014) 'Doing Crime as Doing Gender? Masculinities, Femininities and Crime', in R. Gartner and B. McCarthy (eds), *The Oxford Handbook of Gender, Sex and Crime*, Oxford University Press: Oxford.

Mohanty, C. (1984) 'Under Western Eyes: Feminist Scholarship and Colonial Discourses', *Boundary 2*, 12(3): 333–358.

Mohanty, C. (2003) *Feminism without Borders: Decolonising Theory, Practicing Solidarity*, Duke University Press: Durham and London.

Naffine, N. (1987) *Female Crime*, Allen & Unwin: Sydney.

Naffine, N. (1991) *Law and the Sexes*, Allen & Unwin: Sydney.

Naffine, N. (1997) *Feminism & Criminology*, Allen & Unwin: Sydney.

Potter, H. (2015) *Intersectionality and Criminology: Gender, Race, Class and Crime* (New Directions in Critical Criminology), Routledge: London & New York.

Rafter, N. (2000) 'Preface', in N. H. Rafter (ed.), *Encyclopedia of Women and Crime*, ORYX Press: Phoenix, AZ, xxv–xxx.

Renzetti, C. (1999) 'The Challenge to Feminism of Women's Use of Violence in Interpersonal Relationships', in S. Lamb (ed.), *New Versions of Victims*, New York University Press: New York, 42–56.

Renzetti, C. (2013) *Feminist Criminology*, Routledge: London.

Renzetti, C., Miller, S. and Gover, A. (eds) (2013) *Routledge International Handbook of Crime and Gender Studies*, Routledge: London & New York.

Rice, M. (1990) 'Challenging Orthodoxies in Feminist Theory: A Black Feminist Critique', in L. Gelsthorpe and A. Morris (eds), *Feminist Perspectives in Criminology*, Open University Press: Buckingham.

Russell, D. (1975) *The Politics of Rape: The Victim's Perspective*, Stein and Day: New York.

Sandoval, C. (1991) 'U.S. Third World Feminism: The Theory and Method of Oppositional Consciousness in the Postmodern World', *Genders*, 10: 1–24.

Scutt, J. (1983) *Even in the Best of Homes: Violence in the Family*, Penguin: Australia.

Simon, R. J. (1975) *Women and Crime*, D. C. Heath: Lexington, MA.

Smart, C. (1976) *Women, Crime and Criminology*, Routledge: London.

Smart, C. (1989) *Feminism and the Power of Law*, Routledge: London.

Smart, C. (1990) 'Feminist Approaches to Criminology – or Postmodern Woman Meets Atavistic Man', in L. Gelsthorpe and A. Morris (eds), *Feminist Perspectives in Criminology*, Open University Press: Buckingham.

Stanko, E. (1990) *Everyday Violence*, Pandora: London.

Stanley, L. and Wise, S. (1983) *Breaking Out: Feminist Consciousness and Feminist Research*, Routlege & Kegan Paul: London.

Sumner, C. (1990) 'Preface', in L. Gelsthorpe and A. Morris (eds), *Feminist Perspectives in Criminology*, Open University Press: Buckingham.

Taft, A. (2000) 'Violence against Women in Pregnancy and after Childbirth', *Australian Domestic and Family Violence Clearinghouse*, Issues Paper 6, Sydney.

Tanesini, A. (1999) *An Introduction to Feminist Epistemologies*, Blackwell Publishers: Massachusetts.

Thayer, M. (2010) *Making Transnational Feminism*, Routledge: New York.

Threadgold, T. (1993) 'Critical Theory, Feminisms, the Judiciary & Rape', *Australian Feminist Law Journal*, 1: 7–25.

UN Women (2011) *Women's Police Stations in Latin America Case Study: An Entry Point for Stopping Violence and Gaining Access.* www.endvawnow.org/uploads/browser/files/security_wps_case_study.pdf

Walklate, S. (2007a) *Imagining the Victim of Crime*, Open University Press: Maidenhead.

Walklate, S. (ed.) (2007b) *Handbook on Victims and Victimology*, Willan: Cullompton.

Walklate, S. (2011) 'Reframing Criminal Victimisation: Finding a Place for Vulnerability and Resilience', *Theoretical Criminology*, 15(2): 175–192.

Walmsley, R. (2015) *World Female Imprisonment List, Third Edition*, Institute for Criminal Policy Research, University of London.

Young, A. (1992) 'Review of Feminist Perspectives in Criminology', *Journal of Law and Society*, 19: 289–292.

Young, A. (1996) *Imaging Crime: Textual Outlaws and Criminal Conversations*, Sage: London.

Young, A. (1998) 'The Waste Land of the Law, the Wordless Song of the Rape Victim', *Melbourne University Law Review*, 22(2): 442–465.

Young, J. (1998) 'Breaking Windows: Situating the New Criminology', in P. Walton and J. Young (eds), *The New Criminology Revisited*, Macmillan: London; St Martins: New York.

Zedner, L. (2003) 'Victims', in *The Oxford Handbook of Criminology* (2nd edn), Oxford University Press: London.

8

QUEERING CRIMINOLOGY

Clara Moura Masiero

Introduction

This chapter seeks to present possibilities for the development of queer criminologies, that is, criminological perspectives making use of queer 'theories' to propose new approaches for research subject matters specific to criminology, and also new ways of thinking about criminologies themselves. At issue is not specifically a theory, since, in relation to queer, one cannot speak about an organic corpus or a dogmatic system of thinking, but only about a plurality of theoretical perspectives. The decision to use 'criminologies' in the plural was taken because, as shall be seen in this article, there are various possibilities for criminological approaches within this field. Furthermore, the use of the term 'queer criminology' would give a sense of singularity and solidity that is not appropriate to the intersection between queer studies and criminology. The best option might even be to use the expression, 'queering criminology', so as to remove the unyielding idea of a fragmented field of knowledge and allow, instead, an idea of ongoing intersection with criminology. For, in the same way as a series of new criminological approaches has been developed, focused on specific individuals or groups left aside historically by criminological studies – such as black and feminist criminologies – queer criminologies have arisen to supplement the already-fragmented and stimulating field of critical alternative criminologies.[1]

Queer criminologies can be considered critical because queer concepts involve, par excellence, a critical thought, a critical attitude or a critical view. In the same way that critical criminology once challenged some criminological orthodoxies, so do queer criminologies seek to destabilise conventional identities, social rules, heteronormativity and sex–gender binarism. And queer criminologies can be considered as alternatives because they entail new ways of thinking about criminology and respective subject matters, in a manner that is sensitive and aware as to sexual diversities and gender identities. Until now this approach has been non-existent or only incipient in criminological research. Worse, there has been a long history of actually criminalising and pathologising homosexuality and transgenderism or transexuality ('gender identity disorder', according to medical literature) globally, which, as will be seen, continues today. But first, a note on how the word transgender is being used in this chapter.

The word transgender is used in this chapter to refer, in general terms, to transvestites, transexuals, cross-dressers and drag queens, though it is recognised that there are particularities differentiating these categories. The term transgender started to become popular from the end of the 1990s, and made reference to various groups of people who use, either at specific moments or constantly, clothes and accessories conventionally held to belong to the opposite sex. The use of the term arose with particular vigour as part of homosexual militancy where it referred to the problem of gender identity. Its use attempted to satisfy specific demands from transgender people for space and rights within the homosexual movement (Vencato, 2009). Transgender may relate to feelings and activities that psychiatry used to label transvestism and/or to the constant toing-and-froing between one gender and another, though not every cross-dressing habit indicates the existence of a transgender identity, and one cannot even say that the passage between masculine and feminine is what defines them. Transgender people transform themselves 'in the ways in which one views, interprets, incorporates or rejects signs of masculinity and femininity as available socially' (Vencato, 2009, p. 26).[2]

Many countries still criminalise homosexual acts between consulting adults in public while more than a third of countries still criminalise homosexual relations between consenting adults in private. There are even countries – such as parts of Nigeria and Somalia, Mauritania, Sudan, Iran, Saudi Arabia and Yemen – that provide for punishment in the form of the death penalty or imprisonment for life. Only recently, Uganda, for instance, approved a law which transformed any promotion of homosexuality into a crime (ILGA, 2013). As concerns pathologisation, it was as late as 1995 that the World Health Organisation (WHO) removed homosexuality from the list of mental disorders (International Classification of Diseases (ICD)). Until then it considered 'homosexuality' to be a sexual disorder or deviance. Transexuality remained defined as a 'gender identity disorder' in the *Diagnostic and Statistical Manual of Mental Disorders* (DSM) until 2013, whereafter it came to be referred to as 'gender dysphoria'. This latter is not viewed as being so serious as a gender disorder, but it remains a mental disorder. These criminalising or pathologising norms give rise to controls on behaviour and a repressive system causing violence against those who do not fit in.

The stigma of being deviant or abnormal that is ascribed to people not following the binary norms (whether social or legal) of sexuality and gender identity persists and even the most advanced and critical approaches have failed to identify and deconstruct the normative discourses which establish and impose just one sex–gender–sexuality sequence. Centred on heterosexuality and strictly governed by gender norms, such heteronormative discourses ultimately give rise to violently homophobic and transphobic societies in which sexually related crimes are committed. That is why there is a need to intersect queer studies and criminology; to suggest that repressive or rigid identity regimes are criminogenic (about homophobia, see more at Borillo, 2010).

This article is engaged in exactly this struggle for change, and focuses on the presentation of possibilities for the development of queer criminologies or queering criminology. It is divided into three parts: in the first part, the term queer is discussed as a concept, a theory and a social movement; in the second part, a case is made for placing a queer criminological approach within the scope of critical alternative criminologies; and, lastly, the third part presents the possibilities for lines of research that can be undertaken as part of a queer criminological approach. Certainly, this exposition will not cover all possibilities – which are numerous – but it will illustrate, by example, how the queering criminology approach might develop.

Queer as a critique

It is difficult to define what queer is. Is queer a theory, a social movement, an academic movement or a form of activism? Maybe this difficulty exists because queer is all of that and also because queer is peculiarly indefinable. Sara Salih (2013) would even say that part of the radicalism of queer lies in its resistance to easy definition. Eve Sedgwick (1994), a theorist considered queer, characterises queer as undistinguishable, indefinable, unstable; or even: 'Queer is a moment, a movement, an on-going, recurring, perturbing, troublant [unsettling]' cause, highlighting that the Latin root of the word means sideways (Salih, 2013, p. 19).

The emergence of this theoretical and political perspective dates back to the end of the 1980s, in the United States, in the gay and lesbian intellectual culture which was in opposition to sociological studies about sexual and gender minorities (Miskolci, 2009). It therefore proposed both a new critical theory and a new form of struggle. It was an academic movement that produced both theoretical constructions and political engagement.

Queer estrangement with respect to the social theory that was being produced in the 1990s resulted from the fact that social sciences dealt with the social order as a synonym of heterosexuality (Miskolci, 2009). The queer movement, therefore, criticised gay and lesbian movements at the time for their uncompromising conception of identity, their tendency to allow themselves to be assimilated by mainstream culture and their commercialisation. This was the perception of López Penedo (2008, p. 49) when she wrote that: 'these young [queer] activists accuse gay culture of having abandoned that intention of questioning heterosexual society and of having fallen into a replica of its privileges'.

Aware that a stable and fixed identity policy can become an accomplice to the system which it seeks to rise against, so-called queer theorists, both male and female, nowadays suggest a post-identity theory and policy. The objective of this policy and of this theory is to critique heterosexual/homosexual opposition which dichotomy is understood as the central category that organises social customs, knowledge and relations between subjects. Indeed, Miskolci (2009) would say that, despite their good intentions, some sexuality studies and some actual social movements have also ended up maintaining and naturalising the heterosexual norm. In opposition, queer perspectives have striven to destabilise some of these cultural zones of comfort created by heterosexism and that are established as a means of social control and regulation. Queer perspectives have thus attempted to deconstruct some monolithic gay and lesbian identities in order to demonstrate that they also have had superimposed upon them power relations generated on the basis of static conceptions of heterosexuality, race, gender or ethnicity (López Penedo, 2008). Thus, queer perspectives seek a sexual revolution with broad reach to transform sexuality in ways that will benefit both homosexuals and heterosexuals.

Meanwhile, and according to Judith Butler (2005), one of the most cited queer theorists, gender operates as a regulatory construction favouring heterosexuality. This is because, according to Butler, each gender is a representation, it is not an essence, but rather a series of rites that, when repeated, build up an identity. Societies construct norms governing and materialising sex and these norms need to be repeated and reiterated to be realised as effective, because bodies do not fully conform with norms. And societies constantly and only repeat gender norms from a heterosexual point of view. Accordingly, heterosexuality, 'far from arising spontaneously from each new-born body, must be re-instilled or re-instructed by way of constant repetition and recital of (male and female) codes socially accepted as natural' (Preciado, 2014,

p. 26). Yet even though these norms always reiterate heterosexuality, they cannot force all bodies to conform to them. The latter are accordingly held as 'wretched' subjects, as those falling outside the norm.

In this deconstruction, the rupture proposed by the queer perspective is characterised by a removal of sex from the natural order of things, and it is, instead, placed in the much more malleable territory of discourses, institutions and customs (Corrêa, 2006). Similarly, there is a break with a whole series of opposing dichotomies: homosexuality/heterosexuality, man/woman, male/female, nature/technology and their respective effects such as hierarchy, domination and exclusion since they reject identity pigeonholing as to sexual orientation and gender identity (Welzer-Lang, 2001, p. 473).

The use of the term queer to refer to this academic and social movement is symbolic. The word queer did not take on a sexual connotation until 1920, at which point it started to be used habitually to refer to homosexuals. The term then became popular among homosexuals themselves, who made use of it for self- definition until 1930, until the use of the term 'gay' began to spread (López Penedo, 2008). It is curious that the term 'gay' arose as the result of a rebellion by younger homosexuals who sought to

> designate a separation between their way of understanding homosexuality and the sexual deviance that queer implied at the time, and that now, in a sort of a return journey ... the term queer has taken this role in the resistance process.
>
> *(López Penedo, 2008, p. 36)*

For, in the 1920s queer started to be used as an insult and form of abuse directed at homosexuals, and within the framework of the stigmatising qualifiers used in everyday speech to refer to homosexuals (Carrara and Simões, 2007). It was a signifier of what constitutes human sexuality: something strange (Assis, 2011, p. 149). The term is invoked now, however, with all its baggage of strangeness and mockery, by the so-called queer movements, specifically to characterise their perspective of opposition and challenge towards the normalisation and stability proposed by identity policy. It is interesting to observe how the term itself already constitutes a political tool. After all, queer has also transformed itself into the subject of deviant sexuality (post-modern sexual pluralism): bisexuals; homosexuals; transsexuals; drag queens. Based on the questioning of the concept of identity, queer theorists seek to focus on sexual customs, including, in this way, cross-dressers and drag queens, as well as sadomasochists and bisexuals (Furlani, 2009). Thus, from being an insult at the end of the 1980s, the term queer gradually took on a new affirmative meaning, with inputs from academics which included both theoretical constructions and political engagement. Above all, queer is nowadays affirmation of a post-identity identity (Butler, 2005).

The favoured and fundamental policy tactic for the queer movement is the questioning of the thinking found behind the terms, 'deviant' and 'normal'. The US activist group, Queer Nation, from the 1990s, was one of the first to put into action this form of struggle. Its intention was to transform the public discourse on sexuality by destabilising the boundaries of both public and private space, thereby dismantling the idea that sexuality was something to be confined to the private realm. For this, they employed tactics going from the 'invasion' of bars and shopping centres frequented by heterosexuals, to the staging of large-scale 'kiss-ins' in public spaces. In this way, they sought to demonstrate that naturalisation of a space as belonging to heterosexuals necessarily depends upon the invisibility of gays (López Penedo, 2008).

The queer movement, it should be noted, seeks to go beyond the analysis and critique of identities and sexual differences to new ways of knowing and being. For this reason, one can speak about queer epistemology, that is, a new way of thinking about power, culture, knowledge and education. This is the perception of Guacira Lopes Louro (2009, pp. 91–92):

> Queer is a way of thinking and of being that does not covet the centre or want it as a reference; a way of thinking and being that challenges society's regulatory norms, which accepts the discomfort of ambiguity, of being 'between places'.

Queer criminologies as critical alternative criminologies

The intersection between queer studies and criminological studies has the potential to give rise to new fields of reflection: so-called queer criminologies. This theoretical alliance has much to contribute to criminological thought, to the extent that it opens up new perspectives for research that until now have been explored very little or not at all by criminology. This section will seek to introduce the emergence of this dialogue between queer perspectives and criminology, justify its theoretical pertinence and, furthermore, contextualise this criminological perspective among critical alternative criminologies.

The founding insight on the possibility and/or need for queer criminology is usually credited to the article, 'Perverse criminologies: the closet of Doctor Lombroso', by Nic Groombridge (1999) (see also Sorainen, 2003; Ball, 2014). Groombridge, in this article, challenged criminologists to take criminology 'out of the closet'. He observed that criminology 'has a long record of selectively ignoring deviance associated with new social movements and insights from other disciplines' (Groombridge, 1999, p. 532). Until the 1970s, homosexuality and various non-cisgender gender identities[3] were labelled as criminal, psychopathic, sinful and perverted outlooks; and criminological studies were engaged in determining whether or not being lesbian, gay, bisexual or transgender was a form of deviance (Woods, 2014). After 1970, according to Jordan Blair Woods (2014, p. 15), a period began marked by invisibility in discussions relating to sexual orientation and gender identity in criminology and it is not difficult to establish that there was (and is) very little or no theoretical engagement in this subject in 'each of the four major schools of criminology: biological, psychological, sociological, and critical'.

The time has now come for criminology to open up to new ways of thinking, including queer conceptions, feminist thought and gender studies; and to search for new ways of bringing together theory and empirical investigation (Sorainen, 2003). This criminological proposal responds to the call for critical alternative criminological perspectives. After all, and as Ball (2014) highlights, critical alternative criminologies and queer perspectives share a common attitude of opposition towards orthodoxy in knowledge, in politics and in ways of thinking, above all when dealing with matters relating to crime and justice, or sexuality and gender.

Given that queer criminologies have come to question heteronormativity to the extent that they conceive human relations, identities and concepts as specificities contingently and historically marked by relations of power and political interests, then it seems logical that they fall within the scope of critical alternative criminologies, as proposed in this book, which, in the words of Pat Carlen (Chapter 1) seek, ultimately, to 'deconstruct the meanings of crime and criminal justice so as to expose the relationships between social structural inequalities, criminal injustices, laws and human identities' (p. 4). For, as Ball, Buist and Woods (2014, p. 4) emphasise, the project of queer/ing criminology is always unfinished and must remain an open space in which such diversity of perspectives, methods, critiques, and reflections can flourish. Queer criminology can speak to a number of people and communities. It can take us down multiple paths, and it can remain an open space of intellectual and political contestation. And, like all critical criminologies, it can, and indeed should, remain engaged in a constant struggle to achieve justice, eliminate inequality, and challenge subordination.

In the following section it will be suggested that there are a multiplicity of perspectives and lines of research that can be examined via queer perspectives in criminology.

Queering criminology research perspectives

Ball, Buist and Woods (2014) define queer criminology as a diversified range of criminological research, critiques, methods, perspectives and reflections involving a fluid notion of queer. Agreeing that queer is a fluid term that can be used in various manners and in view of the work already undertaken within this field (for example, Groombridge, 1999; Sorainen, 2003; Carvalho, 2012; Woods, 2014; Buist and Stone, 2014; Ball, 2016), the proposal is made here to divide queer criminology into three significant lines of research, based on three different uses made of the term queer: (i) as a noun relating to identity; (ii) as a set of theoretical concepts intended to destabilise concepts, categories and heterocentric social norms; and (iii) as a verb, relating to a process or activity.

A noun relating to identity

Those using queer to refer to identity categories make it into an umbrella term covering all people with non-heterocentric sexual orientations or with gender identities that do not follow the protocol established for obtaining the expected identity, such as gay, lesbian, bisexual, transgender, among others[4] (traditionally represented by the 'LGBT' acronym).[5] In this way, they conceive of queer criminology as a project to include LGBT [lesbian, gay, bisexual transgender] people in criminological research, in order to produce knowledge about the experience of such people with crime and criminal justice. This is the approach taken by the criminologists, Carrie L. Buist and Codie Stone (2014, p. 45), when they affirm:

> Criminology and criminal justice researchers need to thoughtfully include transgender individuals in their research and continue to add to the knowledge of the entire LGBTQ population. This is indeed the reason why there is a need for queer criminology. As the LGBTQ [lesbian, gay, bisexual, transgender, queer/questioning] community in the US slowly but surely marches forward towards full equality, the transgender community has become more vocal and demanding of full inclusion in society.

In the same way, this is the approach of Jordan Blair Woods (2014, p. 32):

> Queer criminology must equip criminologists with the tools to explore how various circumstances shape LGBTQ people's experiences of crime without inherently labelling them as victims, or as criminals, on account of their sexual orientations and gender identities. This task is not easy given that the treatment of LGBTQ people in the field

of criminology has been shaped largely by their perceived statuses as criminal sexual deviants.

Research undertaken along these lines will aim to: explore the ways in which non-heterocentric or transgender people are treated by the justice system, whether as victims or as perpetrators of criminal infractions; explore the experiences of transgender people as agents of criminal justice; and identify discriminatory heteronormativity in the criminal justice system.

A set of theory-destabilising concepts

The second line of enquiry encompasses work making use of concepts from queer theories in order to comprehend/destabilise categories of sexual and gender diversity and explore them in criminological research, especially to bring to light the various forms of normative regulation that produce injustices for those not seen to be complying with dominant sexual norms. A revealing research reversal might be that proposed by Groombridge: a replacing of the conventional assumption that sexual diversity is a deviant outlook with analysis, instead, of patterns of heteronormativity and of homophobic and transphobic culture (Sorainen, 2003; Carvalho, 2012). In other words, instead of taking for granted existing patterns of normative sexuality, researchers could take on the task of understanding and then destabilising the means of control engendered by heteronormative logic.

To queer – a verb

The third line of research is presented by Matthew Ball (2014) and is based on a critical analysis with respect to the first two lines set out. Ball recognises the importance of the first two approaches but warns about their limits and about how in focusing on sexuality and gender they may close off other lines of investigation. Ball's (2014) proposal is inspired in a particular conception of critique, developed by Michel Foucault and Judith Butler (2000), which conceives of it as a virtue, an activity that involves pushing beyond the limits or, simply, 'the art of not being governed' (Foucault, 2007, p. 44). He therefore proposes an uncoupling of the term queer from sexuality and gender, so as to avoid presumptions that queer relates to something (such as an identity category) and instead to advance towards an approach conceiving of queer as a verb, or an attitudinal process with respect to what is held as 'normal'. Queer criminology developed in these terms 'might help people to detach themselves from the way their lives have been inscribed (or not) in particular discourses, and in the truths, orderings, and ethical precepts that are installed in forms of government' (Ball, 2014, p. 31). Being queer would thus involve the maintenance of a constant interrogative stance towards what is taken for granted as being normal. And here it is important to note that queering criminology can be more than a project for inclusion of LGBTQ people, sexuality and gender in criminological studies – even if this alone would be no small feat – but rather a way of rethinking varied norms governing our lives and our bodies – a project at the service of society as a whole.

Conclusions

When working with a queer approach, one of the fundamental challenges may appear to lie in the actual definition of the term. But it is both difficult and undesirable to ascribe to queer a precise definition because it is a fluid and open concept, covering a diverse range of ideas and knowledges, as well as political projects… all united by a critical attitude. This attitude goes beyond a critical analysis of identities and sexual diversity to involving a new form of thinking about power, culture and knowledge itself.

Queer approaches are critical exercises that seek to expose the limits, contingencies and instabilities of existing norms (Salih, 2013), thereby gambling on the multiplication of differences that can subvert all-encompassing, hegemonic or totalitarian discourses. Despite resisting regimes of normality, queer politics recognise the need for an 'epistemology of the wretched, based on intersectional studies' (Miskolci, 2009, p. 173). There are no limits to queer research possibilities.

One of the main focuses of queer analyses are sexualities, since queering them leads to the identification of the limits of the various forms of governance of the body and of sexuality and of the exclusions that they generate. Queer researches seek to break with binary reasoning resulting in the establishment of hierarchies and subordination within the current sexual order and, in light of this, queer theories think about sexuality, genders and bodies in a plural, multiple and changing sense. Therefore, queer approaches can both unmask the notion that sex, gender and sexuality are essential and fixed concepts, as well as challenge the stability of concepts, methods and assumptions of conventional researches in social sciences. Yet dialogues between queer and criminological research are possible. Queering criminologies engender a criminological field of new criminological perspectives seeking to understand and unveil violences, exclusions and stigmata generated by the regimes of normalisation (above all, heteronormative sexual orders).

Unlike feminist criminology which addresses the hierarchies established between female and male, queer seeks to transcend the dichotomy of gender. It tends towards the deconstruction of gender dichotomies so as to emphasise understandings that identities and ideas of normalities must not be taken as stable and fixed. The experiences of LGBT people with crime and the criminal justice system is one of the first targets of research that can be identified in this plural field of queer criminologies. It will be innovative in tackling full-on – and anywhere in the world – any conception of homosexuality or transgenderness as deviant or pathological conducts.

Queer criminology must take the field forward beyond the framework of sexual deviance and consider sexual orientation and gender identity and expression as non-deviant differences in conjunction with other differences, such as race, ethnicity, class and religion. They become of concern to criminology when they influence victimisation, involvement in crime and experiences in the criminal justice system more broadly. It is already possible to identify advances in the recognition of sexual and gender diversity in many western societies. Sadly, however, in my home country of Brazil, and despite numerous pending bills seeking the acknowledgement of rights for homosexuals and transgenders, no such emancipatory legislation has yet been approved, and there are still enormous challenges. Queering criminology is offered as a small contribution to this struggle.

Notes

1   For Brazilian readers, this field has been very well covered by this book, thanks to Pat Carlen and Leandro Ayres França, to which this author would like to express her gratitude for accepting the proposal of this chapter and, as such, the great honour of being part of this publication. I would also like

to thank the members of the Study Group on Contemporary Criminologies for their careful reading of the first version of this article, for the opportunity to discuss the text and for their contributions to its improvement.

2 Non-English references were translated by the author.

3 Non-cisgender identities are all those that do not identify with the gender corresponding to their sex as ascribed biologically.

4 'Gender identities are multiple and varied and even the actual terminology used in defining non-normative genders is multiple and varied. It may even depend on the cultural context' (Masiero, 2014, p. 26).

5 The LGBT label used here follows the formula approved by the 1st Brazilian National LGBT Conference, thereby referring to Lesbians, Gays, Bisexuals and Transgenders (transvestites, transexuals and transgenders). Sometimes it takes on other variations, which invert the order of the letters, double the 'T' or add new letters that allude to other identities (such as 'I' from Intersexual or 'Q' from Queer). It is stressed, therefore, that this label is open and subject to challenges, variations and changes (Simões and Fachini, 2009, p. 15).

References

Assis, Cleber Lizardo de (2011). 'Teoria *queer* e a Resolução CFP n° 1/99: uma discussão sobre heteronormatividade *versus* homonormatividade'. *Bagoas*, 6, pp. 145–155.

Ball, Matthew (2014). 'Queer criminology, critique, and the "art of not being governed"'. *Critical Criminology*, 22, pp. 21–34.

Ball, Matthew (2016). *Criminology and Queer Theory: Dangerous Bedfellows?* London: Palgrave Macmillan.

Ball, Matthew; Buist, Carrie L.; Woods, Jordan Blair (2014). 'Introduction to the special issue on Queer/ing Criminology: New Directions and Frameworks'. *Critical Criminology*, 22, pp. 1–4.

Borillo, Daniel (2010). *Homofobia: História e crítica de um preconceito*. Translated by Guilherme João de Freitas Teixeira. Belo Horizonte: Autêntica.

Buist, Carrie L.; Stone, Codie (2014). 'Transgender victims and offenders: failures of the United States criminal justice system and the necessity of queer criminology'. *Critical Criminology*, 22, pp. 35–47.

Butler, Judith (2000). 'What is critique: an essay on Foucault's virtue'. Available at: http://eipcp.net/transversal/0806/butler/en. Accessed January 2015.

Butler, Judith (2005). *Cuerpos que importan: sobre los límites materiales y discursivos del 'sexo'*. Buenos Aires: Paidós.

Carrara, Sérgio; Simões, Júlio Assis (2007). 'Sexualidade, cultura e política: a trajetória da identidade homossexual masculina na antropologia brasileira'. *Cadernos Pagu*, 28, pp. 65–99.

Carvalho, Salo de (2012). 'Sobre as possibilidades de uma criminologia *queer*'. *Revista Sistema Penal & Violência*, 4(2), pp. 151–168.

Corrêa, Sonia (2006). 'Cruzando a linha vermelha: questões não resolvidas no debate sobre direitos sexuais'. *Horizontes Antropológicos*, 12(26), pp. 101–121.

Foucault, Michel (2007). 'What is critique?' In S. Lotringer (ed.) *The Politics of Truth*. Los Angeles: Semiotext(e), pp. 41–81.

Furlani, Jimena (2009). 'Direitos humanos, direitos sexuais e pedagogia *Queer*: o que essas abordagens têm a dizer à educação sexual?' In Rogério Diniz Junqueira (ed.) *Diversidade sexual na educação: problematizações sobre a homofobia nas escolas*. Brasília: Ministry of Education/UNESCO, pp. 293–323.

Groombridge, Nic (1999). 'Perverse criminologies: the closet of doctor Lombroso'. *Social & Legal Studies*, 8(4), pp. 531–548.

ILGA (International Lesbian, Gay, Bisexual Trans and Intersex Association) (2013). *Homofobia de Estado: un estudio mundial jurídico sobre la criminalización, protección y reconocimiento del amor entre personas del mismo sexo*, 8ª ed.

López Penedo, Susana (2008). *El laberinto queer: la identidad en tiempos de neoliberalismo*. Barcelona, Madrid: Egales.

Louro, Guacira Lopes (2009). 'Heteronormatividade e homofobia'. In Rogério Diniz Junqueira (ed.) *Diversidade sexual na educação: problematizações sobre a homofobia nas escolas*. Brasília: Ministry of Education/UNESCO, pp. 85–93.

Masiero, Clara Moura (2014). *O movimento LGBT e a homofobia: novas perspectivas de políticas sociais e criminais*. Porto Alegre: Criação Humana.

Miskolci, Richard (2009). 'A teoria *Queer* e a sociologia: o desafio de uma analítica da normalização'. *Sociologias*, 11(21), pp. 150–182.

Preciado, Beatriz (2014). *Manifesto contrassexual: práticas subversivas de identidade sexual*. Translated by Maria Paula Gurgel Ribeiro. São Paulo: n-1 edições.

Salih, Sara (2013). *Judith Butler e a teoria queer*. Translated and notes by Guacira Lopes Louro. Belo Horizonte: Autêntica.

Sedgwick, Eve (1994). *Tendencies*. London: Routledge.

Simões, Júlio Assis; Fachini, Regina (2009). *Na trilha do arco-íris: do movimento homossexual ao LGBT*. São Paulo: Fundação Perseu Abramo.

Sorainen, Antu (2003). 'Queering criminology'. In *3rd Annual Conference of the European Society of Criminology 'Crime and Control in an Integrating Europe'*, University of Helsinki.

Vencato, Anna Paula (2009). *'Existimos pelo prazer de ser mulher': uma análise do Brazilian Crossdresser Club*. Rio de Janeiro, 277 f. Tese (Doutorado em Antropologia Cultural) – Post-Graduate Programme in Sociology and Anthropology at the Universidade Federal do Rio de Janeiro.

Welzer-Lang, Daniel (2001). 'A construção do masculino: dominação das mulheres e homofobia'. *Estudos Feministas*, 9(2), pp. 460–482.

Woods, Jordan Blair (2014). '"Queering criminology": overview of the state of the field'. In D. Peterson and V. R. Panfil (eds) *Handbook of LGBT Communities, Crime, and Justice*. New York: Springer Science+Business Media, pp. 15–40.

9

THE POLITICS OF SEXUALITY

Alternative visions of sex and social change

Jo Phoenix

It is the twenty-first century. Gay weddings are legal. Women's sexual agency is recognised. Geo-social networking apps are used by women and men for recreational sex. Diverse sexualities, e.g. LGBTQi (Lesbian, Gay, Bisexual, Transgendered, Queer, intersexed) proliferate. Cosmopolitan sexualities, furries and fetish clubs have entered the sexual market place; sexting (that is, sending sexually explicit messages or images using smart phone technology), grooming (that is, an adult befriending or establishing a relationship in order to lower a child's resistance to or inhibition regarding future child sexual abuse), child sexual exploitation, historic sex abuses, prostitution, human trafficking and female sex offenders have become more visible. Such is the twenty-first-century landscape of sex, sexualities and sex regulation in most anglophone countries. It is an exciting landscape, but it is also full of contradictions. For, while law reforms have led optimistic commentators to claim that, freed from traditional bonds, sexuality is on the road to unqualified liberation, critical analyses of the relationships between sex and social structure (especially the structural sources of gender-based inequalities) have resulted in the more pessimistic critical commentaries in which sexual activities are pictured in contradictory fashion. Scenarios focused on a victimology of sex and social exchange depict the practice and purveyance of sex as being essentially exploitative under present social conditions and therefore (and for a variety of reasons) in need of stricter, rather than more relaxed, regulation. Scenarios more concerned with the apparent freeing up of previously suppressed sexual identities claim that, despite limited law reform and limited cultural recognition of a diversity of sexual identities, the notion of 'normal sex' remains dominant and that, as a result, Other sexual identities are still as open to demonisation and punitive regulation as they ever were.

Sociological, cultural and criminological research and writings on sex and its regulation since the early 1980s are far too voluminous to be adequately covered here. This chapter, therefore, is limited to presenting a brief overview of criminology's early focus on female prostitution before delineating four contrasting visions of sex and social change in late modernity. It aims only to show how the critical interrogation of sexual politics has been dominated by the three following questions: what is normal sex? What determines the definitional boundaries between permitted and unpermitted sexualities? Who are the winners and losers in normal and abnormal sexual transactions? Readers interested in other theorisations of sexualities, therefore, should also consult Chapter 8 on queering criminologies as well as Chapter 10 on the criminology of mobility and Chapter 16 on hate crimes. Meanwhile, the basic terminology used in this chapter is as follows: terms like sex, sexual activities, behaviours or practice denote the range of embodied experiences that most people would associate with the common sense use of the word 'sex'. 'Sexual identities' refers to the sense of sexual self an individual might possess and that which in common parlance is associated with words like heterosexual, homosexual, lesbian, gay, transgendered and so on. 'Sexual regulation' is a broad term used to include the following: formal legal regulation via criminal justice; and less formal regulation via other governmental and non-governmental organisations and agencies that provide personal and welfare support, such as health, education and child welfare services as well as normative controls present in discourses and constructions of sex, sexual behaviours and sexual identities. 'Sexuality', following Foucault (1979), Rich (1980), Weeks (1989) and Plummer (2002), is to be understood less as a set of embodied experiences and more as a force or energy that is given shape, meaning and effect within specific social, political, economic and material contexts.

Sexual regulation and criminology in the twentieth century: a tale of victims, the righting of sexual wrongs and the regulation of economically and culturally marginalised women's and girls' sexual lives

Twentieth-century criminology showed only a passing interest in sex, sexuality or sexual behaviours, and typically only in relation to explorations of girls' promiscuity, women's prostitution, men's homosexuality and rape of women by men. Early questions posed were about the connections between women's and girls' *pathological* promiscuity and their criminality (Lombroso and Ferrero 1898, Glueck and Glueck 1934). Later work sought to shed light on the deviant subcultures and identities of those whose sexual behaviours – mostly women in prostitution and homosexuals – either placed them in conflict with the law or in conflict with then dominant, gendered norms and values about sex (Humphreys 1972, 1975, Sion 1977, Cohen 1980, McHugh 1980, Marshall 1981). Studies exploring victim precipitation were particularly interested in rape and hypothesised that women's overt sexual behaviours or sexual reputations had a part to play in hastening any eventual rape (Amir 1968, Curtis 1974, Schultz 1975). Shaping the connections that were made between sex, crime and justice were the then dominant discourses of gender and sex that constituted normal, respectable women as being sexually chaste and submissive and normal men as heterosexual and possessed of an active sex drive that demanded satisfaction, attention and regular release (Kinsey et al. 1948) and which, if frustrated, provided the explanation for both rape and the demand side of prostitution.

Towards the end of the twentieth century, the study of prostitution, homosexuality ('sluts and perverts'; Liazos 1972) and sexual victims became more academically critical and politically radical when scholars started challenging biological and naturalistic constructions of sex, sexualities and sexual behaviours. Radical critique stemmed partly from sociological perspectives describing the ways in which 'sexuality' varies according to social and historical context (Gagnon and Simon 1973, Plummer 1981, Weeks 1989); partly from a proliferation of feminist scholarship challenging ideologies of gender as they impact on sex and sexuality (Brownmiller 1976, McIntosh 1978, Smart and Smart 1978, Daly 1979, Eisenstein 1979, Shulman 1980, Dworkin 1981, Barry 1984); and, predominantly, from Michel Foucault's (1979) claim that the notion of sexuality is an historical construct, rather than a biological concept with an essential and unvarying empirical reality. Together, this body of work opened an anti-essentialist theoretical space in which it became possible to reconceptualise sexual violence, prostitution and homosexuality. Rape was no longer seen only as a form of deviant or pathological sex but, additionally, was reconceived as an act of social and political power (Kelly 1988). Prostitution was reconceived as labour in a materially unequal society rather than an individual act of delinquency or immorality (McIntosh 1978, McLeod 1982). The pathology of homosexuality was challenged (Porter and Weeks 1991). In this new, more critical, theoretical space, all kinds of alternative connections were drawn between crime, justice, sex and sexuality. Questions were asked about how dominant discourses of sex, sexualities or specific sexual behaviours (like prostitution or homo-sex) shape institutional processes of criminalisation and punishment as well as individuals' conceptions of self and sexual identity.

A commitment to investigating and explaining the experiences, self-identities and victimisation of previously demonised groups of people and to listening to the silenced voices of lesbians and gay men, sex workers and other victims of sexual violence formed the basis of a second set of alternative criminological connections between sex, sexuality, crime and justice. The key questions posed were as follows. How does the policing of sex, sexualities and sexual behaviours relate to extant power relations and economic, social and political inequalities? How, and to what effect, are infractions of legal rules and governmental policies about sexuality and sex policed? In addressing these two questions, many of the studies produced at the end of the twentieth century described historically and socially specific cultures of sexual regulation (Weeks 1989, 2007, Evans 2013). They traced the infinite variety of ways that discourses about age, class, gender, sexualities, ethnicity and culture have shaped the designation of some (but not other) sexual behaviours as crime (Chapkis 1997, Bernstein 2001, Davidson 2005, Little 2008, Rubin 2009, Sanders et al. 2009, Hester et al. 2010, Bernstein 2012, Samons 2013), the policing of different (but legal) expressions of sexuality (Waites 2003, 2005, Dwyer 2011, Johnson and Dalton 2012) and the prosecution, conviction and punishment of those who break sex-related laws (Ward and Hudson 2001, McAlinden 2005, Phoenix 2007, 2008, 2012, Hebenton and Seddon 2009).

Overall, two main findings stood out from the late twentieth-century critical studies of the politics of sex. First, that victimhood and legal protection were routinely being denied to crime victims (e.g. homosexuals or prostitutes) whose sexual practices or identities were either not those permitted within discourses of 'normal' or legitimate sex; or to women whose victimisation occurred within a pre-existing sexual relationship such as happened in date rape or rape within marriage (Cowling 1998, McGlynn and Munro 2011). Second, that people seen as sexual 'Others' (i.e. 'not like us') because their sexual activities were not legitimated by dominant sexual mores were frequently over-policed and criminalised in situations where it was doubtful that any crime had been committed at all. An iconic case in the UK that highlighted these issues was the prosecution, conviction and punishment of 16 gay men involved in sado-masochistic sexual practices for the offence of assault occasioning actual bodily harm in December 1990. Their defence was that sado-masochistic sexual practices were (and remain) legal and that they had all consented to the activities in which they were engaged. However, the Court of Appeal, the Law Lords and the European Court of Human Rights all upheld the original ruling: that an individual cannot consent to the harms committed against them. Arguably, it is particular meanings of vulnerability, victimhood, morality and sexuality that have facilitated a situation in which 16 gay men were given prison sentences or fined for their sado-masochistic sexual practices. It is rumoured that the policing operation cost in excess of £4 million. To date, no similar policing operation has yet occurred in England in relation to heterosexual sado-masochistic clubs and practices. The new critical writings on sex, sexualities, sexual behaviours and crime and justice of the late twentieth century informed some of the very complex politics of sex, gender and victimhood of the early twenty-first century. How the initial reform of prostitution policies widened to provide protection to children provides an interesting case study.

Since the 1990s there has been a fundamental shift across Europe and in many anglophone countries in how prostitution has been regulated and policed. Whereas until the last decades of the twentieth century the policing of prostitution was directed almost entirely at women sex workers themselves, recent legislative and policy change has focused policing on those who victimise and exploit sex workers. In 1999, Sweden, for example, criminalised the clients of sex workers by making the purchase of sex illegal. They also offered sex workers intensive social pedagogy and welfare interventions (see Skilbrei and Holmstrom (2013) on the Swedish model). After the United Nations ratified the *Protocol to Prevent, Suppress and Punish Trafficking in Persons Especially Women and Children* in November 2014, all national governments were required to report on the efforts made to accomplish the aims of the protocol. Meanwhile in England and Wales, the Sex Offences Act 2003 (SOA 2003) had been passed and implemented. SOA 2003 made it illegal for anyone at any age to facilitate or engage in sexual activities or behaviours of any kind with someone under the age of sexual consent (that is, 16 years old), including sexual exploration between two 15-year-olds. Although prostitution was not included in either the review of previous sexual offences or in the part of those offences that were modernised, one new crime was created: the commercial sexual exploitation of children. The rationale was that age of consent legislation made it illegal, by definition, to involve anyone under the age of sexual consent in any commercial sexual behaviour, but that such protection did not apply to those still legally defined as children (i.e. under the age of 18) but over the age of consent (16). During the following five years, new provisions were added. They related to child sexual exploitation, the online grooming of children for sexual exploitation and the production and distribution of pornography – including child pornography. Meanwhile, and as a result of growing concern about the relationships between the global movement of women and children and their enslavement in prostitution, the Immigration Act 1971 had already criminalised the 'smuggling' (by immigration avoidance) of people into the UK and the SOA 2003 and the Asylum and Immigration Act 2004 had criminalised both human trafficking for the purposes of sexual exploitation and 'internal trafficking', i.e. the movement of a woman or child for the purposes of sexual exploitation from one local authority within England and Wales to another.

At the same time as these legal changes were seeking to strengthen the protection of women and children vulnerable to sexual exploitation, theoretically informed feminist and criminological studies began to explore the meanings of prostitution for the women involved. The main debate provoked by these innovative investigations focused on: the possible relationships between women's economic circumstances and their involvement in prostitution; and the relationship between men's violence and women's involvement in prostitution. Were both prostitution and men's violence against women social institutions resulting from patriarchy (Høigård and Finstad 1992, Barry 1996, O'Neill et al. 1997)? Or, could women's experiences in prostitution be better explained by reference to class- and labour-based inequalities (Davidson 1998, Agustín 2001, 2007)? Or both (Phoenix 1999)? This debate, about how to view prostitution, has become increasingly polarised between those who support a 'prostitution-as-work approach' (and therefore craft a politics focusing on sex workers' rights and labour protection) and those who support a 'prostitution as exploitation and violence' perspective (and therefore argue for an abolitionist approach which should, as a beginning, at least criminalise those who buy sex-workers' services). At the most fundamental level, this debate is a continuation of the age-old argument about to what extent people should have the right to develop their sexual identities and pursue their sexual desires independently of the effect on (and possibly the exploitation of) other people. And this debate about the oppositions between sexual agency and sexual victimisation continues – even though the theoretical lens and empirical stories have changed.

Today, in academic and campaigning writings on sexuality, the focus is much more on the discursive strategies which are permissive of some tales rather than others. Yet, in tracing out how 'trafficked women' are discursively distinguished from 'migrant sex workers'; how young sex workers become defined as victims of childhood sexual exploitation; or how exploited or prostitute women are distinguished from 'consensual' sex workers (Phoenix 2002, Chapkis 2005, Agustín 2006, Sanders et al. 2009, Phoenix and Oerton 2013) the division into agents who choose their destinies and victims who are targeted – by either punitive welfare agencies or predatory and exploitative males – persists. But they persist in a reversal of the nineteenth- and twentieth-century moral drama wherein 'bad women' were portrayed as being a threat to young men's health, young women's morals and family inheritances. Nowadays, too, the dramatic characters in the eternal sexual morality play have changed and the threat is seen to come not from 'fallen women' but from 'otherwise respectable' predatory and powerful male 'sexual abusers' and 'sexual exploiters' – both historical and contemporary.

In the twenty-first century, critical and alternative imaginations have also sought to draw new and radically different links between sex, sexualities, crime and justice. Instead of focusing mainly on prostitution, academics now write and discuss sex, sexual behaviours and sexualities from a variety of perspectives. They have questioned the old, taken-for-granted 'victimisation and vulnerability' discourses that previously brought so many sexual practices under official surveillance and made them over-vulnerable to subsequent prosecution and criminalisation. They have demonstrated how 'victimisation and vulnerability' discourses work in a range of contexts to sustain (or, occasionally, destabilise) the operation of material, gendered, cultural or state-based inequalities. (For how discourses on human trafficking help to underpin increasingly repressive immigration regimes, see Turner and Kelly 2009, O'Connell Davidson 2011, Anderson 2013.) And they have highlighted how the rhetoric of exploited and/or prostituted women may engender and sustain austere welfare policies which women and girls experience as punishment rather than protection (Phoenix 2009). In short, early twenty-first-century commentators have recognised a plethora of sexualities of infinite variety and meaning – a recognition that is the life-force of queer criminology. For criminologists, however, the old focus on regulation via the legal construction of 'offender' and 'victim' necessarily remains central in explanations of the prosecution and reform of sexual regulation – even though at times the offending causes of sexual Othering or injustices may be seen to inhere in a socio-economic system such as 'patriarchy' or capitalism. The rest of the chapter will therefore examine four very different visions of sex and social control in later modernity in order to support its central argument: that the opposing concepts of sexual liberation and sexual victimisation remain central in criminological explanations of both sexual regulation and sex regulation reform.

Sex and social change: four visions of sex and social change in late modernity

Historical studies have repeatedly demonstrated that discourses on sex, sexualities and sexual behaviours are not only about sex but also a means by which other anxieties can be expressed and, once expressed, regulated (see, for example, Walkowitz (1980) for a fine analysis of the relationships between industrial capitalism, prostitution and the regulation of women in nineteenth-century England and Wales. See also Finnegan (1979) and McHugh (1980)). Contemporary discourses on sex and sexualities are no different. They are dominated by anxieties about the meanings and directions of social change and their implications for sexual regulation and sexual expression. Several critical scholars, for example, have argued that there have been changes in the social construction of sex, sexualities and sexual behaviours subsequent to the shift into a late modern period (Weeks et al. 2003, Butler 2011, Bernstein 2012, Beck and Beck-Gernsheim 2013, Attwood 2014, Weeks 2016) and for several decades it has been assumed that today's (anglophone) cultures are marked by a more permissive attitude towards sex, sexualities and the sexual than was prevalent, say, half a century ago – even though sex, sexualities and sexual behaviours periodically still become causes of public concern. The remainder of the chapter focuses on just four of the many different perspectives whence these changes have been discussed in the anglophone world. Two of the perspectives agree that there has been a degree of sexual liberation but disagree about both the level of benefits and the beneficiaries (Giddens 1992, Bauman 2013). The third perspective, in analysing the relationships between sex and consumption, argues that sex has become devalued by its commodification under neo-liberal capitalism. Finally, the fourth perspective discussed, takes a much darker view, seeing the permeation of the previously non-sexual by the sexual as a descent into the obscene in which sex is devalued and debased through deregulation and vulgarisation.

Sex and liberation

A number of empirical studies conducted in the 1980s charted what they saw as dramatic changes in both the normative values shaping sexual behaviours as well as the behaviours themselves (Rubin 1984). The traditional values ascribed to female virginity and chasteness were seen to have given way to an acceptance of women's sexual agency and to women's sense of entitlement to sexual activity. Noting these changes, Giddens (1992) argued that they were the result of transformations in broader social structures subsequent to a shift from modernity into late modernity and that, as such, they had redefined experiences of both gender and, importantly, intimacy. Part of a wider thesis (that, as societies modernise, aspects of social existence that have previously been seen as 'natural' become reconstituted as matters of 'lifestyle' choice) Giddens' argument here was that 'intimate life' had been gradually transformed from containment within the tightly constrained and fundamentally unequal conjugal relationships between men and women of traditional societies, through to the semi-structured eighteenth- and nineteenth-century notions of intimacy and romantic love (which were nevertheless circumscribed by gender scripts that constrained women) and, most recently, into modern day notions of confluent love in which intimacy and sex become matters to be mutually negotiated between two seemingly equal partners. He argued that modern scientific advances in relation to birth control broke the link between sex, intimacy and motherhood, which meant that in late modernity 'sexuality' has an independent and free-floating social existence. The quest for sexual pleasure and/or freedom has moved from women who, by definition, were previously seen to occupy the margins of social existence (courtesans, for instance) and has been taken up by any and all women as part of their search for a 'pure relationship'. This quest has taken place within a wider social context where the loosening of social constraints brought about by modernity has generated the problem of managing the new sexual freedoms. For, late modernity generates new uncertainties in place of the old constraints. These new uncertainties find expression in an ontological insecurity and a new pedagogy based on a proliferation of experts instructing how the new uncertainties are to be managed. In this way, late modernity has shaped a form of sexual expression that becomes the modern embodiment of the search for personal fulfilment and meaning – what Giddens (1992) termed 'plastic sexuality' (see also Evans 2013, Plummer 2015). The 'revolution in female sexual autonomy' and the 'flourishing of homosexuality' (Giddens 1992: 28) are exemplars par excellence of a plastic sexuality wherein people make their own sexuality and manage it according to their own sexual self-concepts. Thus Giddens and those writing within the same vein (Plummer 2015, Weeks 2016) make the case that the social shape of sex has become 'more democratic', and in terms of intimacy there now exists a new found equality between men and women and between heterosexual and homosexual. What takes precedence is 'the individual' and the individual making of a self (Beck 1992, Beck and Beck-Gernsheim 2013).

Those writing within a tradition of critical sexuality studies now routinely start with the assumption that, in twenty-first century late modern societies, individuals are somehow more free to pursue, construct and create their own unique sexual identities (see Weeks 2011, Butler 2015, Plummer 2015) in a sexual landscape that has been variously described as effervescent with possibilities, marked by diversity and with a growing attitude of tolerance (see Seidman et al. (2010) for a more thorough description of this 'new' sexual landscape). One of the taken-for-granted assumptions prevalent in this discourse is that there has been a democratisation of sex and of desire. In other words, it is assumed that there is expanded popular access to sexual expression which, in turn, has facilitated a sexual culture, pluralistic in nature and driven by individuals' expression of their 'authentic' sexual selves – whether those sexual selves are contained within the sexual and gender binaries structured by twentieth-century modern social institutions (family/work; public/private; heterosexuality/homosexuality) or the free floating, always emergent, multiplicity of sexualities unleashed from the binaries of the twentieth century – but still bringing with them the ever pervasive binary of predator/victim.

Sex and consumption

A more dystopian view of sex and social change than that of Giddens (1992) which celebrates the liberation of sex from the confines of traditional institutional and normative frameworks is to be found in the work of Bauman (2013) and others (Illouz 2012, Attwood and Smith 2013). Bauman, like Giddens, sees a relationship between sexual mores, sexual practices and social change. However, rather than focusing on intimacy, he focuses on the changing nature of human relationships. For Bauman, modernity (as a social formation) is dualistic in nature, and characterised by both order and rationality on the one hand and radical social, economic and cultural change on the other. Late modernity, by contrast, is marked by the failure of order and control and the capacity of capitalism to generate constant change – two conditions which both separately and together produce a less solid and more liquid form of social life (liquid modernity). When they combine with the advances of medical, reproductive technologies of the late twentieth century, the conditions that effect change in individuals' social and sexual lives are incrementally increased. So, for Bauman as for Giddens, contemporary social life is marked by the dissolution of constancy in social relations. But, apart from that initial agreement, their analyses differ. Giddens sees the dissolution of constancy as ushering in a democratisation of intimacy and sex where individuals are enabled, or perhaps compelled by their own ontological insecurities, to express their authentic sexual identities. Bauman, by contrast, views the severance of sex both from biology, via reproductive technologies, and from traditional forms of intimacy in marriage and family life, as limiting sex in late modernity – to serving no purpose other than pleasure. Yet, at the same time, he argues, sex is not freed from a density of other expectations – those, for example, relating to love, erotic desire and existential meaning via reproduction. Unable to meet any or all of these expectations, sex and intimacy in liquid modern societies, far from being repositories of pleasure and personal fulfilment, become sources of distress, grievance and anxiety.

There is, however, more to Bauman's dystopian vision than the idea that liberated sex ('free love') cannot fulfil the expectations individuals bring to it. He further argues that the same social processes which help to sustain consumer capitalism ensure that sex stays caught in a tension characteristic of modernity where consumption, rather than production, becomes the principal means of both social organisation and personal identity formation. Such a change has required a shift from what might have once been called 'the work ethic' to an aesthetic of consumption where individuals are groomed into a constant state of unsated desire in order to stimulate continuous consuming activities. To meet this unsated desire 'the market' produces an endless variety of new experiences, new pleasures and new products to purchase. The essence of consumption is not, therefore, product acquisition; it is the compulsion to consume the next thing. Consumption thus is not an end in itself. In the unending quest to assuage its appetite, consumption becomes the essence of social existence and identity. In this context, the tension that sex gets caught within is the opposition between its expectation overload and a consumption ethic that constantly denies durability to what is consumed. The individual, let loose from kinship ties and his/her identity as a producer, is left to create ties that are both provisional (i.e. to be 'free' to be oneself) and not provisional (i.e. at least durable enough to give identity and ontological security). It is not that sex becomes yet another experience to consume (although it does become that), rather it is that love and sex are transfigured into human relationships based in and around consumption. Twenty-first-century technologies, especially as instanced by the internet and smart phones, facilitate the quantity and turnover, and are also the hallmarks, of consumable sex. In the age of internet dating and geo-social networking for sex, these technologies suddenly appear not as *new* social phenomena *per se* but as ultra-expedient ways to achieve virtual connectedness and proximity in a world of otherwise consumable love and sex. (In this context, see also the concept of 'leisured sex' in Attwood and Smith (2013).)

Law reform and the markets

In many countries, the last 15 years has been a period of extraordinary reform to criminal and civil law concerning LGBTQ people. When Northern Cyprus repealed its laws in 2014, Europe became the first region in the world where homo-sex is not illegal in any of its countries. Additionally, many countries have also taken the opportunity to equalise the age of sexual consent for homo-sex and hetero-sex and to provide full legal equality and protection for LGBTQi people. In England and Wales, for example, there have been year on year legal reforms which culminated with the Equality Act 2010 that conferred the status of 'legally protected' on LGBTQ people alongside any other group likely to experience discrimination (on grounds of ethnicity, religion or gender). In 2013 gay marriages in England and Wales became legal.[1] However, where some have seen an era of reform based on an increasingly progressive culture of sexual regulation, others have seen the myriad sexualities now possible as having been shaped by a neo-liberal economic rhetoric of choice and the emergence of a political economy of intimacy, desire and sexual experience (Bernstein 2001, Illouz 2007, Harvey and Gill 2011). These latter critics characterise the shift in cultures of sexual regulation as being less to do with a relaxation of punitive regulation, and more to do with economic exploitation in a newly developing sexual market place. Take, for instance, the drive to provide equality for LGBTQ people. Since the end of the twentieth century, 'the market' has responded to the lesbian and gay community in ways undreamed of 30 years ago, providing everything from specialist magazines, to rainbow weddings, LGBTQ law firms specialising in LGBTQ laws, LGBTQ greeting cards, towels, travel companies and so on. Gay Pride and Lesbian Strength political marches of the 1980s and 1990s have given way to Mardi Gras style celebrations that, in the words of a journalist for queerty.com, are 'giant excuses for corporate marketing' and a chance for such companies to demonstrate both their commitment to LGBTQ equality as well as a chance to sell their goods (www.queerty.com/gay-pride-parades-are-giant-excuses-for-corporate-marketing-get-over-it-20100218). This is so much the case that Ulster Television reported that the legalisation of gay marriage in Ireland could, literally, be worth millions to the economy. The news channel also cited a report produced by the World Travel Market in 2014 which claimed that the global annual spend by LGBT people exceeded 182 billion euro. Within a week of the legalising of lesbian and gay marriage in Ireland, Tourism Ireland launched a major advertising campaign promoting LGBT weddings and honeymoons in Ireland for couples around the world, using the tag line 'Ireland says "yes" to love' (http://utv.ie/News/2015/05/25/Pink-pound-could-be-worth-millions-to-Irish-economy-37883).

Prostitution and pornography 'markets' have changed as well. Global capitalism and new technologies facilitate a vast and ever-expanding range of commercially available sexual experiences and products: from live sexual shows and a variety of sexually explicit texts to videos and imagery in print and online; from fetish clubs to sexual venues specialising in lap dancing and striptease; and from escort agencies, telephone and internet sexual encounters to sex tourism in developing countries and global cities. The size and scale of the industry is almost impossible to determine but Forbes estimated the size of the pornography industry in 2010 to be worth $520 million (www.forbes.com/2001/05/25/0524porn.html). In comparison the Office for National Statistics estimated that prostitution in the UK was worth £5.3 billion in 2014 (www.statslife.org.uk/economics-and-business/1865-is-prostitution-really-worth-5-7-billion-a-year). Such is the scale and growth of this industry that it has prompted some academics to attempt to 'map' it or at the very least describe and characterise it in global terms (see, for instance, McNair 2002, Davidson 2005, Brents and Hausbeck 2007, Brents and Sanders 2010).

Cybersex, with its attendant monetisation of individuals' sexual lives, can nowadays be added to the more traditional commercial sexual market. Geo-social networking apps and dating websites operate as for-profit organisations and companies that earn profits in two different ways. Dating websites, for instance, typically earn profit from the subscription fees that they charge clients. Others, like TINDR, GRINDR and BLENDR and other geo-social networking apps, do not ask for subscription fees. Instead, they make their profits from the big data that they own – data generated by individuals' use of their apps. Thus, part of today's concern about 'consumable sex' is not merely and only about the commercialisation of sexual products or services. Rather it is also about how individuals' private sexual lives and sexual identities become monetised in the form of big data. Surplus value is not extracted from the labour of private individuals. Instead, in the digital age, private lives and sexual identities become monetised and enmeshed in a broader political economy of intimacy, desire and sex.

Descent into the obscene

A different dystopian vision of sex, consumerism and commodification has been advanced by critical sexualities scholars who argue that, alongside the reconfiguration of intimacy, love, sex and the erotic in line with consumption, there has been a concomitant collapse between 'the everyday' and the obscene. There are many different versions of this dystopian vision of twenty-first-century western societies saturated by pornographic images and messages. One variant is the *pornographication* thesis (McNair 1996, 2002) in which 'the obscene' (as in sexually explicit and pornographic imagery) is portrayed as being increasingly more visible and accessible in the mainstream cultures from which it has traditionally been excluded. Central to the pornographication thesis is the claim that at the same time as wider social changes relating to digital technologies have disrupted the boundaries between private and public realms, media consumer trends have given primacy to the confessional, to lifestyle and to interactivity. As a consequence, in the most popular social media (TV reality shows for one example) images and topics that have previously been excluded from, or remained on the margins of public space, flood into the mainstream. By some writers supporting the 'pornographication' thesis, these shifts are seen as being a logical extension of the commodification of sex and sexual consumerism in an age of consumer capitalism (see McNair's (2002) concept of 'strip-tease culture'; and Attwood 2004, Rubin 2009, Smith 2010).

A second variant of this vision is the *sexualisation* thesis. Feminist cultural studies academics and critical sexualities scholars have raised political concerns about the manner in which everyday use of pornographic imagery is a form of 'retrosexism' (Whelehan 2000) and a hostile response to feminist cultural critique (see also Attwood 2006, Levy 2006, Evans et al. 2010, Renold and Ringrose 2011). Thus, both variants of the descent into obscenity thesis make assumptions about the corrupting effect of sex. And once more sex has a victim. Whereas in McNair's pornographication thesis, 'the obscene' corrupts both popular and high culture, in Whelehan's sexualisation thesis, 'the obscene' (i.e. masculinist sexual ideology) corrupts the possibilities of women's sexual agency. However, the more common and more popular version of the sexualisation thesis is less about the corruption of culture in general and women's sexual freedom in particular. It is much more concerned about the sexualisation of children and teens.

From the first decade of the twenty-first century, popular concern was being expressed about the extent to which sexualised images of children were becoming increasingly common in advertising and marketing material (see Rush and La Nauze 2006). This unease later developed into a more generalised concern about media, sex, children and young people. In the UK and as part of a government consultation investigating violence against women and girls, a report into childhood sexualisation highlighted the following areas of concern: sexualised imagery across different media (magazines, advertising, marketing, television, film, music);

the 'mainstreaming' of pornography (with an emphasis on the easy availability of pornography on the internet); the ways in which smart phone technology supports new social practices, such as sexting; and the increasingly pornographic content of digital and online games (Papadopoulos 2010). Around the same time, popular and professional concern was being expressed in Australia, Canada and the USA about the supposedly new phenomenon of 'sexting' and what could or should be done about it (Benotsch et al. 2013, Burkett 2015). Furedi (2013) asked whether these anxieties about childhood sexualisation was a moral panic born of a newly accelerated anxiety about the changing nature of childhood combined with the older twentieth-century fear about the corrupting influence of media on childhood innocence. To aggravate all these fears, there were increasing reports from many anglophone countries about accusations of, and prosecutions for, contemporary and historic sexual abuse now revealed to have been practised in a variety of established institutions, and especially in church, educational and medical establishments previously seen to be the trustworthy guardians of, rather than threats to, childhood innocence.

In the Republic of Ireland, a series of criminal cases in the late 1990s and government inquiries in the opening decade of the twenty-first century demonstrated that hundreds of children had been subjected to sexual abuse by clerics in the previous decades (cf. www. hiainquiry.org/). Similarly, and in response to a series of reports about child sexual abuse in the church and across a range of public institutions, the Australian government set up the Royal Commission into Institutional Responses to Child Sexual Abuse in 2014. Media coverage of the Jerry Sandusky case in 2013 in the United States fomented popular concern about historic child sexual abuse in sporting and coaching contexts. And, as a final example, in the United Kingdom, the Jimmy Savile case of 2011 exposed the extent to which historic sexual abuse had occurred in other types of public institutions such as the British Broadcasting Corporation, hospitals and schools (NSPCC 2013). The UK policing operations that followed revealed a mass of historic sexual abuses by celebrities, politicians, teachers, music masters, sports coaches and so on. As a result of police and public investigative zeal, it appeared by the end of 2010 that the sexual abuse of children was everywhere, that no child was safe anywhere and that none of the institutions previously thought to safeguard children were to be trusted. The institutions traditionally assumed to protect children, like religious organisations or public bodies, were demonstrably not safe. Worse, modern modes of communication, particularly the internet and smart phones, provided novel opportunities for sexual predators to exploit and abuse children. Yet, underlying the shock of the new were all the old assumptions about the essentially corrupting influence of sex and sexuality on the essential innocence of children (Evans 2013, Faulkner 2011). What was different, however, was that the new paedophiles and sex offenders were not drawn from traditional stereotypes of sexual 'others' but from high status sex offenders and paedophiles who could be either male or female (new phenomenon). These newer embodiments of sexual threat are currently being portrayed as being much more dangerous to their potential victims than previous generations of 'perverts' because, having never been seen as Other, they are, despite their offences, seen as being driven by a normal sexuality corrupted in a context of power. Far from ever having previously been Othered, they appear as normal men and women, successful and established in their careers. Theirs is the dark side of normal sexuality. However, because they are seen as being 'not Other' but, rather, 'like us' they threaten everyone's sexual identities and securities. Not being Other, they might, indeed, be Us! For, as this chapter has attempted to demonstrate via a detailed analysis of the regulation of prostitution prior to the twentieth century and the explication of four visions of sex and social change in the twenty-first century, the changing governance and practices of sexualities are forever rooted in an always and already alternative and unending politics of sex. The main task of criminologists is to provide ever-alternative analyses of the social, cultural and economic conditions in which the governance of sexualities and sexual identities takes the form it does in specific societies and at specific points in time.

Note

1   That said, male and female homosexuality is still illegal across large parts of the globe. The International Lesbian and Gay Association lists 79 countries where lesbian or gay sex (or both) are illegal (see www.ilga.org for a detailed interactive map demonstrating what homosexual acts are illegal where and how they are punished).

References

Agustin, L. M. (2001) 'Sex workers and violence against women: Utopic visions or battle of the sexes?' *Development* 44(3): 107–110

Agustín, L. M. (2006) 'The disappearing of a migration category: Migrants who sell sex.' *Journal of Ethnic and Migration Studies* 32(1): 29–47

Agustín, L. M. (2007) *Sex at the margins: Migration, labour markets and the rescue industry.* London: Zed Books

Amir, M. (1968) 'Victim precipitated forcible rape.' *Journal of Criminal Law, Criminology & Police Science* 58: 493

Anderson, B. L. (2013) *Us and them? The dangerous politics of immigration control.* Oxford: Oxford University Press

Attwood, F. (2004) 'Pornography and objectification.' *Feminist Media Studies* 4(1): 7–19

Attwood, F. (2006) 'Sexed up: Theorizing the sexualization of culture.' *Sexualities* 9(1): 77–94

Attwood, F. (2014) *Mainstreaming sex: The sexualization of western culture.* London: I. B. Tauris

Attwood, F. and C. Smith (2013) 'More sex! Better sex! Sex is fucking brilliant! Sex, sex, sex, SEX.' In T. Blackshaw (ed.) *Routledge Handbook of Leisure Studies.* Abingdon: Routledge, 325–336

Barry, K. (1984) *Female sexual slavery.* New York: NYU Press

Barry, K. (1996) *The prostitution of sexuality.* New York: NYU Press

Bauman, Z. (2013) *Liquid love: On the frailty of human bonds.* New York; London: John Wiley & Sons

Beck, U. (1992) *Risk society: Towards a new modernity.* London: Sage Publications

Beck, U. and E. Beck-Gernsheim (2013) *Distant love.* Cambridge: Polity

Benotsch, E. G., D. J. Snipes, A. M. Martin and S. S. Bull (2013) 'Sexting, substance use, and sexual risk behavior in young adults.' *Journal of Adolescent Health* 52(3): 307–313

Bernstein, E. (2001) *Economies of desire: Sexual commerce and post-industrial culture.* Berkeley: University of California Press

Bernstein, E. (2012) 'Carceral politics as gender justice? The "traffic in women" and neoliberal circuits of crime, sex, and rights.' *Theory and Society* 41(3): 233–259

Brents, B. G. and K. Hausbeck (2007) 'Marketing sex: US legal brothels and late capitalist consumption.' *Sexualities* 10(4): 425–439

Brents, B. G. and T. Sanders (2010) 'Mainstreaming the sex industry: Economic inclusion and social ambivalence.' *Journal of Law and Society* 37(1): 40–60

Brownmiller, S. (1976) *Against our will: Men, women and rape.* Harmondsworth: Penguin Books

Burkett, M. (2015) 'Sex (t) talk: A qualitative analysis of young adults' negotiations of the pleasures and perils of sexting.' *Sexuality & Culture* 19(4): 835–863

Butler, J. (2011) *Bodies that matter: On the discursive limits of sex.* London: Taylor & Francis

Butler, J. (2015) *Notes toward a performative theory of assembly.* Cambridge, MA: Harvard University

Chapkis, W. (1997) *Live sex acts: Women performing erotic labour.* London: Routledge

Chapkis, W. (2005) 'Soft glove, punishing fist: The Trafficking Victims Protection Act of 2000.' In W. Chapkis (ed.) *Regulating sex: The politics of intimacy and identity*. New York: Routledge, 51–65

Cohen, B. (1980) *Deviant street networks: Prostitution in New York City*. Lexington, MA: Lexington Books

Cowling, M. (1998) *Date rape and consent*. Aldershot: Ashgate

Curtis, L. A. (1974) 'Victim precipitation and violent crime.' *Social Problems* 21(4): 594–605

Daly, M. (1979) *Gyn/ecology: The metaethics of radical feminism*. London: The Women's Press

Davidson, J. O. C. (1998) *Prostitution, power and freedom*. London: Routledge

Davidson, J. O. C. (2005) *Children in the global sex trade*. Oxford: Polity

Dworkin, A. (1981) *Pornography: Men possessing women*. London: Women's Press

Dwyer, A. (2011) 'Policing lesbian, gay, bisexual and transgender young people: A gap in the research literature.' *Current Issues in Criminal Justice* 22(3): 415–433

Eisenstein, Z. R. (1979) *Capitalist patriarchy and the case for socialist feminism*. New York; London: Monthly Review Press

Evans, A., S. Riley and A. Shankar (2010) 'Postfeminist heterotopias.' *European Journal of Women's Studies* 17(3): 211–229

Evans, D. (2013) *Sexual citizenship: The material construction of sexualities*. London: Routledge

Faulkner, J. (2011) *The importance of being innocent: Why we worry about children*. Cambridge: Cambridge University Press

Finnegan, F. (1979) *Poverty and prostitution: A study of Victorian prostitutes in York*. Cambridge: Cambridge University Press

Foucault, M. (1979) *The history of sexuality*. London: Allen Lane

Furedi, F. (2013) *Moral crusades in an age of mistrust: The Jimmy Savile scandal*. Basingstoke: Palgrave Macmillan

Gagnon, J. H. and W. Simon (1973) *Sexual conduct: The social origins of human sexuality*. Chicago: Aldine

Giddens, A. (1992) *The transformation of intimacy: Sexuality, love and eroticism in modern societies*. Cambridge: Polity Press

Glueck, S. and E. Glueck (1934) *500 Delinquent Women*. New York: Alfred Knopf

Harvey, L. and R. Gill (2011) Spicing it up: Sexual entrepreneurs and The Sex Inspectors'. In R. Gill and C. Scharff (eds) *New femininities: Postfeminism, neoliberalism and subjectivity*. Basingstoke: Palgrave Macmillan, 52–67

Hebenton, B. and T. Seddon (2009) 'From dangerousness to precaution: Managing sexual and violent offenders in an insecure and uncertain age.' *British Journal of Criminology* 49(3): 343–362

Hester, M., C. Donovan and E. Fahmy (2010) 'Feminist epistemology and the politics of method: Surveying same sex domestic violence.' *International Journal of Social Research Methodology* 13(3): 251–263

Høigård, C. and L. Finstad (1992) *Backstreets: Prostitution, money, and love*. Oxford: Policy Press

Humphreys, L. (1972) *Out of the closets: The sociology of homosexual liberation*. Englewood Cliffs, NJ: Prentice-Hall

Humphreys, L. (1975) *Tearoom trade: Impersonal sex in public places*. London: Aldine Transactions

Illouz, E. (2007) *Cold intimacies: The making of emotional capitalism*. Oxford: Polity

Illouz, E. (2012) *Why love hurts: A sociological explanation*. Oxford: Polity

Johnson, P. and D. Dalton (2012) *Policing sex*. London: Routledge

Kelly, L. (1988) *Surviving sexual violence*. Oxford: Polity Press

Kinsey, A. C., W. B. Pomeroy and C. E. Martin (1948) *Sexual behavior in the human male*. Indiana: Indiana University Press

Levy, A. (2006) *Female chauvinist pigs: Women and the rise of raunch culture*. New York: Simon and Schuster

Liazos, A. (1972) 'The poverty of the sociology of deviance: Nuts, sluts, and perverts.' *Social Problems* 20(1): 103–120

Little, S. (2008) 'Challenging changing legal definitions of family in same-sex domestic violence.' *Hastings Women's Law Journal* 19(2): 259

Lombroso, C. and E. Ferrero (1898) *The female offender*. New York: D. Appleton and Company

Marshall, J. (1981) 'Pansies, perverts and macho men: Changing conceptions of male homosexuality.' In K. Plummer (ed.) *The making of the modern homosexual*. London: Hutchinson, 133–154

McAlinden, A.-M. (2005) 'The use of "shame" with sexual offenders.' *British Journal of Criminology* 45(3): 373–394

McGlynn, C. and V. Munro (2011) *Rethinking rape law: International and comparative perspectives.* London: Routledge

McHugh, P. (1980) *Prostitution and Victorian social reform.* London: Croom Helm

McIntosh, M. (1978) 'Who needs prostitutes? The ideology of male sexual needs.' In C. Smart and B. Smart (eds) *Women, sexuality and social control.* London: Routledge and Kegan Paul, 53–64

McLeod, E. (1982) *Working women now.* London: Croom Helm

McNair, B. (1996) *Mediated sex: Pornography and postmodern culture.* New York: Hodder Arnold Publication

McNair, B. (2002) *Striptease culture: Sex, media and the democratization of desire.* Hove: Psychology Press

NSPCC (2013) *Giving victims a voice.* www.nspcc.org.uk/globalassets/documents/research-reports/yewtree-report-giving-victims-voice-jimmy-savile.pdf

O'Connell Davidson, J. (2011) 'Moving children? Child trafficking, child migration, and child rights.' *Critical Social Policy* 31(3): 454–477

O'Neill, M., G. Scambler and A. Scambler (1997) 'Prostitute women now.' In: G. Scambler and A. Scambler (eds) *Rethinking prostitution: Purchasing sex in the 1990s.* London: Routledge, 3–29

Papadopoulos, L. (2010) *Sexualisation of young people review.* http://webarchive.nationalarchives.gov.uk/+/ http://www.homeoffice.gov.uk/documents/sexualisation-of-young-people.pdf

Phoenix, J. (1999) *Making sense of prostitution.* Basingstoke: Macmillan Press

Phoenix, J. (2002) 'In the name of protection: Youth prostitution policy reforms in England and Wales.' *Critical Social Policy* 22(2): 353–375

Phoenix, J. (2007) 'Governing prostitution: New formations, old agendas.' *Canadian Journal of Law and Society* 22(2): 73–94

Phoenix, J. (2008) 'ASBOs and working women: A new revolving door?' In P. Squires (ed.) *ASBO Nation: The criminalisation of nuisance.* Bristol: Policy Press, 289–303

Phoenix, J. (2009) *Regulating sex for sale: Prostitution, policy reform and the UK.* Bristol: Policy Press

Phoenix, J. (2012) *Out of place: The policing and criminalisation of sexually exploited girls and young women.* London: Howard League for Penal Reform

Phoenix, J. and S. Oerton (2013) *Illicit and illegal: Sex, regulation and social control.* Cullompton, Devon: Willan.

Plummer, K. (1981) 'Building a sociology of homosexuality.' In *The making of the modern homosexual.* London: Hutchinson, 17–29

Plummer, K. (2002) *Telling sexual stories: Power, change and social worlds.* London: Routledge

Plummer, K. (2015) *Cosmopolitan sexualities.* London: Polity

Porter, K. and J. Weeks (1991) *Between the acts: Lives of homosexual men, 1885–1967.* London; New York: Routledge

Renold, E. and J. Ringrose (2011) 'Schizoid subjectivities? Re-theorizing teen girls' sexual cultures in an era of "sexualization".' *Journal of Sociology* 47(4): 389–409

Rich, A. (1980) 'Compulsory heterosexuality and lesbian existence.' *Signs* 5(4): 631–660

Rubin, G. (1984) 'Thinking sex: Notes for a radical theory of the politics of sexuality.' In P. Nardi and B. Schneider (eds) *Social Perspectives in Lesbian and Gay Studies.* Abingdon: Routledge, 100–133

Rubin, G. (2009) 'The traffic in women: Notes on the "political economy" of sex.' In E. Lewin (ed.) *Feminist anthropology: A reader.* Malden, MA: Blackwell, 87–106

Rush, E. and A. La Nauze (2006) *Corporate paedophilia: Sexualisation of children in Australia.* Manuka: Australia Institute

Samons, C. (2013) 'Same-sex domestic violence: The need for affirmative legal protections at all levels of government.' *Southern California Review of Law and Social Justice* 22(3): 417

Sanders, T., M. O'Neill and J. Pitcher (2009) *Prostitution: Sex work, policy and politics.* London: Sage Publications

Schultz, L. G. (1975) *Rape victimology.* Springfield, IL: Charles C. Thomas

Seidman, S., N. Fischer and C. Meeks (2010) *Introducing the new sexuality studies.* London: Routledge

Shulman, A. K. (1980) 'Sex and power: Sexual bases of radical feminism.' *Signs* 5(4): 590–604

Sion, A. A. (1977) *Prostitution and the law*. London: Faber

Skilbrei, M. and C. Holmstrom (2013) *Prostitution policy in the Nordic region*. Farnham: Ashgate

Smart, C. and B. Smart (1978) *Women, sexuality and social control*. London: Routledge & Kegan Paul

Smith, C. (2010) 'Pornographication: A discourse for all seasons.' *International Journal of Media and Cultural Politics* 6(1): 103–108

Turner, J. and L. Kelly (2009) 'Trade secrets: Intersections between diasporas and crime groups in the constitution of the human trafficking chain.' *British Journal of Criminology* 49(2): 184–201

Waites, M. (2003) 'Equality at last? Homosexuality, heterosexuality and the age of consent in the United Kingdom.' *Sociology* 37(4): 637–655

Waites, M. (2005) *The age of consent: Young people, sexuality, and citizenship*. Basingstoke: Palgrave Macmillan

Walkowitz, J. R. (1980) *Prostitution and Victorian society: Women, class and the state*. Cambridge: Cambridge University Press

Ward, T. and S. M. Hudson (2001) 'Finkelhor's precondition model of child sexual abuse: A critique.' *Psychology, Crime & Law* 7(1): 291–307

Weeks, J. (1989) *Sex, politics, and society: The regulation of sexuality since 1800*. London; New York: Longman

Weeks, J. (2007) *The world we have won: The remaking of erotic and intimate life*. London; New York: Routledge

Weeks, J. (2011) *The languages of sexuality*. Abingdon, Oxon; New York: Routledge

Weeks, J. (2016) *What is sexual history?* Cambridge: Polity Press

Weeks, J., J. Holland and M. Waites (2003) *Sexualities and society: A reader*. Cambridge: Polity Press

Whelehan, I. (2000) *Overloaded: Popular culture and the future of feminism*. London: Women's Press

10

THE CRIMINOLOGY OF MOBILITY

Sharon Pickering, Mary Bosworth, and Katja Franko

The purpose of this chapter is to consider how criminological interest in migration and crime has been taken up by critical scholars within an emerging part of the discipline known as 'the criminology of mobility'.[1] Drawing together theoretical and empirical accounts, authors in this subfield focus on the non-citizen and the global governance of and through migration control. The control of mobility, in this view, has become not just an adjunct to crime control, but intertwined with it.

Overview

Criminological theories address some of the most central issues concerning the constitution of societies and their moral beliefs. How we deal with law breakers and victims, as well as those who respond to them, tells us a lot about the places in which we live, its membership, limits, goals and ideas. The ways in which societies think about punishment and deviance illuminate questions of social order and solidarity. How they respond to victims, and what they define as crime, reveals ideas about vulnerability, desert and safety.

The relationship between immigration and crime is also arguably a foundational aspect of criminology, particularly for scholars influenced by the Chicago School and attentive to the US context. Yet, while other settler societies like Australia and Canada, and the former colonial powers of Europe, have been shaped by migration, until recently little criminological attention has been given to such matters. Instead, much of post-war criminological scholarship was defined by, and confined to, the boundaries of the nation state and its citizenry.

Recently, however, a growing number of scholars have argued that our understanding of society needs to change, as under conditions of globalization and mass mobility, boundaries of the social have become blurred and unstable. In this light, the new subfield known as the criminology of mobility has been established for scholars interested in citizenship, race, gender, ethnicity and immigration control (Aas and Bosworth 2013). The criminology of mobility is interested in the processes of inclusion and exclusion at the borders of and within states which draw from and extend arsenals usually reserved for the criminal justice system, law enforcement and the military without their usual protections. Lines of inquiry have traced existing inequalities (gender, race and class) and their acceleration in new alignments of power and belonging. As Bowling (2013: 291) has noted, these processes are a portent of global racial segregation in a worldwide system of 'pass-laws, stronger and longer walls and fences, databases of suspected and unwanted persons, and prisons filled with "foreign nationals" who have transgressed criminal or immigration law'.

This chapter will first consider *where has the criminology of mobility come from?* In answering the question it identifies three interdependent lines of scholarly inquiry – criminological concern with identity, scholarship on mobility and the border, and research around the global migration control industry. It will trace mobility in criminology over the past decades, considering how this early work approached the study of migration and the shifting categories of migrant, citizen, non-citizen in order to understand the recent turn to mobility. It will then examine how the border has come to be central in criminological work concerned with mobility. The border is both symbolically and instrumentally powerful in shaping and responding to global mobility. It is the site at which significant and far-reaching institutional change in law enforcement and incarceration practices has taken place. It is also a site for increasing harms. At the end of this section, we will identify how the criminology of mobility has concentrated on the migration control industry and its role in global governance and social control.

This chapter will then ask *where is the criminology of mobility heading?* To answer this question the chapter needs to identify silences in the criminology of mobility literature as well as some of its challenges. It will note the points at which mainstream literature has effectively responded to the terrain and insights of criminology of mobility as well as where they remain politely disengaged. A discussion of the theoretical, empirical and disciplinary resources required to redress these silences will draw the chapter to a close.

Traces of mobility

Generating a genealogy of a field is challenging. While, for the most part, the criminology of mobility has a relatively short history, earlier vestiges of it can be found in a number of corners of criminological inquiry seemingly unrelated to one another. From the earliest days of the Chicago School to contemporary feminist and postcolonial accounts, scholars have been interested in matters of exclusion, integration and identity, all factors in which we can find traces of mobility.

The starting point for any consideration of mobility in criminology can be found in George Simmel's (1950) essay 'The stranger', parts of which were translated into English and included in Robert Park and Ernst Burgess' textbook, *Introduction to the science of sociology* (Park and Burgess 1921).[2] For Simmel and the Chicago School, the foreigner was inherently an illusive figure, who brought with him (and their attention was squarely on men) (Deegan 1990) certain cultural practices and expectations, which the host society either had to deflect or integrate. He was difficult to understand, potentially a threat.

Whereas Simmel's interest was largely a philosophical one, Park and Burgess (1921) adapted his ideas to empirical study. How did migrants assimilate, they wanted to know. Where did they live? Were foreigners more criminal than citizens? Drawing on ethnographic and later statistical models, these early US criminologists spent considerable time debating such matters, mapping the various shifts within and between new migrant groups and their concomitant effect on the burgeoning urban centres, a tradition which has been in recent years taken up by Robert Sampson and others (Graif and Sampson 2009).

Seemingly removed from such accounts, there are evident connections between contemporary studies of mobility and earlier accounts of race and ethnicity. The two scholarly traditions share an interest in, and a concern with, questions of membership and belonging. The diverse nature of contemporary social membership has been historically shaped both by international migration and various imperial and colonial projects. Given the relationship between contemporary migration and the history of colonialism, there are therefore important connections to be made with postcolonial criminology.

Criminology has a long-standing yet limited relationship with postcolonialism and critical race theory (Agozino 2003). In the 1970s it was, briefly, part of the vanguard of studies in this area when Stuart Hall and his colleagues at the Birmingham Centre for Contemporary Cultural Studies published *Policing the crisis*, a damning critique of the racialized nature of 'moral panics' and policing in Britain. Building on Stanley Cohen's (1972) notion of 'moral panic', Hall et al. (1978) explored the ties between social disorder, immigration and urban life in postcolonial Britain. According to them, the agents of state power and young people were acting out and drawing on decades-long assumptions about belonging, rights and race. *Policing the crisis* forcefully brought to attention the racial and ethnic stereotyping, stigmatization and prejudice within the police and criminal justice – topics which have been of central concern to contemporary scholars of borders and migration control.

In other disciplines, postcolonial theory flourished, offering an historically grounded critique of state power, and a new conceptual framework of understanding that championed the voices and experiences of those in the Global South in a radical challenge to the orthodox politics and scholarship on the Left. In feminist and literary theory, scholars such as Gayatri Spivak (1988) and Edward Said (1979) coined new terminology, the 'subaltern' and 'Orientalism', to capture the distinct experience of those from former European colonies, while pointing to the constitutive nature of such individuals for the West itself. In their work postcolonialism is presented as both an historical period and a relationship; any institution can be considered through this lens.

Feminist criminology offers, in its attention to gender, and in its concern with methodological issues and the study of vulnerable groups, a key part of contemporary analyses of mobility, a topic to which we shall return at the end of this chapter. Responding to many of the same pressures that underpinned postcolonial studies, scholars in gender theory have been debating questions of membership, identity and belonging for some decades. In the 1990s, for instance, arguments disputed the constitution of the subject 'woman', a figure whose membership and utility came under question as lesbians and women of colour challenged the white, heterosexual and middle-class control of the women's movement (Schor and Weed 1994). In legal studies, Kimberlé Crenshaw (1989) championed the notion of 'intersectionality' to capture the multi-layered experience of identity, while feminist philosopher Judith Butler (1990, 1993) first articulated the idea of 'performativity' in which 'gender' is a part played out and made real in the contours of daily life. Identity norms, in this view, are performed and attached to power within a social system. Though partly conceptual, and, in Butler's view, subject to challenge and transformation, identity is made real through actual bodies.

While Butler was primarily influenced by the work of Michel Foucault and psychoanalysis, other theorists like Seyla Benhabib, Iris Marion Young and Nancy Fraser mined different traditions to develop more explicitly normative and political accounts of gender and identity (see for example, Young 1990, 1997; Benhabib et al. 1996). For these scholars, it was not a huge jump to examining citizenship and social exclusion. Benhabib (2004) has thus developed a cosmopolitan ethics, while Fraser (1997) seeks to balance recognition and redistribution, retaining some of her roots in the Frankfurt school of critical theory. Young (1997) deliberated on the constitution of citizenship under conditions of multiculturalism.

Such theoretical work, within and outside criminology, in its attention to the links between identity and power, laid the foundation for the criminology of mobility. Identity, this scholarship attests, is an important conduit for power, both its product and its effect; its subject and its object. While the figure of the migrant or foreigner fades in and out of view in this work, its attention to the intersecting aspects of subjectivity recognized the existence of various axes of belonging, among which citizenship is placed.

Border sightings

A systematic review of criminological scholarship reveals three distinct domains of border-related concern. The first can be found in attention to the border as a passing referent to the location of offending – spatially demarcating offending. In the late 1960s, for example, articles on the cross-border importation of drugs began appearing (Chappell 1967). The opportunity was missed, however, to concentrate on the physical site. Rather, in the decades to follow most work remained concerned with domestic responses to offending and harms (often addiction) or domestic informal economies and illicit markets (Ruggiero and Vass 1992; Vaughn, Huang and Ramirez 1995; Odergard 1995; Farrell, Mansur and Tullis 1996; Paoli 2002).

The second domain of criminological scholarship that we can identify, considers the border as a framing device for crime and of state and supra-state responses. Quietly the border became increasingly important for studies of various forms of transnational crime and crime control, such as drug trafficking, cybercrime and counter-terrorism – offending that seemingly paid little respect to national boundaries. However it is important to note that as borders came in for increased, albeit still limited, attention, the criminological focus arguably contributed to a sense of the border as an exceptional topic of concern. Studies in the 1990s, for example, depicting borders as a matter of the exotic (which tended to focus on Northern Ireland, Africa, Asia and the Middle East) (e.g. Pearson 1990; Mapstone 1992), postcolonial arrangements in the Global South (e.g. Vagg 1992; van zyl Smit 1999; Korn 2000) or the end of the Cold War (Arnold 1995; Dunkel 1995). In the rare cases where the border in question was closer to home it was considered an exceptional criminological topic (most notably in relation to terrorism) rather than routine (Hills 1995).

An early example is Geoffrey Pearson's (1990) account in the *British Journal of Criminology* of an academic study tour to Israel and his reflection on crime and politics during the first *Intifada*. Borders were not the focus of this account, however they loomed large in a criminological attempt to consider the geopolitical context of the Israeli–Palestinian conflict. Importantly this article raised the irreconcilable intersections of geography, vocabulary, migration and politics and highlighted the need to criminologically question the high rate of foreign national imprisonment, the relationship of delinquency and political participation in the *Intifada*, security force harassment, the difficulty of defining deviance in the absence/compromise of the rule of law as well as the need/desire to advance more detailed ethnographic work.

Although these kinds of questions did not immediately disturb standard criminological fare in Europe or North America or sharpen the discipline's focus on borders themselves, this era confirmed the border as a topic of analysis for scholars of transnational crimes, where it was often identified as an impediment in the policing and prosecution of supply as offenders moved cargo from one state to another. Following crime across borders did not always necessitate a sustained interest in the border either – in as much as the border was becoming central in these studies it did not present new or different normative concerns for scholars. It was not until transnational policing scholars came to identify its role in producing a broader range of criminal activities and their challenges for national and transnational policing (e.g. Sheptycki, 1995, 1998) that the border came to more regularly feature in criminological concerns and accelerate the foregrounding of current work. It was really taking its cue from this concern with transnational policing that the border moved from being a secondary consideration to a primary concern for criminological inquiry and a discernable third line of scholarship that we refer to as the criminology of mobility.

The first article in the *British Journal of Criminology* to directly and substantively identify borders in relation to crime and social control was Ben Bowling's (1990) article concerning race and migration in Europe. He argued that 'the relationship between black people and crime will be an undercurrent in debates concerning policies to control migration in Europe and between European countries' (1990: 483). He accurately forecast that 'internal border controls' would come to feature which indeed they have although the bulk of the article was dedicated to challenging the methodological weaknesses in research on race and crime. The first study to focus specifically on the border in the same journal was Vagg's (1992) analysis of the Hong Kong–China boundary and the ways the frontier shaped the definition and production of crime. From this time, criminological study of the border, its enforcement and its unauthorized crossing (or even its authorized crossing for reasons other than those given and accepted in processes of authorization) have generated sustained interest around the experiences of harms (Munro 2006) and the expansion of control and enforcement agencies and powers (Sheptycki 1995). Even so, it was not until criminology began to draw on the resources of cognate fields that authors asked normative questions about the border or considered it in terms of criminological concepts.

The border has long been a central concern of political scientists and international relations scholars, particularly critical international relations theorists (see McCulloch and True 2014; Anderson 1996; Andreas and Snyder 2000; Torpey 2000; Andreas 2000), geographers (Rajaram and Grundy-Warr 2007), surveillance scholars (Zureik and Salter 2005; Lyon 2009) and anthropologists (Donnan and Wilson 1999; de Genova and Peutz 2010) so it is not surprising that early criminological work drew on ideas developed and shared amongst these disciplines (see Pickering and Weber 2006). In drawing on insights from cognate fields we can see how the shift in criminological concern for borders fundamentally changed. For example, concern for drug trafficking across borders has closely followed the literature on organized crime. Unsurprisingly, early concern for human trafficking across national borders followed suit (see Weitzer 2009 for critique of these). By contrast, more critical work on trafficking that drew on gender studies and international relations identified the centrality of the border in preventing authorized mobility for those considered undesirable (Segrave, Milivojevic and Pickering 2009; Lee 2007). Studies of human smuggling that draw on anthropology, international relations and sociology (see, for example, Sanchez 2014; Grewcock 2014) have followed a similar trajectory, focusing on smuggling not as another/new 'high policing' issue for the mainstream criminological list but as an outcome of border control. Such accounts argue that criminologists need to engage in broader interdisciplinary debates around sovereignty, identity and power.

While criminologists studying the border were indebted to scholars in other disciplines they brought key criminological concepts to bear on border issues that enabled sharp interventions in both domestic and international realms. In particular they were adept at identifying and responding to the performative and symbolic border (Wonders 2007) in criminalization processes (Aliverti 2013), expansionist criminal justice programmes and moving responses into more nuanced and regulatory responses. Most importantly they were important contributors to upsetting the narrow focus on victimization which failed to engage in broader structural and agentic features of irregular mobility and harm which brought into sharp relief the ways borders were physically and legally negotiated. Arguably the most important contribution to the criminological study of borders has been to identify the mobile character of borders and the changing forms of criminalization which occur at a range of border 'sites' that may or may not neatly map onto the territorial nation state (Weber 2006).

The symbolic and instrumental power of the border (as fixed and as ever changing) has been central to populist debate around illegal migration, heightened levels of fear of outsiders (which always has racial inflection), and has seen the ready and often unquestioned application of labels of illegality to the unauthorized crossing of a border. Criminological work concerned with border crossing has highlighted the dangers inherent in applying familiar and convincing language of domestic crime control to non-citizens without authorized migration status. It has identified the ways the language and labels of criminality mobilized in the name of border control have been central to destabilizing international norms capable of protecting non-citizens especially in states with weak human rights cultures and mechanisms.

The border has been reconceived in some criminological study as a frontier, a borderland (see Pickering and Weber 2006) and/or a no-man's land (Barker 2013). It has also been identified as transformative of key criminal justice institutions relied upon for its symbolic and instrumental performance (Pratt and Thompson 2008). Scholars have identified an expansion/extension of existing agencies and exercise of powers (see Aas and Bosworth 2013) while others have shown the symbiotic relationship between border enforcement, illegal cross-border activity and the generation of harms (Gerard and Pickering 2014). Work in this field has included studies of border-related deaths (Weber and Pickering 2013; Pickering and Cochrane 2013), widespread use of incarceration in the form of immigration detention and imprisonment of foreign nationals (Bosworth 2011, 2012; Ugelvik and Ugelvik 2013; van Kalmthout, Hofstee-van der Meulen and Dünkel 2007; Lee 2007) and the use of summary type powers including 'turn-arounds' at border sites (Aas 2011a).

The criminology of mobility literature has, in particular, paid attention to the ways the policing of borders has drawn in a multitude of agencies and techniques especially in shared border policing arrangements such as those around the European Union (Aas 2011b). The relationship between borders and changing European identities (Green and Grewcock 2002) and the political and material resources amassed by border policing agencies has been highlighted by criminologists working in a range of contexts. Equally and rather cheekily a significant proportion of what may be regarded as criminological work on the border does not self-identify as criminology at all (see, for example, Andreas 2000; Nevins 2002). Regardless, it points to a rich inter-disciplinary milieu from which a study of borders in an age of mass mobility can not only study what is happening, but can increasingly contribute to the conversation around what needs to happen in 'a world in motion' (Aas 2007). It has been in this space that the criminology of mobility has identified the development of the migration control industry and its centrality in the global governance of social control.

The migration control industry

The lively recent attention paid to borders within criminology reflects the increased focus on border security by state agencies and private entities. Borders, and migration more generally, have become in the post-9/11 climate hotly contested political issues and intrinsically connected to notions of security and fear. A series of rhetorical and political moves have established a clear nexus between migration and insecurity or what has been termed the securitization of migration (Huysmans 2006; Guild 2009). The trend has spurred a series of governmental and private security initiatives, which aim to secure the potentially risky flows of people and to distinguish between 'good' and 'bad' mobility, trustworthy and untrustworthy travellers. The development of what might be termed (paraphrasing Christie 2000) a migration control industry has been extensively documented, particularly within the surveillance scholarship (Adey 2004; Zureik and Salter 2005; Amoore 2006; Pickering and Weber 2006; Aas 2011b). The industry produces a vast technological paraphernalia, which includes soft-end solutions, such as large-scale IT systems, biometric identification and airport surveillance, as well as more militarized approaches at the maritime and territorial borders, including unmanned aerial vehicles (UAVs), military and police vessels, airplanes, helicopters, surveillance cameras, etc. As pointed out above, this political and technological framing places migrants as a source of insecurity (and as potential criminals), rather than people who are exposed to considerable dangers on their migratory journeys, and therefore deserving of protection and assistance. The notions of threat are intrinsically connected to the fear of waning state sovereignty under conditions of globalization and to the contestations over shrinking welfare resources for citizens.

Criminology of mobility has sought to destabilize the migration–security nexus, and to problematize its political, practical and ethical implications. In particular, it has pointed out how the shift of focus has affected the patterns of legal regulation of migration. In past decades, irregular migratory activities have been progressively subjected to stricter penalties and criminalization. While previously unauthorized movement of people across state borders mainly fell under the auspices of administrative law, in recent years criminal law has become a prominent tool used by states in the Global North for the purpose of immigration control. These processes of 'making people illegal' (Dauvergne 2008) have been charted in several seminal contributions, among others, in Ana Aliverti's (2013) study of 'crimes of mobility' in the UK. While there are great jurisdictional differences, and much comparative work which remains to be done, the criminalization of immigration offences has had a considerable impact, both in terms of symbolic politics and actual enforcement. In the USA, 54 per cent of all federal prosecutions are for immigration crimes (Vázquez 2011). The sheer size of the development has drawn a new generation of scholars to examine the criminological and socio-legal implications of immigration law and enforcement. Consequently, a growing body of scholarship is addressing the progressive intertwining of the two, previously distinct, fields of asylum/immigration law and criminal law. In the US context, the development has been termed 'crimmigration law' (Stumpf 2006; Pickering and Ham 2014b; Vázquez 2011); the term which has lately also found resonance within Europe and Australia, where attention is being paid not only to legal but also to the criminological aspects of the phenomenon (Aas 2011b; Guia, van de Woude and van der Leun 2012).

The criminology of mobility has needed to overcome large silences in criminology, and has drawn eclectically from other disciplines, such as law, as it moves from theoretical concern to empirical endeavour. What are the key concepts and ideas of criminology that have been applied successfully or have proved insufficient in this new landscape? One of the traits of the field is that as it qualitatively and quantitatively maps the forms of penalty applied to non-citizens, and what distinguishes them from the more traditional forms of crime control, it is also transforming our understanding of social control and punishment. For example, how is policing different when directed at the populations of non-citizens? As shown by Weber (2013) and others (van der Leun 2003; Weber and Bowling 2008, 2012; Pickering and Weber 2013) policing of migrant populations involves novel forms and rationalities of policing, which are openly focused on the task of border control (identifying aliens, denial of entry, deportation, etc.). It also requires unprecedented levels of international cooperation and data exchange, thus destabilizing the traditional connections between the police, citizens, the nation state and its territory.

One of the strengths of criminology of mobility is that it offers an informed and nuanced understanding of law and criminalization and their impact on the lives of migrants, particularly the most vulnerable ones. The field has outlined a complex set of conditions of precariousness to which migrants, living in the shadow of the law, are exposed in their everyday realities. The precariousness includes not only the physical dangers of the journey, but also social marginality upon arrival, economic hardship and exploitation, as well as intrusive policing, surveillance and the threats of deportation and detention. Kitty Calavita's study *Immigrants at the margins* (2005) gives, among others, an account of conditions of severe economic exploitability which are a result of the contingent legal status of many immigrants in Southern Europe. The condition of the immigrant as a source of cheap labour has also inspired some neo-Marxist accounts of immigration control (De Giorgi 2010; Melossi 2013).

Economic exploitability is intrinsically connected to the condition of deportability – the threat of forced removal – which accompanies and stalks irregularity. An extensive body of work has documented the emotional and social hardship of deportees and their families, as well as the extensive state apparatus dedicated to the creation of deportable subjects and their actual expulsion (Kanstroom 2007; de Genova and Peutz 2010; Brotherton and Barrios 2011). Particularly criminologically relevant is the fact that criminal convictions have become in several countries the fastest path leading to deportation. In the USA, deportation became, after several legislative changes, 'the consequence of almost any criminal conviction of a non-citizen' (Stumpf 2006: 371). According to the data provided by the US Immigration and Customs Enforcement, the numbers of so-called criminal aliens removed from the country have risen dramatically in the past decade. Over 400,000 individuals were removed from the United States in 2012, twice as many as housed in the Federal Bureau of Prisons. Not only rhetorically, but also practically, the blurred categories of a 'criminal alien' and an 'illegal alien' are serving as an aggressive justification for reaffirmation of state sovereignty. The non-citizen has been designated not only as a deportable, but also as a detainable subject, inhabiting the spaces of immigration detention as well as a growing proportion of the more traditional spaces of imprisonment (Ugelvik and Ugelvik 2013; Bosworth 2014).

While deportation and immigration detention are not forms of penal power which have been so far a frequent topic of criminological study, there is a deepening acknowledgement that they represent an expression of the state's will to control, to inflict pain upon, and often, to punish its non-members. By doing so, penal power is no longer a domain of internal domestic relations, but also enters inter-state relations and becomes one of the mechanisms of global social control and governance. The label 'illegal' and 'illegal alien' is therefore, as Dauvergne

(2008: 18) points out, not only applied nationally, but has become a 'globally meaningful identity label' which distinguishes the insiders in the prosperous Global North from the intrusive outsiders from the Global South.

Where is the criminology of mobility heading?

The criminology of mobility directs its critical gaze at the heart of unequal global social relations. By producing categories of 'legal' and 'illegal aliens' – worthy and unworthy migrants – Northern states are using the power of criminal law, and the sovereign prerogatives of policing and detention, for the purpose of protection of their territorial integrity. By doing so they are setting in motion complex processes of daily re-entrenchment of global inequalities through criminal justice. In the US context, Latinos are disproportionately affected by the intertwined relationship of criminal law and immigration control. They represent over 90 per cent of those in immigration detention; 94 per cent of those removed; and 94 per cent of those removed for criminal violations (Vázquez 2011). In these trends, the racial inequalities which have historically shaped the US imprisonment surge become reframed as global inequalities structured along citizenship lines.

With some exceptions, most of scholarship in the field has been produced by scholars in the Global North, and thus pertains to Northern empirical realities. This is an imbalance which marks most social science scholarship (Aas 2012). However, just as the criminology of mobility thematically addresses the unequal subject positions of citizen and non-citizen, so does it also – through its focus on gender, race and ethnicity – aim to address the inequalities of academic knowledge production within the field. The marginalized position of the non-citizen within Northern societies is to some extent replicated by the peripheral status that scholarly knowledge about non-citizens occupies within the existing hierarchies of knowledge production. There are considerable empirical challenges in studying global phenomena and cross-border flows, as most of official data sets relate to phenomena within nation states. Official statistics therefore often do not collect data on people with unclear and irregular immigration status, or data related to the immigration status. In the United Kingdom, for instance, the government rarely publishes details about those held in prison under Immigration Act powers (Aas and Bosworth 2013). The lack of data, and their unavailability, is often also a result of the politically charged nature of the phenomena at hand, the most blatant example of which is the lack of systematic knowledge about border-related deaths (Weber and Pickering 2011). Under such circumstances, providing quantitative and qualitative accounts of the hidden and invisible populations, and hidden forms of victimization, becomes an important function of academic research.

Related to the invisibility within official knowledge production, the non-citizen has been also auspiciously absent in the prevailing criminological theoretical conceptions which by and large do not address citizenship issues. The established notions of domestic penality address predominantly forms of penal power exercised over citizens and seldom, for example, examine deportation as a punitive measure, or immigration detention centres as penal institutions. These forms of penal power differ from the ones usually discussed in criminological and penological texts and textbooks, in which punishment tends to be inextricably linked to the idea of imprisonment and which take prison figures as the main indicator of societal punitiveness. In such texts, Western European countries tend to be described as penal moderates, while if we look at the levels of incarceration of foreigners, Western Europe is in fact a penal outlier. These are not only empirical and conceptual gaps, but importantly often also result in gaps in regulation and rights. For example, in crimmigration law, non-citizens do not enjoy the same rule of law protections as citizens, such as the privilege against self-incrimination and eligibility for legal aid in deportation cases (Stumpf 2006), and basic human rights standards are often without reach of socially marginalized migrant populations (Dembour and Kelly 2011).

However, while the emerging fields of criminology of mobility and border studies may be producing a growing body of knowledge, which addresses the above mentioned omissions, there are still important gaps which need to be filled. We know very little about what happens to those who are removed or deported. Moreover, contemporary strategies of mobility control have substantial extraterritorial dimensions (Ryan and Mitsilegas 2010) and an active reach into the countries in the Global South. These developments demand research on the emerging global interconnectedness that is more 'democratically distributed' in epistemo-logical terms (Aas 2012). As such, the criminology of mobility has the potential for shedding light on vital aspects of global inequality and the nature of contemporary power relations, post-colonial struggles and social exclusion, and thereby also for theoretical innovation.

Notwithstanding the traces of feminist, critical race and postcolonial literature that can be found in the criminology of mobility, race and gender continue to be marginalized or under-theorized in the figure of the 'non-citizen' or migrant. So, too, questions remain unasked and unanswered about the methodological and ethical difficulties of studying 'a world in motion' (Aas 2007). For the most part, much of the extant criminological literature on mobility as it is elsewhere, is largely theoretical, perhaps drawing on policy documents and the law. Only sometimes does it draw on firsthand accounts and fieldwork (see, for example, Weber 2013; Bosworth 2014; Pickering 2014; Pickering and Ham 2014a).

While these two matters – methods, ethics and the integration of race and gender – may seem unrelated, they are, in fact, deeply intertwined. Methodologically, both gender and post-colonial theory direct our attention to the actions and deliberations of those subject to power and, for the purposes of this project, to the affective nature of mobility and border control itself. In terms of intersectionality and performativity, what are the connections and disjunctions between the citizen and the prisoner or between the asylum seeker and the criminal? Thinking about embodiment, how should we understand punishment under the deportation regime, where foreign bodies are no longer reformed but banished? What of those making asylum claims for whom their body is the evidence? What of cosmopolitan justice? How effective are universal human rights in pursuing concrete gendered claims for redress and protection?

Focusing on the interplay between subjectivity and power relations emphasizes both the affective nature of penal power and the attempts people make to resist it. The point is not to substitute first-hand or micro accounts with structural or macro ones, but to bring the two into dialogue in order to develop broader understandings of penal power and its effects. In so doing, the criminology of mobility reveals that the empirical focus of inquiry must shift to include those sites, historical and contemporary, where penal power intersects with other forms of state governance. It also calls for methodological innovation.

How might we study those whose languages we do not share? Who are without legal immigration status? Who have been deported? How can we come to an understanding across cultural, religious and economic divides? Is it possible to work with and for those on the move, involving them in the production of knowledge? Or is the criminology of mobility always a view from above?

In many respects criminology is ideally placed to be innovative methodologically since its disciplinary borders are weakly drawn (Bosworth and Hoyle 2011). Characterized some time ago by David Downes as a '*rendezvous* discipline', criminology (or at least parts of it) has long been open to new ideas and approaches. To that end, the criminology of mobility builds on existing disciplinary strengths, adding to work in comparative criminology (Nelken 2010) as well as race, gender and postcolonialism. Unlike many extant accounts, however, the criminology of mobility also seeks to provide a grounded approach to theorizing, making room for the affective nature of power relations, rather than superimposing a grand narrative. In so doing it aspires to transcend the boundary between macro and micro accounts of the state, placing empirical material in dialogue with a theoretical framework. It is interdisciplinary, drawing on gender and postcolonial theory as well as human rights, sociology of punishment, history, migration studies and criminology.

Conclusion

As this chapter has argued, the criminology of mobility is a vibrant, interdisciplinary, form of criminological inquiry. It has experienced a considerable growth over the past decade, and we have seen a shift in focus from the study of immigrant involvement in crime, to the exploration of the mechanism of penal and legal control and exclusion, with a growing awareness of the border as a symbolic and physical site of social control. Despite its apparent newness, the criminology of mobility has its roots in a number of enduring criminological debates about identity, exclusion and social justice and combines sophisticated theoretical analysis with empirical evidence, situated in an historical context.

By drawing attention to the legal and criminological challenges posed by the increasing criminalization of immigration and the securitization of the border, the criminology of mobility demonstrates that mobility and its control are matters central to any understanding of the criminal justice system. Is it at all possible to understand imprisonment in Europe today without understanding the patterns and the role of the remarkable imprisonment of foreign nationals? Can we fully grasp the meaning of penal punitiveness without taking into account the urge to expel and deport unwanted non-citizens? Moreover, can we properly grasp the nature of criminal law in Western societies without seeing it in a global context, in conjunction with immigration law?

The extensive body of work within the criminology of mobility is united by a key underlying concern with rights, law and state power under conditions of globalization. By drawing on related disciplines, such as law, anthropology, border and surveillance studies, it is generating new conceptual and theoretical frameworks to address the legal, organizational and normative responses to the challenges that migration and globalization present to contemporary criminal justice systems.

Notes

1   This chapter first appeared in the 2014 *Routledge Handbook on Crime and International Migration* edited by Sharon Pickering and Julie Ham.
2   Originally published in German in 1908, Simmel's essay was later translated and reproduced in full in an edited collection of Simmel's scholarship published by Karl Wolf in 1950.

References

Aas, KF 2007, 'Analysing a world in motion: global flows meet "criminology of the other"', *Theoretical Criminology*, vol. 11, no. 2, pp. 283–303.

Aas, KF 2011a, 'A borderless world: cosmopolitanism, boundaries and frontiers', in CM Bailliet and KF Aas (eds), *Cosmopolitan justice and its discontents*, Routledge, New York, pp. 134–150.

———— 2011b, '"Crimmigrant" bodies and bona fide travellers: surveillance, citizenship and global governance', *Theoretical Criminology*, vol. 15, no. 3, pp. 331–346.

———— 2012, '"The earth is one but the world is not": criminological theory and its geopolitical divisions', *Theoretical Criminology*, vol. 16, no. 1, pp. 5–20.

Aas, KF and Bosworth, M (eds) 2013, *The borders of punishment: migration, citizenship and social exclusion*, Oxford University Press, Oxford.

Adey, P 2004, 'Surveillance at the airport: surveilling mobility/mobilising surveillance', *Environment and Planning A*, vol. 36, no. 8, pp. 1365–1380.

Agozino, B 2003, *Counter-colonial criminology: a critique of imperialist reason*, Pluto, London.

Aliverti, A 2013, *Crimes of mobility: criminal law and the regulation of immigration*, Routledge, London and New York.

Amoore, L 2006, 'Biometric borders: governing mobilities in the war on terror', *Political Geography*, vol. 25, no. 3, pp. 336–351.

Anderson, M 1996, *Frontiers: territory and state formation in the modern world*, Polity Press, Cambridge.

Andreas, P 2000, *Border games: policing the US–Mexico divide*, Cornell University Press, Ithaca, NY.

Andreas, P and Snyder, T (eds) 2000, *The wall around the west: state borders and immigration controls in North America and Europe*, Rowman & Littlefield, Lanham.

Arnold, J 1995, 'Corrections in the German Democratic Republic: a field for research', *British Journal of Criminology*, vol. 35, no. 1, pp. 81–94.

Barker, V 2013, 'Democracy and deportation: why membership matters most', in KF Aas and M Bosworth (eds), *The borders of punishment: migration, citizenship and social exclusion*, Oxford University Press, Oxford, pp. 237–256.

Benhabib, S 2004, *The rights of others*, Cambridge University Press, Cambridge.

Benhabib, S, Butler, J, Cornel, D and Fraser, N 1996, *Feminist contentions*, Routledge, London.

Bosworth, M 2011, 'Deporting foreign national prisoners in England and Wales', *Citizenship Studies*, vol. 15, no. 5, pp. 583–595.

———— 2012, 'Subjectivity and identity in detention: punishment and society in a global age', *Theoretical Criminology*, vol. 16, no. 2, pp. 123–140.

———— 2014, *Inside immigration detention: foreigners in a carceral age*, Oxford University Press, Oxford.

Bosworth, M and Hoyle, C (eds) 2011, *What is criminology?*, Oxford University Press, Oxford.

Bowling, B 1990, 'Conceptual and methodological problems in measuring "race" differences in delinquency: a reply to Marianne Junger', *British Journal of Criminology*, vol. 30, no. 4, pp. 483–492.

———— 2013, 'Epilogue: the borders of punishment: towards a criminology of mobility', in KF Aas and M Bosworth (eds), *The borders of punishment: migration, citizenship and social exclusion*, Oxford University Press, Oxford, pp. 291–306.

Brotherton, DC and Barrios, L 2011, *Banished to the homeland: Dominican deportees and their stories of exile*, Columbia University Press, New York.

Butler, J 1990, *Gender trouble*, Routledge, London.

———— 1993, *Bodies that matter*, Routledge, London.

Calavita, K 2005, *Immigrants at the margins: law, race, and exclusion in Southern Europe*, Cambridge University Press, Cambridge.

Chappell, D 1967, 'Australian seminars of the problems of drug use', *British Journal of Criminology*, vol. 7, no. 4, pp. 413–417.

Christie, N 2000, *Crime control as industry: towards gulags, western style*, 3rd edition, Routledge, Abingdon.

Cohen, S 1972, *Mods and rockers*, Routledge, London.

Crenshaw, KW 1989, 'Demarginalizing the intersection of race and sex: a Black feminist critique of antidiscrimination doctrine, feminist theory and antiracist politics', *University of Chicago Legal Forum*, 139–167.

Dauvergne, C 2008, *Making people illegal: what globalization means for migration and law*, Cambridge University Press, Cambridge.

Deegan, MJ 1990, *Jane Addams and the men of the Chicago School, 1892–1918*, Transaction Publishers, New Brunswick.

de Genova, N and Peutz, N 2010, *The deportation regime: sovereignty, space, and the freedom of movement*, Duke University Press, Durham.

De Giorgi, A 2010, 'Immigration control, post-Fordism, and less eligibility: a materialist critique of the criminalization of immigration across Europe', *Punishment & Society*, vol. 12, no. 2, pp. 147–167.

Dembour, MB and Kelly, T (eds) 2011, *Are human rights for migrants? Critical reflections on the status of irregular migrants in Europe and the United States*, Routledge, Abingdon.

Donnan, H and Wilson, TM 1999, *Borders: frontiers of identity, nation and state*, Berg, Oxford.

Dunkel, F 1995, 'Imprisonment in transition: the situation in the new states of the Federal Republic of Germany', *British Journal of Criminology*, vol. 35, no. 1, pp. 95–113.

Farrell, G, Mansur, K and Tullis, M 1996, 'Cocaine and heroin in Europe in 1983–1993', *British Journal of Criminology*, vol. 36, no. 2, pp. 255–281.

Fraser, N 1997, *Justice interruptus*, Routledge, London.

Gerard, A and Pickering, S 2014, 'Gender, securitization and transit: refugee women and the journey to the EU', *Journal of Refugee Studies*, vol. 27, no. 3, pp. 338–359.

Graif, C and Sampson, RJ 2009, 'Spatial heterogeneity in the effects of immigration and diversity on neighborhood homicide rates', *Homicide Studies*, vol. 13, pp. 242–260.

Green, P and Grewcock, M 2002, 'The war against illegal migration: state crime and the construction of a European identity', *Current Issues in Criminal Justice*, vol. 14, no. 1, pp. 87–101.

Grewcock, M 2014, 'Reinventing "the stain": bad character and criminal deportation in contemporary Australia', in S Pickering and J Ham (eds), *Routledge handbook on crime and international migration*, Routledge, Abingdon, pp. 121–136.

Guia, MJ, van de Woude, M and van der Leun, J (eds) 2012, *Social control and justice: crimmigration in the age of fear*, Eleven International Publishing, The Hague.

Guild, E 2009, *Security and migration in the 21st century*, Polity, Cambridge.

Hall, S, Critcher, C, Jefferson, T and Clarke, J 1978, *Policing the crisis: mugging, the state and law and order*, Palgrave Macmillan, London.

Hills, A 1995, 'Militant tendencies: "paramilitarism" in the British police', *British Journal of Criminology*, vol. 35, no. 3, pp. 450–458.

Huysmans, J 2006, *The politics of insecurity: fear, migration and asylum in the EU*, Routledge, London.

Kanstroom, D 2007, *Deportation nation: outsiders in American history*, Harvard University Press, Cambridge, MA.

Korn, A 2000, 'Crime and legal control', *British Journal of Criminology*, vol. 40, no. 4, pp. 574–594.

Lee, M (ed.) 2007, *Human trafficking*, Willan Publishing, Devon.

Lyon, D 2009, *Identifying citizens: ID cards as surveillance*, Polity Press, Cambridge.

Mapstone, R 1992, 'The attitude of police in a divided society: the case of Northern Ireland', *British Journal of Criminology*, vol. 32, no. 2, pp. 183–192.

McCulloch, J and True, J 2014, 'Shifting borders: crime, borders, international relations and criminology', in S Pickering and J Ham (eds), *Routledge handbook on crime and international migration*, Routledge, Abingdon, pp. 367–381.

Melossi, D 2013, 'People on the move: from the countryside to the factory/prison', in KF Aas and M Bosworth (eds), *The borders of punishment: migration, citizenship and social exclusion*, Oxford University Press, Oxford.

Munro, VE 2006, 'Stopping traffic: a comparative study of responses to the trafficking of women for prostitution', *British Journal of Criminology*, vol. 46, no. 2, pp. 318–333.

Nelken, D (ed.) 2010, *Comparative criminal justice and globalization*, Ashgate, London.

Nevins, J 2002, *Operation Gatekeeper: the rise of the 'illegal alien' and the making of the US–Mexico boundary*, Routledge, New York.

Odergard, E 1995, 'Legality and legitimacy: on attitudes to drugs and social sanctions', *British Journal of Criminology*, vol. 35, no. 4, pp. 525–542.

Paoli, L 2002, 'The development of an illegal market: drug consumption and trade in post-Soviet Russia', *British Journal of Criminology*, vol. 42, no. 1, pp. 21–39.

Park, RE and Burgess, E 1921, *Introduction to the science of sociology*, University of Chicago Press, Chicago.

Pearson, G 1990, 'Crime and criminology in Israel: a personal account of a British study tour', *British Journal of Criminology*, vol. 30, no. 2, pp. 235–243.

Pickering, S 2014, 'Floating carceral spaces: border enforcement and gender on the high seas', *Punishment & Society*, vol. 16, no. 2, pp. 187–205.

Pickering, S and Cochrane, B 2013, 'Irregular border-crossing deaths and gender: where, how and why women die crossing borders', *Theoretical Criminology*, vol. 17, no. 1, pp. 27–48.

Pickering, S and Ham, J 2014a, 'Hot pants at the border: sorting sex work from trafficking', *British Journal of Criminology*, vol. 54, no. 1, pp. 2–19.

———— 2014b, *Routledge Handbook on Crime and International Migration*, Routledge, Abingdon.

Pickering, S and Weber, L (eds) 2006, *Borders, mobility and technologies of control*, Springer, Dordrecht.

———— 2013, 'Policing transversal borders', in KF Franko and M Bosworth (eds), *The borders of punishment: migration, citizenship and social exclusion*, Oxford University Press, Oxford, pp. 93–110.

Pratt, A and Thompson, SK 2008, 'Chivalry, "race" and discretion at the Canadian border', *British Journal of Criminology*, vol. 48, no. 5, pp. 620–640.

Rajaram, PK and Grundy-Warr, C (eds) 2007, *Borderscapes: hidden geographies and politics at territory's edge*, University of Minnesota Press, Minneapolis and London.

Ruggiero, V and Vass, AA 1992, 'Heroin use and the formal economy: illicit drugs and licit economies', *British Journal of Criminology*, vol. 32, no. 2, pp. 273–291.

Ryan, B and Mitsilegas, V 2010, *Extraterritorial immigration control: legal challenges*, Brill, London.

Said, E 1979, *Orientalism*, Vintage Books, New York.

Sanchez, G 2014, 'Human smuggling facilitators in the US Southwest', in S Pickering and J Ham (eds), *Routledge handbook on crime and international migration*, Routledge, Abingdon, pp. 275–286.

Schor, N and Weed, E 1994, *The essential difference*, Indiana University Press, Bloomington.

Segrave, M, Milivojevic, S and Pickering, S 2009, *Sex trafficking: international context and response*, Willan Publishing, Devon.

Sheptycki, J 1995, 'Transnational policing and the makings of a post-modern state', *British Journal of Criminology*, vol. 35, no. 4, pp. 613–635.

———— 1998, 'Policing, postmodernism and transnationalization', *British Journal of Criminology*, vol. 38, no. 3, pp. 485–503.

Simmel, G 1950, 'The stranger', in K Wolff (ed. and trans.), *The sociology of Georg Simmel*, The Free Press, New York, pp. 402–408.

Spivak, G 1988, 'Can the subaltern speak?', in C Nelson and L Grossberg (eds), *Marxism and the interpretation of culture*, Macmillan Education, Basingstoke, pp. 271–313.

Stumpf, J 2006, 'The crimmigration crisis: immigrants, crime & sovereign power', *American University Law Review*, vol. 56, no. 2, pp. 367–419.

Torpey, J 2000, *The invention of the passport: surveillance, citizenship and the state*, Cambridge University Press, Cambridge.

Ugelvik, S and Ugelvik, T 2013, 'Immigration control in Ultima Thule: detention and exclusion, Norwegian style', *European Journal of Criminology*, vol. 10, no. 6, pp. 709–724.

Vagg, J 1992, 'The border of crime: Hong Kong–China cross-border criminal activity', *British Journal of Criminology*, vol. 32, no. 3, pp. 310–328.

van der Leun, J 2003, *Looking for loopholes: processes of incorporation of illegal immigrants in the Netherlands*, Amsterdam University Press, Amsterdam.

van Kalmthout, AM, Hofstee-van der Meulen, FBAM and Dünkel, F (eds) 2007, *Foreigners in European prisons*, Wolf Legal Publishers, Nijmegen.

van zyl Smit, D 1999, 'Criminological ideas and the South African transition', *British Journal of Criminology*, vol. 39, no. 2, pp. 198–215.

Vaughn, MS, Huang, FFY and Ramirez, CR 1995, 'Drug abuse and anti-drug policy in Japan: past history and future directions', *British Journal of Criminology*, vol. 35, no. 4, pp. 491–524.

Vázquez, Y 2011, 'Where do we go from here? Advising noncitizen defendants on the immigration consequences of a criminal conviction after Padilla', *Fordham Urban Law Journal*, vol. 39, no. 1, pp. 169–202.

Weber, L 2006, 'The shifting frontiers of migration control', in S Pickering and L Weber (eds), *Borders, mobility and technologies of control*, Springer, Dordrecht, pp. 21–44.

———— 2013, *Policing non-citizens*, Routledge, London and New York.

Weber, L and Bowling, B 2008, 'Valiant beggars and global vagabonds: select, eject, immobilize', *Theoretical Criminology*, vol. 12, no. 3, pp. 355–375.

———— (eds) 2012, *Stop and search: police power in global context*, Routledge, London.

Weber, L and Pickering, S 2011, *Globalization and borders: death at the global frontier*, Palgrave Macmillan, Basingstoke.

———— 2013, 'Exporting risk, deporting non-citizens', in F Pakes (ed.), *Globalisation and the challenge to criminology*, Routledge, Abingdon, pp. 110–128.

Weitzer, R 2009, 'Legalizing prostitution: morality in Western Australia', *British Journal of Criminology*, vol. 49, no. 1, pp. 88–105.

Wonders, N 2007, 'Globalization, border reconstruction projects, and transnational crime', *Social Justice*, vol. 34, no. 2, pp. 33–46.

Young, IM 1990, *Justice and the politics of difference*, Princeton University Press, Princeton.

———— 1997, *Intersecting voices: dilemmas of gender, political philosophy and politics*, Princeton University Press, Princeton.

Zureik, E and Salter, MB (eds) 2005, *Global surveillance and policing: borders, security, identity*, Willan Publishing, Cullompton.

11

GREEN CRIMINOLOGIES

Reece Walters

What do criminology and criminologists do to decrease the chances of the extinction of mankind and the destruction of the planet?

(Harding 1983: 82)

Introduction

At the 2003 British Society of Criminology's conference in Bangor I used the above quotation from Richard Harding when delivering a paper entitled 'Crime and genetically modified food'. The words of Harding were greeted by the audience with dismissive facial expressions of cynicism and jocularity. Yet my paper pursued Harding's challenge to the criminological world to cease proving that 'the circle is round and the square has four sides' and explore big-picture issues of global concern (Harding 1983: 90). My presentation critiqued the techno-cratic and genetic monopolisation of food through a political economy of state and corporate power. It drew on the works of Nigel South, Piers Beirne and Michael Lynch, notably their then decade-long debates about the 'greening' of crime and criminology. To my surprise, somewhat cynical and dismissive questions from the audience commenced with, 'what does this have to do with Criminology?'; and 'where is the crime?' I was to experience similar bemused and unwelcome responses at other international conferences and also whilst present-ing public seminars at 'prestigious' universities in both northern and southern hemispheres. I am aware that fellow academics within what is now widely known as 'green criminology' have had similar experiences, however, thankfully, not for some time. Indeed, the last ten years have witnessed a proliferation of books, courses and conferences devoted specifically to this area (South and Brisman 2013a; Walters et al. 2013; Spapens et al. 2014; Lynch and Stretesky 2014; Hall 2015; Sollund 2015). Moreover, panels on 'green criminology' within mainstream criminological conferences have become regular fixtures, as harms and crimes against the environment continue to gather global political and policy prominence. The proliferation of intellectual and policy discussion about environmental crime has also culminated in annual conferences devoted to green criminology and numerous subject specific textbooks (White and Heckenberg 2014).

Indeed green criminology has blossomed into a range of critical discourses examining environmental concerns within notions of power, harm and justice (Walters et al. 2013). Since its emergence in the late 1980s, discourses in the greening of the criminological enterprise have adopted various terms and nomenclature in an attempt to harness and capture evolving debates. As a result, we have witnessed the use of 'green criminology' (Lynch 1990), 'eco-critical criminology' (Seis 1993), 'conservation criminology' (Herbig and Joubert 2006) and 'eco-global criminology' (White 2011), all used in various intertwined ways to explore state and corporate exploitation of the environment for power and profit. There have also been attempts by White (2008) to reclaim the term 'environmental criminology' from existing work on 'crime mapping' or charting the spatial and geographical occurrence of recorded crime (Bottoms and Wiles 2003; Wortley et al. 2008); however, an unspoken consensus has settled among scholars that 'green criminology' be the preferred generic banner for this critical narrative exploring harms against the environment (Hall 2015). Similar debates have occurred regarding the subject matter of a green criminology, as a result 'green crime', 'environmental crime', 'crimes against the environment', 'green harm' and 'eco-crime' are used, often interchangeably (Sollund 2015).

The voices of opposition to a green criminology have been few. However, in 2004, Mark Halsey published his insightful and provocative article 'Against "green" criminology' in the *British Journal of Criminology*. His critique focused more on the veracity and utility of the label 'environmental crime' rather than debunking a dedicated strand of criminological thought. That said, he challenged green criminologists to reconfigure notions of nature within broader philosophical and epistemological discourses, and jettison the term 'green', 'because it does not adequately capture the inter-subjective, inter-generational, or inter-ecosystemic processes which combine to produce scenarios of harm' (Halsey 2004: 835). Throughout the past decade, Halsey's call for theoretically diverse critiques of nature and the environment, and his critique of what he calls 'truth effects' have been somewhat heeded (White 2014). Indeed, for some the emerging connections between green criminology and science 'are precisely where green criminology has eclipsed orthodox criminology' (Lynch and Stretesky 2014: 80).

There are numerous international protocols that provide legal definitions of environmental crime. Many of these topic areas are included within the green criminological agenda. For example, the United Nations Interregional Crime and Justice Research Institute (UNICRI) has established a now widely used categorisation of organised environmental crime based on various international protocols and multilateral agreements. Other organisations including Interpol, the UN Environment Programme and G8 also adopt the following five key areas when referring to transnational and organised environmental crime. The areas are:

- illegal trade in endangered species and wildlife (breach of the 1973 Washington Convention on International Trade in Endangered Species (CITES));
- illegal trade in ozone-depleting substances (breach of the 1987 Montreal Protocol on Substances that Deplete the Ozone Layer);
- illegal dumping, trade and transport of waste and hazardous substances (breach of the 1989 Basel Convention on the Control of Transboundary Movement of Hazardous Wastes and Other Wastes and their Disposal);
- illegal, unregulated and unreported commercial fishing;
- illegal logging and trade in protected woodlands (CITES) (see Hayman and Brack 2002: 5).

Such internationally recognised acts of environmental harm have been adopted within the domestic laws of nation states. In addition, green criminologists draw on sociological analyses of deviance to broaden the subject matter under review and include acts committed by states. For example, White (2008: 99) refers to the 'coloring of environmental crime issues' to differentiate types or 'dimensions' of environmental harm. For him, 'brown issues' involve things such as pollution, oil spills, dumping of toxic waste; 'green issues' relate specifically to conservation matters including loss of biodiversity, species decline and habitat destruction; while 'white issues' focus on genetic modification, animal testing and other lab-based or scientifically orchestrated harms. Other scholars including Carrabine et al. (2004) adopt a typology of primary and secondary green crime. The aforementioned includes pollution, deforestation, species decline and animal rights, whereas secondary green crimes involve symbiotic harms from state and corporate agencies exploiting environmental damage (for example, state violence and oppositional groups, hazardous waste and organised crime). Some authors have also steered away from the state-embedded notion of 'environmental crime' which has been traditionally used by western governments to target street and property offences such as graffiti and vandalism, opting for 'eco-crime', a term used by the environmental movement to encompass acts of state and corporate harm (Westra 2004; Walters 2010). Irrespective of the particular theoretical or ideological persuasion the terms 'environmental crime', 'eco-crime' and 'green crime' are used interchangeably within green criminological narratives to identify those 'harms against humanity, against the environment (including space) and against non-human animals committed by both powerful organisations (e.g. governments, transnational corporations, military apparatuses) and also by ordinary people' (Bierne and South 2007: xiii).

In 2013, Nigel South and Avi Brisman compiled the first *International Handbook of Green Criminology*. In their introduction they describe it as a 'capacious and evolving perspective' where 'diversity is one of its great strengths'. They further add that it includes a:

> set of intellectual, empirical and political orientations towards problems (harms, offences and crimes related to the environment, different species and the planet). Importantly, it is also an 'open' perspective and framework, arising from within the tradition(s) of critical criminology; at the same time, it actively seeks inter- and multi-disciplinary engagement.
>
> *(2013b: 28)*

It is also important to note that South (2010: 242), one of the pioneers of green criminology, rightly argues that analysing emerging environmental harms and injustices requires 'a new academic way of looking at the world but also a new global politics'. This includes an intellectual discourse that moves 'beyond the narrow boundaries of traditional criminology and draws together political and practical action to shape public policy' (2010: 242). Green criminology continues to evolve as a dynamic knowledge of resistance and innovation, one that challenges mainstream crime discourses, and critically examines the policies and practices of contemporary governments and corporations. It is a collection of new and thought-provoking voices within the criminological lexicon, and its engagement with diverse narratives seeks to identify, theorise and respond to environmental issues of both global and local concern. The expansion of green criminological perspectives serves to harness and mobilise academic, activist and governmental interests to preserve, protect and develop environmental issues.

This chapter untangles the intellectual orientations of green criminology by exploring its origins, developments and scholarly trajectories. It examines what's new about this collection of criminological discourses, and in keeping with this edited volume, what's alternative?

Greening the criminological landscape

As is often the case with new intellectual endeavours, questions of genealogy and pedigree are frequently nonlinear and contested. This is true for the origins and emergence of green criminology. It has a trans–Atlantic ancestry, emanating from both the United States and the United Kingdom, and is inspired by eco-activism and environmental sociology. It is widely known that Rachel Carson's critique of agricultural chemicals and ecological harm in her groundbreaking (1962) book *Silent Spring* spawned subsequent environmental movements and intellectual innovation; including Samuel Klausner's 'environmental sociology' – *On Man and His Environment* (1971) and William Catton's (1980) *Overshoot: The Ecological Basis of Revolutionary Social Change*. Against the backdrop of protest and dissent, these pivotal texts drew on classical sociological theory and a growing political and social environmental consciousness, to explore the 'energy crisis', chemical waste, pollution and agricultural risk (Hannigan 1995).

Within the criminological world, these works resonated in the sociology of deviance, and with scholars interested in environmentalism and green-party politics. In the spirit of Raymond Williams and his evolution of culture in his classic piece *Marxism and Literature* (1977), the following section briefly charts those substances, struggles or events from which new knowledges in green criminology were cast. As mentioned above, the genealogy of green criminology is traceable to specific moments during the late 1970s and 1982 in both the USA and the UK, and the intellectual advances of Michael Lynch and Nigel South respectively. The first coining of the term 'green criminology' in a published work is attributed to Michael Lynch in his (1990) article 'The greening of criminology: A perspective on the 1990s'. Lynch was influenced by green social movements, green activism and the rise of green party in Europe. The 1989 European elections that witnessed green politicians capture 26 seats proved a pinnacle moment for Lynch as he describes:

> It was that election that began to affect how I was thinking about radical explanations of crime and my interest in environmental crime … It seemed to me that the focus on class and political economic explanations in European green politics and radical criminology was a good way of integrating these ideas, and lead to the idea that there might be something that could be called green criminology that could be constructed to united political economic theory, social movement research and growing political awareness of green issues.
>
> *(Lynch 2015; cf. Natali 2013: 74–75)*

For Lynch, crimes committed by corporations in the early 1980s that polluted or harmed the environment were acts of 'excessive ecological consumption' – a concept that was further developed in the influential works of ecological Marxism (Foster 2000).

Simultaneously during the mid–late 1980s in the UK, sociologist and criminologist Nigel South (University of Essex), as yet unaware of the works of Lynch (which he did not read until the mid-1990s) began examining a political economy of resource exploitation. In works published in 1984, South and his colleagues, influenced by Rosa Del Olmo's 'eco-bio-geneocide', examined the links between drugs, 'exploitation, legacies of colonialism and how western nations pushed down prices for agricultural cash crops and raw minerals thereby encouraging the growth of profitable informal/illicit drug economies' (South 2015). For South (who compiled the first collection on green criminology – see Beirne and South 1998), this and other high prioritised acts of environmental damage at the time provided the contexts for him developing a 'green agenda' for criminology in the late 1980s.

The state and corporate induced acts of environmental harm that motivated political and social green movements, as well as intellectual criminological developments on both sides of the Atlantic, comprised four key internationally reported events of environmental devastation. These included the 1978 discovery of thousands of drums of toxic waste dumped by Hooker Chemicals in Love Canal near Niagara Falls resulting in birth defects, miscarriages and chromosomal abnormalities to local residents, and declaration of a state-of-emergency by the then US President Jimmy Carter. Second, the 1984 poisonous and negligent gas explosion at Union Carbide's pesticides factory in India that killed many thousands of people and animals and contaminated soils and waterways. Third, the 1984 bombing of Greenpeace's protest ship, the *Rainbow Warrior*, in Auckland, New Zealand. This was an act of French government espionage against a green movement objecting to that nation's illegal nuclear testing. Finally, the nuclear explosion in Chernobyl and the dislocation and death of thousands of people in the Ukraine sparked an international awareness of the dangers of nuclearism.

These acts resulting in environmental destruction, human and non-human victimisation captured international headlines and stirred a public and political consciousness about the abuse of state and corporate power. They also provided the impetus for cross-disciplinary intellectual scholarship that was informed by a growing green politics and social movements of environmental concern. Therefore, when it was first coined and developed within criminology, 'green criminology' was a term designed to harness green environmentalism and green political theories to examine 'environmental destruction as an outcome of the structure of modern capitalist production and consumption patterns' (Lynch 1990: 1). In this sense, green criminology has its theoretical roots embedded within the traditions of radical criminological schools of thought such as feminism, Marxism and social constructionism. (These radical criminologies emerged in the late 1960s and early 1970s in the UK and the USA arguing, among other things, that crime is to be found in relations of power, oppression and selective processes of criminalisation.)

Green criminological theories and perspectives

Green criminology asserts that eco-crimes at an international and domestic level should encapsulate all acts of environmental harm to human and non-human species as well as to the natural environment itself (Lynch and Stretesky 2003; Beirne and South 2007; White 2008). Green criminology remains an undeveloped and evolving criminological narrative, yet its various perspectives aim to provide an interdisciplinary scholarship committed to the protection and conservation of environmental resources and the prevention of illegal and harmful acts that unnecessarily threaten or damage the natural environment. As mentioned above, early green criminological thinking was influenced 'theoretically' by political economy, environmental politics and the radical traditions within criminology. This remains true today with various green criminologists exploring corporate and state exploitation of the environment and utilising the analytical tools of feminism, masculinities, Marxism and other traditions within the critical criminological lexicon (see Lynch and Stretesky 2014; South and Brisman 2013b).

That said, White (2008: 15) argues that there is no one green criminological theory but rather a series of 'perspectives' that draw on various philosophical, sociological, legal and scientific traditions. He argues that the three 'theoretical tendencies' that inform green criminology are 'environmental justice', 'ecological justice' and 'species justice'. These three perspectives have been widely adopted and integrated into a range of green criminological topics.

Environmental justice is a human-centred or anthropocentric concept that emerged out of the US civil rights movement. In 1979 the Texan case of *Bean v Southwestern Waste Management Corporation* applied civil rights law to challenge the construction of a dumping facility near an African American community in Houston. This landmark case highlighted the discriminatory corporate practice of placing hazardous and toxic waste in landfills abutting the homes of ethnic minorities in what became known throughout the US as acts of 'environmental racism' (Bullard 2005: 19–20). In 1991 the 'principles of environmental justice' were established by delegates to the First National People of Color Environmental Leadership Summit held in Washington, DC. This gathering, which would become known as Summit 1, included 1000 culturally diverse representatives from social movement organisations who argued that 'environmental hazards were disproportionality imposed upon people of color' (Johnson 1996: 376). The Summit asserted that indigenous peoples and ethnic minorities experienced alarming rates of environmental dislocation, contamination and pollution as employees, residents and migrants. In addition, the benefits of a safe, healthy and mineral rich environment were deprived of 'people of color' in preference to powerful and privileged classes who exploited resources for maximum political and financial return (see Heiman 1996; Goldman 1996). As a result, the earliest expressions of environmental justice comprise two dimensions. The first relates to capitalism and racism and explores the ways in which the financially marginalised and powerless experience the majority of all deleterious and dangerous residues and discards of neo-liberal market economie (Capek 1993). The second critiques the inequity of access and use of environmental resources across social and cultural divides (Foreman 1998). Who has access to the benefits and profits of natural resources and why? What factors prevent all people from equally sharing in the environment? Such analyses identified that environmental injustice was widespread, with the socially, politically and economically underprivileged and disenfranchised routinely denied access to environmental benefits (Holifield et al. 2010).

The European Court of Human Rights has since ruled that all member states and their subjects have a 'right to a safe environment' (Mularoni 2003). Subsequently, a growing body of green criminological scholarship has examined actions that prevent, jeopardise or compromise this right. It explores how the poor and powerless people are affected by climate change, toxic dumping, chemical spills, industrial pollution, nuclear testing, illegal fishing and wildlife poaching and contamination of drinking water (White 2009; Hall 2015; Lynch and Stretesky 2014). All have adverse side-effects but do not victimise all people equally. It is indigenous people, ethnic minorities, the poor, and often women, who are most affected. For White (2014), environmental justice focuses on 'harms to humans', and has evolved to explore the ways in which policy and law can enable equitable access to environmental benefits whilst limiting disproportionate distribution of environmental damage and dislocation. For example, the United States Environmental Protection Agency (2015) defines environmental justice as:

the fair treatment and meaningful involvement of all people regardless of race, color, national origin, or income with respect to the development, implementation, and enforcement of environmental laws, regulations, and policies. EPA has this goal for all communities and persons across this Nation. It will be achieved when everyone enjoys the same degree of protection from environmental and health hazards and equal access to the decision-making process to have a healthy environment in which to live, learn, and work.

Ecological justice focuses on the relationship or interaction between humans and the natural environment; its focus is 'harm to nature' (White 2014). When humans develop the environment for material needs (housing, agriculture, business, consumption) an ecological justice approach insists that such actions be assessed within the context of damage or harm to other living things (non-humans) as well as inanimate objects (such as rocks, soil, water and air). This position is often referred to as an 'eco-centric' understanding of human and nature interaction. It is widely known that humans have bestowed moral and ethical value upon nature's flora and fauna. An ecological justice perspective ensures that policies, laws and treaties are utilised to create 'stewardship' over the preservation and responsible development of the environment for mutual human and non-human benefit (Baxter 2005). When humans damage or destroy nature for the purposes of productivity or what Peter Dauvergne (2008) refers to as the 'shadows of consumption', they do so with irresponsible disregard of humans' co-existence with the natural environment. These 'ecological shadows' or 'death by consumption' (VanDeveer 2011: 325) provide the underlying contexts for examining and explaining environmental harm. For Scholsberg (2001: 12) ecological justice,

> that is, doing justice to nature to allow the sustainability of natural capital, the protection of irreplaceable nature, or the protection of natural 'value' or processes of nature generally, demands an extension of recognition to nature. As with social justice generally, we need to examine structures, mores, norms, language, symbols that mediate our relation with nature. Much of this has been done in the vast literature of green theory.

Some may criticise this position because it lacks acknowledgement that the reality of harm, existence, development, progress and so on will always be defined and responded to, by humans (Holifield 2010). Yet ecological justice argues that an environmentally centred perspective which upholds the importance of living creatures as well as inanimate and non-living objects provides useful insights for guiding future economic and developmental decisions. It upholds the intrinsic value and equal status of non-humans and explores the potential for sustainability while utilising environmental resources for fundamental human needs.

Species justice is a non-human or biocentric discourse that emphasises 'harms to non-humans' (White 2014). It asserts that human beings are not the only creatures with rights, nor are humans superior beings. In other words, there is no hierarchy of existence with human beings at the pinnacle. All 'living things in existence' share an equal status of importance. This perspective has its roots in 'speciesism', a term developed by British psychologist Richard Ryder in 1970 at Oxford University's Animals, Men and Morals Group. The essence of Ryder's argument is that moral distinction should not be drawn between animals and humans as the two groups fundamentally share similar biological characteristics. He was moved at the time by the vast exploitation of animals in experiments that he dubbed both cruel and unnecessary.

As a result he argued that, just like sexism and racism, speciesism should be recognised as one species' domination and control of another (Ryder 2010). This thinking has its roots embedded in the utilitarian ideology of Jeremy Bentham and his widely cited work on the suffering of non-human animals in his *Introduction to the Principles of Moral and Legislation* (1823). For Bentham (1823: 16):

> the question is not, Can they reason? nor, Can they talk? but, Can they suffer? Why should the law refuse its protection to any sensitive being? ... The time will come when humanity will extend its mantle over everything which breathes...

The subsequent development of discourses in animal welfare and animal rights emerged in philosophical studies, most notably Peter Singer's influential book *Animal Liberation* (1975). Within green criminology, Beirne and South (2007) argue that to prohibit or disregard non-human creatures as not of equal standing within the natural environment denies the value and worth of those species. Conversely it may be argued that existence or survival, and indeed evolution itself, is dependent upon one species consuming another. Linked closely to this, is the notion of 'ecological extension' where the importance of human beings is considered no more significant in the long-term existence of the environment than that of all other creatures that combine to form the natural environment. As White (2008: 17) argues, an analysis from this perspective aids a critique of how rights are constructed. It allows us to question the bases from which rights are created and protected. It follows that if rights are about ensuring health and well-being while minimising pain and suffering, then humans are not the only species to experience such emotions. For Reagan (2004) this was the basis for promoting a case for animal rights. Since then we have witnessed a flourish of university courses, as well as law firms practising in 'animal law' (Miller 2011).

The above perspectives centre critical attention on the key issues of how and why certain things come to be called criminal and others not. In doing so, it opens up debate over whether certain harms should be criminalised. Importantly, green criminology is not only a response to official and scientific evidence about environmental damage and species decline, but also an engagement with emerging social movements and public opinions of resistance. As such, green criminology moves away from a sole reliance on risk and measurement as presented by government, and incorporates social and cultural meanings of harm as defined by ordinary citizens. In these ways, green criminology itself can be considered an evolving knowledge base that challenges mainstream disciplinary discourses as well as neo-liberal governing rationalities. It questions the moral and ethical bases upon which contemporary laws permit the exploitation of nature and examines the conditions in which co-existence and inter-species co-operation can be achieved. Moreover, its globalising of the criminological lens permits the involvement of movements and organisations which are outside the state to contribute to emerging notions of environmental justice.

Therefore, the three green criminological perspectives of 'environmental', 'ecological' and 'species' provide the trunk from which topics branch out and are theorised through established critical lenses. For example, within green criminology environmental, ecological and species 'injustices' have been explored by Stretesky et al. (2014). Drawing on Allan Schnaiberg's (1980) ecological Marxism and his Treadmill of Production (ToP) theory, Stretesky et al. (2014) demonstrate how market-oriented, advanced neo-liberal societies are responsible for ongoing environmental harm. Central to ToP is that capitalism, with its expanding technologies, is intrinsically environmentally destructive. For Schnaiberg (1980) and Gould et al. (2004), the extraction of natural resources, the deforestation of woodlands and habitats, and the exploitation of flora and fauna, are essential ingredients in the capitalist ToP process that results in 'ecological disorganisation'. The treadmill is driven by a perpetual need to service consumer society, with the supply and demand of expanding markets and trade-oriented economic policies underpinning contemporary globalised international relations and providing the fabric and essence of environmental despoliation. The ongoing commercialisation and commodification of products, resources and global commons, for example, fuel the treadmill through expanding trade and consumption. Thus, governing rationales premised on capitalist ideologies are, according to Stretesky et al. (2014), both responsible for environmental destruction and incapable of redressing ongoing harm. The inability to reverse environmental damage or the 'law of entropy' is crucial to their critique of ecological disorganisation. According to this critique, the commercial processes of production exploit and manipulate the natural environment for power and profit and, as a result, disrupt, reorganise and disfigure the ecological balance that sustains environmental stability and development (cf. Johnson et al. 2016).

Others such as Wonders and Danner (2015) have applied feminism to analyses of the deleterious effects of climate change on women; some have explored risk society and political economy analyses to the contamination and exploitation of food, water and air (Croall 2013; Stretesky et al. 2014; White 2003) and recently connections have been made between environmental crime and social conflict theory (Brisman et al. 2015). As Nigel South identified back in 1998, it was essential for the foundations of a green criminology to be established first through an examination of 'regulation, disasters and violations, second, legal and social censures, and third, social movement and environmental politics' (1998: 445). It is evidently clear that Nigel South provided a platform that he and others have built on during the last two decades. The consolidation of research in animal rights, wildlife trafficking and deforestation, to mention only a few, have provided alternative criminological voices that are multidisciplinary, transnational and theoretically rich (see Sollund 2013; Wyatt 2013; and Boekhout van Solinge and Kuijpers 2013). The intellectual exchange between green criminology, environmental sociology, ecophilosophy, environmental law and environmental science has created an exciting, evolving and dynamic blend of discourses that critique political ideologies and environmental policy on a local, national and global scale. Such exchanges have ensured that green criminology continues to devolve with the advantage of theoretical and scientific expertise from the sciences, social sciences and humanities. Underpinning these emerging narratives is a commitment to alternative, unorthodox and critical engagement. This requires analyses that challenge agents of state and corporate power, and harness and mobilise voices of resistance and dissent. Green criminological issues often involve discussions of state and corporate power.

Power, harm and towards a 'green justice'

There is much criminological writing about injustice and powerlessness; and green criminology continues to unravel the relevance of power, injustice and discrimination. Indeed, many green criminologists have discussed the influence of Paul Gilroy's classic text *There Ain't No Black in the Union Jack* (1987), on the development of their environmental research agendas premised on institutional bias, state power and prejudice. Indeed some green criminologists attempt to bind topics of environmental, ecological and non-human research topics with a conceptual twine made from debates about power, harm and justice. We witness 'coercive power' or 'power over' or what Bachrach and Baratz (1970: 43) referred to as the mobilisation of bias; in acts where corporations exploit, plunder and pollute natural resources to the peril of indigenous communities and developing societies (Schmidt 2004; Green et al. 2007). Here we observe individuals in positions of state and corporate authority systematically reinforcing predominant values through institutional practice. Those who benefit are placed in a preferred position to defend and promote their vested interests.

At another level, various forms of 'influential power' are utilised for commercial and political gain. Here networks of position are used to manipulate pressure and sway specific events for desired outcomes. The bribing of political officials, the falsification of documentation, flexing diplomatic or market muscle or setting political agendas are brought about by having the resources and 'strategic power' to influence outcomes (Clifford 2014). Influential power often operates in partnership with the subject or object of influence, unlike coercive power which denies the disempowered access to processes, practices and decisions. This form of 'ambassadorial or soft power' is based on a combination of political and economic interest, and combined with charm, persuasion and entrepreneurism (Nye 2004). Here, those in elite or influential positions are able to present, construct and promote their desired outcome through methods and images that appear to favour multiple parties. For example, the images of corporate green responsibility and environmental regeneration projects from oil companies are persuasive ways to curry favour with sceptical and critical voices (Smandych and Kueneman 2010); similarly, the adoption of genetic technologies in food (Walters 2011); or the transference and dumping of toxic harms (Heckenberg 2010).

The concept of harm has also been widely adopted with green criminologies (Sollund 2015). The discourses defining and assessing harm in environmental law are diverse and complex. While environmental laws and regulations are designed to 'protect' the environment, in practice they work to assign value to harm already caused, in order to measure the consequences of some action, and thus measure and apply sanctions. To sanction harm, the law must assess penalties for inflicting harm, and to do this the law must measure those harms to assess the level of sanction to apply. The necessity to assess harm and regulate sanctions has become necessary with the global increase in environmental law which, since the 1970s, has regulated and legislated outcomes of behaviour and actions which impact upon 'the environment', another concept which is rarely defined and infrequently considered other than to generalise about ecosystems. Such legal requirements have produced a theoretically robust narrative about ecological harm, environmental harm and species harm (discussed above). Yet the notion of the environment itself is theorised much less, and the law struggles to include any real definitions of the environment or indeed of any prevention of harm to the environment, instead focusing on the impact of human actions which cause harm to the health or business of humans, from a very anthropocentric and economic perspective.

In legislation and policy, a discourse of sustainability has reigned supreme. This discourse is all about allowing development, economic sustainability and the continuance of human activities which may harm the environment. The sustainability discourse has subsumed and overtaken any understanding of protecting the environment for moral or ethical reasons, instead focusing on economic and developmental concerns. Examples of this economic and anthropocentric perspective abound, in United Nations declarations, the USA and European laws (Westerhuis 2013). The definitions we do have of 'harm and the environment' are generally derived from United Nations conventions or treaties, and then transposed to diverse national and local legislation and regulation which are intended to support international agreements. In all these narratives, the extent to which environmental harm is considered is limited to those harms which affect the resources and processes in natural ecosystems, but only those from which we are able to extract or gain benefit. Other impacts are rarely, if ever, considered or sanctioned. This anthropocentric focus is upon 'ecosystem services', a concept which describes benefits to humans which can be obtained from the environment. These are then linked to risk, harm and the future of food availability, rather than to any concerns about animals other than humans. When these other animals are considered, it is in the context of advantages to humans, or future generations of humans, or to the resources or services that they offer – albeit to the detriment or harm, in many cases, of non-human animals. For White (2012: 63–64) green criminologies must continue to reconfigure such notions of environmental harm and recognise what he calls 'paradoxical harms' that arise

> out of an apparent contradiction (for instance, we have to pollute certain parts of the planet in order to save it from other types of pollution). Such examples of paradoxical harm include the adoption of compact fluorescent light globes to save energy (but contain toxic mercury), promotion of nuclear energy (but which involves disposal of nuclear waste), and carbon emission storage (that penetrates and despoils the subterranean depths of land and sea).

White's critique of environmental harm is a network theory of neo-liberalism that identifies how new technologies developed with an environmental consciousness but underpinned by fiscal imperatives can be damaging and destructive to nature. For him, green criminologies must continue to engage in critical debates about production and consumption to understand the ways in which the environment is continually compromised by policies and practices that promote social and economic good.

Kibert (2001) has asserted that a 'green justice' should seek to redress the discrimination of ethnic and socially disadvantaged minorities who experience 'environmental racism and victimology' and the disproportionate effects of air pollution and advanced capitalism. As a concept, 'green justice' has been used by activists and left scholars to examine environmental injustice, namely, the plight of the poor and powerless at the hands of affluent, industrial economies (Alier 2000). Others have used the phrase to discuss environmental law and policy and the use of court processes (Hoban and Brooks 1996; White 2013; Walters and Westerhuis 2013). Therefore, the usage of the term 'green justice' resonates not only in discourses of protest, resistance and anti-capitalism, but also within legal debates about the role of law. For example, emerging within philosophical and political science discourses, and more specifically related to emissions and climate change, is the concept of 'atmospheric justice' (Vanderheiden 2008). This position recognises that the vast majority of air pollution and greenhouse gas emissions is caused by fossil fuel combustion, deforestation and the industrial activities of the world's most economically wealthy and powerful nations. This productivity continues to have devastating consequences for the world's lowest producing emission countries. The concept is based on principles of Rawlsian concepts of liberal egalitarian justice (Rawls 2001), as well as cosmopolitan justice and political realism. Vanderheiden (2008) proposes an international climate change regulatory regime based on equity, responsibility and compensation. In essence, he advocates the 'polluter pays principle' within a framework of 'fault-based liability' that includes historical emissions. He calls for internationally agreed-upon air pollution targets with a system for compensating low emitting nations for the environmental and human impacts of atmospheric injustices not of their doing. Unlike Kyoto and the carbon credit system, he asserts that a new international independent climate change committee, with representatives from various nations, could collect and analyse air quality data and policies from individual countries.

Whatever shape a green justice may take, it will need to include transnational justice in a form that can assert a central place within criminological discourse across the globalised landscapes of contemporary organised, corporate and state crime (see Reichel 2005). International justice and transnational legal processes are emerging through protocols and inter-state agreements that seek to regulate and prevent illicit corporate activity within the complex webs of global markets (Likosky 2002). Environmental offences including air pollution are often seen as administrative matters rather than crimes. That said, the enforcement of international environmental protocols and treaties for both EU and non-EU countries may take place in the International Court of Justice. With increasing concerns about climate change, ecological degradation, ozone depletion, food and water security, and sustainable development, it is imperative that a legally constituted and representative system of justice should exist. The expansion of international environmental law and policy has also witnessed an increase in processes to mitigate and adjudicate cases of environmental concern. The recognition of anthropocentric environmental damage and the need for ecological sustainability has ensured that discourses of risks, rights, harm, responsibility and liability have become part of green criminology (Hamman et al. 2015).

There has been a steady growth in both developed and developing countries of specialist environmental frameworks which often include specialist Environmental Courts or Tribunals (ECTs). It is reported that some 350 ECTs operate across 41 countries, facilitating various forms of environmental due process and justice (White 2013; Walters and Westerhuis 2013). The growth of ECTs can be attributed to 'continual [pressure] worldwide for effective resolution of environmental conflicts and/or expanding recognition of the need for procedural and substantive justice vis-à-vis environmental matters' (White 2013: 268). These burgeoning fora for settling environmental disputes can inculcate both civil and criminal jurisdictions and resolve a variety of claims from more administrative matters such as planning permits to serious prosecutions involving environmental contamination. The diversity and complexity of environmental cases increasingly requires innovative approaches based on 'problem-solving' before judicial officers with specialised knowledge (White 2013). Moreover, a range of innovative policing and prevention initiatives continue to emerge that harness the knowledges and experiences of environmental activists and local communities (Walters 2013; Spapens et al. 2014).

Indeed, the involvement of citizens in environmental activism has been pivotal to the progression and development of environmental policies and regulation (Clifford and Edwards 2012). Environmental movements are becoming central in the identification, detection and prevention of environmental crime. Their resources, technologies, databases and personnel are increasingly utilised by law enforcement agencies to police, regulate and prosecute both organised and localised environmental crime. Here, environmental activism, through technology and networks of action, local alliances, as well as appeals to citizens and officials elevate the social movement to a reliable and reputable status that is inculcated into government and regulatory structures. Environmental activism becomes not mere representative democracy but participatory democracy with both a visible presence and impact. As such, with public and political integration it becomes a new and important form of environmental governance. The momentum created by environmental movements is, to quote Foucault, a source of mobilised power. Emerging from alliances with local institutions of governance, and knowledges have come to be relied upon as accepted and trusted regimes of truth (Foucault 1979).

Networks of green activists, therefore, have become important in environmental law enforcement and are increasingly drawn upon by official agencies for intelligence. They are the coalface frontier of new and emerging forms of 'green justice'. On the other hand, environmental or green activism has become a threat to corporate and governing elites that seek power and profit through the exploitation of natural resources. It is widely known that environmental activists have long been the targets of corporate spying, police infiltration and state espionage (Lubbers 2012). As such, the plight of those seeking to protect and preserve the environment through vocal and direct public action has been both risky and dangerous. Global Witness reports that between 2002 and 2013, a total of 908 environmental activists were killed across 35 countries with only ten reported convictions (Lakhani 2014). It concludes that two environmental activists are killed every week, stating, 'Many of those facing threats are ordinary people opposing land grabs, mining operations and the industrial timber trade, often forced from their homes and severely threatened by environmental devastation' (Global Witness 2015: 4).

Conclusion

Green criminology continues to emerge and evolve as knowledge of resistance, one that challenges mainstream crime discourses, and critically examines the policies and practices of contemporary governments and corporations. It is a collection of new and innovative voices within the criminological lexicon, and its engagement with diverse narratives seeks to identify, theorise and respond to environmental issues of both global and local concern. The expansion of green criminological perspectives serves to harness and mobilise academic, activist and governmental interests to preserve, protect and develop environmental issues. In doing so, it examines international agreements and policy within diverse environmental discourses of sociology, criminology and political economy.

Green criminology, in its 'pursuit of social justice and human rights', is capable of identifying and exposing 'environmental problems' and converting them to 'historical facts' (South and Brisman 2013a: 99, 2013b: 19). Such an agenda inevitably involves examination of the intersection of the concepts of harm, power and justice; and also of the ways in which power is mobilised to justify a market model of capitalism with unjust and harmful consequences for the environment and the world's most vulnerable peoples. It is thus that green criminologies extend critical rethinking of the parameters and horizons of the criminological landscape. Such a rethinking requires a reflection on how humans relate to the environment and what constitutes acceptable and unacceptable exploitations of flora, fauna and natural resources. While legal interventions seek to protect the environment, the imperatives of market economies and free trade perpetuated by powerful institutions and governments provide the impetus for the continuance of eco-crime. To analyse and explain the complexities of eco-crime, green criminologies will continue to require ongoing criminological imagination and scholarship.

References

Alier, J. (2000) 'Retrospective environmentalism and environmental justice movements today', *Capitalism, Nature, Socialism*, 11(4), 45–50.

Bachrach, P. and Baratz, M. (1970) *Power and Poverty: Theory and Practice*. New York: Oxford University Press.

Baxter, B. (2005) *A Theory of Environmental Justice*. London: Routledge.

Beirne, P. and South, N. (eds) (1998) 'Special issue on green criminology', *Theoretical Criminology*, 2(2).

Beirne, P. and South, N. (eds) (2007) *Issues in Green Criminology: Confronting Harms against Environments, Humanity and Other Animals*. Devon: Willan.

Bentham, J. (1823) *An Introduction to the Principles of Morals and Legislation*. Oxford: Oxford University Press.

Boekhout van Solinge, T. and Kuijpers, K. (2013) 'The Amazon rainforest: A green criminological perspective', in South, N. and Brisman, A. (eds) *Routledge International Handbook of Green Criminology*. London: Routledge, pp. 199–213.

Bottoms, A. and Wiles, P. (2003) 'Environmental criminology', in Maguire, M., Morgan, R. and Reiner, R. (eds) *The Oxford Handbook of Criminology*, 3rd edition. Oxford: Oxford University Press.

Brisman, A., South, N. and White, R. (2015) *Environmental Crime and Social Conflict: Contemporary and Emerging Issues*. Abingdon: Routledge.

Bullard, R. (2005) 'Environmental justice in the twenty-first century', in Bullard, R. (ed.) *The Quest for Environmental Justice: Human Rights and the Politics of Pollution*. San Francisco: Sierra Club Books.

Capek, S. (1993) 'The "environmental justice" frame: A conceptual discussion and an application', *Social Problems*, 40, 5–24.

Carrabine, E., Iganski, P., Lee, M., Plummer, K. and South, N. (2004) *Criminology: A Sociological Introduction*. London: Routledge.

Carson, R. (1962) *Silent Spring*. New York: Houghton Miffin Hardcourt.

Catton, W. R., Jr (1980) *Overshoot: The Ecological Basis of Revolutionary Social Change*. Champaign: University of Illinois.

Clifford, M. (2014) 'The corporation as villian and victim: Reflections on privilege, complicity, awareness and accountability', in Spapens, T., White, R. and Kluin, M. (eds) *Environmental Crime and Its Victims: Perspectives within Green Criminology*. London: Ashgate, pp. 41–62.

Clifford, M. and Edwards, T. (2012) *Environmental Crime*, 2nd edition. Burlington: Jones and Bartlett Learning.

Croall, H. (2013) 'Food crime', in South, N. and Brisman, A. (eds) *Routledge International Handbook of Green Criminology*. Abingdon: Routledge.

Dauvergne, P. (2008) *The Shadows of Consumption*. Cambridge: MIT Press.

Environmental Protection Agency (2015) 'What is environmental justice?', www3.epa.gov/environmentaljustice/ (accessed 2 November 2015).

Foreman, C. (1998) *The Promise and Peril of Environmental Justice*. Washington, DC: Brookings Institution Press.

Foster, J. (2000) *Marx's Ecology – Materialism and Nature*. New York: Monthly Review Press.

Foucault, M. (1979) 'Truth and power: An interview with Michel Foucault', *Critique of Anthropology*, 4, 131–137.

Gilroy, P. (1987) *There Ain't No Black in the Union Jack: The Cultural Politics of Race and Nation*. London: Routledge.

Global Witness (2015) 'How many more?', www.globalwitness.org/campaigns/environmental-activists/how-many-more/ (accessed 23 August 2015).

Goldman, B. (1996) 'What is the future of environmental justice', *Antipode*, 28, 122–141.

Gould, K., Pellow, D. and Schnaiberg, A. (2004) 'Interrogating the treadmill of production: Everything you wanted to know about the treadmill but were afraid to ask', *Organization & Environment*, 17(3), 296–316.

Green, P., Ward, T. and McConnachie, K. (2007) 'Logging and legality: Environmental crime, civil society, and the state', *Social Justice*, 34(2), 94–110.

Hall, M. (2015) *Exploring Green Crime: Introducing the Legal, Social and Criminological Contexts of Environmental Harm*. London: Palgrave.

Halsey, M. (2004) 'Against "green" criminology', *British Journal of Criminology*, 44(4), 833–853.

Hamman, E., Walters, R. and Maguire, R. (2015) 'Environmental crime and specialist courts: The case for a "one-stop (judicial) shop" in Queensland', *Current Issues in Criminal Justice*, 27(1), 55–79.

Hannigan, J. (1995) *Environmental Sociology*, 2nd edition. London: Routledge.

Harding, R. (1983) 'Nuclear energy and the destiny of mankind – some criminological perspectives', *The Australian and New Zealand Journal of Criminology*, 16(2), 81–92.

Hayman, G. and Brack, D. (2002) 'International environmental crime: The nature and control of environmental black markets: Workshop report', www.chathamhouse.org. uk/files/3050_riia_environmental_crime_workshop_report.pdf.

Heckenberg, D. (2010) 'The global transference of toxic harms', in White, R. (ed.) *Global Environmental Harm: Criminological Perspectives*. Cullompton: Willan, pp. 37–61.

Heiman, M. (1996) 'Race, waste, and class: New perspectives on environmental justice', *Antipode*, 28, 111–121.

Herbig, F. and Joubert, S. (2006) 'Criminological semantics: Conservation criminology – vision or vagary', *Acta Criminologica*, 19(3), 88–103.

Hoban, T. and Brooks, R. (1996) *Green Justice: The Environment and the Courts*, 2nd edition. Boulder: Westview Press.

Holifield, R. (2010) 'Actor-network theory as a critical approach to environmental justice: A case against synthesis with urban political ecology', in Holifield, R., Porter, M. and Walker, G. (eds) *Spaces of Environmental Justice*. Chichester: Wiley-Blackwell, pp. 47–69.

Holified, R., Porter, M. and Walker, G. (2010) 'Introduction: Spaces of environmental justice – frameworks for critical engagement', in Holifield, R., Porter, M. and Walker, G. (eds) *Spaces of Environmental Justice*. Chichester: Wiley-Blackwell, pp. 1–22.

Johnson, B. (1996) *Environmental Policy and Public Health*. Boca Raton: CRC Press.

Johnson, H., South, N. and Walters, R. (2016) 'The commodification and exploitation of fresh water: Property, human rights and green criminology', *International Journal of Law, Crime and Justice*, 44, 146–162.

Kibert, N. (2001) 'Green justice: A holistic approach to environmental injustice', *Journal of Land Use and Environmental Law*, 17(1), 169–182.

Klausner, S. (1971) *On Man in His Environment*. New York: Jossey-Bass.

Lakhani, N. (2014) 'Surge in deaths of environmental activists over past decade, report finds', www.theguardian.com/environment/2014/apr/15/surge-deaths-environmental-activists-global-witness-report (accessed 1 October 2015).

Likosky, M. (ed.) (2002) *Transnational Legal Processes: Globalisation and Power Disparities*. London: Butterworths.

Lubbers, E. (2012) *Secret Manoeuvres in the Dark: Corporate and Police Spying on Activists*. London: Pluto Press.

Lynch, M. (1990) 'The greening of criminology: A perspective on the 1990s', *The Critical Criminologist*, 2(3), 1–12.

Lynch, M. (2015) Email communication, 13 October 2015.

Lynch, M. and Stretsky, P. (2003) 'The meaning of green: Contrasting criminological perspectives', *Theoretical Criminology*, 7(2), 217–238.

Lynch, M. and Stretesky, P. (2014) *Exploring Green Criminology: Toward a Green Criminological Approach*. Farnham: Ashgate.

Miller, G. (2011) 'The rise of animal law', *Science*, 332(6025), 28–31.

Mularoni, A. (2003) 'The right to a safe environment in the case-law of the European Court of Human Rights', in Postiglione, A. (ed.) *The Role of the Judiciary in the Implementation and Enforcement of Environmental Law*. Rome: International Court of the Environmental Foundation.

Natali, L. (2013) 'The contemporary horizon of green criminology', in South, N. and Brisman, A. (eds) *Routledge International Handbook of Green Criminology*. London: Routledge, pp. 73–84.

Nye, J. (2004) *Soft Power: The Means to Success in World Politics*. New York: Public Affairs.

Rawls, J. (2001) *Justice as Fairness: A Restatement*. Cambridge: Belknap Press Harvard.

Reagan, T. (2004) *The Case for Animal Rights*. Berkeley: University of California Press.

Reichel, P. (ed.) (2005) *Handbook of Transnational Crime and Justice*. London: Sage.

Ryder, R. (2010) 'Speciesism again: The original leaflet', *Critical Society*, 2(Spring), http://homepage. ntlworld.com/amacguru/Critical%20SocietyJournal/Archives_files/1.%20Speciesism%20Again.pdf (accessed 2 November 2015).

Schmidt, C. (2004) 'Environmental crimes: Profiting at the Earth's expense', *Environmental Health Perspectives*, 112(2), 96–103.

Scholsberg, D. (2001) 'Three dimensions of environmental and ecological justice', http://ecpr. eu/Filestore/PaperProposal/5ef89598-7149-4b8d-82b3-567750b392f6.pdf (accessed 9 November 2015).

Schnaiberg, A. (1980) *The Environment: From Surplus to Scarcity*. New York: Oxford University Press.

Seis, M. (1993) 'Ecological blunders in US clean air legislation', *Journal of Human Justice*, 10(2), 22–42.

Singer, P. (1975) *Animal Liberation*. New York: Harper Collins.

Smandych, R. and Kueneman, R. (2010) 'The Canadian-Alberta tar sands: A case study of state–corporate environmental crime', in White, R. (ed.) *Global Environmental Harm: Criminological Perspectives*. Cullompton: Willan, pp. 87–109.

Sollund, R. (2013) 'The victimization of women, children and non-human species through trafficking and trade: Crimes understood through an ecofeminist perspective', in South, N. and Brisman, A. (eds) *Routledge International Handbook of Green Criminology*. London: Routledge, pp. 317–330.

Sollund, R. (ed.) (2015) *Green Harms and Crimes: Critical Criminology in a Changing World*. London: Palgrave.

South, N. (1998) 'Corporate and state crime against the environment: Foundations for a green perspective in European criminology', in Ruggiero, V., South, N. and Taylor, I. (eds) *The New European Criminology: Crime and Social Order in Europe*. London: Routledge, pp. 443–461.

South, N. (2010) 'The ecocidal tendencies of late modernity: Transnational crime, social exclusion, victims and rights', in White, R. (ed.) *Global Environmental Harm: Criminological Perspectives*. Devon: Willan, pp. 228–247.

South, N. (2015) Email communication, 2 October 2015.

South, N. and Brisman, A. (2013a) 'Critical green criminology: Environmental rights and crimes of exploitation', in Winlow, S. and Atkinson, R. (eds) *New Directions in Crime and Deviance*. London: Routledge, pp. 99–111.

South, N. and Brisman, A. (eds) (2013b) *Routledge International Handbook of Green Criminology*. London: Routledge.

Spapens, T., White, R. and Kluin, M. (2014) *Environmental Crime and Its Victims: Perspectives within Green Criminology*. Aldershot: Ashgate.

Stretesky, P., Long, M. and Lynch, M. (2014) *The Treadmill of Crime: Political Economy and Green Criminology*. London: Routledge.

VanDeveer, S. (2011) 'Consumption, commodity chains and the global environment', in Axelrod, R., VanDeveer, S. and Downie, D. (eds) *The Global Environment: Institutions, Law and Policy*, 3rd edition. Washington, DC: CQ Press, pp. 311–332.

Vanderheiden, S. (2008) *Atmospheric Justice: A Political Theory of Climate Change*. Oxford: Oxford University Press.

Walters, R. (2010) 'Eco crime', in Muncie, J., Talbot, D. and Walters, R. (eds) *Crime: Local and Global*. Devon: Willan, pp. 173–208.

Walters, R. (2011) *Eco Crime and Genetically Modified Food*. London: Routledge.

Walters, R. (2013) 'Ecomafia and environmental crime', in Carrington, K., Ball, M., O'Brien, E. and Tauri, J. (eds) *Crime, Justice and Social Democracy*. London: Palgrave, pp. 281–294.

Walters, R. and Westerhuis, D. (2013) 'Green crime and the role of environmental courts', *Crime, Law and Social Change*, 59(3), 279–290.

Walters, R., Westerhuis, D. and Wyatt, T. (eds) (2013) *Emerging Issues in Green Criminology: Exploring Power, Justice and Harm*. London: Palgrave.

Westerhuis, D. (2013) 'A harm analysis of environmental crime', in Walters, R., Westerhuis, D. and Wyatt, T. (eds) *Emerging Issues in Green Criminology: Exploring Power, Justice and Harm*. London: Palgrave, pp. 197–217.

Westra, L. (2004) *Ecoviolence and the Law (Supranational Normative Foundations of Ecocrime)*. Ardsley, NY: Transactional Publishers.

White, R. (2003) 'Environmental issues and the criminological imagination', *Theoretical Criminology*, 7(4), 483–506.

White, R. (2008) *Crimes against Nature: Environmental Criminology and Ecological Justice*. Oregon: Willan.

White, R. (2009) *Environmental Crime: A Reader*. Devon: Willan.

White, R. (2011) *Transnational Environmental Crime: Toward an Eco-Global Criminology*. London: Routledge.

White, R. (2012) 'Climate change and paradoxical harm', in Farrall, S., Ahmed, T. and French, D. (eds) *Criminological and Legal Consequences of Climate Change*. Oxford: Hart, pp. 63–78.

White, R. (2013) 'Environmental crime and problem-solving courts', *Crime, Law and Social Change*, 59(3), 267–278.

White, R. (2014) *Environmental Harm: An Eco-Justice Perspective*. Bristol: Policy Press.

White, R. and Heckenberg, D. (2014) *Green Criminology: An Introduction to the Study of Environmental Harm*. London: Routledge.

Williams, R. (1977) *Marxism and Literature*. London: Oxford.

Wonders, N. and Danner, M. (2015) 'Gendering climate change: A feminist perspective', *Critical Criminology*, 23(4), 401–416.

Wortley, R., Mazerolle, L. and Rambouts, S. (eds) (2008) *Environmental Criminology and Crime Analysis*. Devon: Willan.

Wyatt, T. (2013) 'Uncovering the significance of and motivation for wildlife trafficking', in South, N. and Brisman, A. (eds) *Routledge International Handbook of Green Criminology*. London: Routledge, pp. 303–316.

12

CYBER-CRIMINOLOGIES

Leandro Ayres França[1]

Introduction

The title of this chapter is a neologism and has been coined by the author without any intention of attempting to brand the academic study of cybercrimes an entirely new criminology. It is proffered both as denoting just one set of *alternative* criminologies and as a way of underlining the main point of this essay: that the distinctiveness of crimes born of (rather than merely facilitated by) cyber technologies engenders new modes of thinking about crimes and punishments. These new modes of criminological thought are both demanded by, and engendered by, cyber technology-provoked philosophical issues of culpability; and by new practical problems of criminal definition, deterrence, regulation and enforcement. Already, however, criminologists are creating explanations of emergent cybercrimes that are dependent upon, and transformative of, the existing criminological canon. It is therefore to emphasise that not only are cybercrimes essentially new, but that new criminologies are required to conceptualise and explain them that the term cyber-criminologies is being used here.

In recent years, and in current discourse, *cyber* has been used to refer variously to information technology culture, computers and virtual reality or (with reference to the internet) to futuristic concepts. The ease of combining *cyber* with other words and the resultant directness of connotation have also encouraged me to propose the title of *cyber-criminologies* to denote scientific studies of the perpetration, control and punishment of delinquent behaviour in a telematic context. Already other terms have been proposed. Jaishankar (2007) argues for a new academic 'sub-discipline' that explains and analyses crimes on the internet, proposing that it be called *cyber criminology*. Brown (2013) prefers the term *virtual criminology*. Both terms are very similar to cyber-criminologies. However, as I have already said, I will argue that the distinctiveness, complexity and novelty of emergent cyber phenomena justify a *variety* of *pluralistic* and *alternative* perspectives able to debate the rapid emergence of previously unknown and unknowable crimes.

When the plural is chosen to refer to a field of study, it is already presupposed that this field is able to adapt to the realities that inspire it and that are unveiled by it. But does criminology have this ability to change, adapt and transform? According to Zedner (2007: 267) criminology has, historically, shown itself able to respond to the 'seismic shifts in its substantive terrain' and to grasp diversity through the development of kaleidoscopic frameworks. Perhaps, she goes on to argue, criminology possesses this ease of adaptation because it is an interstitial discipline and inhabits spaces in and between other longer-established social sciences. As a result, criminology is able to develop borrowed analytical tools according to its purpose and, while remaining free from disciplinary institutionalisation, is able to redefine its postulates, values and methods in order to adapt to the 'changing topography' of what is new and what needs to be explained (Zedner 2007: 268, 275; see also Carlen: Chapter 1). It is in adopting such a perspective that I speak of criminologies, but I also do so in recognition that a diversity of alternatives does not exclude potential synergies nor the development of shared views.

Cyber-criminologies currently exemplify a range of alternatives, synergies, and ever-changing neologisms born of new understandings and experiences. Even so, and as I have already indicated, not all theorists writing on cybercrime agree that a new concept is necessary to depict the terrain and the activities referred to in this chapter as cyber-criminologies. The rest of this chapter will therefore argue the need for distinctive criminological approaches to the study of cybercrimes, and it will be divided into three main parts. First, I will outline the different perspectives on the debate as to whether a distinct criminology of cybercrime can be justified. In the second part I will attempt justification of the term 'cyber-criminologies' by arguing that they are constituted by previously unknown phenomena not easily apprehended by already existing criminological perspectives. Third, I will address the question 'What is *cyber* about cybercrimes, and what are their distinctive relationships to the legal subject?'

Cyber-criminologies contested

Traditionalists

At the beginning of this century some authors (e.g. Brenner 2001; Grabosky 2001; Lévy 2001) concluded that there is presently no need for a new and distinct criminology that comprehends the phenomenon of cybercrimes. Virtual criminality, they argued, is basically the same as the terrestrial crimes with which we are already acquainted; it differs only in its techniques. Brenner (2001), for example, questioned the implicit presumption, promoted as a reaction to an unprecedented phenomenon, that there is something new, distinct from the traditional comprehension of crime, and argued that such a presumption does not even manage to conceal a lot of 'old wine in new bottles'. Grabosky (2001: 243) was also cautious: 'While the technology of implementation, and particularly its efficiency, may be without precedent, the crime is fundamentally familiar.' Similarly, Lévy (2001: 185) pointed out that gangsters, terrorists, paedophiles and pornographers (all traditional criminals) may make as much use of the internet as they do of other methods for lawbreaking. Yet, he points out, even though all types of criminals use airplanes, motorways and telephones during crime commission, nobody has thought of identifying these other technological networks as demanding a distinct criminology. Thus, all three theorists, Brenner (2001), Grabosky (2001) and Lévy (2001), argue that already-existing criminological categories can be legitimately used to inform understanding of crimes committed within cyberspace; and that at least some of the current criminological knowledge can be applied to virtual reality or information technologies. In arguing thus, however, these authors appear to overlook the specificity of some of the most important features of cybercrimes: the capacity of cyber technology to create crimes which cannot exist outside cyberspace.

Adaptationists

While not arguing the need for an entirely new criminology, other authors have argued for an adaptation of criminology to inform analysis of emergent phenomena which might or might not attract a criminal label. Brown (2006, 2013), Capeller (2001) and Wall (2007) have all argued for a revision of criminological concepts and theoretical frameworks on the grounds that the criminological universe has become incapable of explaining the new deviations that have provoked demands for the creation of new (cyber)crimes. Central to the arguments of all three has been an either explicit or implicit notion of discontinuity with the old and emergence of the new.

In 2001 Capeller argued for a revision of existing criminological models with the aim of explaining the movement within cyberspace towards newly immaterial deviations from informal social rules and pre-legal norms. According to her (Capeller 2001: 230) criminology has become incapable of explaining newly perceived rule-deviations that possibly have the potential to be legally defined as cybercrimes. In arguing thus, Capeller, therefore, *explicitly* uses the concept of *(dis)continuity*: while there is a *continuity* of the traditional forms of criminal activities, including those increasingly using virtual space as their support, the emergence of a new criminal phenomenology peculiar to information technology establishes a *discontinuity* in relation to the traditional phenomena (Capeller 2001: 230).

Making a different adaptive argument (though still one *implicitly* based on discontinuity), Brown (2006) defends a criminology of *hybrids* (humans plus techniques) that concerns itself with mapping the techno-social networks, its actants and assemblages. For Brown (2006: 236) it is not enough to apply old laws to new technologies, nor to evoke simple analogies between 'embodied crime' and cybercrime. Thus, in a more recent article Brown (2013) defines as *virtual criminology* a variety of works that have emerged since the mid-1990s, and which have been concerned with the implications of current technocultures in the way we understand crime, justice, law and social control. According to her, virtual criminology challenges two (embodied) features of traditional criminology: first, the focus on the deviant body and mind as subject and object of crime and control; and second, the notion that technology is a medium, an external appendage, a mere tool, in criminal endeavour and social control.

According to Brown, virtual criminology justifies itself firstly by reference to the uniqueness of its object: it allows for the absorption of behaviours that are not necessarily defined as criminal and of areas that are not regarded by traditional criminology as part of its domain – precisely because they are 'virtual'. Relatedly, the modes of order, control and deviation within virtual environments are not necessarily the same as those in the real or embodied world. Secondly, cybercultures display complex patterns and new forms of informal punishment (the punishments for rule-breaking for example, vary from textual sanctions to taking down of servers and information-bombing). Thirdly, virtual criminology is justified by its focus on simulation and disembodied relationships: 'What is at stake theoretically in virtual criminology', argues Brown (2013: 487, emphasis in original), 'is the notion of the *interface* between the human and the software/hardware; the human sensorium extends into virtuality and makes the human being and the machine co-constituents.' Thus, whereas traditional criminology (and traditional law) rest on the presumption that human agency, motivations and culpability are distinct from non-human things and from technology, virtual criminology is alert to the fusion of the human with the technical, to the dissolution of the body into information, disembodied identities and simulated consciousness.

There are obviously areas of agreement about cyber technology's plethora of emergent meanings and modes of understanding between Brown and Capeller. Wall (2007), however, offers opportunity for a more nuanced analysis by developing a generational approach to questions concerning the potential of existing criminologies to mediate the changing historical and cultural challenges and meanings of cyber activities. By categorising cybercrimes according to their dates of generation, he argues that different technological developments demand different criminological explanations, some of which can use existing criminologies, some of which cannot. While traditional cybercrimes use information technology as a means to the preparation of crimes and hybrid cybercrimes use it to carry out crimes, there are also crimes that are totally mediated by technology, products of the opportunities created by the internet and only possible within cyberspace (true cybercrimes). Accordingly, while first and second generation cybercrimes may be understood through the application of conventional criminological theories and concepts, third generation cybercrimes demand the development of new theoretical approaches. In similar vein, Yar (2013: 19) also claims that criminology needs to start searching for 'new tools' for 'new crimes'.

The point has often been made that criminology has continuously been challenged by social transformations and has repeatedly risen to the challenge (Garland and Sparks 2000; Zedner 2007). It is in that tradition, therefore, that this essay adopts the presupposition that the development of a new and distinctive social environment, cyberspace, with its own ontological and epistemological structures, interactional forms, roles and possibilities (Yar 2005: 408) may well provide the opportunity for the emergence of unprecedented criminal phenomenologies which can justify the neologism, cyber-criminologies. The following phenomenological novelties are listed in support of this argument.

The spatial distinctiveness of cyberspace

Cyberspace challenges physical spatial limits, making geography irrelevant (Jaishankar 2010; Lévy 2001: 31) when facing an experience of equidistance (Wall 2007: 37). Even if constant spatial references are identified – navigation, sites, portals, chat rooms, sending and receiving (e-)mails – the descriptors used reveal themselves as convenient metaphors that help us contextualise an environment that is inherently different from the physical world (Yar 2005). Take for instance the word 'page' to indicate the plane on which one writes information. Whereas the *physical* page, like the sheet of paper, is a limited field on which content is fixed (the Latin heading *pag-* indicates fixing: pact, pagan, pay [pacare], peace [pax]), the *virtual* page is a unit of flow, subject only to the limitations of the network connection (Lévy 2001: 139).[2]

Inspired by the ideas of Manuel Castells, Yar (2005, 2013) argues against the notion of the disconnectedness of cyberspace from socio-cultural constraints. For Yar, although cyberspace is different to the material world, it is, none the less an interactional social-technically generated environment that is rooted in the real world of political, economic, social and cultural relations. Cyberspace thus translates or reproduces real world characteristics onto the virtual space. Yar also counters the idea of equidistance in cyberspace: distance, for him, exists and is measured by the expenditure of time and effort to reach a certain content, in a calculation that should be punctuated by the number of clicks. Cyberspace is a special challenge for criminologists because a significant part of the tradition of criminological perspectives is based on, implicitly or explicitly, ecological theories – which have related crime occurrence, its patterns and distributions, to the social-spatial arrangement of specific places, and have made possible such concepts as mapping, criminogenic environment identification and prevention programmes (Yar 2013: 17). It is important to highlight, too, that, despite being an environment different from the physical world, cyberspace has a feature in common with it: architecture. When identifying political properties in cyberspace technological experience, Lessig (1998) states that cyberspace has its own architecture: the *code*, that is, the set of protocols and coded and implemented rules that determine how people interact (or exist) in this space. So, just as a physical architectural structure can in part structure human behaviour (and inspires ecological analysis), the cyberspace code structures and conditions behaviours, and establishes restrictions and permissions. It is this architectural base which allows us to envision an ecological cyber-criminology.

The temporal distinctiveness of cyberspace

Time has also been transformed in cyberspace. The most common understanding of time is as a quantifiable flow of events with a dynamic that varies from the expectation (future), the happening (present) and the loss (past). In cyberspace, however, the experience of communication at the speed of light provides a feeling of immediacy that baffles an understanding used to perceiving a sequence of physical actions. What is the interval, in cyberspace, between the moment of action and the production of the result? Besides, temporal compression offers another phenomenon: the annihilation of the past (loss) by the permanent remembrance. If oblivion has always been the natural consequence of time, challenged by the historical registries of written narratives and representations – which we call memory or remembrance – information storage and recovery techniques today allow for the past to be present; what has happened in the past is immediately within reach. Remembering thus becomes absolute, comprehensive and permanently available even to the point that forgetting has been recently elevated to a right to have personal information deleted from some second party's electronic records or databases, already called upon in courts around the world (Souza 2016).

Actants' autonomy and empowerment

Seemingly free from control by governments or corporations, internet users experience a new autonomy. Thus it is, Lévy (2001) argues, that cyberspace breaks from the idea of *society of the spectacle*, reported by the situationists as the context in which interpersonal relationships are crystallised by media characterised by centralised nodes distributing messages to isolated receivers unable to answer. In cyberspace, by contrast, communication is inherently free from compulsory media intervention because it is communal, non-hierarchical and reciprocal (Lévy 2001: 206). The internet, Lévy (2001: 208) argues, is 'anarchist' – not *in spite of* its military origin, but *because* of it (the dispersed structure of the network was designed to resist eventual enemy attacks).

In the context of criminal manifestations, the individual empowerment provided by the internet generates greater control of criminal activity by acting individuals. This empowerment is due to the ability technology possesses to be a force multiplier, allowing individuals with minimum resources to generate potentially great negative effects (Wall 2007: 39–40; Yar 2005, 2013: 11). A single spammer, for example, can reach millions of addressees and it has been estimated that over 80% of global spams were originated by fewer than 200 known spammers in the United States (see Wall 2007: 145; see also note 4 in this chapter).

New identities and feelings of anonymity

Interactions in cyberspace allow for individuals to reinvent themselves, adopting new virtual personae potentially quite distant from their 'real world' identities (Yar 2005, 2013: 11). Moreover, feelings of anonymity enable individuals to employ behaviours that, in non-cyber social worlds, would be limited by distinct levels of control (psychological brakes, social rules, legal norms) and that, if performed, would be defined as being illicit or, at least, deviant. A commonplace and non-criminal example portrays well this distinction: it is not uncommon that individuals, for various reasons, follow other people's lives on social media and sometimes do so with a dedication that, together with different applications (Facebook, Twitter, Foursquare) enables them to trace the routine of the observed being. The same following and observing practice of a third party's life, if applied in the real world (it suffices to imagine a constant observer outside the person's home, at the window), would imply the identification of an impertinent, aggressive, deviant conduct, to which the first reaction by any observer or victim would be to call the police.

New aspects of victimisation

New modes of association and exchange in cyberspace, characterised by instantaneity and apparent equidistance of the interactions between users, make everyone vulnerable to a variety of 'predators' that can reach them instantly, without the normal restrictions of physical distance (Yar 2005, 2013: 11). This generalised perception of real or potential victimisation is a characteristic of late modernity and was described by Garland and Sparks (2000) as the late modern *crime complex*: a cultural formation characterised by a distinct set of attitudes, beliefs and practices, derived from the perception of high crime rates as a normal social fact that makes crime avoidance a daily life-guiding principle. Cyberspace architecture enhances the possibility of this reality and intensifies feelings of potential victimisation. There is also clear evidence that the psychological and behavioural effects of this increased perception of cybercrimes have resulted in daily habits of prevention.

Grabosky (2001), however, argues that the possibilities of victimisation in the physical world and in cyberspace are similar. He claims that, in traditional reality, people are also aware of their vulnerability to crime. They are aware that, when they are victims of theft or burglary, for example, the chances of recovering their lost possessions are slim; they are aware that it is almost certain that the perpetrators are not going to be brought to justice and that the role of the police is going to be limited to registering the incident, giving a few words of comfort and perhaps some advice on preventing future crimes; and, finally, they are aware that they are on their own and that only a change of habit (and maybe a structural renovation – for those who can afford it) may reduce their degree of vulnerability. He concludes therefore that the 'necessity of self-reliance in crime prevention is no more in cyberspace than in one's physical neighbourhood' (2001: 245).

Virtual equidistance without the corresponding physical proximity to the victim may also be an incentive to deviant behaviours in cyberspace. David Wall (2007: 64) reported that an internet fraudster told him in interview that it was the lack of direct contact with the victim that had become the drive for his conduct. Virtual fraud, in particular, attracts perpetrators because of the (mistaken) belief that it is an infraction without victims and, consequently, that the financial loss is borne by banks. It is a neutralisation strategy which also hides the reality that financial institutions pass their losses on to traders, who then compensate by transferring the cost of these operational risks to consumers (Wall 2007: 81).

Transnationality (and the irrelevance of territorial jurisdictions)

Social norms enforcement and criminal prosecutions, traditionally linked to territorial jurisdictions, have become problematic with the advent of cybercrime. As Lévy (2001: 187) has claimed, it is as if national laws on information and communication have become 'irrelevant'. Owing to cybercrime globalisation, effective law enforcement requires a reasonable level of common ground and expensive co-operation between national legal systems. Yet even if there were sufficient commonality of legal structures, a very high commitment from governments and their police agencies would be required for successful prosecutions to be brought, and it is unlikely that local agencies such as police and courts would prioritise the task of assisting distant victims.

A fluid constant

The biggest challenge of all to understanding cyber activities is that everyday life technological transformation is a continuous dynamic process that grows more intense with each new moment. This feeling of accelerated movement is clear, for example, in the unprecedented microphenomena of cybercrimes: the length of time for a cybercrime opportunity to turn into a cybercrime wave has been measured in hours and minutes instead of in months and years, as happens with traditional crimes (Wall 2007: 2–3). Capeller (2001: 238) argues that, besides *transnationality*, two other characteristics of the internet have direct impact in terms of control: *fleetingness* and the *volatile nature* of the internet's content and its user strategies. A user can simultaneously be a server, an editor or a consumer, creating vast confusion in the various roles in the virtual community. This confusion of roles sometimes makes it impossible to determine which legal rule to apply and to whom to apply it. Think, for instance, about the difficulty of defining a *spammer*: is it he who compiles the addressee list? She who sells the list? He who buys the list? She who distributes the messages? He who abuses the advertising of their product? All of them?

Lévy (2001: 9) argues that although this fluid and constant movement gives the impression that digital technology lacks any stable essence, the rate of change is, in itself and paradoxically, a constant in cyberculture; and this *fluid constant* partially explains the sensation of impact, exteriority and strangeness that afflicts us when we venture to grasp the contemporary movement of technology.

What is distinctive about the relationships of cybercrimes to law?

Cybercrime exists as a legal object, as legislative agenda, as a news topic, literary theme and it is shared in people's daily communication. Yet what characterises the crime as *cyber*, as possibly justifying new and alternative criminologies?

It has been said that, when so-called cybercrime cases get to police stations or courts, they reveal themselves more in terms of their traditional aspects than as 'cyber' (Wall 2007: 8–9).

There is, of course, a clear issue of epistemological divergence between academic and popular definitions. With the purpose of guiding construction of a cyber-criminological theory, this essay proposes the following definition: cyber-criminologies study the criminal phenomenon originating in temporal, dynamic and ontological realities structured and conditioned by information technology.

Historically,[3] traditional and modern concepts of technique are different: whereas traditional technique was a way of poetic revelation, the modern technique, or technology, is a mathematical framework, constituted as a system and articulated increasingly more objectively, not as a material apparatus or the social-technical networks that end up forming themselves, but as 'the knowledge that allows all this not only to work, but to impose itself as a new and radical form of world' (Rüdiger 2014: 127).

In the 17th century the purpose of technology was the study of techniques – that is, the study of knowledges, the exposure of the rules of an art. From the 19th century onwards, however, the term technology began to refer to the synthesis between technique and science, the scientific technique of operable scientific knowledge. But even if such a definitional change may seem a huge leap from the Greek understanding of *tékhnē*, the Greek meaning still shows us something essential about the modern 'technology'. As Heidegger (1953/1977: 13) wrote, 'Technology is a mode of revealing; it comes to the presence where truth happens.'

Defining cyber activities as crime

The term *cybercrime* is not the most useful for close analysis of the different types of social and legal infractions committed in cyberspace. In the analysis of a global phenomenon, the reference to crime cannot presuppose any legal sanction being imposed on the basis of only (a local) legal description of the act as socially harmful and a (local) legal provision of penalty (cf. Sutherland 1945 on the difficulties of arguing for the criminalisation of as yet not recognised crimes). Perhaps it is possible formally to differentiate three dynamic categories of cyber deviations from either law or social rules: *cybercrime* as the violation of a legal norm via reference to legally prohibited uses of information technology in some states but not of a legal rule universally recognised in jurisdictions worldwide;[4] *cyber violation*, or *cyber deviance* as the violation of a social rule (but not of a legal rule) via new uses of information technology seen as being socially unacceptable; *neo-cyber threat* as the practice of a newly harmful act, newly possible solely via cyber technology, but against which there is not (yet) any universal or local rules under which it can be categorised (made sense of). In other words: while a *neo-cybercrime* does not constitute criminal conduct in some jurisdictions, a neo-cyber *threat* is more generally treated as a technical problem or a novelty, and its meaning tends to generate neither immediate social reprobation nor immediate understanding as *crime*. Consequently, Yar (2005: 409, 2013: 9, emphasis in original) argues that rather than trying to define the states of emergence and recognition of different degrees of what might be called cyber-criminalisation, 'it might be better to view the term cybercrime as formally signifying a *range* of illicit activities whose "common denominator" is the central role played by networks of ICT [Information and Communications Technology] in their commission'.

More substantively also, the dynamism that is characteristic of information technology influences the conceptual comprehension of cybercrimes. For Wall (2007: 10), cybercrimes are 'criminal or harmful activities that are informational, global and networked' and 'that involve the acquisition or manipulation of information for gain'. He thus limits cybercrimes to those activities that are products of network technology and that have changed the division of criminal labour, offering entirely new crime opportunities. He justifies his option of displaying cybercrimes in a framework of time instead of organising them according to a spatial perspective by arguing that in this way one can show how succeeding cyber-generations were defined by different stages of technological development. In order to distinguish the various offensive manifestations of information technology, Wall proposes a 'transformation test', that questions what is left, in the whole that we call cybercrimes, if those same network technologies are removed from the equation. The test, he says, does not claim to be scientific; instead, it concerns a heuristic device, a rule of thumb (Wall 2007: 34). The notion of transformation allows him (i) to offer the prospect of reconciling apparently distinct accounts of cybercrime by categorising them as different phases in the process of change, and (ii) to understand that study of the same technologies which create cybercrimes can also suggest unique opportunities for their regulation and control.

Hollinger (2001), like Wall, usefully periodises the development of cybercrimes. The first period covers the three decades from 1946 to 1976. In these years of mainframe systems, the most common violations concerned property: computers were vandalised, destroyed and stolen. With the development of personal computers, theft, via unauthorised transfers, together with various internet scams in the form of fraudulent billing invoices, became more common. The second period, from 1977 to 1987, was marked primarily by scaremongering predictions about the potential of cybercrimes to wreak global havoc. Even though few really damaging crimes were, in fact, perpetrated, various scares about the technological potential for mischievous young hackers to deliberately promote institutional chaos, or perhaps accidentally start a Third World War, became the main activity of this second period, together with calls for the 'correction' of countless deficiencies and inadequacies in penal law and the criminalisation of the illicit use of information technology. However, even with the promulgation of a plethora of legal statutes in relation to cybercrimes, in many countries the general public still did not see cybercrime as a burning social problem and relatively few offenders were prosecuted.

The third period, between 1988 and 1992, was characterised by vigorous efforts at law enforcement against individuals considered virtual offenders. Now it was the moment of demonisation of hackers and crackers. Finally, the last phase started in 1993 and lasted almost a decade (Hollinger's analysis limits itself up to its publishing year), and Hollinger labelled it as the censorship period, when attention turned to limiting computer user access to various 'dangerous' materials available on the internet. Despite being historically enlightening, Hollinger's methodology is structured on the social reaction to the cybercrimes phenomenon and each phase indicates why and towards what the criminalisation process had turned. Both Hollinger and Wall present sociological analyses but, whereas Hollinger's focuses on the social reaction to the new world of cyber technology, Wall's focuses more on the relationships between technique and knowledge. The following categorisation of cybercrimes is informed (with a few adaptations) by the generations framework elaborated by Wall (2007).

First generation: traditional (or ordinary) cybercrimes

First generation cybercrimes occurred (and still occur) within distinct computation systems and are characterised by the criminal exploitation of mainframe computers and their operating systems. They concern *traditional* (Wall 2007) or *ordinary* (McQuade 2006) crimes, in which computers are used in the preparation stage of the crime as communication tools obtaining preparatory information, in short, to assist traditional violations. Cybercrimes categorised as traditional are those committed in the so-called real world: the conduct for committing the crime, the circumstances involved in the act and its results happen in the physical world. They are delineated by the modern penal law itself which, as a fundamental premise, limits account-ability to the conduct, active or omissive, that takes place in the physical world, excluding from its scope non-externalised actions, such as thoughts (Brenner 2001: para. 10). In the crimes of this first generation the actual crime committed is not dependent upon technology (for instance, a computer may have been used instead of a map for locating a crime scene) and is easily perceived to have been a violation of the criminal code independently of the technology used (Wall 2007: 44–45).

Second generation: hybrid (or adaptive) crimes

Second generation cybercrimes are those committed through networks. They are *hybrid* (Wall 2007) or *adaptive* (McQuade 2006) crimes, though it is also possible to describe them as traditional crimes for which new globalised opportunities have arisen. Once the internet is removed from the equation, the offending behaviour remains; however, where it can be argued that hybrid or adaptive crimes are different from traditional crimes is that for hybrid crimes, when technology is removed new offending opportunities disappear; and though much the same criminal effects may be achieved they will be promulgated by other means, in smaller numbers and on a reduced scale (Wall 2007: 45–47). Under the heading of hybrid or adaptive (cyber) crimes, the following can be included:

Hacking concerns the unauthorised access to spaces over which ownership or access rights have already been established, by means of taking advantage of security breaches, with a broad variety of motivations and activities (Wall 2007: 53). Unauthorised access may result in: use of the resources of breached computers (file storage, bandwidth usage, botnet creation); data subtraction; alteration, sabotage and destruction of systems; defacement and 'spoofing' (falsification) of websites (Yar 2013: 28–30). When the unauthorised acts crack the code of a security system or inflict some kind of damage, the activity is called *cracking*.

Cyber-espionage also involves unauthorised access. However, unlike hackers and crackers, cyber-spies do not seek public acknowledgement for their activities and work with discretion in their trespass to obtain restricted information.

Cyber-blackmail is extortion made via ransomware (see below). The data of a system are illicitly cryptographed and the payment of a 'ransom' (or the agreement in distributing the malicious software) is demanded in exchange for the cryptograph key.

Cyber-terrorism uses information technology to attack critical infrastructure (see below) with *the aim of causing social or generalised terror*, exposing people or assets to hazard and, thus, manipulating political agendas. Examples include attacks to water and food supplies, energy supplies, telecommunication systems, to train and airplane traffic control, to hospital systems, to financial transactions, to security and emergency systems and to material assets of significant symbolic content.

Input frauds, unlike the crimes that use violence or coercion, extract assets or money from victims through misinformation or cheating. They happen on the internet in many ways, but generally reproduce traditional scam schemes. An adapted form is fraud committed through entry data, which refers to 'fraudulently obtaining information to apply for credit facilities, including making illicit credit card applications or using the stolen personal information to take over the owner's account' (Wall 2007: 72). Personal financial information can be obtained[5] by means of trashing, phishing or pharming (see all below).

Virtual sting involves the use of counterfeit or cloned credit cards; grey market exploitation; exploitation of reputation management systems (sellers' profiles in e-commerce, Facebook fan pages); financial pyramid schemes; direct investment scams ('work from home', etc.).

Appropriation of intellectual properties and *piracy*: digital property has the peculiarity of being able to be stored as code and, thus, be reproduced in its original format. Differently from analogical copies that lose quality with every copy generation, digital reproductions are identical. This brings a complex novelty: in cases where the victim finds him/herself deprived of the subtracted information, there is a clear variation of the traditional theft crime; when the criminal copies information (a song, a book, a film, software), the result is no longer a 'zero sum' that identifies the classic subtraction. Instead, what happens is an undue dilution of property because the victim is not the only one in possession of the information any more.

Child pornography is not a product of the internet and there is historical evidence indicating that the adult sexual interest in children dates from ancient times. Has the internet, however, had any changing impact on the promotion and organisation of child pornography? Wall (2007: 112) and Brown (2006: 233) both argue that the internet has facilitated the increased distribution of pornography.

Violent and dangerous content broadcast: the expansion of the internet has been accompanied by the *proliferation of hate speech* (promoted by various intolerant groups: extreme right, ultranationalists, supremacists, neo–Nazis, fundamentalist Christians and others); the *dissemination of images of violence* (like videos of deaths); the *appearance of sexting* (see below); the *facilitation of cyber-stalking*; and the *expansion of child sex abuse opportunities*.

True cybercrimes

The third generation of cybercrimes appeared at the turn of the century, with the substitution of the dial-in modem access by broadband, and is comprised of the *true cybercrimes*, of a distributed and automatised nature, almost completely mediated by technology. The cybercrimes of this generation are literally *sui generis*: they are products of the opportunities created solely by the internet and can only be perpetrated within cyberspace. Exclude the technology that allowed them to happen, and true cybercrimes disappear. Yar (2013: 6) agrees. 'It is the Internet that provides the crucial electronically generated environment in which cybercrime takes place' and, without it, cybercrime cannot exist. David Wall understands that this third generation of cybercrimes signifies a new period in which offenders and victims do not know each other and do not intend to get involved with one another, but in which they intertwine due to vulnerabilities and system flaws. Agreeing with this latter interpretation of true cybercrimes, I list below some of the cyber violations exclusive to information technology and which are governed by it.

Hacktivism consists of activism and political protest that makes use of hacking techniques and tools. Brenner (2001: paras 95–98) considers hacktivism as a new form of vigilantism – and it is not rare to find the expression cyber-vigilantism being used. In recent years, this practice received wide publicity when hacking was used as an important tool in the political mobilisations of what was known as the Arab Spring and from the various and varied operations by notorious hacker groups such as the collective Anonymous (Olson 2012: 64; Yar 2013: 47). Hacktivism may express itself in distinct ways, such as: server overload by DDoS (see below); communication congestion by email bombs (see next paragraph); defacement and alteration of websites; and malware use (see next paragraphs).

Cyber-barrage or *blockade*: in direct contrast with hacking, the main objective of this provoked congestion on the internet is to prevent legitimate users from gaining access to network and computer systems by bombarding access gateways with a barrage of data. Effective distributed denial of service (DDoS) attacks may be executed by groups of people with simultaneous access to a system in a short period of time, with the aim of overloading it. The DDoS were initially executed with the objective of extorting sums from companies; however, from the end of the first decade of the 21st century, DDoS became a popular form of cyberactivism, especially and notoriously present in the attacks by the collective Anonymous. Another way of congesting information traffic is used in email bombs, a technique that overloads email systems by the massive emission of messages.

Botnets: robot networks comprehend lists of zombie computer IP (see below) addresses that have been infected by remote administration tools and that, thus, may be controlled by a distant actant. Botnets are generally composed of something between 10,000 and 100,000 computers; some bigger, with enough capacity to shut down servers of big companies and smaller governments, have the capacity of remotely controlling more than a million computers (Olson 2012: 74). This explains why botnets are valuable merchandise (they can be rented for a certain amount of time) and their dimension influences their recognition and, in consequence, the price of renting them. 'In the underground hacker culture, larger botnets translate to greater street cred for the controllers, or botmasters' (Olson 2012: 75).

Spamming (see below) is the mass distribution of unsolicited email. Spamming cannot be compared with the massive distribution of unwanted mail, because whereas the latter supports the postal delivery service, spamming prevents email communication efficiency by smothering bandwidth, reducing access rates and introducing new risks to the addressees. (Interestingly, it is in exactly the same way that legitimate telemarketing is supported by information technology: shared databases of personal information; automated scheduling, dialling and messages by the computer. But all of it is often equally unsolicited.)

Malicious software (or *malware*) distribution: among the strategies used by hackers to achieve their plans are social engineering (a technique to get information and access codes by means of establishing a relationship of trust with those who have them) and using malicious software: logic bombs, spywares, trojans, viruses, worms (see all below). All of them are developed from code, depend on a connection with a computerised system, take advantage of systemic failures and vulnerabilities of the users and are projected to instil damage or gather information.

Leaking: the undue leaking of sensitive information is not something new. The novelty about leaking in the digital era is, firstly, in the public launching of data that should be confidential or restricted to a few individuals or for a certain amount of time. This wide diffusion, justified by the tradition of freedom of information, differentiates leaking from cyber-espionage (warfare/competition) and piracy (economical ends). A second characteristic is the new mode characterising contemporary leaking: instead of direct leakage of who has legitimate access to the information, the information is transmitted through encrypted communication (for source protection) to the organisations that analyse, edit and make available the leaked content. Diplomatic correspondence information, military records, companies' databases are a few of the most leaked contents by hackers. Julian Assange (2014: 205), founder of Wikileaks, when narrating a brief history of the case of the United States *versus* WikiLeaks, so described his organisation:

> It is WikiLeaks' mission to receive information from whistleblowers and censored journalists, release it to the public, and then defend against the inevitable legal and political attacks. It is a routine occurrence for powerful states and organizations to attempt to suppress WikiLeaks publications, and as the publisher of last resort this is one of the hardships WikiLeaks was built to endure.

Assange (2014: 134) also presented justifications for the leaks:

> There are really two fundamental justifications. First of all, human civilization, its good part, is based upon our full intellectual record, and our intellectual record should be as large as possible if humanity is to be as advanced as possible. The second is that, in practice, releasing information is positive to those engaged in acts that the public supports and negative to those engaged in acts that the public does not support.

Conclusion

This chapter has presented a proposal for the study of cyber-criminologies that presupposes technique as a temporal and dynamic ontological reality – a mode of revelation, a mode of knowing – and the essence of technique as a conditioning happening (and not mere means). Without information technology, the programmes listed above as third generation cybercrimes could neither have been created not have had any use; and, accordingly, they could never have existed as activities with rule-breaking dimensions potentially eligible for criminalisation and sanctioning by the criminal law. This is what makes them true cybercrimes. Without technology they could have had no past and no future. In the present their technology renders their relationship to the law emergent rather than already codified.

This proposal in no way should be confused with technological determinism, nor does it imply the defence of a type of mystification in which technologies are considered as a generative element of a constellation of historical events. Technology forms an age, because it expresses a mode of being that opens a world, and it *conditions*, in its own possibilities, all of a human being's attitudes, including the actions he/she performs in the virtual reality that has been built by information technology. Lévy (2001: 7–8) clarifies this issue by explaining that technology *conditions* and does not *determine* society: 'To say that technology conditions is to imply that it provides access to certain possibilities, that certain cultural or social options couldn't seriously be contemplated without its presence. Yet several possibilities remain open, and many are left untouched.' True cybercrimes emerge when individuals activate the criminal opportunities brought up within this framework, and when these acts are considered as threat, deviance or a violation of the law.

New understandings of cybercrimes will be developed in the future. In this chapter, however, I have argued that, in addition to exploration and conceptualisation of new and presently unthought-of cyber technologies, elements of traditional criminological knowledges are also likely to remain pertinent to cyberspaces, able to be transposed and applied to new realities. Meanwhile, it is proposed that, on the basis of the arguments presented in this chapter, studies of cybercrimes can, at least for the time being, justifiably be called cyber-criminologies.

Glossary

Critical infrastructure (CI):   installations, services and assets that are essential for the functioning of a society; CI interruption or destruction may have a debilitating impact on social and economic welfare, and on national security. Examples of CI: electricity generation, transmission and distribution; financial services; food production and distribution; gas and oil production, transport and distribution; public health (hospitals, ambulances); security services (police, military); telecommunication; transportation systems; water supply. CI may include material assets whose symbolic content or inherent meaning is deemed important to national cohesion and welfare (see Yar 2013: 51).

Distributed Denial of Service (DDoS) attack   'is an attempt to make a website inaccessible by sending so many requests for access that the site is unable to respond to them all. This is a way of censoring a website by targeting the source of the website and effectively taking it down' (Assange 2014: 74).

Internet Protocol (IP) address   is the unique identifying number that network devices use to identify themselves and communicate.

Logic bomb   is a type of malicious software that activates once predetermined criteria are met, such as a specific date, setting off a malicious function (e.g., damaging a computer network or wiping hard drives and records). Logic bombs can be used to gain momentum and spread before being noticed.

Pharming   is an automated version of *phishing* that tricks the domain name server (DNS) into automatically accepting incorrect access data. By changing the stored records that the target computer uses, people are automatically redirected to fraudulent websites which seem like the victim's own bank site. *Pharming* does not rely upon social engineering to trick people.

Phishing   is the use of internet communications to socially engineer people (trick people) out of personal financial information. Usually, victims are asked to voluntarily log onto the URL given in the email and confirm their personal information details. It is common for *phishing* and *spam* emails to use *spoofing* (the creation of email messages with a forged sender address) to mislead the recipient about the origin of the message; the creation of credible forged 'From' fields in the emails make them more likely to be opened.

Ransomware   is a malicious software that hijacks a computer system through code encryption until a ransom is paid (preferably via cryptocurrency, like Bitcoin) or the victim agrees to infect other systems; the decryption code is then released by the blackmailer.

Sexting   is the exchanging of sexually explicit messages, photographs or images, primarily between mobile phones. It has been promoted further by messaging applications like Snapchat and WhatsApp.

Spamming is the distribution of unsolicited bulk emails that deliver invitations to participate in schemes to earn money, purchase/obtain products and services, etc. The term 'spam' is said to be derived from the Monty Python *Spam Song* sketch in which spam (Hormel Foods' canned ham) dominated a café menu and was sung repeatedly by a group of Vikings (Wall 2007: 133).

Spyware is software that covertly surveys the user's computer files to obtain (by keeping a log of the victim's key-strokes or seeking out financial information stored on the hard-drive) and return personal information about the user to the infector.

***Trashing* (or *dumpster diving*)** is the practice of going through trash bags to obtain discarded documents and personal information for identity theft.

Trojan horse is 'a program that appears to perform a benign or useful function, but in fact has some hidden destructive capabilities that only become apparent after a user has downloaded and installed the software' (Yar 2013: 31).

Viruses are malicious software (malwares) which install themselves without user consent. When executed (activated by human action), they self-replicate, copying their own source code or infecting other computer programs by modifying them.

Worms are 'independent pieces of software capable of self-replication and self-transmission' (Yar 2013: 31). Unlike viruses, worms have the capability to spread without any human action.

Notes

1   Translation from its original in Brazilian Portuguese by Leandro Ayres França and Monica Monawar. The author thanks Paulo Torres, Rodrigo Cavagnari, Clara Masiero and Pat Carlen for their comments on previous drafts.
2   The metaphorical resource of the paper page is old; in *Computer Machinery and Intelligence*, Turing (1950: 441) had already written: 'The [digital] computer includes a store corresponding to the paper used by a human computer. It must be possible to write into the store any one of the combinations of symbols which might have been written on the paper.'
3   The most accurate form would be 'Historically, (…)'. In Heidegger's literature, *Historie* corresponds to the mere chronological listing of events, the expression of a 'calculating thought', whereas *Geschichte* has a different relationship to temporality (i.e. not as an object of historiography), proper to a 'meditative thought'. English translations have not drawn the distinction between their adjectives *historisch* and *geschichtlich*, and have translated both as 'historical'. In other versions (e.g. French, Portuguese), *geschichtlich* has been rendered *historial*.
4   A case, cited by Yar (2013: 2), is paradigmatic: the two Filipino computer programmers who developed the ILOVEYOU worm (see glossary), which attacked tens of millions of computers, causing US$7 to 10 billion in damages worldwide, were released with all charges dropped by state prosecutors since there were no laws in the Philippines against writing malware at the time.
5   'Identity theft' is commonly used to characterise fraudulent use of credit card data, subtracted or falsely obtained, in order to commit retail theft against online vendors; it has been argued, however, that it would be best to apply the expression 'fraud due to impersonation'.

References

Assange, Julian. (2014) *When Google Met WikiLeaks*. New York: OR Books.

Brenner, Susan W. (2001) 'Is There Such a Thing as "Virtual Crime"?', *California Criminal Law Review*, v. 4, n. 1.

Brown, Sheila. (2006) 'The Criminology of Hybrids: Rethinking Crime and Law in Technosocial Networks', *Theoretical Criminology*, v. 10, n. 2, pp. 223–244.

Brown, Sheila. (2013) 'Virtual Criminology', in McLaughlin, Eugene; Muncie, John (eds), *The SAGE Dictionary of Criminology*, 3. ed. London: SAGE, pp. 486–488.

Capeller, Wanda. (2001) 'Not Such a Neat Net: Some Comments on Virtual Criminality', trans. Serena Barkham-Huxley, *Social & Legal Studies*, v. 10, n. 2, pp. 229–242.

Garland, David; Sparks, Richard. (2000) 'Criminology, Social Theory and the Challenge of Our Times', *British Journal of Criminology*, v. 40, n. 2, pp. 189–204.

Grabosky, Peter N. (2001) 'Virtual Criminality: Old Wine in New Bottles?', *Social & Legal Studies*, v. 10, n. 2, pp. 243–249.

Heidegger, Martin. (1953/1977) *The Question Concerning Technology, and Other Essays*, trans. William Lovitt. New York/London: Garland Publishing/Harper & Row Publishers.

Hollinger, Richard Clifton. (2001) 'Computer Crime', in Luckenbill, David; Peck, Denis (eds), *Encyclopedia of Crime and Juvenile Delinquency (Vol. II)*. Philadelphia: Taylor and Francis, pp. 76–81.

Jaishankar, K. (2007) 'Cyber Criminology: Evolving a Novel Discipline with a New Journal', *International Journal of Cyber Criminology*, v. 1, n. 1, pp. 1–6.

Jaishankar, K. (2010) 'The Future of Cyber Criminology: Challenges and Opportunities', *International Journal of Cyber Criminology*, v. 4, n. 1&2, pp. 26–31.

Lessig, Lawrence. (1998) *The Laws of Cyberspace: Draft 3*. Taipei: Taiwan Net '98.

Lévy, Pierre. (2001) *Cyberculture*, trans. Robert Bononno. Minneapolis: University of Minnesota Press.

McQuade, Sam. (2006) 'Technology-Enabled Crime, Policing and Security', *Journal of Technology Studies*, v. 32, n. 1, pp. 32–42.

Olson, Parmy. (2012) *We Are Anonymous: Inside the Hacker World of LulzSec, Anonymous, and the Global Cyber Insurgency*. New York: Back Bay Books.

Rüdiger, Francisco. (2014) *Martin Heidegger e a questão da técnica: prospectos acerca do futuro do homem*, 2. ed. Porto Alegre: Sulina.

Souza, Bernardo de Azevedo e. (2016) *Direito, tecnologia e práticas punitivas*. Porto Alegre: Canal Ciências Criminais.

Sutherland, Edwin Hardin. (1945) 'Is "White Collar Crime" Crime?', *American Sociological Review*, v. 10, n. 2, pp. 132–139.

Turing, Alan Mathison. (1950) 'Computing Machinery and Intelligence', *Mind*, v. LIX, n. 236, pp. 433–460.

Wall, David S. (2007) *Cybercrime: The Transformation of Crime in the Information Age*. Cambridge: Polity.

Yar, Majid. (2005) 'The Novelty of "Cybercrime": An Assessment in Light of Routine Activity Theory', *European Journal of Criminology*, v. 2, n. 4, pp. 407–427.

Yar, Majid. (2013) *Cybercrime and Society*, 2 ed. London: SAGE.

Zedner, Lucia. (2007) 'Pre-Crime and Post-Criminology?', *Theoretical Criminology*, v. 11, n. 2, pp. 261–281.

PART II
Critical issues for the 21st century

13

CRIME AND MEDIA

Eamonn Carrabine

It is often said that we live in a media-saturated world, and this chapter will explore how some of the dynamics between crime and justice are conceived in an era of global interconnectedness.[1] The transformations in media technology wrought by print, telegraph and wireless communication, which gave birth to the electronic age from the mid-twentieth century, have led to the phenomenon of mediatization. Defined as a powerful force eroding divisions between 'fact and fiction, nature and culture, global and local, science and art, technology and humanity' to the extent that 'the media in the twenty-first century have so undermined the ability to construct an *apparent* distinction between reality and representation that the modernist episteme has begun to seem somewhat shaky' (Brown 2003: 22, emphasis in original). In other words, the advent of postmodernity has meant that it is becoming increasingly impossible to distinguish between media image and social reality (Osborne 1995: 28). This blurring of boundaries is captured well in the following passage:

> Today, as criminals videotape their crimes and post them on YouTube, as security agents scrutinize the image-making of criminals on millions of surveillance monitors, as insurrectionist groups upload video compilations (filmed from several angles) of 'successful' suicide bomb attacks and roadside IED (Improvised Explosive Device) detonations, as images of brutality and victimization pop up on office computer screens and children's mobile phones, as 'reality TV' shows take the viewer ever deeper inside the world of the beat cop and prison setting, there can be no other option but the development of a thoroughgoing *visual* criminology.
>
> *(Hayward 2010: 2, emphasis in original)*

It is significant that Keith Hayward is drawn to the concept of 'Mediascape' (Appadurai 1996) in his efforts to develop a visual criminology that can grasp how the power of images plays a decisive role in shaping the social imaginary. Of course, the 2011 protests and revolutions in the Middle East were also characterized by distinctive forms of cyber-organizing through social media like Facebook, Twitter and YouTube, which helped shape grassroots political activism while also enabling new forms of surveillance dedicated to countering dissent.

These are important arguments for understanding the relationships between crime and the media, not least since the very reach of global media networks is now unparalleled. Of course, it is not simply that there are many more media technologies consumed all over the world, but that these developments are breaking down conventional understandings of time and space by making events instantly available to us wherever we are. The 'speed' of modern communication is not a politically neutral occurrence (Virilio 1986), as the acceleration of perception does not necessarily bring us closer together but can reinforce the distance between neighbours and strangers. In a classic essay on television news Michael Ignatieff (1999: 25) has described how this tendency has prompted 'one of the dangerous cultural moods of our time', the belief that the world is so out of control and so dreadful that all we can do is disengage from it.

This experience of dislocation and fatalism is far removed from the optimism of the earliest media theorists, who saw the growth in electronic communications in positive terms. Marshall McLuhan (1964/1994), for example, coined the term 'global village' to describe how modern media could transcend the divisive nationalisms of the past, increasing mutual responsibility and uniting us all. As we will see, these diametrically opposed understandings continue to shape debates on the nature of the global public sphere and its significance for the future of the human condition. Indeed, the concept of 'mediapolis' has been developed to convey 'both the reality and the possibility of global communication' (Silverstone 2007: 22) and we will shortly be exploring how mediated space offers certain possibilities, while curtailing others. The chapter begins by setting out how the implications of the proliferation of global media have been understood, before turning to how the concept of moral panic has been developed by criminologists to grapple with the force of representation. It then describes how media theorists have sought to understand the social relations fostered by increasingly networked societies. In order to further unravel the politics of representation the chapter turns to the controversies and debates surrounding how pornography infiltrates and proliferates in modern media culture.

Given that global interdependence between societies has reached the levels it has, there are growing debates over how this new world should be lived in, which have been approached through the lens of cosmopolitanism and the idea that the media provide a global civic space. Roger Silverstone (2007: 22) has termed this space the 'mediapolis', as one of the most important roles the media, in all their diversity, perform is the setting of boundaries and in doing so it poses important questions on how 'the relations between self and other are to be conducted in a global public sphere'. It then follows that such topics as media justice, compassion, hospitality and responsibility emerge as key conditions shaping a more ethical media culture in which the 'mediated other will be listened to and heard' (Silverstone 2007: 24). Like the *polis* of ancient Greece, modern mediated space offers one thing but often delivers another less than virtuous social environment, reinforcing social divisions and typically stifling critical debate.

Silverstone (2007: 19) emphasizes just how much of the media's work is concerned with constructing and maintaining boundaries – from micro to macro levels their 'primary cultural role' is a ceaseless 'playing with difference and sameness'. Beginning in the nineteenth century with the newspaper press and then cinema, radio and television there emerged a mass media; as each of these technologies grew from initial uncertainty and intense competition with older, more established media they eventually forged equally advantageous relationships in many instances. This is what he describes as a 'centripetal phase' where each medium 'articulated the boundaries of national and linguistic cultures', whereas now we live in an era where the media are more 'centrifugal' and developments like the Internet have profoundly changed the shape of communication, reaching out to the 'social margins' and making 'boundary work … even more significant, if not more challenging and complex' (Silverstone 2007: 19). The rise of digital media and technoculture have certainly seen a vast expansion of global cultural flows, with a greater emphasis on interactivity, but a key question remains over the kinds of connectivity encouraged in increasingly networked societies. The dominant preoccupations of criminologists in this area over the last forty years or so has been with the distinctive moral force of the media, and it is here we begin with the concept of moral panic.

Moral panics in an age of anxiety

The concept of moral panic is one of the few terms from the social sciences that have entered into popular vocabulary. From its initial formulation in the early 1970s the concept has been adapted, criticized and dismissed in equal measure by criminologists, sociologists and other commentators. Yet, at the same time, the social processes described by moral panic theory are now so well known to journalists, politicians and within the culture industries generally that certain reactions are entirely predictable and greeted with cynical weariness, or even ridicule, when the scaremongering becomes all too transparent.

Although the experience of fear is universal to the human condition and felt by every living creature, the actual sources of dread are socially distributed. It was only in the 1930s that the social sciences began to draw attention to the specific problems posed by anxiety when the impact of Freudian psychoanalysis started to register in the broader intellectual climate. Indeed, the key insight is that anxiety is the price we pay for possessing a sense of self. Ever since the publication of W. H. Auden's (1948) epic poem *The Age of Anxiety*, written just after the terror of world war, numerous commentators have used the title to describe the existential fate of modern times. By the end of the twentieth century terms like 'culture of fear', 'fear of crime' and 'risk society' had been coined – each announcing that we live in an era of intense worry, while many of the debates surrounding 'postmodernism' have been understood as a kind of '*fin-de-siècle* neurosis' (Wilkinson 2001: 4). Even though commentators were initially reluctant to describe the aftermath of the 11 September 2001 attacks as a form of 'repressive hysteria' (Garland 2008: 25) there is evidence that this has begun to change, with work appearing that now describes the social reaction from within a broad moral panic framework (Weber and Lee 2009).

Moral panics can be analysed from a range of theoretical perspectives. These include the symbolic interactionism of the original definitions, later Marxist revisions, various postmodern challenges as well as more orthodox attempts to tame the concept in American sociology through the study of collective behaviour. Yet what is lost in this migration is any sense of the urgent politics of anxiety that is crucial to the development of the concept in Britain. Indeed, here all of the recent attempts to update the concept are drawn to the risk society thesis, while across the Atlantic North American scholarship has focused on social problem construction in ways that have often required the analyst to suspend any 'particular political or ideological assumptions' (Best 2008: ix). However, I will argue that the concept remains a crucial one and needs to reconnect more thoroughly with the sociology of modernity to make sense of the fears haunting our social worlds. I begin by outlining the sociological origins of moral panics, before describing the criticisms the concept has received and then insisting that contemporary media spectacles do still foster distinctive moral relations in quite fundamental ways.

From the outset the concept of moral panic has been concerned with societal reactions and their symptomatic character – how they are rooted in major underlying structural changes and the impassioned outrage they can provoke – reveals much about the contours of normality, tolerance and repression endured in a society. The founding texts are Jock Young's (1971) *The Drugtakers* and Stanley Cohen's (1972/2002) *Folk Devils and Moral Panics*. They both innovatively built on developments in the American sociology of deviance tradition. These, combined with the British statistician Lesley Wilkins's (1964) understanding of 'deviancy amplification', were crucial to how the concept developed in Britain. Both acknowledge the influence of Marshall McLuhan's (1964/1994) celebrated account of the consequences of the shift from print to electronic media, captured in his iconic phrase that the 'medium is the message'.

McLuhan (1964/1994) argued that the world initially expanded through urbanization and transport developments, but has now 'imploded' as the mass media bring the world closer together again. It is this 'implosive factor' that Cohen and Young (1973: 340) find essential for the 'media are the major and at times the sole source of information about a whole range of phenomena' and thereby 'points to continual bombardment by images of phenomena that otherwise could be conveniently forgotten'. The model used to explain how moral panics occur is deviancy amplification and versions of it are to be found in all the classic studies. Cohen (1972/2002) uses the notion to show how the petty delinquencies of rival groups of mods and rockers at seaside resorts were blown up into serious threats to law and order, and he goes to some lengths to situate the moral panic in social context. In particular, the hostile reaction revealed much about how post-war social change was being experienced. The new affluence and sexual freedom of teenage youth cultures in the 1960s fuelled jealousy and resentment among a parental generation who had themselves grown up experiencing the hungry depression of the 1930s, traumatic world war and subsequent drab austerity.

Young (1971) also used the idea of deviancy amplification in his study of drug use in bohemian London, describing how the mass media transformed marijuana use into a social problem through sensationalist and lurid accounts of hippie lifestyles. Crucially, he notes how the high pitched indignation contains a potent mix of fascination and repulsion, dread and desire that moral guardians exhibit towards the objects of their anxiety. There is a strong Durkheimian theme here, in that the boundaries of normality and order are reinforced through the condemnation of the deviant and thereby generating powerful feelings of 'collective effervescence'. But what Cohen (1972/2002) and Young (1971) both were emphasizing was that this process only occurred in modernity through a considerable distortion of reality.

This emphasis on how the media distort the reality of social problems was developed by Stuart Hall and his colleagues at the Birmingham Centre for Contemporary Cultural Studies in their *Policing the Crisis: Mugging, the State, and Law and Order* (1978). In this book an explicitly Marxist account of crime is developed that stands in some contrast to this Durkheimian sociology of deviance tradition. The book draws together the Birmingham Centre's work on youth subcultures, media representation and ideological analysis in a magisterial account of the hegemonic crisis in Britain that began in the late 1960s and anticipates the victory of Margaret Thatcher's authoritarian 'law and order' programme in the 1980s. The book ostensibly explores the moral panic that developed in Britain in the early 1970s over the phenomenon of mugging. Hall and his colleagues demonstrate how the police, media and judiciary interact to produce ideological closure around the issue through a signification spiral. Black youth are cast as the folk devil in police and media portrayals of the archetypal mugger – a scapegoat for all social anxieties produced by the changes to an affluent, but destabilized society.

Critical issues

In mainstream criminology the moral panic concept has received extensive criticism. Some took issue with the empirical evidence presented by Hall and his colleagues (Waddington 1986) and for overstating the extent to which the criminality crisis was contrived by elites for dominant interests (Goode and Ben-Yehuda 1994). Sympathetic critics have applauded the theoretical sophistication of the analysis, but worry about the consequences this has had for the study of street crime (Hallsworth 2008). By the 1990s the complaint had become that the concept of moral panic is used indiscriminately and 'applied to anything from single mothers to working mothers, from guns to Ecstasy, and from pornography on the Internet to the dangers of state censorship' (Miller and Kitzinger 1998: 221). Meanwhile, others warned against eliding all anxieties under a single heading 'of some (hypothetically universal, endlessly cyclical) feature of social life, namely panickyness' (Sparks 1992: 65).

In his wide-ranging review of the concept Cohen (2002: xxvii) acknowledged that the term 'panic' has caused much trouble, but remains 'convinced that the analogy works'. The term does still convey well the drama, urgency and energy of certain media narratives, but problems persist in the contrast between an 'irrational' panic and the supposedly 'rational' analysis of it. It is this last difficulty that lies at the centre of Simon Watney's (1987/1997) perceptive critique. He argued that the gradual and staged creation of folk devils as described in classic moral panic theory was incapable of grasping how the entire field of sexuality is saturated with 'monstrous' representations. Nor can it distinguish between different degrees of anxiety or explain how sexuality is regulated through a multiplicity of overlapping and competing institutions.

These ideas were developed by Angela McRobbie and Sarah Thornton (1995) in their influential attempt to update moral panic theory in the light of multi-mediated social worlds. Their argument emphasizes that contemporary moral panics now have an extremely short shelf life and a rapid rate of turnover, making it extremely difficult to cling to a model that emphasizes their episodic quality, spirals and flows. In addition to their increase in frequency moral panics are also now far more likely to be contested, while the 'hard and fast boundaries between "normal" and "deviant" would seem to be less common' (McRobbie and Thornton 1995: 572–573). On their reckoning these changes result from the vast expansion and diversification of the mass media, which for Garland (2008: 17, emphasis in original) heralds a significant 'shift *away* from moral panics as traditionally conceived (involving a vertical relation between society and a deviant group) towards something more closely resembling American-style "culture wars" (which involve a more horizontal conflict between social groups)'.

The extent of pluralism should not be overstated here. While it is clear that there has been a proliferation of communication technologies encouraging new spaces for diverse niche interests, there has also been a broader tendency towards the merging of news and entertainment. Arguably it is conflict rather than consensus that is the decisive change. This is due to the bitterness of contemporary identity politics, which not only provokes deeply polarized reactions to most social issues but suggests a significant normative shift in the status of many deviant groups has taken place. Though clearly not all, as the pariah figures of the paedophile and terrorist continue to testify in very different ways. Likewise, Young (2009: 13) has recently described how indignant moral outrage is still stoked by powerful feelings of *ressentiment*:

> the alarm about pit-bulls may well be vested in the fears of an underclass, of 'chavs', the pronouncement on the dangers of binge drinking may well relate to a moral dislike of the hedonism of modern youth, and the 'dissolute' nature of the night-time economy.

It is highly significant that much of the earlier commentary on the underclass relied on characterizing certain groups in the working class as suffering from a pathological relationship to *production* (the world of socially useful labour), whereas 'chavs' are defined through a pathological relationship with *consumption* – as manifest in dire forms of taste poverty (Hayward and Yar 2006).

At the same time there have arisen new sites of social anxiety generated by the pace and scale of industrial advances in western societies. Since the mid-1980s particular fears have built up around nuclear, chemical, biological, environmental, genetic and medical hazards. Some well-known examples include global warming, nuclear fallout, toxic pollution, BSE, bird flu and other food scares that have made us acutely aware of the catastrophic potential of scientific and technological developments. Many have turned to the concept of 'risk society' (Beck 1986) to understand the anxieties provoked by these transitions to late modernity. According to Beck the pace of technological innovation generates global risks, such as nuclear war and environmental catastrophe, which outstrip our ability to control them, creating new hazards and uncertainties that previous generations did not have to face. Yet accompanying these global risks is a more pervasive 'ambient fear' that 'saturates the social spaces of everyday life' and 'requires us to vigilantly monitor even the banal minutiae of our lives' (Hubbard 2003: 52). Urban fortress living, manifest in the protection of privileged consumption places (private homes, retail parks, heritage centres, leisure complexes) distinguishes between those who belong and those who threaten. Each of these defensive responses to insecurity only serves to heighten our awareness of unforeseen danger lurking around every corner.

The increased frequency of dramatic moral narratives in the mass media over the last two decades is partly a response to the increased pressures of market competition, but is also a key means by which

> the at-risk character of modern society is magnified and is particularly inclined to take the form of moral panics in modern Britain due to factors such as the loss of authority of traditional elites, anxieties about national identity in the face of increasing external influences and internal diversity.
>
> *(Thompson 1998: 141)*

Moral panics are now an integral dimension of modern media culture. They have become an institutionalized part of social life and are a routine part of governing through crime – encouraging a new kind of political subjectivity that sees danger and menace everywhere. Malcolm Feeley and Jonathan Simon (2007: 51) contend that 'moral panics are now part of the manufactured background, a feature of the larger order of knowledge and power that never goes away or recedes, and that must be constantly guarded against'. In this they share the diagnosis that the 'problem of uncertainty' (Ericson 2007: 204) has become the dominant principle organizing political authority and social relations in neo-liberal societies.

What is missing though is an account of the implosive character of contemporary media spectacles and the distinctive moral relationships that the media impose upon audiences. These are crucial points, as indignant denunciation is only one way of responding to what is seen and read – indeed, one of the fundamental requirements of viewing is that we are obliged to take sides. The act of not looking, or changing channels, if a story is too disturbing is to ignore the pain experienced by others. To turn away, feel pity, get angry or be overwhelmed by the horror of it all are each dispositions that a culture of spectatorship encourages. In what follows I develop these arguments through a consideration of the different moral relations the modern mass media cultivate and their place in public life.

Understanding media

Both Jock Young and Stan Cohen have made clear their indebtedness to the famous Canadian media theorist Marshall McLuhan. Although McLuhan remains a somewhat controversial figure his overall contribution is one that emphasizes how different media fundamentally change social life. Throughout his career McLuhan remained convinced that developments in media technologies brought many benefits, especially with 'cool' media – like television, hi-fi systems and telephones – that require high levels of audience participation to complete meaning. In doing so these media reconnect our senses, encourage intense involvement and bring us together to produce social bonds enabling the 'human family' to become 'tribal once more' (McLuhan 1964/1994: 172). One of the examples he uses is how televised events like President Kennedy's funeral illustrate the 'unrivalled power of TV' to unite 'an entire population in a ritual process' (McLuhan 1964/1994: 337). The key significance then of the 'implosion' of electric media is that they do not just bring us physically closer together, but emotionally move us to communally participate in human solidarity. This is an understanding of the media that sees the possibilities of a global conscience united in emotional empathy towards the suffering of distant strangers. Had he lived to see the public responses to the Ethiopia famine in 1984, the Asian tsunami in 2004 and the Haiti earthquake in 2010 then he may well have found encouraging evidence for this internationalization of responsibility that media coverage makes possible.

Of course, the early moral panic theorists shared this Durkheimian understanding of the power of the mass media to ritually unite communities in emotionally charged ways, but the shared indignation generated in response to certain kinds of deviance was regarded as not only unhealthy but intensely neurotic. In highlighting the collective hostility moral panics unleash the new deviancy theorists were also echoing other critics of McLuhan's optimistic understanding of the media. One of the earliest rebukes came from Guy Debord (1967/ 1977: 29) who maintained that far from unifying humanity in a network of communication the global village marks the triumph of capitalism as a 'global spectacle' that shatters the 'unity of the world'. Raymond Williams (1974/1990: 127–129) took issue with McLuhan's technological determinism and criticized his 'idealist model of human history'. Even those who are clearly influenced by McLuhan reverse his central claims:

> Much of the time we are witnesses to what is rightly called a 'pseudo' public sphere, where politicians and docile politicians act out a travesty of democratic debate. No wonder, as Jean Baudrillard (1983) suggests, the masses are generally turned off from 'serious' politics and turned on to something else that is much more entertaining.
>
> *(McGuigan 2005: 429)*

Ever since Baudrillard's (1967/2001) review of *Understanding Media*, he has been regarded as a postmodern proponent of McLuhan's vision. Yet he utterly rejects neo-tribal optimism, while taking the idea that the 'medium is the message' beyond anything envisaged by McLuhan. Baudrillard (2001: 42) follows McLuhan by seeing the message of television as lying not in its content, but in 'the new modes of relations and perceptions that it imposes' and its destructive replacement of lived relations with semiotic relations. Too much is seen obscenely fast. As he puts it, we 'are no longer a part of the drama of alienation; we live in the ecstasy of communication' and 'this ecstasy is obscene' (Baudrillard 1985: 130). Baudrillard's is clearly a hyperbolic voice, but his overall point is that the contemporary media transform social experiences in quite damaging ways – where the banal becomes serious, democracy turns into show business and incoherence is privileged over meaningful debate.

In this pessimistic assessment of the mass media he is joined by Jürgen Habermas (1962/1989) who influentially described how the formation of a bourgeois public sphere in the eighteenth century marked a decisive stage in the development of rational debate. The transition from feudalism to capitalism brought with it the commodification of culture and opened up the liberal, democratic possibility of well-informed individuals resolving their differences through enlightened reason rather than brute force. Yet by the nineteenth century the public sphere had become contaminated and weakened through 'refeudalization' – in that advertising, public relations and other techniques of information management have returned the public sphere to trivial spectacle and subordinate to selective commercial interests. Extending this argument to the early twenty-first century we can see how political spin doctors, global media corporations and tabloid celebrity marketing have replaced monarchs, church and nobility as the patrons and sponsors of much mass communication.

Of course, critics have disputed the appropriateness of the feudal analogy to contemporary media, whereas others claim that he has idealized the bourgeois public sphere. Habermas initially responded by acknowledging that social interests shape communication, but he insists the Enlightenment remains an unfinished project as the possibilities of communicative rationality have yet to be realized. More recently he has suggested that there may well be some cosmopolitan potential in mediated communication, but in the final analysis he retains the pessimistic verdict (Habermas 2006: 9–10). There are evidently parallels with Silverstone's (2007) own understanding of the mediapolis, which he describes is:

> both more and less than the Habermasian public sphere. It is more because within it communication is multiple and multiply inflected: there is no rationality in an image, and no singular reason in a narrative ... The mediapolis is less than the public sphere, in its modesty. There is no expectation that all the requirements for fully effective communication can be met by those responsible for its initiation, and those, in good faith, who contribute to it.
>
> *(Silverstone 2007: 33)*

Clearly there are some fundamental differences here. Arguably the real power of contemporary media lies in the way each of these forces neutralize one another – rendering audiences almost helpless before the endless flow of mediated misery encountered in their daily lives. It has even been noted that the most profound moral demand television makes on spectators is to place us as witnesses of human suffering, without giving us the option to act directly on it (Ellis 2000: 1). However, there are many ways spectators respond to, and actively involve themselves with, what they see on screen, read in newspapers or browse online.

Ethics, rhetoric and spectatorship

A central claim of this chapter is that the discourses produced by mediated moral panics should be understood as rhetorics of indignant denunciation – these are typically directed at the scapegoats, but the persecutors could also find themselves angrily accused of prejudice. In his account of how modern media use images and language to render distant suffering not only intelligible but also morally acceptable to the spectator Luc Boltanski (1999) identifies three rhetorical 'topics' in which audiences engage with mediated misfortune. The distinctive argument is that ever since the end of the eighteenth century, when pity became central to politics, the topics of 'denunciation', 'sentiment' and 'aesthetics' have become the ethically proper ways of responding to the disturbing spectacles of distant suffering. In doing so they provide an invaluable starting point for understanding how mediatized events can, at times, unleash great social change; while at others produce little more than banal indifference amongst media audiences. Each involve competing ways of organizing emotions and, by extension, the norms that govern the ethics of cosmopolitan citizenship.

Although indignant denunciation is motivated by anger it 'can be criticised as an empty substitute for action' (Boltanski 1999: 70) and is often discredited for the ways it appeals to vindictive desires like revenge, envy and resentment. A second way in which spectators can sympathize with the unfortunate is through 'sentiment', which provokes a 'tender-heartedness' that recognizes the suffering of another, so as to be moved to compassion. However, it is the very sentimentalism itself that has been condemned and disqualified as an indulgence. To take an example, ever since the 1960s the image of a starving African child, with pleading eyes, had become a powerful symbol of human suffering and was used by agencies like Oxfam and Save the Children in appeals to western adults for charitable donations.

By the 1980s the images had become more shocking – pictures of emaciated bodies of starving young children, only hours from death, featured in a number of campaigns – accompanied with text explaining that 'While you're eating between meals, he's dying between meals' and 'You're not the only one with weight problems' (Holland 2006: 153–155). At the same time neo-colonial critics attacked this kind of imagery for stressing helplessness and dependence, which sustains 'a patronizing, offensive and misleading view of the developing world as a spectacle of tragedy, disaster, disease and cruelty' (Cohen 2001: 178). From the 1990s onward such imagery was denounced as 'aid pornography' while hiding the close relationships between western affluence and the increasing poverty in the rest of the world. New codes of practice were drafted in response and most agencies pursued a strategy of 'positive images' where recipients are not seen as feeble beneficiaries of charitable donations.

Problems remain though about the reality behind, and the rhetoric, of the image – too much 'information can confuse the power of the image, and an understanding of political complexities deflects emotional response' (Holland 2006: 155). Of course, these humanitarian organizations are acutely aware of 'compassion fatigue' and have developed sophisticated ways of renewing campaigns in response to criticism and apathy. One recent policy, favoured among a number of international development charities, has been to use celebrities as a way of attracting popular media coverage and personalizing complex situations so that foreign affairs are made accessible to the ordinary public. The worry is that by transforming politics into entertainment the difficulties surrounding development issues are submerged beneath the banalities of celebrity lifestyle, brand identity and show business.

It is also the case that new media technologies themselves have generated distinctive anxieties, which should not be simply reduced to a fear of the new, but rather that a certain paranoid disposition structures much of the debate. It is one that has been described as a 'hermeneutics of paranoia' that arises in 'a particular context of self to technology and the visual' (Fuery 2009: 70), and thereby governs much of the mistrust, threat and uncertainty surrounding new technology. This is especially evident in how the mainstream media have tended to depict the Internet, which has been through the 'rhetoric of "moral panic"' where digital culture is depicted in 'negative terms' where threats like viruses, spam, fraud, stalking and various other kinds of electronic harassment proliferate, while the users are 'pathologized' and typically described in distinctive ways: 'the excessive female body, the abused female body, the "pirate" teenager, the tech-savvy Al-Qaeda operative' are just some of the examples that have been identified (Gournelos and Gunkel 2012: 10).

Yet the most prevalent focus of public concern over new media technology centres on the problems posed by pornography, which take a number of forms and are worth exploring in more detail. Not least since the issue enables a consideration of specific policy implications, and will allow a more nuanced account of the politics of representation to emerge. Newspaper editors have long been aware of how sex sells – from the sexualization of mundane events, through the detailing of celebrity sex scandals, to the salacious reporting of violent sex crime – yet today a porn aesthetic has become firmly 'mainstreamed' (Attwood 2010a) across a broad range of social activities. Alongside the 'pornification' (Paasonen et al. 2007) of modern media culture, much attention has also focused on images thought to exist at the edges of culture that are seen as increasingly extreme and shocking.

Pornography, sexualization and regulation

The origins of modern attitudes to pornography have been traced back to the merging of two very different events occurring in the late eighteenth century: the creation of 'secret museums' for objects classified as obscene and the growing volume of writing about prostitution (Kendrick 1987). Historians have shown how literary and visual representations of 'sex' have varied over time, as have ideas of what to regulate and prohibit. But it is clear that by the nineteenth century the definitions of what was pornographic, obscene or indecent depended on who could access the material, which was largely restricted to erudite men. The assumption was that only a privileged few specialists could read and look at a class of objects, while the great many could not. Pornography as a distinctive form of regulation emerges in 'response to the perceived menace of the democratization of culture' (Hunt 1996: 13). By the middle of the century states across Europe increasingly turned to the moral surveillance of their subjects and the first major obscenity trials were conducted initially in France, then England and Germany, before the United States embarked on their own crusades against pornography.

It was the Victorians who influentially defined obscenity as material that had the capacity to 'deprave and corrupt' in legislation that still shapes contemporary debates (Kendrick 1987: 121). The history of censorship and obscenity laws reveals that state control was justified in the name of protecting the weak – particularly the young, poor and female – from the dangers of immorality. Once the trade moved from being just between gentlemen, but circulated on the unruly metropolitan streets, it was then that obscenity became a social problem, driven by concerns of the availability of such material for mass consumption and advances in print media.

Producers have always been adept at exploiting the latest technology and it is clear that the invention of photography considerably changed the nature of sexual imagery and secured the place of sexuality in modern, commodity culture. The traffic in illicit images flourished from the medium's inception. Louis Daguerre patented the daguerreotype in 1840 and within ten years the French government were sufficiently alarmed by the circulation of explicit photographs to introduce legislation prohibiting the sale of obscene photographs (Kendrick 1987: 248). In an important essay on photographic history Abigail Soloman-Godeau (1991: 233–237) maintains that amidst all this 'sexually coded imagery' there is an important 'shift from a conception of the sexual as an activity to a new emphasis on specularity – the sexual constituted as a visual field' which is intimately linked to other cultural developments, like the newly invented department stores organized around the fetishistic display of goods and the enormous popularity of 'illusionistic spectacles' produced by stereoscopes, magic lanterns and dioramas in the Victorian era. In her account, photography produces an 'erotics of the fragment', especially of female body parts, and it is this commodification of women – closely tied to the eroticizing of commodities – that is the hallmark of consumer culture.

It is also clear that as long as the pornographic market was restricted to the upper classes, it articulated their obsessions: libertine, scientific and objectifying the subordinated (Sigel 2002). One example is the 'occidental fascination with the harem' which depicted a 'microcosm of empire where sexual conquest was commensurate with imperial conquest' (Colligan 2006: 23). Developments in print technology were crucial, as they enabled texts and images to be consumed by a wider public, eventually reaching the masses in cheap visual form by the 1880s through the invention of photolithography, which permitted the inexpensive manufacture of pornographic picture postcards and distribution on an international scale. One estimate has it that some 140 billion postcards were sent around the world between 1894 and 1919, while many more were collected and never sent through the mail (Sigel 2002: 122). These illicit images recycled already well-established conventions and reproduced social divisions, emphasizing racial and sexual subordination for a mass market. Ultimately, it was the expansion of empire in the nineteenth century that enabled the traffic in pornography, informing its fantasies and facilitating its movement around the world.

The invention of motion pictures in the 1890s enabled further displays of nudity and cinematic pornography is credited as emerging in France, but with others quick to follow – notably Argentina, Austria, Italy and the United States. These 'stag films' were shot in 10 minute lengths so as to fit on 'a single, easily smuggled reel' and featured 'hard-core intercourse interspersed with raucous intertitles' (Milter and Slade 2005: 173). Alongside film, inexpensive paperbacks, illustrated pamphlets, slot machines and the burgeoning postcard trade further enabled the distribution of pornography across the class structure and national markets. Although various states countered the expansion of consumer pornography by organizing censorship campaigns and passing new legislation, these measures did little to stall the trade. After World War II the American cultural influence in Western Europe proved to be decisive, especially with the arrival of 'pin-up girls' then ubiquitous in the popular culture of the 1940s and 1950s, allowing a very 'public model of sexuality' to flourish, which was then followed by the American 'porno' film and magazine (Sigel 2005: 15). By the 1960s and 1970s many European governments began to partially legalize pornography in response to a more 'permissive' mood of sexual liberation, while new legal definitions of artistic, historical and literary merit emerged in the landmark obscenity trials of the era.

Technological innovations have always been crucial to the development of the pornography industry, and the example of the battle between VHS and Betamax video formats in the late 1970s is often used to illustrate the case. Betamax eventually lost out to VHS, despite having a superior picture and sound quality, and this defeat is attributed to their refusal to license pornography. Of course, other factors played an important role and while the history of porn can be regarded as a journey from print to film, video, CD-ROM, DVD and up to the Internet, with an increasing emphasis on the visual image over the written word, it is important to note that the industry today makes use of commercial strategies based on convergence. That is the content and distribution are managed in such a way that the same product can be marketed across different formats and platforms, while media mergers have seen single corporations now owning what were previously distinct and separate areas of commercial activity. Companies that initially made their fortunes from magazines, like Larry Flint Publishing and Playboy, have moved into DVD and Web production and distribution, pay-per-view TV and retailing to increase profits and exert greater control over the industry (Paasonen et al. 2007: 6). Indeed, it has been argued that just like mainstream media corporations 'porn companies with global ambitions regard mastery of distribution as more crucial than increased production' (Milter and Slade 2005: 176) when it comes to profit maximization.

Nevertheless, the 'video revolution' heralded a vast increase and change in the production and distribution of hardcore pornography. Although adult theatre releases of feature-length films had enlarged mainstream markets, it was home video technology that enabled the expansion of pornographic media into more private spaces of consumption from the 1980s. This development was further facilitated by the rapid growth of the Internet, where online pornography was crucial in demonstrating the commercial promise of the new technology. Certainly, the industry 'pioneered deluxe online shopping mall designs, secure payment systems and video streaming' (O'Toole 1998: 369) and the increased accessibility of porn, alongside the anonymity of online consumption, has transformed sexuality in quite profound ways (Dines 2010). These technological developments have also been accompanied by changes in media regulation, which has seen many countries relaxing censorship laws and thereby enabled the mainstreaming of pornography, which has been accompanied by a broader sexualization of popular culture over the last three decades. The changes are far from straightforward and are multi-faceted, so it is worth examining them in more detail.

Mainstream culture

One distinction has it that the sexualization of culture describes a wide array of phenomena, where sex permeates practically every aspect of existence, while pornification is a more specific term referring to the blurred boundaries between pornography and mainstream media (Paasonen et al. 2007: 8). The latter describes the proliferation of sexually explicit imagery from the late 1980s onwards. As porn became 'chic' across the worlds of high art and popular culture, where artists like Robert Mapplethorpe and Cindy Sherman deliberately deployed a pornographic aesthetic in their work, while pop stars including Madonna, Lady Gaga and Britney Spears have drawn on imageries from the commercial sex trade to bring an illicit edge to their performances, so the codes and conventions of pornographic representational practice have 'become acceptable, even fashionable' (McNair 2010: 55). Since the 1990s there has been a significant change in how women's bodies have been represented in advertising, with the accent on fun, pleasure and empowerment, which now presents women as active, desiring sexual subjects – rather than the passive, mute objects of the past.

By incorporating porn into mainstream media products the intention is clearly to use some of the 'dirty glamour' and 'sense of danger' associated with porn, but in doing so the media legitimate and normalize sexual imagery in the fabric of everyday life (Poynor 2006: 132). More recently Lee clothing and American Apparel have run controversial advertising campaigns that deploy the aesthetics of amateur pornography in ways that are 'not always "lighter" or less extreme' (Neely 2012: 102) than that featured in hard-core imagery. The visual references are typically deployed through an ironic, knowing tone of address that marks out the parody as a question of style, taste and sensibility in an effort to undermine potential criticisms. Those who do take the issues too seriously are unable to get how porn revels in artificiality, excess and pastiche. It is this logic that informs how advertisers have come to produce commercials ridiculing the vocabulary of their own trade. In some respects, this is simply repackaging old sexual stereotypes in a new brash language of female empowerment. In others, it is an attempt to address hip, young, urban consumers who are regarded by advertisers as sceptical and knowing, with a postfeminist emphasis on women gaining power and control through the commodification of their appearance. This is a subtle, but decisive shift, not least since it makes 'critique much more difficult' as Rosalind Gill (2010: 107) has shown in her analysis of how 'porn chic' has become normalized in advertising imagery.

More generally sex has become increasingly visible in mainstream western culture, changing the meanings of sexuality, developing new forms of 'public intimacy' (McNair 2002), and now an important site of leisure and consumption. In the British context, where commercial sex had been restricted to seedy backstreet sex shops or the top shelves of newsagents the landscape has changed considerably:

> today the places, products and performances associated with sex for its own sake are becoming more visible. Commercial sex is gaining a toehold in the high street and being gentrified. Strip joints have become gentlemen's clubs. The Rampant Rabbit vibrator is now almost as well known as that much older sign for sex, the Playboy bunny girl, signifying a new interest in women as sexual consumers. Porn shops have been joined by the cheap and cheerful sexual paraphernalia of the Ann Summers empire and by elegant and expensive boutiques selling lingerie, toys and erotica. Pole dancing is being repackaged as a form of keep-fit, and burlesque is undergoing a revival, producing new stars such as Dita von Teese.
>
> (Attwood 2010a: xiv–xv)

This passage conveys how commercial sex products, services and experiences have become an almost ubiquitous presence in contemporary culture.

Yet there have been some challenges from campaign organizations contesting the sexual objectification of women. These anti-sexualization movements are important and they chime with a growing literature condemning the social processes normalizing pornography in contemporary culture. Much of the literature is North American, addressing the rapid growth and size of the porn industry in the country, which generates more revenue than Hollywood and all the major league sports combined (Williams 2004: 2). The proliferation of pornography has generated a number of critical interventions in recent years. They include Ariel Levy's

(2005) account of *Female Chauvinist Pigs*, which highlighted the rise of 'raunch culture' to describe how commercial sex had acquired such normative status that women incorporated its aesthetics so as to present themselves as strong, independent and exciting. According to Levy, this is not a sign of empowerment, but yet another way in which women are objectified and a further indication of how desire and desirability are increasingly governed by commerce. A similar diagnosis is detailed by Pamela Paul (2005) in her discussion of how American culture has become *Pornified*, where the increased accessibility and acceptability of porn, particularly on the Internet, has detrimental effects on consumers and their relationships. A report by the American Psychological Association (2007) is also regarded as significant for elaborating a distinctly negative understanding of 'sexualization' (Wouters 2010: 724–725), while Gail Dines (2010) has continued the critique in her mapping of the alienating and corrosive consequences of *Pornoland*. Clearly each of these publications condemn the commercialization of sexuality, whether this be in the spread of porn, pole dancing, sex toys or striptease, but all frame the problem largely in moral terms.

In many respects these arguments mark the revival of anti-pornography feminism that had been so influential in the 'sex wars' of the 1970s and 1980s. In this radical movement the slogan 'pornography is the theory and rape the practice' (Morgan 1980) caught the mood of the times. The leading representatives included Andrea Dworkin, Susan Griffin and Catherine Mackinnon who each argued that pornography degraded women and reproduced violent male sexuality. Although their positions on censorship varied, they shared the view that porn oppresses women and controversially formed uneasy alliances with neo-conservatives and Christian groups to generate a new form of 'legal moralism'. Other feminists highlighted the problems and contradictions in the anti-pornography position. Elizabeth Wilson (1992) accused the movement of fundamentalism: intolerance, denial, preacher style harangues, living life through repressive rules, and above all else a profound suspicion of sexuality.

Moreover, it was argued that anti-pornography feminism is based on an unhelpful distinction between male sexuality as violent and lustful whereas female sexuality is gentle and tender, which upholds the 'notion that women are victims of sex and that sex is degrading to women but not to men' (Turley 1986: 89). In turn, some recent feminist scholarship has defended pornography, especially if it encourages sexual freedom or challenges heteronormativity, while denouncing the language of martyrdom and victimhood associated with the movement's activism. Both sides situate the problem in moral terms: pornography is 'either degrading therefore bad *or* it is enjoyable and thus morally good' (Power 2009: 45, emphasis in original) and while the debate remains entrenched in such questions it lacks a more nuanced account of cultural variation and historical specificity. It is to such matters that Cas Wouters (2010) directs attention, arguing that too narrow a view has prevailed, missing deeper and broader shifts in human interactions gathering pace since the late nineteenth century. Anti-pornography and anti-sexualization movements are seen as part of a broader reworking of the ideal of monogamy, where changing taboos surrounding sexual practices are especially significant. The analysis demonstrates how sex is bound up with a set of manners governing our intimate lives and social relationships, which echoes Michel Foucault's (1979) influential writings on the *History of Sexuality* and Anthony Giddens's (1992) study on the *Transformation of Intimacy* in late modernity (Attwood (2010b). By contextualizing the commercialization of sexuality in a broader historical and theoretical framework, the approach reveals much about the social and political conditions underpinning cultural life.

Extreme media

Such an approach is also useful for understanding contemporary anxieties about the role of the Internet in disseminating increasingly 'extreme' images. The debates condense a range of anxieties about the increasing sexualization of society and the role played by media technologies in enabling the dissemination of this material. A well-known example is how the term 'pornography' has been used to describe a recent cycle of horror films including *Saw* (2004), *Hostel* (2005) and *Wolf Creek* (2005), which have been dubbed 'torture porn' on account of their gruesome depictions of torture, mutilation and nihilistic cruelty (Edelstein 2006). At around the same time Jean Baudrillard (2005) coined the term 'war porn' to describe the infamous Abu Ghraib photographs taken by American troops in Iraq.

These different uses of the term suggest a crisis over the meaning of 'porn', and indicate that it may be less concerned with images of sexual pleasure than with various attempts to make a spectacle of the body. This theme is developed by Steve Jones and Sharif Mowlabocus (2009: 622) where they discuss how numerous 'representations of body rupture have become immensely popular in western culture' across a broad range of factual and fictional media where scenes of 'opening up' the body are now commonplace. What unites these otherwise diverse images is their focus on extreme experiences and the visceral sensations they provoke. Similarly, Feonna Attwood (2011: 19) situates these extreme forms of representation in a 'broader cultural trend towards the depiction of humiliation, suffering and terror', which raises pressing new questions on 'the ways in which the body, technology and the self are represented and experienced in contemporary Western societies'. It is by examining these wider processes we can understand why it is that the boundaries of the forbidden, taboo and illicit have reconfigured in recent times. If these boundaries are policed through the regulation of audiences, as Kendrick (1987) maintains, then the conclusion to be drawn is that the greatest threat will be posed by those media technologies that permit the greatest circulation.

Although liberals defend pornography on the grounds of free speech, it is clear that the producers are not remotely concerned with sexual liberation but with making large profits. And as Nina Power (2009: 51, emphases in original) puts it, the 'sheer *hard work* of contemporary porn informs you that, without delusion, sex is just like everything else – grinding, relentless, boring (albeit *multiply* boring)'. By highlighting the capitalist tendencies of pornography she reminds us that the scale of the business has far reaching ramifications. A key factor driving the growth of the industry has been the development of digital technologies enabling cheaper, easier and faster access to porn. The point can be further developed by pursuing the implications of what has been termed the 'pathological public sphere' (Seltzer 1997). In Habermas's influential account, the public sphere arose in the eighteenth century as an arena of rational debate that was an alternative to despotic state violence, yet today there is 'a radical mutation of and relocation of the public sphere', which is now focused, Seltzer (1997: 4) maintains, on the 'shared and reproducible spectacles of pathological public violence'.

In his analysis of contemporary 'wound culture', Seltzer (1997: 3) demonstrates how a fundamental reconfiguration of individual and collective understandings of suffering, trauma and witnessing has recently taken place, which 'takes the form of a fascination with the shock of contact between bodies and technologies'. It is here that the concerns over increasingly 'extreme' forms of representation can be situated, which would enable a more critical understanding of the kind of social relations encountered in the mediapolis and would connect with the arguments presented earlier in this chapter. It remains the task of future work to develop these points considerably further, but the material presented here should be seen as part of an ongoing project dedicated to unravelling the power of images in contemporary societies.

Note

1 This chapter is an edited version of Carrabine, E. (2013) 'Crime, Culture and the Media in a Globalizing World', in Arrigo, B. and H. Bersot (eds.) *The Routledge Handbook of International Crime and Justice Studies*, New York, Routledge.

References

American Psychological Association (2007) *Report of the APA Task Force on the Sexualization of Girls*, Washington, DC: American Psychological Association.

Appadurai, A. (1996) *Modernity at Large*, Minneapolis: University of Minnesota Press.

Attwood, F. (2010a) 'Introduction: The Sexualization of Culture', in Attwood, F. (ed.) *Mainstreaming Sex*, London: I. B. Taurus.

Attwood, F. (2010b) 'Sexualization, Sex and Manners', *Sexualities*, Vol. 13, No. 6, pp. 742–747.

Attwood, F. (2011) 'The Paradigm Shift: Pornography Research, Sexualization and Extreme Images', *Sociology Compass*, Vol. 5, No. 1, pp. 13–22.

Auden, W. H. (1948) *The Age of Anxiety*, London: Faber and Faber.

Baudrillard, J. (1967/2001) 'Review of Marshall McLuhan, *Understanding Media*', in Genosko, G. (ed.) *The Uncollected Baudrillard*, London: Sage.

Baudrillard, J. (1985) 'The Ecstasy of Communication', in Foster, H. (ed.) *Postmodern Culture*, London: Pluto Press.

Baudrillard, J. (2001) *The Uncollected Baudrillard*, ed. G. Genosko, London: Sage.

Baudrillard, J. (2005) 'War Porn', *International Journal of Baudrillard Studies*, Vol. 2, No. 1, Online. Available www.ubishops.ca/baudrillardstudies/vol2_1/taylor.htm (accessed 22 April 2012).

Beck, U. (1986) *Risk Society*, London: Sage.

Best, J. (2008) 'Foreword', in Waiton, S. *The Politics of Antisocial Behaviour: Amoral Panics*, London: Routledge.

Boltanski, L. (1999) *Distant Suffering: Morality, Media and Politics*, Cambridge: Cambridge University Press.

Brown, S. (2003) *Crime and Law in Media Culture*, Buckingham: Open University Press.

Cohen, S. (1972) *Folk-Devils and Moral Panics: The Creation of the Mods and Rockers*, London: McGibbon and Kee.

Cohen, S. (2001) *States of Denial: Knowing about Atrocities and Suffering*, Cambridge: Polity.

Cohen, S. (2002) 'Moral Panics as Cultural Politics: Introduction to the Third Edition', in *Folk Devils and Moral Panics*, 3rd edn, London: Routledge.

Cohen, S. and Young, J. (eds.) (1973) *The Manufacture of News*, London: Constable.

Colligan, C. (2006) *The Traffic in Obscenity from Byron to Beardsley: Sexuality and Exoticism in Nineteenth-Century Print Culture*, Hampshire: Palgrave Macmillan.

Debord, G. (1967/1977) *Society of the Spectacle*, Detroit: Black & Red Books.

Dines, G. (2010) *Pornoland: How Porn Has Hijacked Our Sexuality*, Boston: Beacon Press.

Edelstein, D. (2006) 'Now Playing at Your Local Multiplex: Torture Porn', *New York Movies*, Online. Available http://nymag.com/movies/features/15622/ (accessed 2 April 2012).

Ellis, J. (2000) *Seeing Things: Television in an Age of Uncertainty*, London: I. B. Tauris.

Ericson, R. (2007) *Crime in an Insecure World*, Cambridge: Polity.

Feeley, M. and Simon, J. (2007) '*Folk Devils and Moral Panics*: An Appreciation from North America', in Downes, D. et al. (eds.) *Crime, Social Control and Human Rights: From Moral Panics to States of Denial, Essays in Honour of Stanley Cohen*, Devon: Willan.

Foucault, M. (1979) *The History of Sexuality, Volume One: An Introduction*, London: Allen Lane.

Fuery, K. (2009) *New Media: Culture and Image*, Hampshire: Palgrave Macmillan.

Garland, D. (2008) 'On the Concept of Moral Panic', *Crime, Media, Culture*, Vol. 4, No. 1, pp. 9–30.

Giddens, A. (1992) *The Transformation of Intimacy*, Cambridge: Polity Press.

Gill, R. (2010) 'Supersexualise Me! Advertising and the "Midriffs"', in Attwood, F. (ed.) *Mainstreaming Sex*, London: I. B. Taurus.

Goode, E. and Ben-Yehuda, N. (1994) *Moral Panics: The Social Construction of Deviance*, Oxford: Blackwells.

Gournelos, T. and Gunkel, D. (2012) 'Introduction: Transgression Today', in Gunkel, D. and Gournelos, T. (eds.) *Transgression 2.0: Media, Culture, and the Politics of a Digital Age*, London: Continuum.

Habermas, J. (1962/1989) *The Structural Transformation of the Public Sphere*, Cambridge: Polity Press.

Habermas, J. (2006) *Times of Transition*, Cambridge: Polity Press.

Hall, S., Critcher, C., Jefferson, T., Clarke, J. and Roberts, B. (1978) *Policing the Crisis: Mugging, the State and Law and Order*, London: Macmillan.

Hallsworth, S. (2008) 'Street Crime: Interpretation and Legacy in *Policing the Crisis*', *Crime, Media, Culture*, Vol. 4, No. 1, pp. 137–143.

Hayward, K. (2010) 'Opening the Lens: Cultural Criminology and the Image', in Hayward, K. and Presdee, M. (eds.) *Framing Crime: Cultural Criminology and the Image*, London: Routledge.

Hayward, K. and Yar, M. (2006) 'The "Chav" Phenomenon: Consumption, Media and the Construction of a New Underclass', *Crime, Media, Culture*, Vol. 2, No. 1, pp. 9–28.

Holland, P. (2006) *Picturing Childhood: The Myth of the Child in Popular Imagery*, London: I. B. Tauris.

Hubbard, P. (2003) 'Fear and Loathing at the Multiplex: Everyday Anxiety in the Post-Industrial City', *Capital and Class*, Vol. 27, No. 2, pp. 51–75.

Hunt, L. (1996) 'Introduction', in Hunt, L. (ed.) *The Invention of Pornography: Obscenity and the Origins of Modernity, 1500–1800*, New York: Zone Books.

Ignatieff, M. (1999) *The Warrior's Honor: Ethnic War and the Modern Conscience*, London: Vintage.

Jones, S. and Mowlabocus, S. (2009) 'Hard Times and Rough Rides: The Legal and Ethical Impossibilities of Researching "Shock" Pornographies', *Sexualities*, Vol. 12, No. 5, pp. 613–628.

Kendrick, W. (1987) *The Secret Museum: Pornography in Modern Culture*, New York: Viking.

Levy, A. (2005) *Female Chauvinist Pigs: Women and the Rise of Raunch Culture*, New York: Free Press.

McGuigan, J. (2005) 'The Cultural Public Sphere', *European Journal of Cultural Studies*, Vol. 8, No. 4, pp. 427–443.

McLuhan, M. (1964/1994) *Understanding Media: The Extensions of Man*, London: Routledge.

McNair, B. (2002) *Striptease Culture: Sex, Media and the Democratisation of Desire*, London: Routledge.

McNair, B. (2010) 'From Porn Chic to Porn Fear: The Return of the Repressed', in Attwood, F. (ed.) *Mainstreaming Sex*, London: I. B. Taurus.

McRobbie, A. and Thornton, S. (1995) 'Rethinking "Moral Panic" for Multi-Mediated Social Worlds', *British Journal of Sociology*, Vol. 46, No. 4, pp. 559–574.

Miller, D. and Kitzinger, J. (1998) 'AIDS, the Policy Process and Moral Panics', in Miller, D., Kitzinger, J., Williams, K. and Beharrell, P. (eds.) *The Circuit of Mass Communication*, London: Sage.

Milter, K. and Slade, J. (2005) 'Global Traffic in Pornography: The Hungarian Example', in Sigel, L. (ed.) *International Exposure: Perspectives on Modern European Pornography, 1800–2000*, New York: Rutgers University Press.

Morgan, R. (1980) 'Theory and Practice: Pornography and Rape', in Lederer, L. (ed.) *Take Back the Night: Women on Pornography*, New York: William Morrow.

Neely, S. (2012) 'Making Bodies Visible: Post-Feminism and the Pornographication of Online Identities', in Gunkel, D. and Gournelos, T. (eds.) *Transgression 2.0: Media, Culture, and the Politics of the Digital Age*, London: Continuum.

Osbourne, R. (1995) 'Crime and the Media: From Media Studies to Post-Modernism', in Kidd-Hewitt, D. and Osbourne, R. (eds.) *Crime and the Media: The Post-Modern Spectacle*, London: Pluto Press.

O'Toole, L. (1998) *Pornocopia: Porn, Sex, Technology and Desire*, London: Serpent's Tail.

Paasonen, S., Nikunen, K. and Saarenmaa, L. (eds.) (2007) *Pornification: Sex and Sexuality in Media Culture*, Oxford: Berg.

Paul, P. (2005) *Pornified: How Pornography Is Damaging Our Lives, Our Relationships, and Our Families*, New York: Owl Books.

Power, N. (2009) *One Dimensional Woman*, Hants: O Books.

Poynor, R. (2006) *Designing Pornotopia: Travels in Visual Culture*, London: Laurence King.

Seltzer, M. (1997) 'Wound Culture: Trauma in the Pathological Public Sphere', *October*, Vol. 80, pp. 3–26.

Sigel, L. (2002) *Governing Pleasures: Pornography and Social Change in England, 1815–1914*, New Brunswick, NJ: Rutgers University Press.

Sigel, L. (2005) 'Introduction: Issues and Problems in the History of Pornography', in Sigel, L. (ed.) *International Exposure: Perspectives on Modern European Pornography, 1800–2000*, New York: Rutgers University Press.

Silverstone, R. (2007) *Media and Morality*, Cambridge: Polity.

Soloman-Godeau, A. (1991) *Photography at the Dock*, Minneapolis: University of Minnesota Press.

Sparks, R. (1992) *Television and the Drama of Crime: Moral Tales and the Place of Crime in Public Life*, Milton Keynes: Open University Press.

Thompson, K. (1998) *Moral Panics*, London: Routledge.

Turley, D. (1986) 'The Feminist Debate on Pornography', *Socialist Review*, Vol. 16, No. 3–4, pp. 81–96.

Virilio, P. (1986) *Speed and Politics*, New York: Semiotext(e).

Waddington, P. (1986) 'Mugging as a Moral Panic: A Question of Proportion', *British Journal of Sociology*, Vol. 32, No. 2, pp. 245–259.

Watney, S. (1987/1997) *Policing Desire: Pornography, AIDS and the Media*, 3rd edn, London: Cassell.

Weber, L. and Lee, M. (2009) 'Preventing Indeterminate Threats: Fear, Terror and the Politics of Preemption', in Lee, M. and Farrall, S. (eds.) *Fear of Crime: Critical Voices in an Age of Anxiety*, London: Routledge-Cavendish.

Wilkins, L. (1964) *Social Deviance: Social Policy, Action and Research*, London: Tavistock.

Wilkinson, I. (2001) *Anxiety in a Risk Society*, London: Routledge.

Williams, L. (2004) 'Porn Studies: Proliferating Pornographies On/Scene: An Introduction', in Williams, L. (ed.) *Porn Studies*, Durham and London: Duke University Press.

Williams, R. (1974/1990) *Television: Technology and Cultural Form*, London: Routledge.

Wilson, E. (1992) 'Feminist Fundamentalism: The Shifting Politics of Sex and Censorship', in Segal, L. and McIntosh, M. (eds.) *Sex Exposed: Sexuality and the Pornography Debate*, London: Virago Press.

Wouters, C. (2010) 'Sexualization: Have Sexualization Processes Changed Direction?', *Sexualities*, Vol. 13, No. 6, pp. 723–741.

Young, J. (1971) *The Drugtakers*, London: Paladin.

Young, J. (2009) 'Moral Panic: Its Origins in Resistance, Ressentiment and the Translation of Fantasy into Reality', *British Journal of Criminology*, Vol. 49, No. 1, pp. 4–16.

14

CRIME AND RISK

Pat O'Malley

Introduction

Crime and risk have long been associated. In the 19th century, governments and social reformers across Europe and America were obsessed with the supposed failure of the working classes to adopt the bourgeois habits of industry and thrift. For the great penal reformer Jeremy Bentham (1789/1962) the most important task of government was to persuade the masses to take on what he called 'the yoke of foresight': the burden of looking to the future, assessing its possible dangers and opportunities, and thus accumulating wealth and avoiding harm. For the masses, this risk-orientation meant a life of self-denial not only with respect to work and domestic budgeting, but also with respect to leisure and pleasure. The poor were to avoid gambling, which both exposed them to the risk of destitution and undermined belief in thrift and industriousness. Alcohol likewise was regarded as an evil. Drinking represented the unproductive pursuit of pleasure that in inebriation robbed workers of their will and ability to labour. Money spent on alcohol should have been saved to guard against future risks. As will be seen shortly, criminology accepted these moral judgements about risk into its identification of criminal traits, turning them into 'scientific' truths.

Likewise, risk played a key part in the emergence of modern crime control. In Robert Peel's 19th-century design for the Metropolitan Police, the key police function was that of prevention. Police were to recruit informers in order to thwart planned crimes and to build up a preventive knowledge. In practice, this role came to be marginalised in favour of more dramatic and visible practices of detection and capture, but it makes clear that we should not think that, in policing, the crime and risk nexus is a new phenomenon (O'Malley and Hutchinson 2007). Even notions of crime deterrence, which informed 19th-century police and punishment, were risk-based. Returning to Jeremy Bentham's reforms (similar to those of other 'classical' criminologists such as Beccaria), punishment was not to be random and spectacular, but disciplined, certain and measured. Police should not focus on occasional high-profile cases, but rather should provide constant surveillance and thus generate high probabilities of capture. Given such policing, punishments need only slightly exceed the gains of crime in order to deter effectively. Rational choice actors, Bentham supposed, would avoid crime because the high risk of capture and of the cost of punishment made offending unattractive.

While risk and crime were thus closely intertwined in the formation of modern criminology and crime control, it is clear that the last half-century has witnessed major changes both in how risk is understood and applied to understanding offenders, and closely related to this, how risk is applied to crime control.

Risk and criminal activity

Positivist criminology has a long history of attending to crime as risk-taking. Usually, it does so in a way that regards risk-taking as pathological. Thus 'short term hedonism' produced by poor socialisation, or 'thrill seeking' produced by the boredom of lower class working life, are explanations for crime that have been deployed by positivist criminologists (e.g. Miller 1958). Such criminological work can readily be accused of class bias. For example, while some criminologists see crime arising from risk-taking as a response to the boring lives of workers, it is hard to believe that the lives of many conformist white collar males are very different when it comes to day-to-day excitement. Indeed, evidence abounds of white collar workers engaging in binge drinking and illicit drug consumption on the night club circuit (Winlow and Hall 2006).

More sophisticated variants of this kind of criminology go on to argue that working class risk-taking is linked to crime largely because there are fewer legitimate outlets for risky excitement open to the poor. While this may be true, it seriously underestimates the extent to which middle class people, and especially middle class youth, may engage in crimes associated with risk-taking. One response, as argued by Jack Katz in *Seductions of Crime* (1988), is that the experience of risk can be analysed as a form of resistance and creativity. Common-or-garden shoplifting, vandalism or joy-riding for example, are too widespread across class lines to be explained in conventional terms as either the poor attempting to eke out a living or as evidence of the working classes trying to escape from the tedium of factory jobs. Katz explores the experiential phenomenology of such activities rather than trying to reduce them to an effect of some determining variable. He attempts to render these experiences intelligible as a form of risky flirting with the humiliation of capture that generates 'sneaky thrills', and thus provides excitement available to all. Perhaps the children of the middle class, standing to lose more, would find this even more thrilling, no matter how supposedly less boring are their lives than those of their working class peers. Some crime therefore can be understood as 'embracing risk' (Baker and Simon 2002).

Yet Katz's thesis still retains a pathologising claim. While class factors are held not to explain risky crimes, for Katz the explanation lies in the pathology of mundane modern urban life in which personal worth is constantly challenged and humiliation becomes a central emotional experience. With the shoplifter, Katz posits flirting with risks of humiliation as the generator of thrills. But surely there are many things other than (or as well as) humiliation 'at risk': the risk of losing money through fines, of receiving other punishment such as probation and perhaps imprisonment, the risk to one's future job prospects, maybe the risk of a physical beating from an irate parent. It could equally be argued that what generates excitement here is *fear*. Taking risks, at least in the present, is intelligible as a source of excitement in part because of the adrenaline rush released by a kind of vertigo – of being on an edge where one's future existence itself seems at stake. The same applies, perhaps, with the example of young men confronting other young men in street fights. It is quite plausible to suggest that it is not the humiliation of life in the barrios that is the issue, as Katz argues, but rather the opportunity for excitement associated with the risk of pain or injury, even death, mixed perhaps with an excited liking for inflicting these fearful possibilities (Jackson-Jacobs 2004).

Such crimes may emerge as not needing a pathological, determinist explanation. After all, the current world of consumer culture constitutes excitement as normal and desirable (Lyng 2005). Risk takers who end up committing crimes in pursuit of excitement may thus embrace actions that embody mainstream values. Of course, this kind of personal orientation to risk and excitement is not new. Yet perhaps the expansion of consumer culture, coupled with the neo-liberal political emphasis on risk-taking as valued attribute in the 'entrepreneurial' society, combine to produce an environment in which crimes embracing risk become more attractive to many people, and especially young people.

Crime, risk and control

In what follows, I wish to argue that crime and risk management, and crime as risk-taking need to be considered together because their convergence has marked the years at least since the 1970s and probably earlier. Broadly speaking, this conjunction can be seen to emerge out of a broader contingency – the rise of consumer capitalism since World War II, and the development and ascendancy of neo-liberal politics since the 1970s.

Together, these two influences have done much to erode, or at least significantly change, the world of the closed disciplinary institutions and the ethos of self-denial and deferred gratification that characterised the period before World War II. While Margaret Thatcher (1992) liked to talk of the rediscovery of such Victorian virtues, their take-up has been restricted to matters of individual responsibility and to the valorisation of competition and markets. Self-denial and self-sacrifice have not notably been embraced in everyday life and politics. The expansion of commodification in the neo-liberal period has been associated with a loosening of moral constraints so that increasingly markets cater to (and form) what have come to be called 'lifestyles' (Rose 1999). Discipline, of course, survives but increasingly is inflected by hedonism – indeed Mike Featherstone (1994) has referred to the emergent ethos as 'controlled hedonism'. It is good to consume, and conspicuous consumption is the sign and reward of success. And the measure of one's success, perhaps more than ever, is income and the possession of expensive commodities – for these are the rewards delivered by the market to those who take risks and make prosperous enterprises of their lives.

Not only does this development break down many pre-existing moral barriers, but it creates an environment of constant change, in some senses an exciting milieu in which 'all that is solid melts into air' (Berman 1983). A cultural emphasis on the value of novelty, self-gratification and expressiveness erodes or qualifies one of emotional containment and rational utilitarianism. This has created conditions for the emergence of new forms of regulation, of the sort described by Deleuze (1995) as 'control'.

In 'control societies' concern with individuals and their conformity to narrow moral precepts, and the centrality of closed disciplinary institutions, is increasingly displaced by the immanent regulation of behaviours. We might take as a crude example the imposition of taxes on cigarettes as a way of channelling behaviour away from unwanted directions. Prices 'modulate' the frequency of actions, deflect them into other areas or activities, while at the same time being an almost taken for granted aspect of everyday life. But there is more to it than this. The driver's licence, for example, is not merely a licence to drive. It is almost the required means for providing proof of age or identity, or such other details as home address, that are so frequently required to guarantee our credentials to enter this or that site, or to purchase this or that commodity (alcohol and tobacco for example). Likewise the credit card may now be a taken for granted part of anyone's wallet. But like the driver's licence it is also a passport, at least for those domains where access is a commodity. It acts as a sign that we have good credit and thus provides an impersonal and highly portable warranty of riskiness or trustworthiness in a world in which life is more than ever lived and expressed through commodities. Even these instruments of access and identity are themselves commodities. We purchase the credit card and even the driver's licence – and part of their price is the cost of a series of other security checks and verifications, carried out by credit agencies, police and so on, which they embody. Unlike cash, which as Simmel (1895/1990) says is 'undifferentiated' and anonymous, each time these instruments are used, an electronic trace is left behind. They are the perfect risk-managing collateral in a consumer society that is also a society permeated by risk consciousness, for they are at one and the same the means of access to commodities and risk management technologies. This is why, as urban myths have it, the Mafia always pay in cash.

While constraining in new ways, nevertheless at the same time through such means individuals are freed to 'float' morally within constraints that work through consumption and 'choice'. The boundaries of acceptability are patrolled by such devices and the principal contours of the perimeter are coming to be associated with risks created for others (Simon 1988). Within this security perimeter, a good deal of the moral restriction of the Victorian age has been eroded. Of course, in this process, there is regulation. The commodities we purchase very largely have been approved and themselves governed by a grid of risk. Safety standards and inspections filter that which appears in the market. A broad form of censorship has selected out those objects or services considered unacceptable. But the range of moral tolerance would be appalling to the Victorian moralist.

In complex ways, crime both is shaped by and helps to shape this state of affairs. Consumption has become a much more salient domain for offending, especially where associated with crimes of the risk-embracing sort. Crimes and lesser offences associated with motor vehicles are one example, from speeding and dangerous driving to car theft and street racing. Drug consumption, graffiti, vandalism and other activities are older forms of offending that are linked to excitement that have been given new life and new prominence in consumer society. The response to these has been Janus-faced. On the one hand are those former crimes of excitement that once exercised the police and courts, such as gambling. Very largely these have been commodified and corporatised so that now gambling is no longer a crime but a key part of those new inventions the 'leisure industry' and 'financial services'. Once criminal and officially despised, now gambling is highly valued as a source of employment, capital growth and state revenue (O'Malley 2004). It is assumed that, very largely, individuals should be given responsibility for their own risk management, and a paternalistic state should not interfere in pleasures *that do no harm to others*. Hence the emergence of new images such as that of 'responsible gamblers' and 'drinking responsibly': a freedom is bestowed – both on producers and consumers – but hedged around by a moral perimeter that self-governing consumers are supposed to internalise. In many jurisdictions, especially outside the United States, even 'illicit' drug consumption has been extensively decriminalised on similar grounds.

As this suggests, the risk-control cuts in especially where crimes of excitement create harms or risks for others. Here the margin for tolerance has, if anything, been closed down. Through various forms of anti-social behavioural order, often using on-the-spot fines, all manner of 'acting out' and 'thrill seeking' that may once have been ignored or at least tolerated, now fall into the penumbra of criminal justice. And of course, much of the increased tolerance applies only to those who are 'in' the market. For the vast bulk of offenders, even in this era of the culture of control, sanctions are primarily fines, or at worst some form of risk management in the community. Prisons are not the principal sanction. Rather, their inmates fall into two classes. First are the 'failed consumers'. These include a large number of those who cannot afford to pay fines, the consumer society penalty par excellence, and who in many jurisdictions may be imprisoned in default (O'Malley 2009). Through much of the 20th century they supplied up to a third or even more of prison admissions. The other principal category is made up of those who present risks of a magnitude that are deemed inappropriate to be governed through market techniques. And among these are many who present only a small risk, but – as Feeley and Simon (1992) put it – have so little to lose that they are deemed to fall below the threshold of deterrence.

Risk and crime control

Beginning about the mid-1980s, criminologists began remarking on the ways in which the governance of crime – from policing and crime prevention to sentencing and prison organisation – had moved away from a focus on reforming offenders towards preventing crime and managing behaviour using predictive techniques. Some noted that whereas the principal concern of 20th-century 'penal modernism' had been to understand and scientifically correct offenders, increasingly that was being abandoned in favour of focusing on managing their behaviours (Cohen 1985, Simon 1988). No-one was much interested any more in the motives and meanings of these people. Instead what was at issue was what they did, how to control them and how to minimise the harms they generated. Offenders and their offences were coming to be reframed less as the pathological products of societal and psychological breakdowns who needed to be therapeutically reformed, and more as bundles of harmful behaviours and potentialities.

At the same time, other criminologists observed that new techniques and new concerns were emerging in crime control. Reflecting the focus on behaviours, they detected a new emphasis on shaping the environment, and especially the built environment, in order to make crime difficult or impossible (Shearing and Stenning 1985, Reichman 1986). Increasingly, crime was seen as a matter of people taking opportunities rather than in terms of their inappropriate attitudes or disadvantaged backgrounds. Crime prevention accordingly was moving away from building up supportive environments and improving economically deprived neighbourhoods. The new focus increasingly was on designing crime-proof buildings, crime-preventing streetscapes and communities. As David Garland (1996) was later to term it, interest was focused on 'criminogenic situations'. Reducing crime opportunities by creating 'gated communities', and the widespread installation of closed circuit television (CCTV) to monitor public spaces, were seen to create a paranoid society in which intervening against the different, the unwanted and the merely annoying is a principal means whereby we are creating an 'exclusive security' (Young 1999). Pre-emptive intervention against 'pre-delinquents' and 'at risk' young people, 'threatening' gangs of youths or 'anti-social' groups of teenagers congregating in shopping malls inflict restrictions on those who may not yet have done anything dangerous or illegal. Crime awareness campaigns aimed at improving public safety are often regarded as increasing the sense of insecurity and adversely affecting the quality of life for all citizens. Programmes such as Neighbourhood Watch and the 'Safer Cities' movements mobilised community members into collaboration with police, providing alerts concerning suspicious strangers or activities, and being 'empowered' to increase the security of their homes through fitting hardware (such as deadlocks, security screens and alarms) and developing crime conscious practices such as disguising any absence from home and enlisting neighbours to watch while they were away. While prudent in themselves, the net effect of these measures was seen to create a sense of a society beleaguered by crime, in which outsiders appeared as sources of risk.

There were other, linked, changes also being reported in the criminal justice system. Penal modernism – the optimistic reformative correctional approach dominant until about the 1970s – had been vitally interested in offenders' pasts in order that they could be understood as individuals. However, while the emerging risk techniques in crime control were also interested in offenders' pasts they used statistical techniques for other purposes: to identify correlations between pre-existing conditions and criminal action, and to treat these conditions as 'crime-risk factors'. These factors could be used especially to identify potential offenders and change their ways before they offended. This had been tried since the 1930s. But it was the use of statistical risk factors to assign a person to a certain risk pool, rather than for understanding the unique individual, that was the novel development.

This had been a phenomenally successful model in the medical sciences, of course, and nearing the end of the 20th century, risk had become a predominant 'impersonal' way of governing all manner of problems – for example through improving diet, mandating safety equipment and so on. The model of risk itself – the use of predictive statistical knowledge linked to techniques of harm prevention – overwhelmingly has been regarded as one of the benefits bestowed by science. However, with respect to the governance of crime, this is not altogether how things have gone, and especially not in criminology. For critical criminologists, by the late 1990s risk-based approaches were seen to have played a key role in the emergence of the 'culture of control' in which the reformist and socially inclusive optimism of modernist penal policies has been submerged beneath an exclusionary and punitive approach to crime. Because of its focus on controlling behaviour rather than therapeutic correction, and on offenders as risks to others rather than as people struggling with the challenges of life, the new risk techniques were seen by critics to mesh well with an emerging 'new punitiveness' (Garland 2001, Pratt et al. 2000). Examples that support this view are not hard to find. For example, 'three strikes and you're out' and similar tariff-based sentencing policies focus on the risk that an offender represents rather than on the seriousness of the particular offence at issue. For quite minor offences – but for offences that are seen to be part of a pattern of activity that indicates a high risk of future crime – offenders could be imprisoned for long periods. These approaches to sentencing collide with almost taken for granted principles of proportionality between wrong and punishment, for a relatively minor offence may result in a lengthy risk-based sentence. They also fly in the face of therapeutic thinking that sentences should reflect the correctional needs of the offender as judged by experts.

Other examples exist in abundance. Curfews imposed on troublesome teenagers and electronic tagging of sex or violent offenders in the name of risk reduction, are condemned as doing nothing to reform the offender while limiting the freedom of many people whose offences are often minor. They are also viewed as turning the community into an extension of the prison system. Other prominent instances are 'Megan's laws' and 'Sarah's laws', where in the name of risk minimisation the identities and often the residences of former sex and violence offenders are made public. The stated aim is to warn people in the neighbourhood to take extra precautions in view of this risk in their midst. These laws have become associated with accusations that they promote vigilantism and victimisation of past offenders who may be trying to reform themselves or whose offences may in fact be quite mild. They may also create living hells for the families of the offenders.

Such ways of using risk to reduce crime are viewed as extending punishment into an indefinite future after release from prison, and as making unbearable the lives of former offenders and their families without this technique actually being proven to reduce crime victimisation (Levi 2000). On top of this, a 'new penology' or 'actuarial justice' based on risk is seen to be shifting emphasis from correction to risk reducing incapacitation or warehousing (Feeley and Simon 1992, 1994). A prime example is taken to be the imprisonment of many of those incarcerated under 'three strikes' laws, who are imprisoned in the name of reducing risk to the community but who receive little or nothing by way of correctional services while they are inside. The goal is simply to remove these 'risks' from society. As Feeley and Simon (1992) suggested, the rationale of imprisonment changed, so that managerial models concerned with the 'throughput' of offenders displaced concerns with recidivism and the 'failure' of the prison to reform. If prisoners are understood as risks, then the more there are in prison, the more risks have been removed from the community. Indeed, recidivism no longer appeared as a sign of failure, but rather as proof that the right people had been imprisoned and that prisons did 'work' as risk reduction mechanisms.

Such problematic and often obviously worrying developments are viewed by critics as exemplary of risk techniques' *characteristic* forms. In what has become a new orthodoxy in critical criminology, risk appears overwhelmingly as a negative development in crime control and criminal justice, driving out the inclusive model of criminal correction and installing in our midst segregating practices and technologies.

Such critical criminological views reflect social theory's abiding pessimism about the present. It is epitomised by works such as Bauman's (2000) and Young's (1999) sociologies of the 'exclusive society' and Agamben's (2005) apocalyptic vision of the state of exception. For Agamben, those who pose threats to security are consigned to a vulnerable form of humanity increasingly stripped of the rights and protections others take for granted, living a life deemed not worthy of living. In these accounts, criminal justice, public security and social exclusion blur together, and in the post-9/11, post-social-welfare state there seems little hope of change except for the worse. It is hard to disagree with many of the points they make, substantiated as they are by copious research.

However, these pessimistic analyses pick up and maybe overemphasise just one trend, albeit a powerful one, and they rarely suggest any way out of the nightmare they depict. Perhaps nowhere is this more clear than with respect to police. In the late 1990s, the publication of Ericson and Haggerty's *Policing the Risk Society* (1997) made an enormous impression on critical criminology. The authors put forward the striking thesis that the work of police had been revolutionised by the rise of the risk society as delineated by Beck (1992). In this vision, the emergence of new and massive risks such as global warming and global terrorism – that were neither predictable nor limited in impact – shattered existing forms of modernity. All of the old institutions of risk management, such as national governments, trade unions and even the family became obsolete because they could not deal with such threats. Moreover, Beck argued that existing forms of modern consciousness, focused on class, gender and race, were consequently displaced by an overriding obsession with these new risks that Beck called 'risk consciousness'. Accepting Beck's thesis that the risk society reframed government around risk consciousness, Ericson and Haggerty proposed that police were shifting ground from a focus on moral transgression and reactive crime control towards governing problems in terms of their probabilistic nature and potential harms. The insatiable demand for knowledge created by this concern with risk (Beck referred to risk society as 'knowledge society') placed police in a socially strategic position, for they were traditionally organised both to gather security-related knowledge, and to mobilise this in relation to a wide network of institutions and agencies. Police were depicted as 'knowledge brokers'.

The risk society thesis transformed this knowledge-brokering from being one among many roles, to being the defining function of police in reflexive modernity. In turn, as the main function of police became that of providing risk information to other institutions so they come to be 'governed by the risk formats of those other institutions'. Such formats transform police because they 'establish the criteria through which institutional participants understand risks and articulate their preferred courses of action ... Alternative meanings are either seen as unrealistic or are not seen at all' (Ericson and Haggerty 1997: 127). Primary among these institutions is the insurance industry, itself now transformed into the pivotal institution of risk society. And it is this industry that has acted as the key agent changing police, through its irresistible demands for police to provide information about security aspects of criminal events and its promotion of police involvement in crime prevention programmes such as Neighbourhood Watch and situational crime prevention more generally.

Ericson and Haggerty thus introduced into criminology a revolutionary thesis that was innovative, striking and systematic. They posited a complete and thoroughgoing transformation of police in form and function, connected this to a detailed exposition of the increasingly influential risk society thesis, and provided a very extensive mapping of empirical exemplars in the study of Canadian police. In so doing, *Policing the Risk Society* delivered a new perspective on police to an academic audience already alerted to the growing importance of risk in the criminological domain.

However, it would not appear that things have unfolded quite as Ericson and Haggerty envisioned. To begin with, there are policing domains where risk-orientations may not have penetrated a resistant police culture. Indeed, there is evidence aplenty that despite Ericson and Haggerty's assertions to the contrary, traditional policing styles and values remain in place despite informatics and related 'revolutions' (e.g. Chan 2001: 156; Harris 2007: 181). In this way, a key possibility – that the police take-up of risk frameworks has been uneven – could not be explored (cf. Mythen 2014: 62–63). In this respect, key research by Ferret and Spenlehauer (2009) deserves close attention. Their work focuses on the field of traffic policing, which has become (by volume) perhaps the largest field of offending, one that costs many lives and much property damage, and also one that engages considerable amounts of police resources. From a study of the development of road traffic policing in several countries, Ferret and Spenlehauer (2009) conclude that it is difficult to detect any simple ruptural change, especially not change focused on the insurance industry and its supposed domination of police in the risk society. Quite to the contrary, they suggest that insurers were more influential in 'riskifying' police in the *early* part of the 20th century. During later years other interest groups came to be involved in governing road risks, producing a form of democratisation of risk. In this process, the kinds of knowledge demanded by insurers became no more than one form of information required, while much transformational pressure on police was not concerned with risk. Second, Ferret and Spenlehauer (2009) reject the vision of police as simply forced to respond to outside demands for risk knowledge. Even within the field of road risk policing, police have to deal with crises of legitimacy. These include claims that they are focusing on drivers when they ought to be policing major crimes – a view police on the beat may share – and that road cameras are sources of revenue rather than risk reduction. Police hierarchies thus have to compromise between various demands, not all of which fall into line with the pressures for risk society policing.

To this could be added further refinements to the general point at issue. In one of the Australian states (New South Wales) taken to illustrate their critique, things have moved to a point not taken up by the authors. The impact of 'riskification' with respect to policing road traffic offending has led to the almost complete automation of large sectors of the domain (O'Malley 2010b). Speed and red-light cameras record offending, while linked computers match their readings with predetermined calibrations equating speed, risk and penalty. Penalty notices are issued by mail. At no point in this process are police necessarily involved. Even the collection and enforcement of penalties is overwhelmingly effected by the State Debt Recovery Office: a branch of Treasury. The sheer volume of traffic offending has meant that reliance on police became too cumbersome and expensive. Even where mobile speed cameras are used, these are often operated and managed by (cheaper) private contractors – sometimes also the case with fixed cameras. The emerging governmental 'logic' of risk, together with economic pressures, has not so much transformed police, but rather has transformed *policing*, externalising this most risk-focused police work to other agencies. In turn, this has not been resisted by police, perhaps precisely because it has not meant reductions in staffing so much as the 'freeing up' of police officers to engage in more traditional forms of police work.

As this suggests, critical studies of risk and crime have tended to exaggerate the pervasiveness of changes and the absence of effective resistance to the spread of risk-based techniques and practices. In practice, however, failure and frustration seem to have been as much a characteristic of risk-based developments as they have been for any other governmental process. Hazel Kemshall (2003) for example has mapped out the ways in which probation and prison staff have been able to resist the displacement of their professional judgement by risk schedules, particularly with respect to parole decisions. In part simple subversion has been one tool, whereby workers make their decisions on parole, and then fill out the risk schedule in such a way that it conforms to their preferred course. In part, the fact that senior staff are frequently professionals themselves has meant that strict risk-based regimes have been watered down so that the score on risk assessment schedules becomes only one factor to be considered, and is normally subject to professional interpretation.

Elsewhere, risk-based programmes have been developed that reassert some of the central values and knowledges of the penal modernist agenda. Kelly Hannah-Moffat (1999, 2005) has analysed the development and operation of 'risk-needs' programmes introduced into prisons from the 1980s onwards. Now dominant in many penal contexts, risk-needs is a response to the 'nothing works' mindset of the 1970s penal reformers who argued that correctionalism had failed, and that prison's only valid purpose was therefore risk containment and punishment. Risk-needs proposed to restore many correctional programmes, but subjected them to rigorous evaluation regarding their focus on reducing crime risks. As Hannah-Moffat shows, the result was often quite negative, and in many instances risk-needs were used to increase the sentence of prisoners and/or to reduce their access to benefits. But at least according to its proponents (Andrews and Bonta 2006) the important thing to attend to was that risk-needs served to reconnect prisoners to services that were often identical to the kinds of reformative programmes that had been available under penal modernism.

Of course, as David Garland (2001) argues, such developments may still be regarded as part of the culture of control, for they subordinate correctional reform and social assistance to techniques of crime prevention. And as this implies, correctional reform and social assistance will only be provided to the extent that they are shown to reduce crime risks. This is a valid and important point. But these developments can also be seen as sites of resistance by the 'social' professions – psychologists, social workers, psychiatrists and so on seeking to maintain or defend the welfare orientations and the therapeutic corrections that so many criminologists complain are being swept away. More significantly, they can be seen as points from which more promising initiatives can be explored or launched. In this way they are possibly Janus-faced, offering at least *ambiguous* risk-based alternatives to the apparently desolate culture of control. 'Drug harm minimisation' is likewise dangerous but promising. It offers therapeutic services and efforts to reintegrate and accommodate drug users in society in the name of reducing the total array of harms illicit drug use creates. In this process, much less emphasis is placed on punishment and policing in favour of a more public-health orientation. Ordinary users and even street-level dealers may thus experience less demonisation and harassment, although increased moral pressure and criminal justice penalties are directed at those identified as drug 'smugglers' and high-end dealers – who are regarded as creating societal drug risks. Certainly harm minimisation does impose expert domination and subjects services to the test of reducing those actions and behaviours judged by experts to be harmful and risk-laden. It also has the potential to extend the net of social control, for example by the use of methadone programmes as a 'chemical leash' for users. Whatever their other benefits, methadone programmes are intrusive and constraining, requiring users to report at frequent intervals to an approved drug agency, and often making them submit urine tests to detect illicit drug use. All of these risk-related formations have dangerous potentials. But as sites where 'socially' oriented expertise has attempted to reshape risk, they may also offer the potential for the reconfiguring of risk in more optimistic, socially inclusive and constructive fashion than is imagined by many of those opposed to crime control through risk techniques.

It could be anticipated that the hardest test of such optimism about risk would be the burgeoning field of biocriminology. Many criminologists responded to Eysenck's 1970s resurrection of Lombroso's 19th-century deterministic biological approaches to criminology with disdain and sometimes ridicule (Eysenck 1978). However, by the early 1990s alarm was beginning to spread, especially with the rise of more sophisticated risk-based genetic and neurogenetic approaches. For some (e.g. Duster 1990), this had the potential to create a new preventive eugenics of crime. In one of the most influential responses, Nelkin and Lindee (1995) regarded the rise of genetic approaches to crime as consigning offenders – and more problematically 'pre-offenders' – to a genetically determined life course from which they could not escape. As a corollary, they assumed that risk-based interception would displace reform and reintegration and the welfare orientations of penal modernism – the culture of control would never be reined in. Again, risk appears as part of the forces driving, rather than being shaped by, the broader framework of the government of crime. In science fiction, works such as Phillip Kerr's *A Philosophical Investigation* (1996) fanned the flames, with his vision of a 'Lombroso programme' which could use DNA to identify and control pre-killers.

In practice, however, almost no genetics researchers envisaged any such possibility, arguing that genetic determinism would never produce anything like a gene for crime, inter alia because of the social construction of criminal law. While, for example, there may be links between genetics and violent or aggressive behaviours, the overwhelming tendency was to see genetic factors as creating 'susceptibilities' rather than acting as determinants (Rose 2007: 244–247). In this much more conditional framework, emphasis is put most heavily on what kinds of interventions and techniques of the self can reduce or ameliorate the risks of offending. Immediately, the temptation is to leap to an incapacitation model. This is by no means the only possibility: it *is* a possibility – and a very strong possibility – where the culture of control is unchecked. But at least equally possible, and at least as readily identifiable among the current programmatic responses to biocriminology, have been therapeutic responses much along the lines of the welfare sanctions of 30 years ago. Thus Rose (2000) emphasises that 'the contemporary biologization of risky identities in the name of public health offers biological criminologists a role as therapeutic professional'. Again, this may not always be the ideal course. It is itself risky and dangerous, creating opportunities for technocratic domination. But it also creates new possibilities for some more positive interventions than incapacitation and incarceration. Risk itself is not the problem.

In sum, as Nicole Rafter (2008: 246) has argued, the problem of biocriminology

> lies not with the scientists who are investigating biological causes of crime but rather with simplistic or politically manipulative understandings of their work. To avoid the misappropriation of biocriminology for political ends … we need to learn how to question science intelligently and acknowledge our own ignorance.

More generally, I would suggest, this implies that criminologists abandon their pessimism, especially on this question, and begin to engage proactively to appropriate risk for positive initiatives, and to counter the conservative politics of control with a democratisation of risk itself.

The uncertain promise of risk

Even in the domains of criminal justice, security and safety, risk appears as a contested technology and discourse of governance. Indeed, some opponents, such as Ulrich Beck (1992) have called for a democratisation of risk. Confronted by a world in which, it is argued, ungoverned technological development has created risks to the entire planet, Beck calls for democratic controls to be applied to science: for in many respects risk has become a technology dominated by scientific expertise. This democratisation does not involve the subordination of scientific findings to populist politics. Rather, the democratic concern is with defining which problems should be defined as risks, which risks to govern and by what means? What would a government of crime and security risks look like if governed democratically along such lines?

The issue can only be gestured towards in this chapter. But one answer has been the subject of experimentation by Shearing (2001) and his colleagues (Johnston and Shearing 2003). People in the township environment in South Africa were audited on what they regarded as the main risks to their security. Perhaps surprisingly, these did not overwhelmingly relate to crime, and in some degree police were regarded as a security threat rather than a solution. The researchers persuaded the ruling ANC to redirect some of the funding for police to 'peace committees'. This involved a participatory and informal approach along the lines of restorative justice in which communities addressed the resolution of conflicts that they felt threatened security. In this democratised risk-oriented environment, Shearing notes that 'justice' took on a rather different meaning from that familiar to courts. While the procedures strongly resembled restorative justice, justice was not so much about the backward-looking moral condemnation of offenders, the attribution of blame and the delivery of punishment. Rather people focused on forward-looking questions of risk – on the attempt to ensure that unwanted events and actions did not happen again. In this process expertise was subordinated to the task of developing and proposing solutions to problems of risk defined by the communities. The proposals they made were in turn subject to debate and approval. Crime prevention was being reshaped as a democratic process of risk reduction.

The point is not whether one likes or dislikes the approach taken by Shearing or of any brand of restorative or re-integrative justice. Nor is it meant to understate the difficulties of such a course. It is rather that this illustrates a kind of 'risky' innovation that opened up new directions and took 'risk' away from a pre-set course in which expert definitions went unchallenged. Such work pursued new directions that could offer an alternative to the present (see O'Malley 2003). In their nature such innovations in risk are dangerous: any change we advocate may be co-opted, may be blocked or may open up developments that have unanticipated negative consequences. One possibility is that unpopular minorities may get still more marginalised. But to argue that this is inevitable should make us question the point of a 'critical' discipline.

Post-risk security and the 'new terrorism'

Risk has thus been seen to take on a wide variety of forms with respect to crime control and criminal justice. Indeed, it may be argued that the potential for diversity within risk frameworks is so great that no generalisations may be made concerning their form, function or effects (O'Malley 2010a). Even so, the general reliance of risk on statistical modelling has come to be regarded as an Achilles Foot when it comes to the governance of new and unforeseen forms of criminal threat.

In the current era, it is impossible to think about the deployment of discourses and technologies of risk and crime without immediately turning to the problem of governing the 'new terrorism'. Terrorism is understood to have been transformed in the past twenty years, creating new problems for preventive government. Terrorist groups are said to be characterised by semi-autonomous groups and individuals that are less predictable and traceable than are 'old' terrorist centralised and hierarchical arrangements. Access to new internet-based technologies has increased the array of ways in which terrorists may recruit membership and spread their messages, while increasing the array of targets through informatics-based sabotage of many kinds. Civilians and everyday life have ceased to become incidental to terrorist tactics, and are now depicted as principal targets. Linked to all these shifts, terrorism is seen as creating new risks through globalised networking. Whereas once terrorism was largely focused on particular national struggles, now more globally generalised causes emerge – of which 'radical Islamisation' is currently the principal example. All these changes associated with 'new' models of terrorist strategies are said to render older responses based on risk inadequate. While the associated 'politics of catastrophe' has been challenged – together with much of the assumed novelty of the 'new' terrorism (Walklate and Mythen 2014) – its impact on discourses and technologies of risk is hard to gainsay.

Thirty years ago, it was possible to see the dawning of a new age of predictive governance of crime and security based on probabilistic modelling. Now, many challenges are argued to be generating new 'post-risk' responses. Probabilistic risk techniques rely on two related conditions: the building up of a large body of data from which statistically based predictions may be calculated; and an environment that is sufficiently stable into the future for such predictions to apply. As Ulrich Beck (1992) suggested some time ago, these conditions are no longer to be relied upon. For example, terrorist incidents are said to be too few in number and too dispersed and diverse in nature to permit the required accumulation of mass statistical data; the increased autonomy of terrorist cells and individuals renders surveillance and interception much harder; and terrorists take steps to avoid conforming to predictable patterns – for example by selecting operatives who do not fit risk-profiles (Beck 2002). Faith in preventive government appears to have given way to the emergence of an array of non-probabilistic manoeuvres that do not rely on prevention – or that change its meaning considerably. On the one hand, non-probabilistic ('uncertain') techniques have come to be deployed in place of statistical risk. In the identification of 'risky' passengers passing through airports, for example, security agencies are using such cues as combining how the ticket was paid for and where the journey originated, to trigger further 'uncertain' investigation (de Goede 2008). On the other hand, prevention is increasingly giving way to mitigation, as in the proliferation of advice to citizens on responding to terrorist attacks (Collier 2008). These 'post-risk' forms of governance can be grouped into several broad, and increasingly familiar, categories.

'Preparedness' is perhaps the most straightforward. By this, Collier and Lakoff (2008: 11) mean 'a form of planning for unpredictable but catastrophic events … the aim of such planning is not to prevent these events from happening, but rather to manage their consequences'. They argue that while this is not a new form of governance, it has increasingly been foregrounded and enhanced as an institutionalised response to the uncertain environment post-9/11. Collier outlines enactment as a key technique of preparedness, in which expertise is not so much drawn upon to calculate as to *imagine* catastrophic futures and plan optimal responses. Here, vulnerability and loss are deployed through the development of computer modelling based on analogous past events, rather than accumulated statistical data (Collier 2008: 242).

'Precaution' is a second major response to increasing uncertainty, operating through imagining worst case scenarios. As Francois Ewald (2002: 288) suggests, precaution is not just inviting one 'to take into account doubtful hypotheses and simple suspicions' but even 'to take the most far-fetched forecasts seriously, predictions by prophets, whether true or false'. Since the turn of the 20th century it has been argued that waiting for sufficient evidence to establish a calculable risk to emerge is a luxury that cannot be afforded. Thus the US '9/11 Commission' noted that before 9/11 there had been considerable speculation about catastrophic scenarios, including that of the destruction of the Twin Towers. Given this, the Commission asked why no preventive measures had been taken. In response it argued that imagination should be bureaucratised in the name of governing terrorist risks. If it can be imagined, it must be governed (Bougen and O'Malley 2009, Carlen 2009). In a highly uncertain environment, imagination thus directs or even replaces the calculation of risk.

This is closely related to 'speculative pre-emption', used for example in justifying the war in Iraq. Of course pre-emptive strikes as such are not new, but these have largely been based on clear evidence of threats. However, as the US National Security Strategy makes quite explicit, recent developments offer a radical departure from conservative risk models:

> The greater the threat, the greater is the risk of inaction – and the more compelling the case for taking anticipatory action to defend ourselves, *even if uncertainty remains as*

to the time and place of the enemy's attack. To forestall or prevent such hostile acts by our adversaries, the United States will, if necessary, act pre-emptively.

(National Security Council 2002 quoted by Cooper 2006: 125)

Speculative pre-emption relies precisely on high uncertainty for its rationale and this is argued to differentiate it from historical precursors. Previously, pre-emptive strikes would be founded on clear evidence that an attack was imminent. In 'the risk society', however, high uncertainty has become a justification in its own right. Cooper (2006: 125–127) has argued that the logic of post-9/11 speculative pre-emption – to intervene in emerging events precisely *because of their uncertainty* – is clearly illustrated by the Iraq war, and by the subsequent furore over the relevant governments' lack of evidence of the existence of weapons of mass destruction.

It cannot be disputed that such terrorism-related 'post-risk' discourses and techniques dominate much of contemporary political debate and awareness, at least in the West. But thus far these new and revived manoeuvres against illegalities directly impact on a relatively small number of people, although admittedly even this is out of proportion to the miniscule numbers of people in the West actually harmed by terrorist actions (Walklate and Mythen 2014). Risk regimes, on the other hand, have played and continue to play a major role in reshaping key institutions of everyday security, particularly with respect to criminal justice, policing and crime prevention. Even in terms only of impacts on imprisonment – the tip of the penal iceberg – risk technologies have drastically affected the lives of hundreds of thousands in the English-speaking world alone (Garland 2001). As seen earlier risk-based preventive justice has not been swept aside by techniques and discourses of high uncertainty. Far from it, they have been paralleled by an even more far-reaching risk-based shift – from 'preventive' to 'mass preventive' justice – epitomised by risk-based mass surveillance of traffic offending.

Such a continuing, risk-based and consequential revolution in criminal justice should not be allowed to slip into the shadow of the discourses of securitisation associated with the politics of terrorism.

References

Agamben, G. (2005) *State of Exception*, Chicago: University of Chicago Press

Andrews, D. and J. Bonta (2006) 'The recent past and near future of risk/need assessment', *Crime and Delinquency* 52: 7–27

Baker, T. and J. Simon (eds.) (2002) *Embracing Risk*, Chicago: University of Chicago Press

Bauman, Z. (2000) 'Social issues of law and order', *British Journal of Criminology* 40: 205–221

Beck, U. (1992) *Risk Society: Toward a New Modernity*, New York: Sage

Beck, U. (2002) 'The terrorist threat: World risk society revisited', *Theory, Culture and Society* 19: 39–55

Bentham, J. (1789/1962) 'Principals of penal law' in John Bowring (ed.) *The Works of Jeremy Bentham Vol. I*, New York: Russell and Russell, pp. 365–580

Berman, M. (1983) *All That Is Solid Melts into Air*, London: Verso

Bougen, P. and P. O'Malley (2009) 'Bureaucracy, imagination and US domestic security policy', *Security Journal* 22: 101–118

Carlen, P. (ed.) (2009) *Imaginary Penalities*, Devon: Willan

Chan, J. (2001) 'The technological game: How information technology is transforming police practice', *Criminology and Criminal Justice* 1: 139–159

Cohen, S. (1985) *Visions of Social Control*, London: Polity Press

Collier, S. (2008) 'Enacting catastrophe: Preparedness, insurance, budgetary rationalization', *Economy and Society* 37: 224–250

Collier, S. and A. Lakoff (2008) 'Distributed preparedness: Space, security and citizenship in the United States', *Environment and Planning D: Society and Space* 26:7–28

Cooper, M. (2006) 'Pre-empting emergence: The biological turn in the war on terror', *Theory, Culture and Society* 23: 113–135

De Goede, M. (2008) 'Beyond risk: Premeditation and the post-9/11 security imagination', *Security Dialogue* 39: 155–176

Deleuze, G. (1995) 'Postscript on control societies' in G. Deleuze (ed.) *Negotiations 1972–1990*, New York: Columbia University Press, pp. 177–182

Duster, T. (1990) *Backdoor to Eugenics*, London: Routledge

Ericson, R. and K. Haggerty (1997) *Policing the Risk Society*, Toronto: University of Toronto Press

Ewald, F. (2002) 'The return of Descartes's malicious demon: An outline of a philosophy of precaution' in T. Baker and J. Simon (eds.) *Embracing Risk*, Chicago: University of Chicago Press, pp. 273–301

Eysenck, H. (1978) *Crime and Personality*, London: Paladin

Featherstone, M. (1994) *Consumer Culture and Postmodernism*, London: Sage

Feeley, M. and J. Simon (1992) 'The new penology: Notes on the emerging strategy of corrections and its implications', *Criminology* 30: 449–474

Feeley, M. and J. Simon (1994) 'Actuarial justice: The emerging new criminal law' in D. Nelken (ed.) *The Futures of Criminology*, New York: Sage, pp. 173–201

Ferret, J. and V. Spenlehauer (2009) 'Does *Policing the Risk Society* hold the road risk', *British Journal of Criminology* 49: 150–164

Garland, D. (1996) 'The limits of the sovereign state: Strategies of crime control in contemporary society', *British Journal of Criminology* 36: 445–471

Garland, D. (2001) *The Culture of Control*, Oxford: Oxford University Press

Hannah-Moffat, K. (1999) 'Moral agent or actuarial subject: Risk and Canadian women's imprisonment', *Theoretical Criminology* 3: 71–95

Hannah-Moffat, K. (2005) 'Criminogenic needs and the transformative risk subject', *Punishment and Society* 7: 29–51

Harris, C. (2007) 'Police and soft technology: How information technology contributes to police decision making' in J. Byrne and D. Rebovich (eds.) *The New Technology of Crime, Law and Social Control*, New York: Criminal Justice Press, pp. 153–183

Jackson-Jacobs, C. (2004) 'Taking a beating: The narrative gratification of fighting as an underdog' in J. Ferrell, K. Hayward, W. Morrison and M. Presdee (eds.) *Cultural Criminology Unleashed*, London: Glasshouse Press, pp. 231–245

Johnston, L. and C. Shearing (2003) *Governing Security: Explorations in Policing and Justice*, London: Routledge

Katz, J. (1988) *The Seductions of Crime*, New York: Basic Books

Kerr, P. (1996) *A Philosophical Investigation*, Harmondsworth: Penguin

Kemshall, H. (2003) *Understanding Risk in Criminal Justice*, Milton Keynes: Open University Press

Levi, R. (2000) 'The mutuality of risk and community: The adjudication of community notification statutes', *Economy and Society* 29: 578–601

Lyng, S. (ed.) (2005) *Edgework: The Sociology of Risk Taking*, London: Routledge

Miller, W. (1958) 'Lower class culture as a generating milieu of gang delinquency', *Journal of Social Issues* 14: 5–19

Mythen, G. (2014) *Understanding the Risk Society: Crime, Security and Justice*, London: Palgrave Macmillan

Nelkin, D. and M. Lindee (1995) *The DNA Mystique: The Gene as a Cultural Icon*, New York: Freeman

O'Malley, P. (2003) 'The uncertain promise of risk', *The Australian and New Zealand Journal of Criminology* 37: 323–343

O'Malley, P. (2004) *Risk, Uncertainty and Government*, London: Glasshouse Press

O'Malley, P. (2009) 'Theorizing fines', *Punishment and Society* 11: 67–83

O'Malley, P. (2010a) *Crime and Risk*, New York: Sage

O'Malley, P. (2010b) 'Simulated justice: Risk, money and telemetric policing', *British Journal of Criminology* 50: 795–807

O'Malley, P. and S. Hutchinson (2007) 'Reinventing prevention: Why did "crime prevention" develop so late?', *British Journal of Criminology* 47: 439–454

Pratt, J., D. Brown, M. Brown, S. Hallsworth and W. Morrison (eds.) (2000) *The New Punitiveness: Trends, Theories and Perspectives*, Devon: Willan

Rafter, N. (2008) *The Criminal Brain: Understanding Biological Theories of Crime*, New York: New York University Press

Reichman, N. (1986) 'Managing crime risks: Toward an insurance based model of social control', *Research in Law and Social Control* 8: 151–172

Rose, N. (1999) *Powers of Freedom: Reframing Political Thought*, Cambridge: Cambridge University Press

Rose, N. (2000) 'The biology of culpability: Pathological identity and crime control in a biological culture', *Theoretical Criminology* 4: 5–34

Rose, N. (2007) *The Politics of Life Itself*, Princeton: Princeton University Press

Shearing, C. (2001) 'Transforming security: A South African experiment' in H. Strang and J. Braithwaite (eds.) *Restorative Justice and Civil Society*, Cambridge: Cambridge University Press, pp. 15–34

Shearing, S. and P. Stenning (1985) 'From panopticon to Disneyland: The development of discipline' in A. Doob and E. Greenspan (eds.) *Perspectives in Criminal Law*, Toronto: Canada Law Book Co

Simmel, G. (1895/1990) *The Philosophy of Money* (enlarged edition), New York: Routledge

Simon, J. (1988) 'The ideological effects of actuarial practices', *Law and Society Review* 22: 771–800

Thatcher, M. (1992) *The Downing Street Years*, London: Harper Collins

Walklate, S. and G. Mythen (2014) *Contradictions of Terrorism: Security, Risk and Resilience*, London: Routledge

Winlow, S. and S. Hall (2006) *Violent Night: Urban Leisure and Contemporary Culture*, New York: Berg

Young, J. (1974) *The Drugtakers*, St Albans: Paladin

Young, J. (1999) *The Exclusive Society: Social Exclusion, Crime and Difference in Late Modernity*, New York: Sage

15

THE CRIMINAL PURSUIT OF SERIOUS WHITE-COLLAR CRIMES

Michael Levi

This chapter is dedicated to the memory of my former student Maxwell Nkole, who prosecuted former President Chiluba of Zambia for embezzlement and who, despite the instructions of the then President not to, insisted on appealing against the acquittal in 2009. After this, he was fired and spent several years in the wilderness before his eventual return to public service. The Zambian government never enforced the $57 million order against Chiluba that the English High Court awarded to it in an earlier civil case.

Introduction

This chapter examines the tensions involved in the policing, prosecution and non-prosecution and sentencing of serious economic crimes, focusing principally upon the UK but referring also to other jurisdictions such as Brazil and the USA. It examines the organisational and political tensions surrounding the process of making cases more efficient as well as the criminalisation process itself. Using some case illustrations, I review the political dimensions surrounding prosecutions and non-prosecutions and of sentencing, and asks how and whether we can develop a system that is – and is seen to be – politically impartial, vigorous and fair to defendants.

People have varied ideas of what they are including when they use terms such as white-collar crime, corruption and economic crime. Some mean all crimes of deception, which increasingly have become the most common form of non-violent crimes for economic gain; others think primarily of crimes of exploitation by elites and extortion by the economically and politically powerful. In previous work (Levi, 2009) I explored the question of why fraud and corruption are not more strongly reacted to by the criminal justice process, and why moral panics about aspects of them are managed away from the standard rituals of retributive punishment which still preoccupy reactions to major and even much minor crime. But the austerity impacts of economic crises since 2007 have led to street demonstrations, to movements such as UK/US Uncut, Occupy Wall Street/London and – in several Brazilian cities – to massive protests over the mensalão/*lava jato* (car wash) scandals involving elite political and business corruption (as well as over the use of scarce tax revenues for vast expenditures on the

World Cup and the Olympics, much of which has been linked to corruption in construction contracts). Political tensions (as well their own alleged misconduct) have led to the indictment of the past two Presidents of Brazil and of the previous President of Argentina; to the resignation of the Prime Minister of Romania in 2015 and to that of the Justice Minister and others in 2017;[1] to the final conviction of Prime Minister Berlusconi of Italy, etc. Counter-pressures have inhibited the indictment of many other business and political figures who, for fear of defamation lawsuits, are not named here.

Unlike after previous economic crises, not a single elite financier in the USA or the UK has been jailed for the misconduct and reckless lending that precipitated the global financial crisis from 2007 onwards. However, not directly connected to the economic crises, some of the largest banks in the world have received very large regulatory fines and/or Deferred Prosecution Agreements (DPA) for money laundering and economic sanctions breaches; others like Barclays, Citigroup, Credit Suisse, JPMorganChase, BNP Paribas, RBS and UBS have been criminally convicted for violating international sanctions and for market rate-rigging. Global banks paid the enormous sum of $162.2 billion in fines and legal settlements with US regulators from the financial crisis in 2008–July 2015 (http://blogs.ft.com/ftdata/2015/07/22/bank-fines-data/). In 2016, 27 companies paid some $2.48 billion to resolve US Foreign Corrupt Practice Act (FCPA) cases, the largest annual total in history. The four largest FCPA settlements in 2016 were Teva Pharmaceutical ($519 million), Odebrecht/Braskem ($419.8 million in the USA), Och-Ziff ($412 million) and VimpelCom ($397.6 million).

Corruption scandals have been very prominent in many Latin American and Caribbean countries, often linked to political finance (Levi and Nelken, 1996) and political vendettas (Conaghan, 2012) as well as to personal venality and otherwise unaffordable lifestyles. Conaghan (2012: 650) notes that from 1980 to 2010, 34 former Presidents were indicted in Latin America, partly to stop them from returning to power. The assumption in much English legal literature that prosecutions are based around objective investigations and are adjudicated dispassionately is at best contestable in Latin America, and in many other parts of the world likewise: but this does not mean that *all* prosecutions and convictions there or elsewhere are motivated by political and/or personal opposition rather than by evidence.

Partly due to the efforts of investigative journalists, the exposure of elite misconduct has had less dramatic but still significant consequences in major Western countries. In addition to the major international scandal arising from the 'Panama Papers' leaks in 2016 and regular scandals over decades in French, Italian and Irish politics, an example is the LuxLeaks scandal in which revelations by a former PriceWaterhouseCoopers staff member, Antoine Deltour, exposed the 'sweetheart deals' on taxation that have done much to enable the world's major corporations to avoid paying much corporation tax: he received a 12-month suspended sentence – cut to 6 months on appeal – and was fined €1,500 after conviction on charges including theft and violating Luxembourg's strict professional secrecy laws. (A journalist co-accused was acquitted.) There have been an increasing number of such whistleblowing cases involving banks in jurisdictions like Liechtenstein and Switzerland where leaking customer information is regarded as economic espionage: HSBC employee Hervé Falciani was sentenced to five years' imprisonment in absentia in November 2015 in Switzerland for passing on to foreign tax authorities data on foreign tax evading account-holders. How seriously, though, when we label acts as white-collar crimes or not, should we take the issue of whether the criminal law has been broken, the traditional boundary between criminology and other areas of social control?

The level of present and future trust in law enforcement agencies is a powerful influence on views about the legitimacy of crime control. This chapter focuses upon a particular sub-set of 'the trust issues', the prosecution of serious fraud and allied financial crimes. In some countries, mostly but not exclusively poor ones, in which economic and social power are highly concentrated, anger at fraud and corruption can manifest itself in demands for prosecution of elites as well as recovery of the proceeds of their frauds and bribes. Similar allegations of kleptocracy are made against the incoming administrations, demonstrating the weakness of criminal law alone as an instrument of prevention in countries of the South and North. After the financial collapse of 2007–2009, this public rage has been directed in the USA against Wall Street elites (and, after the Gulf of Mexico environmental disaster, to BP; or after the 2015 Samarco mine and environmental disaster, to BHP Billiton, Vale and the Brazilian government). The locus of blame is influenced by socially constructed values and media campaigns, etc., and can focus on 'criminals', crime non-preventers, investigators, prosecutors, judges and/ or juries in those countries that have them.

Feeley and Simon (2007) and Garland (2008) suggest that the *general* social construction of crime has changed since the 1960s, with the cultural temperature being raised frequently to target fear of different crimes and criminal groups. Cullen et al. (2006) discuss attempts to criminalise what they term 'business violence', and the history of criminal regulation of business activities has always been contested space (Levi, 1987/2013). Yet even at times of economic crisis such as that experienced in many countries in the late 'noughties', Western governments have regularly sought to defuse the risk of a social movement against white-collar crimes (broadly defined to include both elite and non-elite[2] commercial crimes), preferring to deal with them more softly and – they claim – more effectively by regulation and occasional symbolic prosecution. The USA has historically had a more vigorous approach to the prosecution and regulatory sanctioning of elites, assisted by easier rules for founding corporate criminal liability than has had the UK. Moreover, some US prosecutors (and an occasional investigative judge/prosecutor from France – Eva Joly – and Italy – Antonio di Pietro) have been able to base political careers around white-collar crime fighting, even if, as former New York Attorney-General Eliot Spitzer found, they can come crashing down again later, due to his attempt to hide his interstate electronic payments for high class prostitutes, which was picked up and reported by his bank, and followed up both by Republican private investigators and the police. Spitzer had to resign both his office and high political ambitions, to the relief of the financial institutions who had been pursued by him, though he was not replaced by business-friendly successors.

By contrast, UK prosecutors have not sought political careers, and none of those who have 'rocked the boat' by suggesting an aggressive approach to prosecution have been appointed to top fraud prosecutorial positions. In Brazil, prosecutors have shown an independent spirit in pursuing cases against politicians (the *mensalão* scandal) and against politicians and businesspeople involved in the serious mismanagement of the oil company Petrobras, to the extent that they and some judges have been accused by the Left of being part of a right wing conspiracy or coup.[3] But Brazilian regulators of environmental permits have not usually shown independence from collusive business and political elites, allegedly because of corruption; nor did national prosecutors develop any cases against Brazilian FIFA leaders accused of notorious corruption. Case complexity, the need for financial information from secrecy or even from non-secrecy jurisdictions and limited competence are further reasons why this non-aggressive approach is difficult to shift: but it may be argued that these are convenient pegs upon which to hang other reasons for inaction. However, it is interesting to explore the aspects of change and continuity through the lens of transformations (and non-transformations) in the elements that make up the prosecution of serious fraud, and it is this to which we now turn.

First, some background. One of the problems that surrounds terms like 'serious fraud', 'white-collar crime', 'economic crime', 'financial crime' and even 'corruption' is that they misleadingly aggregate a set of quite disparate phenomena, which are more meaningfully ana-lysed in terms of variations in victim and offender status and interests. We should review not just the social composition of prosecuted offenders but also the status of their victims in order to assess the social meaning of prosecutions for corruption and fraud. It is helpful to see fraud and corruption prosecutions as an attrition process that passes or does not pass through the successive filters of awareness, reporting, recording, investigation, prosecution and conviction. Unless a 'case' passes through all of these filters, criminal justice sanctions cannot be applied, though there remain important alternatives such as regulatory fines, occupational disqualifica-tion and bad publicity that may be imposed if the corporate or individual actor is subjectable to those sorts of penalties. In addition, some countries have the possibility of civil forfeiture, and all have civil lawsuits, though these may require substantial funding or 'no win, no fee'/ class action arrangements. This review will not examine the merits and demerits of criminal versus regulatory modes of control – important though that debate is – but will focus on the criminal route.

The more complex a case is, the more it needs resources and competence at all of these stages. Thus resource starvation can indirectly destroy the willingness to take on major cases, since the opportunity cost of doing so is high. On the other hand, as alleged in the prosecu-tion of Putin's opponent Mikhail Khodorkovsky, former CEO of Yukos Oil, and some other Russian émigré 'oligarchs', financial investigation resource abundance can be directed in a politically partisan way, to prosecute the regime's opponents and to let off the regime's sup-porters, and this is especially easy if there is not *de facto* independence by prosecutors and/or judges. However, prosecuting elite cases also needs a mind-set of seeing 'what happened' as criminal and a willingness to tackle it via the criminal law, and it is this mind-set that is often far from natural. We are used to seeing criminals as 'not like us' so if someone is (or appears to be) 'like us', it is difficult for us to treat them as a 'real' criminal. So the composition of 'the fraud problem' depends partly on the flow of complaints/investigations and partly on the pragmatic assessment of 'political' (with a small or large 'p') difficulties within the resources available.

A short history of the prosecution of serious white-collar crimes in England and Wales

Resources act as an upper limit on prosecutions. In the early 1970s, for example, a third of the entire Fraud Division of the Office of the Director of Public Prosecutions plus a large per-centage of the Metropolitan Police Fraud Squad were working full-time on the Poulson local government corruption case that caught the then Home Secretary, Reggie Maudling, within its ambit (Gillard, 1974). In the late 1970s, the Department of Trade – the main vehicle for the prosecution of misconduct by company directors rather than of fraud by outsiders – had only eight lawyers working on company fraud.

Three particular periods of prosecutorial crisis in the UK suggest themselves. The first was in the early 1980s; the second in the early–mid 1990s; and the third in the aftermath of the BAE transnational bribery investigations and global financial crisis. It remains to be seen whether there will be a fourth crisis following proposals to close down the Serious Fraud Office and to merge it with the National Crime Agency and the Crown Prosecution Service.

Unlike civil law countries such as Brazil, the tradition in common law countries is for the police to lead all criminal investigations, with a stronger prosecutorial involvement in the USA than elsewhere. Nevertheless, a series of unsuccessful prosecutions and scandals in the early 1980s culminated in the Fraud Trials Committee (1986) and, as part of a push for the international credibility of London as the premier global financial services centre, it was felt that some higher profile was needed to show the international community that the British were competent and serious about tackling fraud, and thus, the Serious Fraud Office was created. As the Home Secretary Douglas Hurd expressed it in the Parliamentary debate on the Fraud Trials Committee report:[4]

> We intend to create and seize every opportunity for stern action against fraud. We think this is crucial for the City and for the country so that private enterprise can flourish in a clean environment. It is crucial for public confidence, and our competitive position in international markets that the probity of our financial institutions, especially in the City, should be beyond doubt. Those who save and invest, whether grand or small, should be well protected by our law from dishonest practices, however complicated the transaction. We are determined that the pursuit and the bringing to justice of fraudsters should be carried out with commitment and skill. If our present instruments for cutting our fraud are blunt we must manufacture a new carefully directed scalpel ... Early detection of irregularities can often prevent serious fraud and as with all crime, prevention is our first aim. If prevention fails then the machinery for dealing with fraud must be effective.

Although no-one at the time raised questions about prosecutor independence from government, the police ensured that they retained discretion over resource allocation for fear that they might have to give too many officers to fraud investigations, and this has remained a source of tension ever since, though in principle, the Director-General of the National Crime Agency can direct policing resources from other forces to investigate fraud, corruption or other offences. (To date, this has not happened, at least formally.) The Criminal Justice Act 1987 did create a separate body with non-specific accountability to Parliament via the Attorney-General parallel to the Director of Public Prosecutions (DPP), who retained the discretion to prosecute (or not) police-investigated fraud cases and corruption cases. At that time, transnational bribery cases were not contemplated, and the Organisation for Economic Co-operation and Development (OECD) transnational bribery convention – which later was to generate such problems for the Serious Fraud Office (SFO) and led to the dynamic Bribery Act 2010 with its extraterritorial jurisdiction – was not contemplated. It also inaugurated for the first time in England and Wales (though not Scotland, which had them already) lawyer-headed investigations, aiming to reduce the cost and time wasted on police investigations on lines that the prosecution counsel later considered inappropriate, or not investigating things that counsel later considered essential.

The SFO led to an increase in major fraud prosecutions generally and an upsurge in cases involving otherwise legitimate company executives. In the first seven years of its operation, an average of only 16 cases *per annum* involved organisational frauds committed through otherwise legitimate companies; fewer still, an average of only four cases *per annum*, involved chief executive officers working for financial institutions situated in London's financial markets or public limited companies (Fooks, 2003). Fooks assumes that this is *disproportionately* small, but this conclusion is not self-evident as there may be disagreement about the appropriate metrics.

The first few major SFO prosecutions gave little reason to suspect lack of prosecutorial courage. Compared with the sorts of prosecutions into marginal figures that had gone before, the prosecution of the chief executive of Guinness, a partner in a major brokerage firm, a lawyer (and some more 'entrepreneurial' City of London figures) looked like a serious attempt to deal with elite crime (though in the event, the elite professionals were not convicted – see Levi, 1991). This was followed by a prosecution of County NatWest Bank, brokers Phillips & Drew (by then bought by UBS), and a range of fairly elite lawyers and investment advisers (who in organised crime discourse would be termed 'professional enablers'), in relation to the hiding of problems in a corporate takeover. This generated concern in some financial services circles about the non-accountability (to business elites) of the SFO, even though most defendants were acquitted, and then the remaining defendants had their convictions quashed by the Court of Appeal.

November 1992 and early 1993 witnessed two extraordinary events. The first was the prosecution by HM Customs & Excise of three directors of a company called Matrix-Churchill for allegedly violating prohibitions on the export of arms components to Iraq by *deceiving* the Department of Trade and Industry into granting export licences. The second was the scandal surrounding the flight to North Cyprus of Asil Nadir, who had been charged by the SFO with defrauding Polly Peck International of over £30 million: he was eventually extradited and jailed for ten years in 2012, 19 years after his flight. *Inter alia*, these and some other fraud cases involving powerful defendants and potential defendants have opened up interesting issues such as the relative autonomy of the *prosecution* as well as the *policing* process from 'the government'. This was to re-emerge over BAE.

Especially before the Human Rights Act, legislation on powers to investigate white-collar crime seemed often to diverge from that of 'ordinary' crime, largely because it is seen as analytically separable from it, businesspeople's rights do not interest many on the political left, and because of their social status and articulateness, they have usually not been seen to be at risk of miscarriages of justice in the UK (Levi, 1993, 1987/2013).[5] They are, in a sense, the most unappealing group among those who might lay claim to 'victim of miscarriage status'. For these reasons, paradoxically, there have been relatively few challenges from the civil libertarian left to the model to combat 'white-collar crime'. In contemporary Brazil and elsewhere in Latin America, this may not be the case, as former leaders of parties of the Left have been targeted for prosecution and this is seen by some Brazilians as a right wing coup using the criminal justice system.

Fairness in serious fraud prosecutions

McConville et al. (1991) argue that cases are *constructed* by the prosecutor on the basis of police reports and perceptions of 'what happened', in which the police re-form witnesses' statements into their own mixture of conviction-supporting material. Hypothetically, serious fraud cases – to which they make no reference – would not be expected to look like this, for their density and the elite status of suspects should protect them from the strong arm of the law. Except where there is a political 'fix', under Rule of Law principles, serious fraud would be expected to involve lengthy negotiation over access to documents, over interpretations of what happened and over the decision to prosecute itself rather than to impose administrative penalties or other measures such as Deferred Prosecution Agreements.

Police influence over *witness* statements can de-complexify reality, minimising witness culpability while sometimes exaggerating the suspect(s)'s culpability. It is also an article of faith rather than evidence that professional status will immunise interviewers against taken-for-granted 'frames' within which the evidence and their interviews are viewed. What the SFO regime does is to ensure that interviews with key professional witnesses are taped and are conducted by lawyers and accountants, removing one layer of such unsupervised steering. However, it remains deeply problematic in complex organisational settings to know which witnesses are telling the truth and, more especially, how 'blameworthiness' is distributed. For example, accountants may find it convenient for their position in defending themselves from later professional misconduct or negligence charges if it is believed that they were told lies by the directors than if they failed to check things without being told lies or even suggested various 'dodgy' manoeuvres; it is also less damaging professionally to their reputations for competence. What is *anyone* who was not actually there at the time to make of conflicting interpretations of what was said (given that, unlike ordinary police cases, the SFO can make them *have* to say *something* unless they have a – tightly circumscribed – 'reasonable excuse' not to answer)?[6] Simply because fraud has a lot more documentation than other crimes does not mean that the interpretation of roles and who knew (or was told) what is unproblematical. One of the most public illustrations of this is the undercurrents about the drafting of witness statements by civil servants and Ministers that emerged from that portion of the Tribunal of Enquiry by Lord Justice Scott (1996) that dealt with the Matrix-Churchill export licences. Whatever the disputes about Lord Justice Scott's interpretation of 'what happened', it is clear that prosecution witnesses radically re-framed events in order to fit the prosecution's theory to enable conviction to take place. If the background documentation that the Ministers' Public Interest Immunity certificates covered (and sought to hide) had not been made available to the defence, as it eventually was, there is every probability that the Matrix-Churchill directors would have been wrongly convicted for deceiving the Department of Trade and Industry export licence department into believing that the arms components were made for civil use.[7] This is not an issue restricted to serious fraud: it also arose, for example, in the prosecution of News International executives for alleged conspiracy to intercept mobile voicemails, alongside others connected to the newspaper.

The second crisis for the SFO arrived in 1992–1995, when it came under increasing attack from defence lawyers and in the media both for 'over-prosecution' and for failing to obtain convictions in high profile cases, culminating in the acquittal of the public 'folk devils' Kevin and Ian Maxwell (Corker and Levi, 1996; Levi, 2009). One basis (or pretext) for these attacks was allegations that the SFO produced 'scattergun' charges: such allegations of overcharging are often made against the US Department of Justice.

Meanwhile the tax agencies – which have never been under the control of the SFO – continued with their focus on financial settlements as an alternative to prosecution except where they regard it as strategically important for deterrent (and long run revenue-maximising) purposes (Levi, 2010). In cases where their targets were (offshore) donors, this preference for money recovered over criminal convictions is obviously 'sensitive'. Despite various actual and anticipated pressures, however, the prosecution of Conservative donor Octav Botnar (and a co-director and auditors, who were convicted, by the Inland Revenue), Nadir (by the SFO) and the Matrix-Churchill directors (by HM Customs & Excise) lends support to those who argue that British law enforcement officials enjoy relative autonomy from the government, at least under most circumstances, despite the complex liaison between heads of prosecution departments and the politically appointed Attorney-General.

No fraudsters are targets of police/populist retributive sentiments to the extent of terrorists or drugs traffickers, but those who defraud 'widows and orphans' are certainly not viewed more favourably than 'ordinary decent criminals'. Anyone observing the public and US presidential excoriation of BP over the Gulf of Mexico oil spillage might wonder how the company or its chief executive could get a fair criminal or civil trial (for jury prejudice in a UK context, see Corker and Levi, 1996; Honess et al., 2002); whether the Brazilian Samarco disaster would receive similar treatment is unknown. In several cases in the 1980s and since, there were very high profile arrests in the glare of publicity, accompanied by allegations that 'the SFO' *deliberately* used what the Americans call 'the perp walk' as a prejudicial PR stunt. Alternatively/additionally, these may be viewed as attempts to enhance the legitimacy of prosecutors and of government efforts to deal with public scandals and allegations against elites.

In every realm of criminal justice, even where there is undercover infiltration or covert surveillance (particularly without video-recording),[8] imperfect approximations are made regarding 'what happened'. The police and regulators have their interpretations, which may reflect their cynical lack of empathy with the 'commercial community'; in countries with jury systems the jury have theirs, which may reflect dislike of rich Jews or 'foreigners', or excessive respect for their social superiors as much as the evidence.[9] (In some civil law systems, judges may be under pressure from governments to convict, and/or may be conditioned to accept prosecutorial perspectives without searching hard for counter-arguments.) There is more pressure from British Police and Crime Commissioners and the Home Secretary to deal with crime on the streets than crime in the suites, but in addition to problems of dealing with blue-collar or 'organised' cybercrimes, the place of Britain in a global economy, as well as the security of retirement pensions and redundancy payments, depends also on Britain's reputation for dealing with financial misconduct. That, of course, creates its own pressures to get convictions, to show other countries that 'we' deal with our fraudsters effectively, as well as to demonstrate the 'effectiveness' of individual and agency decisions to prosecute. Although Brazil is not a major international financial services centre, analogous arguments can be applied to its need to show there is no '*impunidade*', which pressures were more easily resisted in earlier times and obviously under military dictatorship. International reputation and political pressures can change the balance of political interests in taking (or not taking) action, including action only against political opponents.

Reasonable people can disagree over whether or not they have discovered a 'smoking prosecutorial gun' in overt political motivation for white-collar prosecutions. Conaghan (2012) details how and why politicians, prosecutors and judges 'went after' Ecuadorian Presidents and ex-Presidents and the political machinations that underlay these decisions. Nelken (1996) shows how the legal and political autonomy of Italian investigating judges can give rise to tectonic clashes between the Rule of Law/Judges and the pragmatic compromises that may be needed to operate the economic and political system in Italy. Concern has been expressed domestically and internationally about Turkey's prosecutions of alleged Gulenists and the non-prosecution of family and associates of President Erdogan (despite covert videotapes of them published on YouTube) in the current decade. There are relatively few British or North American studies of the elite prosecution or non-prosecution process, though Eichenwald's (2001) fascinating study of the failed handling of an embezzling insider who acted as informant against conglomerate ArcherMidlandDaniels for sustained price fixing; the dissection of the problems of the FBI's undercover operation on the Chicago futures markets (Greising and Morse, 1991), which led to many convictions and many acquittals of the 46 people indicted; and Cullen et al.'s (2006) study of the Ford Pinto case are rich in detail. However they show the skilful use of procedural and evidential law, and mistakes made by prosecutors, rather than political 'fixes'. As for the UK, Turkish-origin millionaire entrepreneur Asil Nadir failed to come up with the tapes or records that would have substantiated his claim that 'they' (i.e. the UK and US governments) wanted him out of the way to promote a peace settlement regarding the Turkish Republic of North Cyprus. Likewise, how did the interests of the Conservatives in cracking down on City crime (and in forestalling commercially competitive US leaks about 'untouchable' British City crooks, arising out of US Securities and Exchange Commission and US Department of Justice interviews with insider trader Ivan Boesky) lead senior officers in the Metropolitan Police Fraud Squad to arrest Guinness Chairman Ernest Saunders, but not to arrest other 'City criminals' who presumably could equally have been selected to satisfy the Conservatives' alleged pre-1987 election political white-collar blood-lust? If such prosecutions are necessary to legitimate capitalism then, why were there no similar prosecutions following the financial crisis of 2007–2010? These functionalist 'explanations' of prosecution decision-making in white-collar crime cases do not appear to work at the level of agency.

This brings us to the third crisis for the prosecution of white-collar crimes, the BAE case and its aftermath. The history of the case is elegantly set out in *R (on the application of Corner House Research and others) v Director of the Serious Fraud Office* [2008] UKHL 60. Suffice it to state that when the SFO investigation got close to obtaining information it needed from Switzerland to mount a prosecution of BAE for transnational bribery in relation to the Saudi Al Yamamah contract, the Saudis threatened to withdraw counter-terrorist assistance, which – doubtless fortuitously – placed it beyond the 'national economic benefit' issues outlawed by s. 5 of the OECD Convention as a reason for not prosecuting. On the face of it, the Law Officers behaved wholly properly in requiring representations by BAE and by the Saudis to be referred first to the SFO Director, and the Attorney-General examining the issues *qua* the most senior lawyer, even if the SFO Director disagreed with his judgment on the strength of the case. The SFO Director eventually agreed that the threat to UK national security overrode the benefit of continuing that particular case against BAE. In the highest court ruling, Lord Bingham added (para. 32) that:

> the discretions conferred on the Director are not unfettered. He must seek to exercise his powers so as to promote the statutory purpose for which he is given them. He must direct himself correctly in law. He must act lawfully. He must do his best to exercise an objective judgment on the relevant material available to him. He must exercise his powers in good faith, uninfluenced by any ulterior motive, predilection or prejudice.

Notwithstanding the legal arguments, this produced an international outcry, stimulated by Cornerhouse and other NGOs, and by the OECD itself which continued to question the UK government's sincerity in its commitment to the OECD Convention and its slowness in passing modern anti-bribery laws. Questions continued to be raised about the role of the Attorney-General as a Cabinet member and supervisor of the DPP and SFO Director, though the SFO Director insisted that he had taken the decision personally to allow national security considerations to override the desirability of a prosecution, preserving constitutional propriety.

The (then) Labour Attorney-General, Baroness Scotland, insisted that Labour reject the proposal not to allow her to overrule the DPP or SFO Director. This was an issue that did not excite the public but continues to raise important questions about the objectivity of decisions to prosecute and not to prosecute (as also in the USA, though the Federal authorities have a Congress-approved Special Prosecutor arrangement that seeks – not always successfully as in the Clintons and the 'Whitewatergate' manufactured scandal – to de-politicise prosecution decisions about political elites).

The closest fit for the British conspiracy theorists of prosecution decisions might appear to be Matrix-Churchill, at least in terms of reflecting the desire to show the public that Britain had *not* willingly provided the weapons used to kill its own soldiers in the Gulf War.[10] Some support for this explicitly political 'reading' is that in an earlier case, Prime Minister Margaret Thatcher sent her best wishes for the success of their 'sting' operation to Customs & Excise, which were conveyed to the undercover agents nine months *before* they arrested Daghir and Speckman, who were successfully prosecuted for allegedly supplying arms components to Iraq.[11] Yet even the determination to go ahead with the prosecution of Matrix-Churchill directors seems to have more to do with the resentment of Customs & Excise at what they viewed as political interference with their earlier planned prosecution over the supply of 'Supergun' components to Iraq[12] than with national politics: in this sense – and somewhat ironically, in view of its miscarriage of justice potential – it represents the triumph of legal over political values. But how can we properly decide on whether or not a prosecution or non-prosecution decision is affected by explicit political factors (or, for that matter, by the cultural attitude more common in Britain than in the USA or Australia – the desire not to 'rock the boat')? 'Methodic suspicion' often leads to the ignoring of counter-evidence, but even insider researchers are confronted with the classic Cicourel (1968) problem of being torn between our personal judgement that x would never have conspired to do y, and the risk that we too have 'gone native' and have been misled by excessive familiarity with our research subjects. If John Le Carré had written up the Matrix-Churchill affair in the form of a novel, many might have found it to be an unrealistic portrait of shiftiness and ineptitude on the part of some civil servants and Ministers.

But to demonstrate that state institutions sometimes behave like that does not mean that *all* paranoid or self-serving allegations of political conspiracies are true. Though far less is involved in the specimen charges in the indictment, the amount of money missing from Polly Peck – whose absence has still not been explained and some of which has not been satisfactorily traced – was equivalent to the total net losses from automobile crime in England and Wales that year. It is unsurprising that prosecutors and investigators at the SFO should have come up with the hypothesis that a man who transferred so many millions to an offshore company acting on lawful authority but without any apparently good business reason might have been intending to steal it! Eventually Nadir was extradited from North Cyprus and failed to cause enough doubt about his guilt to convince the jury to acquit him, but it is possible that the jury believed *both* that there was a political motivation to prosecute him *and* that he was guilty.

The SFO Director has financial limitations in pursuing investigations to prosecution and a need to leverage its efforts via a more general 'fraud and corruption reduction' strategy, involving attempts to pursue American-style Deferred Prosecution Agreements, though the current Director (David Green QC) displayed far more commitment to prosecute than did his predecessor (Richard Alderman). This shift away from reliance on the criminal justice process generated much criticism, and difficulties in the courts over plea negotiations; in addition there are tensions over which approaches are more or less 'effective' (Lord, 2014a, 2014b; Lord and Levi, 2015). In November 2015, the SFO concluded its first ever DPA, over corruption in Tanzania   (www.sfo.gov.uk/press-room/latest-press-releases/press-releases-2015/sfo-agrees-first-uk-dpa-with-standard-bank.aspx):

> As a result of the DPA, Standard Bank will pay financial orders of US$25.2 million and will be required to pay the Government of Tanzania a further US$7 million in compensation. The bank has also agreed to pay the SFO's reasonable costs of £330,000 in relation to the investigation and subsequent resolution of the DPA.
>
> In addition to the financial penalty that has been imposed, Standard Bank has agreed to continue to cooperate fully with the SFO and to be subject to an independent review of its existing anti-bribery and corruption controls, policies and procedures regarding compliance with the Bribery Act 2010 and other applicable anti-corruption laws. It is required to implement recommendations of the independent reviewer (Price Waterhouse Coopers LLP).

Others followed, most notably to date the DPA with Rolls Royce which led to its agreement to pay the SFO £497.2 million – a record British fine for criminal conduct by a company. Rolls Royce also agreed to pay $170 million to the US Department of Justice and $25.6 million to Brazil's Ministerio Publico Federal. The agreed facts were that Rolls Royce had committed systematic corruption between 1989 and 2013 in a range of countries including those not settled in the DPA (*SFO v Rolls Royce*, 17 January 2017, www.judiciary.gov.uk/judgments/serious-fraud-office-v-rolls-royce/). The SFO announced that it was also going after the individuals involved. The settlement raises issues about how far prosecutors and judges should take into account symbolic messaging, fairness and the bargaining power afforded by collateral damage to jobs: but in the reasoning of the judge, Sir Brian Leveson – a former Chairman of the Sentencing Council – a key issue was that though Rolls Royce had not self-reported to the SFO, it had given an extraordinary degree of cooperation to the SFO and none of those involved in the previous misconduct were still on the Board.

The emotional contradiction many people experience when reviewing the prosecution of white-collar crime is that convicting 'the suits' may be seen as a necessary prerequisite of 'equal justice'. This is brilliantly captured in the American novel (and movie) *Bonfire of the Vanities*, where the prosecutors long to put some rich white guys in jail instead of the poor blacks whom they feel deep down have little real alternative to crime (Wolfe, 1987). Serious fraud and corruption prosecutors might get it wrong either in imagining possible lines of defence or in imputing culpability.[13] On the other hand, the depth of prejudicial publicity which follows a corporate collapse (as in Enron or Maxwell) or a major fall in profitability (as in Petrobras) is a powerful impetus to carry people forward to prosecution, fuelled by media suspicions of 'cover up' if they do not do so. The prosecution of white-collar crime, as much as any other, entails the perpetual refrains of 'was s/he behaving dishonestly?' and 'what did s/he know and what was s/he told about this transaction?' Our judgements of plausibility may differ as between (a) a hi-tech engineering firm in which senior management were professional hardware/software engineers and (b) a bank in which the senior management were ignorant of banking. The criminal law bifurcates people into the crude binary division of 'guilty' or 'innocent' (or at least insufficient certainty of guilt, which then gets read politically as innocent or 'got off though probably guilty'), and in the complex world of corporate actions where there are so many people who are potentially indictable, this yields strange and bitter fruit, in which many of the prosecution witnesses are as unattractive and prone to generate disinformation as are the defendants (see Levi, 1993; Eichenwald, 2001).

Even before SFO Director Richard Alderman announced the policy of seeking to get corporate bribers to volunteer confessions in return for more lenient treatment (which he was unable to guarantee),[14] there was debate about the role of informants in the criminal justice process. But it is a very rare case where, as in the first Guinness trial in 1990, the judge has to give a massively complex set of jury instructions which revolve around whether the Finance Director, Olivier Roux, was really an unindicted accomplice or was merely a key witness (source: trial transcript). Likewise, it is a curious system in which, because the Serious Fraud Office – which determines its own workload – considers itself to be 'full up' with large cases, a vast fraud is dealt with by the police under ordinary police powers with less access to specialised accounting advice or witness compulsion: but this is an inevitable organisational and economic reality, especially in times of austerity. The business plans of the Serious Fraud Office and of the Crown Prosecution Service stress independence and accountability for performance (www.sfo.gov.uk/download/annual-report-2015–2016; www.cps.gov.uk/publications/docs/cps_2020.pdf; www.cps.gov.uk/publications/docs/annual_report_2015_16.pdf), but how these declarations will generate legitimacy is unclear. These prosecution bodies (plus the Financial Conduct Authority) collaborate with the National Crime Agency's Economic Crime Command, the City of London Police Economic Crime Department, local Trading Standards investigators, and other police and non-police bodies. The then Chancellor of the Exchequer observed (16 June 2010, www.hm-treasury.gov.uk/press_12_10.htm): 'We take white collar crime as seriously as other crime and we are determined to simplify the confusing and overlapping responsibilities in this area in order to improve detection and enforcement.' But perceptions that elites are dealt with on different criteria than ordinary people are not shifted by declarations alone.

In Brazil, allegations of corporate corruption have not been rare (Lazzarini, 2010; Margolis, 2015; Cuadros, 2016), but they have received greatest publicity in relation to sport (soccer and volleyball), going back at least to the era of ex-FIFA President Joao Havelange and his former son-in-law Ricardo Teixeira, and remaining current (Jennings, 2015). In all sectors, they appear to relate to networks of patron–client relationships. On 12 December 2014, José Hawilla, the owner and founder of the Traffic Group, the Brazilian sports marketing conglomerate, waived indictment and pleaded guilty in the USA to a four-count information charging him with racketeering conspiracy, wire fraud conspiracy, money laundering conspiracy and obstruction of justice. He also agreed to forfeit over $151 million, $25 million of which was paid at the time of his plea. Other Traffic companies pleaded guilty to fraud. Odebrecht channelled almost $788 million to politicians and officials across a dozen countries, as an 'unparalleled bribery and bid rigging scheme' as the US, Brazilian and Swiss authorities fined Odebrecht at least $3.5 billion. By the end of 2016, the Petrobras investigation led to 82 people – ranging from former PT treasurer João Vaccari Neto to Marcelo Odebrecht himself – being convicted in the lower courts on charges ranging from corruption to money laundering while the Supreme Court, which is responsible for trying serving politicians, was processing a further 74 cases (*Financial Times*, 28 December 2016).

The scandals have generated legislative change: the Brazilian Clean Companies Act (Lei n. 12.846/2013) entered into force in 2014, creating an anti-corruption system similar to but less ambitious than the US Foreign Corrupt Practices Act and the UK Bribery Act. The law imposes strict civil and administrative liability upon Brazilian companies for acts of domestic and international corruption, and on foreign companies operating in Brazil. The Clean Companies Act prohibits facilitation payments and makes no exception for small bribes. It also prohibits fraud, data manipulation and the obstruction of government investigations. Unlike the UK legislation, the Clean Companies Act does not provide a defence that a company had 'adequate procedures' in place to prevent corruption. Under severe political pressure, on 18 March 2015, then President Rousseff issued a presidential decree (Decreto n. 8.420/2015) specifying the responsible investigative and enforcement agencies and providing guidance regarding corporate anti-corruption procedures. So far, the Brazilian authorities have adopted US-style tactics of trying to get defendants to 'roll over' and incriminate other more senior figures to reduce sentences and perhaps avoid conviction and severe asset forfeiture: there may also be an element of score-settling by those who consider that if they are 'going down', others should too!

The progress of some prosecutions was interrupted by the death of Judge Teori Zavascki in a plane crash in January 2017 and by the time anyone reads this chapter, the situation is likely to have changed further: but the *lava jato* (Car Wash) enquiries have been variously interpreted as an attempt by the traditional economic elites to use an ambitious prosecutor to remove a constraint on their powers, at one extreme, to a heroic attempt of independent prosecutors to demonstrate that there is no impunity for current elites, at the other. Empirically, this issue remains contested: much may depend on whether equal vigour is exercised in the prosecution of important conservative politicians and their business allies as has already been exercised against Rousseff and Lula. It is difficult for outsiders to assess the strength of the evidence 'objectively' or even to agree what objectivity would look like.

Sentencing

Do 'the powerful' receive more lenient treatment than others? Analytically this is difficult because for the most part, they do not commit easily comparable 'like for like' offences: the exceptions are personal frauds against the government (such as tax versus social security fraud). Elsewhere, it is not obvious how we adjudicate rationally between hypotheses that (1) there is an ideological and/or social bias against imprisoning the powerful, and (2) inequality of treatment is an *un*intended (and often unseen) product of wider criminal justice processes such as plea bargaining that are uneven in their application because better defence counsel and greater case complexity gives elites in complex business and governmental organisations more grounds for denying culpability. We also need to consider the conditions under which 'respectable offenders' may become targets for status degradation, e.g. at times of general 'moral panic' about corruption or white-collar crimes, or 'victor's justice' efforts to get rid of elite rivals or troublesome critics (as discussed earlier). In other words, we need both to examine sentencing data themselves and to interpret how to make sense of them (Levi, 2002, 2016).

Note also that bias can occur (or be believed to occur) in how offenders are allocated to categories of prison, parole decisions and pardons: this is part of the sanctioning process, if not formally of the sentencing process. President Clinton was much criticised from many parts of the political spectrum for pardoning a number of people in jail for fraud and money laundering, plus especially Marc Rich and Pincus Green, who had been fugitives (in Switzerland) after their indictment in 1983 on charges of racketeering and of mail and wire fraud arising out of their oil business; Rich had been indicted for evading $48 million in taxes. Clinton felt obliged to try to defend his decision-making and his reputation, not least against suggestions that donations by Rich's ex-wife to the Presidential Library and Democratic campaigns had facilitated the pardon (see www.propublica.org/article/the-shadow-of-marc-rich).

One area where there are few parallels with most 'ordinary' offenders is that professional sanctions can also create the possibility of 'incapacitation without custody' (Levi, 1987/ 2013): this can serve as a rationale for light formal sentencing because they no longer consti- tute a threat to others. However it is much harder to cut off from crime opportunities those who defraud the government and banks as *external* actors (from credit card fraud to hacking) so readily as it is those people who need authorisation as 'fit and proper persons' to practise their professions (like lawyers and senior bankers); and though some payments to social secu- rity fraudsters can be cut off, other opportunities to defraud might be available to them. We need also to consider the impacts in reality: if someone is no longer on the Board of FIFA or the International Olympic Committee (IOC), does it mean that they exert no influence any more? Someone who is banned from politics (or whose presidential maximum term has expired), from being a company director, or from the securities market can exert influence as a shadow director and it is hard to know what the probability is of their being discovered. The effect of shaming depends on how much the particular business wants to continue operating. Few pre-planned fraudsters will care, unless the publicity somehow incapacitates them – after all, they have already successfully neutralised their crimes to their own ethical satisfaction; and though others may try to disturb or break those neutralisations, they may regard the moral claims of what Al Capone called 'the respectable rackets' as unrealistic or hypocritical. Those who turn to fraud when their businesses are about to go bust may not care anyway, if they are focused narrowly on keeping going (though there are personality and cognitive dimensions here). The main people who care about shaming are (a) those whose social lives are embedded in respectability, and (b) those who fear that they may be excluded economically from markets because others distrust them or fear that by associating with them, they themselves will attract unwelcome attention from regulators or police.

Conclusions

Compared with the voluminous literature on police accountability (Reiner, 2010; Lister and Jones, 2015), prosecutorial accountability has been largely neglected, at least prior to the BAE scandal. This is not true in France, Italy, Spain or even Switzerland, where some high profile investigating magistrates have gone after political elites at home and abroad, and where there have been highly politicised attempts to restrain this vigour by bringing them under more central governmental control. Nor is it true of Latin America. The important issues of accountability raised by serious fraud and corruption prosecutions – and, perhaps even more importantly, by *non-prosecutions* and (in the USA) *Deferred Prosecution Agreements* (used against business and professional elites to avoid the collateral damage from felony convictions) are unlike most faced in other arenas, and arise principally because of the political (with a small or large 'p') ramifications of particular cases, exaggerated by the potential for asset recovery from the corrupt. These controversies include party political donations (including alleged 'cash for honours') from businesspeople – on which political parties became highly dependent from the 1980s onwards – who sought favours such as well-photographed dinners with the Prime Minister and other leading figures, used by them for subsequent Public Relations purposes to impress people overseas as well as in the UK. They also include broader conceptions of 'public interest' which are difficult to unpack. In theory, prosecution decisions are made by the Directors of Public Prosecutions and of the Serious Fraud Office, autonomously from their political heads. However, they are also answerable to the Attorney-General who in turn is answerable to Parliament. In practice, it is rare for answers to be given to current cases, but concern from MPs (including Ministers) can transmit across to those dealing with the case, and prosecutors are dependent on the government for funding (HMCPSI, 2016; see also the Parliamentary debate at https://hansard.parliament.uk/commons/2017-02-07/debates/ 17020768000006/SeriousFraudOffice(ContingenciesFundAdvance)). There is no clear evidence whether the non-prosecution of senior industry or governmental persons in some UK cases was due to 'influence' or merely to the well-attested fact that remoteness from actual decisions makes it hard to convict people for crimes committed in a complex corporate context and therefore, consistent with the Code for Crown Prosecutors, it is arguably improper to prosecute them.

The SFO's overall conviction rate (including guilty pleas) varies between one-third and over 90 per cent: between 2012 and 2016, the conviction rate was 65 per cent by defendant and 81 per cent by case, with 49 out of 75 defendants in 25 cases convicted. However the low conviction rate in 'famous name' SFO prosecutions makes the Law Officers of the Crown as well as the case lawyers look bad, and this is something they normally seek to avoid. Bureaucracies need the support of politicians (including the Attorney-General) for resources, and there have been major campaigns against the Serious Fraud Office under the rubric of insufficient courage and cost-effectiveness: some might argue that there may be ambivalent feelings of politicians and businesspeople about the *desirability* of the effective prosecution of some elite fraud and corruption, but there is no evidence of that, at least outside cases where corruption wins business for national corporations.

Looking at these issues comparatively, what sort of system would plausibly provide the kind of transparency of decision-making that might reassure people that decisions were *not* influenced directly or indirectly by 'political' considerations is too major a task for our existing knowledge, but it seems unlikely that any system, even in theory, would meet all the necessary and sufficient conditions for 'true independence'. My object here has been to try to integrate some themes in 'white-collar crime control' with the mainstream of literature on police and prosecutorial accountability, and, in an arena unfamiliar to many criminologists, to raise some issues of major practical as well as ideological importance about the methodology of equal justice and impartiality. How to ensure high levels of motivation, skill and courage among prosecutors while giving them the independence that can mean freedom *not* to do enough remains a difficult issue of balance to which there is unlikely to be a universal 'correct solution'.

Notes

1   A decree to decriminalise abuse of office where the losses were less than $47,200 was reversed after hundreds of thousands demonstrated in the streets of Bucharest.
2   This binary distinction is used for reasons of simplicity – socio-economic status should be viewed in a more variegated way, even in more unequal societies such as Brazil.
3   In November 2015, a leading banker was alleged to have taken part in a conspiracy with the ruling Workers' Party leader in the Senate and two others to try to suppress testimony being offered by a former Petrobras director, Nestor Ceveró, to prosecutors in exchange for leniency. There have followed many arrests and indictments, most prominently those of the former Presidents Lula da Silva and Dilma Rousseff on a range of hotly disputed issues.

4 HC Deb 13 February 1986 vol. 91 cc1148.

5 Contentious issues have arisen mainly in the context of extradition of white-collar defendants to the USA, where it has been alleged they are unfairly disadvantaged, by the well-funded PR campaigns of 'the NatWest Three', later cases such as price-fixer Ian Norris (www.supremecourt.gov.uk/decided-cases/docs/UKSC_2009_0052_Judgment.pdf) – eventually extradited to the USA and jailed for 18 months; and the (blue-collar status) computer hacker Gary McKinnon, whose extradition was refused and who was not in the end charged in the UK either, a decade after his arrest.

6 I am not arguing here for the sort of libertarian 'freeze' that (by inference) McConville et al. (1991) get into, where because one cannot be certain that x did y, we should prosecute or convict almost no-one. That might simply lead to mass vigilantism, with even less respect for due process and evidence.

7 The vendors of arms to Iraq, whether encouraged by the security services or not, made unlikely heroes for civil libertarians.

8 Even such recordings can be disputed as products of tampering, and a sophisticated industry has been developed in testing them. Well publicised recordings include those of President Erdogan allegedly discussing corrupt deals and hoards of cash with his son. For the transcripts in English, see www.ibtimes.co.uk/turkey-youtube-bantranscript-leaked-erdogan-corruption-call-son-1442150.

9 Although on balance, Thomas' (2010) research gave the jury system a clean bill of health, her study did not focus on what happens in accusations against elites.

10 It is hard to believe that this prosecution decision, taken by HM Customs & Excise, was undertaken with top-level governmental approval, since many outside that department appreciated the risk that 'the wheel would come off' (as it did), and would have judged it not worth that symbolic gain. Once taken, it may have seemed too hard to work out how to stop the prosecution. However, what is crucial is that the charges required proof of *deception* of the Department of Trade and Industry officials, and it is clear that they were not deceived about the export licence applications.

11 The convictions were later quashed by the Court of Appeal: *R v. Daghir*, the *Guardian*, 25 and 26 May 1994.

12 The overlap between political interference and 'legal advice' arises from the dual role of the Attorney-General as chief legal officer and member of the Cabinet.

13 As Braithwaite (1984) and Fisse and Braithwaite (1993) demonstrate, it is astonishing how lines of accountability that are clear for managerial purposes suddenly become opaque when interrogated critically by outsiders. The apparent ignorance displayed by all senior Cabinet Ministers except Michael Heseltine of the change in policy over the supply of arms to Iraq is another case in point.

14 See the important cases of *R v Dougall* [2010] EWCA Crim 1048; and *R v Innospec* [2010] EW Misc 7 (EWCC), which represent the determination of the judiciary not to allow the SFO Director to agree specific sentences with the accused in return for their cooperation. See Lord (2014a, 2014b) for an excellent dissection.

References

Braithwaite, J. (1984) *Corporate Crime in the Pharmaceutical Industry*, London: Routledge.

Cicourel, A. (1968) *The Social Organisation of Juvenile Justice*, New York: John Wiley.

Conaghan, C. (2012) Prosecuting Presidents: the politics within Ecuador's corruption cases, *Journal of Latin American Studies*, 44: 649–678.

Corker, D. and Levi, M. (1996) Pre-trial publicity and its treatment in the English courts, *Criminal Law Review*, September: 622–632.

Cuadros, A. (2016) *Brazillionaires: The Godfathers of Modern Brazil*, London: Profile.

Cullen, F., Cavender, G., Maakestad, W. and Benson, M. (2006) *Corporate Crime under Attack: The Fight to Criminalize Business Violence*, 2nd edition, London: Routledge.

Eichenwald, K. (2001) *The Informant*, New York: Broadway Books.

Feeley, M. and Simon, J. (2007) Folk devils and moral panics: an appreciation from North America, in D. Downes, P. Rock, C. Chinkin and C. Gearty (eds.), *Crime, Social Control and Human Rights*, Cullompton: Willan.

Fisse, B. and Braithwaite, J. (1993) *Corporations, Crime, and Accountability*, Cambridge: Cambridge University Press.

Fooks, G., Contrasts in tolerance: the curious politics of financial regulation, *Contemporary Politics*, 9(2): 127–142.

Fraud Trials Committee (1986) *Report*, London: HMSO.

Garland, D. (2008) On the concept of moral panic, *Crime, Media, Culture*, 4: 9–30.

Gillard, M. (1974) *A Little Pot of Money*, London: Private Eye and Andre Deutsch.

Greising, D. and Morse, L. (1991) *Brokers, Bagmen, and Moles*, New York: John Wiley.

HMCPSI (2016) *Inspection of the Serious Fraud Office Governance Arrangements*. www.justiceinspectorates. gov.uk/hmcpsi/wp-content/uploads/sites/3/2016/05/SFO_May16_rpt.pdf.

Honess, T., Barker, S., Charman, E. and Levi, M. (2002) Empirical and legal perspectives in the impact of pre-trial publicity, *Criminal Law Review*, September: 719–727.

Jennings, A. (2015) *The Dirty Game: Uncovering the Scandal at FIFA*, London: Century.

Lazzarini, S. (2010) *Capitalismo de Laços – Os Donos do Brasil e Suas Conexões*, Rio de Janeiro: Elsevier.

Levi, M. (1987/2013) *Regulating Fraud: White-Collar Crime and the Criminal Process*, London: Routledge.

Levi, M. (1991) Sentencing white-collar crime in the dark? Reflections on the Guinness Four, *The Howard Journal of Criminal Justice*, 30(4): 257–279.

Levi, M. (1993) *The Investigation, Prosecution and Trial of Serious Fraud*, Royal Commission on Criminal Justice Research Study No. 14, London: HMSO.

Levi, M. (2002) Suite justice or sweet charity? Some explorations of shaming and incapacitating business fraudsters, *Punishment and Society*, 4(2): 147–163.

Levi, M. (2009) Suite revenge? The shaping of folk devils and moral panics about white-collar crimes, *British Journal of Criminology*, 49(1): 48–67.

Levi, M. (2010) Serious tax fraud and noncompliance: a review of evidence on the differential impact of criminal and noncriminal proceedings, *Criminology and Public Policy*, 9(2): 449–469.

Levi, M. (2016) Sentencing respectable offenders, in Shanna Van Slyke, Michael Benson and Francis T. Cullen (eds.), *The Oxford Handbook of White-Collar Crime*, New York: Oxford University Press.

Levi, M. and Nelken, D. (1996) The corruption of politics and the politics of corruption: an overview, *Journal of Law and Society*, 23(1): 1–17.

Lister, S. and Jones, T. (2015) Plural policing and the challenge of democratic accountability, in M. Rowe and S. Lister (eds.), *Accountability of Policing*, London: Routledge, 192–213.

Lord, N. (2014a) Responding to transnational corporate bribery using international frameworks for enforcement, *Criminology and Criminal Justice*, 14(1): 100–120.

Lord, N. (2014b) *Regulating Corporate Bribery in International Business: Anti-Corruption in the UK and Germany*, Andover: Ashgate.

Lord, N. and Levi, M. (2015) Determining the adequate enforcement of white-collar and corporate crimes in Europe, in Judith van Erp, Wim Huisman, Gudrun Vande Walle (eds.), *The Routledge Handbook of White-Collar and Corporate Crime in Europe*, London: Routledge, 39–56.

McConville, M., Sanders, A. and Leng, R. (1991) *The Case for the Prosecution*, London: Routledge.

Margolis, M. (2015) How low can Brazil's scandal go?, 1 December, www.bloombergview.com/articles/ 2015-12-01/how-low-can-brazil-s-scandal-go-.

Nelken, D. (1996) The judges and political corruption in Italy, *Journal of Law & Society*, 23: 95–112.

Reiner, R. (2010) *The Politics of the Police*, 4th edition, Oxford: Oxford University Press.

Scott Report (1996) *Report of the Inquiry into the Export of Defence Equipment and Dual-Use Goods to Iraq and Related Prosecutions*, London: HMSO.

Thomas, C. (2010) *Are Juries Fair?* Research Series 1/10, London: Ministry of Justice.

Wolfe, T. (1987) *Bonfire of the Vanities*, London: Paladin.

16

HATE CRIMES

Stevie-Jade Hardy and Neil Chakraborti

Introduction

'Hate crime' is a politically and socially significant term that cuts across disciplines, across communities and across borders. With problems of bigotry continuing to pose challenges for societies across the world, a growth in hate crime scholarship and policy has promoted collective awareness of extreme and 'everyday' acts of hate alongside collective action amongst a range of different actors including law-makers, law-enforcers, non-governmental organisations and activists. The need for such action is clear in the context of a now substantial body of empirical evidence that demonstrates the multiple layers of harm associated with hate crimes (Iganski, 2001; Perry, 2001; Walters, 2011). These harms cause both physical and emotional damage, and have been described by the Office for Democratic Institutions and Human Rights (ODIHR, 2009) as harms which violate human rights between members of society; intensify the level of psychological hurt experienced by the individual victim; transmit an increased sense of fear and intimidation to the wider community to whom the victim 'belongs'; and which create security and public order problems as a result of escalating social tensions.

These harms distinguish hate crimes from other types of crime and have generated an improved understanding across many parts of the world. This has required greater prioritisation from within practitioner and academic communities. Iganski (2008) has highlighted the advantages of thinking of hate crime as both a policy and a scholarly domain: the first domain where elements of the political and criminal justice systems have united – in response to a succession of progressive social movements and campaigns – to combat bigotry in its various guises; and the second where scholars – ostensibly from diverse fields of study but unified by their focus upon the synergies and intersections between different forms of targeted violence – generate new knowledge to inform the development of effective interventions. Progress within both of these spheres has been strengthened by increased legislation. Within the United Kingdom we have seen a succession of laws introduced by consecutive governments covering different strands of hate crime, as well as a wealth of criminal justice policy and guidance and relentless campaign group activism. These developments have been mirrored across the world, with the United States, Canada, Australia and many states across Western and Eastern Europe introducing their own sets of laws which treat hate crime either as a substantive offence or which offer the option of enhanced penalties for convicted hate crime perpetrators.

Similarly, the volume of theoretical and empirical developments in hate crime scholarship over recent years has helped to develop a significantly more nuanced picture of these multi-layered and complex offences. Put simply, we now know more about hate crime than ever before: more about the people who suffer hate crime as well as those who perpetrate hate crime; more about the nature, extent and impact of victimisation; and more about the effectiveness, or otherwise, of different interventions. These developments have shaped thinking across a number of academic disciplines, including criminology, psychology, sociology, history, political science and legal studies; within statutory, voluntary and private sectors; and amongst senior figures in political and criminal justice spheres 'down' to activists, campaigners and community volunteers working at a grassroots level (Chakraborti and Garland, 2014).

But despite this progress, we would suggest that there is much about hate crime that remains peripheral to scholars and practitioners alike. One way of evidencing this claim is through reference to the official hate crime figures that are presented by different countries within the Organisation for Security and Co-Operation in Europe (OSCE) region. Figures collated by ODIHR show substantial disparity between OSCE member states: for instance, the number of hate crimes recorded by police in England and Wales in 2015 – 62,518 – is far greater than the corresponding numbers provided by Germany (3,046), Spain (1,328), Italy (555) and Greece (60) (ODIHR, 2016). Evidently, these figures are not an accurate measure by which to gauge the true scale of hate crime in each respective country; they are more a reflection of how hate crimes are defined, recorded, reported and statistically collated by different states, than of any genuine disparity in levels of hate crime. They also highlight how much variation there is between the way in which hate crime policy has been developed and prioritised in different parts of the world.

Moreover, it is important to remember that recorded figures tell only a partial story when it comes to quantifying levels of hate crime. For instance, while the number of hate crimes recorded by police in England and Wales referred to above provides a more realistic picture than that offered by most other states, it still falls short of capturing anything like the full picture. Recently the Crime Survey for England and Wales, which accounts for experiences of victimisation not necessarily reported to the police, estimated that approximately 222,000 hate crimes are committed each year (Corcoran and Smith, 2016), a number which is nearly six times the 'official' figure cited above. Moreover, the 'real' figure of hate crimes taking place is likely to be higher still, as many cases of hate crime are simply not recognised as such by criminal justice agencies, non-governmental organisations or by victims themselves.

These are key issues confronting criminologists and criminal justice professionals across the world, and their implications will be explored further in due course. Within this chapter we consider a series of important questions that form a central part of debates around hate crime. What does the term 'hate crime' refer to and is there a single universal definition? What groups of people can fall victim to hate crime? Why do people commit hate crime and what characteristics have been associated with hate crime perpetrators? And finally, how should we respond to hate crime? As we shall see, hate crime is an evolving and highly subjective concept, and while much progress has been made in terms of improving levels of understanding, awareness and practical support for victims, a number of conceptual and operational challenges remain which can hinder the 'real-life' value of empirical research and policy development.

Defining hate crime

Before considering some of these challenges in greater depth, it is important to reflect first on what the term 'hate crime' actually means. When asked to define hate crime, one's most immediate and obvious response might be to suggest that the term refers to crimes motivated by hatred. Curiously though, 'hate' is not a prerequisite for an offence to be classified as a hate crime. Rather, most academic definitions are consistent in referring to a broader range of factors than hate alone to describe the motivation that lies behind the commission of a hate crime (see, *inter alia*, Chakraborti *et al.*, 2014; Hall, 2013; Gerstenfeld, 2004; Petrosino, 2003; Jacobs and Potter, 1998; Sheffield, 1995). In particular, terms such as 'prejudice', 'bias' and 'targeted hostility' have all been used interchangeably by criminologists as a way of highlighting that the presence of 'hate' is not central to the commission of a hate crime.

While there is no single definition of hate crime that has universal approval, the framework proposed by the Canadian criminologist Barbara Perry (2001: 10) has garnered arguably the strongest support from those working within this field:

> Hate crime … involves acts of violence and intimidation, usually directed towards already stigmatised and marginalised groups. As such, it is a mechanism of power and oppression, intended to reaffirm the precarious hierarchies that characterise a given social order. It attempts to re-create simultaneously the threatened (real or imagined) hegemony of the perpetrator's group and the 'appropriate' subordinate identity of the victim's group. It is a means of marking both the Self and the Other in such a way as to re-establish their 'proper' relative positions, as given and reproduced by broader ideologies and patterns of social and political inequality.

Perry's framework acknowledges the complexity of hate crime victimisation by highlighting the relationship between structural hierarchies, institutionalised prejudices and acts of hate. It gives primacy to the idea that violent and intimidatory behaviour is qualitatively different when it is motivated by bigotry and directed towards already disempowered and marginalised populations. Moreover, it recognises that hate crime is not a static or isolated problem but one that is historically and culturally contingent, the experience of which needs to be seen as a dynamic social process involving context, structure and agency (see also Bowling, 1993, 1999). For Perry, the experience of hate crime does not just begin or end with the commission of an offence, nor does it occur in a social or cultural vacuum.

Another key factor within Perry's conceptual framework is the emphasis on the group, and not individual, identity of the victim. Within this context individual victims of hate are interchangeable with other potential victims from that same minority group. Hate crimes are therefore acts of violence and intimidation directed not just towards the victim in question, but towards the wider community to whom he or she belongs; crimes which are designed to convey a message to that wider community that they are somehow 'different' and 'don't belong' (see also Hall, 2013). As 'message' crimes, acts of hate reach 'into the community to create fear, hostility and suspicion' and in so doing reaffirm 'the hegemony of the perpetrator's and the "appropriate" subordinate identity of the victim's group' (Perry, 2001: 10). Finally, and perhaps not surprisingly given the symbolic relevance of hate crime within her framework, Perry (2001: 29) sees these offences as most commonly perpetrated against strangers with whom the offender has had little or no personal contact, with the victim simply representing the 'other' in generic terms through their membership of a demonised group.

Although Perry's definition of hate crime helps us to recognise that acts of violence and harassment can be influenced by wider social, political and historical factors, it does restrict our understanding of how hate crime can play out in the 'real world' by suggesting that victims and perpetrators will almost invariably be strangers to each other. Mason (2005), for instance, contests this assumption by drawing from British Crime Survey data and other research evidence to show that a substantial proportion of racially motivated and homophobic incidents are committed by perpetrators who are in fact *not* strangers to their victims (see also Ray and Smith, 2001; Moran, 2007). Mason's (2005: 856) findings challenge the popular notion of hate crime as a form of 'stranger-danger' and the 'one size fits all' method of describing perpetrator–victim relationships. Clearly, hate crimes may take the shape envisaged by Perry of message crimes being targeted towards the wider subordinate community, but by the same token they may also include acts where the perpetrator is known to the victim in some capacity, as a neighbour, a colleague, a classmate or a carer to name just some examples. This is an important but often overlooked reality that has started to form a central theme within contemporary hate crime discourse (see, for instance, Asquith, 2010; Garland, 2010).

Other scholars have observed that hate crime is a more expansive notion than even Perry's framework allows. For instance, Chakraborti *et al.* (2014) have used a simpler, and in some ways wider-ranging definition in their own research, which sees hate crimes as acts of violence, hostility and intimidation directed towards people because of their identity or perceived 'difference'. The rationale for framing hate crime in these broad terms will become clearer over the course of this chapter. However, it is worth noting at this juncture that this definition covers forms of targeted hostility and anti-social behaviour which might not be criminal acts in themselves but which can have just as significant an impact upon the victim, their family and wider communities. Equally, whilst this definition is deliberately concise, it acknowledges that some victims can be subjected to hate not exclusively because of their membership of a particular identity group but also because they are seen as vulnerable or somehow 'different' in the eyes of the perpetrator. Moreover – and crucially from the perspective of making the concept of hate crime operationally viable – the more long-winded definitions that we academics are inclined to use sometimes feel rather too complex, too ethereal and too detached from the everyday realities confronting those who deal with hate crime cases in the 'real world' (Chakraborti, 2014).

Some laudable attempts to develop a common understanding that can generate workable responses to hate crime have emerged outside of the academic domain. One such attempt has come from the Office for Democratic Institutions and Human Rights (ODIHR), whose guidance for OSCE states describes hate crimes as 'criminal acts committed with a bias motive' (2009: 16). In line with the academic definitions described above, this bias does not have to manifest itself as 'hate' for the offence to be thought of as a hate crime, nor does 'hate' have to be the primary motive. Rather, bias in this sense refers to acts where the victim is targeted deliberately because of a 'protected characteristic … shared by a group, such as "race", language, religion, ethnicity, nationality, or any other similar common factor' (2009: 16). Importantly, ODIHR's guidance does not seek to specify which protected characteristics should form the basis of a member state's hate crime policy, aside from making reference to aspects of identity that are 'fundamental to a person's sense of self' and to the relevance of 'current social problems as well as potential historical oppression and discrimination' (2009: 38).

This broad, pan-national framework for understanding hate crime was developed in response to an increased awareness of hate crime and its associated problems, and the pressing need for states, statutory and non-governmental organisations across Europe to respond more effectively to these forms of victimisation. However – and as illustrated by the divergence in hate crime statistics collated by different countries referred to above – there is little evidence of a shared understanding of the concept across nations. As such, there remain vastly differing interpretations of what a hate crime is, who the potential victims are and what type of legislative response is most appropriate (Garland and Chakraborti, 2012). To some extent, such inconsistency is inevitable given the way in which different countries' histories have shaped their conceptualisation of hate crime. In countries such as Germany, Austria and Italy, for example, the association of the term 'hate crime' with right-wing extremism and anti-Semitism is a legacy of tragic events in the 20th century, while at the other end of the spectrum left-wing extremism is also a significant area of concern in some states (FRA (European Union Agency for Fundamental Rights), 2013). Although a universal consensus on the implementation and prioritisation of hate crime policy may be unachievable, ODIHR's guidance encourages law-makers and law-enforcers to think broadly when framing the parameters of hate crime.

Within the UK, the key source of policy guidance on hate crime comes from the College of Policing, the professional body responsible for setting standards in professional development across English and Welsh police forces. Their interpretation of hate crime is especially relevant in the context of the present discussion as it illustrates both the broad application of the hate crime concept and the practical ways in which criminal justice agencies can respond to this conceptual ambiguity. For example, the guidelines provided by the College of Policing include a requirement for all hate incidents to be recorded by the police even if they lack the requisite elements to be classified as a notifiable offence later in the criminal justice process. This means that at the recording stage, any hate incident, whether a *prima facie* 'crime' or not, is to be recorded if it is perceived by the victim or any other person (such as a witness, a family member or a carer) as being motivated by hostility or prejudice. Conceiving of hate crime in such a way enables the police to respond to the more 'everyday' forms of targeted hostility which many victims are routinely subjected to, including harassment, online abuse or other forms of intimidatory behaviour, in addition to more violent expressions of hate.

The College of Policing guidance also stipulates that the police are obliged to record an offence as a 'hate crime' if the incident was motivated by hostility on the grounds of any one of five monitored strands of identity: namely, disability, gender-identity, race, religion and sexual orientation. This recording procedure enables police forces to collate statistics on these strands of hate crimes, which can then be used to identify trends and to make comparisons between different regions and different countries. Most hate crime policy and research within the UK is based around these five strands, although as we shall see shortly the process of deciding what forms of prejudice to define as 'hate crime' is one that is fraught with difficulty. However, there is a degree of flexibility in how the boundaries of hate crime are framed within UK policy, with official guidance stating that the five monitored strands 'are the minimum categories that police officers and staff are expected to record' (College of Policing, 2014: 7). This permits police forces to record other forms of targeted hostility as hate crime in addition to those five strands, and has been developed as a result of tragic cases and an emerging body of research highlighting the targeting of 'other' identities and groups who have not routinely been considered as hate crime victims. These issues are explored in the following section.

It is worth pausing a moment at this stage to reflect upon what we know about hate crime from this inspection of definitions. As this section has demonstrated, there is no one universal definition of hate crime and the plurality of interpretations illustrates the elasticity of the concept. What also becomes clear from this brief discussion is that the presence of 'hate' is not central to the commission of a hate crime, and that the label itself is an inaccurate descriptor of the majority of offences that blight the lives of hate crime victims. For the purposes of this chapter, the following discussion has been framed around the simpler but broader definition outlined above, which refers to hate crimes as acts of violence, hostility and intimidation directed towards people because of their identity or perceived 'difference'.

Hate crime victims

As with attempts to define hate crime, the process of deciding upon which groups of victims to protect through hate crime policy is highly subjective. Not surprisingly, there has been much debate among scholars and practitioners with regard to the identity or lifestyle characteristics that should be recognised within hate crime legislation and therefore afforded special protection. Figures collated by ODIHR (2014) reveal that the most commonly monitored type of identity among member states is race and ethnicity, with a total of 21 countries recording data on racist/xenophobic crimes. This level of recognition is unsurprising given that racist hate crime remains the strand of hate crime with which commentators are most familiar; indeed, politicians, journalists, practitioners and academics sometimes still fall into the trap of describing hate crime exclusively in terms of racist crime.

The sheer weight of academic literature and policy reports devoted to race and racist victimisation in comparison to the relatively small (but growing) body of work on alternative strands of hate crime is illustrative of how criminologists and professionals have tended to prioritise issues around racist hate crime over other forms of targeted hostility. However, one of the shortcomings of existing literature within the field has been a common failure to see beyond simplistic and naïve constructions which depict ethnic minorities as one seemingly homogeneous victim group. This approach dismisses, or at best underplays, the differences in experiences and need between people grouped together within such a framework, as well as those who are typically excluded from such a framework. A notable example is mixed-race families and relationships, with what little research evidence there is suggesting that those from a mixed heritage background face a higher risk of racist victimisation (Home Office *et al.*, 2013) and that white partners in mixed-race relationships face a real, but seldom recognised, risk of being the target of abuse (Garland *et al.*, 2006). There are also many other victim groups, including Gypsies and Travellers (James, 2014), foreign nationals, refugees, asylum seekers and migrant workers (Burnett, 2013; Fekete and Webber, 2010), who suffer racist violence and harassment on a regular basis but yet still remain peripheral to academic and policy debates about racially motivated hate crime.

Although issues relating to faith may in the past have been overshadowed by the propensity to focus predominantly, and sometimes exclusively, upon 'race' and ethnic identity, events over the past decade or so have seen religiously motivated hostility occupy a much more significant role within political and academic thought. The escalating level of prejudice directed towards Muslim communities in particular has given a higher profile to religiously motivated hate crime, and has been a significant factor in the creation of explicit legislative protection against attacks upon religious identity across a number of countries (Chakraborti and Garland, 2015).

However, Muslim communities are not the only faith group to have experienced an increase in targeted hostility. The number of attacks perpetuated against South Asians in general – and not just against Muslims – has risen steeply, prompting fears that anyone ostensibly 'looking Asian', for instance through wearing a turban, sporting a beard or simply by virtue of being 'dark-skinned', has become increasingly susceptible to the risk of physical assault or verbal abuse (Chakraborti and Garland, 2015). There has also been a sharp rise in the number of anti-Semitic incidents across most countries with a sizeable Jewish presence (FRA, 2013), with a range of factors contributing to this rise including the deep-rooted religious mistrust between Jews and other faith groups, resentment of the perceived socio-economic success enjoyed by Jewish communities in the West, the 'transfer of tensions' from the Middle East to other countries and an increase in anti-Zionist or anti-Israeli sentiment (Chakraborti and Garland, 2015; Gerstenfeld, 2004).

More recently we have also seen greater scholarly attention focused on uncovering the targeted violence and intimidation experienced by other groups of victims, including people with learning and/or physical disabilities, the lesbian, gay and bisexual population, and transgender people. Unfortunately, the increased recognition of these strands within criminology has not been replicated within political and criminal justice systems across the world. Of the 41 member states who submitted information to ODIHR in 2015, only 12 were found to record homophobic and transphobic hate crime, and a worryingly low figure of just eight record disablist hate crime (ODIHR, 2016). And it is these inconsistencies that form the basis of a now-familiar criticism of conventional hate crime policy (see, *inter alia*, Mason-Bish, 2010; Jacobs and Potter, 1998) but one which has not been adequately resolved. It is often said that hate crime policy creates and reinforces hierarchies of identity, where some victims are deemed worthy of inclusion within hate crime frameworks and others invariably miss out. As Mason-Bish (2010: 62) notes:

> hate crime policy has been formed through the work of lobbying and advisory groups who have had quite narrow remits, often focusing exclusively on one area of victimisation. This has contributed to a hierarchy within hate crime policy itself, whereby some identity groups seem to receive preferential treatment in criminal justice responses to hate crime.

Activists and campaigners have undoubtedly played a key role in exposing the violence and hostility experienced by certain victims groups, and in stimulating the debate and momentum necessary to influence law making and policy enforcement (Lancaster, 2014; Perry, 2014). This is a process that has been crucial to the maturation of hate crime as an issue of international significance, but there is a downside to this process too: namely, that the parameters of what we cover under the hate crime 'umbrella' can be contingent upon the ability of campaign groups to lobby for recognition under this umbrella. Whether because of greater resources, a more powerful voice, public support for their cause or a more established history of stigma and discrimination, campaigners working to support certain strands of hate crime victim will invariably be able to lobby policy-makers more effectively than other potential claim-makers (Chakraborti, 2015a). This explains why there are certain 'others' who can find themselves marginal to or excluded from hate crime policy and scholarship despite being targeted because of characteristics fundamental to perceptions of their sense of self.

Wachholz (2009), for instance, questions the failure to recognise the all-too-common acts of hostility directed towards the homeless within the USA as hate crime, whilst a growing body of research in the UK has questioned the lack of support for a range of victims who are regular targets of violent and intimidatory behaviour, including members of alternative subcultures (Garland and Hodkinson, 2014), sex workers (Campbell, 2014) and those with mental health issues (Chakraborti *et al.*, 2014). These groups have much in common with the more familiar groups of hate crime victims in that they too are often singled out as targets of hostility specifically because of their 'difference'. However, lacking either the support of lobby groups or political representation, and typically seen as 'undesirables', criminogenic or less worthy than other more 'legitimate' or historically oppressed victim groups, they are commonly excluded from conventional hate crime frameworks (Chakraborti, 2015a). For these marginalised victims, the process of inclusion and exclusion is much more than simply a thorny conceptual challenge; it is a fundamental human rights and equality issue which has life-changing consequences in the context of experiences of targeted violence that go unnoticed and unchallenged in the absence of policy recognition.

At present these experiences of hostility tend to fall between the cracks of existing conceptual and policy frameworks, as does another dynamic central to the process of hate crime victimisation: the intersectionality of identity characteristics that can be targeted by perpetrators of hate crime. Conceiving of hate crimes simply as offences directed towards individual strands of a person's identity fails to give adequate recognition to the interplay of identities with one another and with other personal, social and situational characteristics. Research by Chakraborti *et al.* (2014) found that as many as half of their survey sample of 1,106 hate crime victims had been targeted on the basis of more than one identity or lifestyle characteristic. Indeed, many felt that they had been victimised because of their race *and* their religion; their mental ill-health *and* their physical or learning disability; or their sexual orientation *and* their dress and appearance (Chakraborti *et al.*, 2014). Hate crime victim groups are not homogeneous categories of people with uniform characteristics and experiences (see also Garland, 2012), and therefore it is essential that we capture the differences within and intersections between a range of identity characteristics, including sexual orientation, ethnicity, faith, disability and gender identity.

Similarly, it is important to recognise the interplay between hate crime victimisation and socio-economic status. Hate crimes can often be triggered and exacerbated by socio-economic conditions, and some potential targets of hate crime will invariably be better placed than others to avoid persecution by virtue of living at a greater distance from prejudiced neighbours or in less overtly hostile environments (Walters and Hoyle, 2012; Chakraborti *et al.*, 2014). To date, the relevance of class and economic marginalisation to the commission of hate crime has rarely been a central line of enquiry to scholars and policy-makers. However, these nuances need to feature much more prominently within scholarship and policy-formation in order to reflect the lived realities of victim selection, and to adequately represent the broad range of victim groups affected by hate crime.

Hate crime perpetrators

Much of the academic endeavour within this field has focused upon the processes, forms and impact of hate crime victimisation. Far less attention has been paid to the motivation of hate crime perpetrators. While there have been a number of studies of far-right parties, mainly by political scientists, there has been comparatively little criminological examination of the causes and patterns of hate-related offending perpetrated by those who do not identify with such groups. Official data on the demographics of hate crime perpetrators are equally sparse. There are no published data from Australia or New Zealand, and those which have been published by Canada and the United States are limited. Similarly in Europe, with the exception of three members states – Finland, Sweden and the UK – there are few official data on hate crime offenders (Roberts *et al.*, 2013).

Despite the relative paucity of official data and empirical evidence, some significant research has been conducted which enables us to paint a picture of who commits hate crimes and why they do it. The most influential work to date on hate offender profiles has been produced by McDevitt, Levin, Nolan and Bennett (see McDevitt *et al.*, 2002, 2010). Their typology, based on analysis of 169 hate crime cases investigated by the Boston Police Department, suggests that the majority (two-thirds of the cases assessed) of hate crime perpetrators would fall into the category of 'Thrill Offenders'. These individuals are commonly teenagers or young males who, acting in a group, commit hate crimes in search of a viscerally exciting experience. Key characteristics of this type of offending include the perpetrator(s) venturing from their neighbourhood in search of someone to victimise, and selecting victims based on an underlying prejudice towards their group affiliation (McDevitt *et al.*, 2010). This profile is supported by official data published in Canada (Dauvergne *et al.*, 2008), Sweden (Brå, 2009) and the UK (Creese and Lader, 2014), which suggests that the majority of hate offenders are male and under the age of 25. Similarly, a number of academic studies, although focusing on the different strands of targeted victimisation, have found that most hate crimes are committed by young males acting in groups (Hardy, 2014; Franklin, 2000; Byers *et al.*, 1999). Within these studies, perpetrators targeted those who possessed identifiable traits of 'difference' in order to satiate the desire for thrills, thereby providing empirical evidence to support the claims of McDevitt *et al.*

The second group of offenders identified by McDevitt *et al.* are those labelled 'Defensive Offenders' (these cases made up around a quarter of the total). Although this group have a similar demographic profile to those perpetrators categorised as 'Thrill Offenders', they typically commit hate crimes as a means of 'protecting' their neighbourhood from perceived intruders, in contrast to the motivation underpinning 'thrill' cases. Within this context the victim, or more aptly the community to which the victim is perceived to belong, is seen to be as posing a threat, whether this be socially, culturally or economically. 'Retaliatory Offenders' are the third group in McDevitt *et al.*'s typology (fewer than one in ten of the overall cases), and these perpetrators typically travel to the victim's territory in order to avenge a previous incident which they perceive that the victim, or the victim's social group, has committed (McDevitt *et al.*, 2010). In the case of both 'defensive' and 'retaliatory' offenders, the motivation underpinning the commission of hate crime conforms to the framework proposed by Perry (2001) in that hate crimes can be deployed as 'message crimes', designed to transmit a sense of fear and intimidation to the victim as well as to the wider community.

The final category identified by McDevitt *et al.* (only around 1 per cent of the sample) includes those offenders who are motivated by an overarching 'mission' when perpetrating a hate crime. These perpetrators are considered to be hate-fuelled individuals, and in comparison to the offenders within the other three categories are often far-right sympathisers (McDevitt *et al.*, 2010). Some of the most notorious perpetrators of violent hate-related acts, such as David Copeland in England and Anders Behring Breivik in Norway, would be categorised as 'Mission Offenders'. Although the perpetrators who fall within this category conform to the archetypal idea of a hate crime offender, in reality the vast majority of hate crime perpetrators fit within the other three categories. The fact that such a large proportion of incidents are motivated by a desire for 'thrills' within everyday contexts suggests that much of what we think of as 'hate crime' is worryingly 'routine', and not exceptional, from the perspective of both offender and victim (Iganski, 2008).

One of the shortcomings of much of the academic literature on hate crime perpetration is that it often fails to recognise the 'ordinariness' of much hate crime: ordinary not in relation to its impact upon the victim but in the sense of how the offence is conceived of by the perpetrator (Chakraborti, 2015a). A consistent theme running through much of the literature is the use of hate crime as a mechanism of subordination, designed to reinforce the perceived superiority of the perpetrator whilst simultaneously keeping the victim in their 'proper' inferior place within society. Whilst this structural framework may account for some expressions of hate crime, it overlooks those that occur in the context of spontaneous, 'trigger' situations (Iganski, 2008; McGhee, 2007). A growing evidence base suggests that many hate crimes tend to be committed by relatively 'ordinary' people in the context of their 'ordinary' day-to-day lives (Hardy, 2017; Iganski, 2008; Ray et al., 2004). These offences are not always driven by entrenched prejudices or hate on the part of the perpetrator but may instead arise as a departure from standard norms of behaviour; or through an inability to control language or behaviour in moments of stress, anger or inebriation; or from a sense of weakness or inadequacy that can stem from a range of subconscious emotional and psychological processes (Gadd, 2009; Dixon and Gadd, 2006).

Similarly, the foundations of much hate crime scholarship and policy have been built on the assumption that these are exclusively majority-versus-minority crimes, but this understanding ignores the capacity for the latter to be the protagonist in such incidents. Racist attacks, for instance, can arise from disputes between members of different minority ethnic groups, while victims of homophobic and transphobic hate crimes are sometimes targeted by religious minorities (Chakraborti et al., 2014), to cite another example. The kinds of biases, prejudices and stereotypes that form the basis of hate crimes are not the exclusive domain of any particular group. Such an assumption fails to account for the acts of hate, prejudice and bigotry committed by minorities against fellow minorities, or indeed against those who might be described as majority group members. Equally, our reliance on the labels 'victim' and 'offender' assumes dichotomous roles in hate crime offences, but research has shown that this reinforces a de-contextualised picture of some cases, particularly neighbourhood conflicts, where both parties can share culpability for the anti-social acts which form the basis for the broader conflict and hate offence (Walters and Hoyle, 2012). All of these points are too significant to remain peripheral to the domains of scholarship and policy. As Mason (2005: 844) suggests, when conceiving of hate crime perpetration there is no 'one size fits all' explanation for the motivation for such behaviour; rather, we need to resist drawing neat, overly simplistic conclusions based around what we think we know and instead use these multiple realities to inform our understanding conceptually and empirically.

Responding to hate crime

As the preceding discussion illustrates, hate crime is a highly complex and divisive subject area, and the further we take our analyses in order to seek conceptual clarity the more likely we are to find ourselves confronted with operational challenges. Learning how best to tackle hate crime is a difficult, ongoing task, but one which has formed a unifying theme within contemporary criminological enquiries (see, *inter alia*, Chakraborti, 2010; Perry, 2009; Iganski, 2008). This final section seeks to highlight the differing ways in which hate crime responses are being developed and deployed around the world. Often the 'job' of responding to hate crime is designated to criminal justice agencies; however, as we shall see, the effectiveness of this approach in terms of addressing offending behaviour or the support needs of victims is questionable.

As noted throughout this chapter, many jurisdictions have erected a legislative framework in order to respond to incidents of hate crime. Countries including the United States, Canada, Australia and many states across Western and Eastern Europe have introduced their own sets of laws which enshrine hate crime as a substantive 'stand-alone' offence or which offer the option of enhanced penalties for convicted hate crime perpetrators. Although the scope, implementation and effectiveness of hate crime provisions can vary from country to country, hate crime laws – and specifically the enhanced sentencing framework that accompanies these laws – have significant value in terms of their capacity to express collective condemnation of prejudice; to send a declaratory message to offenders; to convey a message of support to victims and stigmatised communities; to build confidence in the criminal justice system within some of the more disaffected and vulnerable members of society; and to acknowledge the additional harm caused by hate offences (Chakraborti and Garland, 2015; Walters, 2014a; ODIHR, 2009).

Within this context effective legislation and enforcement is important, both for individual freedoms and security and for cohesive communities. Nevertheless, the principles underpinning the creation of hate crime laws have been contested by academics, lawyers, politicians and the public. This is particularly evident in relation to the symbolic value of hate crime legislation, with critics questioning the capacity of hate crime provisions to have a declaratory and deterrent impact on the general public (Dixon and Gadd, 2006). Further concerns have been expressed over the rationale for criminalising thoughts, and not merely actions; the process of criminalising certain forms of prejudice and not others; and the potential for hate crime laws to create and reinforce hierarchies of victimisation which prioritises some groups of victims over others (for an overview see Jacobs and Potter, 1998). While concerns over the framing of hate crime laws are understandable, it is equally important not to become unduly alarmist about the implications of such laws. As Hall (2013: 35–6) notes, having hate crime laws in place does not make it a crime to harbour prejudiced attitudes nor is it a crime to hate: that prejudice or hate needs to be manifested through some form of behaviour or action before criminal justice agents can decide whether it constitutes a hate crime and deserves to be dealt with in accordance with the laws in place to punish perpetrators of such offences.

There are also question marks over the appropriateness of criminal justice responses to punish and rehabilitate offenders. Hall (2013) provides three criticisms of the use of imprisonment for hate crime offenders. First, he suggests, prison has limited deterrent value to these offenders; second, prisons are often divided along the lines of race and religious affiliation and may therefore simply reinforce intolerant attitudes and inadvertently encourage hate-related activity and recruitment; and third, the overcrowded prison environment offers little opportunity for the kind of rehabilitation that is necessary to truly address prejudicial beliefs. Therefore, while imprisonment and the use of enhanced sentences may be entirely appropriate in certain contexts, there are equally many forms and perpetrators of hate crime for which and for whom such punishment might not be especially effective. This point is supported by Burney (2002) who notes that prosecuting an offender using hate crime laws might in one sense symbolise the importance of confronting expressions of hate, but at the same time punishing and labelling offenders as 'hate offenders' does little to challenge hate-motivated behaviours. In this regard Walters (2014b) suggests that restorative approaches may offer an alternative and more effective way of punishing offenders, as it offers a form of dialogue which can help to break down the fears, stereotypes and prejudices that give rise to hate crimes.

Conventional punitive approaches to dealing with hate crime have also been criticised for failing to adequately address the legal justice needs of hate crime victims. Williams and Tregidga (2013) describe the gap between victim-centred reporting mechanisms and evidence-driven criminal justice prosecution processes which can leave victims – and in particular vulnerable victims of persistent 'low-level' hate incidents – frustrated and additionally traumatised by the absence of stringent evidential proof required for prosecution. Similarly, Chakraborti *et al.*'s (2014) research has challenged prevailing assumptions about hate crime victims' inclinations for enhanced prison sentences by revealing an overwhelming preference – shared by victims of different types of violent and non-violent hate crime and from different communities, ages and backgrounds – for the use of community education programmes and restorative interventions as a more effective route to challenging underlying prejudices and preventing future offending.

Fortunately, there are promising signs of change in the way in which responses to hate crime are becoming less prescriptive and more victim-centred (Iganski, 2014; Perry and Dyck, 2014). Within the UK specifically there has been a growing recognition of the importance of challenging prejudicial attitudes before they fully develop, and in this context education and early intervention within and beyond the classroom has an important role in raising awareness of the harms of hate (Walters and Brown, 2016; Chakraborti, 2015b). Equally, health and social care services can offer crucial support and treatment to victims, and their capacity to recognise and respond to hate crimes is pivotal given that such crimes often have severe consequences for physical and emotional health and well-being (Hardy and Chakraborti, 2017, 2016; Chakraborti *et al.*, 2014; Sin, 2014). Non-governmental organisations (NGOs) also play a key role in a variety of ways, not least by monitoring and reporting incidents, acting as a voice for victims and campaigning for action and improvements to legislation (ODIHR, 2009).

These developments are illustrative of the need for a more holistic, collective approach to hate crime. And it is essential that these developments continue, but this can only happen through better synergy between academic knowledge and policy making. This chapter has demonstrated that the value of academic theorising becomes more evident when it accounts for the lived realities of hate crime victimisation and perpetration, and so equally the value of policy-intervention is clearer when such interventions are grounded in empirical evidence (Chakraborti, 2015b). At present, many responses to hate crime are ill-informed due to a lack of synergy between criminological research, criminal justice policy and civil society. If such disconnects remain unchallenged they can have other dangerous implications not least with respect to the ongoing lack of appropriate support for victims and lack of recognition of their justice needs, and the ongoing problems of effectively preventing hate crimes and rehabilitating hate crime offenders.

Conclusion

This chapter has illustrated that the concept of hate crime is more complex and multi-layered than many might imagine. We have seen that the term 'hate' is a problematic, ambiguous and in many cases inaccurate descriptor of the offences with which it is commonly associated, and there is considerable disparity between the ways in which hate crime is conceived of by academics, and political and criminal justice systems around the world. Despite (or perhaps because of) these conceptual and operational challenges, hate crime is a burgeoning topic within criminology and in recent years we have seen the emergence of new knowledge, new ideas and new policies that have been used to tackle forms of targeted violence and hostility. This has facilitated some degree of change in academic, political and cultural attitudes towards the prejudice suffered by a range of minority groups, and of the most appropriate and effective ways to respond to hate offences.

However, we have also seen that a number of themes remain un- or under-explored and they highlight some of the limitations evident within hate crime scholarship and policy. Research and policy frameworks have traditionally sidelined acts of hate directed towards certain groups of 'others' who are not associated with recognised hate crime victim groups. This has contributed to a failure to capture 'hidden' victim groups and forms of victimisation. Similar criticisms can be directed towards hate crime perpetration, where a lack of empirical research and official data, and simplistic assumptions about the nature of hate crime offending, have skewed our understanding of the underlying factors and situational contexts that give rise to hate crime perpetration. Moreover, in operational terms there is uncertainty surrounding the effectiveness, or otherwise, of existing provisions to deal with hate crime and the enforcement of those provisions. In particular, scholars have observed the shortcomings of conventional criminal justice responses to hate crime and the merits of alternative approaches which seek to address the root causes of offending behaviour and to repair the harms of hate.

Crucially, the problems posed by hate crime – and the corresponding challenges for scholars, policy-makers and practitioners – are all the more sizeable in the context of prevailing economic, political and social conditions which act as enabling factors for the continued demonisation of 'marginal' communities, dwindling opportunities for young people and savage public spending cuts. Hall (2013: 197) makes reference to the importance of political prioritisation within this context, noting that the 'political inclinations of the state (and its institutions) can have serious implications for shaping an environment in which hate can potentially flourish' (see also Perry, 2001). Within this context a collaborative response from the corridors of policy, scholarship and activism offers the best chance of success. Encouragingly, there are very real signs of progress evident within each of these domains and this is starting to deliver tangible outcomes for victims of hate. Ultimately, however we conceive of the hate crime label across disciplines, across domains, across borders – and however we choose to prioritise the many challenges ahead – this progress can be maintained if we share a commitment to tackling hate, prejudice and targeted hostility in all its guises, and to developing sustainable ways of supporting those most affected. These common values are ones which can underpin future progress within this field.

References

Asquith, N. (2010) 'Verbal and Textual Hostility in Context', in N. Chakraborti (ed.) *Hate Crime: Concepts, Policy, Future Directions*, London: Routledge.

Bowling, B. (1993) 'Racial Harassment and the Process of Victimisation', *British Journal of Criminology*, 33 (2): 231–50.

Bowling, B. (1999) *Violent Racism: Victimisation, Policing and Social Context*, Oxford: Oxford University Press.

Brå (2009) Hatbrott 2008. Polisanmälningar där det i motivbilden ingår etnisk bakgrund, religiös tro, sexuell läggning eller könsöverskridande identitet eller uttryck, Report No. 2009:10 English summary, Stockholm: Swedish National Council for Crime Prevention (Brå).

Burnett, J. (2013) 'Britain: Racial Violence and the Politics of Hate', *Race and Class*, 54 (4): 5–21.

Burney, E. (2002) 'The Uses and Limits of Prosecuting Racially Aggravated Offences', in P. Iganski (ed.) *The Hate Debate: Should Hate Be Punished as a Crime?*, London: Institute for Jewish Policy Research, pp. 103–13.

Byers, B., Crider, B.W. and Biggers, G.K. (1999) 'Neutralization Techniques Used against the Amish Bias Crime Motivation: A Study of Hate Crime and Offender', *Journal of Contemporary Criminal Justice*, 15 (1): 78–96.

Campbell, R. (2014) 'Not Getting Away with It: Linking Sex Work and Hate Crime in Merseyside', in N. Chakraborti and J. Garland (eds) *Responding to Hate Crime: The Case for Connecting Policy and Research*, Bristol: The Policy Press, pp. 55–70.

Chakraborti, N. (2010) 'Crimes against the "Other": Conceptual, Operational and Empirical Challenges for Hate Studies', *Journal of Hate Studies*, 8 (1): 9–28.

Chakraborti, N. (2014) 'Introduction and Overview', in N. Chakraborti and J. Garland (eds) *Responding to Hate Crime: The Case for Connecting Policy and Research*, Bristol: The Policy Press, pp. 1–9.

Chakraborti, N. (2015a) 'Framing the Boundaries', in N. Hall, A. Corb, P. Giannasi and J. Grieve (eds) *The Routledge International Handbook of Hate Crime*, London: Routledge, pp. 226–36.

Chakraborti, N. (2015b) 'Mind the Gap! Making Stronger Connections between Hate Crime Policy and Scholarship', *Criminal Justice Policy Review*, available via OnlineFirst at http://cjp.sagepub.com/content/early/2015/08/10/0887403415599641.full.pdf?ijkey=pzuAAJlkzXZaJGb&keytype=finite.

Chakraborti, N. and Garland, J. (2012) 'Reconceptualising Hate Crime Victimization through the Lens of Vulnerability and "Difference"', *Theoretical Criminology*, 16 (4), 499–514.

Chakraborti, N. and Garland, J. (eds) (2014) *Responding to Hate Crime: The Case for Connecting Policy and Research*, Bristol: The Policy Press.

Chakraborti, N. and Garland, J. (2015) *Hate Crime: Impacts, Causes and Consequences* (2nd edn), London: SAGE.

Chakraborti, N., Garland, J. and Hardy, S. (2014) *The Leicester Hate Crime Project: Findings and conclusions*, Leicester: University of Leicester.

College of Policing (2014) *Hate Crime Operational Guidance*, Coventry: College of Policing.

Corcoran, H. and Smith, K. (2016) 'Hate Crimes, England and Wales, 2015/16', Home Office Statistical Bulletin 11/16. London: Home Office.

Creese, B. and Lader, D. (2014) *Hate Crimes, England and Wales, 2013/2014*, London: Home Office.

Dauvergne, M., Scrim, K. and Brennan, S. (2008) *Hate Crime in Canada*, Ottawa: Canadian Centre for Justice Statistics.

Dixon, B. and Gadd, D. (2006) 'Getting the Message? "New" Labour and the Criminalisation of "Hate"', *Criminology and Criminal Justice*, 6 (3): 309–28.

Fekete, L. and Webber, F. (2010) 'Foreign Nationals, Enemy Penology and the Criminal Justice System', *Race and Class*, 51(4): 1–25.

FRA (European Union Agency for Fundamental Rights) (2013) *Discrimination and Hate Crime against Jews in EU Member States: Experiences and Perceptions of Antisemitism*, Luxembourg: Publications Office of the European Union.

Franklin, K. (2000) 'Antigay Behaviors among Young Adults: Prevalence, Patterns, and Motivators in a Noncriminal Population', *Journal of Interpersonal Violence*, 15 (4): 339–63.

Gadd, D. (2009) 'Aggravating Racism and Elusive Motivation', *British Journal of Criminology*, 49 (6): 755–71.

Garland, J. (2010) '"It's a Mosher Just Been Banged for No Reason": Assessing the Victimisation of Goths and the Boundaries of Hate Crime', *International Review of Victimology*, 17 (2): 159–77.

Garland, J. (2012) 'Difficulties in Defining Hate Crime Victimization', *International Review of Victimology*, 18 (1): 25–37.

Garland, J. and Chakraborti, N. (2012) 'Divided by a Common Concept? Assessing the Implications of Different Conceptualizations of Hate Crime in the European Union', *European Journal of Criminology*, 9 (1): 38–51.

Garland, J. and Hodkinson, P. (2014) 'Alternative Subcultures and Hate Crime', in N. Hall, A. Corb, P. Giannasi and J. Grieve (eds) *The Routledge International Handbook of Hate Crime*, London: Routledge, pp. 226–36.

Garland, J., Spalek, B. and Chakraborti, N. (2006) 'Hearing Lost Voices: Issues in Researching "Hidden" Minority Ethnic Communities', *British Journal of Criminology*, 46 (3): 423–37.

Gerstenfeld, P.B. (2004) *Hate Crimes: Causes, Controls, and Controversies*, Los Angeles: SAGE.

Hall, N. (2013) *Hate Crime* (2nd edn), London: Routledge.

Hardy, S. (2017) *Everyday Multiculturalism and 'Hidden' Hate*, London: Palgrave Macmillan.

Hardy, S. and Chakraborti, N. (2017) *A Postcode Lottery? Mapping Support Services for Hate Crime Victims*, Leicester: University of Leicester.

Hardy, S. and Chakraborti, N. (2016) *Healing the Harms: Identifying How Best to Support Hate Crime Victims*, Leicester: University of Leicester.

Home Office, Office for National Statistics and Ministry of Justice (2013) *An Overview of Hate Crime in England and Wales*, London: Author.

Iganski, P. (2001) 'Hate Crimes Hurt More', *American Behavioural Scientist*, 45 (4): 626–38.

Iganski, P. (2008) *'Hate Crime' and the City*, Bristol: The Policy Press.

Iganski, P. (with Ainsworth, K., Geraghty, L., Lagou, S. and Patel, N.) (2014) 'Understanding How "Hate" Hurts: A Case Study of Working with Offenders and Potential Offenders', in N. Chakraborti and J. Garland (eds) *Responding to Hate Crime: The Case for Connecting Policy and Research*, Bristol: The Policy Press, pp. 231–242.

Jacobs, J. and Potter, K. (1998) *Hate Crimes: Criminal Law and Identity Politics*, Oxford: Oxford University Press.

James, Z. (2014) 'Hate Crimes against Gypsies, Travellers and Roma in Europe', in N. Hall, A. Corb, P. Giannasi and J. Grieve (eds) *The Routledge International Handbook on Hate Crime*, London: Routledge, pp. 237–48.

Lancaster, S. (2014) 'Reshaping Hate Crime Policy and Practice: Lessons from a Grassroots Campaign', in N. Chakraborti and J. Garland (eds) *Responding to Hate Crime: The Case for Connecting Policy and Research*, Bristol: The Policy Press, pp. 39–54.

Mason, G. (2005) 'Hate Crime and the Image of the Stranger', *British Journal of Criminology*, 45 (6): 837–59.

Mason-Bish, H. (2010) 'Future Challenges for Hate Crime Policy: Lessons from the Past', in N. Chakraborti (ed.) *Hate Crime: Concepts, Policy, Future Directions*, London: Routledge, pp. 58–77.

McDevitt, J., Levin, J. and Bennett, S. (2002) 'Hate Crime Offenders: An Expanded Typology', *Journal of Social Issues*, 58 (2): 303–17.

McDevitt, J., Levin, J., Nolan, J. and Bennett, S. (2010) 'Hate Crime Offenders', in N. Chakraborti (ed.) *Hate Crime: Concepts, Policy, Future Directions*, London: Routledge, pp. 124–48.

McGhee, D. (2007) 'The Challenge of Working with Racially Motivated Offenders: An Exercise in Ambivalence?', *Probation Journal*, 54 (3): 213–26.

Moran, L.J. (2007) 'Invisible Minorities: Challenging Community and Neighbourhood Models of Policing', *Criminology and Criminal Justice*, 7 (4): 417–41.

ODIHR (Office for Democratic Institutions and Human Rights) (2009) *Hate Crime Laws: A Practical Guide*, Warsaw: Author.

ODIHR (Office for Democratic Institutions and Human Rights) (2016) *Hate Crimes in the OSCE Region: Incidents and Responses – Annual Report for 2015*, Warsaw: The OSCE Office for Democratic Institutions and Human Rights.

Perry, B. (2001) *In the Name of Hate: Understanding Hate Crimes*, London: Routledge.

Perry, B. (ed.) (2009) *Hate Crimes Volume 1: Understanding and Defining Hate Crime*, Westport: Praeger.

Perry, B. and Dyck, D.R. (2014) 'Courage in the Face of Hate: A Curricular Resource for Confronting Anti-LGBTQ Violence', in N. Chakraborti and J. Garland (eds) *Responding to Hate Crime: The Case for Connecting Policy and Research*, Bristol: The Policy Press, pp. 185–97.

Perry, J. (2014) 'Evidencing the Case for Hate Crime', in N. Chakraborti and J. Garland (eds) *Responding to Hate Crime: The Case for Connecting Policy and Research*, Bristol: The Policy Press, pp. 71–83.

Petrosino, C. (2003) 'Connecting the Past to the Future: Hate Crime in America', in B. Perry (ed.) *Hate and Bias Crime: A Reader*, London: Routledge, pp. 9–26.

Ray, L. and Smith, D. (2001) 'Racist Offenders and the Politics of "Hate Crime"', *Law and Critique*, 12 (3): 203–21.

Ray, L., Smith, D. and Wastell, L. (2004) 'Shame, Rage and Racist Violence', *British Journal of Criminology*, 44 (3): 350–68.

Roberts, C., Innes, M., Williams, M., Tregidga, J. and Gadd, D. (2013) *Understanding Who Commits Hate Crime and Why They Do It*, Merthyr Tydfil: Welsh Government Social Research.

Sheffield, C. (1995) 'Hate Violence', in P. Rothenberg (ed.) *Race, Class and Gender in the United States*, New York: St Martin's Press, pp. 432–41.

Sin, C.H. (2014) 'Using a "Layers of Influence" Model to Understand the Interaction of Research, Policy and Practice in Relation to Disablist Hate Crime', in N. Chakraborti and J. Garland (eds) *Responding to Hate Crime: The Case for Connecting Policy and Research*, Bristol: Policy Press, pp. 99–112.

Sophie Lancaster Foundation (2011) *The Sophie Lancaster Foundation Educational Game for Schools, Youth Groups and Other Young People's Organisations*, available at www.sophielancasterfoundation.com/index. php?option=com_content&vie w=article&id=73&Itemid=16 (accessed 28 August 2015).

Wachholz, S. (2009) 'Pathways through Hate: Exploring the Victimization of the Homeless', in B. Perry (ed.) *Hate Crimes: The Victims of Hate Crime*, Westport: Praeger, pp. 199–222.

Walters, M. (2011) 'A General Theories of Hate Crime? Strain, Doing Difference and Self Control', *Critical Criminology*, 19 (4): 313–30.

Walters, M. (2014a) 'Conceptualizing "Hostility" for Hate Crime Law: Minding "the Minutiae" when Interpreting Section 28(1)(a) of the Crime and Disorder Act 1998', *Oxford Journal of Legal Studies*, 34 (1): 47–74.

Walters, M. (2014b) *Hate Crime and Restorative Justice: Exploring Causes, Repairing Harms*, Oxford: Oxford University Press.

Walters, M. and Brown, R. (2016) *Preventing Hate Crime: Emerging Practices and Recommendations for the Improved Management of Criminal Justice Interventions*, Brighton: University of Sussex.

Walters, M. and Hoyle, C. (2012) 'Exploring the Everyday World of Hate Victimization through Community Mediation', *International Review of Victimology*, 18 (1): 7–24.

Williams, M. and Tregidga, J. (2013) *All Wales Hate Crime Research Project: Research Overview and Executive Summary*, Cardiff: Race Equality First.

Zempi, I. (2014) 'Responding to the Needs of Victims of Islamophobia', in N. Chakraborti and J. Garland (eds) *Responding to Hate Crime: The Case for Connecting Policy and Research*, Bristol: The Policy Press, pp. 113–25.

17

CRIMINOLOGY AND TERRORISM

Toward a critical approach

Gabe Mythen

Introduction

Terrorism is a social problem which has endured over several centuries, involved multiple aggressors and led to a troubling number of human casualties (see Martin, 2012; Maras, 2013). Over the course of the twentieth century, it is estimated that over 500,000 people were killed in terrorist attacks (see Ahmad, 2012). Into the second decade of the twentieth century, there is little to suggest that this figure is likely to lessen in upcoming years. Indeed, the magnitude and the ubiquity of political and religiously motivated violence in the modern world has led some commentators to proclaim that terrorism is one of the defining markers of the contemporary epoch. To this end, Borradori (2003) has suggested that we live in 'a time of terror', while Beck (2009) alludes to the configuration of a 'terroristic world risk society' beset by uncontrollable security threats. Yet, while terrorism is certainly a worrying feature of the contemporary age, I will be counseling in this chapter against exaggerating the scale and novelty of the problem. Rather, what we criminologists need to do is to take a step back from the representation of terrorism in the media, politics and popular culture and make a balanced assessment of the threat based on the most reliable evidence available to us. In so doing, we can make an informed rather than an emotive judgment about the nature and causes of pre-meditated and organized violence and reflect on the most effective ways of tackling it. In this chapter, I wish to address three core issues around the definition, assessment and regulation of terrorism. Having contextualized the threat of terrorism in the modern age, I wish to bring to the surface some of the problems that arise when we attempt to define terrorism. Second, I wish to examine the extent of terrorism in the contemporary world, flagging up the ambiguities that occur in calibrating or measuring the problem of terrorism. Third, I will be connecting up the representation of the terrorist threat to dominant modes of control and regulation introduced to combat the threat.

In academia, terrorism has been a longstanding topic of study in many subject areas, including peace studies, politics, security studies and international relations. Yet, in criminology there has historically been a lack of attention to the problem of terrorism. Analyses of terrorism have picked up pace somewhat since the 9/11 attacks and discrete strands of research have developed around the role of institutions involved in the social construction of terrorism, the governance of terrorism and legal forms of regulation. Post 9/11 critical criminologists have engaged with the impacts of pre-emptive counter-terrorism interventions (see McCulloch and Wilson, 2015; Poynting and Whyte, 2012; Zedner, 2007), the deleterious effects of such interventions for targeted groups (Mythen, Walklate and Khan, 2013; Spalek and Lambert, 2008) and the implications of counter-terrorism laws for the constitution of justice (Zedner, 2009; Hudson and Ugelvik, 2012). However, larger questions around the root causes of terrorism have largely remained outside the ambit of mainstream debate. This elision matters for at least three reasons. First, as we shall see, if dominant political constructions of terrorism are accepted as just and objective, a simplistic agenda on terrorism which deals only in opposites becomes set as the norm: good/evil, friend/foe, aggressor/victim. Second, if we accept a narrow definition of what terrorism is and means, we enable certain acts that produce terror to evade the lens of scrutiny. Third, if we are to understand the motivations which drive individuals to resort to it, we must begin by fully engaging with the reasons that those involved in violence cite as drivers for their actions. As I shall argue, such an engagement requires facing up to some unsettling questions about the role of nation-states and governments in the production of terrorism, most notably through aggressive and reckless military action. In thinking about what an alternative criminology might contribute to our understanding of the problem of terrorism, taking heed of these issues and pressing them into the purview of those with the power to change law and security policy is but a starting point.

Defining terrorism: problems and issues

The problem of terrorism is centuries old (see Ahmad, 2012). Indeed, the roots of the English word 'terrorism' derive from the French word *terreur* first used to describe the bloody period of upheaval in France in the final quarter of the late eighteenth century. *La terreur* was the collective term used at that historical juncture to describe the gruesome methods of violence exacted during the violent conflict between rival Girondin and Jacobin factions. During the 'reign of terror', thousands of citizens were killed by barbaric means including the guillotine, poisoning and death by flogging (see Ayto, 1990: 524). Interestingly, although the noun terrorism was originally used to describe organized methods of violence exacted by the ruling French State, terrorism is applied in contemporary society to describe the actions of non-State groups and actors (see Jackson and Sinclair, 2012; Maras, 2013). While there is no universally accepted definition of terrorism, the term is commonly deployed to describe violence by non-State actors that is politically and/or religiously motivated and intended to cause widespread harm (Hoffman, 2012: 4). Although imperfect, in following Hoffman's definition what is perhaps striking is the sheer ubiquity of terrorism across time and space. Of the world's 196 recognized countries, 146 have suffered terrorist attacks since 1970 (Global Terrorism Database, 2015). Putting aside for the moment, issues of labeling and the methods by which these attacks are counted, such statistics do indicate the international nature of organized violent acts which are driven by religious and/or political beliefs. Being motivated by political and/or religious values, terrorist acts are also intended to induce fear and anxiety amongst populations (see Schmid, 2011: 56). It is thus easy to see why terrorism has long been a fundamental concern for government. In effect, terrorist attacks destabilize the cherished notion that the State is able to ensure the safety of its citizens.

While the factors documented above are common in instances in which the label terrorism is attached, there is no universally accepted definition that crosses continents. Further, there are perceptible gaps in terms of what may be excluded in the category. For instance, in focusing exclusively on non-State actors, common definitions presuppose that States cannot and do not commit terroristic acts. As those advancing semiological approaches have argued, history shows us that State actors are capable of conducting atrocities and engaging in military violence with huge human costs, whether these fall under the legally defined ambit of terrorism or not (see Ciocchini and Khoury, 2012; Hillyard, 2009). In a world scarred by violent militaristic incursions by the State – from the United States to Israel, Syria to Colombia – we must appreciate that defining terrorism is a contested and contestable enterprise. Far from being a neutral and objective process, a range of factors affect whether a particular act is classified as terrorism. Acknowledging the ways in which terrorism is *socially constructed* leads us on to ask exactly who it is that has power to influence the definitional process. Here, we are entering the turf of institutional analysis and grappling with prickly issues that arise when security experts, academics, lawyers, politicians and journalists make sense of and represent terrorism. While I will return to this kind of analysis later, it is first necessary to quantify the problem of terrorism.

Assessing the terrorist risk: who counts?

I have implied above that there are important problems and issues to consider which stem from ways in which terrorism is defined. In particular, the exclusion of State acts that could otherwise be classified as terroristic is a point of contention that has led some criminologists to deploy the phrase 'State terrorism' to describe such acts. Nevertheless, despite the limitations of official definitions of terrorism, it is worth analyzing the available evidence in order to gain a sense of the scale of the problem. This enables us to grasp historical changes in the frequency of religious and politically motivated violence and differences in regional patterning over time.

In contemporary society, security analysts are agreed that the global terrorist threat is largely constituted by a collection of Islamist extremist groups, including ISIS (Daesh), Al Qaeda, Boko Haram, Al Shabaab and Lashkar-e-Taiba (see Burke, 2015; Martin, 2012). As we shall see, in recent times, these groups have been responsible for a large number of human casualties in Africa and the Middle East. The upsurge in violence committed by Islamist extremist groups partly arose as a consequence of the fracturing of nations such as Iraq and Syria in the Middle East and escalating tensions between Sunni and Shia Muslims in the region. Yet in the 1970s Western Europe experienced the highest number of casualties as a result of terrorism and in the latter decades of the twentieth century the most affected region was Latin America (Global Terrorism Database, 2015). In the 1980s and 1990s several secular left wing organizations – including the Shining Path in Peru, FARC (Revolutionary Armed Forces of Colombia) and the Farabundo Marti National Liberation Front (FMLN) in El Salvador – were effectively at war with the State and the human loss as a result of these conflicts was high. According to the Global Terrorism Database (2015), in the 1980s Latin America experienced more terrorist attacks (17,293) than Western Europe, North America and Asia combined (13,643). While the death toll in Latin America has fallen since this time, it is important to note that – despite very limited coverage in the Western media – serious attacks continue to occur in Colombia, Peru and Mexico. This tells us that organized violence is not only a common problem, it is one which tends to spike, recede and migrate over time.

Focusing on the present, data compiled by the Institute for Economics and Peace (2015: 2) show a troubling escalation of terrorism in the twenty-first century, with the number of deaths attributed to attacks increasing nine-fold from 3,329 in 2000 to 32,686 by 2014. Alarmingly, there was an 80% rise in the number of recorded deaths by terrorism between 2013 and 2014 alone, as a consequence of intense conflicts in several countries. Of the 32,686 deaths that occurred as a direct result of terrorism in 2014, the large majority of these are attributed to attacks by four Islamist militant groups: ISIS, Al Qaeda, Boko Haram and the Taliban (Institute for Economics and Peace, 2015: 2). Although critical data analysts would doubtless want to ask some searching questions about the methodology deployed in the study, the regional patterning of casualties is palpable. While the fact that terrorist attacks occurred in 93 of the world's 196 countries may provide some grist to the mill of politicians and security analysts that insist that the terrorist threat is 'global', the geographical layering of incidents is telling. In total, 78% of deaths attributed to terrorism occurred in just five countries: Iraq, Syria, Afghanistan, Pakistan and Nigeria (Institute for Economics and Peace, 2015: 2). So, how can we interpret the statistics above? What do they tell us about the problem of 'global' terrorism? In responding to these questions from the perspective of critical criminology a number of points stand out.

First, while terrorism might well be a global problem in the sense that it occurs in many countries, the threat level in terms of likelihood of harm is uneven and unequal. While sizeable public resources have been ploughed into countering domestic terrorism in Western nations, if the statistics show anything it is that Western countries have suffered remarkably few deaths on home soil as a result of terrorism over the last two decades. In the UK for instance, the number of people killed in the last two decades as a result of terrorist attacks is 60, making an average of three deaths per annum. Thus, without trivializing or denying the severity of the threat, we should be rightly troubled by the British Prime Minister David Cameron's (2011) assessment that: 'the biggest threat that we face comes from terrorist attacks'. Unsurprisingly, given the wide range of harms that exist – from the environmental and health related to the economic and social – such a position has been questioned. Indeed, following on from archival and statistical analysis, the UK Government's appointed Independent Reviewer of Terrorism legislation, David Anderson QC (2012: 26) compared the average of five deaths per annum caused by terrorism in England and Wales in the last century with 'the total number of accidental deaths in 2010 of 17,201, including 123 cyclists killed in traffic accidents, 102 personnel killed in Afghanistan, 29 people drowned in the bathtub and five killed by stings from hornets, wasps and bees'. Anderson (2012: 26) concludes that terrorism is 'an insignificant cause of mortality in the United Kingdom'.

Second, and relatedly, we might want to ask why – given the relative paucity of attacks in the West – the focus within Western criminology has predominantly been trained on issues of national rather than international security. While the lens of criminology has focused on issues of domestic security and the global media have concentrated attention on the terrorist threat in the West, the statistics point in different directions. Excluding 9/11, just 0.5% of terrorist attacks have taken place in Western countries in the last 15 years (see Institute for Economics and Peace, 2015: 3). Further, despite exhaustive coverage of the 'existential' threat posed by ISIS, the group causing the highest number of deaths in 2014 (6,664) is actually Boko Haram (Institute for Economics and Peace, 2015: 4). This forces us to reflect hard on the degree of attention afforded to the domestic terrorist threat in Western nations post 9/11 relative to the level of risk. Following on, we might ask how many criminology scholars orient their work toward the key sites and regions at which terrorism predominantly manifests itself, such as Nigeria and Iraq? Here it would seem that while all victims of terrorism are equal, some remain more equal than others.

Third, in terms of omissions, we might want to ask some barbed questions about the number of indiscriminate deaths caused by systemic and organized violence that fall outside the ambit of data gathering, such as those resulting from drone attacks, State genocide and assassinations by paramilitary groups. In focusing specifically on non-State violence, otherwise terroristic acts are elided and the plight of victims of these acts becomes muted. If, for instance, the barbaric acts of ISIS in Syria are counted on the abacus, why not the atrocities sanctioned by the President of Syria, Bashar al Assad, which have included the use of weaponized chlorine (see Ross and Malik, 2015)? The technical answer to this would doubtless be that formally democratically elected leaders of States engage in 'just war' rather than terrorism (see Alayo, 2012). Nevertheless, the sheer numbers of innocent civilians killed as a direct result of war – latterly in response to the terrorist threat – serve as a poignant reminder that deaths by terror come in more than one guise. It is estimated, for example, that the documented number of civilians killed in Iraq since the invasion and occupation by United States forces in 2003 stands at a staggering 171,306 (see Iraq Body Count, 2015). A critical analysis of the findings from global databases that document casualties of terrorism shows that the facts do not always speak for themselves. Rather than professionals in the media, academia and politics mirroring the data, a creative process of social construction is involved which shapes the representation of terrorism. We will follow this thread further now as we unravel the ways in which the threat of terrorism has predominantly been presented and understood by powerful groups in the West post 9/11.

Constructing the 'new terrorism': who speaks?

While political violence is a historically omnipresent phenomenon, the assumption that 'the world changed' with the events of 9/11 has been commonplace in media and political circles. This view has significance beyond the observational, having been instrumental in underpinning sweeping changes in national security and counter-terrorism measures in the West. Nevertheless, the view that 9/11 served as a historical break point is somewhat myopic and tends toward Westocentrism. Even the most cursory glance through the history books shows that large-scale terrorist acts are a longstanding part of the global landscape. It thus becomes incumbent on us to ask first, whether Western nations are at an unprecedented risk from terrorist attacks, and second, whether the focus in criminology has been and is sufficiently broad and inclusive. Whilst I will return to these issues later, I want now to address the ways in which the threat level has been institutionally articulated in the West post 9/11.

In the final decade of the twentieth century – and, indeed, *prior to* the 9/11 attacks – a group of security studies scholars (see Arquilla, Ronfeldt and Zanini, 1999; Laqueur, 1996, 1999; Lesser et al., 1999) collectively asserted that the nature of terrorism had fundamentally altered. While these assertions initially attracted limited attention within academia and in intelligence communities, what became known as 'the new terrorism thesis' gained much wider currency in the aftermath of 9/11. At this juncture, the scramble for explanations led to the consolidation of a discourse of 'new terrorism' which was commonly used to emphasize the novelty of the threat posed by extreme Islamist groups, such as Al Qaeda (see Burnett and Whyte, 2006). This discourse of new terrorism – widely propagated in media, political and intelligence circles – suggests that the threat presented by Islamist extremist groups is distinct in nature and scale (see Bolanos, 2012; Neumann, 2009). Due to a combination of global reach, fluid organizational structure and access to extensive weaponry capability, groups such as Al Qaeda and ISIS are said to be engaged in a unique and highly lethal form of violence (see Burke, 2005; Parker, 2013). These new terrorist groups are distinguished from traditional terrorist organizations such as the IRA and the ETA that were involved in local and national struggles for power. Where traditional terrorism groups were inspired by nationalism or communism, the new terrorism is driven by religious fanaticism (Laqueur, 1996). While traditional terrorist groups acted under united ideological objectives and within strict organizational hierarchies, new terrorist groups are said to be defined by their scattered aims, disparate organizational structure and their capacity to launch attacks in countries across the globe (see Morgan, 2004). For proponents of the new terrorism thesis, ideologically motivated and radicalized individuals are preparing in organized cells to launch 'high-lethality' attacks with the intention of maximizing civilian casualties (see Lesser et al., 1999: 42; Hoffman, 2012: 9). The active pursuit of chemical, radiological or nuclear bombs amongst extremist groups, ratchets up still further the potential threat (see Cole and Gurr, 2012; Quinn, 2015). For proponents of the new terrorism thesis, the process of globalization underpins many of these transformations. Rather than drawing on local sources for economic support, new terrorist groups receive donations from benefactors from around the globe, including private financiers, charities and non-governmental organizations (see 9/11 Commission Report, 2004: 57). The global structure of terrorist networks thus means that they are favorably positioned to exploit new media technologies in order to analyze data, disseminate information and to recruit new members (see Martin, 2012: 40; Vertigans, 2010: 29). As Burke (2015) notes, the use of new media as a propaganda tool has been crucial in ISIS's recruitment of so-called 'foreign fighters' from all continents.

It is easy to see why the new terrorism narrative of transformation found favor in intelligence, policing and government circles after 9/11 and subsequently informed counter-terrorism and security policy making in the USA in particular (Duyvesteyn and Malkki, 2012: 36). While there is more than a grain of truth in the new terrorism thesis, the key claim that a radical transformation has occurred is highly questionable (Copeland, 2001; Walklate and Mythen, 2015). Given that dominant understandings of the terrorist threat feed directly into the formation of security and military policy, this matters for reasons more important than academic debate. In interrogating the new terrorism thesis, it becomes clear that assertions regarding transformation are unstable. Clearly the tactics of terrorist groups differ over time and place and modes and chosen methods of attack can reasonably be expected to evolve, in line with resources, capability and technology. At the risk of simplification, it would seem expectable that engaged terrorist groups would want to make use of whatever technological weapons were at their disposal. The fact that these may differ from those previously available does not in itself signal uniqueness. The methods of attack used by terrorist groups in the twentieth century were themselves very different from those popularized during *la terreur*. As the guillotine gave way to the gun, so too the mortar bomb may be supplanted by the dirty bomb. As we shall see, while these transformations occur recursively over time, the new terrorism thesis heralds a seismic change and one which necessitates what Bourke (2005) refers to as 'a new paradigm of resistance'. The new terrorism thesis also implies a process of historical change that is not linear. For example, while a capillary structure is attributed to modern terrorist groups, the anarchist movement in the nineteenth century worked via a loose network. The IRA, for instance, made use of new weapons technologies, operated a cell system and targeted areas of civilian use. Similarly, while fears about chemical, biological and radiological (CBR) attacks are commonly reproduced in political debates, broadcast media and popular culture artefacts, the only case of note conducted by a terrorist group is the Sarin gas attack on the Tokyo subway by Aum Shrinko which occurred in 1995. Some 20 years later, guns and bombs remain the standard mode of terrorist attack across the globe. While it would be churlish to dismiss the extent of the terrorist threat, what we can say with confidence is that the threat level in the West has been exaggerated relative to the risk (see Burnett and Whyte, 2006; Duyvestyn, 2004). At the same time, major terrorist attacks which occur routinely in other parts of the globe have been largely overlooked in Western academic, media and political circles. Having outlined the features and characteristics of 'new terrorism' I will go on to ask what the new terrorism thesis *does* at an ideational level and which policy interventions it permits. The logic of the new terrorism thesis suggests that the enemy is knowable and presents an existential threat to social order. As Burnett and Whyte (2006) argue, this provides the State with a mandate for a range of processes geared toward ordering and controlling populations which would otherwise be considered illegitimate. As we shall see, the assumptions regarding the crystallization of a new and more deadly form of terrorism have served as an ideological prop for the development of a reoriented calculus of risk chiefly focused on the catastrophic impacts of upcoming threats.

Countering terrorism: who is targeted?

Notwithstanding the problems that emerge when we speak about terrorism and difficulties in calibrating the extent of the terrorist threat, one of the thorniest issues we face is how to confront the problem of terrorism. One of the clear requisites for determining an effective response to terrorism is a detailed and cultured understanding of the root causes of terrorism. In this section, I will be arguing that such an understanding has been sadly lacking in the majority of State responses in recent history, compounding the problem and leading to the production of iatrogenic effects. In line with the trajectory of the chapter our key focus will be the threat posed by Islamist terrorist organizations and, more particularly, the response to this that has materialized after 9/11 through the 'war on terror'.

As discussed above, the events of 11 September 2001 have produced geopolitical reverberations that have endured to the present day. The 9/11 attacks were conducted by 19 men – 15 from Saudi Arabia, two from the United Arab Emirates, one from Lebanon and one from Egypt – inspired by the philosophy of Al Qaeda. Four passenger planes were hijacked in flight. Two were flown into the Twin Towers of the World Trade Center in New York, one into the US military headquarters at the Pentagon in Washington and the final fourth plane crashed in Shanksville, Pennsylvania after a struggle between passengers and the hijackers. Almost 3,000 people were killed in the biggest single terrorist attack in modern history. In the days that passed after 9/11 the question of how to respond to these attacks was widely debated. Given that the enemy was constituted by a small and geographically scattered group of individuals committed to a radical belief system rather than a nation or an army, this question yielded few satisfactory answers. What is clear is that the United States government was under a fair degree of pressure – by some of its citizens and certainly sections of the media – to react strongly to the attacks. The response by George Bush Junior, then President of the United States, was to launch what he referred to as 'a war on terror'. The range of this war was unprecedented, involving military action, sweeping powers of surveillance, mass incarceration, changes to immigration regulations and intensified policing at borders and in urban areas (see Walklate and Mythen, 2015; Welch, 2006). A similar, if less extensive range of measures were also launched in Britain by the Prime Minister Tony Blair under the moniker of 'the war against terrorism'. Before we discuss the impacts of these measures, it is again worth noting the ways in which the threat was socially constructed. In attempting to justify wide-ranging interventions, the political rhetoric of both Bush and Blair drew heavily on particular under-standings of discourses of risk, which accented the possibility of future harms as a basis for intervention in the present. In his State of the Union Address Bush (2002) stated that 'America must not ignore the threat gathering against us. Facing clear evidence of peril, we cannot wait for the final proof – the smoking gun – that could come in the form of a mushroom cloud.' Such statements sought to prop up what was described as a pro-active approach based on early intervention as an effective tool to disrupt terrorist attacks in the planning as opposed to the execution stages. A parallel approach of stressing dystopic possibilities was also adopted in the UK by Tony Blair (2001): 'we know, that they (the terrorists) would, if they could, go further and use chemical or biological or even nuclear weapons of mass destruction'. The appeal to worst case scenarios served as a longstanding linguistic device designed to garner public sup-port for military forays and the introduction of stringent domestic counter-security policies (McCulloch and Pickering, 2009; Zedner, 2007). The former were underpinned by binaries that flattened the complexity of the situation, with the language of George Bush Junior in the immediate post 9/11 period being saturated with polar opposites: good and evil, safe and risky, righteous and immoral. These binaries served to ideationally construct a conflict in which there were only two sides. As Bush (2001) declared: 'either you are with us, or you are with the terrorists'. Despite their crudity and ineptitude, in some respects, these responses highlight the difficulties that States have in responding to transnational security threats that are rooted in identity, culture and faith rather than affiliation to a nation or political organiza-tion. Although the majority of the individuals that undertook the 9/11 attacks were Saudi Arabian nationals inspired by the philosophy of the Islamist extremist group Al Qaeda, the initial course of military action ordered by the United States government under 'Operation Enduring Freedom' was to invade Afghanistan. The main objectives of this first phase of the 'war on terror' were to attack the Taliban and to destroy the training camps sanctioned by them that had been established by Al Qaeda in southern and eastern Afghanistan. By 2002, the President of the United States, George Bush, expressed his desire to extend the 'war on terror' to tackle what he referred to as an 'axis of evil' including the 'rogue states' of Iraq and Iran (see Mythen, 2014: 99).

During the occupations of Afghanistan and Iraq the US military was assisted by foreign allies – including the UK, Australia and Poland – whose leaders were apparently persuaded that the 'war on terror' was necessary and just to eliminate future threats to Western nation-states (see Rogers, 2012: 145). The role of risk in both the decisions made by political leaders and the presentation of these decisions to the public should not be understated. The invasion of Iraq by US and UK forces was based on the premise that Saddam Hussein supported Al Qaeda's mission to destabilize the West and that he had been assembling Weapons of Mass Destruction (WMD) that could be used against Western nations. A similar process of deploy-ing risk to accent potential future harms to national security was in operation across the Atlantic, where the now infamous intelligence dossier – *Iraq: Its Infrastructure of Concealment, Deception and Intimidation* – was being presented by the British government to publicly justify its decision to be involved in the invasion of Iraq. This document was littered with inaccurate assumptions that overstated the risk to the West posed by Saddam Hussein, most notably that he had the capacity to fire WMD at Western targets within 45 minutes of issuing an order (see Taylor-Norton, 2011). The fit between these imaginings of a threat of great magnitude and the discourse of new terrorism is snug. The articulation of the new terrorism thesis and the hyperbolic language of the 'war on terror' served as a political lever through which a case was made for the necessity of exceptional security measures, based on hypothetical risk (see Amoore, 2013). In many respects this tendency to ask 'What if?' questions gained traction after the findings of the 9/11 Commission (2004) reported that the attacks on the United States represented 'a failure of imagination'. The inability of security personnel to predict such an attack led to a major shake-up in the intelligence services and an increased emphasis on horizon scanning to prevent future attacks.

The move toward more pre-emptive forms of intervention is one of the most notable features of counter-terrorism policy since 9/11. As Zedner (2007: 269) explains: 'pre-emption stands temporally prior to prevention of proximate harms: it seeks to intervene when the risk of harm is no more than an unspecified threat or propensity as yet uncertain and beyond view'. In the context of counter-terrorism, pre-emptive policies are underpinned by the belief that waiting for absolute proof may allow terrorists the time and space to attack (see Maras, 2013: 127). In his testimony to the UK Iraq War Inquiry, Blair himself claimed that 'a new calculus of risk' was required to deal with the scale of the threat posed by Islamist fundamentalist networks (see Sparrow, 2010). This is consistent with his stance after the 7/7 bomb attacks in London, in which Blair heralded a new phase of struggle against Islamist extremism, declaring that 'the rules of the game' had changed (see Wintour, 2005). While there is nothing inherently bad about considering possible events that may occur in the future as a precautionary tool, at times worst case hypothetical scenarios – which may or may not eventuate – appear to have driven legislation and policy making. As we shall see, here the balance of risk can become inordinately skewed, such that security is not augmented but rather undermined by infringements to human rights and civil liberties (see Mythen, 2014: 99).

While the (contorted) principles of pre-emptive risk clearly acted as a motor for the decisions made to invade both Afghanistan and Iraq, the question that we need to ask is whether these interventions have been successful in reducing the threat of terrorist attacks and whether security has actually been enhanced in the two nations. In the light of the recently launched military interventions by the United States, Britain, Russia and France in Syria, this is a critical question to answer. In terms of the internal security within these nations the answer is, regrettably, a resounding 'no'. However dictatorial and brutal the regimes of Saddam Hussein in Iraq and the Taliban in Afghanistan were, one would be hard pressed to make the case that the military invasions and occupations have improved security along any measure. In the early stages of the war in Afghanistan Taliban control was initially weakened after the cities of Kabul and Kandahar were taken by coalition forces in 2001 and in 2004 Hamid Karzai was democratically elected as the country's president. However, far from the military occupation destroying the organization, the Taliban have conducted an unceasing insurgency that continues some 15 years after US and allied forces first invaded the country. Throughout the bloody conflict the Taliban have successfully used guerrilla war tactics – such as landmines, improvised explosive devices (IEDs), roadside shootings and suicide attacks – leading to high numbers of military and civilian casualties. Between 2001 and 2014 over 26,000 civilian deaths directly associated with the conflict were recorded with 29,900 civilians being wounded (see Crawford, 2014: 7). In total more than 91,000 Afghans – including civilians, soldiers and militants – have perished, with the number of people killed through indirect causes estimated to be around 360,000 (see Crawford, 2014: 42). Despite failing to stabilize the country, NATO announced the withdrawal of international forces from Afghanistan by 2014 and a handover to a new Afghan army (ANA) and police force.

The security situation in Afghanistan remains highly dangerous, with a fragile State and little sign that the insurgency by the Taliban will abate. In the case of Afghanistan, it is pertinent to remember that the military skills and expertise of Taliban fighters are partly a product of historical and organizational learning acquired during the occupation of the country by the USSR from 1979 to 1989. At this time, the United States government directly funded and armed the Afghan Mujahideen in its fight against the USSR. Through 'Operation Cyclone' the United States Central Intelligence Agency was involved in supporting militant Islamic groups through extensive flows of capital thought to run from around 30 million dollars in 1980 up to 630 million dollars by 1987 (see Bergen, 2001: 68). The ironies need not be spelt out further, but suffice it to say that many Mujahideen fighters and their families became involved with the struggle waged by the Taliban. This suggests, with the benefit of hindsight, that the United States may have been somewhat hoist by its own petard.

In Iraq, the total number of deaths as a consequence of the war – including those classified as either State military or insurgents – totals 242,000 (Iraq Body Count, 2015). Aside from the sheer number of casualties, what is tragic in the case of Iraq was the failure to foresee the impact of premature coalition troop withdrawal in a period of post-war instability. Not only did this signal a failure in terms of the objectives of the allied States involved in the occupation, it produced a power vacuum that was seized by terrorist groups, including Al Qaeda and ISIS.

Aside from the decline in security resulting from the occupations of Afghanistan and Iraq, the large scale public opposition to these acts is of relevance. Notwithstanding the major public demonstrations that took place in many countries against military action, the deaths of so many innocent Muslims as a result of the conflicts is likely to have bolstered rather than reduced the recruitment campaigns of terrorist groups such as Al Qaeda and ISIS. It is no coincidence that the so-called 'martyrdom videos' appearing on the internet after the death of individuals committing terrorist acts inspired by radical Islamism point to aggressive foreign and military policies of Western nations as a motivating factor for their actions. Mohammad Siddique Khan, one of the terrorists involved in the 7/7 attacks in London in 2005 that killed 52 people, described his motives thus:

> Your democratically elected governments continuously perpetuate atrocities against my people all over the world. And your support of them makes you directly responsible, just as I am directly responsible for protecting and avenging my Muslim brothers and sisters. Until we feel security, you will be our targets. And until you stop the bombing, gassing, imprisonment and torture of my people we will not stop this fight.

While it is unlikely that Khan himself wrote the script, it is probable that the misguided military ventures that were a direct response to 9/11 have served to exacerbate feelings of hostility, alienation and frustration amongst Muslims (Burke, 2015). As Gregory and Wilkinson (2005) argue, it is likely that military and foreign policies – in particular the invasion of Iraq – were a factor in the radicalization of the individuals that committed the 7/7 attacks. In a similar vein, the German journalist and former politician Jürgen Todenhöfer (2015: 6) asserts that the failed wars in Iraq and Afghanistan have served to inflame rather than reduce tensions, raising rather than reducing the risk presented by radical Islamists: 'In 2001 there were roughly a couple of hundred terrorists in the mountains in the Hindu Kush, now after the war on terror claimed so many innocent lives, we are facing some 100,000 terrorists.' Drawing on a concept developed by his compatriot Ulrich Beck (1992: 50), Todenhöfer (2010) asserts that the violent actions undertaken by Western countries in Afghanistan, Iraq and Libya have led to a 'boomerang effect' in which the problems created by Western nations come back to confront them. To this end, Sandra Walklate and I have cautioned elsewhere about the effects of the 'law of inverse consequences' whereby security interventions can aggravate rather than reduce the situation and thus increase rather than decrease the level of risk (see Walklate and Mythen, 2015). While the iatrogenic effects of military interventions and counter-terrorism measures that jeopardize human rights are doubtless unintentional, it is probable that an intensified focus on Muslims and the widespread ideational assault on Islam are only likely to have exacerbated embedded historical grievances (see Awan, 2013; McGovern, 2010). In the UK over-zealous policing, hasty military interventions and less than strategic foreign policy are well-documented issues of concern for British Muslims, yet insufficient attention is paid to these 'elephants in the room' at a policy level (see Kundnani, 2009, 2015). In as much as such factors are likely to be sources of disquiet for many rather than direct motors of radicalization, there can be little doubt that some of the measures implemented under the auspices of enhancing security have been sources of alienation and frustration for Muslims (see Heath-Kelly, 2013; Pantazis and Pemberton, 2009; Parmar, 2011). While many Western nations – such as the United States, France and the United Kingdom – have invested heavily in national strategies to counter Islamist radicalization via programs oriented toward education and integration, these are unlikely to achieve positive impact in circumstances in which foreign and domestic policies are seen to discriminate against, antagonize and threaten Muslims around the globe. In terms of reducing the threat of terrorism, the collection of processes, practices and interventions implemented under the 'war on terror' have spectacularly failed.

Conclusion

In the course of this chapter, I have sought to provide a critical overview of the major problems that arise in relation to the definition, representation and regulation of terrorism. In bringing the chapter to a close, I wish to underscore three key points that relate to each of these areas in turn. First, in relation to definitions of terrorism, we need to recognize that terrorism is a contingent and contestable label. It is clear that views about the legitimacy or otherwise of groups that use systematic violence in search of their ends can shift over time, as the adage 'one person's terrorist is another person's freedom fighter' illustrates (see Rehn, 2003). While it is unlikely that Al Qaeda or ISIS will, in future, be seen as organizations pursuing legitimate methods in search of peace, we need to remember that organizations previously classified as terroristic – such as the African National Congress (ANC) in South Africa and Sinn Fein in Ireland – have later been accepted as legitimate political parties. This suggests that criminologists need to think seriously about how far they are willing to travel in terms of accepting or rejecting the term 'terrorism'. For some, the term should be disbanded forthwith (see Bolanos, 2012), while others have called for far greater scrutiny of the systematic violence enacted by elected governments, under the analytical frame of 'State Terrorism' (see Poynting and Whyte, 2012). The long- and short-term harms caused by the violent enforcement of the 'war on terror' reinforce the need for wider and deeper scrutiny of State violence. Second, I have emphasized the crucial role of politicians, media professionals and academics in the public representation of terrorism. The State, mass media and academics have all been complicit in the reproduction of a flawed discourse of 'new terrorism' that exaggerates the magnitude of the present threat and conceals historical continuities in forms of organized violence. It has been argued here that representations of the terrorist threat making recourse to future imagined attacks have been used instrumentally as a rationale for an unprecedented wave of military intervention and securitization. While members of the public do not uncritically accept the observations of appointed experts, it is fair to say that agendas on terrorism are set by those with the power to widely articulate their ideas. This matters as it tends to mute or silence otherwise important discussions about the grievances of terrorist groups and the root causes of violence.

Third, as the examples discussed here suggest, careful management of political and religiously motivated violence is crucial in establishing a safer world. In this chapter I have expressed concern about a shift in risk regulation strategies around counter-terrorism, from an emphasis on retrospective probabilistic estimations of harm to a pre-emptive approach based directed by the possibility of soon to materialize harms. The increasing reliance on pre-emptive measures solidifies and amplifies the process of 'social sorting', where dangerous classes are separated out from safe groups and subjected to the intense focus of the surveillant lens (see Wall, 2010). The extent to which pre-emptive counter-terrorism measures are effective in reducing the terrorist threat in the long term is questionable. Insofar as proponents of 'stamp hard, stamp fast' (Gill, 2009: 152) approaches would point toward the thwarting by security services of numerous attacks in the planning stages, wide casting of the net based on dubious risk profiling across populations appears to have at best limited and at worst detrimental effects so far as countering terrorism is concerned. As Daalgard-Nielsen (2012: 800) reasons: 'the question of whether anti-terrorism laws have in themselves become a significant factor in violent radicalization in Europe remains an open question – a question with obvious policy implications'.

In a climate of political manipulation and anxiety around national security, it is incumbent on criminologists to specify what it is that is 'new' or otherwise about 'new terrorism' and to question the extent to which attempts to regulate political violence by Western nation-states have been either socially just or materially effective. In this chapter I have argued that the discourse of 'new terrorism' has acted as an ideological lever for the vortex of measures and interventions that have emerged nationally and globally under the rubric of the 'war on terror'. The erroneous use of the term 'war' in this context notwithstanding, the military excursions in Afghanistan and Iraq and the multiple forms of national counter-terrorism legislation have led to the deaths of countless civilians in the first instance and the reduction of basic rights and liberties in the second. In thinking about what criminology can contribute to future debates about terrorism, it is imperative that security is considered in the round. This means focusing on questions of ideology and issues of power rather than meekly accepting that the security of some is simply more important than that of others.

References

Ahmad, I. (2012) 'How the War on Terror Is a War of Terror', *Al Jazeera News*, 11 September. Viewable at: www.aljazeera.com/indepth/opinion/2012/09/201294115140782135.html (accessed 14 January 2016).

Alayo, E. (2012) 'Just War Theory and the Last of Last Resort', *Ethics and International Affairs*, 29(2): 187–201.

Amoore, L. (2013) *The Politics of Possibility: Risk and Security Beyond Probability*. Durham: Duke University Press.

Anderson, D. (2012) *Report on the Terrorism Acts in 2011*. London: HMSO.

Arquilla, J., Ronfeldt, D. and Zanini, M. (1999) 'Networks, Netwar and Information-Age Terrorism' in I. Lesser, B. Hoffman, J. Arquilla, D. Ronfeldt, M. Zanini and B. Jenkins (eds) *Countering the New Terrorism*. Santa Monica: RAND.

Awan, I. (2013) 'Let's Prevent Extremism by Engaging Communities Not by Isolating Them', *Public Spirit*, December Edition.

Ayto, J. (1990) *Dictionary of Word Origins*. London: Bloomsbury.

Beck, U. (1992) *Risk Society: Towards a New Modernity*. London: Sage.

Beck, U. (2009) *World at Risk*. Cambridge: Polity Press.

Bergen, P. (2001) *Holy War Inc.* London: Free Press.

Blair, T. (2001) Speech to Parliament, 14 September. Reproduced in full by BBC news at: http://news.bbc.co.uk/1/hi/uk_politics/1543558.stm.

Bolanos, A. (2012) 'Is There a New Terrorism in Existence Today?' in R. Jackson and S. Sinclair (eds) *Contemporary Debates on Terrorism*. London: Routledge.

Borradori, G. ed. (2003) *Philosophy in a Time of Terror: Dialogues with Jürgen Habermas and Jacques Derrida*. Chicago: University of Chicago.

Bourke, J. (2005) 'The Politics of Fear Are Blinding Us to the Humanity of Others', *Guardian*, 1 October. Viewable at: www.theguardian.com/world/2005/oct/01/terrorism.politics (accessed 12 December 2014).

Burke, J. (2005) *Al-Qaeda: The True Story of Radical Islam*. London: I.B. Taurus.

Burke, J. (2015) 'There Is No Silver Bullet: ISIS, Al Qaeda and the Myths of Terrorism', *Guardian*, 19 August.

Burnett, J. and Whyte, D. (2006) 'Embedded Expertise and the New Terrorism', *Journal for Crime, Conflict and the Media*, 1(4): 1–18.

Bush, G. (2001) Speech to Joint Session of Congress, 20 September.

Bush, G. (2002) Speech delivered at Cincinnati Union Terminal, Cincinnati, Ohio, 7 October.

Cameron, D. (2011) Speech delivered at Munich Security Conference, 5 February. Viewable at: www.gov.uk/government/speeches/pms-speech-at-munich-security-conference (accessed 31 July 2014).

Ciocchini, P. and Khoury, S. (2012) 'The War on Terror and Spanish State Violence against Basque Political Dissent' in S. Poynting and D. Whyte (eds) *Counter Terrorism and State Political Violence*. London: Routledge.

Cole, B. and Gurr, N. (2012) *The New Face of Terrorism: Threats from Weapons of Mass Destruction*. London: I.B. Taurus.

Copeland, T. (2001) 'Is the New Terrorism Really New? An Analysis of the New Paradigm for Terrorism', *Journal of Conflict Studies*, 21(2): 1–16.

Crawford, N. (2014) *The Costs of War*. Providence: Watson Institute.

Daalgard-Nielsen, A. (2012) 'Violent Radicalization in Europe: What We Know and What We Do Not Know', *Studies in Conflict and Terrorism*, 9(1): 797–814.

Duyvestyn, I. (2004) 'How New Is the New Terrorism?', *Studies in Conflict and Terrorism*, 27(5): 439–54.

Duyvesteyn, I. and Malkki, L. (2012) 'The Fallacy of the New Terrorism Thesis' in R. Jackson and S. Sinclair (eds) *Contemporary Debates on Terrorism*. London: Routledge.

Gill, P. (2009) 'Intelligence, Terrorism and the State' in R. Coleman, J. Sim and S. Tombs (eds) *State, Power, Crime*. London: Sage.

Global Terrorism Database (2015) Viewable at: www.start.umd.edu/gtd (accessed 7 January 2016).

Gregory, F. and Wilkinson, P. (2005) 'Riding Pillion for Tackling Terrorism Is a High-Risk Policy', *Security, Terrorism and Risk*, ISP/NCC 05/01 Briefing Paper. London: Chatham House.

Heath-Kelly, C. (2013) 'Counter-Terrorism and the Counterfactual: Producing the Radicalisation Discourse and the UK PREVENT Strategy', *British Journal of Politics and International Relations*, 15(3): 394–415.

Hillyard, P. (2009) 'The Exceptional State' in R. Coleman, J. Sim, S. Tombs and D. Whyte (eds) *State, Power, Crime*. London: Sage.

Hoffman, B. (2012) *Inside Terrorism*. New York: Columbia University Press.

Hudson, B. and Ugelvik, S. (2012) *Justice and Security in the 21st Century*. London: Routledge.

Institute for Economics and Peace (2015) *Global Terrorism Index*. Sydney: IEP.

Iraq Body Count (2015) Viewable at: www.iraqbodycount.org (accessed 7 January 2015).

Jackson, R. and Sinclair, S. eds 2012 *Contemporary Debates on Terrorism*. London: Routledge.

Kundnani, A. (2009) *Spooked: How Not to Prevent Violent Extremism*. London: Institute of Race Relations.

Kundnani, A. (2015) *A Decade Lost: Rethinking Radicalisation and Extremism*. London: Claystone.

Laqueur, W. (1996) 'Postmodern Terrorism: New Rules for an Old Game', *Foreign Affairs*, September Edition.

Laqueur, W. (1999) *The New Terrorism: Fanaticism and the Arms of Mass Destruction*. Oxford: Oxford University Press.

Lesser, I., Hoffman, B., Arquilla, J., Ronfeldt, D., Zanini, M. and Jenkins, B. eds (1999) *Countering the New Terrorism*. Santa Monica: RAND.

Maras, H. (2013) *Counterterrorism*. New York: Jones and Burlington.

Martin, G. (2012) *Essentials of Terrorism: Concepts and Controversies*. London: Sage.

McCulloch, J. and Pickering, S. (2009) 'Pre-Crime and Counter Terrorism: Imagining Future Crime in the War on Terror', *British Journal of Criminology*, 49(5): 628–45.

McCulloch, J. and Wilson, D. (2015) *Pre-Crime: Pre-Emption, Precaution and the Future*. London: Routledge.

McGovern, M. (2010) *Countering Terror or Counter-Productive?* Liverpool: Edge Hill.

Morgan, M. (2004) 'The Origins of New Terrorism', *Parameters*, Spring Edition.

Mythen, G. (2014) *Understanding the Risk Society: Crime, Security and Justice*. London: Palgrave.

Mythen, G., Walklate, S. and Khan, F. (2013) 'Why Should We Have to Prove We're Alright? Counter-Terrorism, Risk and Partial Securities', *Sociology*, 47(2): 382–97.

9/11 Commission Report (2004) *Final Report of the National Commission on Terrorist Attacks upon the United States*. Washington, DC: National Commission on Terrorist Attacks.

Neumann, P. (2009) *Old and New Terrorism*. Cambridge: Polity Press.

Pantazis, C. and Pemberton, S. (2009) 'From the Old to the New Suspect Community', *British Journal of Criminology*, 49(1): 664–66.

Parker, A. (2013) Speech by the head of MI5 to the Royal United Services Institute, 8 October.

Parmar, A. (2011) 'Stop and Search in London: Counterterrorist or Counterproductive?', *Policing and Society*, 21(4): 369–82.

Poynting, S. and Whyte, D. (2012) *Counter Terrorism and State Political Violence*. London: Routledge.

Quinn, B. (2015) 'UK Government Feared Terrorists Would Weaponise Ebola', *Guardian*, 2 February: 3.

Rehn, E. (2003) 'Excessive Reliance on the Use of Force Does Not Stop Terrorism' in T. Hoeksema and J. ter Laak (eds) *Human Rights and Terrorism*. Holland: NHC/OSCE.

Rogers, P. (2012) 'Wars of Terror': Learning the Lessons of Failure' in R. Jackson and S. Sinclair (eds) *Contemporary Debates on Terrorism*. London: Routledge.

Ross, A. and Malik, S. (2015) 'Syrian Doctors to Show the US Evidence of Assad's Use of Chemical Weapons', *Guardian*, 16 June: 1.

Schmid, A. (2011) *The Routledge Handbook of Terrorism Research*. London: Routledge.

Spalek, B. and Lambert, R. (2008) 'Muslim Communities, Counter-Terrorism and Counter-Radicalisation: A Critically Reflective Approach to Engagement', *International Journal of Law Crime and Justice*, 36(4): 257–70.

Sparrow, A. (2010) 'Tony Blair at Iraq Inquiry', *Guardian*, 29 January: 1.

Taylor-Norton, R. (2011) 'Iraq Dossier Drawn up to Make Case for War – Intelligence Officer', *Guardian*, 12 May.

Todenhöfer, J. (2010) 'I Know ISIS Fighters', *Guardian*, 27 November: 6.

Todenhöfer, J. (2015) 'ISIL Is the Baby of George W Bush', *Euronews*, 16 January: 6.

Vertigans, S. (2010) 'British Muslims and the UK Government's "War on Terror" Within: Evidence of a Clash of Civilizations or Emergent De-Civilizing Processes?', *British Journal of Sociology*, 61(1): 26–44.

Walklate, S. and Mythen, G. (2015) *Contradictions of Terrorism: Security, Risk and Resilience*. London: Routledge.

Wall, D. (2010) 'From Post-Crime to Pre-Crime: Preventing Tomorrow's Crimes Today', *Criminal Justice Matters*, 81(1): 22–3.

Welch, M. (2006) 'Seeking a Safer Society: America's Anxiety in the War on Terror', *Security Journal*, 19: 93–109.

Wintour, P. (2005) 'Blair Vows to Root Out Extremism', *Guardian*, 6 August: 1.

Zedner, L. (2007) 'Pre-Crime and Post-Criminology?', *Theoretical Criminology*, 11(2): 261–81.

Zedner, L. (2009) *Security*. London: Sage.

18

VIOLENCE AGAINST WOMEN

Nicole Westmarland

Introduction

While violence committed within the home, by intimate partners or family members, used to be viewed as a private matter to be resolved between the parties concerned, there is increasing recognition across the world that this is an issue that requires state involvement. Anglo-American feminists in the 1970s started to link various forms of men's violences against women – particularly rape and domestic violence/battering – with gender inequality, and it is this understanding that now guides the thinking of some of the world's most powerful institutions.

For example, the United Nations Declaration on Violence Against Women confirmed violence against women to be an obstacle to the achievement of equality, development, and peace:

> Violence against women is a manifestation of historically unequal power relations between men and women, which have led to domination over and discrimination against women by men and to the prevention of the full advancement of women, and that violence against women is one of the crucial social mechanisms by which women are forced into a subordinate position compared with men.
>
> *(UN General Assembly, 1993, p. 2)*

Similarly, Action Aid (2010) names violence against women and girls as 'one of the starkest collective failures of the international community in the 21st century' (p. 1), describing it as a means of social control which maintains unequal gender power relations and reinforces women's subordinate status.

In Europe, the Council of Europe Convention on preventing and combating violence against women and domestic violence (known as the 'Istanbul Convention') also takes as its starting point the link between women's inequalities and the violences committed against them. It recognises that violence against women is both structural in nature and one of the social mechanisms that forces women into a subordinate position in comparison to men. It requires parties ratifying it to put in place a broad range of measures to eliminate all forms of discrimination against women, to promote substantive equality, to empower women, and to develop a comprehensive framework to protect and provide assistance to all victims of violence against women and domestic violence.

Viewing violence against women as a cause and consequence of women's inequality links it to men's power in society. Although there exists debate as to the usefulness of the term 'patriarchy' in modern society, few would doubt that there exists what Connell and Messerschmidt (2005) call a 'gender hierarchy'. The concept of 'gender hierarchy' explains how there can be subordinated and marginalised as well as hegemonic masculinities, and that these different forms of masculinities are relational to real or imaginary models of femininity.

Forms of violence against women

There are many different forms of violence against women. Many forms are based on traditional cultural expectations of women and girls, and so vary in nature depending on when and where the violence takes place. For example, a lot of threats, abuse and harassment now take place via the internet, which is a major change in how violence against women is perpetrated. Similarly, some forms of violence against women are contained to particular cultural backgrounds, for example countries such as Sierra Leone have very high levels of female genital mutilations whereas this is very rare or non-existent for women from other cultures. This chapter describes some of the forms of violence against women, based on the categorisation developed in my recent book *Violence against Women: Criminological Perspectives on Men's Violences* (Westmarland, 2015). These categories are: men's violences in relationships, in the family, in public spaces, and in institutions.

Men's violences in relationships

Men's violences in relationships are sometimes called 'domestic violence' summarised to 'DV' (most common in the UK), wife battering (common in the USA), or 'intimate partner violence', summarised to IPV, or simply 'partner violence' (terms increasingly being used globally). The term partner violence is probably the clearest one to use, acknowledging that this also includes people who have previously been in a relationship and are now separated – i.e. ex-partners. Sometimes the phrase 'and abuse' is added onto the end – for example domestic violence and abuse (DVA) to show that partner violence often includes elements of abuse that are not directly physically violent. However for many the term 'violence' is understood symbolically – to emphasise that all forms of violence, abuse, harassment, control, and coercion are a form of violence against women.

Four forms of men's violences within relationships are: partner homicide; physical violence; sexual violence; and psychological (including financial) abuse. These are discussed below. It is important first to note though that ethnicity as well as gender plays an important role in terms of the perpetration and responses to men's violences within relationships. Aisha Gill and others have argued that Black, Asian, Minority Ethnic, and Refugee women are 'doubly victimised' in relation to domestic violence – not only are they victimised by the violence that is perpetrated against them, they are also victimised by a societal response that fails to provide them with appropriate support that would be empowering to them (Gill, 2004; see also Imam, 2002; Gupta, 2003; Hampton et al., 2003). For example women may face racist responses if they ask for protection from the state (Patel, 2003). Other barriers may include financial dependence on abusive partners because of no recourse to public funds, lack of access to an interpreter, previous experiences of poor police responses for other crimes, community pressure, and a lack of accessible information about women's legal entitlements in the UK (McWilliams and Yarnell, 2013).

Partner homicide

Men's fatal violence against women in relationships – also known as domestic homicides – refer to the offences of murder, manslaughter, and infanticide. It is also related to the term 'femicide', which Jill Radford and Diana Russell (1992) argued is a useful alternative term to the gender-neutral term 'homicide'. They defined femicide as the 'misogynistic killing of women by men' (p. xi) and the 'killing of women by men *because* they are women' (p. xiv, their emphasis). Therefore, femicide includes but is not restricted to homicide by partners.

In a systematic review of the global prevalence of intimate partner homicide, Stöckl et al. (2013) found that an estimated 38% of all women killed globally are murdered by an intimate partner compared to just 6% of men killed by an intimate partner. In nearly every country they looked at, the number of intimate partner homicides of females was far higher than for males, with the exceptions of Panama and Brazil, where the figures were nearly equal. They found differences between regions, with intimate partner homicide being highest in the South-East Asia region (55% of all women killed were murdered by an intimate partner) and the high-income (some European countries such as France and the UK) region (41%). The African Region (40%) and Region of the Americas (38%) were a little lower, but the authors suggest that while these regional differences could represent differences in the cultural acceptability of violence against women and be 'real' difference, they could also be correlated with the quality of data among countries and regions. This shows that care must be taken when interpreting statistics on violence against women. They also highlight that all the prevalence rates are likely to underestimate the problem, since the victim–offender relationship was not always recorded.

In the USA, Campbell et al. (2003) looked at the risk factors for homicide in abusive relationships based on research across 11 US cities. They compared the circumstances of 220 women who were killed with a sample of 343 abused women who had not been killed. Both an abuser's access to a firearm and his use of illicit drugs were most strongly associated with intimate partner homicide. The abuser's use of alcohol was not significantly associated with homicide, and nor was alcohol or drug use by the victim. The period during which a woman was separating from an abusive partner after living together was linked to a higher risk of homicide, as was ever leaving or asking the abuser to leave the home. They also found that if the victim had a child living at home that was not the biological child of the abuser, the woman's risk of homicide was more than doubled. The risk of partner homicide was found to increase where the abuser was highly controlling, and increased nine-fold with the combination of a highly controlling abuser *and* separation after previously living together. When threatening behaviour was considered in addition, previous threats with weapons and threats to kill were both associated with substantially higher homicide risks. Finally, they found that there was a link (approaching statistical significance) between abusers' use of forced sex (rape) and partner homicide. Where an abuser had previously used a gun in the worst incident of abuse, the risk of homicide was increased 41-fold.

Physical partner violence

Non-fatal physical forms of partner violence include acts such as pushing, slapping, hitting with a fist or other object, biting, kicking, scratching, burning, strangulation, asphyxiation, stabbing, hair pulling, arm or finger twisting, and bone breaking. Although injuries may be visible, they are often hidden. Perpetrators often confine physical signs of injury to the torso and lower body that can be hidden by clothing.

Women with disabilities may be at a higher risk of experiencing partner violence including physical partner violence. This is because where a woman's partner is also her carer, this can increase the net of control that surrounds her. Hague et al. (2008) found many examples of this within their research, including unplugging the battery from a woman's wheelchair, pushing a woman over, taking a phone out of a woman's reach so she could not call anyone for help, putting a woman on the stairs where she would be stuck, grabbing a woman's hair, repeatedly raping a woman, and attempting to suffocate a woman by putting a hand over her mouth.

Although it is a controversial topic, some research has found that domestic violence perpetrator programmes, or 'batterer intervention programmes' can reduce men's use of physical partner violence. In a large study in the USA, Ed Gondolf (2002) conducted a multi-site evaluation of 600 men who had attended well-established perpetrator programmes. He compared those who completed the programme with those who dropped out of the programme in the early stages and asked their female partners/ex-partners whether violence and abuse continued or not. He found that men who completed the programme were far more likely to stop using violence than men who dropped out, and that the majority of men who completed the programme were no longer using violence within a relationship at the four year follow-up point.

Similarly optimistic findings have been found in the UK as part of 'Project Mirabal' – named after the three Mirabal sisters murdered in Dominican Republic who became symbols of popular and feminist resistance to violence in South America. In this multi-site study of 12 well-established domestic violence perpetrator programmes Kelly and Westmarland (2015) looked at 100 women over a 15 month period and asked them about six different 'measures of success', of which 'safety and freedom from violence and abuse for women and children' was one of the measures. They also conducted a range of interviews including with women partners/ex-partners, men on programmes, children of men on programmes, programme staff, and other partner organisations.

Kelly and Westmarland found that, for the majority of women whose partners or ex-partners attended a domestic violence perpetrator programme the physical and sexual violence stopped completely. Many of these findings were dramatic – for example 'made you do something sexual that you did not want to do' fell from 30% before the programme down to 0% 12 months after; 'used a weapon against you' fell from 29% down to 0%; tried to strangle, choke, drown, or smother you, and punched, kicked, burnt, or beat you also fell dramatically, from around half the women reporting this happened before the programme down to almost zero – just 2% – afterwards.

When it came to non-contact physical violence, 'punched or kicked walls or furniture, slammed doors, smashed things or stamped around', this started off as one of the most common forms – with 94% of women saying it happened before the programme. This did reduce significantly – but only to 23%. This pattern – of non-contact physical violence, harassment, and abuse reducing, but not to the same extent as the contact physical and sexual violence – was replicated throughout the research findings; for example financial abuse reduced only very marginally. In some cases men described how they were reducing or ceasing their violence not only towards their partners but also in other areas of their lives, for example in this quote from 'Ivan' who attended one of the programmes:

> To be fair, the longer I've been on the course … the more knowledge that I've gathered and gained on how I was and how I reacted … So I'm basically eradicating it slowly if you know what I mean? A couple of months ago someone knocked my wing-mirror off while [partner] was in the car and, maybe last year I would have reacted, I would have stopped the car, made a u-turn and chased this person who knocked my wing-mirror off. But the first thing I thought of was 'Is she okay?', the first thing I thought of was our safety and I thought 'Well everything's fine, it's okay, it's just a wing-mirror that's replaceable' and [partner] was surprised of that … she did notice the change in me.
>
> *('Ivan', quoted in Kelly and Westmarland, 2015, p. 22)*

While physical forms of partner violence therefore might be the forms that many stereotypically associate with violence in relationships, it may be that the physical forms of violence are more quickly changed than other forms of partner violence such as harassment, coercive and controlling behaviours, isolation, and threats.

Partner sexual violence

Partner sexual violence is best thought of as an umbrella term that consists of a range of acts, including but certainly not limited to: rape (sexual intercourse without consent); forcing someone to watch pornography against their will; taking photographs or making videos without consent; unwanted sexual touching; sexualised name calling (slag, whore, etc.); reproductive coercion; and pressurising or forcing her to sell sex for money or other benefit. The World Health Organisation defines sexual violence within the context of intimate partner violence as being: 'Physically forced to have sexual intercourse when you did not want to, having sexual intercourse because you were afraid of what your partner might do, and/or being forced to do something sexual that you found humiliating or degrading' (WHO, 2013, p. 6). Some of these forms of sexual violence will be criminal offences – for example, rape and attempted rape are criminal offences in most countries now including within marriage, but McOrmond-Plummer (2014) points out that calling a partner names such as 'slut' or 'whore' are forms of sexual violence that are used to degrade or control the victim. Similarly, McOrmond-Plummer argues, that reproductive coercion has severe consequences for women whose individual wishes about childbearing are disregarded, but that this is not a criminal act.

Some have argued that partner sexual violence, or intimate partner sexual violence (IPSV as it is sometimes abbreviated to) has fallen through a gap at the intersection of domestic violence and sexual violence movements. On the one hand, it happens within partner relationships, but on the other hand, the nature of it and its impacts could be argued to be better understood and dealt with by rape and sexual violence services. For example, Bergen (1996) writing from a US perspective found that, when the women in her study of battered women who were raped received services from domestic violence services, the trauma left by the sexual violence often went unaddressed. Similarly, Williamson (2014) argues that some issues are addressed while others are marginalised and silenced in service provision, highlighting that 'sexual violence within domestically abusive intimate relationships is often annexed and considered in isolation rather than as part of an ongoing and systematic pattern of abuse' (p. 81).

Psychological abuse by partners

Psychological abuse – including financial abuse, technology-enabled abuse, threats, and harassment – is often perpetrated alongside physical and sexual forms of violence. They operate to restrict women's lives and narrow what Nordic researcher Eva Lundgren (2004) calls 'life space'. These concepts describe how, as threats and fears become more central and embedded into a woman's everyday life, she further restrains her own behaviour in an attempt to manage the violence. This, in turn, is used by abusive men to further control and restrict women's behaviour. It is why so many women talk about feeling as though they were 'walking on eggshells' while in a partner violent relationship.

Men's violences in the family

Violence can occur within a family or extended family unit which is not restricted to partners/ex-partners and includes: violence against mothers and grandmothers; forced marriage; 'honour'-based killings and violence; female genital mutilation; and familial rape and abuse. Just as partner violence is connected to how women are 'expected' to act within different communities as wives and partners, wider family violence is also connected to expectations around how women fulfil the gender roles ascribed to them. This often varies depending on factors including but not limited to: ethnicity; tradition; culture; sexuality; age; class; asylum status; and dis/ability. This can lead to the marginalisation of some women's experiences of violence – for example Crenshaw (1991) argued there had been a failure to consider intersectionality. In a highly influential essay called 'Mapping the margins: Intersectionality, identity politics, and violence against women of color', Crenshaw (1991) argues that the experiences of women of colour are frequently the product of both racism and sexism intersecting. Both the feminist and the anti-racist movement, she argues, have resulted in the marginalisation of women of colour's experiences of violence.

Violence against mothers and grandmothers

Harbin and Madden (1979) are usually credited with being the first to identify 'parent abuse' as a form of family violence. While parental abuse is now increasingly being studied, violence against grandparents is still seldom discussed. Parent abuse is generally used now to describe a pattern of behaviours, for example in the following definition by Holt (2013, p. 1):

> a pattern of behaviour that uses verbal, financial, physical or emotional means to practice power and exert control over a parent. The parent may be a biological parent, step-parent or a parent in a legal capacity, and the son or daughter is still legally a child (i.e. under 18 years) and is usually living in the family home with their parent(s).

Although, as with partner violence, violence can of course also be perpetrated against male members of the family including fathers and grandfathers, family violence, as with partner violence, is gendered. Hunter and Nixon (2012, p. 213), for example, concluded that 'scrutiny of the international evidence suggests that parent abuse is both increasingly prevalent and a gendered issue, with mothers more likely to be abused by their (most frequently male) adolescent children'. Similarly, Karen Ingala Smith (2014) argues that fatal homicide within the family is gendered and that they should be classed as sexist crimes. In her Counting Dead

Women project, she counted a minimum of 16 women killed by their adult sons in 2012, and 12 in 2013. For grandmothers over the same period, the figures were one for 2012 and three in 2013 (including one case of a step-grandmother). The most common method of killing was stabbing, which accounted for eight of the men who killed their mothers and three of the men who killed their grandmothers. Ingala Smith found no cases of women killing their fathers over the same time period and only two cases of women who killed their mothers.

Forced marriage

A forced marriage is one where either the bride, the groom, or both parties, do not freely consent to getting married. Forced marriages continue across the world despite being outlawed by a number of international human rights instruments. For example, Gill and Anitha (2011) point out that forced marriage violates the 1948 Universal Declaration of Human Rights which states under Article 16 that both parties must give their free and full consent to marriage.

It is consent, therefore, that is central to understandings of whether a marriage is forced or not. This is echoed through international human rights instruments as above, but also through domestic law and policy (Gangoli et al., 2011). Consent is used to try to draw a clear line between arranged marriage and forced marriage. However, this apparently clear distinction does oversimplify matters to some extent. Gangoli et al. (2011) argue that slippage occurs between what are classed as 'forced' and what are classed as 'arranged' by rendering invisible more subtle forms of coercion. In Gangoli et al.'s (2006) study of 37 women and 32 men in South Asian communities in the North-East of England, they found that of the 16 women who self defined as having an arranged marriage, 11 described some form of coercion having taken place. This was sometimes through social expectations, for example one interviewee talked about having it 'drummed into her' that marriage is what she should be working towards because it is what girls do in life.

There are overlaps between most forms of violence against women, and this is particularly the case in relation to forced marriage. For example, once forced into marriage, partner violence including sexual violence may be used against women. In some cases, the refusal to marry has resulted in family members plotting to kill because the refusal was seen as bringing dishonour on the family. In one high profile case in the UK, Shafilea Ahmed was murdered by her parents in 2003 when she was aged 17. One of the reasons given for the murder was that she was refusing to agree to a marriage they were arranging for her. After being taken to Pakistan, Shafilea drank bleach and was hospitalised for ten weeks on her return to England, and on her release from hospital was subjected to violence and abuse from her parents. However, no one intervened to support Shafilea, and she was smothered to death by her parents, who forced a plastic bag down her throat. It took nearly ten years for her father Iftikar Ahmed and her mother Farzana Ahmed to be convicted and sentenced for her killing.

'Honour'-based violence and killings

'Honour'-based violence or 'honour'-based killings are a form of violence against women where violence and abuse are used under the guise of family 'honour'. Meetoo and Mirza (2007) define 'honour-based violence' as: 'extreme acts of violence perpetrated upon a woman when an honour code is believed to have been broken and perceived shame is brought upon the family' (p. 187). Faqir (2001) defines 'honour' killings as 'the killing of women for suspected deviation from sexual norms imposed by society' (p. 66). The term 'honour' is usually written with inverted commas around it, or alternatively referred to as 'so-called honour'-based violence to show that, of course, there is nothing honourable about violence against women, and no honourable basis for its use. Some have argued the term 'honour' should not be used at all. However, most agree that the term 'honour' is a useful one to retain to show that the violence or homicide is linked in some part to the role of 'honour' (Welchman and Hossain, 2005).

Examples of perceived dishonour that led to 'honour'-based violence recorded by the Iranian and Kurdish Women's Rights Organisation (IKWRO), a London women's organisation, include seeking a divorce, refusing an arranged marriage, beginning a relationship that the family does not approve of, or even being the victim of a sexual assault. They cite one 15-year-old girl who was beaten and placed under house arrest after her father found she had been texting male school friends (IKWRO, 2011).

Unlike partner violence and homicide, there is often more than one person involved in 'honour'-based violence and killings. A wide set of family members – including in-laws – as well as the woman's husband or partner are often involved in the acts of violence and abuse, for example fathers, brothers, sons, and extended family members. Sometimes a woman's female family members are also involved, for example her mother or mother-in-law. Most victims are women. Gill (2010) notes that while the victimisation of men through 'honour'-based violence does exist, men represent a tiny minority of cases – and these are often linked to being seen with women who are considered to be transgressive.

Female genital mutilation

Female genital mutilation, or 'FGM', refers to the altering or injuring of a girl or woman's genitals for non-medical reasons. It is sometimes referred to as either 'female circumcision' or 'female cutting' by those who are concerned about naming a cultural practice 'mutilation'. However, for many people FGM is thought of as a harmful cultural practice. FGM can vary quite substantially in terms of what it consists of and also the conditions in which it takes place. The World Health Organisation (2001) breaks FGM down into four major types.

- Type 1 is 'Clitoridectomy', which is the partial or total removal of the clitoris.
- Type 2 is 'Excision', which is the partial or total removal of the clitoris and the labia minora, with or without excision of the labia majora.
- Type 3 is 'Infibulation', which is the narrowing of the vaginal opening through the creation of a covering seal which is formed by cutting and repositioning the inner, or outer, labia (with or without removal of the clitoris).
- Type 4 is 'Other', which covers all other harmful procedures to the female genitalia for non-medical purposes (e.g. pricking, piercing, incising, scraping and cauterising the genital area).

FGM is thought to be prevalent in 28 countries in Africa, the Middle East and Asia. Egypt, Ethiopia, Somalia, and Sudan are thought to have particularly high rates of up to 98% (FORWARD, n.d.). It is estimated that around 100–140 million women and girl children worldwide have been subjected to FGM, and a further 3 million are actively at risk (Female Genital Mutilation/Cutting: Data and Trends: Update 2010, Population Reference Bureau, Washington, DC, USA, 2010).

The children's charity, Plan, is one of the groups that work internationally to end FGM, particularly focusing on working with children in the world's poorest countries. The fact that FGM is often committed against children rather than adult women, at least in the first instance of FGM, firmly places it as a priority area for many international children's organisations. Plan argues that the overarching reason for FGM practices is the existence of power imbalances between men and women. For example, it is often linked to being key to a 'good marriage match' because of its perceived links with 'purity' and 'virginity'.

Despite the contemporary focus on gender inequality, it is nearly always women rather than men who directly perpetrate FGM. The perpetrators are most often mothers, aunts, grandmothers, or female neighbours (Hemmings and Khalifa, 2013). Much of the work around ending FGM is around the creation of new social norms where FGM is not seen as a 'rite of passage' and women's sexual freedom and enjoyment is promoted.

Familial rape and abuse

The rape and abuse of children within the family environment (whether or not by a family member) covers a range of acts that is also variously known as child sexual abuse, incest, or intra-familial sexual abuse. It happens to boy and girl children, but the focus of this chapter is on girls. It is difficult to estimate the prevalence of any forms of violence against women because so much goes unreported, but this is particularly the case in relation to familial child sexual abuse. Radford et al. (2011) found that more than one in three of the children in their UK study who had experienced a direct form of sexual abuse by an adult had not told anyone about it.

Most research on the effects of child sexual abuse does not differentiate by perpetrator type – i.e. whether the perpetrator is within or external to the family. However, where research has differentiated between types of perpetrator, it has tended to find that victims of familial rape and abuse suffer greater physical and emotional symptoms because of the breach of the relationship of trust with the perpetrator (Horvath et al., 2014). In their review into the impact of familial child sexual abuse, Horvath et al. (2014) found that the short-term impacts tended to be damaging but 'hidden', making it difficult to intervene early. The longer-term impacts were found to be profound psychological damage over an extended period of time. For example, Carter et al. (2006) found that almost half of female in-patients with anorexia nervosa had a history of child sexual abuse. Kendler et al. (2000) found that women who had been raped as children were over four times more likely than those who had not been sexually abused to develop an alcohol misuse disorder. Similar findings have been reported in relation to illicit drug use (Hayatbakhsh et al., 2009).

Men's violences against women in public spaces

Most research on violence against women focuses on violence within the home and private spaces, perpetrated by partners, ex-partners, or by family members. As this chapter has shown so far, these forms of violence and abuse take a number of different guises. However, this focus on violence in 'private' life by known men has contributed to some forms of violence and abuse such as those perpetrated in public spaces being sidelined. This has been particularly the case for those that are more 'routine' (ironically more prevalent) and normalised. Elvines (2014) suggests that one reason for the relative silence in comparison to the expansion of knowledge of other forms of violence against women is the difficulty in naming it. Similarly, Kelly (2012) states that it is because the everyday, routine intimate intrusions have dropped off so many agendas that domestic violence is now seen to be the most common form of violence against women. In addition, as online public spaces continue to grow and be public spaces where people spend long periods of time, more violence and abuse is likely to be perpetrated within or be linked to this space. To date, this has particularly been seen in relation to sexualised threats against women, particularly those who speak out about gender and inequality.

United Nations Women have a Safe Cities initiative that seeks to create safer public spaces for women. They highlight that both the fear and in many cases the reality of violence against women in public spaces leads to a reduction in women's and girls' freedom of movement and also reduces their ability to access services, enjoy cultural and recreational opportunities, and ability to fully participate in school, work, and public life. They recognise that violence and abuse such as sexual harassment in public spaces remains a neglected area with few laws and policies in place to combat it.

Sexual violence and harassment in the workplace

According to the European Union, sexual harassment is defined as: 'any form of unwanted verbal, non verbal or physical conduct of a sexual nature occurs, with the purpose or effect of violating the dignity of a person, in particular when creating an intimidating, hostile, degrading, humiliating, or offensive environment' (European Parliament, Equal Treatment Amendment Directive, 2002, Article 1). When these unwanted acts take place within the workplace it is sexual violence or harassment. Examples of sexual harassment given by the legal organisation Rights of Women (2010) include name-calling (e.g. calling someone a 'typical woman'), making direct sexual remarks (e.g. about a woman's body or looks), sexual touching, punching, or patting, sexual innuendo or suggestions, demanding that women take clients to a lap dancing club, or displaying sexist or pornographic material.

Sexual violence and harassment take place within almost all organisations, and even (or maybe particularly) has been found to occur within 'respectable' high profile workplaces including Parliament and the police. There are many reasons why women might not report sexual harassment. They may feel it is not 'serious' enough to complain about, and may feel they should be able to take it as a 'joke'. Often it is brushed off not as harassment but as 'banter'. Research by Blackstone et al. (2014) shows that younger workers often did not define their early experiences as sexual harassment at the time, but were more likely to define it as such when they were older and looking back at what had happened.

Sexual harassment has a range of impacts, including emotional and physical symptoms such as anger, anxiety, depression, tiredness, and headaches (O'Donohue et al., 1998). It is also related to workplace problems, such as decreased performance, low job satisfaction, high levels of absenteeism, and ultimately resignation (Hunt et al., 2007). Internationally, different studies have found contradictory findings in terms of whether sexual harassment in the workplace is increasing or decreasing. However, most would agree that there is not enough research on the topic. Where findings seem more consistent is in relation to the impact that an organisational climate or environment has. Willness et al. (2007), amongst others, found that having an organisational climate that is conducive to sexual inequality and harassment is central to understanding different organisations' rates of sexual harassment. Given this knowledge, they argue that organisational policies and procedures should play an important role in the prevention of sexual harassment.

Street and public space violence

The term 'everyday harassment' was first used by Schneider in 1987 to refer to a broad range of seemingly 'banal' behaviours which are actually focused around power and the maintenance of the status quo. Some of the earliest feminists to explicitly link gender, violence, and abuse to the 'everyday' and 'the routine' were Stanko (1990) and Kelly (1988).

Stanko (1990) argued in her influential book *Everyday Violence: How Women and Men Experience Sexual and Physical Danger* that violence can be viewed as an ordinary part of life, and described the techniques that the women she interviewed had developed in order to try to manage the possibility of this violence. Stanko showed that for women in her interviews in North America, the danger of violence crossed the public and private spheres. At the time this was quite a diversion from the 'malestream' criminologists who tended to write about the threat of violence as something that came more from strangers.

Similarly, Kelly (1988) was also shattering the illusion that violence occurred as individual, rare attacks and that the main threat to women was male strangers. She developed a 'continuum of sexual violence', based on the UK women that she interviewed who described experiencing different forms of violence and abuse at different points in their lives. The continuum is not a severity scale, but rather is used to describe a 'continuous series of elements or events that pass into one another and cannot be readily distinguished' (p. 76). Kelly's continuum continues to be influential today.

Kelly's continuum has more recently been applied by Kanyeredzi (2014) to the experiences of African and Caribbean heritage women who have lived for most of their lives in the UK. She found that there exists a 'continuum of oppression' which reflected violence and abuse to body or concept of self. She found that the impacts were indistinguishable and included experiences of racism and the abuse of other family members, arguing that: 'Women in this study carried narratives of intergenerational trauma faced by their mothers, including how legacies of historical migration formed the sociocultural context to their experiences of violence and abuse' (p. 186). Elvines (2014) highlights that the lack of agreed definition and naming of street harassment means it is difficult to measure, and even more difficult to make meaningful comparisons across research. Despite this, the findings of different studies are remarkably consistent insofar as they show that nearly all women have experienced some form of street harassment and that most women see this as a problem. The largest study conducted to date was by the European Union Agency for Fundamental Rights (FRA, 2014). They conducted an EU-wide survey of violence against women and did interviews with 42,000 women across the 28 member states. Although they did not specifically ask about street harassment, approximate figures can be gathered from the locations where violence happened and whether the violence was from someone who was not a partner. In terms of all forms of sexual harassment (they measured 11 types), it was found that 55% of women had experienced some form of sexual harassment since the age of 15, and 21% had experienced some form in the last 12 months. Very few women – just 4% – had reported the harassment to the police. It is worth noting that these figures do not only refer to public space violence by strangers but also to other forms of sexual harassment including that perpetrated by friends and acquaintances and in the workplace.

A number of campaigns have been set up to log and 'shout back' against street and other public space violence and harassment. One good example of this is Hollaback (www.ihollaback.org). This is an international non-profit-making organisation and a movement to end street harassment. At the time of writing (October 2015) they had activist groups operating in 84 cities in 31 countries. On an international level, Hollaback argue that street harassment is simultaneously one of the most pervasive forms but least legislated against forms of gender-based violence. They link street harassment to gender – being female – but also to LGBTQ (lesbian, gay, bisexual, transgender, and queer) communities. They argue it is culturally accepted and rarely reported as it is seen as 'the price you pay' for being a woman and/or gay. Hollaback challenges this by crowd sourcing incidents of gender-based street harassment – through the sharing of stories and compiling of 'hotspots'. This information is then used to document and name street harassment, to present findings to policy makers, and to create new cultural norms, to show that people are not alone in experiencing street harassment, and to 'hollaback' (shout back). Their overall vision is 'a world where street harassment is not tolerated and where we all enjoy equal access to public spaces' (Hollaback, n.d.).

Stranger and acquaintance rape

Most feminist research and campaigns have not been focused on stranger rape – rather they have sought to dismantle the myth of 'real rape', to show that rape often happens by people known to the victim and does not adhere to the myth of a 'stranger down a dark alley'. However, this means that stranger rape specifically has been the focus of relatively little feminist research. Rape is defined differently in different places, but generally broadly refers to sexual intercourse without consent. At first sight, 'stranger' and 'acquaintance' rape might seem to be two very different categories. However, in reality very few rapes are committed by complete strangers. In England and Wales, the National Policing Improvement Agency (2010) define a stranger rape as one where the victim is either unable to name or identify the offender (these tend to be known as 'stranger one' rapes) or where there was only a brief or a single encounter so the victim would be able to identify them but they would not call them an acquaintance ('stranger two' rapes). Acquaintance rapes are where the victim can identify the suspect as someone they know – for example a neighbour, friend, or – increasingly – someone they have met through an online dating website.

For all types of rape, victims may be reluctant to report to the police, although women raped by strangers are probably the most likely to be reported. Kelly et al. (2005) summarise the reasons that women are reluctant to report as falling into two categories: personal reasons (e.g. feelings of shame/embarrassment, belief about own culpability, loyalty to the perpetrator) and criminal justice reasons (e.g. expectation of ill-treatment by the police, lack of confidence they will be believed, fear of court proceedings).

Although now dated, Scully's (1990) research remains possibly the most in-depth study of rapists from a feminist perspective. She interviewed 114 men convicted for rape and 75 men convicted for other offences in North America. Given it was an incarcerated sample the majority of the rapes in it were stranger rapes. From her interviews, Scully developed her socio-cultural model of rape, in which sexual violence is an acquired, learned behaviour which is supported by societies and cultural groups where men's use of sexual violence is broadly supported and women are generally subordinated. Scully was particularly interested in comparing the men who were convicted for rape with the men convicted for other offences in order to look at their similarities and differences – given that not all men who grow up in rape supportive cultures choose to perpetrate sexual violence against women. In her results, she found very few differences between the two groups of men in terms of their backgrounds or in terms of their family, sexual, psychological, and criminal histories. She also found few differences between the two groups of men in terms of their views on women and equality – being surprised at how liberal some of the men were (although this was more pronounced in relation to equality for women in the public sphere, e.g. pay and education than in the domestic sphere, e.g. housework and childcare). She found that both groups tended to put 'women on a pedestal' – the idea that women should be more virtuous than men and need male protection and guidance. Both groups also had similar attitudes towards the acceptability of violence against women. Although she found a slight difference between the groups, the differences were not as great as she expected. She argued this could be for methodological reasons – the men convicted for other offences could also have been unreported/un-convicted sexual offenders as well.

For the stranger rapists, just over half had planned the rape and said that rape was their original intent. For the others, their plan had been to commit a different crime such as robbery or burglary or they had originally planned something else – for example, to stop and help fix a car. When Scully asked the men how they decided who they were going to rape, the most striking commonality was that they were 'just there' – going about their day to day business, travelling to work, college, or at home. As one man put it: 'Didn't have to be her, she was just there at the wrong time' (p. 175). In terms of the acquaintance rapists, their offences tended to be less planned and more spontaneous. The men tended to meet women with the intention of having sexual intercourse with them, but if the woman did not consent then force was used. However, she found that these were not 'gentle seductions' that then overstepped a thin line. Rather, she found that a third of these rapes involved weapons such as knives from the woman's own kitchen and were often associated with threats, injuries, or even death. However, she does acknowledge that this level of associated physical injury may be partly linked to it being an incarcerated sample.

Men's violences within institutions

Violence and abuse within institutions overlaps with other sections within this chapter, for example sexual harassment in the workplace and child sexual abuse. However, there are a range of institutions that have had specific 'scandals' associated with them. In these institutions the damage caused/still being caused goes beyond the immediate violence and abuse experienced, as this abuse is then compounded by the institutions' responses or lack of responses to the allegations. Some institutions are deliberately not listed below because both boys and girls were abused in similar proportions. In the case of the Catholic Church it is likely that more boys than girls were sexually abused. The umbrella term 'institutional child sexual abuse' – ICSA – is often used to describe some of these forms of abuse. However, this term tends to obscure the fact that violence within institutions does not only happen to children but adults – overwhelmingly women – as well. It also obscures the fact that not all the abuse was sexual, but physical violence was also perpetrated.

Sexual violence, celebrity culture, and public institutions

In the UK there has been a huge scandal surrounding celebrity culture and institutions, such as the British Broadcasting Corporation (BBC), which acted as a protective bubble around a group of celebrities. Children's entertainer, television DJ, and charity fundraiser Jimmy Savile, for instance, emerged as one of the most prolific sex offenders known to the police. The news that he had sexually abused girls and young women first emerged when five women were interviewed in a documentary. There was an immediate backlash against the women, given Savile had since died and was therefore not able to defend himself from the allegations. However, these backlash voices were soon drowned out as more and more women particularly, but also some men, came forward to testify to the abuse they too had had perpetrated by Savile. The investigations that have been published to date have found that Savile sexually assaulted people aged between five and 75 across 28 hospitals during decades of 'unrestricted access' – including both staff and patients – adults and children (Gray and Watt, 2013).

Despite over 600 people coming forward after Savile's death, only seven incidents had been reported to the police about Savile in his lifetime. Because of Savile's celebrity status, some of these reports were restricted, and police forces were not able to 'join the dots' and see the pattern of Savile's offending. Even where some of the dots were joined, for example when three individual reports from women unknown to each other all made allegations against Savile to Surrey police, these three victims were not made aware that it was not just them who had been assaulted (HMIC, 2013).

Institutional sexism within large institutions, and the overlaps it has with sexual harassment, needs to be brought back into the picture in relation to understanding sex offending within institutions. The abuse perpetrated by Savile was found to have been ignored by many officials, across the BBC and a number of hospitals in particular. Many more abusers have since been named and convicted as part of connected police investigations – including Rolf Harris – and it is hoped that the culture of immunity has been ended.

Institutional abuse in residential care

Women and girls may face abuse throughout their lifespan if receiving some form of residential care. They may be abused in the looked-after care system, for example in children's care homes, in prison, in mental health care, or in residential care for the elderly. This section will focus on violence against older women in care homes, as it is an area that is often classed as 'elder abuse' and therefore not properly considered from a violence against women perspective.

The most comprehensive research to date was conducted in Australia in 2014 and was named 'Norma's Project' – after the sexual assault of the mother of one of the authors while in respite care in an aged care facility (Mann et al., 2014). In their study they found a range of examples where women had been abused sexually in the aged care sector – on some occasions by women but most often by men. In one of the examples in their report they cite a woman whose 86-year-old mother was being showered by a man who sexually assaulted her, made sexually offensive comments, and asked 'vulgar' questions. When she went to the management of the residential aged care home they agreed not to allow a man to shower her again, but seemingly took no further action. No official report was ever taken, and the woman felt that she let her mother down, saying: 'I wish I could have protected her better from this horrible experience' (family member of woman abused in rehabilitation centre, in Mann et al., 2014, p. 29).

Mann et al. also found that a diagnosis of dementia was used by some as a way of avoiding and denying abuse. In these cases, reports of current abuse were explained away as the recollection of past abuse, for example in childhood. While it is of course possible that past trauma could and does re/surface during later life, the fact that some people were not even considering the possibility of current abuse was problematic. They also found that the social context and how ageing bodies are understood was important in understanding the inappropriate responses from some service providers. Older bodies were seen as asexual, meaning that service providers often fail to connect older people with sexuality generally, as well as with sexual assault. They found respondents talked about a general reluctance from service providers to see older women as attractive or sexual, and tended to link sexual assault with sex rather than with power.

Violence against women in higher education institutions

It is increasingly being recognised that a range of violences against women are prevalent on university campuses from a range of perpetrators including staff – but mainly by other students. In North America, this has been acknowledged for some time, given a major study into the topic was published 30 years ago by Mary Koss. In her study, across 32 campuses across the USA, she found that 6% of undergraduate female students had been raped within the last year, and 15% had been raped since they were aged 14 (Koss, 1988). A further 12% had experienced attempted rape, meaning that one in four university students in the USA had experienced attempted or completed rape (Koss, 1988).

More recently, the National Union of Students published a national survey called the 'Hidden Marks' study in England and Wales, consisting of over 2000 female students' experiences of harassment, stalking, violence, and sexual assault (NUS, 2010). They found that violence against women in college and university settings was commonplace. Some of the headline findings from the Hidden Marks study were that:

- One in seven students experienced a serious physical or sexual assault during their time at college or university.
- Over two-thirds (68%) said they had experienced some form of verbal or non-verbal harassment in or around their institution – for example groping, flashing, or unwanted sexual comments.
- Most perpetrators were already known by the victim.
- Nearly half (four in ten) victims of serious sexual assault had told no one about what had happened to them.

Participants in the Hidden Marks survey also complained about sexual comments made by staff – one student recounted a lecturer joking about how to cover up spiking a drink with a rape drug, and another recalled being shown a picture of a former student where the lecturer said he fantasised about what could have happened between them.

Many connect sexual assault on university campuses to 'lad culture', which consists of a subculture which is at best tolerant and at worst actively supportive of male violence against women and is common in universities, particularly when linked to sport and alcohol. However, student-led campaigns and staff, student, and voluntary sector bystander intervention collaborations are working to try to counteract some of this cultural denial (university level) and acceptance/promotion (lad culture and rape culture) of violences against women on campus. Bystander education programmes aim to empower women and men to intervene to change the social norms in their peer group and to proactively intervene to divert sexual assaults from being perpetrated. Examples of these might include challenging someone in a group telling 'rape jokes' or intentionally moving a male friend away from a female who seems intoxicated to the extent she seems unable to consent. Rather than seeing participants on a bystander intervention programme as potential victims or perpetrators, as traditional training programmes have tended to do, they are seen as potential allies for change.

Chapter summary

As is evident from the nature, extent, and range of violences discussed in this chapter, from workplace harassment to femicide, it is clear that male violence against women and girls is both multi-faceted and endemic. It is crucial that all forms of violence against women and girls are recognised as a violation of human rights, and that work continues to be undertaken in order to challenge gender and other forms of inequalities that allow violence against women and girls in all its manifestations to thrive.

References

Action Aid (2010) *Destined to Fail? How Violence against Women Is Undoing Development*, London: Action Aid.

Bergen, R. (1996) *Wife Rape: Understanding the Response of Survivors and Service Providers*, Thousand Oaks, CA: Sage.

Blackstone, A., Houle, J. and Uggen, C. (2014) '"I didn't recognize it as a bad experience until I was much older": Age, experience and workers' perceptions of sexual harassment', *Sociological Spectrum: Mid-South Sociological Association*, 34 (4), pp. 314–337.

Campbell, J., Webster, D., Koziol-McLain, J., Block, C. et al. (2003) 'Risk factors for femicide in abusive relationships: Results from a multisite case control study', *American Journal of Public Health*, 93 (7), pp. 1089–1097.

Carter, J.C., Bewell, C., Blackmore, E. and Woodside, D.B. (2006) 'The impact of childhood sexual abuse in anorexia nervosa', *Child Abuse & Neglect*, 30, pp. 257–269.

Connell, R.W. and Messerschmidt, J.W. (2005) 'Hegemonic masculinity: Rethinking the concept', *Gender and Society*, 19, pp. 829–859.

Crenshaw, K. (1991) 'Mapping the margins: Intersectionality, identity politics, and violence against women of color', *Stanford Law Review*, 43 (6), pp. 1241–1299.

Elvines, F. (2014) *The Great Problems Are in the Street: A Phenomenology of Men's Stranger Intrusions on Women in Public Space*, London Metropolitan University, unpublished PhD thesis.

European Parliament and the Council of the European Union, The European Equal Treatment Directive, 2002/73/EC. Available at: http://eur-lex.europa.eu/LexUriServ/LexUriServ.do?uri=OJ:L:2002:26 9:0015:0020:EN:PDF.

Faqir, F. (2001) 'Intrafamily femicide in defence of honour: The case of Jordan', *Third World Quarterly*, 22 (1), pp. 65–82.

FORWARD (n.d.) 'Female Genital Mutilation (FGM) | FORWARD' [online]. Available at: www. forwarduk.org.uk/key-issues/fgm (accessed 7 October 2014).

FRA (2014) *Violence against Women: An EU-Wide Survey – Main Results*, Luxembourg: Publications Office of the European Union.

Gangoli, G., Razak, A. and McCarry, M. (2006) *Forced Marriage and Domestic Violence among South Asian Communities in North East England*, Bristol: University of Bristol.

Gangoli, G., Chantler, K., Hester, M. and Singleton, A. (2011) 'Understanding forced marriage: Definitions and realities', in Gill, A. and Anitha, S. (eds.) *Forced Marriage: Introducing a Social Justice and Human Rights Perspective*, London: Zed Books, pp. 25–45.

Gill, A. (2004) 'Voicing the silent fear: South Asian women's experiences of domestic violence', *The Howard Journal*, 43 (5), pp. 465–483.

Gill, A. (2010) 'Reconfiguring "honour"-based violence as a form of gendered violence', in Idriss, M. and Abbas, T. (eds.) *Honour, Violence, Women and Islam*, London and New York: Routledge-Cavendish, pp. 218–231.

Gill, A. and Anitha, S. (2011) 'Introduction: Framing forced marriage as a form of violence against women', in Gill, A. and Anitha, S. (eds.) *Forced Marriage: Introducing a Social Justice and Human Rights Perspective*, London: Zed Books, pp. 25–45.

Gondolf, E.W. (2002) *Batterer Intervention Systems: Issues, Outcomes and Recommendations*, California: Sage.

Gray, D. and Watt, P. (2013) *Giving Victims a Voice: Joint Report into Sexual Allegations Made against Jimmy Savile*, London: Metropolitan Police and NSPCC.

Gupta, R. (2003) *From Homebreakers to Jailbreakers: Southall Black Sisters*, London: Zed Books.

Hague, G., Thiara, R.K., Magowan, P. and Mullender, A. (2008) *Making the Links: Disabled Women and Domestic Violence*, Bristol: Women's Aid Federation of England.

Hampton, R., Oliver, W. and Magarian, L. (2003) 'Domestic violence in the African American community', *Violence Against Women*, 9 (5), pp. 533–577.

Harbin, H. and Madden, D. (1979) 'Battered parents: A new syndrome', *American Journal of Psychiatry*, 136, pp. 1288–1291.

Hayatbakhsh, M.R., Najman, J.M., Jamrozik, K., Mamun, A.A., O'Callaghan, M.J. and Williams, G.M. (2009) 'Childhood sexual abuse and cannabis use in early adulthood: Findings from an Australian Birth Cohort Study', *Archives of Sexual Behavior*, 38 (1), pp. 135–142.

Hemmings, J. and Khalifa, S. (2013) *'I Carry the Name of My Parent': Young People's Reflections on FGM and Forced Marriage. Results from PEER Studies in London, Amsterdam and Lisbon*, London: Options UK.

HMIC (2013) *'Mistakes Were Made': HMIC's Review into Allegations and Intelligence Material Concerning Jimmy Savile between 1964 and 2012*, London: HMIC.

Hollaback (n.d.) 'Hollaback! You have the power to end street harassment' [online]. Available at: www.ihollaback.org/ (accessed 7 October 2014).

Holt, A. (2013) *Adolescent-to-Parent Abuse: Current Understandings in Research, Policy and Practice*, Bristol: Policy Press.

Horvath, M.A.H., Davidson, J.C., Grove-Hills, J., Gekoski, A. and Choak, C. (2014) *'It's a Lonely Journey': A Rapid Evidence Assessment on Intrafamilial Child Sexual Abuse*, London: Office of the Children's Commissioner.

Hunt, C., Davidson, M., Fielden, S. and Hoel, H. (2007) *Sexual Harassment in the Workplace: A Literature Review*, Working Paper No. 59, Manchester: Equal Opportunities Commission.

Hunter, C. and Nixon, J. (2012) 'Introduction: Exploring parent abuse – building knowledge across disciplines', *Social Policy and Society*, 11, pp. 211–215.

IKWRO (2011) 'Nearly 3000 cases of "honour" violence every year in the UK', IKWRO website, 3 December. Available at: http://ikwro.org.uk/2011/12/nearly-3000-cases-of-honour-violence-every-year-in-the-uk/ (accessed 1 October 2014).

Imam, U. (2002) 'Asian children and domestic violence', in Humphreys, C. (ed.) *Children's Perspectives on Domestic Violence*, London: Sage.

Ingala Smith, K. (2014) 'Counting Dead Women campaign'. Available at: http://kareningalasmith.com/counting-dead-women/.

Kanyeredzi, A. (2014) *Knowing What I Know Now: Black Women Talk about Violence Inside and Outside of the Home*, London Metropolitan University, unpublished PhD thesis.

Kelly, L. (1988) *Surviving Sexual Violence*, Cambridge: Polity Press.

Kelly, L. (2012) 'Standing the test of time? Reflections on the concept of the continuum of sexual violence', in Brown, J. and Walklate, S. (eds.) *Handbook on Sexual Violence*, London: Routledge.

Kelly, L. and Westmarland, N. (2015) *Domestic Violence Perpetrator Programmes: Steps towards Change*, Project Mirabal Final Report, London and Durham: London Metropolitan University and Durham University.

Kelly, L., Lovett, J. and Regan, L. (2005) *A Gap or a Chasm? Attrition in Reported Rape Cases*, Home Office Research Study 293, London: Home Office.

Kendler, K.S., Bulik, C.M., Silberg, J., Hettema, J.M., Myers, J. and Prescott, C. (2000) 'Childhood sexual abuse and adult psychiatric and substance use disorders in women: An epidemiological and co-twin control analysis', *Archives of General Psychiatry*, 57 (10), pp. 953–959.

Koss, M. (1988) 'Hidden rape: Sexual aggression and victimisation in a national sample of students in higher education', in Wolbert Burgess, A. (ed.) *Rape and Sexual Assault II*, New York: Gardland Publishing.

Lundgren, E. (2004) *The Process of Normalising Violence*, Stockholm: ROKS.

Mann, R., Horsley, P., Barett, C. and Tinney, J. (2014) *Norma's Project: A Research Study into the Sexual Assault of Older Women in Australia*, Melbourne Australia: Australian Research Centre in Sex, Health and Society, La Trobe University.

McOrmond-Plummer, L. (2014) 'Preventing secondary wounding by misconception: What professionals really need to know about intimate partner sexual violence', in McOrmond-Plummer, L., Easteal, P. and Levy-Peck, J.Y. (eds.) *Intimate Partner Sexual Violence: A Multidisciplinary Guide to Improving Services and Support for Survivors of Rape and Abuse*, London: Jessica Kingsley Publishers, pp. 30–40.

McWilliams, M. and Yarnell, P. (2013) *The Protection and Rights of Black and Minority Ethnic Women Experiencing Domestic Violence in Northern Ireland*, Belfast: Northern Ireland Council for Ethnic Minorities.

Meetoo, V. and Mirza, H.S. (2007) '"There is nothing 'honourable' about honour killings": Gender, violence and the limits of multiculturalism', *Women's Studies International Forum*, 30, pp. 187–200.

National Policing Improvement Agency (2010) *Guidance on Investigating and Prosecuting Rape (Abridged Edition)*, Bedfordshire: NPIA.

NUS (National Union of Students) (2010) *Hidden Marks: A Study of Women Students' Experiences of Harassment, Stalking, Violence and Sexual Assault*, London: NUS.

O'Donohue, W., Downs, K. and Yeater, E.A. (1998) 'Sexual harassment: A review of the literature', *Aggression and Violent Behaviour*, 3 (2), pp. 111–128.

Patel, P. (2003) 'The tricky blue line: Black women and policing', in Gupta, R. (ed.) *From Homebreakers to Jailbreakers: Southall Black Sisters*, London: Zed Books, pp. 160–187.

Radford, J. and Russell, D.E.H. (eds) (1992) *Femicide: The Politics of Woman Killing*, Buckingham: Open University Press.

Radford, L., Corral, S., Bradley, C., Fisher, H., Bassett, C., Howat, N. and Collishaw, S. (2011) *Child Abuse and Neglect in the UK Today*, London: NSPCC.

Rights of Women (2010) *A Guide to Sexual Harassment in the Workplace*, London: Rights of Women.

Schneider, B.E. (1987) 'Graduate women, sexual harassment and university policy', *Journal of Higher Education*, 58, pp. 46–65.

Scully, D. (1990) *Understanding Sexual Violence: A Study of Convicted Rapists*, London: Unwin Hyman.

Stanko, E.A. (1990) *Everyday Violence: How Women and Men Experience Sexual and Physical Danger*, Sheffield: Pandora.

Stöckl, H., Devries, K., Rotstein, A., Abrahams, N., Campbell, J., Watts, C. and Garcia Moreno, C. (2013) The global prevalence of intimate partner homicide: A systematic review, *The Lancet*, 382 (9895), pp. 859–865.

United Nations General Assembly (1993) *Declaration on the Elimination of Violence against Women* (A/RES/48/104 of 19 December 1992).

Universal Declaration of Human Rights (adopted 10 December 1948) UNGA Res. 217A(III) (UDHR) art. 16(2).

Welchman, L. and Hossain, S. (eds.) (2005) *'Honour': Crimes, Paradigms and Violence against Women*, London: Zed Press.

Westmarland, N. (2015) *Violence against Women: Criminological Perspectives on Men's Violences*, London: Routledge.

WHO (2001) *Female Genital Mutilation: Integrating the Prevention and the Management of the Health Complications into the Curricula of Nursing and Midwifery*, WHO: Geneva.

WHO (2013) *Responding to Intimate Partner Violence and Sexual Violence against Women: WHO Clinical and Policy Guidelines*, Geneva: WHO.

Williamson, E. (2014) 'Reproductive coercion', in McOrmond-Plummer, L., Easteal, P. and Levy-Peck, J.Y. (eds.) *Intimate Partner Sexual Violence: A Multidisciplinary Guide to Improving Services and Support for Survivors of Rape and Abuse*, London: Jessica Kingsley Publishers, pp. 76–87.

Willness, C., Steel, P., and Lee, K. (2007) 'A meta-analysis of the antecedents and consequences of workplace sexual harassment', *Personnel Psychology*, 60, pp. 127–162.

19

ATROCITY

The Latin American experience

Susanne Karstedt

Contemporary atrocity

In 1995 the German public was confronted with an exhibition of crimes committed by the German Armed Forces in East Europe in the Second World War. Photos were on display that showed in graphic detail the killings committed by German soldiers, and documented the direct involvement in mass murder by many men (and some women). In 2015, an exhibition of photos of torture and murder by security forces in Syria were shown in the United Nations' headquarters in New York and later in the European Parliament in Brussels; the photos had been taken by a photographer working for the Syrian security forces and later been brought out of the country. Stephen Ferry's (2012) *Violentology: A Manual of the Colombian Conflict* is a collection of images of massive and persistent violence. These are all images of atrocious crimes; they are also documentations of atrocity crimes.

Mass atrocity affects millions of people worldwide; still, atrocity crime remains an under-examined area within criminology (Hagan & Rymond-Richmond 2009a). However, as criminology is entering this field, the contours of these crimes have decisively changed, as has the terminology. In fact the term "atrocity crime" is a signal of these changes that started during the last decades of the previous century, when the new global landscape of mass violence and mass atrocity crimes emerged. Latin America as a region epitomised these ongoing changes. This required new perspectives and new tools to address and prevent these crimes, new instruments of justice, as well as data and analyses that would underpin such endeavours. Three developments were decisive in this process: terminological innovation; adoption of new analytical frameworks; and a focus on micro-level processes in local contexts (see Karstedt 2012, 2013a).

The terminological innovation is the introduction of the term atrocity crime by David Scheffer in 2002 (also 2006, 2007). Within a decade, the term has been widely adopted, e.g. by the Task Force on the EU Prevention of Mass Atrocities (2013) and in 2014 by the United Nations (2014) with its new *Framework of Analysis for Atrocity Crimes*, as well as by the UN Secretary General in his Report (United Nations 2015) and Scott Straus (2016) in an overview over preventive measures. In its global spread it has pervaded scientific as well as vernacular language and has been translated. Since about 2005, the term is increasingly used in scholarly work on Latin America and other regions (e.g. Osiel 2005/1999, 2009; Drumbl 2007), and has become vernacular in Latin American media and on the websites of non-governmental organisations (NGOs), including international ones like Human Rights Watch (2005) in their country reports.[1] The term provides a conceptual framework independent of both legal definitions and the straitjacket of characteristics which reify a particular type of crime, group of perpetrators and structural environment in which such crimes happen, as e.g. the label of "state crime" would suggest, or "hate crime" by indicating a specific motivation (Alvarez 1999).

New analytical frameworks sought to account for the fact that even in the course of the violent decades of the second half of the 20th and the beginning of the 21st century "mega-genocides" (Levene 2004, 163) were rare events, but massive atrocities were not. The majority of these events are of a smaller scale and reiterated, but account for millions of victims across the globe. Christian Gerlach's (2006, 2010) concept of "extremely violent societies" aims at de-constructing the conventional understanding of mass atrocity as state-driven violence and at re-contextualising it within a larger framework of conflict. These are societies where an "overall acclimation to violence" (Gerlach & Werth 2009, 172) has occurred that facilitates and precipitates events of mass atrocity crimes. Atrocities emerge from the "grassroots nature" (ibid.) of other types of violence, and conditions where violence becomes "multi-polar" (Gerlach 2010, 149). Importantly, an array of perpetrator groups gets into the spotlight, among them militias and paramilitary groups, rebel groups or warlord armies.

Finally, as more data on historical as well as more contemporary mass atrocity events have become available, not the least from victim-witnesses' and perpetrators' accounts before truth commissions and international criminal tribunals, understanding of these dynamics has transcended the model of top–down state action. According to this model, which was mainly derived from the Holocaust, a "select group of government elites" (Alvarez 1999, 467) mobilises, and orchestrates large numbers and groups of perpetrators, building on the common motivation of hatred against another group, and authoritarian obedience among the perpetrator group. In particular, evidence from the Rwandan genocide showed that as genocidal violence unfurled, prevalence and involvement processes were operating that defied hierarchical models and clear-cut typologies of perpetrators, bystanders, collaborators and victims (Des Forges 1999; Straus 2006; Fujii 2009).[2] Thus the emphasis moved towards understanding the realisation of violence by different actors, and in local dynamics, and away from the top–down model of master plans, and strategic intentions.

As the centres of mass atrocities moved around the globe from Asia in the 1960s and 1970s, to Latin America from the 1970s onward, to Europe and finally Africa in the 1990s and first decade of the 2000s, Central America and the South American subcontinent were the first region where the changes in the contexts and dynamics of mass atrocities became visible. These campaigns included unambiguously genocidal events but also waves of different types of indiscriminate and selective violence and atrocity crimes in the course of repressive action by states and their subsidiaries, as well as rebel groups. The protracted civil war in Guatemala from 1978–96 involved different actors – military, security forces and militias, waves of different atrocity crimes, including torture, disappearances, extrajudicial killings and genocide, and targeted different groups in its course (Sanford 2004; Higonnet 2009; Rothenberg 2012). The sinuous character of genocide and mass atrocities, with "peaks and lulls" of violence (De Waal 2007), where campaigns of massive and targeted violence alternate with lower levels, where indiscriminate violence has different objectives and victimises successive groups in waves, have been equally observed for Peru (Mucha 2013) and Colombia. Colombia in particular is an exemplary case of links between atrocity crimes, other types of violence and organised crime, as well as the involvement of different and in particular non-state actors, ranging from paramilitaries to organised crime (Civico 2016).

The vantage point in understanding such extreme violence has been moved closer to the violence that is committed and goes on in wars, civil wars and gang wars, to collective and other forms of political violence, or to organised crime and violence committed by these actors. Contextualising atrocity in these ways does not deny involvement of the state nor its potential nature as "state crime". However, it pays more attention to the different types of violence involved, the temporal and spatial patterns and the micro-dynamics of singular events. Extreme violence and atrocity crimes thus become comparable to other settings, where violence spirals out of control in "Hobbesian" spaces and environments of civil conflict.

This chapter will chart these changes with a focus on the Latin American experience. It starts with an exploration of the concept and characteristics of atrocity crimes. What types of crimes are these? It then moves to the analysis of contextual features of atrocity crimes, actors and their strategies, and the two "paradoxes" of state-led atrocities which shape incidences and prevalence (Karstedt 2014a). In each section, the Latin American experience over the past decades will be explored, and situated within global and regional developments. Latin America stands out as it has embarked on a successful process of curbing atrocity crimes, and ending impunity for the perpetrators through an array of judicial and extrajudicial transitional procedures. A brief overview over these procedures will conclude the chapter.

Atrocity crimes: the progress of a concept

The term "atrocity" has its origin in military penal law; states prohibit in their military penal codes "atrocious and aberrant acts", which are blatantly and manifestly violations of and in "evident contradiction to all human morality" as the International Military Tribunal at Nuremberg stated when dealing with Nazi Germany's crimes committed against the peoples of Europe and the European Jews (cited in Osiel 2005/1999, 46). In 2014, the United Nations' Atrocity Crimes Framework (2014, 1) defines atrocity crimes: "the term 'atrocity crimes' refers to three legally defined international crimes: genocide, crimes against humanity and war crimes", independent of whether they are committed in international conflict, internal conflicts or even in a peaceful country, like e.g. torture or extrajudicial killings. Since 2005, the crime of ethnic cleansing is counted among atrocity crimes (United Nations 2014, 1; Hagan 2009); while not defined as an independent crime under international law, it crosscuts the broad categories and includes acts that are serious violations of international human rights and humanitarian law that may themselves amount to one of the recognised atrocity crimes, in particular crimes against humanity.

With these definitions the international community finally acknowledged and put into practice the proposal by former US Ambassador-at-Large for War Crimes Issues, David Scheffer, first forwarded in 2002, of a "new crimes category that would be called 'atrocity crimes' and a new category of international law" (Scheffer 2002, 398). "Atrocity law" would comprise the range of laws – from the law of wars to human rights law – that lay the foundation for the contemporary prosecution of such crimes by international tribunals and national courts.[3] Scheffer's aim was threefold: first, he wanted to facilitate the prosecution of those who commit such crimes, and second, to improve communication and outreach to the general public both at home and abroad through "easily comprehensible terms" (ibid.). Finally, and importantly he wanted to move away from the centrality of genocide, and to lift the heavy burden of connotations with legal, political and moral action, which appeared increasingly dysfunctional for the task of the international community to prevent, intervene and to prosecute, and its practical operation. He thus aimed at coining a term for a category of crimes beyond and above legal categories, but which would have a clear and, in particular, moral meaning.

As a concept, atrocity crime disconnects an ultimate legal judgment (e.g. on genocide) from preventive and protective action, which necessarily has to precede it. Here, Scheffer (2007, 92) addresses in particular the needs of the international community to meet the challenges of mass atrocity crimes "during the early phases of such crimes … thereby standing a better chance of influencing the development of effective responses to massive death, injury and destruction". Atrocity crimes can also be

> precursors of genocide … occurring immediately to and during possible genocide that can point to an ultimate legal judgment of genocide but which should be recognized and used in a timely manner to galvanize international action to intervene, be it diplomatically, economically or militarily.
>
> *(Scheffer 2006, 232)*

Precursors such as forced displacement, illegal use of force by security forces, looting and forced disappearances in this sense can be markers of dangerous situations, signals of increasing tensions or expanding use of illegal force by security forces or engagement of militias (Hagan 2009; Hagan & Kaiser 2011). The term "atrocity crime" thus captures the processual character of mass atrocities, both from a long-term and macro-perspective as well as from the micro-perspective of single events of mass atrocities.

Scheffer's conceptualisation epitomised a change in terminology and conceptualisation that was already on its way, but has gathered momentum since then, as demonstrated by the Task Force on the EU Prevention of Mass Atrocities and their report in 2013, and the UN Framework report in 2014. For Schabas it was an "idea whose time has come" (2007, 32) as international law moved "towards greater coherence and more simplicity" (ibid., 31). Today genocide, crimes against humanity and war crimes constitute a "seamless body of 'atrocity law' covering all serious violations of human rights" (ibid., 34).

The nature and characteristics of atrocity crimes

The nature and characteristics of atrocity crimes are shaped by their origins in international law, however they are not confined by it. This implies four defining features: magnitude and large-scale commission; systematic commission; being commissioned as part of a collective or "joint enterprise"; and being organised as part of institutionalised, or group activities (see also Scheffer 2002, 399; Osiel 2005/1999). These features are not fixed in terms of e.g. precise numbers of individual acts or harm done, but rather define degrees and scales, thresholds and tipping points. They signify the organised and collective nature of atrocity, particular types and groups of perpetrators, and types of acts (Karstedt 2014b). Nonetheless, atrocity crimes are individual acts, and are prosecuted as such. Some atrocity crimes like torture or illegal killings are mostly committed by individual perpetrators, while others like ethnic cleansing need a more collaborative effort on the part of the perpetrators, and include different types of involvement, from direct violence against members of the target group at the lowest level to planning, orders and finally tacit collusion at the higher ranks.

When outlining the characteristics of atrocity crimes Scheffer (2002, 399) had in mind prosecution by international criminal tribunals, and those crimes which increasingly are excluded from domestic amnesty "deals". He clearly followed the Rome Statute of the International Criminal Court which in its definition of crimes against humanity is the most explicit of all legal documents on the particular defining features of atrocity crimes. Individual acts should be "committed as part of a widespread or systematic attack ... with knowledge of the attack"; the crime itself should involve "multiple commissions" of such acts. The Statute also states the non-individual character and motivation of such atrocity crimes beyond individual goals, emotions and material gains, though all of these come into play in the perpetration of individual acts of atrocity: atrocity crimes are committed "pursuant to or in furtherance" of a state policy or the goals of an organised group like e.g. a rebel group or militia (Rome Statute of the International Criminal Court Rome Statute, Article 7; UN General Assembly 1998). Atrocity crimes are not confined to times of war; they can occur equally in times of peace, or – and this applies to most contemporary atrocities, in particular in Latin America – in times of civil strife and conflict, and "of violent societal upheaval of some organized character" (Scheffer 2002, 399).

These legally defined characteristics imply that atrocities are crimes of "significant magnitude", and they are "part of a large-scale commission of such crimes". "Significant magnitude" refers to the victims of murder, forced disappearances, torture and other crimes, and implies numerous deaths, and severe harm and injury inflicted upon them (Scheffer 2002, 399). Next, they transcend individual motives, planning and knowledge and are part of an organised and "joint enterprise" (Karstedt 2014b). Scheffer (2002, 400) describes them as "high impact crimes ... of an orchestrated character that shock the conscience of humankind, that result in significant numbers of victims". Both sides of this equation – the impact of the crime on the one hand and the context on the other – pose major dilemmas. What are the thresholds and definitions of a significant magnitude or numbers of victims, and what makes a crime of "extreme gravity"? On the other hand, what can count as organisation and collaboration of the perpetrators in a joint enterprise, and what as typical motivation by state governments and group interests?[4] Are elites part and parcel of such collaboration, and a necessary correlate of such crimes as argued by Scheffer (2002, 399)? Scheffer (ibid., 400) stresses that atrocity crimes are neither "isolated (n)or aberrant events", and thus can be precursors to major mass atrocities as well as part of an ongoing system of terror and torture. The UN Framework (2014, iii) confirms that they are part of "processes, with histories, precursors and triggering factors which, combined, enable their commission". What makes atrocity "systematic" is both the continuous and serial usage across a considerable period as e.g. in the civil war in Guatemala and the conflicts in Colombia, and the planning and commission of a singular massive violent attack on victims.

The list of crimes included in the bodies of law that Scheffer (2002, 2006) labels "atrocity laws" is long. The majority of these are direct acts of violence against life and person, deprivation that causes serious bodily and mental harm, and particularly humiliating and degrading treatment ("committing outrages upon personal dignity"). Incriminated acts also include attacks on individual and collective property and wilful destruction of cultural and religious goods, mainly in times of war and internal conflict. The crimes against humanity, as defined by the Rome Statute of the International Criminal Court in Article 7, define the core of atrocity crimes and include besides lethal violence (murder, extermination) enslavement; forcible transfer of populations; imprisonment in violation of fundamental rules of international law; torture; sexual violence, including rape, slavery, enforced prostitution, forced pregnancy or sterilisation; enforced disappearances of persons; persecution of specific groups on grounds of national, ethnic, religious or other characteristics, including gender; and any other similar act causing "great suffering" and "serious injury to body or to mental and physical health".[5] The range of crimes also includes the most serious, genocide.

Most of these incriminated acts are atrocities committed by state agents like the military and the police, or by state bureaucracies (Karstedt 2014a; Alvarez 1999). The definition of state crime by Kramer, Michalowski and Rothe (2005, 56) clearly comprises atrocity crimes as outlined above:

> State Crime is any action that violates public international law, international criminal law, or domestic law when these actions are committed by individuals acting in official or covert capacity as agents of the state pursuant to expressed or implied orders of the state, or resulting from state failure to exercise due diligence over the actions of its agents.

This might include subsidiaries like militias and paramilitary groups with close links to state agencies, however it does not capture those who act more independently. Even if state agencies and their auxiliaries are the dominant perpetrators, it is important to note that atrocity crimes are committed by a range of different actors in often fluid and changing alliances, and are not defined by the type of perpetrators who commit them.

Wars, conflict and extreme violence: the context of atrocity crimes

Contemporary atrocity crimes are embedded in trajectories of long-term conflict, and the majority of mass killings since the Second World War have been part of civil wars and ethnic conflicts (Krain 1997; Human Security Report Project 2011). They typically occur within nation states and independent of their boundaries, and are embedded in the environment, social formations and actor configurations of societies that have a history as well as trajectory of violent conflicts. Societies become "extremely violent" during such periods, creating an environment where violence becomes "multi-polar" (Gerlach 2010, 149). Different groups are victims of massive attacks of physical violence, including mass killings, systematic sexual violence and enforced displacement, and atrocity crimes oscillate between these different forms of violence. In many incidents of atrocities systematic sexual violence is dominant (Hagan & Rymond-Richmond 2009b; Letschert et al. 2011; De Brouwer et al. 2012; Braithwaite 2013; Leatherman 2011). Perpetrator participation in these events spreads across the boundaries of different groups and blurs the lines between different types of involvement and non-involvement (Fujii 2009, 2011; Straus 2011). Diverse groups of perpetrators participate, ranging from state government forces to militias (Alvarez 2006; Colombia: Arjona & Kalyvas 2011; Civico 2016; Guatemala: Schirmer 1998; Higonnet 2009; Latin America: Huggins 1991), and engage in complex and shifting alliances. Organised violent actors like, for example, paramilitary groups, become increasingly involved, whether encouraged, funded and trained by state actors or other powerful actors (e.g. Colombia: Amnesty International 2008; Sherman 2015; Dugas 2012; Hristov 2009). Engagement of military and paramilitary forces, as well as of the police in paramilitary action result in forced disappearances, widespread torture and sexual violence (Mitchell, Carey & Butler 2014; Argentina: Crenzel 2013; Guatemala: Rothenberg 2012; Higonnet 2009). Mass atrocities are often linked to other criminal activity, including weapons and drugs trafficking or illegal natural resources exploitation (Richani 2007; Braithwaite 2012, 2013). Actors engage in atrocity crimes for a multitude of reasons, and the power of violence stems from the mixture of attitudes, interests and motives, that brought them together in the first instance.

In particular between 1970 and 1990, Latin American countries were major contributors to the global level of conflicts, civil wars, political violence and state repression, and the sites of mass atrocities.[6] The surge in conflict and atrocities is embedded in the global context of the Cold War, and the "technologies of war" that it generated (Kalyvas & Balcells 2010). The Cold War's "system polarity" was conducive to irregular or guerrilla wars, which were turned into "robust insurgencies" through massive material support from one of the two competing powers, spread of ideological doctrine and build-up of a military and political organisation. This favoured the strategic use of excessive and "indiscriminate" violence by state actors – both directly and indirectly through militias and paramilitary groups – in campaigns against the rebels and their supporting bases, in all Latin American conflicts during the 1970s and 1980s (Kalyvas 2004; Carey, Colaresi and Mitchell 2015).

As in other parts of the globe, the majority of mass atrocities in Latin America are part of protracted conflicts and violent societal upheaval (Krain 1997). Table 19.1 gives an overview of conflicts in Latin American countries, which shows that the majority were involved in both state conflicts and non-state conflicts. Non-state conflicts are those where none of the parties

TABLE 19.1 State-based and non-state conflicts in Latin America

Country	State-based conflict 1980–2014	Non-state conflict 1990–2014
Bolivia		2000
Brazil		1994–2011
Colombia	1980–2014	1990–2005
Ecuador		2003
El Salvador	1980–91	
Guatemala	1980–95	2005
Haiti	1989–91, 2004	1991
Honduras		2010
Jamaica		2001
Mexico	1994–96	1993, 2002–14
Nicaragua	1981–90	
Panama	1989	
Paraguay	1989	
Peru	1982–99, 2007–10	
Suriname	1986–88	
Trinidad & T.	1990	
Venezuela	1982, 1992	

Source: UCDP (2015) Battle-Related Deaths Dataset; UCDP (2015) Non-State Conflict Dataset; own computation; see Appendix.

is a state; these are mostly conflicts between ethnic groups, or landowners/businesses (and their militias) and such groups, or, as in the case of Mexico, between organised crime groups and their auxiliaries.[7] Genocide Watch (2010) lists atrocity events and mass violence from 1945 to 2010. Central and South American states such as Guatemala (1950s–1996), El Salvador (1980–92), Nicaragua (1970–79, 1980–89), Colombia (1948–58, 1975–2010) and Brazil (since 1964) experienced extended periods of mass violence and atrocities, with hundreds of thousands of victims in systematic atrocity crimes. The recorded death toll, which does not include all other types of violent atrocities, testifies to the widespread and large-scale commission of atrocity crimes: 200,000 in Guatemala; more than 200,000 in Colombia in both periods; 75,000 in El Salvador; 69,000 in Peru; 60,000 in Nicaragua during both periods; 20,000 in Argentina; 10,000s in Chile.

It is in this context that Latin American countries became extremely violent societies. According to the Violent Societies Index (VSI) which combines measures of state violence, terrorist attacks and conflict battle deaths, six of the 20 most violent countries in 1980–89 were Latin American countries including El Salvador, Guatemala, Colombia, Peru, Chile and Nicaragua.[8] Table 19.2 first demonstrates that extremely violent societies are at a high risk of major mass atrocities, or have a history of such mass violence (as indicated by †). Next, it shows that while indeed the 1980s were the most violent in Latin America, violence subsided

TABLE 19.2 Top 20 violent societies (Violent Societies Index (VSI))

Rank	1980–89		1990–99		2000–12	
	Country	VSI	Country	VSI	Country	VSI
1	**El Salvador†**	**20.1**	**Colombia†**	**16.7**	Iraq†	17.8
2	**Peru†**	**15.1**	Algeria†	14.0	Afghanistan†	17.1
3	Uganda†	14.7	India†	13.5	India†	13.0
4	**Colombia†**	**12.7**	Afghanistan†	12.7	Sudan†	12.8
5	**Guatemala†**	**12.1**	Turkey†	12.6	**Colombia†**	**12.6**
6	Afghanistan†	11.6	**Peru†**	**12.3**	Pakistan†	12.0
7	Ethiopia†	11.5	Bosnia & H.†	12.1	Sri Lanka†	12.0
8	**Nicaragua†**	**11.4**	Sri Lanka†	12.0	Somalia†	11.9
9	Iran†	10.7	Angola†	12.0	Israel†	11.7
10	**Chile†**	**9.9**	Sierra Leone†	11.5	Burundi†	10.9
11	Sri Lanka†	9.6	Somalia†	10.9	Russia†	10.4
12	Iraq†	9.5	Pakistan†	10.8	Congo, DR†	10.2
13	India†	9.4	Iraq†	10.7	Nepal†	10.1
14	South Africa†	9.3	Sudan	10.4	Philippines†	9.8
15	Angola†	9.1	Rwanda†	10.4	Algeria†	9.7
16	Philippines†	8.9	South Africa†	10.2	Myanmar†	9.3
17	Syria†	8.2	Burundi†	10.0	Uganda†	8.7
18	Mozambique†	8.1	Myanmar†	9.7	Chad†	8.6
19	Myanmar†	7.4	Philippines†	9.4	Thailand	8.1
20	Turkey†	7.4	Korea, North†	9.0	Nigeria†	8.1

† Previous mass atrocities according to Genocide Watch 1945–2009; N = 162. Bold: Latin/Central American countries.
Source: Karstedt (2012); Genocide Watch (2010); own computation.

during the following decades. In the 1990s, only Colombia and Peru remain in this group; at the beginning of 2000, only Colombia remains in this group.

State-led atrocities are a constitutive element and integral part of extremely violent societies. This type of repressive violence is a driver of other types of violence that coalesce in the context of extremely violent societies. In fact, the state and its loyalist arms (militias, paramilitary groups) account for the majority of atrocity crimes as e.g. in Guatemala. As Gerlach and Werth (2009, 136) point out, state violence is both public and secret in the development of repressive policies and mass atrocities. Killings, deportation of people and sexual violence are more public, while enforced disappearances, torture and illegal imprisonment are often concealed. Nonetheless, both public and secret violence instil fear and terror in the population. As atrocity crimes are predominantly committed by state agents, a reasonably reliable measurement of atrocity crimes is a scale of state-led violence, the Political Terror Scale (PTS). The scale includes extrajudicial killings by security forces, enforced disappearances, torture and political/illegal imprisonment. The PTS used here throughout is combined from two sources, the country reports of the US State Department and Amnesty International; both are ranked from 1 (no state violence) to 5 (has expanded to the whole population) and are provided separately. Both values were added up, resulting in a scale from 0 to 9, which covers the period from 1976–2014. This scale does not capture the full amount of atrocity crimes committed by all actors, however it is highly correlated to other measures that include such actors.[9]

Table 19.3 shows the level of atrocity crimes committed by state agents in Latin American countries during three decades from 1980 to 2014. Countries with high levels of state violence and atrocity crimes also have a history of mass atrocity and violence (indicated by †). This demonstrates a rather fluid transition from state repression to massive violence. High levels of state violence are related to conflict, both to state and non-state conflicts (indicated by bold print). In the group of the 25% of countries with the highest levels of state-led atrocities, nearly all are experiencing a conflict at the time; in contrast, in the 25% with the lowest level of state atrocities, conflict is an exception. As Kalyvas and Balcells (2010) point out, the typical conflicts and internal wars ravaging Latin America since the 1970s were characterised by high levels of state repression, atrocities and mass violence. Figure 19.1 shows that in particular during the 1980s and 1990s, levels of state-led atrocity crimes in countries with conflicts (both state and non-state) hugely exceed those in countries without conflicts. However, even in countries without conflict levels of state-committed atrocities are generally high in the region. As the gap between the two groups closes at the beginning of this century, this is predominantly caused by a significant drop of state-led atrocities in conflict countries.

The dynamics of atrocity crimes: global, regional and local trajectories

Extremely violent societies are not defined by structural or cultural characteristics that are conducive to massive violence and atrocity (Gerlach 2006, 460). Rather they have moved into a violence-prone and dangerous situation, which they can leave behind again. Atrocity crimes are embedded in trajectories of violence: they act as triggers and create such trajectories as repressive measures mount, the pool of perpetrators widens and violence is used in an increasingly indiscriminate way against different victim groups. State-led atrocities are major drivers in this process. Even when the conflict ends, they leave "societies of fear" in their wake where citizens distrust institutions and each other, and breakdown of social relations is widespread (Koonings & Kruijt 1999; Karstedt 2013b; Guatemala: Green 1995).

TABLE 19.3 State-led atrocities in Latin America

Rank	1980–89		1990–99		2000–14	
	Country	PTS	Country	PTS	Country	PTS
1	**El Salvador†**	**7.8**	**Colombia†**	**8.8**	**Colombia†**	**7.9**
2	**Guatemala†**	**7.6**	**Peru†**	**7.2**	**Brazil†**	**6.9**
3	**Colombia†**	**6.8**	**Brazil†**	**7**	**Mexico†**	**5.9**
4	**Peru†**	**6.7**	**Guatemala†**	**6.9**	Venezuela†	5.5
5	Chile†	6.4	**Haiti**	**6**	**Jamaica**	**5.5**
6	**Nicaragua†**	**6.2**	**Venezuela**	**5.9**	Dominican Rep.	5.2
7	**Paraguay†**	**5.4**	**Mexico†**	**5.8**	**Haiti**	**5.1**
8	Honduras	5.3	**Nicaragua†**	**5.2**	**Honduras**	**4.9**
9	**Haiti**	**5.2**	**El Salvador†**	**5.2**	Guatemala†	4.8
10	Cuba†	5.1	Cuba†	5.1	Cuba†	4.7
11	Brazil†	5	Honduras	4.4	**Ecuador**	**4.3**
12	**Suriname**	**4.9**	Ecuador	4.3	**Peru†**	**4.1**
13	Mexico†	4.9	Paraguay†	4.2	Paraguay†	4.1
14	Bolivia	4.8	Jamaica	3.8	El Salvador†	4
15	Argentina†	4.3	Dominican Rep.	3.8	Nicaragua†	3.7
16	Uruguay	4.1	Chile†	3.7	Guyana	3.6
17	**Panama**	**4**	Bolivia	3.5	**Bolivia**	**3.5**
18	Ecuador	4	Argentina†	3.5	Argentina†	3.5
19	**Venezuela**	**3.9**	Panama	3.2	Trinidad & T.	3.4
20	Guyana	3.9	Guyana	2.9	Suriname	2.7
21	Dominican Rep.	3.1	Uruguay	2.6	Chile†	2.5
22	Jamaica	2.2	Suriname	2.6	Panama	2.1
23	Costa Rica	1.2	**Trinidad & T.**	**2.3**	Costa Rica	2
24	Trinidad & T.	1.1	Costa Rica	1.3	Uruguay	1.4

† Previous mass atrocities according to Genocide Watch 1945–2009; Bold: Countries with state-based conflict or non-state conflict.
Source: Gibney, Cornett and Wood (2015); Genocide Watch (2010); own computation; see Appendix.

State atrocity in Latin America has declined since 1980, in contrast to an upward global trend. Table 19.4 shows that between 1980 and 2014, the global level of atrocity crimes rose, mainly due to a significant increase in both Africa and Asia. The level in the global region of the Americas dropped, mainly due to a quite substantive decrease in the 24 Latin American states. Amidst a global wave of state atrocity, Latin American countries were successful in curbing it.

However, this was neither an even development, nor did it take hold in all countries. Table 19.5 gives an overview over Latin American countries with increasing, decreasing or mixed trajectories of state-led atrocities between 1980 and 2014, and shows the size of the trend as well as its significance. Nearly half of the countries curbed state violence. Among these were countries that cut state atrocity by nearly or more than 50%, as e.g. Uruguay, Chile, El Salvador and Panama. The population of the majority of these countries had experienced mass atrocities at the hands of the state and governments (indicated by †). In contrast, we see considerable and significant upward trends of state-led atrocity crimes in one-third of all countries. In three of these – the Central American states Jamaica, Trinidad and Tobago,

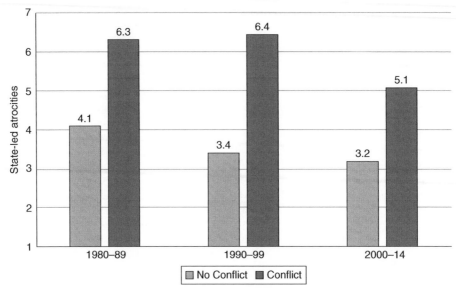

FIGURE 19.1 State-led atrocities: conflict and non-conflict countries (1980–2014)
Source: Gibney, Cornett and Wood (2015); UCDP (2015) Battle-Related Deaths Dataset; UCDP (2015) Non-State Conflict Dataset; own computation; see Appendix for state and non-state conflict; threshold for Conflict ≥ 100 battle-related deaths (1980–2014)

TABLE 19.4 State-led atrocities: global regions and Latin America

	1980–89	1990–99	2000–14
Africa	3.98	4.89	4.95
Americas	4.47	4.29	4.10
Asia & Oceania	4.23	4.40	4.60
Europe	2.34	2.21	2.35
Global level	3.83	4.06	4.12
Latin America	4.75	4.55	4.22

Source: Gibney, Cornett and Wood (2015); own computation.

and Costa Rica, the level of state atrocity about doubled from fairly low levels. In the other countries, including Mexico, Brazil, Venezuela and Colombia, even more repressive violence by the state and atrocity crimes were added to already high levels; among these, Colombia was immersed in a conflict between state, rebel groups and organised crime, while Mexico became increasingly involved in a non-state conflict between warring organised crime groups who themselves committed systematic and serial atrocity crimes (Sundberg, Eck & Kreutz 2012).

In which ways are atrocity crimes embedded in these trajectories? Who are the predominant perpetrators and targeted victims as these events unfold? When is atrocity "selective", and when does it become "indiscriminate" (Kalyvas 2004)? The well-documented temporal and spatial pattern of the Guatemalan civil war is exemplary of other cases: a spatial concentration

TABLE 19.5 Country trajectories of state-led atrocities (1980–2014)

Country	1980–89	1990–99	2000–14	Trend	Sig.
Increasing violence					
Jamaica	2.2	3.8	5.5	+0.114	★★★
Dominican Rep.	3.1	3.8	5.2	+0.078	★★★
Trinidad & T.	1.1	2.3	3.4	+0.076	★★★
Venezuela	3.9	5.9	5.5	+0.072	★★★
Brazil†	5	7	6.9	+0.064	★★★
Colombia†	6.8	8.8	7.9	+0.063	★★
Mexico†	4.9	5.8	5.9	+0.050	★★★
Costa Rica	1.2	1.3	2	+0.039	★★★
Decreasing violence					
Uruguay	4.1	2.6	1.4	−0.161	★★★
Chile†	6.4	3.7	2.5	−0.147	★★★
El Salvador†	7.8	5.2	4	−0.125	★★★
Guatemala†	7.6	6.9	4.8	−0.107	★★★
Argentina†	4.3	3.5	3.5	−0.098	★★★
Nicaragua†	6.2	5.2	3.7	−0.094	★★★
Suriname	4.9	2.6	2.7	−0.067	★★
Peru†	6.7	7.2	4.1	−0.064	★
Paraguay†	5.4	4.2	4.1	−0.055	★★★
Bolivia	4.8	3.5	3.5	−0.055	★★★
Panama	4	3.2	2.1	−0.050	★★★
Mixed trajectories					
Cuba†	5.1	5.1	4.7	−0.015	ns
Ecuador	4	4.3	4.3	+0.015	ns
Guyana	3.9	2.9	3.6	+0.006	ns
Haiti	5.2	6	5.1	−0.018	ns
Honduras	5.3	4.4	4.9	+0.029	ns

★ p<0.05; ★★ p<0.01; ★★★ p<0.001; ns = not significant.
† Previous mass atrocities according to Genocide Watch 1945–2009.
Source: Gibney, Cornett and Wood (2015); own computation.

of indiscriminate state violence, alternating patterns of types of violence, irregular temporal patterns, and changing strategies and targets of violence. Mass atrocities were concentrated in a few areas, with one region suffering nearly 50%, and four areas accounting for 75% of all human rights violations and atrocity crimes committed between 1962 and 1996 (Gulden 2002; Rothenberg 2012). Executions, forced disappearances and torture all peak between 1980 and 1984, and are indicative of the ongoing genocide against the Maya population. However a period of lower-level atrocities from 1962 to 1977 precedes this escalation of violence during which "arbitrary executions", forced disappearances and torture alternate, indicating a pattern of violence switching back and forth between selective and indiscriminate strategies (Kalyvas 2004). Fear and threat were strategically used by government forces and their subsidiaries, who were responsible for more than 90% of all atrocity crimes (Rothenberg 2012, appendix 1; Schirmer 1998). In particular in rural Guatemala, this led to a paralysis and widespread breakdown of social relations (Green 1995).

Actors and strategies

Large-scale and systematic commission, being part of a collective or "joint enterprise", and organised as part of institutionalised activities are the four defining features of atrocity crimes. These characteristics privilege the state, its agencies and agents as actors, and as we have seen these were the predominant perpetrators of atrocities in Latin America – from Argentina to Guatemala. However, militias and paramilitary local groups were an integral part of these campaigns, and played an increasing role in particular in the conflicts in Guatemala, Nicaragua and Colombia. Often their original rationale and justification was the protection of local populations from insurgent groups. However, most of these were "pro-government groups" with close connections to the government and sometimes directly incorporated with semi-legal status, whilst others were loosely linked and ties remained hidden and secret (Carey, Mitchell & Lowe 2013). Civico (2016, 23) describes the Colombian paramilitary groups as "war machines acquired by the state to produce violence". They form part of an overall strategy of the government to evade accountability for human rights violations and atrocity crimes by delegating repression to other actors (Carey, Colaresi and Mitchell 2015). Both paramilitary groups and rebel groups joined forces with organised crime groups and engaged in shifting alliances in several conflicts (Civico 2016). As drug cartels waged an "open warfare" with the Colombian government in the area around Medellin, the ties between the Colombian Armed Forces and paramilitary groups tightened (Sherman 2015, 458).

Paramilitary groups are perpetrators of numerous atrocity crimes, from displacement to systematic killings; when they enter a conflict this generally raises the level of atrocity crimes, in particular torture, disappearances and killings (Mitchell, Carey & Butler 2014; Civico 2016). Militias commit atrocity crimes not only against civilians, but also within their own groups in order to enhance cohesion within the group (Jentzsch, Kalyvas & Schubiger 2015). Paramilitary groups which have child soldiers in their ranks are particularly involved in sexual violence, as are those which are trained by the regular army (Cohen & Nordås 2015). Latin American countries were forerunners in the engagement of a multitude of non-state actors that later took hold in Africa.[10] Figure 19.2 shows that both state actors and non-state actors were involved in "one-sided violence", i.e. atrocities against non-combatants/civilians.[11] State-led atrocities are dominant until the mid-1990s, when non-state actor atrocity increases exponentially, and supersedes state action until 2010. The peak as well as the continuously higher level of non-state actor atrocity is exclusively caused by non-state actors in Colombia, with an overall death toll of 1,500 victims and uncounted non-lethal atrocity crimes during this short period.

This probably is a low estimate and underestimates the actual level, given the strategies used by state and non-state actors to evade responsibility (for estimates see Restrepo, Spagat & Vargas 2006; Sherman 2015; Tate 2007). The 2008 report by Amnesty International on Colombia estimates that in 2002 4,000 civilians were killed by all parties to the conflict, which decreased to about 1,400 in 2007. State-led atrocities, in particular extrajudicial killings by security forces increased after 2003 when the paramilitary demobilisation process started testifying to the close and subsidiary relationships between the state and paramilitary groups. Enforced disappearances are estimated at between 15,000 and 30,000, and during the 2000s, there were several hundred victims each year (Amnesty International 2008, 30). Forced displacement in Colombia is one of the highest in the world exponentially increasing after 2005 and presently estimated at more than 4 million people (World Bank 2015). Because of

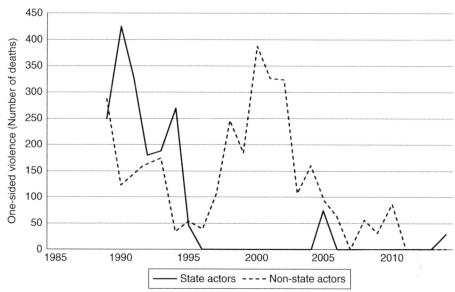

FIGURE 19.2   One-sided violence in Latin America: state and non-state actors (1989–2014)
Source: UCDP (2015) One-Sided Violence Dataset; own computations; see Appendix

its secretive character, cases of torture are particularly hard to document. Of 80 reported cases where the perpetrator was known, state security forces were responsible for 60%, paramilitary groups for 27% and guerrilla groups for 11% (Amnesty International 2008, 40).

As these reports from Colombia demonstrate, the involvement of state and non-state actors fuels the violence from a mixture of varying and variable interests and motives that brought them together in the first instance. These are embedded in local and regional political economies, and local motives converge with supra-local imperatives when the interests of landowners and transnational business are involved, making the latter complicit in atrocity crimes (Kalyvas 2003; Colombia: Avilés 2006; overview Dugas 2012). Jasmin Hristov (2009, 124–6) alleges that "all of Colombia's paramilitary human rights violations are motivated by the need to protect and advance the wealth and the interests of the upper classes" (Dugas 2012; Brewer Norman 2012). Organised crime actors were motivated by economic and territorial interests (Sherman 2015). Paramilitary organisations persist in particular, where they have close links with the executive and legislature and act in the shadow of the state (Colombia: Acemoglu, Robinson & Santos 2009). In Colombia, paramilitaries infiltrated state institutions on a large scale, and politicians colluded with them, thus becoming complicit in atrocity crimes through arming and financing these groups (Amnesty International 2008, 19; for Guatemala: Schirmer 1998).

The concurrence of conflicting and overlapping interests and motives shapes the regional distribution of state and non-state actor activity and simultaneously of atrocity crimes. Like all violence, extreme and even indiscriminate violence does not spread uniformly across a city, region or country, but is highly concentrated in "hot spots". In Guatemala, atrocity crimes were concentrated in a few areas, with one region suffering nearly 50%, and four areas accounting for 75% of all atrocity crimes (Gulden 2002; Rothenberg 2012). In Colombia, paramilitary presence and activity was concentrated in the regions on the west coast, with a violence hub in the region of Antioquia (Civico 2016, chap. 3).[12]

Beneath the master-narratives of elite interests and state power are those of "ordinary men" who participate in armed groups and finally become involved in atrocity crimes for a variety of reasons and motives. Insurgent as well as militia groups resemble each other in forced or voluntary recruitment (Jentzsch, Kalyvas & Schubiger 2015, 758; Colombia: Gutiérrez Sanín 2008). Members are recruited through local networks of proximity and influence among neighbours; incentives and opportunities to participate are shaped at the local level, not the least because of proximity to violence. Some militias recruit from the same social groups as insurgents, which seems to inhibit violence against civilians (Stanton 2015; Colombia: Gutiérrez Sanín 2008). Paramilitary groups in Haiti associated with President Aristide were recruited from street gangs (Adams 2002).

The proximity of reasons and motives between both groups is demonstrated for Colombia. Arjona and Kalyvas (2011) report from a survey with demobilised fighters, that "defending society" is a most common motive for rebel as well as paramilitary groups. Economic motives (escaping from poverty) is a predominant motive, followed by ideology and revenge for harms done. This is mirrored by an ethnographic life course study of two members of paramilitary death squads; rather, the leader of one such group came from a privileged background and had military training (Civico 2016, 55–88). All three were involved in atrocities. By contrast, state agents who engage in systematic torture, disappearances and killings are specialised, trained and selected for the task as Martha Huggins and her colleagues found in interviews with Brazilian torturers (Huggins, Haritos-Fatouros & Zimbardo 2002).

Atrocity crimes are both public and secret in the development of repressive policies and massive violence; in a way many of them can be classified as semi-public, as the signs of torture or enforced disappearances can hardly be hidden. However, as such crimes are excluded from the open public space of communication and thus turn into subterranean "public" knowledge, they become a continuous source of fear. The forced disappearances during the years of the Dirty War in Argentina exemplify these strategies and their long-term detrimental impact on society (Osiel 2005/1999; Crenzel 2013). In Guatemala, evidence of the sheer scope of atrocities committed by the police and security forces was discovered in a warehouse which stored police files, in 2005 (Doyle 2011). Even if atrocity crimes are hidden from public view they are widely known within the confined spheres of the groups, state agencies and armed forces that are involved in atrocities. In fact such involvement and the secrecy surrounding it is used as a tool for building up group cohesion.[13] With increasing pressure from the international human rights regime, evading accountability and denying involvement become integral elements of campaigns of state repression and state-led atrocity crimes; paramilitary auxiliaries are a welcome tool for governments plausibly to deny any involvement (Alvarez 2006; Campbell & Brenner 2002; Bueno de Mesquita, Down & Smith 2005; Mitchell, Carey & Butler 2014).

Colombia is an exemplary case of the use of both secret and public atrocity crimes by state agencies and paramilitary auxiliaries, and the strategies related to both. Media, NGO reports and reports from Amnesty International (2008) concur in describing subterfuge tactics in order to evade accountability not only by police, armed and security forces, but equally by paramilitary organisations. Among these, forced disappearances are the most obvious way of denying responsibility and involvement. In Colombia, "encounter killings" were widely and systematically used; these are extrajudicial killings ostensibly in a fake encounter which links the victim to an enemy group or other violence (Amnesty International 2008, 25). Other subterfuge and cover-ups used by leaders of paramilitary groups and other security forces included orders not to leave more than three victims so that they and their groups could not be made accountable for atrocity crimes (Tate 2007; Bouvier 2009). In contrast, paramilitary groups used what Civico (2016, chap. 3) terms "spectacular violence" in an open display of atrocity crimes. In the region of Antioquia paramilitary groups in cooperation with police and security forces committed massacres and used systematic and "spectacular violence" in order to assure their dominance over the region, and to gain legitimacy among the population. Such open display of atrocity included checkpoints, where local leaders were killed, searches of houses and the murder of targeted victims, as well as establishing headquarters in a hotel in the city, where torture, sexual violence and disappearances were conducted on a regular and systematic basis and with knowledge of the population (Civico 2016, 98–100). In this spectacle of violence, corpses were publicly exposed; it was "a ritual in which power was manifested and expanded" (ibid., 118).

The paradoxes of state-led atrocity

Two paradoxes set atrocity crimes, in particular as state-led or state violence, apart from all other types of crime (Karstedt 2014a, 2014b). The first of these can be termed the "paradox of state and crime". This is the paradox of the state as a guardian against its own crimes and those committed by its own agents: states and governments hardly "police themselves" and prosecute their own agencies (Jorgensen 2009; Ross & Rothe 2008). The second of these paradoxes is the "paradox of state strength and weakness". Modern states have the capacity and muster powerful institutions to provide security to their citizens and equally to decrease the security of targeted groups. It is this Janus-face of contemporary states that shows itself in their capacities to protect the lives, rights and properties of citizens and equally violate, confiscate and destroy them. However, if state institutions lose the capacity to control in particular security forces, and states lose their monopoly of force, they lose the capacity to act as guardians against atrocity crimes. Both state strength and weakness are therefore related to high levels of atrocity crime.

Accountability to citizens and for actions of state agents is the "critical feature" that makes states and governments respect human rights and refrain from violations, and to police their own agents (Mitchell, Carey & Butler 2014). Full-fledged democracies have a comparative advantage as their institutional patterns foster accountability on all levels, where institutions control each other and citizens have the rights and space to control institutions; the rule of law is the lynchpin of accountability structures. In contrast, authoritarian states are characterised by low accountability and in addition highly coercive structures (Karstedt 2013b). Established authoritarian states thus have significantly higher levels of atrocity crime than stable and mature democracies: strong states and regimes thus make good as well as unwilling guardians against atrocity crime in their territory.

Figure 19.3 shows the relationship between regime type and state-led atrocity. Regime types were classified according to the Polity Index, which ranks countries on a scale from –10 (autocratic) to +10 (fully democratic) using a number of formal characteristics of regime change and accountability.[14] Across three decades since 1980 autocratic states in Latin America had twice as high levels of atrocity crimes than the fully democratic countries in the region. However, autocratic regimes share little respect for human rights and high levels of atrocity with mixed, as well as nearly, democratic regimes. As in other global regions, it needs a

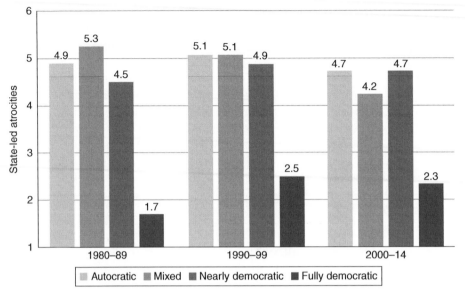

FIGURE 19.3 State-led atrocities and regime type (1980–2014)
Source: Gibney, Cornett and Wood (2015); Marshall and Jaggers (2014); own computation; see Appendix

fully democratic institutional pattern to curb state-led atrocities in Latin America (Bueno de Mesquita, Down & Smith 2005). Compared to the 1980s, Latin American democracies had a considerably worse record of atrocity crimes during the following decades. The gains in terms of reduction of state-led atrocities in the region as shown in Table 19.4 were achieved by the more autocratic and less stable democracies rather than by the full-fledged democracies in Latin America.

Two mechanisms of accountability generate the significantly better record on atrocity crimes of Latin American democracies. These are first, strong rule of law institutions, in particular independent judiciary and non-corruptible justice institutions, and second political participation and interaction between citizens and governments, indicating a stable pattern of representation and mediation between state and society, and the extent of civil society inclusion. As numerous Latin American countries were transitional societies on the road to democracies during this period, both indicators were taken from the Bertelsmann Transformation Index (BTI, Bertelsmann Stiftung 2012) which measures transitions to democracy.[15] As Figures 19.4 and 19.5 show, both indicators of stable and successful patterns of accountability significantly reduce the level of state-led atrocity crimes. Where rule of law institutions were built and consolidated, and where patterns of representation for civil society were firmly in place since 2000, levels of state-led atrocity crimes are lowest.[16] Both indicators represent types of "state strength" which are decisive for the control of state-led atrocity. Strong democratic state institutions are capable of enforcing the rule of law among the agents of the state. Manifold and viable relations between state and civil society, where different groups articulate and promote their interests and where approval of democratic norms and procedures is high, provide the mechanisms for controlling state atrocity "externally" (Ross & Rothe 2008).

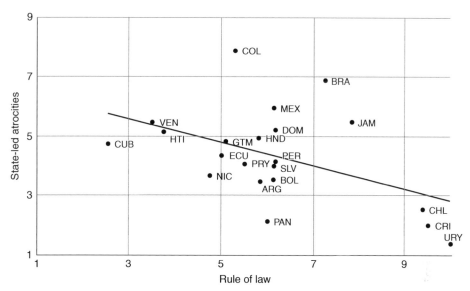

FIGURE 19.4 State-led atrocities and rule of law (2000–14)

R-square: 0.23; $F_{(1, 19)}$ = 5.51*; $p < 0.05$

Source: Gibney, Cornett and Wood (2015); Bertelsmann Stiftung (2014) Bertelsmann Transformation Index 2003–14; own computation; see Appendix

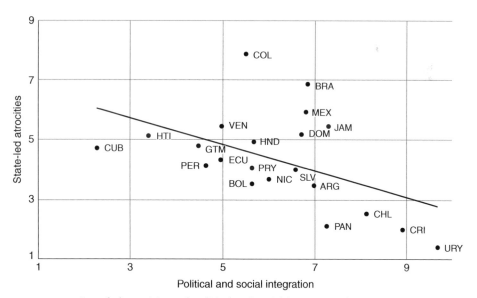

FIGURE 19.5 State-led atrocities and political and social integration (2000–14)

R-square: 0.23; $F_{(1, 19)}$ = 5.73*; $p < 0.05$

Source: Gibney, Cornett and Wood (2015); Bertelsmann Stiftung (2014) Bertelsmann Transformation Index 2003–14; own computation, see Appendix

Colombia is an outlier with high levels of atrocity crimes despite medium level rule of law credentials as well as participation and mediation mechanisms. During this period, as well as before, the country is in the group of "nearly democratic countries" which according to Figure 19.3, share high levels of atrocity violence with autocratic and "mixed regimes". This group includes a high number of countries which recently made the transition to more democratic rule, and are at risk of high instability and weakness of their flagging institutions (Esty et al. 1998). State fragility implies a breakdown of the functioning, authority and legitimacy of core institutions of the state (Rotberg 2004). Powerful groups and elites capture vital institutions and exploit these for their own interests. As the monopoly on force that modern states possess unravels, security forces start to act without control, pursue their own interests or are subject to the demands of powerful groups. True, the monopoly on force offers the opportunities for states, governments and their agents to commit the most atrocious crimes; however, when a fragile state loses control, other groups step in, from armed forces to paramilitary groups, and as has been shown above, this sends state-led atrocity skyrocketing (generally: Jentzsch, Kalyvas & Schubiger 2015). Thus, the 20 most fragile states also have highest levels of state-led atrocities (Karstedt 2015), and the United Nations' Framework (2014, 12) lists "weakness of state structure" as a major risk factor for atrocity crimes. If a state's strength is little restrained by accountability mechanisms, as in authoritarian states, and if weak states are incapable of securing the monopoly of force and thus do not muster the capacity of protecting the human rights and security of their citizens, both will result in high levels of state-led atrocities. This constitutes what has been termed "the paradox of state strength and weakness", and the high levels of atrocity found for autocratic states as well as nearly democratic ones in Latin America are a convincing demonstration.

Acemoglu, Robinson and Santos (2009) show how the loss of the monopoly of force in a near-democracy contributes to the persistence of paramilitary groups. Their in-depth study of different regions of Colombia demonstrates in which ways the continuous presence of paramilitary groups distorts the democratic processes of accountability and ultimately facilitates and unleashes atrocity crimes (see Dugas 2012). As they have strong links to interest groups and socio-economic elites, paramilitaries influence elections as well as the executive, and assist in rigging elections. Policies in areas with a strong paramilitary presence favour these groups rather than benefitting citizens. The ensuing "symbiotic relationships" became evident when more than 60 parliamentarians were investigated, charged and sentenced for their associations with paramilitary groups and their complicity in atrocity crimes (Amnesty International 2008, 19).

The Latin American "justice cascade": an end to impunity?

Latin America is the only global region where state-led atrocity decreased over the past decades and defied the global trend, even if still remaining on high levels (Table 19.4). It is an exemplary case of the impact of regional and international human rights instruments on the level of state-led atrocity crimes, Europe being the other one. After half a century of massive state violence, culminating in genocide, Europe established its regional human rights regime as early as the 1950s, and European states adopted a supra-national legal and normative order that was crucial in targeting state-led atrocity. Presently, Europe is the global region with the lowest level of state-led atrocity crime, and the transitional countries of Eastern and Central Europe have continuously and successfully reduced the level of such violence (Karstedt 2014a).

The contemporary human rights regime and its global and regional supra-national institutions have been established to guard citizens and protect them against atrocity crimes at the hands of states, governments and their agents, as well as against non-state actors, if states and governments fail in their responsibility to "police themselves". According to Kathryn Sikkink (2011) Latin American countries owe the achievements in reducing atrocity crimes to the establishment of the regional Latin American human rights regime at the beginning of the 1980s when the first Latin American countries emerged from a past of massive human rights violations and atrocity crimes. The Inter-American Court of Human Rights, established in 1979 became a major force in addressing atrocity crimes in the dynamic development that Sikkink describes as a "justice cascade" (Sikkink 2011; Sikkink & Kim 2013). This is the "emergence of a decentralised, interactive system of global accountability" (Sikkink 2011, 97), which integrates three streams: international prosecutions; domestic and foreign (i.e. transnational) institutions, and "hard laws" (ibid.) which besides the above-mentioned atrocity law includes the Convention against Torture (1987) and the Inter-American Convention on Forced Disappearances (1996). Between 1979 and 2009, half of all domestic prosecutions for atrocity crimes took place in Latin America, and one-third of all Truth Commissions (Olsen, Payne & Reiter 2010; Hayner 2011; own computations). The 1982 and 1983 Truth Commissions in Bolivia and Argentina were the first in Latin America, and some count them as the first globally (e.g. Sikkink 2011; Wiebelhaus-Brahm 2010).[17] The first domestic trial of a former head of state charged with atrocity crimes including genocide took place in Guatemala in 2013. Even with this record since the 1980s, and a decrease in amnesties, Latin America still has considerable periods of impunity between the commission of atrocity crimes and the start of criminal proceedings (Karstedt 2014c). However, the history of the region gives reason for hope, and provides lessons for the prevention and reduction of atrocity crimes globally.

Acknowledgements

I am grateful to Johanna Schönhöfer, University of Leeds, and Lucy Strang, Cambridge, for research, and to Lorena Rivas, Griffith University, Australia, for Spanish language support. I thank Michael Koch, University of Magdeburg, Germany, for data collection, analysis and graphics. I thank my Colombian students in the 2016 Master Course at the International Institute for the Sociology of Law, Oñati, Spain for sharing invaluable knowledge and experience with me.

Notes

1   Newspaper report 2014: www.elnuevoherald.com/noticias/mundo/america-latina/article3998537.html; 2010: www.elmundo.es/elmundo/2010/02/03/solidaridad/1265214137.html; reports: Human Rights Watch (2005); website 2013: www.kienyke.com/politica/las-atrocidades-de-las-farc/.
2   Simultaneously, the established narrative of the Holocaust was challenged by in-depth studies of local events and the dynamics of mass violence (e.g. Browning 1992; Kühne & Lawson 2011).
3   These include the 1948 Convention on the Prevention and Punishment of the Crime of Genocide, the 1949 Geneva Conventions and their 1977 Additional Protocols, and the 1998 Rome Statute of the International Criminal Court, among other treaties. In the 2005 World Summit Outcome Document on the "Responsibility to Protect" (paragraphs 138 and 139), United Nations member states made a commitment to protect populations from genocide, war crimes, ethnic cleansing and crimes against humanity.

4 At the International Military Tribunal in Nuremberg, legal tools (conspiracy) that had been developed in the fight against organised crime in the United States in the 1930s, were used and refined to capture the organisation of the Holocaust and in particular the involvement of different elites of the Nazi regime. Thus, the SS, SA, the Nazi Party Leadership Corps, but also the High Command of the Armed Forces were charged as "criminal organisations" (Karstedt 2014b).

5 Article 7 of the Rome Statute includes the "crime of apartheid"; Scheffer (2002) includes "terrorism" as an atrocity crime; neither are discussed in this article.

6 See Table 19.A for countries included.

7 See Appendix Measurement for the definition of conflict and non-conflict countries, and Table 19.A for categorisation of countries across three decades.

8 For the construction of the VSI see Appendix Measurement and Karstedt (2012). If homicides are included in the Violent Societies Index, nine out of the 12 most violent societies are Latin American countries, now including Brazil, Mexico and Paraguay (Karstedt 2012). However, due to a lack of reliable data on homicides, this Index includes only a very small number of African countries, and excludes the most violent ones.

9 See Karstedt (2014a) and Appendix Measurement; ibid. for other measurements of atrocity crimes which also take into account non-state actors. As these are highly and significantly correlated (> .60) with the PTS, only the PTS is used.

10 See the Human Security Report Project (2013) on non-state actors and their involvement globally.

11 See Appendix Measurement.

12 See the map at http://geoactivismo.org/2013/09/22/paramilitarismo/ (accessed 14 January 2016).

13 These processes are well documented for the Holocaust and the murder of disabled people in Nazi Germany; for Brazilian torturers: Huggins, Haritos-Fatouros and Zimbardo (2002, chap. 10); for paramilitary groups and sexual violence: Cohen and Nordås (2015).

14 The Polity Index was used; see Appendix Measurement for details. For each decade, a country was ranked according to its mean value/the most frequent category during the period; for country classification see Table 19A.

15 See Appendix Measurement for details of the BTI.

16 The same was found for European states (Karstedt 2014a).

17 Olsen, Payne and Reiter (2010) define the 1971 Truth Commission in Pakistan as the first one, Hayner (2011) the 1974 Commission in Uganda.

References

Acemoglu D., Robinson J.A. & Santos R. 2009. The Monopoly of Violence: Evidence from Colombia. Working Paper 15578. Cambridge, MA: National Bureau of Economic Research

Adams D. 2002. Haiti: How Nation-Building Has Gone Awry. *St Petersburg Times*, 14 January

Alvarez J.E. 1999. Crimes of States/Crimes of Hate: Lessons from Rwanda. *Yale Journal of International Law* 24(2): 365–483

Alvarez J. 2006. Militias and Genocide. *War Crimes, Genocide & Crimes against Humanity* 2: 1–33

Amnesty International 2008. *Leave Us in Peace: Targeting Civilians in Colombia's Internal Armed Conflict.* London: Amnesty International

Arjona A.M. & Kalyvas S.N. 2011. Recruitment into Armed Groups in Colombia: A Survey of Demobilized Fighters. In Guichaoua Y. (ed.) *Understanding Collective Political Violence*, 143–71. London: Palgrave Macmillan

Avilés W. 2006. *Global Capitalism, Democracy and Civil–Military Relations in Colombia.* Albany: State University of New York Press

Bertelsmann Stiftung 2012. *Transformation Index (BTI) of the Bertelsmann Stiftung. Codebook for Country Assessments.* Gütersloh: Bertelsmann Stiftung

Bertelsmann Stiftung (ed.) 2014. *Transformation Index (BTI) 2014.* Gütersloh: Bertelsmann Stiftung

Bouvier V.M. (ed.) 2009. *Colombia: Building Peace in a Time of War.* Washington, DC: United States Institute of Peace Press

Braithwaite J. 2012. Cascades of Violence and a Global Criminology of Place. *Australian & New Zealand Journal of Criminology* 45(3): 299–315

Braithwaite J. 2013. Relational Republican Regulation. *Regulation & Governance* 7(1): 124–44

Brewer Norman S. 2012. A Tale of Two Paramilitaries. *The Latin Americanist* March: 37–56

Browning C. 1992. *Ordinary Men: Police Battalion 101 and the Final Solution in Poland.* New York: HarperCollins

Bueno de Mesquita B., Down G.W. & Smith A. 2005. Thinking Inside the Box: A Closer Look at Democracy and Human Rights. *International Studies Quarterly* 49(3): 439–57

Campbell B.B. & Brenner A.D. 2002. *Death Squads in Global Perspective: Murder with Deniability.* New York: Palgrave Macmillan

Carey S.C., Colaresi M.P. & Mitchell N.J. 2015. Governments, Informal Links to Militias and Accountability. *Journal of Conflict Resolution* 59(5): 850–76

Carey S.C., Mitchell N.J. & Lowe W. 2013. States, the Security Sector, and the Monopoly of Violence: A New Database on Pro-Government Militias. *Journal of Peace Research* 50(2): 249–65

Civico A. 2016. *The Para-State: An Ethnography of Colombia's Death Squads.* Oakland: University of California Press

Cohen D.K. & Nordås R. 2015. Do States Delegate Shameful Violence to Militias? Patterns of Sexual Violence in Recent Armed Conflicts. *Journal of Conflict Resolution* 59(5): 877–98

Crenzel E. 2013. The Narrative of Disappearances in Argentina: The Nunca Mas Report. In Johnson E.A., Salvatore R.D. & Spierenburg P. (eds) *Murder and Violence in Modern Latin America*, 174–92. Chichester: Wiley-Blackwell

De Brouwer A.M., Ku C., Römkens R. & van de Herik L. (eds) 2012. *Sexual Violence as International Crime: Interdisciplinary Approaches.* Antwerp: Intersentia

Des Forges A. 1999. *Leave No One to Tell the Story: Genocide in Rwanda.* New York/Washington: Human Rights Watch

De Waal A. 2007. Reflections on the Difficulties of Defining Darfur's Crisis as Genocide. *Harvard Human Rights Journal* 20: 25–33

Doyle K. 2011. The Atrocity Files. In Grandin G. Levenson D. & Oglesby E. (eds) *The Guatemala Reader: History, Culture, Politics*, 463–69. Durham: Duke University Press

Drumbl M.A. 2007. *Atrocity, Punishment and International Law.* Cambridge: Cambridge University Press

Dugan L. 2012. The Making of the Global Terrorism Database and Its Applicability to Studying the Life Cycles of Terrorist Organizations. In Gadd D., Karstedt S. & Messner S. (eds) *The SAGE Handbook of Criminological Research Methods*, 175–97. Los Angeles & London: SAGE

Dugas J.C. 2012. Paramilitaries and the Economic Origins of Armed Conflict in Colombia. *Latin American Research Review* 47(1): 205–13

Esty D.C., Goldstone J.A., Gurr T.R. & Harff B. et al. 1998. State Failure Task Force Report. Phase II Findings. Working Papers. 31 July 1998, University of Maryland

Ferry S. 2012. *Violentology: A Manual of the Colombian Conflict.* New York: Umbrage

Fujii L.A. 2009. *Killing Neighbors: Webs of Violence in Rwanda.* Ithaca/London: Cornell University Press

Fujii L.A. 2011. Rescuers and Killer-Rescuers during the Rwanda Genocide: Rethinking Standard Categories of Analysis. In Semelin J., Andrieu C. & Gensburger S. (eds) *Resisting Genocide: The Multiple Forms of Rescue*, 145–57. London: Hurst & Company

Genocide Watch 2010. *Genocide and Politicides, and Other Mass Murder since 1945* (www.genocidewatch. org/genocide/genocidespoliticides.html, accessed March 2014)

Gerlach C. 2006. Extremely Violent Societies: An Alternative to the Concept of Genocide. *Journal of Genocide Research* 8(4): 455–71

Gerlach C. 2010. *Extremely Violent Societies: Mass Violence in the Twentieth-Century World.* Cambridge: Cambridge University Press

Gerlach C. & Werth N. 2009. State Violence: Violent Societies. In Geyer M. & Fitzpatrick S. (eds) *Beyond Totalitarianism: Stalinism and Nazism Compared*, 133–79. Cambridge: Cambridge University Press

Gibney M., Cornett L. & Wood R. 2015. *The Political Terror Scale 1976–2014* (www.politicalterrorscale. org/)

Green L. 1995. Living in a State of Fear. In Nordstrom C. & Robben A.C. (eds) *Fieldwork under Fire: Contemporary Studies of Violence and Survival*, 101–34. Berkeley: University of California Press

Gulden T.R. 2002. Spatial and Temporal Patterns in Civil Violence: Guatemala, 1977–1986. *Politics and the Life Sciences* 21(1): 26–36

Gutiérrez Sanín F. 2008. Telling the Difference: Guerrillas and Paramilitaries in the Colombian War. *Politics and Society* 36(1): 3–34

Hagan J. 2009. Prosecuting Ethnic Cleansing and Mass Atrocity in the Former Yugoslavia and Darfur. *Journal of Scandinavian Studies in Criminology and Crime Prevention* 10(1): 26–47

Hagan J. & Kaiser J. 2011. The Displaced and Dispossessed of Darfur: Explaining the Sources of a Continuing State-Led Genocide. *British Journal of Sociology* 62(1): 1–25

Hagan J. & Rymond-Richmond W. 2009a. Criminology Confronts Genocide: Whose Side Are You On? *Theoretical Criminology* 13(4): 503–11

Hagan J. & Rymond-Richmond W. 2009b. *Darfur and the Crime of Genocide*. Cambridge: Cambridge University Press

Hayner P.B. 2011. *Unspeakable Truths: Transitional Justice and the Challenge of Truth Commissions*. New York: Routledge

Higonnet E. (ed.) 2009. *Quiet Genocide: Guatemala 1981–1983*. New Brunswick/London: Transaction Publishers

Hristov J. 2009. *Blood and Capital: The Paramilitarization of Colombia*. Athens: Ohio State University Press

Huggins M. (ed.) 1991. *Vigilantism and the State in Modern Latin America*. New York: Praeger

Huggins M.K., Haritos-Fatouros M. & Zimbardo P.G. 2002. *Violence Workers*. Berkeley: University of California

Human Rights Watch 2005. Las apariencias engañan: La desmovilización de grupos paramilitares en Colombia. *Human Rights Watch* 17(3): 1–14

Human Security Report Project 2011. *Human Security Report 2009/2010*. Simon Fraser University, Canada

Human Security Report Project 2013. *Human Security Report 2012*. Simon Fraser University, Canada

Jentzsch C., Kalyvas S.N. & Schubiger L.I. 2015. Militias in Civil Wars. *Journal of Conflict Resolution* 59(5): 755–69

Jorgensen N. 2009. Impunity and Oversight: When Do Governments Police Themselves. *Journal of Human Rights* 8: 385–404

Kalyvas S.N. 2003. The Ontology of "Political Violence": Action and Identity in Civil Wars. *Perspectives on Politics* 1: 475–94

Kalyvas S.N. 2004. The Paradox of Terrorism in Civil Wars. *Journal of Ethics* 8(1): 97–138

Kalyvas S.N. & Balcells L. 2010. International System and Technologies of Rebellion: How the End of the Cold War Shaped International Conflict. *American Political Science Review* 104(3): 415–29

Karstedt S. 2012. Extremely Violent Societies: Exploring the Dynamics of Violence and Peace. *European Journal of Criminology* 9(5): 499–513

Karstedt S. 2013a. Contextualizing Mass Atrocity Crimes: Moving towards a Relational Approach. *Annual Review of Law and Social Sciences* 9: 383–404

Karstedt S. 2013b. Trusting Authorities: Legitimacy, Trust and Collaboration in Non-Democratic Regimes. In: Tankebe J. & Liebling A. (eds) *Legitimacy and Criminal Justice: An International Exploration*, 127–56. Oxford: Oxford University Press

Karstedt S. 2014a. State Crime: The European Experience. In Body-Gendrot S., Hough M., Kerezsi K. & Lévy R. (eds) *The Routledge Handbook of European Criminology*. Oxford: Routledge, 125–53

Karstedt S. 2014b. The State as Organised Crime Actor. In Paoli L. (ed.) *Oxford Handbook of Organised Crime*, 303–20. Oxford: Oxford University Press, online DOI: 10.1093/oxfordhb/9780199730445.013.031

Karstedt S. 2014c. The End of Impunity? Global Lawmaking and Atrocity Crimes. *Zeitschrift für Rechtssoziologie*, Special Issue on "Sociology of Penal Law", 34(1&2): 125–48

Karstedt S. 2015. Does Democracy Matter? Comparative Perspectives on Violence and Democratic Institutions. *European Journal of Criminology* 12(4): 457–81

Koonings K. & Kruijt D. (eds) 1999. *Societies of Fear: The Legacy of Civil War, Violence and Terror in Latin America*. London: Zed Books

Krain M. 1997. State-Sponsored Mass Murder: The Onset and Severity of Genocides and Politicides. *Journal of Conflict Resolution* 41(3): 331–60

Kramer R., Michalowski R. & Rothe D. 2005. "The Supreme International Crime": How the U.S. War in Iraq Threatens the Rule of Law. *Social Justice* 32(2): 52–81

Kühne T. & Lawson T. 2011. *The Holocaust and Local History*. London: Valentine Mitchell

Leatherman J. 2011. *Sexual Violence and Armed Conflict*. Cambridge: Polity

Letschert R., Haveman R., de Brouwer A.M. & Pemberton A. (eds) 2011. *Victimological Approaches to International Crimes: Africa*. Antwerp: Intersentia

Levene M. 2004. A Dissenting Voice: Or How Current Assumptions of Deterring and Preventing Genocide May Be Looking at the Problem through the Wrong End of the Telescope, Part I. *Journal of Genocide Research* 6(2): 153–66

Marshall M. & Jaggers K. 2014. *Polity IV Project: Political Regime Characteristics and Transitions 1800–2014, Polity Level 1980–2014* (www.systemicpeace.org/polity/polity4.htm)

Mitchell N.J., Carey S.C. & Butler C.K. 2014. The Impact of Pro-Government Militias on Human Rights Violations. *International Interactions* 40(5): 812–36.

Mucha W. 2013. Prone to Conflict, but Resilient to Violence. Why Civil Wars Sometimes Do Not Happen: Insights from Peru and Bolivia. *Journal of Peace, Conflict and Development* 20(1): 96–114

Olsen T.D., Payne L.A. & Reiter A.G. (2010) *Transitional Justice in Balance: Comparing Processes, Weighing Efficacy*. Washington, DC: United States Institute of Peace Press

Osiel M. 2005/1999. *Obeying Orders*. New Brunswick: Transaction Publishers

Osiel M. 2009. *Making Sense of Mass Atrocity*. Cambridge: Cambridge University Press

Restrepo J.A., Spagat M. & Vargas J.F. 2006. The Severity of the Colombian Conflict: Cross-Country Datasets versus New Micro-Data. *Journal of Peace Research* 43(1): 99–115

Richani N. 2007. Caudillos and the Crisis of the Colombian State: Fragmented Sovereignty, the War System and the Privatization of Counterinsurgency in Colombia. *Third World Quarterly* 28(2): 403–17

Ross J.I. & Rothe D. 2008. Ironies of Controlling State Crime. *International Journal of Law, Crime and Justice* 36: 196–210

Rotberg R.I. (ed.) 2004. *When States Fail: Causes and Consequences*. Princeton: Princeton University Press.

Rothenberg D. (ed.) 2012. *Memory of Silence: The Guatemalan Truth Commission Report*. New York: Palgrave Macmillan

Sanford V. 2004. *Buried Secrets: Truth and Human Rights in Guatemala*. New York/London: Palgrave Macmillan

Schabas W.A. 2007. Semantics or Substance? David Scheffer's Welcome Proposal to Strengthen Criminal Accountability for Atrocities. *Genocide Studies and Prevention* 2(1): 31–6

Scheffer D. 2002. The Future of Atrocity Law. *Suffolk Transnational Law Review* 25(3): 389–432

Scheffer D. 2006. Genocide and Atrocity Crimes. *Genocide Studies and Prevention* 1(3): 229–50

Scheffer D. 2007. The Merits of Unifying Terms: "Atrocity Crimes" and "Atrocity Law". *Genocide Studies and Prevention* 2(1): 91–6

Schirmer J. 1998. *The Guatemalan Military Project: A Violence Called Democracy*. Philadelphia: University of Pennsylvania Press

Sherman J.W. 2015. Political Violence in Colombia: Dirty Wars since 1977. *History Compass* 13(9): 454–65

Sikkink K. 2011. *The Justice Cascade*. New York: W.W. Norton

Sikkink K. & Kim H.J. 2013. The Justice Cascade: The Origins and Effectiveness of Prosecutions of Human Rights Violations. *Annual Review of Law and Social Science* 9: 269–85.

Stanton J.A. 2015. Regulating Militias: Government, Militias, and Civilian Targeting in Civil War. *Journal of Conflict Resolution* 59(5): 899–923

Straus S. 2006. *The Order of Genocide: Race, Power and War in Rwanda*. Ithaca/London: Cornell University Press

Straus S. 2011. From Rescue to Violence: Overcoming Local Opposition to Genocide in Rwanda. In Semelin J., Andrieu C. & Gensburger S. (eds) *Resisting Genocide: The Multiple Forms of Rescue*, 331–43. London: Hurst & Company

Straus S. 2016. *Fundamentals of Genocide and Mass Atrocity Prevention*. United States Holocaust Memorial Museum, Washington

Sundberg R., Eck K. & Kreutz J. 2012. Introducing the UCDP Non-State Conflict Dataset. *Journal of Peace Research* 49(2): 351–62

Task Force on the EU Prevention of Mass Atrocities 2013. *The EU and the Prevention of Mass Atrocities: An Assessment of Strength and Weaknesses. Foundation for the International Prevention of Genocide and Mass Atrocities* (www.budapestcentre.eu/Home/, accessed March 2013)

Tate W. 2007. *Counting the Dead: The Culture and Politics of Human Rights Activism in Colombia*. Berkeley: University of California Press

United Nations 2014. *Framework of Analysis for Atrocity Crimes: A Tool for Prevention*. New York: United Nations Office on Genocide Prevention and the Responsibility to Protect

United Nations 2015. *General Assembly: Report of the Secretary General*. A/70/1. New York: UN

Wiebelhaus-Brahm E. 2010. *Truth Commissions and Transitional Societies*. London: Routledge

World Bank 2015. Displacement: 1989–2012. Internal Displacement Monitoring Centre (www.internal-displacement.org/)

Appendix

Measurement

Indicators and measurement are listed in the order as they appear in the text.

Violent Societies Index (VSI)

The VSI comprises originally four different types of violence: interpersonal violence measured as the homicide rate; state violence is measured by the Political Terror Scale (PTS) and includes state-sanctioned killings, torture, disappearances and political imprisonment; terrorist attacks comprise of a count of such attacks in each country; battle deaths in state-based internal armed conflicts measures violence by armed groups. These indicators were standardised according to the highest and lowest country values in each year, and converted into scales ranging from 1–10; the VSI was calculated as the combined value of these components. Here a version of the VSI was used that excluded homicide due to a lack of reliable homicide data and was based on three components – state violence, battle deaths and terrorist attacks.

Political Terror Scale (PTS)

The PTS is combined from two sources, the US State Department and Amnesty International Country Reports; both ranked from 1 (no state violence) to 5 (has expanded to the whole population) and are provided separately (www.politicalterrorscale.org). Both values were added up, and rescaled from 1 to 9. If only one of the two sources is available, the available report is double-weighted. The PTS is highly correlated with Extrajudicial Killings from the CIRI Human Rights Data Project (r = .82) and the Freedom from Political Killings Scale of the Varieties of Democracy Project (r = .63).

Battle-related deaths: state-based conflict 1970–2014

Battle deaths in state-based internal armed conflicts measures violence by armed groups, which include the state as well as paramilitary groups and guerrillas. The count of battle deaths (soldiers and civilians killed in combat) is based solely on military action in two types of conflict: (a) internal armed conflicts that occur between the government of a state and one or more internal opposition group(s) without intervention from other states; (b) internationalised internal armed conflicts that occur between the government of a state and one or more internal opposition group(s) with intervention from other states (secondary parties) on one or both sides. In all cases the low estimate of annual battle fatalities is used.

Battle deaths were retrieved from the Peace Research Institute Oslo PRIO Battle Death Dataset (v3.0) for 1976–88 (www.prio.no/CSCW/Datasets/Armed-Conflict/Battle-Deats/), and from the University of Uppsala Department of Conflict and Peace Research (v5) for 1989–2014 (www.pcr.uu.se/research/ucdp/datasets/ucdp_battle-related_deaths_dataset/); rates per 100,000 were based on population statistics from the World Development Indicators (http://data.worldbank.org/indicator/SP.POP.TOTL).

Terrorist attacks

Terrorist attacks were retrieved from the Global Terrorism Database START, and counted per country and year (www.start.umd.edu/gtd/contact/) (Dugan 2012).

Genocide Watch: Mass atrocities 1945–2009

Genocide Watch (2010) *Genocides, Politicides, and Other Mass Murder since 1945* (www.genocidewatch.org/genocide/genocidespoliticides.html).

Conflict and non-conflict countries

Both state and non-state conflicts were included. The classification was based on annual battle-related deaths (see above); if a country had more than 100 battle-related deaths annually between 1980 and 2014, it was classified as a conflict country. Mexico was counted as a conflict country from 1990 onwards.

Non-state conflict

Non-state conflicts are defined as communal and organised armed conflict where none of the parties is the government of a state. For formally organised groups the recording of battle-related deaths follows the exact same criteria as in the state-based armed conflict category i.e. the warring groups must target representatives of the other formally organised group. For informally organised groups instead of coding deaths according to the state-based criteria the dataset records patterns of violent (lethal) interaction between informally organised groups, regardless of whether the targets are civilians or other armed groups. The dataset includes information on start and end dates, fatality estimates and locations. Countries are coded with a non-state conflict if the count of fatalities in such a conflict exceeds 100; if this falls below this threshold for a brief period (up to five years) but then resumes again, this is counted as one conflict.

UCDP Non-State Conflict Dataset; Uppsala Conflict Data Program (UCDP) 1989–2013.

One-sided violence: state and non-state actors

One-sided violence is the use of armed force by the government of a state or by a formally organised group against civilians which results in at least 25 deaths. Extrajudicial killings in custody are excluded. The dataset lists annual information of intentional attacks on civilians by governments and formally organised armed groups: (a) one-sided non-state actor: total number of fatalities resulting from one-sided violence perpetrated by non-state actors; (b) one-sided state actor: total number of fatalities resulting from one-sided violence perpetrated by state actors in a given year.

Provider: Uppsala Conflict Data Program, 1989–2013
(www.pcr.uu.se/research/ucdp/datasets/ucdp_one-sided_violence_dataset/).

Polity Index regime classification

The Polity Index is based on key components of political and regime structures: the competitiveness of political participation, to which the regulation of participation is added for autocracies; the openness and competitiveness of executive recruitment; and constraints on the chief executive. Each regime type is measured on an additive 11-point scale (ranging from 0 to 10); combining the two scales results in a continuous scale which ranges from −10 indicating full autocracies, to +10, indicating full democracies (for details see www.systemicpeace.org/polity/polity4.htm). This scale is divided into four distinct categories, and countries were classified as "fully democratic" (+10), "nearly democratic (+6 to +9), "mixed" (+5 to −5) and "autocratic" (−6 to −10), using their mean level in the respective period. This classification closely follows the Polity Index classification in *autocracies* (−10 to −6), *anocracies* (−5 to +5) and *democracies* (+6 to +10). See Table 19.A for classification of countries.

Bertelsmann Transformation Index (BTI): rule of law and political and social integration

The BTI analyses and evaluates democracy, market economy and political management for 128 developing and transition countries bi-annually since 2003. It is based on 17 individual criteria which are combined for each of the three dimensions, and ranks the countries on each of the criteria from 1 (low) to 10 (high) (Bertelsmann Stiftung 2012), see www.bertelsmann-stiftung.de/en/our-projects/transformationsindex-bti/.

a)   The Rule of Law Index measures the extent of the separation of powers, independence of the judiciary and guarantees and protection of civil rights.
b)   The Political and Social Integration Index measures the capacity of the party system to articulate and aggregate societal interests, of cooperative associations or interest groups, approval of democracy and the extent of social self-organisation.

TABLE 19.A Appendix countries

Country	Abbreviation	1980–9	1990–9	2000–14
Argentina†	ARG	Mixed/Non-conflict	Nearly democratic/Non-conflict	Nearly democratic/Non-conflict
Bolivia	BOL	Mixed/Non-conflict	Nearly democratic/Non-conflict	Nearly democratic/Non-conflict
Brazil†	BRA	Mixed/Non-conflict	Nearly democratic/Non-conflict	Nearly democratic/Non-conflict
Chile†	CHL	Mixed/Non-conflict	Nearly democratic/Non-conflict	Fully democratic/Non-conflict
Colombia†	COL	Nearly democratic/Conflict	Nearly democratic/Conflict	Nearly democratic/Conflict
Costa Rica	CRI	Fully democratic/Non-conflict	Fully democratic/Non-conflict	Fully democratic/Non-conflict
Cuba†	CUB	Autocratic/Non-conflict	Autocratic/Non-conflict	Autocratic/Non-conflict
Dominican Rep.	DOM	Mixed/Non-conflict	Nearly democratic/Non-conflict	Nearly democratic/Non-conflict
Ecuador	ECU	Nearly democratic/Non-conflict	Nearly democratic/Non-conflict	Mixed/Non-conflict
El Salvador†	SLV	Mixed/Conflict	Nearly democratic/Conflict	Nearly democratic/Conflict
Guatemala†	GTM	Mixed/Conflict	Mixed/Conflict	Nearly democratic/Non-conflict
Guyana	GUY	Autocratic/Non-conflict	Mixed/Non-conflict	Mixed/Non-conflict
Haiti	HTI	Autocratic/Conflict	Mixed/Conflict	Mixed/Conflict
Honduras	HND	Mixed/Non-conflict	Nearly democratic/Non-conflict	Nearly democratic/Non-conflict
Jamaica	JAM	Fully democratic/Non-conflict	Fully democratic/Non-conflict	Nearly democratic/Non-conflict
Mexico†	MEX	Mixed/Non-conflict	Mixed/Conflict	Nearly democratic/Conflict
Nicaragua†	NIC	Mixed/Conflict	Nearly democratic/Conflict	Nearly democratic/Conflict
Panama	PAN	Mixed/Non-conflict	Nearly democratic/Non-conflict	Nearly democratic/Non-conflict
Paraguay†	PRY	Autocratic/Non-conflict	Mixed/Non-conflict	Nearly democratic/Non-conflict
Peru†	PER	Nearly democratic/Conflict	Mixed/Conflict	Nearly democratic/Non-conflict
Suriname	SUR	Mixed/Non-conflict	Mixed/Non-conflict	Mixed/Non-conflict
Trinidad & T.	TTO	Nearly democratic/Non-conflict	Fully democratic/Non-conflict	Fully democratic/Non-conflict
Uruguay	URY	Mixed/Non-conflict	Fully democratic/Non-conflict	Fully democratic/Non-conflict
Venezuela	VEN	Nearly democratic/Conflict	Nearly democratic/Conflict	Mixed/Conflict

† Previous mass atrocities according to Genocide Watch 1945–2009.

20

CRIMES AGAINST HUMANITY AND WAR CRIMES

José Carlos Portella Junior

Introduction

With the end of World War II, a new legal order was created with the emergence of international human rights law, at the core of which is the principle of the protection of human dignity at a global level. The international community, shocked by the unspeakable barbarisms committed during the recent history of national states, especially in the first four decades of the 20th century, has, since then, boosted the humanization of international law, placing humankind under the legal protection of international treaties which have elevated the individual to a position of subject of the international law. These activities, in turn, led to the creation of the International Criminal Tribunals for the purpose of prosecuting the most serious crimes committed against humanity. Thus the Nuremberg and Tokyo Tribunals were set up for the trial of Nazi and Japanese officers responsible for crimes committed against humanity and international peace during World War II. These tribunals definitively determined the *locus standi* of human beings in international law.

Inspired by the post-war tribunals and by the ideal of the universality of human rights, the international community has demanded that international law must guarantee the legal and criminal protection of peace and security of humankind. Since the end of the 1940s, several international treaties have been issued, which require states to adopt measures to prevent serious violations of human rights. The International Tribunals of Nuremberg and Tokyo represent a break within the legal tradition and the emergence of a new paradigm: the international criminal responsibility of individuals for gross violations against the universally protected human rights. From this rupture, massacres administered by states or those perpetrated by non-state organizations (so common in the 19th and 20th centuries) come to be understood by international law as international crimes that offend the peace and security of humankind.

State massacres and the paradigm-shift in the legal tradition: moving from the notion of state sovereignty to legal protection of peace and security of humanity by international criminal law

The historical period between the end of the 19th century and the first half of the 20th century was marked by massacres organized and carried out by agents at the service of state. Atrocious acts committed against civilian populations were not considered crimes because they were justified by the idea of sovereignty (*raison d'État*) or because they were inserted in the perspective of the imperialist expansion of the European powers, who did not see the dominated peoples as deserving any legal protection.

At the end of the 19th century, Brazil was the scene of one massacre administered by the state, at a time of political and social turbulence in the transition from the Monarchy to the Republic (1889–1897). During this period, the federal government, seeking to consolidate the newly inaugurated Republic of Brazil, began to repress any popular and elitist demonstrations that could jeopardize the Republican project and the centralization of power around the Federal Union.

Between 1896 and 1897, President Prudente de Morais sent several military expeditions to end the alleged threat that Antonio Conselheiro and the inhabitants of Canudos (located in the hinterland of Bahia) represented to the Republic. From 10,000 to 35,000 *sertanejos* settled in Canudos between 1883 and 1897, under the political and spiritual leadership of the so-called Blessed Antonio Conselheiro, who sought to maintain a traditional style of life devoted to rural work and the Catholic faith, as opposed to the interests of economic and political elites who wanted to impose on all Brazilian territory the liberal ideals of "progress" and the demobilization of social movements that could challenge the authority of the Federal Union (Levine, 1999).

With the aim of ending the leadership of Antonio Conselheiro and appeasing the autonomy of communities in the interior of Brazil, the federal government ordered the Brazilian army to destroy Canudos and exterminate all inhabitants. It took four military expeditions in Canudos to reach the goal of eliminating the "threat" of the *sertanejos* to the young Republic of Brazil. It is estimated that some 25,000 people were killed (including Antonio Conselheiro himself, who died of illness and hunger) in the fighting between the military and the inhabitants of Canudos. The Army used cannons and machine guns against the *sertanejos* in the expeditions, and destroyed all residences and plantations. Women, children and prisoners of conscience were not spared extermination, the latter for the most part subjected to beheading ("red cravat") (Monteiro, 2009).

One of the most emblematic exterminations administered by state organs was promoted by the German colonial regime in Namibia against the Herero people in 1904 and 1905. As a result of the imperialist expansion of the European powers on the African continent, as ratified by the Berlin Conference (1884–1885), the region of South-West Africa (where Namibia is located today) passed to the dominion of Germany in 1884. Several rebellions occurred during the period of German colonial occupation, but the most significant of them were Namas (1893–1894) and Hereros (1904–1905). In order to end the Herero revolt (which also ended up joining the Namas) against the colonial power, General Lothar von Trotha declared himself supreme commander of the German troops and, with the support of Kaiser Wilhelm II, determined that the Hereros and Namas should be annihilated, including those who did not take part in the acts of rebellion, as well as women and children. Those who were not killed in the battle that became known as the Waterberg Massacre were forced by the troops to head to the Omaheke Desert, where they died of hunger, exhaustion and thirst because the Germans had poisoned the wells. The orders of the military command were clear: to annihilate the enemy, because any negotiation was seen by the German military personnel like a defeat. This doctrine would come to be known in World War I as the "*Schlieffen Plan*".[1]

Following orders from Berlin, after pressure from public opinion to halt the massacre, the few survivors were taken prisoner and taken to concentration camps run by German officials, where they were subjected to forced labor, sexual violence and scientific experiments, as well as suffering with hunger, disease and degrading treatment (Magalhães, 2010).

In the first half of the 20th century, other massacres organized by the state and arising from the colonialist, racial, nationalist and genocidal discourses, imposed a paradigm shift in the legal traditions according to which law should respond to this social phenomenon. Historical events such as the Armenian genocide of the Ottoman Empire in 1915, the Holodomor of 1932–1933 and the crimes committed in Europe during the two Great Wars (including the Jewish Holocaust) imposed on the international community the construction of a new legal framework that could prevent new massacres from happening again and through which justice could be brought to the victims.

By the international architecture of protection of human rights, erected on the rubble of World War II, the individual becomes not only a subject of rights at the international level, but also the bearer of duties before the international community. This new reality means a Copernican revolution in the theory of international law advocated since Hugo Grotius, according to which only state entities could be considered as subjects of international law. Violating international human rights standards, individuals can be brought before the International Courts or even the national courts (through the universal jurisdiction paradigm) to be held accountable for their acts that threaten the peace and security of humankind.

In addition to the international responsibility of the state for violation of international norms that protect human dignity, the emergence of this new paradigm also imposes the individual criminal responsibility of those who, even in the service of the state, violate international norms for the protection of human rights. The first examples of the consolidation of this paradigm were the International Tribunals created to judge the crimes committed on the scene of World War II by the Nazi authorities (the Nuremberg International Military Tribunal, created by the London Charter of 1945) and by the Japanese (the Military International Court for the Far East, established in 1946 and also known as the Tokyo International Court).

As the cases of massacres administered and promoted by the state reveal, the idea of "acts of state", linked to sovereignty, could serve to exclude criminal responsibility from those who act within official capacity, even if these acts were committed in the pursuit of a policy for the disposal of human beings. However, in view of the new paradigm, it would not be necessary to speak of the removal of criminal responsibility, since serious violations of human rights are considered international crimes, which could be tried by International Tribunals or by other states for the application of the universal jurisdiction.

The establishment of the Nuremberg and Tokyo International Courts represents the second phase of the development of international criminal law (Gouveia, 2008). The yearning for the creation of an International Court that could judge the crimes committed against the peace and security of mankind goes back to the 15th century. In the year 1474, an *ad hoc* Tribunal was set up to prosecute crimes against "the laws of God and Humanity" committed by Peter von Hagenbach during his tyrannical administration of the city of Breisach. When he was deposed, von Hagenbach was brought to trial by a coalition of independent states such as Austria and France and cities of the Holy Roman Empire; von Hagenbach was found guilty and sentenced to death.

Notwithstanding this remarkable historical event, the international community defended the creation of courts of this nature again only after World War I. The Treaty of Versailles, of 1919, established the possibility of the creation, by the victorious powers, of an *ad hoc* International Court to judge the crimes of war and against peace, committed under the orders of Kaiser Wilhelm II. However, this Court was never installed, because of the refusal of the Netherlands to hand over the Kaiser to the allied powers.[2]

Other unsuccessful attempts were made by the international community in its yearning to create an International Criminal Court, such as the 1920 Treaty of Sèvres, which sought the judgment of the Turkish–Ottoman authorities for the Armenian genocide (but, in 1927, the Treaty of Lausanne granted amnesty to the Turks), as well as the 1937 Counter-Terrorism Convention, which called for the creation of an International Court for the trial of persons accused of terrorist acts, but did not end up having the necessary number of ratifications to enter into force.

In 1990, the UN International Law Commission presented to the General Assembly, after more than 40 years of discussions, a draft court order to prosecute Crimes against Peace and Security of Mankind. However, the creation of this permanent Court was postponed. At the same time, the international community was confronted with new massacres perpetrated against the civilian population in the Balkans and in Rwanda. In order to allow the punishment of those involved in the massacres, the UN created, through a Security Council resolution and based on the interpretation of Chapter VII of the Charter of the United Nations, the International Tribunal for the Former Yugoslavia (Resolution 808 of 1993) and the International Tribunal for Rwanda (Resolution 955 of 1994), both with retroactive jurisdiction, thus raising the same criticisms for the post-war tribunals (Consigli & Valladares, 1998). Only in 1998 did the ideal of creating a permanent International Court for the prosecution of crimes against the peace and security of mankind come true. The International Criminal Court (ICC) was established by the Rome Statute. With the 60th ratification, the treaty entered into force, and the ICC was definitively established on July 1, 2002.

Notwithstanding the fact that the massacres promoted by the state propelled a rupture with the legal tradition, international criminal law also suffered new demands from the massive violations against human rights committed by non-state organizations from the second half of the 20th century.

The atrocities committed by non-state organizations and the new demand for the legal and criminal protection of the peace and security of humanity

With the end of World War II and the emergence of a new world order, the decolonization movements in Africa and Asia were born, as well as the social insurgency of the subjugated classes against the political power of the traditional elites in Latin America. Inspired by the ideal of the self-determination of peoples, endorsed by international law after World War II, and by anti-colonial discourse, in the 1950s and 1960s came the militias that sought the liberation of African countries which were colonies of Europe. The most well-known were the Popular Liberation Movement of Angola, the Portuguese colony, the Congolese National

Movement (the Congo was under Belgian colonial rule), the Mau Mau (which fought for the liberation of Kenya from British rule) and the Union of the African People of Zimbabwe, which at the time was a British colony.

After the independence of the former European colonies, some groups loyal to the newly inaugurated African governments and groups dissatisfied with the new political elite began to wage fratricidal wars, as in Ethiopia (from 1974 to 1991), in Angola (from 1975 to 2002), Congo-Kinshasa (civil war in progress since 1960) and Uganda (from the early 1980s to the present).

In Latin America, from the 1960s onwards, with the intensification of social inequalities during the dictatorships and authoritarian presidencies that imposed the Washington Consensus against popular interests, there emerged socialist-oriented guerrillas who sought to end autocratic regimes in countries such as Colombia, the Dominican Republic, Guatemala, Nicaragua, El Salvador and Peru.

The Colombian case is certainly one of the most emblematic to illustrate how the guerrillas constituted themselves in organizations (hierarchical, with an organizational politics and well-defined responsibilities) that wanted to dispute political power with the state. In order to do so, these organizations have resorted to violence and committed mass atrocities against the civilian population, disrespecting the legal protection of human dignity imposed by both the national and international law. In the Colombian civil war, that lasted more than 50 years, human rights violations committed by the Revolutionary Forces of Colombia (FARC) against the civilian population included large-scale homicides, forced disappearance of persons, kidnapping, sexual violence, inhumane treatment of prisoners and forced displacement of people from the areas dominated by the guerrillas. An estimated 220,000 people, mostly civilians, were killed in Colombia's civil war and more than 5 million Colombians were forced to leave their homes to escape the brutality of the FARC, the official military forces and paramilitary groups (Colombia, 2013).

In the case of Colombia, in addition to massacres against the civilian population committed by the state security forces in the war against the FARC, paramilitary groups (such as the United Self-Defense Forces of Colombia) also participated in these crimes, with tolerance and sometimes open support from the state. Such was the case of the Mapiripán Massacre (July 1997), in which hundreds of civilians allegedly linked to the FARC were murdered, tortured, disappeared and displaced from their lands (Inter-American Court of Human Rights, 2005).

In Peru, according to the report of the Truth and Reconciliation Commission, more than 11,000 murders and more than 1,500 forced disappearances of people committed by the Shining Path (*Sendero Luminoso* movement) were documented during the "dirty war" between the guerrillas and the Peruvian security forces, between the years from 1980 to 2000 (Peru, 2003). Just as in the Colombian case, paramilitary groups operated freely during the "dirty war" in Peru, which persecuted people allegedly linked to the left-wing guerrillas and even worked under the then President Alberto Fujimori, as was the case with the Colina Group, which participated in the massacres of Barrios Altos (in November 1991) and La Cantuta (in July 1992) (Inter-American Court of Human Rights, 2001, 2006).

In Africa, a number of countries have faced or are facing a bleak scenario of recurrent massacres committed by state security forces and pro- or anti-government militias such as the Democratic Republic of Congo, Somalia, Central African Republic, Mali, Côte d'Ivoire, Eritrea, Libya, among others. In the Democratic Republic of Congo (Congo-Kinshasa) for instance, the militia led by Germain Katanga, known as the Ituri Patriotic Resistance Forces

(FRPI), committed massacres in villages in the Ituri region in 2003. In addition to murdering hundreds of people, members of the FRPI raped women and girls, destroyed homes and looted the assets of the region's residents. Another militia, the Congo Patriotic Liberation Force (FPLC), led by Thomas Lubanga, was responsible for the deaths of 60,000 people between 1999 and 2003, as well as other acts of violence such as rape, mutilation and recruitment of child soldiers (Human Rights Watch, 2014).

Faced with this new form of massacres, promoted by non-state organizations that systematically violate human rights on a large scale, often relying on the impunity of their members – because they exercise dominion over a certain territory, or because they paralyze state institutions with their violence or because they have the tolerance and support of the state – the international criminal law has developed its own legal categories to allow the punishment of those responsible for their acts, that jeopardize the peace and security of humanity (Redress, 2006).

In the first phase of the development of international criminal law, it was intended to impose on state agents the obligation to protect, through international treaties, the peace and security of mankind, creating criteria for assigning individual criminal responsibility to those who, pursuing a policy to commit massive violations of human rights, would perpetrate crimes against humanity. The second phase of international criminal law, however, is marked by a new mass criminality engendered by non-state organizations that now rival state authority, sometimes receiving support from the state itself, and whose members often escape criminal prosecution at the local level. Thus, international criminal law began to contemplate new forms of criminality and criteria of criminal imputation that could account for this new form of crime, avoiding impunity, at least in the normative level, of these grave violations of human rights.[3]

One example of this paradigm shift was the inclusion in the jurisdiction of the International Criminal Tribunal for Rwanda of crimes committed by members of non-state organizations who acted in coordination with Rwandan security forces such as the Hutu militia Interahamwe during the 1994 genocide against the Tutsis (Obote-Odora, 2005). The same was true of the Special Court for Sierra Leone. Following the recommendation of the United Nations Security Council (Resolution 1315/2000), the Government of Sierra Leone and the UN signed in 2002 a treaty to establish a criminal court for the prosecution of crimes against humanity and war crimes committed between 1996 and 2002 by state agents and non-state groups, such as the United Revolutionary Front militias and the Revolutionary Armed Forces Council (Perriello & Wierda, 2006).

At the International Criminal Tribunal for the former Yugoslavia, members of the Republika Srpska, a political organization that began to exercise control in parts of Bosnia and Herzegovina after the collapse of Yugoslavia, were convicted of crimes committed during the Balkan War of Independence, such as the genocide of the Bosnian Muslims in Srebrenica in 1995 (Bosnia and Herzegovina, 2004). Given this new phenomenon of massacres perpetrated by non-state organizations, the juridical-international definition of crimes against humanity and war crimes was remodeled to serve the purpose of guaranteeing greater normative protection to human rights.

International criminal law and the legal definition of international crimes

The legal tradition until the emergence of the international law on human rights and international criminal law after World War II was that the responsibility for breach of international obligations was only of the state, since, according to classical thinking, international law sought to regulate relations between sovereign states (Trindade, 2006). For this reason, international treaties that sought to protect human rights from the second half of the 20th century imposed duties only on states to safeguard human dignity vis-à-vis the international community, thus failing to address citizens' obligations toward the international rights.

International treaties such as the Convention on the Prevention and Punishment of Genocide (1948), the Geneva Conventions (1949) and its 1977 Additional Protocols, the Supplementary Convention for the Abolition of Slavery (1956), the International Convention on the Elimination of All Forms of Racial Discrimination (1965), the Convention for the Suppression and Punishment of Apartheid (1973), the Convention against Torture (1984) and the Inter-American Convention on Forced Disappearance of Persons (1994), *inter alia*, obliged states to prevent and to repress serious violations of human dignity, under penalty of international state responsibility. Although these same treaties served to oblige states to implement social and criminal policies at the local level to combat such practices, they could not substantiate individual responsibility at the international level, even if violations were committed according to a state policy (Schabas, 2002). With the statutes of the Courts of Nuremberg and Tokyo, international law began to impose on individuals the responsibility before the international community, notably for acts that violate the peace and security of mankind. In the statutes of the post-war tribunals, international crimes are defined for the first time: crimes against peace (aggression),[4] war crimes[5] and crimes against humanity.[6] International criminal law is thus inaugurated.

According to Stanislaw Plawsky, international crimes are those that grossly violate human rights recognized in treaties. For this reason, crimes of this nature fall within two branches of law: criminal law aimed at the protection of life, bodily integrity, freedom, in short, the dimensions of human dignity, and public international law, which guarantees justice in international relations (Plawsky, 1972, p. 98). On the need to define proper categories for crimes that jeopardize the peace and security of humanity, Hannah Arendt (2003, p. 295) wrote that:

> Nothing is more pernicious for the understanding of these new crimes, nothing further complicates the emergence of an international criminal code to deal with them than the common illusion that the crime of murder and the crime of genocide are essentially the same, and that the latter, therefore, "is not a new crime properly speaking". The problem with this is that an entirely different order is broken and an entirely different community is violated.

Almost 50 years after the trials in the post-war tribunals, it was only in the 1990s, with the *ad hoc* Tribunals for the former Yugoslavia and Rwanda, that international criminal law brought new legal definitions for war crimes, genocide and crimes against humanity, taking into account these phenomena of macro-criminality, while at the same time referring to the paradigm of individual criminal responsibility.[7] The international community has endorsed the creation of such *ad hoc* Tribunals, via the UN Security Council resolutions and Chapter VII of the United Nations Charter, and special courts with mixed composition (with a panel of international judges nominated by the UN and local national judges), created by bilateral treaties between the United Nations and the country where the trials will be held, such as the Special Court for Sierra Leone[8] and the Extraordinary Chambers in the Courts of Cambodia (created by a 2003 treaty between the Asian country and the UN to try the crimes committed during the bloody Khmer Rouge regime in the 1970s).[9] At the same time, there was also a parallel movement within the UN for the creation of an International Code of Crimes against the Peace and Security of Mankind.

In 1947, the UN General Assembly mandated the organization's International Law Commission to design a draft of an International Criminal Code (Resolution 177(II)/1947). Because of disagreements on the best definition for international crimes, the Commission's work was extended until 1996, when the draft of the Code was then presented to the General Assembly. It was this project that served as a basis, although it underwent many changes during the *travaux préparatoires*, to the 1998 Rome Statute, a treaty that created the first permanent criminal court with international jurisdiction (Bassiouni, 1999).

Encouraged by the spirit of the Courts that preceded it, the International Criminal Court consolidates the paradigm of international individual criminal responsibility, which is expressed in Article 25 of the Rome Statute and has jurisdiction over crimes under the Statute: genocide, crimes against humanity, war crimes and crime of aggression (the latter defined by another treaty, the Kampala Declaration of 2010, which will come into force in 2017). According to Article 6 of the Rome Statute, the crime of genocide was defined as the practice of any of the acts mentioned in its paragraphs, provided that it is intended to destroy, in whole or in part, a national, ethnic, racial or religious group.[10] As regards the crime of genocide, the Rome Statute endorsed the definition already enshrined in the Convention on the Prevention and Punishment of Genocide (1948) and the statutes of the *ad hoc* Tribunals for the former Yugoslavia and Rwanda. It is not required for the configuration of the crime of genocide that there is an organizational policy, although proof of *dolus specialis* is required ("with intent to destroy, in whole or in part"), nor is it required that genocidal acts be committed in connection with an armed conflict, as required by the Nuremberg Tribunal statute.[11]

Genocide can be committed through serious offenses against the physical or mental integrity of members of one group, such as through torture, mutilation and sexual violence (as recognized by the jurisprudence of the International Tribunal for Rwanda). The intentional subjection of group members to conditions that could lead to death (slow death) also constitutes genocide. An example of this type of genocidal act is to keep victims in concentration camps subject to starvation, thirst, disease, severe cold, slavery, medical-scientific experiments, physical violence, etc., in order to lead them to death. It is also a genocidal act, recognized by the Rome Statute, to impose measures to prevent births within the group, such as forced abortions, forced sterilization and enforced pregnancy followed by the expulsion of the victim from the group, and the forcible transfer of children from the group to another group (to be assimilated by another group).

Article 6 of the Rome Statute imposes the protection of national, ethnic, racial and religious groups because of the possibility of sharing cultural, political, social and historical identities among the members of these groups. Although groups may be heterogeneous (with members who, in a fluid way, share more than one identity), the massacres of the 20th century reveal that the plan for the annihilation of a group comes from the dissemination of a discourse that essentializes the differences between groups, disregarding the multifaceted identities of their members, to justify the domination of one over another, as in the genocide of the Tutsis in Rwanda in 1994 (Taylor, 2001).

Article 7 of the Rome Statute lists a number of conducts which, if perpetrated in a systematic or widespread attack on the civilian population, provided the perpetrator is aware of this attack, constitute crimes against humanity. They are (provided for in paragraph 1 of Article

7): (a) homicide; (b) extermination (such as subjecting victims to degrading conditions leading to their death); (c) slavery; (d) deportation or forced displacement of a population; (e) imprisonment or other severe form of deprivation of liberty in violation of fundamental rules of international law; (f) torture; (g) sexual violence, sexual slavery, forced prostitution, forced pregnancy, forced sterilization or any other form of sexual violence of comparable gravity; (h) persecution of a politically, racially, nationally, ethnically, culturally, religiously or gender-sensitive group or collectivity, or other criteria universally recognized as unacceptable in international law (differentiated from genocide since *dolus specialis* is not required in the "intention to destroy, in whole or in part"); (i) forced disappearance of persons; (j) apartheid; and (k) other inhuman acts of a similar character which intentionally cause great suffering or seriously affect physical integrity or physical or mental health (e.g. forced marriages between girls and women of an ethnic group with men of another ethnic group) (Human Rights Watch, 1999).

For the characterization of crimes against humanity, it is not necessary to link the attack to an armed conflict, so that these crimes can be committed in times of peace (contrary to the definition of the Nuremberg Tribunal). The Rome Statute requires as an element of context the presence of an "attack against a civilian population" and understands this "attack" as "any conduct involving the multiple practice of acts referred to in paragraph 1 against a civilian population, pursuant to or in furtherance of a state or organizational policy to commit such attack" (Article 7(2)(a)). The context element of the international crimes (attack against a civilian population) differentiates in severity from crimes of homicide or torture committed as part of state policy or an organization from those committed isolatedly (which may even constitute human rights violations, but do not characterize international crimes).[12] It is the perpetration of a systematic or widespread attack against the civilian population, required by the chapeau of Article 7, which represents the violation of the legal protection of human rights imposed by international law, putting at risk the security of mankind. According to the Rome Statute, the attack on the civilian population must be governed by a state policy or that of a non-state organization, since it is this policy that allows crimes to be committed on a large scale and can at times guarantee impunity of its perpetrators at the domestic level.[13]

Article 8 of the Rome Statute defines war crimes, which may be committed in both international and non-international armed conflicts. According to international humanitarian law (a branch of international law regulating conduct in war),[14] international armed conflicts are those in which two or more states are belligerent parties, it being sufficient for their characterization that one of the states employs armed force (of its own or has effective control over an armed group operating in a foreign territory) against another state, even if there is no military resistance from the attacked state and even if the state of war is not officially recognized (Gasser, 1993).

According to Article 3, common to the 1949 Geneva Conventions and Article 1 of Additional Protocol II of 1977, non-international armed conflict is that established in the territory of a state, between government forces and non-governmental armed groups, or only between these groups, without control of one of the groups by a foreign state (this is the case of civil war between state forces and militias or guerrillas, or between these groups), except for riots or internal tensions that do not constitute a prolonged armed conflict.[15] Thus, it is necessary for the non-state groups involved in the conflict to be "belligerent parties", which means that they must have regular and organized armed forces, that is, structured like official military forces, with a defined chain of command and with ability to maintain military operations (Schindler, 1979).

Article 8 of the Statute of Rome defines war crimes as harmful conduct directed at persons and property protected by the Geneva Conventions of 1949 and the two Additional Protocols of 1977 (such as civilians who may be wounded, sick, shipwrecked persons, medical personnel, sanitary and humanitarian assistance, prisoners of war and those who have laid down arms, as well as against goods for strictly civilian use or for religious, educational and scientific purposes, cultural and natural goods, and goods used for humanitarian assistance). Among the conduct defined in the Rome Statute as war crimes, when addressed to persons and property protected by international humanitarian law are: malicious homicide; torture and other cruel or degrading treatment; serious offenses against bodily and mental integrity; looting and destruction of property without necessity for military operations; compelling the prisoner of war to serve the enemy military; deprivation under inhuman conditions of the prisoner of war; deportation; illegal deprivation of liberty; hostage-taking; intentionally directing attacks on the civilian population or those who are out of combat; intentionally directing attacks on civilian assets, such as goods that are not military objectives; intentionally attacking personnel, facilities, equipment, units or vehicles engaged in a peacekeeping or humanitarian assistance mission, in accordance with the Charter of the United Nations, whenever they are entitled to the protection afforded to civilians or to civilian objects by the international law applicable to armed conflicts.

Also criminalized are insidious, cruel, indiscriminate and disproportionate methods of war that can cause serious harm to civilians or excessive damage to protected assets, such as: intentionally launching an attack knowing that it will cause accidental loss of human life or injury to the population; damages to civilian assets or extensive, long-term and severe damage to the environment that is clearly excessive in relation to the concrete and direct global military advantage anticipated (such as the use of Agent Orange, atomic bomb attack and shooting at indiscriminate targets with drones); attack or bombing by any means, cities, villages, dwellings or buildings that are not defended and which are not military objectives; killing or injuring a combatant who has laid down weapons or who, having no more means to defend himself, has unconditionally surrendered; improper use of a flag of truce, the national flag, military insignia or the uniform of the enemy or of the United Nations, as well as the distinctive emblems of the Geneva Conventions, thereby causing death or serious injury; direct or indirect transfer by an occupying power of part of its civilian population to the territory it occupies or the deportation or transfer of all or part of the population of the occupied territory within or outside that territory; intentionally directing attacks on buildings dedicated to religious worship, education, the arts, science or charity, historical monuments, hospitals and places where the sick and wounded are grouped, other than for military purposes; subjecting persons who are under the control of a belligerent party to physical mutilation or to any type of medical or scientific experiment which is not motivated by medical, dental or hospital treatment or is not carried out in the interest of such persons and which causes death or seriously endangers their health; killing or wounding through treason people of that nation or belonging to the enemy army; declaring that no quarter will be given; destroying or seizing enemy property, unless such destruction or seizure is imperatively determined by the needs of war; declaring the rights and actions of the nationals of the enemy party to be abolished, suspended or inadmissible, to compel the nationals of the enemy party to participate in warlike operations directed against his own country, even if they have been in the service of that belligerent party before the beginning of war; plundering a city or a locality, even when taken by assault; using poison or poisoned weapons; using asphyxiating, toxic or other gases or any liquid, material or similar device; using bullets that expand or flatten easily inside the human body, such as hard shell bullets that do not fully cover the inside or have incisions; using weapons, projectiles, materials and methods of combat which, by their very nature, inflict superfluous injury or unnecessary suffering or have indiscriminate effects (such as the use of landmines and incendiary bombs), in violation of international law applicable to armed conflict; outraging the dignity of the person, in particular through humiliating and degrading treatment; committing acts of rape, sexual slavery, forced prostitution, forced pregnancy, forced sterilization and any other form of sexual violence which also constitutes a serious breach of the Geneva Conventions; using the presence of civilians or other protected persons to prevent military points, zones or forces being subjected to military operations (the so-called human shields); directing attacks on buildings, equipment, medical units and vehicles, as well as personnel using the distinctive emblems of the Geneva Conventions, in accordance with international law; deliberately provoke the starvation of the civilian population as a method of warfare, depriving it of the goods necessary for its survival, and even preventing the sending of aid, as provided for in the Geneva Conventions; recruiting or enlisting soldiers who are under 15 years of age (child soldiers) into the national armed forces or using them to participate actively in hostilities.[16]

What is sought with the criminalization of certain conducts on the battlefield is to avoid the annihilation of those identified as enemies, when the belligerent part of the war can suspend the legal protection of human rights in order to deny the enemies the protection of human dignity. From Nuremberg and Tokyo, there is a legal-criminal evolution to adapt definitions of war crimes to contemporary methods of combat, seeking to alleviate the damage caused to those who live the tragic experience of war.

Since the end of the 19th century, wars have incorporated methods of large-scale destruction and unprecedented cruelty, fueled by the industrial and technological revolution (Hobsbawn, 1995), such as the use of mustard gas in World War I, the use of incendiary bombs during World War II and the US atomic bombing of the Japanese population, the use of Agent Orange by the United States in the Vietnam War, the use of sarin gas by Iraq in the Iran–Iraq war and the use of antipersonnel mines by the FARC in the Colombian civil war, although non-technological methods continued to be used systematically, such as torture by French prisoner officers during the Algerian war of independence, the use of sexual violence as a method of warfare during the Balkan conflict and the use of child soldiers by militias in the civil war in Sierra Leone. The criminal prohibition of these methods of combat is justified by the international protection of human rights, which cannot be suspended for warlike reasons or by the absolute will of those who undertake acts of belligerence (using cruel, disproportionate and indiscriminate methods that can impose physical and psychological damages to those who are out of combat). Genocide, crimes against humanity and war crimes are subject to the jurisdiction of the International Courts, such as the ICC. However, treaties dealing with international crimes (such as the Rome Statute) also consolidate states' obligation to prosecute or extradite those who have committed crimes against human rights, as a result of the so-called *aut dedere aut judicare* principle.[17] In the case of an obligation under customary international law, states cannot invoke domestic reasons to avoid it, such as the granting of asylum, refuge or amnesty, or the absence of a prior law criminalizing international crimes. In view of this obligation arising from international *jus cogens*, national courts must, in accordance with their international laws and treaties, judge the perpetrator of the most serious crimes against human rights, even if the crime did not take place in the territory of the state that exercises jurisdiction, and even if the accused or the victim is not its national. In order to do this, the doctrine applied is that of universal repressive jurisdiction or of universal jurisdiction, whose objective is to avoid the so-called "safe haven" for these criminals.

It is a matter of normative construction of international crimes that the state is obliged to hold accountable all perpetrators who commit serious violations of human rights, obliging other states and the International Courts to exercise criminal jurisdiction over such crimes in case of lack of political will or incapacity of the state which should primarily exercise it, because the legal protection of human rights does not depend on the will or capacity of the state (it is an imperative norm). In several emblematic cases, perpetrators of international crimes escaped criminal justice and were able, for political reasons, to ensure *de facto* impunity. However, international criminal law has made it possible to hold responsible those who committed human rights violations on a large scale, whether through International Tribunals or before national courts.

Former Serbian President Slobodan Milosevic was accused of committing genocide, crimes against humanity and war crimes during the Balkan War in the early 1990s at the International Tribunal for the former Yugoslavia.[18] In 1998 Jean Kambanda, the Prime Minister of Rwanda at the time of the 1994 Tutsi genocide, was sentenced to life imprisonment for crimes of genocide and crimes against humanity by the International Criminal Tribunal for Rwanda.

In the ICC, Sudan's current President, Omar al-Bashir, was accused of genocide, crimes against humanity and war crimes committed in the Darfur region. In addition, an ICC arrest warrant has been issued against him, pending compliance since 2005. Also in the ICC, former Ivorian President Laurent Gbagbo has been awaiting his trial since 2011 for crimes against humanity committed against groups that opposed his government.

In 2012, Thomas Lubanga was sentenced to 14 years in prison by the ICC for war crimes ordered by him while he was head of the Patriotic Forces for the Liberation of Congo militia during the civil war of the Democratic Republic of Congo. In 2014, the ICC condemned another militia chief who served in the DR Congo civil war. Germain Katanga was sentenced to 12 years in prison for crimes against humanity and war crimes.

In the Special Court for Sierra Leone, Charles Taylor, the former president of Liberia, was sentenced to 50 years in prison for committing crimes against humanity and war crimes during the Sierra Leonean civil war. Taylor was convicted of exercising control over one of the militias fighting the central government of Sierra Leone and for committing international crimes.

Khieu Samphan, the former president of Cambodia during the tyrannical regime of the Khmer Rouge in the 1970s, was sentenced in 2014 by the Extraordinary Chambers in the Courts of Cambodia for crimes against humanity. Khieu is awaiting a verdict on other charges of genocide and war crimes.

At the national level, stimulated by the development of international criminal law, attempts have been made to hold former heads of state accountable for crimes against humanity as provided in universal jurisdiction: examples are the Augusto Pinochet case and the Hissene Habré case.[19] In the same vein, in the face of obligations contracted with the international community and recognized by the Inter-American Court of Human Rights, national Courts have brought to trial crimes against human rights committed by former heads of state against their own citizens. In Peru, former Peruvian President Alberto Fujimori was tried and sentenced to 25 years in prison for crimes against humanity (for having ordered the Massacres of Barrios Altos and La Cantuta) in 2009. In Argentina, former Argentine dictators Jorge Rafael Videla and Reynaldo Bignone were sentenced in 2010 to life imprisonment for crimes against humanity committed during the military dictatorship. In Uruguay, the Justice condemned to 30 years of prison the former Uruguayan dictator Juan María Bordaberry for crimes against humanity committed during the military regime. In East Timor, former militia commander José Cardoso Ferreira was sentenced in 2003 to 12 years in prison for crimes against humanity committed during the Indonesian war of independence in 1999.

The foregoing examples demonstrate how international criminal law imposes the responsibility of the perpetrators of crimes against human rights, extending the possibility of judging international crimes beyond national jurisdiction. From this perspective, the concept of sovereignty, which, after the emergence of international human rights law, must be seen by the lens of the principle of *ex parte populi*, and not by the lens of *ex parte principis*, is to be re-dimensioned. The legal safeguard of the human status must not anymore find barriers in the "reason of state", but rather it must be projected beyond national borders, guaranteeing its protection at a global level (Lafer, 2003).

Final considerations

Massacres and wars of total destruction deny legal and international protection of human rights, exposing human beings to the irrepressible violence of power relations. International criminal law, when defining the conducts that constitutes international crimes, represents a break with the legal tradition, putting the human being at the center of the international legal order, elevating it to the condition of subject of rights and imposing the legal duty of protection of human dignity. If, at the national level, massacres can pass unpunished, due to sociopolitical or normative factors, by the perspective of the international criminal law, the international community undertakes to repress crimes against human rights, whether through the exercise of jurisdiction by International Courts or by the universal jurisdiction of another state. The 1998 Rome Statute is the main treaty defining international crimes. While the Statute is able to encompass human rights abuses to a certain extent, new forms of macro-criminality in the 21st century pose the challenge for the international community to define them normatively and to make effective the protection of the peace and security of mankind.

In the 20th century international criminal law developed from the social phenomenon of massacres conducted by state or non-state actors. Today the peace and security of humankind must be safeguarded against new threats: for example, the use of inanimate weapons in war (such as robots equipped with missiles); the privatization of military forces, the use of drones that do not discriminate against civilian combatants; methods of cyberwar that collapse vital services to civilian population (such as distribution of energy or water); and serious human rights violations committed by corporations.

Notes

1   Arthur von Schlieffen, chief of the military Germanic cabinet between 1891 and 1906, was one of the idealizers of the so-called "annihilation battle", which means the total destruction of the enemy as a means to achieve victory (Hull, 2005).

2   However, under pressure from the victorious powers, Germany judged its authorities at the Supreme Court of Leipzig in 1921, but of 900 suspects only 12 were tried for war crimes and only six were convicted (Zappalà, 2007).

3 Certainly, the implementation of adequate legislation is not enough to end impunity for international crimes, but it is also necessary to develop public policies aimed at preventing the occurrence of such crimes, as well as the capacity of criminal prosecution agencies to better specific challenges in repressing such crimes. On the factors that must be faced to avoid impunity for international crimes, both normatively and socially, see Ambos (1999).

4 According to Article 6(a) of the Statute of the Nuremberg Tribunal, it is defined as the planning, preparation, initiation or engagement in war of aggression, or a war in violation of international treaties, agreements or warranties, or participation in a common plan or conspiracy to carry out any of the foregoing acts.

5 "Violations of the laws and customs of war include, but are not limited to, murder, ill-treatment or deportation to slave labor or for any other purpose of the civilian population or in the occupied territories, murder or mistreatment of prisoners of war, or people on the seas, hostage-taking, looting public or private property, arbitrary destruction of cities, towns, or villages, or devastation not justified by military necessity" (Article 6(b) of the Statute of the Nuremberg Tribunal).

6 "Murder, extermination, slavery, deportation and other inhuman acts committed against any civilian population, or persecutions for political, racial or religious reasons, when such acts are committed or such persecutions are carried out in connection with any crime against peace or any war crime" (Article 6(c) of the Statute of the Nuremberg Tribunal).

7 See Articles 2, 3, 4 and 5 of the Statute of the International Criminal Tribunal for the Former Yugoslavia (UN Security Council Resolution 827/1993) and Articles 2, 3 and 4 of the Statute of the International Criminal Tribunal for Rwanda (UN Security Council Resolution 995/1994).

8 Under the Statute of the Special Court for Sierra Leone, war crimes and crimes against humanity committed during the civil war that began in 1996 and ended in 2002 should be tried by the court.

9 Under the Statute of the Extraordinary Chambers in the Courts of Cambodia, war crimes, crimes against humanity and genocide committed between 1975 and 1979 are under jurisdiction of the Court.

10 (a) To kill members of the group; (b) serious offenses to the physical or mental integrity of members of the group; (c) intentional subjection of the group to living conditions with a view to their total or partial physical destruction; (d) imposition of measures to prevent births within the group; (e) forcibly transferring children from the group to another group.

11 Genocide, at the Nuremberg trials, was regarded as a form of crime against humanity. It was only in 1948, with the Convention for the Prevention and Punishment of Genocide, that genocide became a legal category of its own.

12 In general, isolated acts, committed by state or non-state actors, for example, do not meet the required degree of gravity for crimes against humanity, notably because, as a rule, they are punished under domestic laws by national courts, not endangering the peace and security of mankind.

13 In the case of perpetrators linked to the state bureaucracy, impunity can be attributed to the fact that they dominate the judicial institutions, have the political support of governments of other states, enjoy immunities as agents of the state, or because they are granted amnesty in the transition of regime. Perpetrators linked to non-state organizations can guarantee their impunity by dominating the official institutions through violence, by winning victory over the current regime or by having been granted amnesty as a condition for ceasing attacks.

14 The International Humanitarian Law is a normative branch that aims to avoid total war or annihilation, guaranteeing the protection of human rights even in the battle scenario. It is ruled by the International Conventions of the Hague – Conventions of 1904 and 1907, the Geneva Conventions of 1949 and their Additional Protocols of 1977, the Treaty on Non-Proliferation of Nuclear Weapons, the Convention for the Prohibition of Chemical Weapons 1993, the 1997 Anti-Personnel Mine Ban Convention and the 2008 Cluster Munitions Convention.

15 The same definition of non-international armed conflict is adopted by Article 8.2f of the Rome Statute.

16 In 2010, during the Rome Statute review conference (Kampala Declaration), additional acts considered war crimes and non-international armed conflicts were added, similar to those already criminalized for international armed conflicts, such as the use of poisonous and chemical weapons.

17 In relation to amnesty laws, international law has accepted them as legitimate only if they are accompanied by other judicial or extrajudicial mechanisms of accountability, are conditioned to the previous investigation of the facts, do not address those most responsible for crimes (notably those who did and planned the crimes); do not include the most serious crimes (such as torture, forced disappearance of persons, murder and sexual violence). Regarding the possibility of amnesty laws being considered legitimate before International Law, aiming at the search for national reconciliation and without neglecting the rights of the victims, see Ambos (2009) and Benvenuti (2014).

18 Slobodan Milosevic was not tried, since he died in prison.

19 In 1998, former Chilean dictator Pinochet was put under house arrest in the United Kingdom after Spain asked for his extradition to respond to crimes against humanity, but the request was denied because of his delicate state of health. The former dictator of Chad Hissene Habré was arrested in Senegal, where he was in exile, on the basis of a request for extradition from Belgium to respond to crimes against humanity. Instead of extraditing him, Senegal decided that it would hold the trial by setting up a special court with the support of the African Union. The trial began in 2015.

References

Ambos, K. (1999) "Impunidad, derechos humanos y derecho penal internacional" in *Nueva Sociedad*, Issue 161, pp. 86–102.

Ambos, K. (2009) "El marco jurídico de la justicia de transición" in K. Ambos, E. Malarino & G. Elsner (eds) *Justicia de transición: informesde América Latina, Alemania, Italia y España*. Montevideo: Fundación Konrad Adenauer, Oficina Uruguay, pp. 23–129.

Arendt, H. (2003) *Eichmann em Jerusalém: um relato sobre a banalidade do mal*. São Paulo: Companhia das Letras.

Bassiouni, M. (1999) *Crimes against Humanity in International Criminal Law*. The Hague: Kluwer Law International.

Benvenuti, P. (2014) "Transitional Justice and Impunity" in *International Studies Journal*, Vol. 1, Issue 1, pp. 119–124.

Bosnia and Herzegovina (2004) *The Events in and around Srebrenica between 10th and 19th July 1995*. Banja Luka: Commission for Investigation.

Colombia. Centro Nacional de Memória Histórica (2013) *¡Basta ya! Colombia: memoriais de guerra y dignidad*. Bogotá: Centro de Memória Histórica.

Consigli, J. & Valladares, G. (1998) "Los tribunales internacionales para ex Yugoslavia y Ruanda, precursores necesarios de la Corte Penal Internacional" in *Revista Jurídica de Buenos Aires*, pp. 55–81.

Gasser, H. (1993) "International Humanitarian Law: An Introduction" in H. Haug (ed.) *Humanity for All: The International Red Cross and Red Crescent Movement*. Berna: Paul Haupt Publishers.

Gouveia, J. (2008) *Direito Internacional Penal: uma perspectiva dogmático-crítica*. Coimbra: Almedina.

Hobsbawn, E. (1995) *Era dos Extremos: o breve século XX (1914–1991)*. São Paulo: Companhia das Letras.

Hull, I. (2005) "The Military Campaign in German Southwest Africa, 1904–1907" in *German Historical Institute Bulletin*, Issue 27, pp. 39–44.

Human Rights Watch (1999) *Human Rights Abuses Committed by RUF Rebels*. Available at: www.hrw.org/reports/1999/sierra/SIERLE99-03.htm (accessed 22 September 2015).

Human Rights Watch (2014) *ICC: Congolese Rebel Leader Found Guilty*. Available at: www.hrw.org/news/2014/03/07/icc-congolese-rebel-leader-found-guilty (accessed 20 September 2015).

Inter-American Court of Human Rights (2001) *"Barrios Altos" v. Peru*, 14 March 2001. Available at: www.corteidh.or.cr/docs/casos/articulos/Seriec_75_esp.pdf (accessed 12 September 2015).

Inter-American Court of Human Rights (2005) *"Mapiripán Massacre" v. Colombia*, 15 September 2005. Available at: www.corteidh.or.cr/docs/casos/articulos/seriec_134_ing.pdf (accessed 12 September 2015).

Inter-American Court of Human Rights (2006) *"La Cantuta" v. Peru*, 29 November 2006. Available at: www.corteidh.or.cr/docs/casos/articulos/seriec_162_esp.pdf (accessed 12 September 2015).

Lafer, C. (2003) *A reconstrução dos direitos humanos: um diálogo com o pensamento de Hannah Arendt*. São Paulo: Companhia das Letras.

Levine, R. (1999) "The Canudos Massacre, a Hundred Years on" in M. Levene & P. Roberts (eds) *The Massacre in History*. New York: Berghahn Books, pp. 185–222.

Magalhães, M. (2010) "Homens e mulheres falando em genocídio: a experiência imperialista alemã (1884–1945)" in *História: Questões & Debates*, Issue 52, pp. 149–171.

Monteiro, V. (2009) "Canudos: guerras de memória" in *Revista Mosaico*, Vol. 1, Issue 1, pp. 83–93.

Obote-Odora, A. (2005) "Rape and Sexual Violence in International Law: ICTR Contribution" in *New England Journal of International and Comparative Law*, Vol. 12, pp. 135–159.

Perriello, T. & Wierda, M. (2006) *The Special Court for Sierra Leone under Scrutiny*. New York: International Center for Transitional Justice.

Peru (2003) *Informe final de la comisión de la verdad y reconciliación*. Lima: Comisión de la verdad y reconciliación.

Plawsky, S. (1972) *Étude des príncipes fundamentaux du droit international penal*. Paris: Libraire Générale de Droit et de Jurisprudence.

Redress (2006) *Not Only the State: Torture by Non-State Actors*. London: Redress Trust.

Schabas, W. (2002) "Punishment of Non-State Actors in Non-International Armed Conflict" in *Fordham International Law Journal*, Vol. 26, pp. 907–933.

Schindler, D. (1979) "The Different Types of Armed Conflicts According to the Geneva Conventions and Protocols" in *Recueil des Cours de Academie de Droit*, Vol. 163, pp. 125–159.

Taylor, C. (2001) *Sacrifice as Terror: The Rwandan Genocide of 1994*. Oxford: Berg Publishers.

Trindade, A. (2006) *A humanização do Direito Internacional*. Belo Horizonte: Del Rey.

Zappalà, S. (2007) *La justice pénale internationale*. Paris: Montchrestien.

21

THE CHALLENGE OF STATE CRIME

Penny Green

Introduction

When I first wrote this chapter, it had become clear that the Myanmar state's long persecution of its Rohingya ethnic minority had entered a new phase. A 12-month study, we conducted, investigating the nature of persecution against the Rohingya[1] concluded that the Myanmar state's crimes constituted genocidal practice (Green et al. 2015). Our research, and that of others[2] confirmed systematic, widespread, and ongoing violations, including: institutional discrimination, torture, sexual violence, arbitrary detention, destruction of communities, apartheid structures of segregation, targeted population control, mass killings, land confiscation, forced labour, denial of citizenship and identity, severe restrictions on freedom of movement and access to healthcare, food, education, and livelihood opportunities; and state-sanctioned campaigns of religious hatred. What we witnessed, documented, and analysed was the culmination of a long history of institutional and organised persecution precisely paralleling the trajectory of other acknowledged genocides.

Our own investigation conceptualised genocide as a process, building over a period of years, involving an escalation in the dehumanisation and persecution of the target group (Feierstein 2014). The Rohingya have been stigmatised as 'illegal immigrants', 'Bengalis', and 'terrorists', deserving of no place in Myanmar society. Following organised and state sanctioned violence in 2012, the Rohingya from Sittwe[3] and surrounding areas were rounded up into detention camps, where they have since remained isolated and impoverished. The Rohingya have been persecuted through disenfranchisement as well as violent and psychological intimidation. Our evidence demonstrated, without any doubt, that the Rohingya are currently experiencing the genocidal stage of systematic weakening wherein state strategies denying access to healthcare, livelihood, food and civic life render a population so physically and psychologically diminished that they are unable to engage in purposeful life.

In October 2016 repression against the Rohingya intensified. As I write now (January 2017), credible evidence of widespread killings, arbitrary detention, mass rape, collective punishment, arson and village clearances – committed by security forces – continues to emerge from Northern Rakhine State (NRS),[4] home to approximately 1.1 million Rohingya.

On-the-ground reports reveal a consistent and chilling picture of a trapped, terrified, and desperate Rohingya community. Tens of thousands have fled across the border into Bangladesh. Reports of abuse are consistent with historical practices of state repression and violence in the region. Evidence suggests a brutal and indiscriminate new phase of state violence is taking place. These events mark a disturbing, yet entirely predictable pattern in the genocidal process. Genocide begins by reducing the target group's strength and undermining moral empathy for the victims, before leading to more violent forms of persecution and eventually, particularly if perpetrators of violence are not held to account, mass killings (Feirestein 2014).

The election of Suu Kyi's National League for Democracy (NLD) in 2015 elicited much global optimism. The Nobel peace laureate has, however, entrenched the persecution of the Rohingya; she has demanded foreign governments refrain from using the term 'Rohingya', and the Myanmar government's public statements continue to simultaneously demonise and deny the existence of the Rohingya identity. An opinion piece which appeared in the 1 November issue of the state run *Global New Light of Myanmar* implicitly referred to the Rohingya as a 'terrorist' 'foreign' threat in NRS and a 'thorn which must be removed'. Myanmar's own Human Rights Commission has refused to acknowledge the existence of the victim group and the domestic criminal justice process is itself being used as an instrument of persecution.

Denial, as Stanley Cohen (1993, 2001) demonstrated, is an enduring feature of state crime practice. Rather than taking allegations of security force abuse seriously, Suu Kyi's government has adopted military dictatorship-era tactics of blanket denial, an absolute ban on international observation, severe limitations on humanitarian access within the region, the muzzling of the press, and the 'blacklisting' and deportation of human rights activists.[5]

Suu Kyi's self-appointed spokesman, U Zaw Htay has claimed that reports of genocide and violence in Rakhine state are part of a conspiracy orchestrated by human rights lobby groups to undermine the state, while the Myanmar military's 'True News Information Team' has deflected blame for the killings, rapes, and village destruction onto its Rohingya victims.[6] The release by Human Rights Watch of satellite imagery confirming 'massive' fire-related destruction across three villages in Maungdaw prompted the Presidential Office headline, 'Military's information team refutes fabrication about massive destruction in Rakhine.' Officials continue to insist that Muslim residents are burning their own houses down, in an attempt to 'tarnish the image of the troops'.[7] Though the government has admitted that violence has taken place, including the killing of Muslims, it insists its military 'clearance operations' are aimed at 'violent attackers' armed with 'machetes' and 'wooden clubs'.[8]

Government officials discredit the veracity of international reports, duplicitously challenging critics to observe the 'actual situation on the ground' before publishing, while simultaneously denying all international attempts to access the region.

I begin with this example not only because much of my recent research has been conducted on the Myanmar state, nor because it brings what is traditionally understood as the world of international relations and genocide studies, so acutely into the domain of critical criminology, but because it encapsulates the complex, interconnected, coordinated, and brutal nature of many forms of state crime.

The questions for scholars of state crime are essentially those major political concerns that have informed critical criminology for at least four decades and relate to the exercise of governance and abuse of power by state agents; the relationship between state, capital, and crime; class relations and conceptions of justice and the challenge to state power from below. Moreover critical criminology has been primarily concerned with exposing and de-mystifying state-defined, and therefore, hegemonic class-based conceptualisations of crime. Critical criminology made clear in the 1980s that the harms of the powerful far outweighed the harms of the powerless, and that the criminal label was often employed by the state as a weapon against those sections of society which challenged it or its corporate allies. It took some time, however, before scholars committed to theoretically examining state criminality and even longer before empirical investigations into state deviance were to be conducted on a serious scale.

We are now witnessing a surge in state crime scholarship that seeks to apprehend, interpret, and expose the orchestrated harms of states and corporations (and often the confluence of both – see below) as crimes. This has involved the repositioning of traditional representations of the protagonists – so that conventional conceptions of the state as 'protector' against, and victim of, crime are replaced by the much more accurate representation of the state as perpetrator of crime. Sophisticated, challenging and courageous methodologies provide an increasingly powerful evidence base for state crime scholarship.

Defining state crime

While crimes of the state are many and varied and include state terror, torture, war crimes, state corporate crime, 'natural' disasters, mass forced evictions and population displacement, ethnic cleansing and genocide – they are all the product of the drive to realise organisational goals through deviant means and as such they are all best understood as processes rather than discrete events.

There are a number of components embodied within the social process definition of state crime employed here – 'organisational deviance, involving human rights violations, in pursuit of state organisational goals' (Green and Ward 2001, 2004) which I will briefly outline below.

The state and organisational deviance

The nature of the modern state is neither unified nor singular in structure, but rather a complex collection of different interconnected agencies (Michalowski 2010). There are, however, a number of general features of state agencies that carry with them a potential for criminal or deviant activity. Green and Ward (2012: 719) have argued that what connects the various agencies of the state into a single overarching organisation, namely the state, is 'some common set of plans and rules'. State agencies are expected to co-ordinate their policies in accordance with directives from a more or less centralised leadership, and to abide by legal and constitutional rules. But state agencies also share a degree of independence from the centralised state – an independence which when exercised may result in plans at odds or divergent with those of the state. This opens up the possibility for organisational deviance from the state's own laws and policies at the local level of state agency. State crime is one very significant form of organisational deviance (Ermann and Lundman 1978).

State crime scholarship has been influenced to a considerable extent by Marxist theory and this is reflected in representations of the state. For Engels (1884/1968) the state was an articulation of the institutions and agencies of coercion. The military, police forces, intelligence agencies, prisons, and detention centres are, under capitalist relations of production, ascribed a monopoly over the legitimate use of force. The legitimacy of that force is based on those agencies adhering to the same rules and laws that apply to the general population (recognised as such by both domestic and international audiences). When coercion is used to advance organisational goals, that coercion can result in 'illegitimate' violence, or violence that breaches legal norms and accepted standards of legitimacy.

States also exercise a significant degree of control over resources in their territory and depend on the revenue derived from those resources. For stable capitalist states, the most efficient way to extract resources is through maintaining a degree of legitimacy (in order that taxation can proceed without direct coercion) and to align their policies with the economic interests of those who control the means of production (Gramsci 1971; Tilly 1990). Liberal capitalist states tend to achieve a high degree of hegemony whereby the contradictions of class divided societies are masked by a shared sense of common interest and legitimacy is secured through consent (Gramsci 1971). This is not true for authoritarian (Khilili and Schwedler 2010) or predatory regimes (Bayart et al. 1999) under which coercion is exercised more extensively and without popular legitimacy.

Human rights

When Julia and Herman Schwendinger (1975) introduced the concept of human rights into the definitional lexicon of crime they unlocked a range of conceptual possibilities for understanding criminal state practice.

Having abandoned legal definitions as inadequate to the task of understanding our subject matter we have instead found the concept of human rights to be a useful, if sometimes problematic, normative standard for determining what states should and should not do. For my colleagues and I, human rights – if they are to be in any sense meaningful for our task – must recognise social and economic rights as well as civil and political rights or as Alan Gewirth (1978) has defined them, the fundamental rights of 'freedom and well-being'.

Rather than base our definitions of state crime on legal arguments surrounding whether a human right has, or has not, been violated we have found greater purchase in the voices of significant (i.e. authentic) social audiences for determining what is illegal or illegitimate state practice. Contested questions of legitimacy must, we argue, be based upon explicitly moral and political grounds and as such we as criminologists must not be afraid of taking sides.

Civil society

The social audience referred to in the previous section is best represented (though not always unproblematically) in the form of civil society. Given that agents of the state – intelligence services, prison authorities, police, military and security forces, government officials – are so frequently responsible for criminal acts it makes no sense at all to imagine that we might look to them for solutions. For the critical scholar of crimes of the powerful, the solutions to state crime lie well outside the frameworks of criminal justice, law, international conventions, domestic or international courts. Instead, as I will argue later, any such solutions are much more likely to be found in the struggles of the state's victims or with those who advocate and organise on their behalf. And it is the organisation of those victims and advocates who not only have the power to challenge state violence and corruption but they are central in defining that corruption and violence as criminal.

While international law may provide a rhetorical framework or campaign goal, for organisations challenging state crime it is wholly inadequate to the task of either defining or challenging these forms of violence and corruption. As the author and her colleague Tony Ward have argued,

> although international law may provide a useful discursive resource, the recognition that what the state proclaims as legality is in reality crime on a grand scale – and some of what it defines as crime is in reality resistance to state crime – is essentially a matter of moral and political consciousness.
>
> *(Green and Ward 2014)*

That consciousness is most visibly and powerfully represented, in organised form, by civil society.

Our research into the varieties of civil society shows it to exist, at least for our purposes, on two scales; the first between militant resistance and complete incorporation in a hegemonic system of government; and the second between 'civil' engagement in established or conventional political discourse and more aggressive or confrontational forms of resistance.

By 'state crime' here we mean, essentially, illegitimate organised violence and corruption. The boundaries between legitimate and illegitimate violence and financial dealings are not always clear and our research suggests it is in drawing and contesting those boundaries that civil society plays one of its most important roles, particularly in liberal democracies where issues of state legitimacy are not as starkly contested as they are under authoritarian regimes. But because our case studies are of states that are (or were, until recently) egregiously illegitimate by international standards, these definitional problems will not be as pressing as they might be in some other contexts.

We have articulated a way of thinking criminologically about the state, in which the concept of civil society plays the most critical role. Our central contention is that the civil society is essential when thinking about crimes committed *by* the state (as well as about state responses to the crimes of others) because of its roles as witness, documenter, disseminator, and challenger. Our definition of civil society captures associations that are not part of the state or of organised political society (i.e. political parties) but which are engaged in some way in seeking to influence or resist the state.

The concept of civil society in this context has a degree of autonomy from its use in other disciplines.

In examining the work and normative aspirations of thirty-five civil society organisations (CSOs) in six states characterised by recent histories of repressive state violence we discovered that remarkably vigorous civil societies can develop in the most unfavourable of circumstances, drawing political and moral nourishment from both the rationalised domains of human rights and democratic discourse and from indigenous, cultural, and religious traditions. Inevitably, many of these civil organisations are fraught with contradictions (see, for example the virulent Islamophobia manifest in Burmese civil society and homophobia in Tunisian human rights organisations) but they are nonetheless vital to developing and sustaining resistance to authoritarian regimes.

Our focus was on the reasons behind the formation of organisations of non-violent resistance; their strategies to challenge and censure state violence and corruption; how they defined state violence and corruption; and their normative vocabularies. In Burma, Turkey, Colombia, and Tunisia we explored the experience of organisations under militaristic or authoritarian rule and their evolution towards greater democracy. In Papua New Guinea (PNG), Turkey, and Kenya, ostensibly democratic states, various forms of illegitimate state violence have been deployed against traditional land-owners, the Kurdish ethnic minority, and Islamic organisations respectively.

In all the states we studied, we found CSOs that systematically and effectively exposed, defined, and challenged state crime. Human rights law was only one among many sets of norms against which state practices were measured. Others included national constitutions, charitable, religious, and spiritual values, and local traditions, including customary law. Only certain CSOs with a strong legal orientation defined their work primarily in human rights terms.

In several countries organised religion, whether Christian, Muslim, or Buddhist, played an important role in the politics of human rights. Some CSOs appealed to what can be categorised as spiritual values (sometimes related to the land), without aligning themselves to a particular religion. Like law, religion often played an ambiguous role: for example that of the Catholic church in Colombia and the Buddhist Sangha (community of Monks) in Burma, with its campaigns against the Muslim minority.

Many civil society groups set out to achieve charitable or religious goals and became engaged in resistance only as a result of the state's repressive reaction to their activities. In Tunisia, for example, social work and fund-raising for the poor formed the organisational base for the more political activism that occurred later during the 2011 revolution.

In several of the countries (Colombia, Kenya, Papua New Guinea, Burma/Myanmar) state violence and repression were closely linked to the efforts of the ruling elite, corporations, and/or criminal enterprise to secure control over land and access to natural resources. Struggles for human rights were closely linked to issues of land ownership and resource exploitation.

The extent to which CSOs relied on formal legal mechanisms varied widely between countries and between organisations. Some organisations were wary of diverting resources into litigation with little eventual result. Some courts, such as the Constitutional Court in Colombia, were seen as enjoying a high degree of independence, while others, particularly in Burma and Turkey, were viewed as tools of the state. But even where the actual operation of a state's legal system was viewed with suspicion or hostility, there was widespread support for – or at least a pragmatic acceptance of – ideals of constitutional government, human rights, and the rule of law. One aim of articulating their struggles in these terms was to reach an international audience which might in turn place pressure on the repressive regime.

It is worth noting that those organisations resisting repressive states are not always faced with a simple binary choice between 'democratic' and 'violent' strategies. The concept of civil society, we have learned from this research, must be flexible enough to include groups that countenance moments of political violence, even if the actual practice of organised violence is, by definition, not a 'civil' activity.

State crime, however, cannot be understood without an appreciation of the strategies states employ to conceal, deflect, and deny their crimes. When Stan Cohen wrote his seminal *States of Denial* in 2001 he was capturing a central defining feature of state crime – the ubiquitous practice of denial and the variety of forms it takes.

As Lasslett has argued, 'state officials are in the privileged position of being able to mobilize significant legal, financial and human resources, to conceal their illicit practices from public scrutiny'. Moreover Lasslett reminds us that civil society remains the most effective means of penetrating and exposing the network of deceits, lies and obfuscation which comprise denial: 'Laying siege to the fortifications that facilitate denial is a difficult and often dangerous process which demands mass-mobilization, an extensive division of labour and considerable auxiliary support' (2012: 126).

State crime scholarship

The study of state crime has become one of the most dynamic and challenging areas within the discipline of criminology. Not only has it opened up a vast arena of the most serious forms of social harm for criminologists but it has also extended the range of responses that can both define, expose, and challenge these crimes (Green and Ward 2004; Stanley and McCulloch 2013).

In the early 1980s Stan Cohen remarked on the tendency towards an increasingly criminal justice-centred character within criminology (Cohen 1981). State-defined categories of criminality and policy needs were defining the research agenda and that agenda very explicitly excluded crimes of the powerful. In 2003 Tombs and Whyte observed that crimes committed by states were, by a significant margin, the least explored of all forms of crime within the discipline and that criminology had long enjoyed 'an extremely intimate, indeed subservient relationship to the state' (Tombs and Whyte 2003: 26). But between 2000 and 2015 the criminological landscape began to change. Criminology 'in the service of the state' is no longer intellectually hegemonic (though it still retains its traditional dominance within the realm of policy and criminal justice practice). And while pragmatic empiricism still defines a significant swathe of criminological research, critical approaches to the state and its role in both punishing and perpetrating crimes are, I would tentatively suggest, in the ascendancy.

No longer is criminology confined only to exploring the offending patterns, backgrounds, motivations, and punishment of young, working class, and disproportionately black men (although that tradition is kept alive in a number of university institutions, state research centres, and the Home Office). Many university criminology courses now incorporate modules on crimes of the powerful (particularly state and corporate crime) and UK research councils have demonstrated a surprising willingness to support research that places states, their proxies, and agents in the criminological dock. Given the scale, harms, and prevalence of state crime and the developed criminological frameworks for interpreting it (Chambliss 1989; Friedrichs 1995; Kramer et al. 2002; Green and Ward 2001, 2004, 2012) this is perhaps not surprising.

Contributing to this excitement is the inter-disciplinarity that now characterises the best theoretical and empirical work in the field. Scholars from a range of disciplines including criminology, anthropology, geography, architecture, international law, human rights, psychology, international relations, political science, and sociology have long worked on issues of state violence and corruption but normally in disciplinary isolation and rarely under the banner of state crime.

Those researching torture, authoritarianism, genocide, disappearances, terror, corporate crime, organised crime, forced evictions, counter-terrorism, state violence, corruption, and resistance have now found a conceptual home in state crime scholarship. It is important to recognise that while criminology is primarily concerned with the violation and enforcement of rules and norms it is not the only discipline to share these concerns. Other disciplines have much to offer in terms of insight into questions of violence, law, democracy, and social order.

William Chambliss is credited as one of the earliest and most significant contributors to the study of state crime and his dialectical approach has certainly influenced my own work and that of my ISCI (International State Crime Initiative) colleagues. His much cited 1988 presidential address to the American Society of Criminology, 'State-Organized Crime' (Chambliss and Seidman 1993) urged scholars to consider 'the contradictions inherent in the formation of states' and to apply that dialectical understanding to what he saw as a 'tendency' for state agents to commit organisational forms of crime (1989: 201). While Chambliss's approach has been an important influence on contemporary scholars his reliance on a traditional criminal law definition of state crime, that is, 'acts defined by law as criminal and committed by state officials in pursuit of their jobs as representatives of the state' was both liberating and inhibiting. Liberating because it placed the state as an institution in the dock, but inhibiting because it restricted inquiry into the state's own definition and construction of crime. This is clearly problematic given the exclusive prerogative of states to make laws, the narrow and class-based conceptions of crime that underpin those laws, and the overwhelming reluctance of states to criminalise their own agencies.

The debate over how state crime should be defined is reflected in two streams of research. The first stream applies to research underpinned by a legally constructed understanding of crime – something defined and punished by domestic and international courts (Kramer and Kauzlarich 1998). The second stream applies to research (the present author's work included) in which crime is essentially a violation of social norms that may or may not reflect legal definitions (Green and Ward 2001, 2004). Crime, from the latter perspective, is not an unyielding legal category but a fluid and contested construct. Importantly, state crime is a process – involving, for the most part, a process rather than the discrete act that law attempts to capture. Precisely because crimes such as genocide, torture, ethnic cleansing, and state terror begin with the stigmatisation, marginalisation, and dehumanisation of certain target groups their harms cannot be understood or adequately challenged by a singular focus on the end stage act or event. Indeed as our work on the genocidal process under way in Burma/Myamar reveals genocide is a process that can evolve over decades (Green et al. 2015). Law has demonstrable difficulty with diffuse, complex, and subtle processes and it has demonstrated little interest or capacity in confronting the crimes of states.

But writing well before Chambliss, was the French Appeals Court judge and writer Louis Proal. His almost unknown thesis, *Political Crime*, published in English in 1898, exhorts us to recognise that:

> There are no greater malefactors than the political malefactors who foment divisions and hatreds by their ambition, cupidity, and rivalries. Ordinary evil-doers who are judged by the courts are only guilty of killing or robbing some few individuals, the number of their victims is restricted. Political malefactors, on the contrary count their victims by the thousand. They corrupt and ruin entire nations.
>
> *(1898: vi)*

Proal's legacy is plainly significant because his focus – unique at a time when the individual was the only site of inquiry – went beyond documenting the crimes of individual powerful political actors to discuss 'crimes committed by political systems, based on craft and violence' (1898: viii). The new wave of state crime scholarship, focusing as it does on the planned and coordinated nature of state violence, corruption, and subsequent denials of those crimes, is very much in Proal's tradition.

The International State Crime Initiative

The International State Crime Initiative (ISCI), based in the School of Law, Queen Mary, University of London (QMUL) has played a pivotal role in providing a structural and intellectual hub for global state crime scholarship. Established in 2009 by the author and her colleagues Thomas MacManus, Tony Ward, and Kristian Lasslett, ISCI is a cross-disciplinary research centre working to advance an empirically based, theoretically informed understanding of state crime. Importantly ISCI's research is driven by emancipatory ideals and focuses on civil society as the most authentic mechanism for exposing, defining, challenging, and sanctioning the crimes of states – a focus that has been explored in theoretical depth in the work of scholars at the Initiative (e.g. Green and Ward 2014; Lasslett et al. 2015).

ISCI quickly became the world's leading centre for state crime scholarship and in 2012 launched the first academic journal devoted to its study, the international journal of *State Crime*. Noam Chomsky, Richard Falk, John Pilger, and Stanley Cohen (until his death in 2013) have supported the Initiative as Honorary Fellows, and scholars and writers including veteran Middle East journalist Robert Fisk, Egyptian writer Ahdaf Soueif, photo journalist Greg Constantine, and Palestinian film-maker Emad Burnat have made major contributions to the public engagement programme which is a central platform of ISCI's research dissemination.

ISCI operates through three primary but inter-related platforms: its website www.state-crime.org; its research programme; and its strategy of public engagement. It is funded by QMUL, the UK Economic and Social Research Council, the British Academy, the Newton Foundation, the Leverhulme Trust, the Miliband Trust, and the Open Society Foundations. Its research endeavours are many and varied but currently include a major comparative study of civil society resistance to state violence and corruption in Burma, Tunisia, Turkey, Colombia, Kenya, and Papua New Guinea; an investigation into the Myanmar state's genocidal practices against its Muslim Rohingya ethnic minority; a study into the role of public relations corporations/reputation managers in state crime denial; a comparative study of Islamist radicalisation, state violence, and civil society in eastern Turkey, Indonesia, and Algeria; forced evictions of Palestinians by the endlessly criminal Israeli state; the role of international actors in facilitating corruption in Uzbekistan; and the relationship between mining corporations, indigenous land rights, and civil war in Papua New Guinea. These inquiries are all driven by a desire to understand the social, economic, cultural, and political relations which inform the state crime-resistance dialectic.

ISCI has also cultivated a thriving community of doctoral researchers working on topics ranging from the struggle for land in post-earthquake Haiti and the limiting practices and discourses of international human rights norms; the layered mechanisms of impunity protecting the Turkish state in eastern Turkey; forced displacement in both rural and urban Myanmar, armed non-state actors, and the adoption of international humanitarian law in Myanmar's border territories; art, civil society, and state crime resistance to digital technology, revolution, and dictatorship in Egypt. Emerging from this new work are ever new and more finely grained questions which challenge and advance our concerns to connect rigorous research with emancipatory activism. Many scholars working on state violence, corruption, and civil society's attempts to combat these crimes, themselves engage in resistance struggles or at the very least engage politically with those activists who lead and define those struggles. ISCI presents an opportunity for both researchers and activists to combine the pedagogical with the emancipatory. One of our primary tasks is to encourage rigorous empirical research so that we may develop the strongest possible evidence base. Understanding and knowledge are fundamental requirements of resistance strategies.

One of the key features of ISCI's field research has been the relationship researchers build with local civil society actors and their struggles against state violence, institutionalised discrimination, and corruption. ISCI has prioritised giving voice to these struggles – and bringing to a wider audience the products of our research through ISCI's website, academic journalism, interactive case studies, photographic exhibitions, and film screenings.

In recent years, considerable attention has been given to the creation of formal legal processes to respond to violations of international criminal law. By contrast and for the reasons stated above, our concern is to explore the potential of informal, non-legal censure employed by civil society rather than censures employed by formal legal institutions.

New directions in research[9]

Some of the most challenging and exciting empirical research in the new wave of state crime scholarship has emerged around the concept of state–corporate crime, that is, crimes that result from the specific relationship between the state and commercially motivated corporations. The term was developed by Kramer and Michalowski in 1990 and employed in the 'integrated model' which encouraged a multi-layered approach to understanding corporate offending within a framework of state complicity – an approach by which the structural, organisational, and psychological interrogation of a deviant event was essential for its understanding (Kramer et al. 2002). The model is based on the proposition that criminal behaviour at the organisational level results from a coincidence of pressure for goal attainment, availability, and perceived attractiveness of illegitimate means, and an absence of effective social control (Kramer et al. 2002: 274).

A distinction was drawn between what Kramer et al. described as state-facilitated corporate crime and state-initiated corporate crime. State-initiated corporate crime occurs when corporations, employed by the government, engage in organisational deviance at the direction of, or with the tacit approval of, the government (Kramer et al. 2002: 271). State-facilitated corporate crime, on the other hand, occurs when government regulatory institutions fail to restrain deviant business activities, either because of direct collusion between business and government or because they adhere to shared goals whose attainment would be hampered by aggressive regulation (Kramer et al. 2002: 271–272).

This approach, however, failed to recognise the existence of state crimes which have been either initiated or facilitated by corporations. Corporate-initiated state crime occurs when corporations directly employ their economic power to coerce states into engaging in deviant actions. Corporate-facilitated state crime, on the other hand, occurs when corporations either provide the means for a state's criminality (e.g. weapons sales), or when they fail to alert the domestic/international community to the state's criminality, because these deviant practices benefit the corporation concerned.

The emphasis of the integrated model is on what state crimes and other kinds of crime have in common. Crimes are rarely if ever committed without a motive, an opportunity, and the failure of some form of control to prevent them (if no control mechanism at all is at work, it hardly makes sense to speak of a crime). Importantly, however, when dealing with crimes of the powerful it is essential to understand that these are not mere individual acts. They are acts committed by people working for organisational units that in turn are part of overarching organisations – states and corporations. Thus, a criminological explanation of state crime needs to study motives, opportunities and failures of control at the structural and organisational level as well as the individual.

The most persuasive and indeed emblematic case study in this model remains Ron Kramer's powerful investigation into the organisational processes that led to the Space Shuttle *Challenger* which he argued was: 'the collective product of the interaction between a government agency, the National Aeronautics and Space Administration (NASA), and a private business corporation, Morton Thiokol, Inc., (MTI)' (Kramer 1992: 271). Here, however, a concentration on the confluence of interests evinced by both state and capital results in both forms interrogated as effectively discrete entities. As Tombs (2012: 177) has argued,

> despite the clearly-stated, and genuinely innovative, conceptual intentions of Michalowski and Kramer – that the focus should be on relationships not acts – the work which has utilized and indeed sought to develop this concept has overwhelmingly focused upon discrete acts and paid inadequate attention to the nature and dynamics of state–corporate relationship.

The case study model, with its template for analysis and narrative sureties has resulted in successive and latterly uninspiring reproductions, particularly in US scholarship – with little change in the case study analysis save the nature of the deviant corporate entity and minor rearrangements of goals, opportunities, and social control (Lasslett 2010).

In the UK the contours of state corporate crime scholarship are, however, changing and this change can be credited to the exciting and challenging work of UK scholars associated with the International State Crime Initiative, in particular that of Steve Tombs, Dave Whyte, Kristian Lasslett, and Thomas MacManus. Underpinning this new work is an understanding that the corporation is not independent of the nation state but rather its creation, and that the nation state plays a central role in supporting and maintaining the corporate form to ensure 'the mobilization, utilization and protection of capital' (Tombs 2012: 176). Moreover state–corporate crime is not atypical but routine and endemic.

In a powerful critique of the extant literature on state–corporate crime Tombs (2012: 177) captures the essence of the new direction in which state crime scholarship is travelling:

> just as states create and sustain markets, so too can and do they create and sustain criminogenic markets, that is, markets that are conducive to, or facilitate, the production of harms and crimes. With this obviousness to the fore, what appear at first sight to be discrete events brought into view by the lens of state–corporate crime are in fact better understood as processes, that is, ongoing, enduring and complex relationships between public and private actors.

One of the key texts encapsulating this shift is Kristian Lasslett's (2014) seminal work on the Bougainville War – a largely hidden conflict that devastated the Melanesian island of Bougainville during the 1990s. At its epicentre Lasslett exposes the mining giant, Rio Tinto, which colluded with the Papua New Guinea and Australian governments to violently suppress indigenous landowner resistance against one of the world's largest copper mines. Employing unparalleled access to senior state–corporate actors and leaked records, *State Crime on the Margins of Empire* uncovers and theorises this powerful conspiracy and the sustained international campaign to deny survivors justice and erase their struggle from memory:

> Internment camps, the mortaring of homes, aerial bombardment, extra-judicial killings, the torture and humiliation of prisoners, rape, and the denial of humanitarian aid, these are just some of the criminal state practices endured by Bougainville residents during 1988 and 1997. Even on the margins of Empire, retribution was cruelly and indifferently applied to those who challenged 'pax Capital'.
>
> *(Lasslett 2014: 178)*

By focusing on the conditional relationship which binds state and corporation, the field of state–corporate criminality has become both wider and more nuanced. The following two examples are indicative of this new wave of scholarship.

The role of public relations corporations in state crime denial presents one of the most significant new developments in state–corporate crime scholarship. Pioneered by Thomas MacManus this area of criminological research explores and describes the interrelationship between the unveiling of state and state–corporate crime by civil society and the counter-campaigning and state crime denial of PR firms on behalf of states. MacManus argues that what he terms 'the combative relationship' between civil society organisations and PR firms is critical in understanding the public-arena process of labelling and counter-labelling state and state–corporate crime (MacManus 2016). In response to civil society claims of crimes against humanity and war crimes, the Sri Lankan government hired the British public relations firm, Bell Pottinger, to write the speech of President Mahinda Rajapaksa delivered at the UN General Assembly in September 2010. The speech incorporated a vehement denial of the allegations. A few years earlier, in 1998 and in the face of public outcry against his presence in the UK, the same PR firm assisted in the campaign for the release of, and continued impunity for, Chile's Augusto Pinochet. The slogan they arrived at, 'reconciliation not retribution', was an attempt to imply a balanced conflict – now over, and in the interests of all to move on replete with the repudiation of years of torture, terror, disappearances, and mass murder.

A second new area of study is that presented by land grabbing and related forced evictions. Forced eviction occurs when the state uses its power, often in the service of speculative capital and regularly under conditions of corruption, to displace residents or farmers who are generally poor, and often have no formal title to land. The forced migration of urban and rural populations is intimately linked with the intensity, and conditions under which capital comes to accumulate in and through landed property. How capital circulates, in this respect, is of course mediated in a significant way by the organisation of state-power within the particular regional context. Through the conduit of urban and rural development strategies, physical planning, and property regimes, states can stimulate the character, pace, and conditions under which capital circulates through land (Green et al. 2014).

Rapid urbanisation, enhanced transnational capital flows, and shifting patterns of growth in emerging market countries have provoked a noticeable rise in development-based, forced evictions in countries as diverse as Azerbaijan, Brazil, Burma, Colombia, India, and Papua New Guinea (Green et al. 2014; Harvey 2012). Development-induced mass forced evictions tend to be highly organised events, underpinned by a range of illicit processes, including: illegal land transactions; corruption; security force violence; illegal use of firearms; the destruction of property; and the displacement of civilians, including vulnerable groups such as children.

Globalisation

Contributing to the expansion of interest in the study of state crime has been what one might best describe as a sense of political mission, commitment to justice, and intellectual adventure. This applies as much to domestic research as it does to research conducted beyond the boundaries of the nation state (see e.g. Phil Scraton's (2013) work on organised police crime arising from the 1989 Hillsborough stadium disaster; and Raphael et al.'s (2016) examination of the UK's role in extraordinary rendition). But where once criminology was almost entirely constrained by domestic concerns, these constraints no longer apply. Globalisation and the immediacy and reach of social media brings the suffering of victims of dictatorship, ethnic cleansing, genocide, torture, state terror, and forced population displacement into the immediate frame of inquiry not only of our imagining but into our lived experience (witness the desperate flight of Syrians from the brutality of the Assad regime and the Muslim minority Rohingya forced to flee genocide in Myanmar). This externalisation of the intellectual gaze, and the comparative ease of modern logistics makes realisable a realm of inquiry hitherto beyond the reach of most scholars. Globalised criminology makes more visible the interconnectedness of state criminal practice, e.g. the state terror inflicted upon the Rohingya in Myanmar and their flight to safer exile resonates on many levels with desperate Syrian refugees seeking safe passage from Bashir Al Assad's brutal and criminal regime.

We can learn much about particular acts of state crime from the violent and corrupt state practices of other states. Globalisation and its possibilities for comparative scholarship have created a limitless horizon for scholars committed to developing an understanding of the complexities of state violence and corruption and the conditions under which they emerge. The future of state crime scholarship depends very much on these comparative studies. Without them we will be far less equipped to draw theoretical generalisations concerning the processes involved in the crimes perpetrated by states, the denials they elicit, and the resistance they engender within communities. Comparative scholarship will also help us to explore the variable criminogenic natures of different state formations and the economic, political, and cultural contexts that shape the character of their crimes. These new comparative horizons allow for the application of concepts, methodologies, and theory, derived within a liberal democratic paradigm, to contexts in which culture, geography, development, and the experience of neo-colonialism may play defining roles in the relational processes involved in state criminality.

Methodology: challenges and opportunities

Researchers in the field are, of necessity, developing new and innovative methodologies in their production of new forms of knowledge (aided by the invaluable data sets offered by Wikileaks and other leaked sources).

Ethnographies of, and research into war (crimes), state terror, 'natural' disasters, genocide, large scale land confiscations/land grabbing, and forced displacement, while to be approached with caution, are now possible as opportunities for fieldwork in hostile environments become more viable. Scholars of state crime are learning much not only from anthropologists and geographers but also from what we might call the 'investigatory' professionals – journalists, war reporters, photographers, documentary film-makers and civil society activists who have in the past had unique access to state crime protagonists. We have learnt from media professionals the value of film and photography not only for personal and scholarly recall but to lend power to the re-telling of our work on more popular platforms with wider popular and policy reach (see for example openDemocracy, Middle east Eye, Al Jazeera, and the more conventional media). Beyond the monographs, book chapters, and journal articles state crime scholars are increasingly informing audiences outside the academy. Most valuable to the researcher are the connections with civil society (now so readily accessible through digital means) both as subjects of scholarship and as a source of local knowledge. State crime researchers have become emboldened as the barriers between the disciplines and the investigatory professions have broken down. Scholars now build in budgets for foreign 'fixers' – well-informed and well-connected individuals on the ground who make research possible for those without the necessary language and cultural skills, traditionally used by journalists and politicians. Academics in the field have always relied on informal assistance but now that assistance is recognised as a legitimate source.

New and digital technologies, the adoption of mapping tools from disciplines like geography, ethnographic immersion in sometimes hostile regions, the use of satellite imagery to monitor troop and displaced population movements and land destruction, and the security and access that NGOs can offer in a country are allowing scholars to develop increasingly nuanced answers to the questions they ask.

Investigating the crimes of government requires stamina, courage, and resolve, particularly when investigations enter the field. Whether interviewing state perpetrators or their victims, confronting the wrongdoings of powerful forces requires a particular kind of fortitude and agility – both intellectual and material.

State crime methodology must be flexible and responsive to the demands and restrictions imposed by these potentially hostile environments. One small example drawn from our Rohingya research is illustrative:

> In early 2015 my colleagues, Thomas MacManus and Alicia de la Cour Venning and I found ourselves in Mrauk U a remote part of Rakhine state, northwestern Myanmar in search of isolated Rohingya IDP [internally displaced persons] camps. Given the official denial of Rohingya identity by the Myanmar authorities and the virtual prohibition on the use of the designator *Rohingya* to describe this ethnic minority, and given the complete segregation which operates in much of Rakhine state locating camps in this region, without drawing undue attention to ourselves we resorted to hiring bicycles to try to locate the camps. With the aid of a GPS and a UNOCHA[10] map we cycled many kilometres across paddy fields and dirt tracks in an effort to find segregated Rohingya willing to discuss their persecution at the hands of the Myanmar state. On the way we were repeatedly encouraged to turn back, told by Rakhine Buddhist villagers and local police that there was nothing of interest in the direction ahead. When we did chance upon the Rohingya village and adjacent IDP camp we found police stationed at its only entrance. Assuming the air of hapless and lost tourists we ignored the police and cycled along the dirt track which led into the village and the camp, whereupon the village administrator immediately notified the authorities in the closest town of our presence by telephone.[11] Within two hours a police vehicle had arrived and we were escorted from the area. In terms of data, however, we had acted quickly in the event that

we would be removed and secured interviews with a wide range of men and women effectively imprisoned in the village and camp.

At the time of writing UK research councils (see especially the UK's ESRC) are favouring large scale, multi-disciplinary, development-led projects and there are increasing funding opportunities for collaborative research between the UK and countries like Brazil, China, India, and Turkey. Large scale international comparative studies exploring state violence, corruption, and resistance, once beyond the financial and logistical reach of academics, are now for the moment at least, feasible. We do not know for how long this situation will last but the more scholarship that exists which pushes the boundaries of comparative research into state violence and corruption the more likely it is that research of this kind will continue to be funded.

Conclusion

Some state crimes are easily recognisable but many others are masked by hegemonic conceptualisations of crime (which effectively exclude crimes of the powerful) and by the discursive processes of state and international denial outlined above. Two egregious examples, of criminal states bolstered in their strategies of 'denial' by the economic, strategic, and political interests of the international community are: (a) Israel with its illegal settlement programme in the occupied West Bank and its endless criminal violence against civilian Palestinians (enabled almost entirely by aid from the USA) and; (b) Myanmar where, as described above, the state is in the process of a genocidal campaign to annihilate its ethnic minority Rohingya population (enabled in particular by regional powers, China and India). The task of scholars then is, not only to demystify the criminal acts of states, but also the wide internal and external networks of support which sustain them. This process, of necessity, involves uncovering, articulating, and understanding the related processes of denial. This is in itself a complex task because the state as I have argued, has at hand a machinery of 'denial producers' – public officials reaching across the range of government agencies, 'independent' experts, public relations spin doctors, and the ideological institutions of hegemony – a compliant media, educational institutions, and the church, and a self-interested international community less concerned with human rights than with markets.

Just how these crimes and state crime more generally are to be addressed, and the responsible criminal agents identified and exposed, depends upon the mobilisation of those forces in civil society who are committed to resisting the violent and corrupt incursions of the state. State crimes, like the states who commit them, are highly contested, fluid, and unstable in character but only because of the challenges that civil society brings to bear.

The criminal label is a powerful discursive and transformative force in the hands of victims and those who resist state crime – as powerful against states as it is against the powerless and possibly more so if civil society draws upon its full force.

Notes

1   The study was based on detailed ethnographic research in Rakhine State and Yangon, Myanmar and included 176 interviews with members of Rohingya, Rakhine, Kaman, and Maramagyi communities; international non-governmental organisations (NGOs); government officials; local Rakhine

civil society actors, activists; diplomats; journalists; lawyers; monks; imams; business-men and women; photographers; and academics.

2 Human Rights Watch (2012, 2013); Allard K. Lowenstein International Human Rights Clinic, Yale Law School for Fortify Rights (2015), https://law.yale.edu/system/files/documents/pdf/Clinics/fortifyrights.pdf; Zarni and Cowley (2014); Al Jazeera, 'Genocide Agenda' (2015).

3 Sittwe is the capital of Rakhine State – the second poorest state in Myanmar. Approximately 1.2 million Rohingya live in Rakhine State, making up one-third of the population. The majority population is ethnic Rakhine.

4 Northern Rakhine State is home to the vast majority of Rohingya. It is a securitised zone to which international observers, journalists, and scholars are denied access by the Myanmar government.

5 On 31 October, a *Myanmar Times* journalist, Fiona MacGregor, was fired, at the instigation of the Ministry of Information and following Facebook denunciations by the President's Office spokesman, U Zaw Htay, for publishing allegations of the rape of dozens of Rohingya women by Myanmar Army soldiers. The leading English language newspaper was forced to suspend reporting on Rakhine state until further notice.

6 *Global New Light of Myanmar*, 14 November 2016, page 1.

7 *Global New Light of Myanmar*, 15 November 2016, page 1.

8 *Global New Light of Myanmar*, 14 November 2016, page 1.

9 This section, 'New directions in research' draws heavily on a piece I wrote for Brisman, A., Carrabine, E. and South, N. (eds) (2017) *The Routledge Companion to Criminological Theory and Concepts*. London: Routledge.

10 United Nations Office for the Coordination of Humanitarian Affairs.

11 Unauthorised international visits, we learned, can result in violent punishments for those deemed responsible. A number of Rohingya in this remote area were, therefore, afraid to be interviewed unless explicit permission was given by the authorities.

References

Bayart, J.-F., Ellis, S. and Hibou, B. (1999) *The Criminalization of the State in Africa*, Oxford: James Currey.

Chambliss, W.J. (1989) 'State-Organized Crime: The American Society of Criminology, 1988 Presidential Address', *Criminology*, 27(2): 183–208.

Chambliss, W.J. and Seidman, R.B. (1993) 'State-Organized Crime', in Chambliss, W.J. and Zatz, M. (eds) *The State, the Law, and Structural Contradictions*, Bloomington: Indiana University Press, 290–314.

Cohen, S. (1981) 'Footprints in the Sand: A Further Report on Criminology and the Sociology of Deviance in Britain', in Fitzgerald, M., McLennan, G., and Pawson, J. (eds) *Crime and Society: Readings in History and Theory*, London: Routledge and Kegan Paul, 183–205.

Cohen, S. (1993) 'Human Rights and Crimes of the State: The Culture of Denial', *Australian & New Zealand Journal of Criminology*, 26: 97–115.

———— (2001) *Human Rights and Crimes of the State: The Culture of Denial in States of Denial: Knowing about Atrocities and Suffering*, London: Polity.

Engels, F. (1884/1968) 'Origins of the Family, Private Property and the State', in Marx, K. and Engels, F. (eds) *Selected Works*, London: Lawrence & Wishart.

Ermann, M.D. and Lundman, R.J. (1978) 'Deviant Acts by Complex Organizations: Deviance and Social Control at the Organizational Level of Analysis', *Sociological Quarterly*, 19: 55–67.

Feierstein, D. (2014) *Genocide as Social Practice: Reorganizing Society under the Nazis and Argentina's Military Juntas*, Brunswick, NJ: Rutgers University Press.

Friedrichs, D.O. (1995) 'State Crime or Governmental Crime: Making Sense of the Conceptual Confusion', in Ross, J.I. (ed.) *Controlling State Crime: An Introduction*, New York: Garland Publishing, 53–80.

Gewirth, A. (1978) *Reason and Morality*, Chicago: University of Chicago Press.

Gramsci, A. (1971) *Selections from the Prison Notebooks*, London: Lawrence & Wishart.

Green, P. (2017) 'State–Corporate Crime', in Brisman, A., Carrabine, E. and South, N. (eds) *The Routledge Companion to Criminological Theory and Concepts*, London: Routledge.

Green, P. and Ward, T. (2001) 'State Crime, Human Rights and the Limits of Criminology', *Social Justice*, 27(1): 101–115.

—— (2004) *State Crime: Governments, Violence and Corruption*, London: Pluto Press.

—— (2012) 'State Crime: A Dialectical View', in Maguire, M., Morgan, R. and Reiner, R. (eds) *The Oxford Handbook of Criminology* (5th edn), Oxford: Oxford University Press.

—— (2014) 'Civil Society and State Crime: Repression, Resistance and Transition in Burma and Tunisia', in Chambliss, W.J. and Moloney, C.J. (eds) *State Crime: Critical Concepts in Criminology*, New York: Routledge, 181-192.

Green, P., Lasslett, K. and Sherwood, A. (2014) 'Enclosing the Commons: Predatory Capital and Forced Evictions in PNG and Burma', in Pickering, S. (ed.) *Routledge Handbook on Migration and Crime*, London: Routledge.

Green, P., MacManus, T. and de la Cour Venning, A. (2015) *Countdown to Annihilation: Genocide in Myanmar*, London: ISCI.

Harvey, D. (2012) *Rebel Cities: From the Right to the City to the Urban Revolution*, London: Verso Books.

Human Rights Watch (2012) *'The Government Could Have Stopped This': Sectarian Violence and Ensuing Abuses in Burma's Arakan State'*, www.hrw.org/report/2012/07/31/government-could-have-stopped/sectarian-violence-and-ensuing-abuses-burmas-arakan.

—— (2013) *All You Can Do Is Pray: Crimes against Humanity and Ethnic Cleansing of Rohingya Muslims in Burma's Arakan State*, www.hrw.org/report/2013/04/22/all-you-can-do-pray/crimes-against-humanity-and-ethnic-cleansing-rohingya-muslims.

Khilili, L. and Schwedler, J. (2010) *Policing and Prisons in the Middle East: Formations of Coercion*, London: Hurst & Co.

Kramer, R.C. (1992) 'The Space Shuttle Challenger Explosion', in Schlegel, K. and Weisburd, D. (eds) *White Collar Crime Reconsidered*, Boston: North East University Press.

Kramer, R.C. and Kauzlarich, D. (1998) *Crimes of the American Nuclear State: At Home and Abroad*, Boston: Northeastern University Press.

Kramer, R.C. and Michalowski, R. (1990) 'State–Corporate Crime', unpublished paper quoted in Aulette, J.A. and Michalowski, R. (1993) 'Fire in Hamlet: A Case-Study in State–Corporate Crime', in Tunnell, K.D. (ed.) *Political Crime: A Critical Approach*, New York: Garland.

Kramer, R.C., Michalowski, R.J. and Kauzlarich, D. (2002) 'The Origins and Development of the Concept and Theory of State–Corporate Crime', *Crime & Delinquency*, 48(2): 263–282.

Lasslett, K. (2010) 'Scientific Method and the Crimes of the Powerful', *Critical Criminology*, 18(3): 211–228.

—— (2012) 'Power Struggle and State Crime: Researching through Resistance', *State Crime Journal*, 1(1): 126–148.

—— (2014) *State Crime on the Margins of Empire*, London: Pluto Press.

Lasslett, K., Green, P. and Stanczak, D. (2015) 'The Barbarism of Indifference: Sabotage, Resistance and State–Corporate Crime', *Theoretical Criminology* 19(4): 514–533.

MacManus, T. (2016) 'The Denial Industry: Public Relations, "Crisis Management" and Corporate Crime', *International Journal of Human Rights*, 20(6): 785–797.

Michalowski, R.J. (2010) 'In Search of "State" and "Crime" in State Crime Studies', in Chambliss, W.J., Michalowski, R. and Kramer, R.C. (eds) *State Crime in the Global Age*, Cullompton: Willan.

Proal, L. (1898) *Political Crime*, London: T. Fisher Unwin.

Raphael, S., Black, C., Blakeley, R. and Kostas, S. (2016) 'Tracking Rendition Aircraft as a Way to Understand CIA Secret Detention and Torture in Europe', *International Journal of Human Rights*, 20(1): 78–103.

Schwendinger, H. and Schwendinger, J. (1975) 'Defenders of Order or Guardians of Human Rights?', in Taylor, I., Walton, P. and Young, J. (eds) *Critical Criminology*, London: Routledge & Kegan Paul.

Scraton, P. (2013) 'The Legacy of Hillsborough: Liberating Truth, Challenging Power', *Race and Class*, 55(2): 1–27.

Stanley, E. and McCulloch, J. (eds) (2013) *State Crime and Resistance*, London: Routledge.

Tilly, C. (1990) *Coercion, Capital and European States 990–1990*, Oxford: Blackwell.

Tombs, S. (2012) 'State–Corporate Symbiosis in the Production of Crime and Harm', *State Crime*, 1(2): 170–195.

Tombs, S. and Whyte, D. (eds) (2003) *Unmasking the Crimes of the Powerful: Scrutinizing States and Corporations*, New York: Peter Lang.

Zarni, M. and Cowley, A. (2014) 'The Slow-Burning Genocide of Myanmar's Rohingya', *Pacific Rim Law and Policy Journal*, 23(3): 683–754.

22

MASS INCARCERATION

David Brown

Introduction

This chapter examines the phenomenon of 'mass imprisonment', more commonly known in the USA as 'mass incarceration', which emerged there from the mid-1970s onwards, and arguably also across a number of other western post-colonial countries. Its chief manifestation is an historically unprecedented rate of incarceration, highly concentrated in specific communities, African American (black) in the USA and Indigenous in Australia, New Zealand and Canada. The chapter will summarise the dimensions of the incarceration explosion in the USA, with brief reference also to Australia, and define the key characteristics of mass incarceration: its magnitude and racial concentration. The effects of mass incarceration on prisoners, their families and communities, its 'collateral consequences', will be outlined, mainly through work in an epidemiological tradition. This is followed by an attempt to identify both the more obvious and direct, and the deeper and more contentious drivers of mass incarceration. The issue of whether mass incarceration has peaked and can and is being wound back through initiatives such as justice reinvestment, and other policies, is briefly addressed. The importance of seeing mass incarceration as a consequence of social and political policy choices rather than simply the operation of criminal law, is emphasised throughout. For while alternative and critical criminologies have pioneered the analysis and critique of mass incarceration, the understandings gained must be carried into the field of democratic politics, in particular within the vulnerable communities most at risk, if the struggle to wind back the debilitating and unjust effects of mass incarceration is to be successful.

The US incarceration explosion

The USA has experienced a 500 per cent increase in its prison population in the last thirty years, as illustrated in Figure 22.1. Note that Figure 22.1 is of prison numbers and not rates and it does not include prisoners in local jails (discussed later) which added a further 744,500 people in 2012, for a total of 2.2 million people incarcerated. Even without including the incarcerated jail populations this is an incarceration rate per 100,000 of 716 in 2012/2013, far and away the highest in the world. With 4.4 per cent of the world population the USA incarcerates 22 per

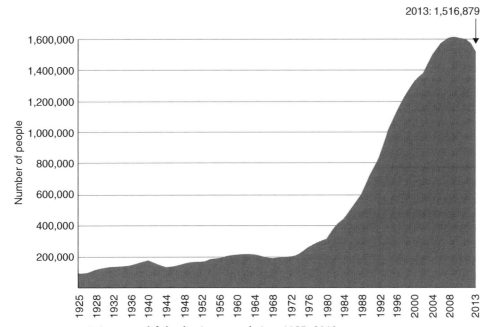

2013: 1,516,879

FIGURE 22.1 US state and federal prison population, 1925–2013

Source: The Sentencing Project, Fact Sheet: Trends in US Corrections: www.sentencingproject. org/publications/trends-in-U-S-corrections (accessed in 2015 and 2016)

cent of the world's prisoners at rates roughly 50 per cent higher than its leading major competitor, the Russian Federation; double South Africa; two and a half times that of Brazil, Uruguay and Chile; roughly five times that of Australia, England and Wales, Bolivia, Argentina, and Spain; six times that of China and Canada, seven times France and Italy; nine times Germany; ten times Sweden, Denmark and Norway; and twenty-three times India (Walmsley, 2013).

Figure 22.1 masks the very significant variation in US incarceration by states, which in 2010 ranged from 867 per 100,000 population in Louisiana to 148 in Maine (Travis et al., 2014: 42). Figure 22.2 shows the wide variation in the ratio of adults subject to some form of correctional supervision in the USA in 2013, highlighting its highly racialised character, a pattern also evident in the jail population (Subramanian et al., 2015: 15). The racial character of US imprisonment rates becomes even starker once age is added in, as demonstrated in Figures 22.3 and 22.4, with both male and female black Americans having higher rates in every age bracket.

For black males aged between 30–39 years, rates of imprisonment exceed 6,000 per 100,000 (Carson, 2014: Table 8) and the rates for black females aged between 25–34 years exceed 250 per 100,000 (Carson, 2014: Table 8). PEW (2008: 5) estimated that one in nine black men aged 20–34 was in prison on any given day in 2008. If those under some form of community supervision (probation and parole) are added to the incarcerated population the result is a correctional population in 2009 of more than seven million people (PEW, 2009). The lifetime likelihood of being imprisoned in the USA is one in three for black men, one in six for Latino men, and one in seventeen for white men. The corresponding figures for women are one in eighteen, one in forty-five and one in 111 (Sentencing Project, 2014: 5).

It is beyond the scope of this chapter to discuss and detail whether and to what extent mass incarceration is only a US phenomenon or applies as well in other countries. The leading

1 in X Analysis: Persons subject to correctional supervision in 2013 in the USA					
TOTAL 1 in 35	WOMEN 1 in 98	MEN 1 in 21	WHITE 1 in 46	HISPANIC 1 in 37	BLACK 1 in 14

FIGURE 22.2 US incarceration – persons subject to correctional supervision in 2013 comparing groups across demographic lines, using a 1 in X analysis
Source: Brown et al. (2016) reproduced with permission of Palgrave Macmillan

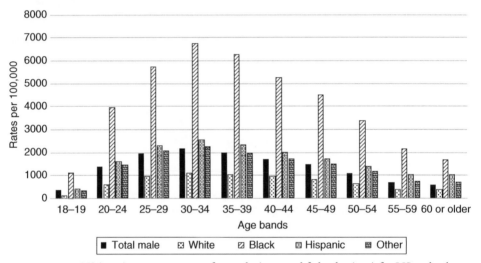

FIGURE 22.3 US imprisonment – rates of custody (state and federal prison) for US males, by age and race/ethnicity in 2013
Source: Brown et al. (2016) based on Carson (2014: Table 8) reproduced with permission of Palgrave Macmillan

contenders are other white settler post-colonial countries like Australia, Canada and New Zealand which all have significantly lower imprisonment rates than those in the USA, but have similarly high or higher levels of racial disparity. To take Australia as an example, the Australian overall rate of imprisonment in 2014 was 185.6 per 100,000 of the adult population (ABS, 2014), which includes unsentenced prisoners and is thus best compared with the US rate inclusive of jails and federal and state prisons of 910 per 100,000 (Glaze and Kaeble, 2014: 4). While the Australian rate is thus around one-fifth of the US, as Figure 22.5 shows it has doubled since the mid-1980s (ABS, 2014). There are also significant variations across the states, as is shown in Figures 22.5 and 22.6, with the Northern Territory having an imprisonment rate of over 800 per 100,000 adult population.

The imprisonment rate for Indigenous Australians is similar to that of black American men and more than double that of black American women (Figures 22.6, 22.7 and 22.8) suggesting

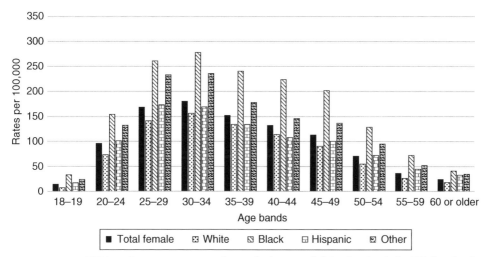

FIGURE 22.4 US imprisonment – rates of custody (state and federal prison) for US females, by age and race/ethnicity in 2013

Source: Brown et al. (2016) based on Carson (2014) reproduced with permission of Palgrave Macmillan

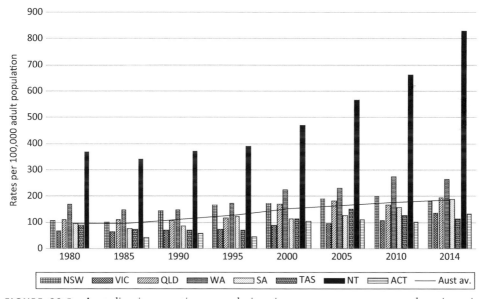

FIGURE 22.5 Australian incarceration – crude imprisonment rates, per state and territory, in increments from 1980–2014

Source: Brown et al. (2016) based on ABS (2014: Table 18) reproduced with permission of Palgrave Macmillan

that a mass incarceration analysis is applicable in Australia. In 2014, the crude Indigenous imprisonment rate was 2,174 per 100,000 (ABS, 2014: Table 19), a national disproportion of fourteen times the non-Indigenous rate. Once age is added in, as illustrated in Figures 22.7 and 22.8, racial disparities and disproportions are even greater. For Indigenous males aged between

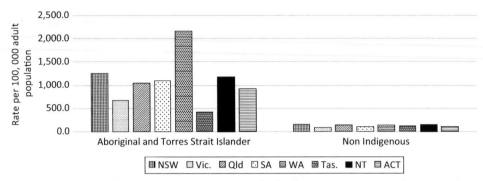

FIGURE 22.6 Australian imprisonment – age standardised imprisonment rates, by state and territory and Indigenous status in 2014

Source: Brown et al. (2016) based on ABS (2014: Table 17) reproduced with permission of Palgrave Macmillan

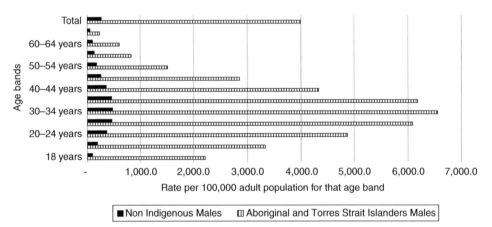

FIGURE 22.7 Australian imprisonment – male rates of imprisonment by age and Indigenous status in 2014

Source: Brown et al. (2016) based on ABS (2014: Table 19) reproduced with permission of Palgrave Macmillan

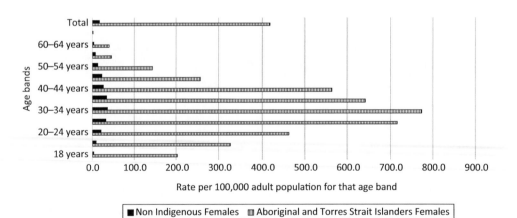

FIGURE 22.8 Australian imprisonment – female rates of imprisonment by age and Indigenous status in 2014

Source: Brown et al. (2016), based on ABS (2014: Table 20) reproduced with permission of Palgrave Macmillan

25–39 years, rates exceed 6,000 per 100,000 adult population and for women 600 per 100,000 (ABS, 2014: Table 20).

'Mass imprisonment'

The term 'mass imprisonment' used to describe the explosion of the US prison population outlined above, came into popular usage with a special issue of the international penology journal, *Punishment and Society* in 2001, later published in book form (Garland, 2001a). In an editorial introducing a range of contributions, David Garland defined the term as involving two key features. These were:

> a rate of imprisonment and a size of prison population that is markedly above the historical and comparative norm for societies of this type. The US prison system clearly meets these criteria. The other feature is the social concentration of imprisonment's effects. Imprisonment becomes mass imprisonment when it ceases to be the incarceration of individual offenders and becomes the systematic imprisonment of whole groups of the population. In the case of the USA, the group concerned is, of course, young black males in large urban centres. For these sections of the population, imprisonment has become normalized.
>
> *(2001a: 1–2)*

A key consequence of adopting a mass imprisonment analysis is to shift the focus from seeing imprisonment rates as an agglomeration of individual instances of criminal behaviour, processed by the police, court and prison systems, towards a recognition of the highly concentrated and systemic effects of criminal justice policies and imprisonment, in particular, mainly racialised, communities. This is not to deny traditional legal categories of individual culpability and responsibility which dominate legal, popular and political discourse, but is to locate them within a much broader systemic analysis of the patterns and effects produced by criminal justice policies and practices, in terms of race, inequalities, vulnerabilities, class, gender, civil rights and citizenship.

As Garland (2001a: 2) put it, imprisonment:

> becomes part of the socialization process. Every family, every householder, every individual in these neighbourhoods has a direct personal knowledge of the prison – through a spouse, a child, a parent, a neighbor, a friend. Imprisonment ceases to be a fate of a few criminal individuals and becomes a shaping institution for whole sectors of the population.

Epidemiologist Ernest Drucker recalls giving a talk to a group of high achieving high school students from the Bronx in New York who had been selected for a specialist medical education programme. When he asked the question: 'How many people here know someone who has been in prison?' all sixty students raised their hands. 'All had a family member, friend, or neighbor who had been in prison' (Drucker, 2011: 76).

From 'mass imprisonment' to 'mass incarceration'

The terminology changed quickly from 'imprisonment' to 'incarceration' to take account of a key feature of the US system not present in many other countries. This is that the term imprisonment in the US context is used to refer to offenders sentenced to federal or state prisons for a term of more than one year (Carson, 2014: 1), omitting short sentence prisoners and those on remand awaiting trial held in local or county level 'jails'. Local jail populations can include a range of state-sentenced inmates awaiting transfer, probationers and parolees awaiting revocation proceedings, immigration detainees and others (Subramanian et al., 2015: 6–7).

The problem then with using the term 'mass imprisonment' in the US context is that leaving out local jail populations considerably understates the levels of 'incarceration'. For example in 2013 the rate of imprisonment for the US adult population was 623 per 100,000 (Carson, 2014: 6); but if we add in the incarcerated jail population the 2013 rate jumps to 910 per 100,000 (Glaze and Kaeble, 2014: 4; Brown et al., 2016) Thus most commentators, at least in the US context, now use the term mass incarceration, which as Simon (2012: 28) notes, can better 'facilitate cross-national comparison' with unified jurisdictions which do not have two or three tiers of incarceration.

It should be noted that even these combined prison and jail populations included in the term 'incarceration' tend to obscure the sheer scale of people cycling in and out of various forms of custody. This is because they are the result of census figures, snapshots taken on one day per year in particular institutions, rather than on overall receptions over one year. For example while there were 731,208 people in jail in the USA on a single day in 2013, nearly 12 million people cycled through jails in that same year (Subramanian et al., 2015: 7; Minton and Golinelli, 2014: 6; Brown et al., 2016). Cunneen et al. (2013: 182–183) note the way imprisonment census figures obscure the larger numbers cycling through custody on short-term sentences for less serious crimes; understate the number of people caught up in the penal system; over-emphasise the seriousness of offences leading to imprisonment; and hide the increased over-representation of Indigenous people and racial minorities amongst these short sentence populations.

Wacquant and 'hyperincarceration'

Leading penal theorist Loïc Wacquant prefers the term 'hyperincarceration', as a way of emphasising the racial and class selectivity that lies behind mass incarceration. Thus:

> the stupendous expansion and intensification of the activities of the American police, criminal courts, and prison over the past thirty years have been finely targeted, first by class, second by race, and third by place, leading not to mass incarceration but to the hyperincarceration of (sub)proletarian African American men from the imploding ghetto. This triple selectivity reveals that the building of the hyperactive and hypertrophic penal state that has made the United States world champion in incarceration is at once a delayed reaction to the civil rights movement and the ghetto riots of the mid-1960s and a disciplinary instrument unfurled to foster the neoliberal revolution by helping to impose insecure labor as the normal horizon of work for the unskilled fractions of the postindustrial laboring class.
>
> *(Wacquant, 2010: 74, footnotes omitted)*

Wacquant's analysis of 'the increasingly tight meshing of the hyperghetto with the carceral system' (2001: 107) and the emphasis on race (see also Wacquant, 2000; 2009a, 2009b) has also been the focus of other scholars such as Michelle Alexander, 2012. (See also Pettit, 2012; Pettit and Western, 2004; Western and Pettit, 2000; Lyons and Pettit, 2011; Mauer and Huling, 1995; Roberts, 2004; Tonry, 2011.)

Michelle Alexander: mass incarceration – *The New Jim Crow*

In *The New Jim Crow: Mass Incarceration in the Age of Colorblindness* (2012) Michelle Alexander places the racial character of mass incarceration in the US context within the history of US racial politics as a new form of racial segregation, in short as a civil rights and equality issue. Jim Crow, named after a character in a black minstrel show, is a term widely used to describe the laws, policies, regulations and practices which achieved racial exclusion, discrimination and segregation, predominantly in the southern states, following the abolition of slavery after the American Civil War, persisting into the 1960s. Tonry (2011: 5) describes them succinctly as 'social practices and conventions and legal forms of segregation [which] kept blacks in their place'.

> By the turn of the twentieth century every state in the South had laws on the books that disenfranchised blacks and discriminated against them in virtually every sphere of life, lending sanction to a racial ostracism that extended to schools, churches, housing, jobs, restrooms, hotels, restaurants, hospitals, orphanages, prisons, funeral homes, morgues and cemeteries.
>
> *(Alexander, 2012: 35)*

The parallel Alexander (2012: 13) draws is that 'like Jim Crow (and slavery), mass incarceration operates as a tightly networked system of laws, policies, customs, and institutions that operate collectively to ensure the subordinate status of a group defined largely by race'.

> Arguably the most important parallel between mass incarceration and Jim Crow is that both have served to define the meaning and significance of race in America. Indeed, a primary function of any racial caste system is to define the meaning of race in its time. Slavery defined what it meant to be black (a slave), and Jim Crow defined what it meant to be black (a second-class citizen). Today mass incarceration defines the meaning of blackness in America: black people, especially black men, are criminals. That is what it means to be black.
>
> *(ibid.: 197)*

In a simple but telling illustration, Alexander (ibid.: 1) opens her book with the story of Jarvious Cotton:

> Jarvious Cotton cannot vote. Like his father, grandfather, great-grandfather, and great-great-grandfather, he has been denied the right to participate in our electoral democracy. Cotton's family tree tells the story of several generations of black men who were born in the United States but who were denied the most basic freedom that democracy promises – the freedom to vote for those who will make the rules and laws that govern one's life. Cotton's great-great-grandfather could not vote as a slave. His great-grandfather was beaten to death by the Ku Klux Klan for attempting to vote. His grandfather was

prevented from voting by Klan intimidation. His father was barred from voting by poll taxes and literary tests. Today, James Cotton cannot vote because he, like many black men in the United States, has been labeled a felon and is currently on parole.

The collateral consequences of mass incarceration

Drawing the parallel between Jim Crow laws and mass incarceration displaces the centrality of crime and the criminal justice system in favour of an examination of the context of race relations, inequality, civil rights and social justice and draws attention to the myriad of what have been called 'collateral consequences' (Mauer and Chesney-Lind, 2002) of mass incarceration. The prison is only one site in the mass incarceration story and the 'punishment' achieved by a sentence of imprisonment radiates far beyond both the prison walls and the prisoners who are enclosed within them. One way of examining these collateral consequences is to adopt an epidemiological approach, that is to analyse mass incarceration as a public health issue through a medical methodology historically used to study epidemics and diseases. Ernest Drucker does this in his book *A Plague of Prisons* (2011) and the analysis is instructive. A key feature of the epidemiological approach is that prison data are viewed as 'collective public events' (ibid.: 68).

Drucker examines US mass incarceration as an 'epidemic' exhibiting the following characteristics. Firstly it has shown a rapid growth rate, a five fold increase since 1970. Secondly it is of a large magnitude, the highest in the world and unprecedented in history. Drucker estimates that 'in total since 1975, about 35 million Americans have been arrested and jailed or imprisoned, probably more than all Americans incarcerated for all offenses in the previous hundred years' (2011: 44). This magnitude is increased when all 'the children, wives, parents, siblings, and other family members are added in' (ibid.). Thirdly mass incarceration has shown persistence and self-sustaining capabilities. Among these are the development of an enormous prison industry involving over 'five thousand federal, state and local prisons and jails', and supporting one full time employee for every one of the 2.3 million people behind bars. (ibid.: 45); the diversion of budgets and resources from health, housing, education and welfare into prisons; and the demoralising effects of mass incarceration on specific communities and neighbourhoods, diminishing social capital and perversely stimulating crime by exacerbating community breakdown, in short proving criminogenic (Rose and Clear, 1998; Clear, 2007a).

Drucker's (2011: 49) argument is that this 'epidemiological paradigm will allow us to see the rapid growth and huge prevalence of mass incarceration in a new way, as a public health and social catastrophe that requires urgent action'. Analogising from an outbreak of cholera in eighteenth-century London, traced by a doctor to a particular water pump in Soho through examining the geographical location of victims, Drucker shows how the Rockerfeller drug laws of 1973 which introduced mandatory draconian penalties for a wide range of drug offences, including possession of small quantities of drugs (sentences in many cases longer than those for violent crimes), were the toxic source, the 'prison pump' of mass incarceration in New York: 'While in 1980 only 10 percent of all New York State new prison commitments were for drug-related cases, drug cases accounted for 45 percent of new prison commitments between 1987 and 1997' (ibid.: 54). Similarly a study of geographic locations showed that almost 50 per cent of the people sent to prison from New York City 'came from about fourteen neighbourhoods in the Bronx, Manhattan and Brooklyn, where only 17 percent of adults in the city reside' (ibid.: 56). Further Drucker's data showed clearly that young black and Hispanic men accounting for 30 per cent of the population accounted for 72.3 per cent of all drug convictions (ibid.: 58) and that this disparity was between '2.5 and 6 times greater than those seen in incarceration for all other offences and that these disparities grew larger between 1990 and 2000' (ibid.: 59).

Drucker describes the long term exposure to the criminal justice system as 'toxic', concluding that 'mass incarceration imposes the same burden for our society as many chronic diseases associated with occupational hazards (for example coal, asbestos, or nuclear radiation), the physical trauma of war, or the depredations of severe poverty and family disintegration' (ibid.: 113–114). Lives lost to drug incarceration in New York State between 1973 and 2008 were three and a half times those lost in the 11 September 2001 terrorist attack on the World Trade Centre in New York in which 2,800 people died (ibid.: 115). The various disabilities of a sentence of imprisonment, what Drucker calls 'the long tail', can be traced through four categories, those pertaining to the prisoner both inside and outside the prison, and the collateral consequences to the children and families of prisoners and to their wider communities.

During the prison term:

> the adverse effects of incarceration on individual prisoners include the ongoing consequences of poor health care services in prisons; failure of prison security to provide a safe environment (the ensuing rape, violence and gang activity that have become a routine part of prison life); serious and persistent mental health problems and inadequate mental health care in prisons; and a paucity of addiction treatment and the absence of effective drug rehabilitation. All this is in addition to the immediate and longer-term psychological implications of trauma associated with overcrowding, poor prison conditions, and many severe disciplinary methods, including isolation and solitary confinement.
>
> *(ibid.: 115)*

The many disabilities suffered after release include restricted access to housing, exacerbated by bars in many states to ex-prisoners living in public housing, leading to frequent homelessness. Restricted access to employment, already difficult given the stigmatising effects of a criminal record and employer reluctance, is exacerbated by bars to employment of ex-felons across a wide range of trades, occupations and professions. Various federal bars exist in relation to access to welfare funds, support programmes for education, employment training and food stamps.

Felony disenfranchisement laws across a number of states variably deny the right to vote to serving prisoners, those on probation and those released but on parole, and in some cases all ex-felons for their lifetime. (See generally on felony disenfranchisement Uggen et al., 2012; Mauer, 2002; Manza and Uggen, 2006; Ewald and Rottinghaus, 2009.) Only two states do not have felony disenfranchisement provisions. The number of voters disenfranchised has blown out from 1.17 million in 1976 to 5.85 million in 2010. Seventy-five per cent of these are living in the community on probation, parole or having completed their sentence. The racial disparity is marked: 2.2 million black citizens are banned from voting. In Florida 23 per cent of black citizens are banned from voting, in Kentucky 22 per cent and Virginia 20 per cent, so that more than one in five black adults in these states are denied one of the most fundamental rights of citizenship (Uggen et al., 2012). The result is a massive racial gerrymander. Were it not for the felony disenfranchisement laws in Florida alone, Al Gore would have defeated George Bush in the 2000 US Presidential election. While access to housing, health, employment and education may be of more immediately practical concern, it is difficult to imagine a starker and more symbolic illustration (unless you are the British PM, David Cameron, who infamously said that the prospect of prisoners being entitled to vote made him feel ill) of the way that mass incarceration goes to the heart of notions of citizenship, and to claims to constitute a democratic polity.

Beyond the serving or released prisoner, in epidemiological terms mass incarceration is 'contagious' (Drucker, 2011: 141), involving inter-generational transmission of disadvantages to children, subsequently 'expressed as school failure, increased health and psychological problems, homelessness, and, ultimately, an increased probability of being arrested and incarcerated themselves' (ibid.: 142). Imprisonment exacerbates pre-existing struggles 'with poverty, unemployment, low wages and unstable housing'; puts a 'huge strain on already unstable marriages' (ibid.: 142); fractures communication and involves the stress of often degrading prison visiting conditions; increases the likelihood of divorce; worsens financial problems and generates 'additional strains on all involved post release. Children of imprisoned parents are more likely to be subject to child removal and foster care placement, and parents can lose their parental rights including rights to contact. Cumulative effects on children include trauma, 'gang membership, delinquency and early involvement in crime' (ibid.: 151). Parental incarceration affects infant mortality, elevating the risk of early death by 29.6 per cent (ibid.: 157). Drucker estimates that 10 to 15 million children have been exposed to parental incarceration over 35 years (ibid.), 'spawning successive generations of prison orphans and young grandmothers in their thirties and forties now caring for children of their imprisoned adult sons and daughters' (ibid.: 159). He concludes that epidemic mass incarceration has become 'one of the most powerful determinants of systematic and intergenerational inequality in our society' (ibid.: 162).

The fourth category of collateral consequences relates to community and neighbourhood consequences and suggests that mass incarceration is counter-productive and criminogenic, contributing to social breakdown and crime (Rose and Clear, 1998; Clear, 2007a; Stemen, 2007; Durlauf and Nagin, 2011; Pritikin, 2008; Vieraitis et al., 2007; Brown, 2010). Based on their pioneering work in Florida where they found that mass arrests and imprisonment in the Tallahassee area of Florida were followed by increasing crime rates, Rose and Clear (1998) argued that there was a 'tipping point' in certain communities, where crime increased once incarceration reached a certain level. This was because:

> high rates of imprisonment break down the social and family bonds that guide individuals away from crime, remove adults who would otherwise nurture children, deprive communities of income, reduce future income potential, and engender a deep resentment toward the legal system. As a result, as communities become less capable of managing social order through family or social groups, crime rates go up.
>
> *(ibid.: 457)*

The 'tipping point' effect in particular marginalised and racialised communities, developed in subsequent work (Clear, 2002, 2007a, 2007b; Clear and Frost, 2014; Clear et al., 2001, 2003; Western, 2002, 2006; Western et al., 2001, 2004; Mauer and Chesney-Lind, 2002), became a significant component in the development of the mass incarceration analysis. It revealed the inadequacies of explanations of imprisonment rates and their effects in terms of an accumulation of individual instances of offending. Rather, the issue was about effects on whole communities. While all this research took place in the USA, it was argued that such effects applied in the Australian context, particularly amongst vulnerable populations and communities, 'such as

Aboriginal communities and certain geographical or "postcode" areas, where we may already have reached that "tipping point" where excessive imprisonment rates are actually causing crime' (Brown, 2010: 141; see also Cunneen et al., 2013).

The 'tipping point' and 'criminogenic' arguments were a direct challenge to the widespread common sense assumption that the significant decreases in crime in the USA and elsewhere experienced from the late 1990s on were a direct result of mass incarceration. This challenge was supplemented by studies which demonstrated the limited role of imprisonment in reducing crime. Western (2006: 7, 168–188) estimates that the growth in US 'incarceration rates explains only one-tenth of the decline in serious crime at the end of the 1990s'. Spelman (2000: 484) concluded that a 10 per cent increase in imprisonment rates will produce at most a 2–4 per cent decrease in crime rates and that only 25 per cent of the US drop in crime rates could be attributed to increased incarceration rates (see also Spelman, 2006; Levitt, 2004; Useem et al., 2001; Pritikin, 2008; Mauer and Chesney-Lind, 2002). Research indicated that:

> incarceration has, at best, a modest effect in reducing crime; that this crime-reduction effect diminishes over time the higher incarceration rates climb; and that in relation to particular communities and groups, such as African Americans in the US and Aborigines in Australia, it is likely to have a negative or crime-producing effect in the long term.
>
> *(Brown, 2010: 142)*

While the foregoing account has given an indication of some of the growing research on the collateral consequences of mass incarceration, with a bias towards the epidemiological, it is important, as Pettit (2012: 102) points out, to note that in the USA 'inmates are excluded from the federal data collection efforts commonly used to generate accounts of the economic, political, and social well-being of the American population, thereby being omitted from consideration in deliberations of social policy and designs of social research', hence the title of her book: *Invisible Men*.

The direct drivers of mass incarceration

Imprisonment rates are in a mechanical sense a function of the content of criminal law, policing policies, arrest rates, numbers of people brought before courts, access to bail, sentencing policies which affect the proportion of convicted persons sent to prison and the length of sentences, remission and parole policies, and rates of revocations from probation and parole. The direct drivers of mass incarceration are relatively easy to identify in the USA in the form of policy shifts in policing and sentencing and most have already emerged in the earlier discussion, especially the role of mandatory minimum penalties in the 'War on Drugs' which increased both rates of prison admissions and the length of sentences. To pick a single significant change and the one most clearly racially targeted, it would be hard to go past the 1986 law that made possession of more than five grams of crack cocaine subject to the same mandatory minimum penalties as that for 500 grams of powder cocaine.

Clear and Frost (2014: chap. 4) identify various phases in the mass incarceration buildup: the targeting of crime in the 1970s, the targeting of drug offences and offenders in the 1980s, the targeting of violent crime and repeat offenders in the 1990s, along with the shift from determinate to indeterminate sentencing and the introduction of sentencing guidelines. Legislation was passed in state and federal legislatures increasing the likelihood of prison and lengthening penalties for certain categories of offences and offenders; mandatory penalties were introduced for serious felonies; 'truth in sentencing' legislation for violent crimes was enacted which required offenders to serve around 85 per cent of sentences before becoming eligible for parole; 'three-strikes' legislation was introduced for recidivist offenders which varied widely across different states, with the most extreme version in California (Zimring et al., 2001); enhanced surveillance and more intensive supervision of people on probation and parole led to increased revocations, often for technical breaches; increased monitoring of those convicted of sex crimes including sex offender registration and notification was introduced; and a range of legislation was enacted which erected barriers to successful reintegration by limiting access to education, public housing, employment and welfare for released offenders. (For a more specific discussion see Clear and Frost, 2014; Clear and Austin, 2009; Cole, 2011; Simon, 2014.)

The deeper drivers of mass incarceration

It is one thing to point to specific policies and specific pieces of legislation that relatively clearly had the effect, whether intended or not, of rapidly increasing both imprisonment rates and their concentration in specific racial communities. It is another to provide clear-cut explanations of the deeper forces which propelled mass incarceration. The explanations developed are multiple, varied and disputed. The architects of many of the policies pointed to rising crime rates and endemic fear of crime; the role of imprisonment in reducing crime (which as we have already seen is true to some extent but massively over-rated); the need to recognise and respond to the plight of victims of crime; the apparent discrediting of rehabilitative efforts reflected in the 'nothing works' mantra; the need to be seen to respond to legitimate public concern over crime; and the responsibility of the state to secure public safety, which it was thought could only be achieved through increased imprisonment.

By way of contrast critics, including many critical criminologists, offered a range of explanations. These included: the media and political appeal and utility of 'tough on crime' politics electorally; mass incarceration as a way in which the state could be seen to be responding to the widespread insecurities and anxieties generated by the rapidly changing economic, social and technological conditions of life; a 'culture of control' response to the increased precariousness of existence in conditions of late modernity; a consequence of the way neoliberalism has proffered the market as the appropriate mechanism for governing social and economic life, undermining older forms of social solidarity partly expressed in social democracy and penal welfarism; a way of utilising crime as a reason for and a means of governing society across myriad sites and vectors; a vehicle for a politics of resentment and a means of controlling, disciplining, warehousing and victimising the unruly and undeserving poor; a mechanism through which racial segregation could be re-enlivened and various forms of racial exclusion, disadvantage and denigration conducted in the 'colour-blind' name of law rather than of race; and a way of stigmatising certain types of law breakers by visiting upon them, their families and communities, a range of civil disabilities and exclusions that severely restrict access to education, employment and other basic attributes of citizenship such as the right to vote; to single out but some. (See generally: Zimring and Hawkins, 1991; Garland, 2001a, 2001b; Beckett and Western, 2001; Mauer and Chesney-Lind, 2002; Pratt et al., 2005; Mauer, 2006; De Giorgi, 2006; Gottschalk, 2006; Clear, 2007a; Stemen, 2007; Lacey, 2008; Miller, 2010; Wacquant, 2001,

2009a, 2009b, 2010; Clear and Austin, 2009; Drucker, 2011; Alexander, 2012; Harcourt, 2012; Pettit, 2012; Cunneen et al., 2013; Raphael and Stoll, 2013; McDowell et al., 2013; Tonry, 2014; Simon, 2014; Clear and Frost, 2014.)

Tonry (2014: 504–505) argues that none of the penal populism, culture of control or neo-liberalism-based accounts provides an 'adequate explanation for American developments', and highlights the unique 'political culture and history' of the USA, concluding 'countries and, within the United States, states, have the policies and prison populations they choose'. This assessment illustrates the difficult and open-ended nature of providing explanatory accounts; the importance of locating explanations in specific local contexts, histories and cultures rather than assuming the inevitability and uniform character of globalising forces and policy transfer; and the argument stressed throughout this chapter, that mass incarceration is an intended and unintended effect of social, political and legal policy choices and not a simple consequence of dealing with crime.

The prospects of winding back mass incarceration

A range of developments in the USA raise the potential prospect of winding back mass incarceration. Prison closures have occurred across at least thirteen states after prison population reductions, some of them substantial, such as the 25 per cent reductions in New York, New Jersey and California, while other states have recorded increases, so that the overall national imprisonment rate has declined slightly since 2009. The US juvenile detention rate has been reduced by 40 per cent since 2001. Some of the collateral consequences of criminal convictions are being wound back across a range of states (Subramaniam et al., 2014). There is strong bipartisan support for justice reinvestment policies and for re-entry programmes following President George Bush's Second Chance Act in 2007. Business leaders (PEW, 2010) and in particular conservative evangelicals, including leading Republican figures, are prominent in supporting these initiatives, arguing on cost, efficiency and redemptive grounds, as are conservative pressure groups such as the influential Right on Crime.

A widespread consensus across the political spectrum in the USA seems to be emerging that the criminal justice is 'broken' (Brown et al., 2016: 205–208). In 2013, then US Federal Attorney General, Eric Holder described it as such, singling out mandatory minimum and recidivist enhancement statutes as having a 'destabilizing effect on particular communities, largely poor and of color' and arguing that 'sweeping, systemic changes', were needed (Reilly, 2013). He went on to describe the US prison population as 'outsized and unnecessarily large', noting that 'we cannot simply prosecute or incarcerate our way to becoming a safer nation'. In April 2015 Presidential aspirant Hillary Clinton called for an 'end to the era of mass incarceration', noting that there is 'something profoundly wrong in our criminal justice system' (Terkel, 2015).

Criminologists such as Clear and Frost (2014), Green (2013) and Simon (2014), have argued that there are signs of a shift in what Green calls 'the penal policy weather' (Green, 2013: 140; see also Cole, 2011). Clear and Frost (2014: 2–3) argue that mass incarceration, which they call 'a kind of grand social experiment' and 'The Punishment Imperative', is 'grinding to a halt' (ibid.: 7) having 'run its course' (ibid.: 16):

> A combination of political shifts, accumulating empirical evidence, and fiscal pressures has replaced the commonsense idea that the system must be 'tough' with a newly

developing consensus that what happened to the penal system can no longer be justified or sustained.

(ibid.: 3)

Green (2013: 142) argues that: 'among the most vocal and active leaders in this shift are those with deeply held religious-moral convictions with long, historical legacies that criminology has often caricatured or overlooked'. Jonathon Simon (2014: 162) argues that: 'like a biblical flood, the age of mass incarceration is finally ebbing'. Simon cites various sources of a 'new commonsense' as: declining crime rates; much less fear of crime; the emergence of better strategies to deal with mental illness; a rediscovery of rehabilitation and re-entry and investment in re-entry strategies and programmes to drive down recidivism rates, programmes often involving former prisoners; and 'the ascendance of dignity as a constitutional value within the legal system' (Simon, 2014: 162; see also Simon, 2012). He stresses the significance of the *Brown v Plata* decision where the US Supreme Court required California to reduce its prison population to 137 per cent of capacity (a potential reduction of 46,000 prisoners) because the gross overcrowding under mass incarceration produced degrading and inhumane health care and mental health care (Simon, 2014: 167).

Other criminologists have begun to investigate the importance of and prospects for 'penal hope', in response to such developments (Currie, 2013; Brown, 2013; Loader and Sparks, 2012). Such accounts provide a counter to the tone of pessimism, inevitability and miserablism in which some of the most sweeping and influential accounts of the 'penal surge' (Wacquant, 2009a; 2009b) are cast, and their lack of attention to contrary assessments (Nelken, 2010; Newburn, 2010; Lacey, 2010; Peck, 2010; Pratt, 2011; Brown, 2012), and to forms of agency and resistance among the marginalised, who tend to figure only as a 'crushed and cringing fragment' (Measor, 2013: 146; see also Piven, 2010; Mayer, 2010; Brown, 2011a, 2011b, 2012; Stenson, 2013, Squires and Lea, 2013).

Citing pressures to control costs (Aviram, 2015), bipartisan and public support for re-entry programmes, the balancing of victims' rights discourse, and increasing recognition that the drug war was a mistake, Clear and Frost (2014: 6) argue that:

> there is a call for correctional programs to be based on 'evidence' rather than ideology. One of the most popular new national programs is 'justice reinvestment', which seeks to control the rising costs of prisons and invest the savings in projects that will enhance, rather than further damage, communities.

They go on to suggest a programme to further the winding back of mass incarceration, including the repeal of mandatory sentences, especially for drug offences; a reduction in the length of sentences by, for example, enabling release on parole at the first eligibility date, and expanded 'good time' (remission) provisions; targeted sentence reduction through winding back truth in sentencing formulas which require 85 per cent time to be served, and the elimination of recidivist sentencing enhancement statutes (two and three strike provisions); the reduction in recidivism through reducing the rate of revocations of probation and parole on technical grounds; and a programme of justice reinvestment, including a focus on incentives, including (more controversially) opening up incentives to the private sector (Clear and Frost, 2014: chap. 7; on justice reinvestment more generally see Tucker and Cadora, 2003; CSG,

2008; 2010a, 2010b; Brown et al., 2012; Austin et al., 2013; Fox et al., 2013; Brown et al., 2016). Other writers (Simon, 2014; Tonry, 2014) and organisations have provided a range of policy suggestions, including ways of addressing racial inequity in criminal justice (Sentencing Project, 2015).

In the Australian context Cunneen and colleagues (2013: 194) raise the question whether 'after nearly 30 years of increasing imprisonment rates we were at something of a conjuncture or turning point, presaging a period of falling imprisonment rates, a movement away from the era of mass imprisonment?' The answer they give is guarded:

> while the moment looks promising in terms of rolling back nearly three decades of increasing imprisonment rates and their drivers, unless reform movements confront the highly selective nature of penality and the way it bears so disproportionately on marginalised groups, then any gains to be made through political and popular attitudinal shifts through widespread adoption of policies such as justice reinvestment or penal reductionism, are likely to be limited in practice.
>
> *(ibid.: 195)*

In a subsequent book length examination of justice reinvestment in the USA and its prospects in Australia, some of the same authors (Brown et al., 2016) take this position as a starting point to advocate and support the emergence of a justice reinvestment groundswell in certain Australian Indigenous communities expressed in terms of Indigenous democracy, a term they use as shorthand for issues of Indigenous governance, empowerment, self determination and nation building. Thus the authors seek to situate their advocacy for justice reinvestment within the local Australian Indigenous context and crucially within a social justice and community development model of justice reinvestment that emanates from within the Indigenous communities that provide such wildly disproportionate prison numbers, as part of a broader democratic political struggle to control their own destinies. Such advocacy by criminologists seeking to support social movement struggles requires, they argue, the ability to hold together three distinct motivations:

> a vision that what currently is, might be otherwise; an appreciation that reforms must be won within existing political possibilities; and a degree of self reflection that movements can only progress if they are able to constantly question and refashion their own foundations, values and claims.
>
> *(ibid.: 240)*

It is not a matter of rejecting advocacy cast in terms of cost savings, 'smart justice' and 'what works' but of attempting to develop a political strategy and programme which builds a new commonsense around criminal justice issues by articulating a range of elements into a narrative for change. 'Such a commonsense', they suggest:

> might be fashioned out of a range of elements, including: appeals to cost savings and 'smarter' justice, data and evidence-based policies; enhanced public safety; reduced recidivism; increased offender accountability to communities; ex-prisoner job creation and other community development programs; redressing racial and other marginalised

group disparities and inequalities; promoting Indigenous democracy; unleashing individual and community potential; creating healthier families; providing a better future for young people; enhancing life chances and building social solidarity.

(ibid.: 249)

However the articulation 'must ultimately be a normative one, conducted in the name of increased social justice, rather than technical or instrumental rationalities or "superior" knowledge claims' (ibid.: 249).

Conclusion

Mass incarceration 'was not a policy that was proposed, researched, costed, debated and democratically agreed. America did not collectively decide to get into the business of mass imprisonment ... Instead ... [it] emerged as the overdetermined outcome of a converging series of policies and decisions' (Garland, 2001a: 2). It was not dreamed up as a grand design to subjugate the black US male underclass, although there were elements of this in particular laws which, as Tonry notes, 'policy makers ... knew would especially damage black people' (Tonry, 2011: 53; see also Simon, 2012: 24), but nor is it simply the end point of an accretion of millions of individual crimes as filtered through the criminal justice system to the prison terminus. It is the patterned and highly selective effect of a series of political, legal, social, cultural and economic policy decisions and choices made by a range of actors and agencies, primarily but not exclusively those with access to political and economic power and influence within the existing structures of government. Decisions made for a variable and sometimes conflicting range of reasons and justifications, explicit and hidden, articulated and unspoken, intended and unintended.

Mass incarceration is a condition of life in racialised, marginalised and vulnerable communities, a lived and shared experience in which incarceration is a structuring force in a field of penality and a penal culture which as Cunneen et al. (2013: 141) put it: 'extends well beyond the prison gates to form part of the defining social conditions of being young, black and male in the USA, the UK, Canada, New Zealand and Australia'. This chapter has left it open to others better qualified, to determine whether and if so to what extent, the notion of mass incarceration is an appropriate, useful and critical one in the South American context and elsewhere.

What I would hope the chapter has contributed to the consideration of those questions, is the understanding that the concept is not one that should be restricted to legal and criminological discourse, to lawyers and criminologists. For while the taken for granted linkage between crime and punishment is historically sedimented in legal and popular thought, mass incarceration is essentially a political construct, an effect of political policy decisions, albeit often expressed in legal form. As such it needs to be discussed and debated as a matter of democratic politics (Barker, 2009, 2013; Good Society Symposium, 2014; Loader and Sparks, 2010, 2012, 2013) and in terms far beyond the limiting constraints of crime and of individual culpability and responsibility. Given that the key characteristic of mass incarceration is its concentration in specific neighbourhoods and in specific racialised communities, policies of redress or prevention must directly confront both the local neighbourhood and community detail, as in the early justice reinvestment concentration on 'million dollar blocks' and its focus on mapping community strengths or 'assets', and the broader structures of racial segregation, inequality and discrimination in access to services such as housing, employment, health care and education, civil rights and citizenship, that mass incarceration enacts. As the discussion of 'collateral consequences' and the epidemiological approach illustrated, the effects of mass incarceration are not confined to the individual prisoner seeking a successful 're-entry', but affect families and whole communities.

Similarly the struggle to wind back, in the USA and in other countries afflicted by mass incarceration, or to prevent its development, in countries not yet scarred, cannot only be waged through appeals to 'evidence led', 'what works' and 'fiscally responsible' policy, however otherwise desirable this might be. A normative commitment to redressing social and racial injustice, and a politics of democratic community engagement from below that can best animate such commitments, are necessary lest success be calculated only in instrumental or managerial terms. While the reduction in prison numbers through reductions in the number and length of sentences, brought about predominantly through criminal justice, policing and sentencing reforms and policies are a necessary part of winding back mass imprisonment, the issue is not simply one of numbers. For this would be to reduce the meaning of mass incarceration to 'a lot' of imprisonment, or at most to the first limb of Garland's definition, a historically unprecedented level. But as we saw, the second part of the definition is the 'social concentration of imprisonment's effects', which can subsist and even worsen within an overall reduction in imprisonment rates. The reduction in numbers is not an end in itself unless it results from strategies consciously redressing drivers that are racially selective and concentrated on communities of vulnerability. The exact nature of such strategies will need to be fashioned according to the specific national, regional and local context and circumstance and the structures of democratic political representation, governance and agency enjoyed (or not) by and within the racial and marginalised communities subject to mass incarceration in those specific contexts. This is always an unfolding and unfinished story and process, in which inspiration can be gained from unlikely sources and the task of imagining the new is conducted with recourse to both the politics of possibility and to dreams of a 'fully social' (Taylor et al., 1973: 275) criminology and future.

References

ABS (Australian Bureau of Statistics) (2014) *Prisoners in Australia, 2014*, catalogue no. 4517.0, Australian Bureau of Statistics: Canberra.

Alexander, M. (2012) *The New Jim Crow: Mass Incarceration in the Age of Colorblindness*, revised edn, The New Press: New York.

Austin, J., Cadora, E., Clear, T.R., Dansky, K., Greene, J., Gupta, V., Mauer, M., Porter, N., Tucker, S. and Young, M.C. (2013) *Ending Mass Incarceration: Charting a New Justice Reinvestment*, http://sentencingproject.org/doc/Charting%20a%20New%20Justice%20Reinvestment%20FINAL.pdf (accessed 8 January 2015).

Aviram, H. (2015) *Cheap on Crime: Recession-Era Politics and the Transformation of American Punishment*, University of California Press: Oakland.

Barker, V. (2009) *The Politics of Imprisonment: How the Democratic Process Shapes the Way America Punishes Offenders*, Oxford University Press: New York.

Barker, V. (2013) 'Prison and the Public Sphere: Towards a Democratic Theory of Penal Order', in D. Scott (ed.) *Why Prison?* Cambridge University Press: Cambridge, 125–146.

Beckett, K. and Western, B. (2001) 'Governing Social Marginality: Welfare, Incarceration and the Transformation of State Policy', *Punishment and Society*, 3(1): 43–59.

Brown, D. (2010) 'The Limited Benefit of Prison in Controlling Crime', *Current Issues in Criminal Justice*, 22(1): 137–148.

Brown, D. (2011a) 'Review Essay: Neoliberalism as a Criminological Subject', *Australian and New Zealand Journal of Criminology*, 44(1): 129–142.

Brown, D. (2011b) 'The Global Financial Crisis: Neo-Liberalism, Social Democracy and Criminology', in Mary Bosworth and Carolyn Hoyle (eds) *What Is Criminology?*, Oxford University Press: Oxford.

Brown, D. (2012) 'Prison Rates, Social Democracy, Neoliberalism and Justice Reinvestment', in K. Carrington, M. Ball, E. O'Brien and J. Tauri (eds) *Crime, Justice and Social Democracy: International Perspectives*, Palgrave Macmillan: Basingstoke.

Brown, D. (2013) 'Mapping the Conditions of Penal Hope', *International Journal for Crime, Justice and Social Democracy*, 2(3): 27–42.

Brown, D., Schwartz, M. and Boseley, L. (2012) 'The Promise and Pitfalls of Justice Reinvestment', *Alternative Law Journal*, 37(2): 96–102.

Brown, D., Cunneen, C., Schwartz, M., Stubbs, J. and Young, C. (2016) *Justice Reinvestment: Winding Back Imprisonment*, Palgrave Macmillan: London.

Brown v Plata (2011) 131 S, Ct. 1910.

Carson, E.A. (2014) *Prisoners in 2013*, BJS Bulletin, September, Bureau of Justice Statistics: Washington, DC.

Clear, T. (2002) 'The Problem with "Addition by Subtraction": The Prison–Crime Relationship in Low-Income Communities', in M. Mauer and M. Chesney-Lind (eds) *Invisible Punishment: The Collateral Consequences of Mass Imprisonment*. New Press: New York.

Clear, T. (2007a) *Imprisoning Communities: How Mass Incarceration Makes Disadvantaged Neighborhoods Worse*, Oxford University Press: New York.

Clear, T. (2007b) 'The Impacts of Incarceration on Public Safety', *Social Research*, 74(2): 613–630.

Clear, T. and Austin, J. (2009) 'Reducing Mass Incarceration: Implications of the Iron Law of Prison Populations', *Harvard Law and Policy Review*, 3(2): 307–324.

Clear, T. and Frost, N.A. (2014) *The Punishment Imperative: The Rise and Failure of Mass Incarceration in America*, New York University Press: New York and London.

Clear, T., Rose, D. and Ryder, J. (2001) 'Incarceration and the Community: The Problem of Removing and Returning Offenders', *Crime and Delinquency*, 47(3): 335–351.

Clear, T., Rose, D., Waring, E. and Scully, K. (2003) 'Coercive Mobility and Crime: A Preliminary Examination of Concentrated Incarceration and Social Disorganisation', *Justice Quarterly*, 20(1): 33–64.

Cole, D. (2011) 'Turning the Corner on Mass Incarceration', *Ohio State Journal of Criminal Law*, 9(1): 27–51.

CSG (Council of State Governments), Justice Center (2008) *Justice Reinvestment – The Strategy: How Justice Reinvestment Works*, 6 October 2008, http://web.archive.org/web/20081006223018/http://justicereinvestment.org/strategy/quantify (accessed 6 October 2008).

CSG (Council of State Governments), Justice Centre (2010a) *Justice Reinvestment: Overview*, www.justicereinvestment.org.

CSG (Council of State Governments), Justice Center (2010b) *Justice Reinvestment – About the Project*, http://justicereinvestment.org/about (accessed 1 September 2010).

Cunneen, C., Baldry, E., Brown, D., Brown, M. Schwartz, M. and Steel, A. (2013) *Penal Culture and Hyperincarceration: The Revival of the Prison*, Ashgate: Farnham.

Currie, E. (2013) 'Consciousness, Solidarity and Hope as Prevention and Rehabilitation', *International Journal for Crime, Justice and Social Democracy*, 2(2): 3–11.

De Giorgi, A. (2006) *Rethinking the Political Economy of Punishment: Perspectives on Post Fordism and Penal Politics*, Ashgate: Aldershot.

Drucker, E. (2002) 'Population Impact of Mass Incarceration under New York's Rockefeller Drug Laws: An Analysis of Years of Life Lost', *Journal of Urban Health*, 79(3): 434–435.

Drucker, E. (2011) *A Plague of Prisons: The Epidemiology of Mass Incarceration in America*, New Press: New York.

Durlauf, S.N. and Nagin, D.S. (2011) 'Imprisonment and Crime: Can Both Be Reduced?', *Criminology and Public Policy*, 10(1): 13–54.

Ewald, A.C. and Rottinghaus, B. (2009) *Criminal Disenfranchisement in International Perspective*, Cambridge University Press: New York.

Fox, C., Albertson, K. and Wong, K. (2013) *Justice Reinvestment: Can the Criminal Justice System Deliver More for Less?*, Routledge: London.

Garland, D. (ed.) (2001a) *Mass Imprisonment: Social Causes and Consequences*, Sage: Thousand Oaks, CA.

Garland, D. (2001b) *The Culture of Control: Crime and Social Order in Contemporary Society*, Oxford University Press: Oxford.

Glaze, L. and Kaeble, D. (2014) *Correctional Populations in the United States 2013*, BJS Bulletin, December, Washington, DC.

Good Society Symposium (2014) 'Symposium on Democratic Theory and Mass Incarceration', *The Good Society* 23(1), Penn State University Press.

Gottschalk, M. (2006) *The Prison and the Gallows: The Politics of Mass Incarceration in America*, Cambridge University Press: New York.

Green, D. (2013) 'Penal Optimism and Second Chances: The Legacies of American Protestantism and the Prospects for Penal Reform', *Punishment and Society* 12(2): 123–146.

Harcourt, B. (2012) 'On the American Paradox of Laissez Faire and Mass Incarceration', *Harvard Law Review*, 125: 54–68.

Lacey, N. (2008) *The Prisoners' Dilemma*, Cambridge University Press: Cambridge.

Lacey, N. (2010) 'Differentiating among Penal States', *British Journal of Sociology*, 6(4): 778–794.

Levitt, S.D. (2004) 'Understanding Why Crime Fell in the 1990s: Four Factors That Explain the Decline and Six that Do Not', *Journal of Economic Perspectives*, 18(1): 163–190.

Loader, I. and Sparks, R. (2010) *Public Criminology*, Routledge: London.

Loader, I. and Sparks, R. (2012) 'Beyond Lamentation: Towards a Democratic Egalitarian Politics of Crime and Justice', in T. Newburn and J. Peay (eds) *Policing, Politics, Culture and Control*, Hart: Oxford.

Loader, I. and Sparks, R. (2013) 'Unfinished Business: Legitimacy, Crime Control and Democratic Politics', in J. Tankebe and A. Liebling (eds) *Legitimacy and Criminal Justice: An International Exploration*, Oxford University Press: Oxford.

Lyons, C. and Pettit, B. (2011) 'Compounded Disadvantage: Race, Incarceration and Wage Growth', *Social Problems*, 58(2): 257–280.

Manza, J. and Uggen, C. (2006) *Locked Out: Felon Disenfranchisement and American Democracy*, Oxford University Press: New York.

Mauer, M. (2002) 'Mass Imprisonment and the Disappearing Voter', in M. Mauer and M. Chesney-Lind (eds) *Invisible Punishment: The Collateral Consequences of Mass Imprisonment*, NYU Press: New York.

Mauer, M. (2006) *Race to Incarcerate*, 2nd edn, The New Press: New York.

Mauer, M. and Chesney-Lind, M. (eds) (2002) *Invisible Punishment: The Collateral Consequences of Mass Imprisonment*, NYU Press: New York.

Mauer, M. and Huling, T. (1995) *Young Black Men and Drug Policy*, The Sentencing Project: Washington, DC.

Mayer, M. (2010) '*Punishing the Poor*, a Debate: Some Questions on Wacquant's Theorizing the Neoliberal State', *Theoretical Criminology*, 14(1): 93–103.

McDowell, D.E., Harold, C.N. and Battle, J. (2013) *The Punitive Turn: New Approaches to Race and Incarceration*, University of Virginia Press: Charlottesville and London.

Measor, L. (2013) 'Loïc Wacquant, Gender and Cultures of Resistance', in P. Squires and J. Lea (eds) *Criminalisation and Advanced Marginality*, Policy Press: Bristol, 129–150.

Miller, L. (2010) *The Perils of Federalism: Race, Poverty and the Politics of Crime Control*, Oxford University Press: New York.

Minton, T.D. and Golinelli, D. (2014) *Jail Inmates at Midyear 2013 – Statistical Tables*, August, Bureau of Justice Statistics: Washington, DC.

Nelken, D. (2010) 'Denouncing the Penal State', *Criminology and Criminal Justice*, 10(4): 331–340.

Newburn, T. (2010) 'Diffusion, Differentiation and Resistance in Comparative Penality', *Criminology and Criminal Justice*, 10(4): 341–352.

Peck, J. (2010) 'Zombie Neoliberalism and the Ambidextrous State', *Theoretical Criminology*, 14(1): 104–110.

Pettit, B. (2012) *Invisible Men: Mass Incarceration and the Myth of Black Progress*, Russell Sage Foundation: New York.

Pettit, B. and Western, B. (2004) 'Mass Imprisonment and the Life Course: Race and Class Inequality in US Incarceration', *American Sociological Review*, 69(2): 151–169.

PEW Centre on the States (2008) *One in 100: Behind Bars in America, 2008*, February, The Pew Charitable Trusts, http://pewtrusts.org/ (accessed 29 September 2015).

PEW Centre on the States (2009) *One in 31: The Long Reach of American Corrections*, March, The PEW Charitable Trusts: Washington, DC, http://pewtrusts.org/ (accessed 28 September 2015).

PEW Centre on the States (2010) *Right Sizing Prisons: Business Leaders Make the Case for Corrections Reform*, www.pewcentreonthestates.org (accessed 26 September 2015).

Piven, F.F. (2010) 'A Response to Wacquant', *Theoretical Criminology*, 14(1): 111–116.

Pratt, J. (2011) 'The International Diffusion of Punitive Penality: Or, Penal Exceptionalism in the United States? Wacquant v Whitman', *Australian & New Zealand Journal of Criminology*, 44(1): 116–128.

Pratt, J., Brown, D., Hallsworth, S., Brown, M. and Morrison, W. (eds) (2005) *The New Punitiveness*, Willan: Cullompton.

Pritikin, M.H. (2008) 'Is Prison Increasing Crime?', *Wisconsin Law Review*, 2008(6): 1049–1108.

Raphael, S. and Stoll, M. (2013) *Why Are So Many Americans in Prison?*, Russell Sage Foundation: New York.

Reilly, R.J. (2013) 'Eric Holder: "Broken" Justice System Needs "Sweeping" Changes, Reforms to Mandatory Minimum', *Huffington Post*, 8 December, www.huffingtonpost.com/2013/08/12/eric-holder-mandatory-minimum_n_3744575.html,2013.

Roberts, D.E. (2004) 'The Social and Moral Cost of Mass Incarceration in African American Communities', *Stanford Law Review*, 56(5): 1271–1305.

Rose, D.R. and Clear, T. (1998) 'Incarceration, Social Capital, and Crime: Implications for Social Disorganisation Theory', *Criminology*, 36(3): 441–480.

Sentencing Project (2014) *Fact Sheet: Trends in US Incarceration*, January, www.sentencingproject.org (accessed 28 September 2015).

Sentencing Project (2015) *Black Lives Matter: Eliminating Racial Inequity in the Criminal Justice System*, 3 February, www.sentencingproject.org/doc/publications/rd/Black-_Lives_Matter.pdf (accessed 21 September 2015).

Simon, J. (2012) 'Mass Incarceration: From Social Policy to Social Problem', in J. Petersilia and K.R. Reitz (eds) *The Oxford Handbook of Sentencing and Corrections*, Oxford University Press: Oxford.

Simon, J. (2014) *Mass Incarceration on Trial*, The New Press: New York.

Spelman, W. (2000) 'What Recent Studies Do (and Don't) Tell Us about Imprisonment and Crime', *Crime and Justice*, 27: 419–494.

Spelman, W. (2006) 'The Limited Importance of Prison Expansion', in A. Blumstein and J. Wallman (eds) *The Crime Drop in America*, 2nd edn, Cambridge University Press: Cambridge, 97–129.

Squires, P. and Lea, J. (eds) (2013) *Criminalisation and Advanced Marginality*, Policy Press: Bristol, 41–60.

Stemen, D. (2007) *Reconsidering Incarceration: New Directions for Reducing Crime*, Vera Institute of Justice, January, www.vera.org.

Stenson, K. (2013) 'The State, Sovereignty and Advanced Marginality in the City', in P. Squires and J. Lea (eds) *Criminalisation and Advanced Marginality*, Policy Press: Bristol, 41–60.

Subramanian, R., Moreno, R. and Gelreselassie, S. (2014) *Relief in Sight? States Rethink the Collateral Consequences of Criminal Conviction, 2009–2014*, New York: Vera Institute of Justice, www.vera.org/sites/default/files/resources/downloads/states-rethink-collateral-consequences-reprint-v3.pdf (accessed 19 September 2015).

Subramanian, R., Delaney, R., Roberts, S., Fishman, N. and McGarry, P. (2015) *Incarceration's Front Door: The Misuse of Jails in America*, February, VERA Institute of Justice: New York.

Taylor, I., Walton, P. and Young, J. (1973) *The New Criminology*, Routledge: London.

Terkel, A. (2015) 'Hillary Clinton to Call for an "End to the Era of Mass Incarceration"', *Huffington Post*, 29 April, www.huffingtonpost.com/2015/04/29/hillary-clinton-mass-incarceration_n_7166970.html,2015.

Tonry, M. (2011) *Punishing Race: A Continuing American Dilemma*, Oxford University Press: Oxford.

Tonry, M. (2014) 'Remodeling American Sentencing: A Ten-Step Blueprint for Moving Past Mass Incarceration', *Criminology and Public Policy*, 13(4): 503–533.

Travis, J., Western, B. and Redburn, S. (2014) *The Growth in Incarceration in the United States*, National Academies Press: Washington, DC.

Tucker, S. and Cadora, E. (2003) 'Justice Reinvestment', *Ideas for an Open Society*, 3(3), Open Society Institute: New York.

Uggen, C., Shannon, S. and Manza, J. (2012) *State Level Estimates of Felon Disenfranchisement in the United States, 2010*, Sentencing Project, July, www.sentencingproject.org (accessed 28 September 2015).

Useem, B., Piehl, A.M. and Liedka, R.V. (2001) *The Crime-Control Effect of Incarceration: Reconsidering the Evidence*, Final Report to the National Institute of Justice, United States Department of Justice: Washington, DC.

Vieraitis, L.M., Kovandzic, T.V. and Marvell, T.B. (2007) 'The Criminogenic Effects of Imprisonment: Evidence from State Panel Data, 1974–2002', *Criminology and Public Policy*, 6(3): 589–622.

Wacquant, L. (2000) 'The New "Peculiar Institution": On the Prison as Surrogate Ghetto', *Theoretical Criminology*, 4(3): 377–389.

Wacquant, L. (2001) 'Deadly Symbiosis: When Ghetto and Prison Meet and Mesh', *Punishment and Society*, 3(1): 95–134.

Wacquant, L. (2009a) *Punishing the Poor: The Neo-Liberal Government of Social Insecurity*, Duke University Press: Durham.

Wacquant, L. (2009b) *Prisons of Poverty*, University of Minneapolis Press: Minneapolis.

Wacquant, L. (2010) 'Class, Race and Hyperincarceration in Revanchist America', *Daedalus*, Summer, 74–90.

Walmsley, R. (2013) *World Prison Population List*, 10th edn, www.prisonstudies.org (accessed 28 September 2015).

Western, B. (2002) 'The Impact of Incarceration on Wage Mobility and Inequality', *American Sociological Review*, 67(4): 526–546.

Western, B. (2006) *Punishment and Inequality in America*, Russell Sage Foundation: New York.

Western, B. and Pettit, B. (2000) 'Incarceration and Racial Inequality in Men's Employment', *Industrial and Labor Relations Review* 54(1): 3–16.

Western, B., Kling, J.R. and Weiman, D.F. (2001) 'The Labor Market Consequences of Incarceration', *Crime and Delinquency*, 47(3): 410–427.

Western, B., Lopoo, L.M. and McLanahan, S. (2004) 'Incarceration and the Bonds between Parents in Fragile Families', in M. Patillo, D. Weiman and B. Western (eds) *Imprisoning America: The Social Effects of Mass Imprisonment*, Russell Sage Foundation: New York.

Zimring, F. and Hawkins, G. (1991) *The Scale of Imprisonment*, University of Chicago Press: Chicago.

Zimring, F., Hawkins, G. and Kamin, S. (2001) *Punishment and Democracy: Three Strikes and You're Out in California*, Oxford University Press: New York.

23

PRISONER REENTRY AS MYTH AND CEREMONY

Loïc Wacquant

The carceral boom in post-Civil Rights America results not from profit-seeking but from state-crafting.[1] Accordingly, we must slay the chimera of the "Prison Industrial Complex" and forsake its derived tale of the "Prisoner Reentry Industry." This murky economic metaphor is doubly misleading: first, most released convicts experience not reentry but ongoing circulation between the prison and their dispossessed neighborhoods; second, the institutions entrusted with supervising them are not market operators but elements of the bureaucratic field as characterized by Pierre Bourdieu. Post-custodial supervision is a ceremonial component of "prisonfare," which complements "workfare" through organizational isomorphism, and partakes of the neoliberal reengineering of the state. Reentry outfits are not an antidote to but an extension of punitive containment as government technique for managing problem categories and territories in the dualizing city. To capture the glaring economic irrationality and bureaucratic absurdities of the oversight of felons behind as well as beyond bars, our theoretical inspiration should come not from the radical critique of capitalism but from the neo-Durkheimian sociology of organization and the neo-Weberian theory of the state as a classifying and stratifying agency.

The varied papers gathered by Douglas Thompkins and his collaborators in the special Forum of *Dialectical Anthropology* on prison reentry offer a kaleidoscopic set of views "from below" of the post-custodial trajectories of American convicts that usefully complements the reigning views "from above" of mainstream criminology, technical penology, and policy-oriented evaluations (e.g., Seiter and Kadela 2003, Petersilia 2003, Travis 2005, Hattery and Smith 2010). But their potential contribution to the much-needed rethinking of this urgent sociopolitical issue and its anthropological ramifications is amputated by three serious conceptual flaws. The first is the impulsive embrace of the demonic myth of the "Prison Industrial Complex" (hereafter PIC), which confuses the reengineering of the state in its dealings with the poor in the postindustrial era with a profit-seeking endeavor. The second is the correlative and inconsiderate invocation of a "Prison Reentry Industry" (hereafter PRI), when the management of felons after their release pertains to bureaucratic ceremony rather than economy. The third is the crippling isolation of penal trajectories from the gamut of state policies that jointly determine the life options of convicts both *before* and *after* confinement, and especially from the regressive transformation of welfare policies (embracing income support, housing, education, job training, health, etc.) that has accompanied, amplified, and complemented criminal justice changes over the past three decades. I briefly take up each of these points *in seriatim* before urging a reorientation of critical approaches to penal policy stressing the perverse circularity, economic absurdity, and political rationale of penalization as a technique for governing urban marginality, as well as the need to integrate "workfare" and "prisonfare" into a single framework for analysis and action.

1. Slay the chimera of the "Prison Industrial Complex"

The editors of the forum and many of the contributors who have come out of the penitentiary frame their (post)custodial experiences and critiques by reference to the "Prison Industrial Complex," an expression that came into vogue among America's criminal justice activists and progressive scholars and journalists after the mid-1990s (Donziger 1996, Davis 1998, Schlosser 1998). The term is, as is too often the case, left undefined and unexplicated, as if its emotional charge and political motive provided sufficient warrant to invoke it. The problem is, to the degree that it can be specified, this wooly notion turns out to be internally incoherent and externally disconnected from the structure and dynamics of carceral expansion in the post-Civil Rights era. Briefly put, four defects suggest that the chimera of PIC must be slayed,[2] and the empirical trends and social dilemmas posed by the peregrination of convicts after prison recast as pertaining to the *revamping of the state* in both its social and penal components (Wacquant 2009).

1.1. PIC is based on a loose analogy with MIC, the "Military Industrial Complex" alleged to have driven the expansion of America's warfare economy during the Cold War era (e.g., Gilmore 2009). Aside from the dubious analytic validity of a notion coined by a speechwriter for a despondent President Eisenhower on the occasion of his farewell address,[3] the claim that PIC parallels MIC in handling security on the home front for the benefit of corporations founders on the fact that there is no justice equivalent for the Pentagon. Whereas the federal Department of Defense is a single decision-making center that manages a single budget and implements military policy through hierarchical command, there exists no bureaucratic lever to direct crime control and submit it uniformly to private interests. Legal punishment in America is meted out through a highly decentralized, disjointed and multilayered patchwork of agencies. The police, courts, and corrections are separate government institutions, subjected to disparate political, funding, and bureaucratic imperatives, that are poorly coordinated and whose relations are riven with tension and conflicts (Neubauer 2005: 6–7)—to say nothing of probation, parole, halfway houses, drug treatment facilities, and assorted outfits entrusted with handling convicts after their release.

In addition to being weakly connected to each other, each of the three components of the penal chain are deeply fragmented across geographic space and political scale. Over 18,000 local and state law-enforcement agencies decide their policing strategies at ground level; some 2,341 distinct prosecutors' offices set their judicial priorities; thousands of counties run their own jail while the 50 states and the federal government each run their separate prison system (and release programs) with little regard for what other administrative units are doing. Moreover, because they are located at the back-end of the penal chain, prisons depend for their key operational inputs on measures and processes set in motion by the police and the courts, over whom they have virtually no pull. The incipient "federalization of crime"

(Waisman 1994), which provides a measure of coordination, has been largely undermined by the diversification of prosecution and corrections philosophies across jurisdictions after the abandonment of indeterminate sentencing (Tonry 2000). In organizational and political terms, then, the government function of punishment is decentralized, fragmented, and horizontal; that is, the polar opposite of the military. The connection between MIC and PIC is purely *rhetorical; it pertains to metaphor and not to analogy.* Even if some malevolent alliance of politicians, corporate owners, and correctional officials wished to harness carceral institutions to the pecuniary aims of "multinational globalization" and foster "a project in racialization and macro injustice" (Brewer and Hetizeg 2008: 625), they would lack the bureaucratic means to do so. Rather than explaining it, PIC precludes posing the crucial question of how and why a *de facto national policy of penal expansion* has emerged out of the organizational hodge-podge formed by criminal justice institutions.

1.2. Advocates of PIC maintain that, due to its stupendous enlargement, incarceration plays a major role in the contemporary capitalist economy of the United States, spurring the accumulation process by offering choice opportunities for profit, an endlessly renewed pool of superexploitable labor, and even the valorization of "surplus land" in rural areas (Gilmore 2007). Nationally prisons are said to "constitute an ever growing source of capitalist growth" (Davis 2003: 96) while internationally "the rise of industrialized punishment has woven mass incarceration into the fabric of the global economy" (Sudbury 2004: 13). This claim borders on the absurd. While it is true that the corrections budget of the United States has increased to outlandish proportions by historical and international standards, it still makes up a tiny and negligible chunk of the domestic economy. The $70 billion the United States spent in 2008 to operate its jails and prisons (adding up the budgets of counties, states, and the federal government) amounts to *less than one-half of 1 percent of its Gross Domestic Product of $14.4 trillion.*

To realize the exaggeration entailed in asserting that prisons have become central to American capitalism (to say nothing of world capitalism), consider that the country's annual expenditures on penal confinement come to about twice the sums Americans disburse for "chocolate, gum, cereal bars and sugar confectionery" (which together generated revenues of $32.9 billion in 2008). They equal the size of the personal products industry which includes "over the counter healthcare, skincare, haircare, makeup, fragrances and others" (with sales of $73.6 billion); and they come to just over one-half of the monies Americans devote annually to soft drinks (with $128 billion).[4] How credible is the notion that the "Soda Industrial Complex" has become a locomotive for the American economy? Prisons have grown as a *government function and a political institution*, as a vehicle for regulating marginality and staging the authority of the Leviathan, but they remain negligible in terms of economic weight and thus non-existent as a vehicle for profit on a national scale—and *a fortiori* on the global stage.

1.3. A related staple of PIC is the strident denunciation of the exploitation of convict labor. The magazine article by Mike Davis that introduced the term "prison-industrial complex" to readers of *The Nation* in 1995 (in quotation marks and without any explication) was appositely entitled "Hell Factories in the Field."[5] Nearly every piece published since by advocates of the PIC perspective complains in florid language that prisons are being turned into "sweatshops" and inmates reduced to "neo-slavery," as they are pushed into the clutches of capitalist firms eager to recruit pliant low-wage workers behind bars who require no medical coverage, no benefits, no vacation pay, and no pension—as if such employment terms were difficult to impose on the contingent workforce outside. The list of companies said to use prison and jail employees is then rolled out: Wal-Mart, Dell, TWA, Toys "R" Us, Chevron, IBM, Boeing,

Nintendo, Starbucks, Victoria's Secret, and so on. The fact that it comprises a Who's Who of corporate America from across economic sectors is presented as definitive proof that inmates have been turned into a coerced reserve army of labor. But the tireless repetition of this list hides the fact that none of these companies ever made more than an incidental or accidental use of prison labor (typically a few hundred staff, hired for short stints through contractors); that none of the industries they lead relies even marginally on convict workers; and that the overwhelming majority of inmates suffer not from labor enslavement but from numbing idleness (Wacquant 2009: 181–184).

Indeed, at peak use around 2002, fewer than 5,000 inmates were employed by private firms, amounting to *one-quarter of 1 percent of the carceral population*. As for the roughly 8 percent of convicts who toil for state and federal industries under lock, they are "employed" at a loss to correctional authorities in spite of massive subsidies, guaranteed sales to a captive market of public administrations, and exceedingly low wages (averaging well under a dollar an hour).[6] Put simply, the notion that convicts constitute a vulnerable labor pool is a *figment of the political imagination*: it is the dream of advocates of the far Right, who wish to turn penitentiaries into "factories behind bars" to fight idleness and lower the carceral bill, and the nightmare of critics of the far Left who fear that carceral factories are already humming. In reality, for a plethora of stubborn economic, legal, and cultural reasons, prison employment on a mass scale has vanished and is a nonstarter in the liberal societies of the advanced West, including the United States (Van Zyl Smith and Dunkel 1999).[7]

1.4. PIC maintains that the profit-motive drives and distorts punishment, on grounds that firms have inserted themselves into an "industrialized" penal process as suppliers of correctional wares and services, designers and builders of prisons, and even managers of for-profit facilities. But there is nothing new or peculiar in this: the intercession of commercial operators is the norm in the provision of public goods in America. Owing to its weak bureaucratic capacities, there is virtually no major function of government—education, welfare, healthcare, housing, transportation, infrastructure, etc.—that does not entail extensive recourse to private entities. In his path-breaking book *The Divided Welfare State*, Jacob Hacker (2002: 6) has shown that American social policy is distinctive among advanced countries, not for its levels of protection and spending (as commonly believed), but for its long-standing reliance on the private sector to deliver protection against life risks through a "hybrid system of social benefits." For instance, two-thirds of Americans get medical coverage through employer-based health plans offered by insurance companies that are closely regulated and heavily subsidized by government through tax concessions. So much so that private expenditures accounted for 55 percent of total healthcare spending in the country circa 2000. The same is true of aid to the poor: long before the "end of welfare as we know it" in 1996, the lion's share of benefits was delivered through nonprofit and commercial outfits (to the tune of 60 percent of expenditures in 1980). The "marketization of welfare" has intensified over the past two decades with the broad expansion of outsourcing for the supervision of workfare recipients, the spread of vouchers, and "the blurring of the distinction between nonprofit and for-profit providers" (Katz 2001: 148–155). Even post-secondary education fits this pattern: 36 percent of the $375 billion paid out to degree-granting tertiary institutions in 2006–2007 went to private schools (Institute of Education Sciences 2009: table 9).

Ironically, the one signal exception to this "mixed economy" of government services is incarceration. In direct contradiction to PIC, what distinguishes punishment in America—as in other advanced societies—is the degree to which it has *remained stubbornly and distinctively public.* After two decades of gusting ideological winds at their back, favorable economic and budgetary circumstances, frantic lobbying, and the pressing need to expand custodial capacity given grotesque overcrowding in existing facilities, private prison firms managed to capture only 6 percent of the "carceral market" at their peak in 2000 (one-fourth of their projected goal of 1995). The bursting of the stock market bubble of 2001 nearly destroyed the sector— its leaders owed their survival to magnanimous new contracts to house immigrant convicts under supervision of the Immigration and Naturalization Service (INS)—and their share is unlikely to grow much further. As for the overseas market, it is equally limited and stagnant: private corrections gets a lot of headlines around the world, but it remains a remarkably marginal "industry" composed of a few small firms whose viability is a brittle by-product of the shifting ideological favors and bureaucratic ineptitude of states.[8]

Incarceration is far and away the one canonical government function that remains firmly in the grip of public officials because penal confinement does not just serve to curb disorder, discipline the unruly and warehouse the supernumerary. It also anchors a core civic theater for dramatizing collective norms, asserting political authority, and staging the sovereignty of the state. *The prison is a core political institution and not an economic one.*[9] PIC obscures the political logic of penal expansion because it inverts cause and consequence: the ring of "prison profiteers" (Herivel and Wright 2007) has enlarged because the penal state has expanded to gargantuan proportions, and not the other way around.

2. Prisoner "reentry" pertains to bureaucratic ceremony and not industrial economy

The penitentiary has returned to the institutional forefront of the advanced societies, not because of its "comprehensive corporatization"—*pace* Angela Davis (Davis and Shaylor 2001: 4)—but because the government has shifted from the social welfare to the punitive management of urban marginality through the simultaneous rolling out of disciplinary workfare and neutralizing prisonfare. The penal boom results *not from profit-seeking but from state-crafting.* Accordingly, it is doubly misleading to invoke murky economic metaphors to speak of a "Prisoner Reentry Industry," as the Forum in *Dialectical Anthropology* does.

2.1. It is misleading to speak of a reentry industry insofar as the vast majority of former convicts experience *not reentry but ongoing circulation between the two poles of a continuum of forced confinement* formed by the prison and the dilapidated districts of the dualizing metropolis (Wacquant 2010a) that are the latter's primary recruiting grounds, as the state deploys the criminal justice apparatus to contain the disorders spawned by economic deregulation and welfare retrenchment in the lower regions of social and physical space. Proof is that seven in ten convicts coming out of the gates of American prisons are rearrested and over half of them are thrown back behind bars within three years (Langan and Levin 2002).[10] For them "reentry" into society would be more accurately described as prelude to another entry into the prison. Similarly, the conventional language of "transition from prison to community" used by practitioners and analysts of "reentry" (e.g., Thompson 2008 for a standard approach) presupposes a clear separation between these two worlds, whereas they increasingly interpenetrate one another under the current regime of hyperincarceration targeted at neighborhoods of relegation—not to mention that these urban wastelands present few of the positive social and moral features commonly associated with the term "community." For lower-class black convicts, who supply the largest contingent of admissions, the bloated prison and the barren hyperghetto stand in a linked relationship of structural continuity, functional surrogacy, and cultural syncretism such that, irrespective of their custodial status, they remain hemmed in social spaces characterized by extreme material denudement, rampant social suspicion, routine violence, and failing public institutions (Wacquant 2001 and 2008: 119–132).

Correlatively, to speak of "pathways of reintegration" (Visher and Travis 2003: 89) disregards the hard fact that there was *no integration prior to incarceration* as evidenced by the social profile of jail detainees in America (Wacquant 2009: 69–72): fewer than half of them held a full-time job at the time of their arraignment; two-thirds come from households living under half of the official "poverty line"; 87 percent have no postsecondary education; and four in ten suffer from serious physical and mental disabilities. Every other jail inmate has an incarcerated family member and six in ten were previously incarcerated themselves. How could former prisoners be "*re*integrated" when they were never integrated in the first place and when there exists no viable social structure to accommodate them outside? How could there be "reentry" when they are enmeshed in a carceral lattice spanning the prison and neighborhoods deeply penetrated and ongoingly destabilized by the penal state?

2.2. It is misleading to speak of a reentry *industry* because the gamut of institutions entrusted with supervising and supporting convicts after their release are not economic institutions. The industrial metaphor applied to the processing of criminals was given its letters of intellectual nobility two decades ago by the widely read book by criminologist Nils Christie, *Crime Control as Industry* (1993, second enlarged edition 1994, third edition 2000, reprinted twice since). Writing from the vantage point of his native Norway, a country with an inmate population under 2,300 at the time, where convicted criminals routinely bide their time on a wait-list for months for a cell to become available in the country's miniscule carceral system, and where rehabilitation is a state religion, Christie could not but be shocked by the mammoth size of America's custodial population (then exceeding 1.5 million), its growing reliance on private suppliers and operators, and its abandonment of correctional treatment for brute neutralization and shrill retribution. The only way to make sense of the sheer scale and penological absurdity of American hyperincarceration was to argue that the "segments of the population" that are "seen as superfluous," due to their "inability to participate in the consumer society," are "given a use function as raw materials for the control industry" (Christie 2004: 7250). But the "control industry," like the reentry industry, is not an industry in any meaningful sense of the term. As with PIC, this economic language obscures that criminal justice outfits are first and foremost public or parapublic organizations entrusted with delivering sanctions, that is, *components of the penal sector of the bureaucratic field* as characterized by Pierre Bourdieu ([1993] 1994).

The gamut of organizations that supervise former prisoners after their release, and either assist them in or hinder them from merging into a household, finding housing and employment, and resolving their medical and other personal troubles (described in detail by Ross and Richards 2009), do not form an economic sector. They do not produce or sell goods in an exchange system where price acts as a clearing mechanism; they do not compete with each other for inputs and vie for segments of a market; and they do not generate profits that would provide an impetus for further expansion.[11] They are "people-processing institutions" entrusted with the management of a tainted population of sub-citizens (owing to the judicial stigma afflicting them), which seek to achieve changes in their clients "not by altering basic personal attributes, but by conferring on them a public status and relocating them in a new set of social circumstances" (Hasenfeld 1972: 256). Now, it is true that reentry outfits contend with one another for contracts with local authorities and cash from philanthropic foundations; that they claim to change the attributes of recipients through moral rearmament, soft skills training, and life coaching techniques; and that they experience the daily scramble over bodies as a form of competition with other human services organizations. But, for all the talk of "marketizing" poor oversight in the post-welfare era, reentry operators remain suppliers of services in a public monopsony, with the government (and associated charities) as sole buyer. Their continued functioning hinges, not on market efficiency, but on bureaucratic clientelism and political patronage. The conceptual vocabulary needed to describe, explain, and eventually transform the institutions handling reentry is not that of the radical critique of capitalism—and even less so of the loosely associated "isms" of racism, sexism, and militarism, ritually invoked by the advocates of PIC—but the tools of the neo-Durkheimian sociology of bureaucratic organization and the neo-Weberian theory of the state.[12]

In their classic essay on "Formal Structure as Myth and Ceremony," John Meyer and Brian Rowan (1977: 346) propose that organizations can be arrayed along a continuum with, at one end, "production organizations under strong output controls" and, at the other, "organizations whose success depends on the confidence and stability achieved by isomorphism with institutional rules." Outfits for postcustodial supervision clearly belong to the latter type, for which "activity has ritual significance: it maintains appearances and validates an organization" (Meyer and Rowan 1977: 354, 355). Such establishments, Meyer and Rowan (1977: 358) point out, are deeply inefficient, but they survive and even thrive by "decoupling" structure and activities, and by following "a logic of confidence and good faith" whereby "delegation, professionalization, goal ambiguity, and the elimination of output data" are enrolled to maintain a "ceremonial façade" (Meyer and Rowan 1977: 358). In short, institutions of penal supervision after incarceration serve less to "reintegrate" convicts who "reenter" society than to cloak the glaring irrationality of the policy of penalization of poverty as the nefarious consequences of hyperincarceration accumulate and fester at the bottom of social and physical space. Denounced upstream and expunged from the prison itself, the welfarist myth of rehabilitation is revived and reactivated downstream *after* custody to help stage the resolve of the state to tackle the crime question on an individual, case-by-case basis. Only now this myth is deployed in a stripped-down, panoptic and disciplinary variant high on symbolism and low on substance, guaranteed to have no more than a marginal impact on the endless recycling of millions of convicts.

For all the excitement it has generated among its advocates since its instigation around 2004 by the Urban Institute and the Open Society Institute (backed by Soros monies), the so-called "reentry movement" is but a minor bureaucratic adaptation to the glaring contradictions of the punitive regulation of poverty. Proof is its measly funding: the Second Chance Act of 2008, ballyhooed by the bipartisan political coalition that passed it and the scholars it subsidizes, has an annual budget of $165 million equal to less than *one-quarter of 1 percent of the country's correctional budget*. Put differently, it provides the princely sum of $20 monthly per new convict released, enough to buy them a sandwich each week. If the authorities were serious about "reentry," they would allocate 20 to 50 times that amount at minimum. They would start by reestablishing the previously existing web of programs that build a bridge back to civilian life—furloughs, educational release, work release, and half-way houses—which has atrophied over the past two decades, and avoid locating "reentry services" in decrepit facilities located in dangerous and dilapidated inner-city districts rife with crime and vice (Ross and Richards 2009: 13–15, 48). They would restore the prison college programs that had made the United States an international leader in higher education behind bars, until convicts were denied eligibility for Pell Grants in 1994 to feed the vengeful fantasies of the electorate, even as government studies showed that a college degree is the most efficacious and cost-effective antidote to reoffending (Page 2004). They would end the myriad rules that extend penal sanction far beyond prison walls and long after sentences have been served—such as the statutes barring "ex-cons" from access to public housing, welfare support, educational grants, and voting—and curtail the legal disabilities inflicted on their families and intimates (Comfort 2007). They would restrain and reverse the runaway diffusion of "rap sheets" through government websites and private firms offering background checks to employers and realtors, which fuels *criminal discrimination* and gravely truncates the life opportunities of ex-offenders years after they have served their sentence and "come clean" (Blumstein and Nakamura 2009). They would expand substance abuse treatment programs both inside and outside prison since the vast majority of convicts suffer from serious alcohol and drug dependency, and yet go untreated by the millions.[13] They would immediately divert low-level offenders who are mentally ill into medical facilities, instead of continuing to subject them to penal abuse and medical neglect in carceral facilities, as consistently recommended by leading public health experts for over two decades (Steadman and Naples 2005). They would stop the costly and self-defeating policy of returning parolees to custody for technical violations of the administrative conditions of their release (Grattet et al. 2008). The list goes on and on.

The twofold point being made here is that, besides serving no productive function, the "reentry industry" is not an industry by dint of its bureaucratic (il)logic and artisanal format. This derives from a signal difference between the military and crime control functions of the state, which PIC and the derivative trope of PRI both ignore and obscure: warfare is a capital- and technology-intensive activity for which the Pentagon necessarily depends on private corporations (in the absence of public sector producers of military wares), whereas justice is a people-intensive activity for which government officials routinely rely on myriad public outfits and their extensions (nonprofit or commercial). And these outfits are not geared toward effecting the "reintegration" of convicts for which budgets, personnel, and political will are lacking, but to performing a simulacrum of rehabilitation after custody while such rehabilitation has been jettisoned in custody. In short, prisoner reentry is *not an industry but a bureaucratic charade*.

3. Post-custodial supervision is a component of prisonfare, which complements workfare and partakes of the neoliberal reengineering of the state

Convict reentry programs activated "downstream" are not only tiny in size, incoherent in design, and grotesquely ineffective—so many properties that would make them a failed industry if they were indeed one. They are also undermined at every turn by the broader set of policies that the state deploys "upstream" on the education, housing, healthcare, welfare, and labor fronts. In all of these domains, over the three decades spanning the dismantling of the Fordist-Keynesian compact, federal and local actions have converged to aggravate inequality and to entrench racialized deprivation in the city.[14] At the same time, the authorities have swung from the social and medical treatment to the penal management of poverty, thus directly fueling admission into the ballooning carceral system and sowing such instability in the nether zones of social and physical space as to render the "reintegration" of convicts after their sentence is served an impractical proposition.

3.1. The multisided and multiscalar involvement of the state in the production and regulation of urban marginality implies that, to properly anatomize the structure and functioning of post-custodial oversight, we must effect three analytic moves: (1) forsake a narrow focus on individual "reentry"—which, for most convicts, is just a step toward repeat incarceration—to capture extended life sequences spanning trajectories before and after prison, using the lineage as unit of analysis and tracking the peregrinations of its members across multiple spells of penal entailment;[15] (2) link social and penal policy since these two variants of poverty policy have become interwoven and coordinated under the same punitive philosophy of moral behaviorism; (3) heed the symbolic purposes and ceremonial logic of post-prison supervision, as opposed to its imagined economic rationale, and trace its socially disintegrative and criminogenic effects as well as its proclaimed supportive role.

The sudden policy and scholarly infatuation with "reentry" as individualized response to the collective predicament posed by the mass return of convicts to the dispossessed districts of the metropolis must not hide the fact that such programs are an integral component of *prisonfare*, defined as the rolling out of the police, the courts, and custodial institutions and their extensions to contain the brewing urban disorders that the state itself has spawned or aggravated by retracting the social safety net and deregulating the low-wage labor market (Wacquant 2009: 16–17, 58–69, 98–109, 135–146). Reentry programs are *not an antidote to but an extension of punitive containment* as government technique for managing problem categories and territories in the dualizing city. They are not a remedy to, but part and parcel of the institutional machinery of hyperincarceration (Cohen 1985), whose reach they stretch beyond bars and over the lifecourse of convicts by keeping them under the stern watch and punctilious injunctions of criminal justice even as they return to their barren neighborhoods. Reentry must therefore be understood as an element in the redrawing of the perimeter, priorities, and modalities of action of the state as a stratifying and classifying agency, and not as an "industry" geared to "reintegrating" a marginalized population that was never socially and economically integrated to start with.

3.2. The recent revamping of post-custodial supervision partakes of the neoliberal reengineering of the state whereby restrictive workfare and expansive prisonfare meet and mesh to impose the discipline of fragmented wage work onto the postindustrial poor, neutralize their more disruptive elements, and project the authority of the Leviathan onto the stage of law and order (Wacquant 2010b). Indeed, the renovated reentry chain is for lower-class criminal men *the penal counterpart and complement to punitive workfare* as the new face of public aid for derelict women and children—who happen to be their mothers, sisters, wives, and offspring, since the welfare and criminal justice arms of the state fasten onto the same households located at the foot of the socioracial hierarchy according to a gendered division of control. Both offer meager and temporary support on condition that recipients submit to disciplinary monitoring pointing them to the substandard employment slots of the service economy. Both use the same case-based techniques of surveillance, moral stigma, the abridgement of privacy, and graduated sanctions to "correct" wayward behavior.[16] Both produce, not material improvement and social incorporation, but forced capitulation to extreme precarity and civic liminality as the normal horizon of life for their clientele. Reentry organizations thus prosper on the penal side thanks to their *organizational isomorphism* with workfare on the social policy side and to their *cultural congruence* with the moral individualism animating a political culture that has splintered between a libertarian, laissez-faire attitude toward those perched at the top and a paternalist and punitive disposition toward those trapped at the bottom. By activating the individualist logic of personal responsibility, post-custodial bureaucracies put the onus of failed "reintegration" on former convicts, thereby screening out the accelerating degradation of the condition of the American working class in the "gloves-off economy" which increasingly consigns them to long-term subemployment and laborious poverty (Kalleberg et al. 2000, Shulman 2005, Bernardt et al. 2008). Lastly, the ceremonial deployment of reentry programs effectively decouples the web of economic, social, urban, and justice policies that absolve the prison from the handling of convicts after incarceration, creating the illusion that the state is not deeply implicated in the entry of convicts. In so doing, it helps legitimize *post festum* the penalization of poverty and the normalization of social insecurity at the bottom of the class structure.[17]

To sum up, the so-called Prison Industrial Complex is organizationally antithetical, not analogous, to its alleged precursor, the Military Industrial Complex; it composes a negligible part of the contemporary economy, and not one of its central planks; it does not exploit convict labor or generate self-sustaining profits (except by way of sideshow), but constitutes a gross fiscal drain; and, far from being "corporatized," punishment remains a distinctively and mulishly public function of government. Because it consistently mistakes a political exercise in state-building for a capitalist quest for profit (stoked by the evils of racism, sexism, and imperialism), PIC supplies no analytic traction on the prison boom in post-Civil Rights America and on the punitive revamping of the neoliberal Leviathan on both the social and penal fronts. Worse, it blinds us to the colossal economic irrationality and Kafkaesque bureaucratic absurdities of hyperincarceration. Consequently, we must jettison the hazy economic metaphor of the "Prison Reentry Industry" and grasp the changing scale, organization, and effects of programs of post-custodial supervision as the ceremonial components of a broader refurbishing of the bureaucratic field in its dealing with the disqualified fractions of the postindustrial working class. Our theoretical inspiration should come not from Karl Marx and Frantz Fanon, but from Emile Durkheim, Max Weber, and Pierre Bourdieu, insofar as the contemporary prison is at core a political institution—a concentrate of material and symbolic violence—and not an economic outfit or a racial organization. More crucially still, we should reaffirm our empirical commitment to tracking the phenomenon of "reentry" as it actually unfolds at ground level, that is, not as satanic mills of punishment for lucre but as a penal morality play and bureaucratic farce.

Notes

1   This essay was previously published in *Dialectical Anthropology* (2010) 34: 605–620 (DOI: 10.1007/s10624-010-9215-5), Forum on "No Exit? The Prison Reentry Industry."

I am grateful for the diligent research assistance of Aaron Benavidez, the sharp analytic comments of Megan Comfort and Reuben Miller, and the patience of the editors of *Dialectical Anthropology*.

2   A chimera is a fire-breathing beast in ancient Greek mythology (first described in Homer's Odyssey), sporting the hind of a snake, the body of a goat, and the head of a lion. It is an apt image for the fearsome triadic combination of astringent justice officials, tough-on-crime politicians and media, and booming private corporations which advocates of PIC imagine propel prison trends.

3   See Moskos (1974) for an early critique pointing to the multiple flaws and limitations of the notion of "Military Industrial Complex."

4   The economic data in this section are taken from the corresponding "Industry Profile" in Datamonitor, Business Source Complete, EBSCOhost (retrieved October 9, 2010).

5   This title is curious since Davis does not describe carceral production units, noting instead "the drastic shortage of work for prisoners, condemning nearly half the inmate population to serve their

sentences idly in their cells watching infinities of television" (Davis 1995: 230).The same Mike Davis compares California prisons to "slave plantations" in his front-cover endorsement of Ruth Gilmore's book *Golden Gulag*, even though Gilmore concedes in the book that "most prisoners are idle" and that "those who work do so for a public agency" (Gilmore 2007: 21).

6 Compare these figures (under 5,000 employed by firms and an estimated 90,000 by government entities, fewer than half of them black, and all working voluntarily) to this statement, typical of the hyperbole of PIC advocates: "Close to a million young Black men suffer the exploitative regime of the modern prison-industrial complex, where their virtually unpaid labor is coerced and extracted for corporate profits ….This is a situation that resurrects the biophysics of spatio-temporal reduction imposed by slavery and segregation" (Juan 2005: 70).

7 Britain's new conservative government will soon (re)discover this as it tries to implement its surreal plan to put English and Welsh inmates to work 40 hours a week (to gain job skills and pay for victim reparations and support). Already, the country's Prison Governors' Association has warned that custodial facilities are not equipped for production; that many inmates are not motivated to do drab work and suffer from serious substance abuse and mental impairments; and that employment will require added supervisory staff, whereas the correctional budget and staff are set to decrease by one-third. Not to mention that providing carceral jobs for convicts will hardly please the 2.4 million Britons who are presently unemployed on the outside (nearly one million of them for over a year).

8 In 2009, Corrections Corporation of America (CCA), by far the largest of only four international firms of incarceration with half of the planet's private prison "beds," sported a profit of $155 million on global sales of $1.7 billion. By comparison, the world's top corporations tallied profits of $10 to $20 billion on sales ranging from $200 to $400 billion. CCA controls assets of $3 billion and employs 17,000; leading multinational companies own assets in the hundreds of billions of dollars (excluding financial conglomerates, whose assets range from $1 to $2 trillion) and employ hundreds of thousands (e.g., Wal-Mart has 1.8 million employees for sales of $408 billion generating a profit of $14 billion; General Electric employs 307,000 for sales of $156 billion and a profit of $11 billion). It is hard to see how CCA, being one-hundredth the size of GE, could be playing more than a decorative role in the global economy.

9 See Wacquant (2009: 287–295, 304–330) for further elaboration. McBride (2007) offers an elegant statement of a germane position from the standpoint of political theory. Harcourt (2011) sketches a provocative historical genealogy of the antinomic opposition between the market economy and the penal state.

10 These figures date from the mid-1990s, concerning convicts released in 1994. Everything suggests that the recapture rate has increased since, given that the overall supply of criminals has decreased steadily since. In California, fully three-fourths of the cohorts entering prison around 2000 were composed of "PVRCs" (parole violators returned to custody).

11 Like other compendia on key economic terms, *The Oxford Dictionary of Economics* defines an industry as "a sector of the economy, in which firms use similar factor inputs to make a group of related products," followed by a second, older, specification: "A group of sectors, mainly in manufacturing and construction, typically producing physical goods rather than services."

12 The only industry that has grown about "reentry" is the tiny subsector of the publishing world devoted to the genre of practical "handbooks" and advice manuals aimed at (ex-) convicts and their family and friends, and the correctional and social work professionals who oversee them after release. See, from the fast-expanding list of titles typically filled with a mix of sensible pointers, painful anecdotes, and dire warnings, as well as lyrical invocations of the moral individualism that undergirds the national commonsense of Americans, Jackson (2008), Bovan (2009), and Boothe (2009).

13 Nationwide, the United States spent $468 billion to handle substance abuse and addiction to tobacco, alcohol, and narcotics in 2005. Less than 2 percent of that sum went to prevention and treatment (Califano 2009).This imbalance is even more pronounced among addicted convicts both behind and beyond bars: the California Department of Corrections offers 750 beds in detoxification wards to its 85,000 parolees known to be alcohol or drug addicts.

14 Wacquant (2008) provides an empirical demonstration in the case of Chicago and Brady (2009) a rigorous international comparison showing, first, that inequality and poverty in the advanced societies are tightly correlated and, second, how both result from power relations and political coalitions institutionalized in the state, not from the behavioral failings or cultural patterns of the lower class (as alleged by those scatty sociologists who periodically rediscover with wonderment the mysterious magnetism of the "culture of poverty").

15 "The dominant model therefore should not be one of people being taken from 'the community' to be incarcerated out of sight and out of mind until they are released and reintegrated back into society. Instead, one sees a continual flow of people moving in and out of correctional facilities, some for short stays and others for long ones, forming various networks that traverse carceral borders and that are subjected to punitive measures in the domestic and communal spheres" (Comfort 2008: 186). This constant churning of the penalized poor in and out of jail and prison exerts a range of disruptive effects on all generations inside a household, and particularly on the children of convicts (Foster and Hagan 2007).

16 This is amply documented by Sharon Hays's (2003) and Collins and Mayer's (2010) lucid accounts of workfare policy at ground level. See also the complementary view offered by Watkins-Hayes (2009) in her portrait of the new-style welfare bureaucrats at work.

17 Peck and Theodore (2009) show how the "job developers" who funnel ex-convicts toward day-labor agencies effect this work of normalization in "Carceral Chicago."

References

Bernhardt, Annette, Heather Boushey, Laura Dresser and Chris Tilly. 2008. *The Gloves-off Economy: Workplace Standards at the Bottom of America's Labor Market.* Champaign, IL: Labor and Employment Relations Association.

Blumstein, Alfred and Kiminori Nakamura. 2009. "Redemption in the Presence of Widespread Criminal Background Checks." *Criminology* 47, no. 2 (May): 327–359.

Boothe, Demico. 2009. *Getting Out and Staying Out: A Black Man's Guide to Success after Prison.* Memphis, TN: Full Surface Publishing.

Bourdieu, Pierre. [1993] 1994. "Rethinking the State: On the Genesis and Structure of the Bureaucratic Field." *Sociological Theory* 12, no. 1 (March): 1–19.

Bovan, Richard. 2009. *The Dedicated Ex-Prisoner's Guide to Life and Success on the Outside: 10 Rules for Making It in Society after Doing Time.* Memphis, TN: Full Surface Publishing.

Brady, David. 2009. *Rich Democracies, Poor People: How Politics Explain Poverty.* New York: Oxford University Press.

Brewer, Rose M. and Nancy A. Heitzeg. 2008. "The Racialization of Crime and Punishment: Criminal Justice, Color-Blind Racism, and the Political Economy of the Prison Industrial Complex." *American Behavioral Scientist* 51, no. 5 (January): 625–644.

Califano, Joseph A. 2009. *Shoveling Up II: The Impact of Substance Abuse on Federal, State and Local Budgets.* New York: National Center on Addiction and Substance Abuse at Columbia University.

Christie, Nils. 1993. *Crime Control as Industry: Toward Gulags, Western Style?* London: Routledge.

Christie, Nils. 2004. "Imprisonment, Sociological Aspects." Pp. 7248–7251 in *International Encyclopedia of the Social and Behavioral Sciences.* Edited by Neil J. Smelser and Paul B. Baltes. London: Pergamon Press.

Cohen, Stanley. 1985. *Visions of Social Control.* Cambridge: Polity Press.

Collins, Jane L. and Victoria Mayer. 2010. *Both Hands Tied: Welfare Reform and the Race to the Bottom in the Low-Wage Labor Market.* Chicago: University of Chicago Press.

Comfort, Megan. 2007. "Punishment beyond the Legal Offender." *Annual Review of Law & Social Science* 3: 271–296.

Comfort, Megan. 2008. *Doing Time Together: Love and Family in the Shadow of the Prison.* Chicago: University of Chicago Press.

Davis, Angela. 1998. "What Is the Prison Industrial Complex? What Does It Matter?" *Colorlines: Race, Culture, Action* (Fall): 13–17.

Davis, Angela Y. 2003. *Are Prisons Obsolete?* New York: Seven Stories Press.

Davis, Angela and Cassandra Shaylor. 2001. "Race, Gender, and the Prison Industrial Complex: California and Beyond." *Meridians* 2, no. 1: 1–25.

Davis, Mike. 1995. "A Prison Industrial Complex: Hell Factories in the Field." *The Nation*, February 20: 229–234.

Donziger, Marc R. 1996. "The Prison Industrial Complex." Pp. 63–98 in *The Real War on Crime*. New York: Harper Perennial.

Foster, Holly and John Hagan. 2007. "Incarceration and Intergenerational Social Exclusion." *Social Forces* 54, no. 4: 399–433.

Gilmore, Ruth. 2007. *Golden Gulag: Prisons, Surplus, Crisis, and Opposition in Globalizing California*. Berkeley: University of California Press.

Gilmore, Ruth. 2009. "From Military Industrial Complex to Prison Industrial Complex." Pp. 1–11 in *Recording Carceral Landscapes*. Edited by Trevor Paglen. Berkeley: The Lef Foundation.

Grattet, Ryken, Joan Petersilia and Jeffrey Lin. 2008. *Parole Violations and Revocations in California*. Irvine, CA: Center for Evidence-Based Corrections.

Hacker, Jacob S. 2002. *The Divided Welfare State: The Battle over Public and Private Social Benefits*. New York: Cambridge University Press.

Harcourt, Bernard. 2011. *The Illusion of Free Markets: Punishment and the Myth of Natural Order*. Cambridge, MA: Harvard University Press.

Hasenfeld, Yeheskel. 1972. "People Processing Organizations: An Exchange Approach." *American Sociological Review* 37, no. 3 (June): 256–263.

Hays, Sharon. 2003. *Flat Broke with Children: Women in the Age of Welfare Reform*. New York: Oxford University Press.

Hattery, Angela and Earl Smith. 2010. *Prisoner Re-Entry and Social Capital: The Long Road to Reintegration*. Lanham, MD: Lexington Books.

Herivel, Tara J. and Paul Wright. 2007. *Prison Profiteers: Who Makes Money from Mass Incarceration*. New York: New Press.

Institute of Education Sciences. 2009. *Digest of Education Statistics, 2009*. Washington, DC: National Center for Education Statistics.

Jackson, Michael B. 2008. *How to Do Good after Prison: A Handbook for Successful Reentry (w/Employment Information Handbook)*. Willingboro, NJ: Joint FX Press.

Juan, E. San, Jr. 2005. "Preparing for the Time of Reparation: Speculative Cues from W.E.B. Du Bois, George Jackson and Mumia Abu-Jamal." *Souls: A Critical Journal of Black Politics, Culture, and Society* 7, no. 2 (April): 63–74.

Kalleberg, Arne L., Barbara F. Reskin, and Ken Hudson. 2000. "Bad Jobs in America: Standard and Nonstandard Employment Relations and Job Quality in the United States." *American Sociological Review* 65, no. 2 (April): 256–278.

Katz, Michael B. 2001. *The Price of Citizenship: Redefining the American Welfare State*. New York: Owl Books.

Langan, Patrick and D.J. Levin. 2002. *Recidivism of Prisoners Released in 1994*. Washington, DC: Bureau of Justice Statistics.

McBride, Keally. 2007. *Punishment and Political Order*. Ann Arbor: University of Michigan Press.

Meyer, John W. and Brian Rowan. 1977. "Institutionalized Organizations: Formal Structure as Myth and Ceremony." *American Journal of Sociology* 83, no. 2 (September): 340–363.

Moskos, Charles C., Jr. 1974. "The Concept of the Military-Industrial Complex: Radical Critique or Liberal Bogey?" *Social Problems* 21, no. 4 (April): 498–512.

Neubauer, David W. 2005. *America's Courts and the Criminal Justice System*. Belmont, CA: Thompson.

Page, Joshua. 2004. "Eliminating the Enemy: The Import of Denying Prisoners Access to Higher Education in Clinton's America." *Punishment & Society* 6, no. 4 (October): 357–378.

Peck, Jamie and Nik Theodore. 2009. "Carceral Chicago: Making the Ex-Offender Employability Crisis." *International Journal of Urban and Regional Research* 32, no. 2 (April): 251–281.

Petersilia, Joan. 2003. *When Prisoners Come Home: Parole and Prisoner Reentry.* New York: Oxford University Press.

Ross, Jeffrey Ian and Stephen C. Richards. 2009. *Beyond Bars: Rejoining Society after Prison.* New York: Alpha Publishing.

Schlosser, Eric. 1998. "The Prison-Industrial Complex." *The Atlantic Monthly* 282 (December): 51–77.

Seiter, Richard P. and Karen R. Kadela. 2003. "Prisoner Reentry: What Works, What Does Not, and What Is Promising." *Crime & Delinquency* 49, no. 3 (July): 360–388.

Shulman, Beth. 2005. *The Betrayal of Work: How Low-Wage Jobs Fail 30 Million Americans.* New York: New Press.

Steadman, Henry J. and Michelle Naples. 2005. "Assessing the Effectiveness of Jail Diversion Programs for Persons with Serious Mental Illness and Co-Occurring Substance Use Disorders." *Behavioral Sciences & the Law* (Special Issue on "Diversion from the Criminal Justice System") 23, no. 2 (March/April): 163–170.

Sudbury, Julia. 2004. "A World without Prisons: Resisting Militarism, Globalized Punishment and Empire." *Social Justice* 31, nos. 1–2: 9–33.

Thompson, Anthony C. 2008. *Releasing Prisoners, Redeeming Communities: Reentry, Race, and Politics.* New York: New York University Press.

Tonry, Michael. 2000. "Fragmentation of Sentencing and Corrections in America." *Alternatives to Incarceration* 6, no. 2 (Spring): 9–13.

Travis, Jeremy. 2005. *But They All Come Back: Facing the Challenges of Prisoner Reentry.* Washington, DC: Urban Institute Press.

Van Zyl Smit, Dirk and Frieder Dunkel (eds.). 1999. *Prison Labour: Salvation or Slavery? International Perspectives.* Farnham: Ashgate.

Visher, Christy A. and Jeremy Travis. 2003. "Understanding Individual Pathways: Transitions from Prison to Community." *Annual Review of Sociology* 29: 89–113.

Wacquant, Loïc. 2001. "Deadly Symbiosis: When Ghetto and Prison Meet and Mesh." *Punishment & Society* 3, no. 1 (Winter): 95–133.

Wacquant, Loïc. 2008. *Urban Outcasts: A Comparative Sociology of Advanced Marginality.* Cambridge: Polity Press.

Wacquant, Loïc. 2009. *Punishing the Poor: The Neoliberal Government of Social Insecurity.* Durham, NC and London: Duke University Press.

Wacquant, Loïc. 2010a. "Class, Race and Hyperincarceration in Revanchist America." *Daedalus* (thematic issue on "The Challenges of Mass Incarceration") 140, no. 3 (Summer): 74–90.

Wacquant, Loïc. 2010b. "Crafting the Neoliberal State: Workfare, Prisonfare and Social Insecurity." *Sociological Forum* 25, no. 2 (June): 197–220.

Waisman, Viviana (ed.). 1994. "Symposium on the Federalization of Crime." *Hastings Law Journal* 46, no. 4 (April).

Watkins-Hayes, Celeste. 2009. *The New Welfare Bureaucrats: Entanglements of Race, Class, and Policy Reform.* Chicago: University of Chicago Press.

24

TOWARDS THE GLOBAL ELIMINATION OF THE DEATH PENALTY

A cruel, inhuman and degrading punishment

Roger Hood and Carolyn Hoyle

The roots of the abolitionist movement

This essay[1] will show how the discourse on capital punishment has, in the last 25 years, been transformed from an issue of criminal justice, crime control, public opinion and culture, to be determined by each state as a matter of national sovereignty, into an issue of universal human rights—namely the right to life and the right not to be subjected to a cruel, inhuman and degrading punishment. It will identify the forces and ideas that have been at work to promote the human rights-based objective of abolishing the death penalty completely in all countries of the world, the extent to which it has so far been successful and what barriers remain to achieving this objective.

Discussion of the case for abolishing the death penalty as the most severe form of punishment that could legitimately be enforced by a state began in Europe during the period of liberal enlightenment in the latter part of the 18th century. Cesare Beccaria's famous treatise *On Crimes and Punishments*, published in 1764, had made a great impression in Europe and America. In one short chapter it had effectively advocated the replacement of the 'bloody code' whereby a vast range of crimes were subject to capital punishment. In England for instance, 220 crimes were still punishable by death in 1810 and methods of execution in European countries in the 17th and 18th centuries had been gruesome and calculated deliberately as a public spectacle to inflict terror and also to convey to the audience the consequences of living an 'immoral' and lawless life.

Beccaria's approach was both humanitarian and utilitarian, but it was not an argument for protecting the *rights* of criminals: abolition of the death penalty was in the interest of the state. He argued that infliction of the death penalty sent out to society the wrong moral message, namely that it extolled and promoted the very practice that the law was trying to prohibit—killing as revenge. He advocated a graduated system of punishments proportionate to the gravity of the crimes committed: one that would, by providing greater certainty and consistency, be a more effective deterrent to crime and recognised as more legitimate by citizens than the arbitrary infliction of excessive punishment. It was illogical to threaten so many crimes of different levels of seriousness where no person had been killed with the same level of punishment as for murder, because this provided no incentive for an offender to choose not to murder but to commit instead a lesser crime—an argument still pertinent today when countries impose the death penalty as a punishment for certain serious non-fatal crimes.

The only exception Beccaria made was for certain political crimes and offenders who, 'even if deprived of their freedom' retain 'such connections and such power as to endanger the authority of the nation, when that is, [they] may threaten and endanger a dangerous revolution in the established form of government'. Even then he advocated capital punishment only as a general deterrent if their death was the 'true and only brake to prevent others from committing crimes'.[2] This distinction between the case for abolishing the death penalty for 'ordinary' criminal offences but for retaining it for crimes that threatened the state, especially during political conflict and in wartime, was for many years widely accepted. As will become evident, since the end of the 1980s, almost all countries that have embraced abolition have accepted the view that no such distinction is justified: even those who engage in terrorism or crimes against humanity are to be protected from a violation of their right to life. However, as mentioned below, the spread of violent terrorist acts in several countries has recently led a few nations to retain capital punishment solely for such offences, and so this could remain a barrier to the total extinction of capital punishment.

Although the question of whether the death penalty should be restricted to fewer crimes and finally abolished altogether was debated widely and with passion in Europe and America, north and south, during the 19th century, progress was only achieved gradually, and usually partially. Hence, by 1948 when the United Nations turned its attention, in the wake of the atrocities committed during the Second World War, to drawing up the Universal Declaration of Human Rights (UDHR), there were still only 15 countries that could claim to be 'abolitionists'. Only eight of them (six being in South America)[3] had abolished capital punishment for all crimes in all circumstances, under civil and military criminal law, in wartime as well as peacetime. Seven others had abolished it for murder, but retained it for offences against the state, four of which carried out executions of traitors immediately after the war.[4] In addition, six German and seven Japanese military and political leaders were executed for 'war crimes' after trial at the Nuremberg and Tokyo Tribunals in 1946 and 1948 respectively. Also, only two (Panama and Uruguay) of the 18 countries represented on the Committee on Human Rights, charged with the task of drafting the UDHR, had already completely abolished capital punishment. Most of the others had not even abolished it for murder, even if some were not unsympathetic to this being an aspiration for the future.

So, although Article 3 of the UDHR proclaimed that '*Everyone* has the right to life …' and Article 5 that '*No one* shall be subjected to torture or to cruel, inhuman or degrading punishment or treatment' (our emphases), no mention was made of whether *everyone* and *no one* should include those convicted of offences that still were subject in law to capital punishment. Two years later, in 1950, the newly created Council of Europe adopted the European Convention on Human Rights (ECHR). This was the first treaty to embody the principles of Articles 3 and 5 of the UDHR. Of the 12 member states of the Council of Europe at that time only two had abolished the death penalty for all crimes (Iceland in 1928 and West Germany in 1949) and an exception was specifically made to the right to life as regards capital punishment in Article 2(1), although not, it should be noted, as regards cruel, inhuman and degrading punishment in Article 3. Article 2(1) stated:

> Everyone's right to life shall be protected by law. No one shall be deprived of his life intentionally *save in the execution of a sentence of a court following his conviction of a crime for which this penalty is provided by law.* (Our emphasis)

This clearly allowed the question of whether or not to abolish the death penalty to be left to the decisions of national governments, notwithstanding that it could have been interpreted as a violation of Article 3 as a species of torture or a cruel, inhuman and degrading punishment. Thus, at this time, those who committed capital offences could be denied these rights in the interests of criminal justice and national security. In particular, there was no enthusiasm in Europe for *complete* abolition so as to include crimes against the state or in time of war. For instance, in 1962 Marc Ancel, the distinguished French jurist and advocate of abolition, in a report for the Council of Europe, wrote:

> Even the most convinced abolitionists realise that there may be special circumstances, or particularly troublous times, which justify the introduction of the death penalty for a limited period … Such questions are outside the scope of a study of capital punishment in relation to ordinary criminal law.[5]

Those who drafted the text of the International Covenant on Civil and Political Rights (ICCPR), which also aimed to embody the principles of the UDHR, had been faced with the same problem. At the time that the right to life provisions embodied in Article 6 were drafted, in 1957, the number of completely abolitionist countries still only amounted to ten, and only three more—all small states—were added to the list by the time the Covenant was adopted by the United Nations General Assembly in 1966 (it came into force in 1976).[6]

In the absence of any likelihood of consensus, a compromise between the abstract right to life ideals of the UDHR and what was still widespread practice in relation to the death penalty was inevitable. Although Article 6(1) of the ICCPR declared that 'Every human being has an inherent right to life', this was qualified by the phrase 'No one shall be *arbitrarily* deprived of his life' (our emphasis). This has come to be interpreted by the UN Human Rights Committee (established to monitor implementation of the Covenant and to make general observations) to mean that no one shall be sentenced to death without a fair trial guaranteed by Article 14 of the Covenant, including not being subject to a mandatory death sentence: but obviously Article 6(1) has not guaranteed a full and unambiguous right to life for *every human being.* Furthermore, Article 6(2) stated that 'In countries which have not abolished the death penalty, sentence of death may be imposed only for the most serious crimes.' However this was not intended to justify and set in stone the continuance of the death penalty, as many retentionist states appeared to have assumed, but to limit its application.

The term 'most serious crimes' was soon given a more restricted interpretation in the Safeguards established to Guarantee Protection of the Rights of Those Facing the Death Penalty, which were adopted with no opposition by the UN Economic and Social Council in 1984. It was to be understood that 'their scope should not go beyond intentional crimes with lethal or other extremely grave consequences'. This still broad and imprecise terminology continues to be regarded by some retentionist countries as justification for the use of the death penalty for crimes which do not involve intentional killing, such as drug trafficking, certain sexual offences, corruption and political and religious offences, on the grounds that each state has the right to determine 'the types of crimes for which the death penalty is applied ... taking fully into account the sentiments of its own people, state of crime, and criminal policy'.[7] However, no *universal* concept of human rights is possible if such cultural and political diversity is allowed to determine this issue. The UN Human Rights Committee has insisted that such crimes cannot be counted among 'the most serious' and that Article 6(2) 'must be read restrictively to mean that the death penalty should be a *quite exceptional measure*' (our emphasis). The UN Special Rapporteur on Extrajudicial, Summary or Arbitrary Executions has adopted the view that this should mean that the death penalty, pending abolition, may only be imposed, 'where it can be shown that there was an intention to kill which resulted in the loss of life',[8] though this should not *justify* its use for such a crime. Indeed Article 6(2) was intended only as a 'marker' to signal that the scope of capital punishment should be *restricted until it had been fully abolished*, as were the other Safeguards in Article 6, such as those protecting persons under the age of 18 at the time of the offence and pregnant women from being executed.

The goal of Article 6 was categorically stated in clause 6(6), namely that: 'Nothing in this Article shall be invoked to delay or to prevent the abolition of capital punishment by any State Party to the present Covenant.' In addition Article 7 of the ICCPR embodied Article 5 of the Declaration, protecting people from torture or cruel, inhuman or degrading treatment or punishment. Thus, the ICCPR was intended to be a 'living document' embodying an aspiration to move towards complete abolition of the death penalty. It provided no justification for states merely to pursue a policy of restricted use of capital punishment, or a justification for judicial executions to continue so long as they followed the fair trial provisions of Article 14 and all the other Safeguards introduced to protect the rights of those facing the death penalty *pending* abolition. Furthermore, as Article 4(2) stipulated—and this was of special significance as regards the question of whether to abolish the death penalty completely in all circumstances or to retain it for 'terrorist crimes'—there could be no derogation from Articles 6 and 7 even 'in time of public emergency which threatens the life of the nation'.

This interpretation of the intent of the Covenant and its vision was fully endorsed by a resolution of the United Nations General Assembly in 1971 and repeated in 1977, the year the ICCPR came into force.[9] It stated that:

> in order *fully to guarantee the right to life*, provided for in Article 3 of the Universal Declaration of Human Rights, the main objective to be pursued is that of progressively restricting the number of offences for which capital punishment may be imposed, with a view to the *desirability* of abolishing this punishment *in all countries*. (Our emphases)

Thus, the issue of the abolition of the death penalty was in the process of being reframed. The traditional arguments about its assumed necessity as a general deterrent and its retributive necessity in response to public demand for 'justice', as judged by governments in relation to culture and national circumstances, were now directly challenged as being incompatible with the right of *all* citizens of the world to be treated with respect for their human dignity and the right to be protected from abuse of state and judicial power and from the vengeful demands of fellow citizens.

Amnesty International was to play a major part in transmitting this message. In 1973, the Council of Amnesty decided to extend its campaign against torture to include abolition of the death penalty, on the grounds that 'it must now be seen as a violation of the human right not to be subjected to cruel, inhuman, or degrading treatment or punishment'.[10]

In December 1977, it convened a major conference in Stockholm attended by over 200 delegates from Asia, Africa, Europe, the Middle East, North and South America and the Caribbean. The resulting *Declaration of Stockholm* called upon the United Nations 'unambiguously to declare that the death penalty is *contrary to international law*' (our emphasis); it being 'the ultimate cruel, inhuman and degrading punishment and [it] violates the right to life'.[11] Franklin Zimring and Gordon Hawkins marked this event as 'the beginning of work on a world-wide scale for the abolition of the death penalty'.[12]

Abolitionists were, however, rather pessimistic that this message would be accepted by political regimes which did not share the 'rights culture' that was becoming ever more firmly entrenched in Western Europe. By the end of 1988 the number of countries that had abolished the death penalty had increased over the previous 40 years from 15 to 52 (including from eight to 17 countries that had abolished only for 'ordinary' offences): an average of less than one new country a year. They now accounted for 28 per cent of the then 180 nation states. But there was fear that the movement had encouraged only those who were 'ready converts' and that the prospects for further significant abolition were rather bleak. In 1986, United Nations staff had concluded a special issue of their *Crime Prevention and Criminal Justice Newsletter* devoted to Capital Punishment with the words: 'it would appear that the goal of the abolition of capital punishment throughout the world remains remote'. Professor Günter Kaiser, the eminent head of the Max Planck Institute for Foreign and International Criminal Law in Freiburg, Germany, in the same issue concluded that: 'Today there appears to be little hope that international bodies, whether private or official, will be able to achieve unanimity [among] the *majority* of countries concerning the restriction or abolition of capital punishment' (our emphasis).[13] The survey for the UN by Roger Hood published in 1988 was just as pessimistic: 'In many regions of the world there is little sign that abolition will occur soon.'[14]

An explosion of abolition

How wrong we were. Beginning in 1989—the year the Berlin Wall came down—the number of countries embracing abolition began to expand at an unprecedented rate. By the end of 2001 the total that had abolished it completely for all crimes in all circumstances had more than doubled from 35 to 75, with another 14 having abolished for all ordinary crimes: making a total of 89. Since then, by the end of December 2016 the 'completely abolitionist' camp has swelled to 104 countries,[15] plus eight countries[16] that are abolitionist for 'ordinary crimes': a total of 112.[17]

This leaves 85 countries that have not committed themselves to abolition. All retain the death penalty for murder, and many of them for other crimes, such as, but not only, for terrorist offences and treason: in 33 countries for example drug trafficking is punishable by death.[18] Forty-nine of these retentionist countries, compared with only 27 at the end of 1988, have not carried out executions for at least a decade and often much longer. They are all classified by the United Nations as 'abolitionist *de facto*', and 30 of them are regarded as 'abolitionist in practice' by Amnesty International, meaning that there appears to be a settled policy not to carry out any executions. Thus, altogether 142 countries (72 per cent) have forsaken the death penalty in law and practice and a further 19 have for various reasons not found it desirable or possible to execute anybody for at least ten years: both Jamaica and Trinidad and Tobago in the

Caribbean are examples of countries that have been thwarted by legal action from carrying out intended executions.

As of 31 December 2016, there were 37 countries (19 per cent of the total) that had carried out an execution in the last ten years since the end of 2006: most of them very infrequently. Whereas in 1998 Amnesty International recorded that 37 countries carried out a judicial execution and 78 imposed at least one death sentence, the number they recorded in 2015 was 25 of the 61 that imposed a death sentence. Only seven (or possibly eight) countries have regularly executed ten or more citizens every year during the past decade (2006 to 2016): China; Iran; Iraq; Saudi Arabia; Somalia; Yemen; the USA; probably North Korea, though there are no reliable data from this country due to restrictive state practice. Of these China,[19] Iran, Saudi Arabia, Iraq and possibly North Korea, execute on a 'grand scale'. These high executing countries were joined in 2015 by Pakistan, following the massacre in December 2014 of children at the army school in Peshawar by the Taliban (see below). According to Amnesty International's report for 2015, the number of executions recorded in Iran, Saudi Arabia and Pakistan accounted for 89 per cent of all executions carried out other than in China. The large number of death sentences imposed in Egypt in the wake of the overthrow of President Morsi may well add Egypt to the ranks of the world's most prolific executioners (see below). While these countries cause considerable alarm to those who campaign for global human rights, very few countries now enforce capital punishment on a scale and with the certainty that would indicate a belief and commitment to it as a deterrent crime control measure. Indeed, the number of executions in many countries has been declining. For example, Singapore which had an annual average rate of executions of 13.57 per million of the population in the years 1994 to 1999—with as many as 74 executions in 1994—has reduced the number drastically. In 2010 only one person was executed, none between 2011 and 2013, and nine in the three years 2014–2016. Meanwhile the number of reported murders in Singapore has not risen but fallen to one of the lowest levels *per capita* in the world—to only 11 in 2012 among a population of over five million.

The mandatory death penalty is being increasingly found to be an unconstitutional form of punishment and the United Nations Human Rights Committee has declared that it is a violation of Article 6(1) of the ICCPR because it is an arbitrary deprivation of the right to life to treat different circumstances and different people as if their actions were all worthy of the same punishment. It is now being replaced in many retentionist countries by a policy which aims to restrict executions to the 'worst of the worst' cases, and only when there appears to be no prospect of rehabilitation of the offender.[20]

The human rights message

Before attempting to identify what the characteristics are of countries that have remained opposed to abolition, it is necessary to try to explain why, within a quarter of a century, such a great advancement has been made by the abolitionist movement and what this suggests about the barriers towards achieving world-wide abolition.

The human rights approach to abolition rejects the most persistent of justifications for capital punishment; namely that it is necessary to meet the needs of *retribution* so as to denounce, expiate and eliminate through execution those whose crimes shock society by their brutality. In contrast, it holds that all human beings have a right to be able to redeem themselves and that a state has *no necessity* and no right to take the life of a *captive* citizen.

The human rights approach has also challenged the view that the death penalty is a *political* necessity because it is demanded by a large majority of the population: a demand that can only be ignored by politicians at their peril and that, without satisfying public opinion, government and the criminal justice system would lose legitimacy, perhaps leading to non-judicial killings. Abolitionists accept that public opinion cannot be entirely ignored but argue that a country concerned for human rights should not merely accept popular opinion as a reason for retaining the death penalty—especially when it may be based on misconceptions about the assumed deterrent effect of capital punishment and the fairness and safety of its application. Research has shown that the majority of persons in retentionist countries support the death penalty because they have become socialised and conditioned to accept it as a legal and cultural norm, the legitimate penalty for murder, rather than on the basis of sound knowledge or principle. Indeed, public opinion surveys carried out in recent years in China, Trinidad, Malaysia, Japan and Taiwan have all shown how limited knowledge is of capital punishment. For example, a large-scale survey in China carried out in 2007 found that only 1.3 per cent of over 3,000 respondents said they had a lot of knowledge and less than a third that they possessed 'some knowledge' of capital punishment; in Malaysia a mere 6 per cent felt they were 'very well informed' about the death penalty in their country and around a half (53 per cent) said that they were not well informed at all. A survey conducted by the National University of Singapore in 2016 revealed that 62 per cent of respondents said they knew 'little or nothing' about its use in Singapore.[21] In Japan also, Mai Sato found that when she presented her respondents with seven items of factual information about the use of the death penalty and asked them to rank their prior knowledge of these facts on a four point scale, ranging from 'I knew all about it' to 'It was new information to me', only two (both abolitionists) of 535 respondents selected 'I knew all about it' for all seven items.[22] Polls in China, Trinidad, Malaysia, and most recently in Singapore, have all shown that when respondents have been asked whether they would be in favour of the death penalty if it were proven to their satisfaction that an innocent person had been executed, the proportion supporting capital punishment fell from between 75 to 90 per cent to between a quarter and a third of the respondents.[23] Surveys that have attempted to test the *strength* of support for capital punishment suggest that although a large majority may claim to favour the death penalty, only a minority would be strongly opposed to abolition. In Taiwan for example, 85 per cent said they opposed abolition of the death penalty but only 32 per cent that they *strongly* opposed it, and in Singapore only 8 per cent said they *strongly* favoured the death penalty.

It has been clear for many years in the USA that asking whether people favour the death penalty will reflect what proportion accepts it as *an appropriate* punishment but not whether they think it is the *most appropriate*, or *necessary* punishment.[24] The large-scale study of public opinion in China in 2007 also found that the proportion favouring death fell from 58 per cent to 38 per cent, if the alternative would be life imprisonment with early release and declined further to 29 per cent if it were life imprisonment without parole and only 24 per cent if the alternative punishment would be life imprisonment without parole plus restitution to the families of victims. The recent Taiwan survey produced very similar findings. Thus the majority favoured alternative punitive penalties that were, in their opinion, *sufficiently severe* to mark the gravity of the crime rather than *demanding* 'a life for a life', while at the same time giving the public protection from the most dangerous offenders.

While methodologically sophisticated public opinion surveys—of the type discussed above—can help to demolish the arguments of retentionist governments who insist that their citizens would not tolerate abolition, the abolitionist stance is that a government committed to human rights should regard its task as informing and leading the general public to appreciate and then to accept the human rights case for abolition. It was of great significance that in post-apartheid South Africa, the newly created Constitutional Court abolished the death penalty in 1995, in face of public opinion in favour of retention. The Court declared that capital punishment was incompatible with the prohibition against cruel, inhuman or degrading punishment and with 'a human rights culture' that would 'protect the rights of minorities and others who cannot protect their rights adequately through the democratic process'.[25] In other words the abolitionist position is that the law should protect the rights of prisoners in the face of outbursts of vengeful emotions—not to satisfy and reinforce such emotions.

In fact no countries have abolished the death penalty because of popular demand as reflected in opinion polls. The public has *followed* political leadership and later shifted towards endorsement of it. Experience shows that a generation that has grown to maturity with no expectation that death will be the penalty for murder is far more likely to regard capital punishment as a barbaric relic of the past, abandoned as civilisation has progressed. For example, in 1948 when West Germany abolished the death penalty completely 74 per cent of the public had favoured its retention, but by 1980 this had fallen to just 26 per cent.[26]

Human rights advocates also challenge the claim that the death penalty must be retained, especially its enforcement through executions, as an essential weapon of criminal justice, without which there would be a *greater incidence* of murder and other capital offences. Promoters of abolition reject this utilitarian argument on both empirical and principled grounds. It may be accepted by some abolitionists that the death penalty could be a deterrent to committing murder in some circumstances, but this is not to say that a lesser penalty, such as life imprisonment, would not also be a deterrent in the same circumstances, nor that in some circumstances threat of death might lead to more murders to escape detection and capture. The real question therefore is whether maintenance of a system of capital punishment enforced through executions leads to a lower incidence of murder than does a penalty system which does not threaten criminals with death. In other words: is capital punishment a *marginally more effective deterrent* than an alternative severe punishment?

The best evidence, based on sophisticated econometric analysis, has failed to provide convincing evidence in support of the assumption that the threat of execution is a uniquely effective deterrent to murder.[27] If capital punishment had a clear deterrent effect, we would expect that when executions cease the number of murders committed *inevitably* increases. In fact there are many examples of falling rates. Prior to the abolition of the death penalty in Canada the homicide rate had been increasing, but 40 years after abolition it was 44 per cent lower than it had been in the year of abolition. Figures in the United Nations Office of Drugs and Crime (UNODC) study of trends in global homicide, published in 2011, show, for instance, that the homicide rate in five countries of central and Eastern Europe (Czech Republic, Hungary, Moldova, Poland and Romania, all of which had abandoned the death penalty in the 1990s) declined by 61 per cent from 4.5 to 1.6 per 100,000 between 2000 and 2008.[28] Furthermore, comparisons between states that have similar demographic and socio–economic profiles show no greater reduction in homicides in those which employ the death penalty. For example, those who claimed that a deterrent effect was proven in the USA when a decline in homicides followed resumption of executions and an increase followed a moratorium, were faced with the fact that almost precisely the same fluctuations were recorded at the same times in Canada where there was no death penalty. A recent review of the literature shows that between 1974 and 2009, the homicide rates of Texas, California and New York followed almost exactly the same fluctuating trends even though Texas had executed 447 people compared with 13 in California and none in New York. A comparative study of Singapore and Hong Kong showed that the homicide rates had declined greatly, in lock step, over the same period in both countries, despite the fact that the former was an executing city and the latter had no death penalty. Even the most sophisticated statistical attempts in the United States to take account of all variables that may affect both the rate of executions and the rate of those 'capital murders' threatened with death (that is, not with all homicides) have failed to provide a clear answer to the deterrent issue. The most recent report by the National Research Council of the USA, after reviewing all available research came to the conclusion that:

> Research to date on the effect of capital punishment on homicide is not informative about whether capital punishment decreases, increases, or has no effect on homicide rates. Therefore the Committee recommends that these studies not be used to inform deliberations requiring judgments about the effect of the death penalty on homicide and … should not influence policy judgments about capital punishment.[29]

Of course, even if a clear deterrent effect could be established in certain jurisdictions, the human rights argument for abolition of capital punishment does not accept that the state should execute convicted persons as a means of affecting the conduct of others. That would be to deny the inherent right of all human beings to be treated with dignity. Furthermore, even if capital punishment could produce a *marginal* deterrent effect, it could only be achieved by high rates of execution mandatorily and speedily enforced. This would increase the probability of innocent or wrongfully convicted persons being executed and also lead to the execution of people who, because of the mitigating circumstances in which their crimes were committed, do not deserve to die. The alternative policy, of restricting executions to the 'worst of the worst' or the 'rarest of the rare' cases, has produced such a low probability of being executed that it not only cannot claim to produce a deterrent effect, but leads inevitably to arbitrary judgements of which cases fall within this class, thus violating the right not to be arbitrarily deprived of life.

Furthermore, the abolitionist movement draws upon a wide swathe of evidence from many jurisdictions (including those that claim to provide what in the USA is called 'super due process') that it has proved to be impossible to devise a *system* of capital punishment which does not inevitably produce error and punishment which is arbitrary, cruel and inhumane.[30]

The acceptance of international human rights norms

The facts laid out above have shown that over the past quarter of a century a 'new dynamic' has been at work to propagate this philosophy by shifting the debate about capital punishment. The view that each nation has, if it wishes, the unchallengeable sovereign right to retain the death penalty as a repressive tool of its domestic criminal justice system on the grounds of its purported deterrent utility or the cultural preferences and expectations of its citizens has been rejected by those who have tried to persuade countries that retain the death penalty that it inevitably, and however administered, violates those human rights embodied in Articles 6 and 7 of the ICCPR which protect citizens, including those who infringe the criminal law, from arbitrary deprivation of their life and from cruel, inhuman or degrading punishments.

Almost all countries that still enforce the death penalty by executions, as well as those that have yet to abolish it in law but are abolitionist in practice, have ratified the ICCPR and therefore have an obligation to abide by the standards it sets in light of the evolving interpretation of Article 6 by the UN Human Rights Committee as well as the Human Rights Council (formerly Commission). At present, only six countries among the 40 that are actively retentionist have not signed or ratified the ICCPR: Malaysia; Oman; St Kitts and Nevis; Saudi Arabia; Singapore; and the United Arab Emirates. China signed the covenant in 1996 but has yet to ratify it. Four countries that are abolitionist in practice, have signed but not yet ratified the ICCPR and another four have neither signed nor ratified it.[31] Nevertheless, all of these countries are subject to the Universal Periodic Review process, carried out by the UN Human Rights Council, of the extent to which they respect their human rights obligations. And all are expected to abide by the *Safeguards Guaranteeing Protection of the Rights of Those Facing the Death Penalty.*[32]

Of great significance during the 1980s was the decision by promoters of abolition to try to commit countries to remove any ambiguity as to whether or not international treaties would permit them to reinstate the death penalty, as appeared to be the case in the wording of Article 2(1) of the European Convention on Human Rights and Article 6(2) of the ICCPR. This was done by establishing protocols to the treaties that embodied such a commitment to abolition. At first, Protocol No. 6 to the ECHR, established in 1983, committed countries that ratified it to abolish the death penalty for all crimes committed in peacetime, which was extended by Protocol No. 13 in 2002 to all crimes in all circumstances. Recently the European Court of Human Rights (ECtHR) has held that the fact that all but two of the 47 Council of Europe states had ratified Protocol No. 13 showed that it 'ranks along with the rights of Article 2 and 3 as a fundamental right, enshrining one of the basic values of the democratic societies making up the Council of Europe' and demonstrated that Article 2 had been (impliedly) amended so as to prohibit the death penalty in all circumstances as an inhuman or degrading treatment or punishment.[33] The European initiative was followed in 1989 by the establishment of Protocol No. 2 to the ICCPR, which also embodied abolition for all crimes (unless a reservation had been made) and did not allow for reintroduction of the death penalty.[34]

The influence exerted by the weight of numbers as more and more countries have embraced the human rights case for abolition has itself strengthened the *normative* legitimacy of the case against capital punishment. Thus the movement has attempted to generate a global *moral* force among the nations of the world, not unlike that which swept away the institutions of slavery in the 19th century. Those countries that maintain the death penalty, being now in the minority, are faced with the knowledge that their international reputation for respecting human rights is now at risk, with all the implications that can have for their diplomatic and trading relations.

Almost two-thirds of the countries that have joined the abolitionist camp since 1989 (and which had not previously abolished it for ordinary crimes) have specifically banned the death penalty in their democratically inspired constitutions. Altogether, 84 countries had, by 31 December 2016, ratified, and four others had signed one or other of the protocols to regional or international treaties or conventions which bar the imposition and reintroduction of capital punishment. It is notable how commitment to abolition as a universal goal has been galvanised by ratification of these treaties. For example, since the UK ratified Protocols No. 6 and 13 to the European Convention on Human Rights and the Second Optional Protocol to the ICCPR in 1999, capital punishment is not only absent from the domestic political agenda but governments of all political parties have been strongly committed to promoting abolition world-wide.

It has needed political leadership on a transnational scale to bring about abolition. Political pressure and political will have been the key and political discourse through human rights dialogues and direct action to try to thwart executions have been forces turning that key. The Council of Europe and the European Union, both of which in the 1990s made membership conditional on abolition of the death penalty, have refused to extradite anyone to a state where there is a 'serious risk that he or she would be subject to the death penalty'.[35] They have also insisted that no goods or services can be exported that could be used to carry out capital punishment.[36] New international bodies have developed alongside of Amnesty International, such as the World Coalition against the Death Penalty; Ensemble Contra la Peine de Mort (Together against the Death Penalty); the International Commission against the Death Penalty, composed of former heads of state of a variety of countries; Penal Reform International; and the Anti-Death Penalty Asia Network. The constitutionality and legality of capital punishment has been successfully challenged in light of international human rights law in the courts of many countries and before national and international courts and tribunals, by NGOs such as the Death Penalty Project, Reprieve and Amicus. They have also made a significant contribution to research and been active in campaigns, such as Reprieve's successful effort to obtain a ban by European countries on the export of drugs (in particular sodium thiopental) to retentionist countries that have been used to execute persons by lethal injection.

The majority of countries that have rejected the death penalty since the end of the 1980s have done so swiftly in recognition that if it is a human rights violation it must be eliminated as a matter of principle (even if they have been influenced also by diplomatic and economic considerations). This has meant that many countries that appeared to be wedded to capital punishment moved quickly to remove it *completely*, especially when political change embodying democratic liberal values became accepted. Turkmenistan, for example, abolished capital punishment in 1999, just two years after the last execution; South Africa in 1995 just four years after. Indeed, the majority (73 per cent) of the countries which abolished the death penalty completely, in all circumstances, since the end of 1988 did so in 'one go' so to speak: not after first abolishing it for all ordinary crimes. This is very different from the pattern in most of those countries that began to abolish the death penalty before the 1980s: for example, in the Netherlands there was a 112 year gap between abolition for murder in 1870 and for all crimes in 1982. Even the few countries that began after 1988 by first abolishing the death penalty for murder soon followed that with complete abolition: for example, Albania did so after seven years, Latvia after three and Turkey after two years. As mentioned above, by the end of 2016 only eight of the 112 abolitionist countries retained the death penalty for crimes against the state, such as terrorism, or in time of war under the military code. Of these, only one, Israel in 1962, executed a person for a politically motivated or war-related atrocity since abolishing the death penalty for all ordinary offences: namely Adolph Eichmann. In other words, even the tiny number of abolitionist countries that have retained the death penalty for political crimes have not found it necessary to carry out executions since doing so.[37]

It is also notable that since 1961 only two nations have reintroduced the death penalty and carried out executions: the Philippines in 1999 and Gambia in 2012. The Philippines abolished it again in 2006 by a huge parliamentary majority. However, President Duterte of the Philippines, who was elected in 2016, has vowed to reinstate capital punishment, despite the Philippines being a party to the Second Optional Protocol of the ICCPR. Gambia withdrew its threat to execute all the other 37 prisoners on death row following international condemnation notably from the African Union (whose Commission on Human and People's Rights favours an Optional Protocol to the African Charter) and has executed no one since. With these rare exceptions, the death penalty once abolished and ratified through international treaties appears to have been permanently consigned to history. Thus, an international movement which began in Europe has now been embraced across the globe by many different political systems, peoples, religious creeds and cultures. This has greatly undermined the argument of those who have taken a cultural relativist's position on this issue and claimed that the abolitionist movement is an imperialist invention and an assault on sovereignty. Although largely European led, it has been embraced throughout almost all of South and Central America,[38] in many parts of Africa, among several secular Muslim states, and is beginning to make headway in Asia.

In Europe only Belarus retains and in some years enforces the death penalty, but there were only three executions in 2012, another three in 2014 and three in 2016 compared with 47 in 1998, and the government has informed the UN Human Rights Council that it will abolish capital punishment after it has moulded public opinion to accept it.[39] Russia has maintained a moratorium since May 1996 and in 2010 its Constitutional Court held that the current legal status and procedures relating to capital punishment were unconstitutional.[40]

At the end of 1988, in the African region south of the Sahara only two island states—Seychelles and Cape Verde—had abolished capital punishment, whereas 17 countries are now completely abolitionist (the most recent being Burundi, Togo, Gabon and Benin; perhaps soon to be followed by Ghana where the Constitutional Review Commission has recommended that the new Constitution should prohibit the death penalty). In addition, Chad and Guinea have abolished capital punishment for all ordinary criminal offences. Another 20 have not executed anyone for at least ten years or have more recently imposed a moratorium. Judicial executions were carried out in 2015 south of the Sahara only in Chad (for terrorist crimes), Somalia, South Sudan and Sudan.

Although all countries in the Middle East and North Africa (the MENA region) where the population is overwhelmingly Muslim, retain the death penalty in law, three of them—Tunisia, Algeria and Morocco—have not carried out any judicial executions for over 20 years. Abolition has also been under consideration in Jordan, Morocco and Lebanon. Furthermore several states elsewhere with Muslim majorities have already joined the abolitionist movement: such as Albania, Azerbaijan, Bosnia-Herzegovina, Djibouti, Kyrgyzstan, Turkey, Turkmenistan and Senegal (for further discussion of the situation in the Muslim world see below).

While only five Asian states (Nepal, Bhutan, Cambodia, Mongolia and the Philippines—though see above) have so far completely abolished the death penalty, five others are now abolitionist *de facto*.[41] Vietnam, 'recognising the global tendency towards scaling back capital punishment'—as a Ministry of Justice official put it in 2014—has made significant progress in reducing the number of crimes subject to the death penalty from 44 in 1999 to 15 in 2015, and has considerably reduced the annual number of *known* executions from at least 63 in 2003 to probably fewer than ten annually in recent years (unfortunately, information on the death penalty remains a state secret).

In August 2015, the Law Commission of India reversed its earlier opinion in 1967 in support of the death penalty and recommended its abolition for all ordinary crimes as the first step to complete abolition (see below pages 415–416). The impact of the human rights dynamic was dramatically evident in Mongolia in 2010 when President Tsakhiagii Elbegdorj called on the Parliament to follow the path of the majority of the world's countries and abolish the death penalty, declaring that 'The road a democratic Mongolia has to take ought to be clean and bloodless.'[42]

This globalisation of the movement is evident from the success of abolitionist countries, led by Italy, in gaining a sufficient number of co-sponsors to bring before the United Nations General Assembly (GA) in 2007 a resolution calling for a moratorium on executions by all countries with a view to abolition. The majority in favour of the resolution has increased on each of the subsequent occasions that it has come before the GA:[43] from 104 (54 per cent) of those voting in 2007 to 117 (62 per cent) of the 188 who voted in December 2016, while the number voting definitely against the resolution has fallen between the same dates from 54 to 40 (from 28 per cent to 21 per cent) of those voting: 31 countries abstained in 2016. Of the 40 countries that rejected the resolution for a universal moratorium, only 24 were among the 37 countries classified as 'actively retentionist' at the end of 2016. Eleven countries that voted against the resolution were Commonwealth Caribbean nations, none of which had executed anyone for more than ten years.[44] Looked at another way, of the 37 countries that had carried out an execution within the past ten years—the active retentionists—25 voted against the universal moratorium on executions. Leaving aside the three that did not vote (Palestinian Authority, Gambia and Taiwan), this meant that nine countries (more than a quarter) that have executed within the past ten years did not oppose the resolution in 2016.[45] This evidence suggests that the number of countries committed to rejecting the goal of a universal moratorium is getting ever smaller.

Countries that objected to the resolution for a moratorium on executions as a prelude to total abolition, led by Singapore and Egypt, sent a *Note Verbale* to the UN Secretary-General after each resolution had been passed,[46] dissenting from it. The stated grounds for dissent were that 'there is no international consensus on whether the death penalty is a violation of human rights', that 'Every State has an inalienable right to choose its … criminal justice systems, without interference in any form by another State', and that there was nothing in the UN Charter that authorised the UN 'to intervene in matters which are essentially within the domestic jurisdiction of any State'. Fifty-eight countries signed this *Note Verbale* after the initial vote in 2007, but by 2014 only 27 (14 per cent of all member states) did so. In fact, of the 39 countries then classed as 'active retentionist', only 18 (9 per cent of all member states) signed the *Note Verbale* in June 2015 after the moratorium vote in December 2014.

How strong is the opposition?

The register of 24 *active retentionist* countries that voted against the moratorium resolution at the UN General Assembly in December 2016 provides a good indicator of which countries, and in which regions of the world, opposition to accepting the human rights case for abolition appears to remain entrenched.[47] *Fifteen* (63 per cent) of them were countries with Muslim majority populations: Afghanistan, Bangladesh, Egypt, Iran, Iraq, Kuwait, Libya, Malaysia, Oman, Pakistan, Saudi Arabia, South Sudan, Sudan, Syria and Yemen; *one* was from the Commonwealth Caribbean (St Kitts and Nevis); *two* were African (Botswana and Ethiopia); *five* Asian (China, India, North Korea, Japan and Singapore); plus the United States. However, Afghanistan, India, Japan, Jordan, South Sudan, St Kitts and Nevis, and the USA had not endorsed the *Note Verbale* sent to the UN Secretary-General in 2015.

There can be no doubt that the greatest barrier to world-wide abolition is the position taken by those Muslim states in the Middle East which claim that Islam permits the infliction of capital punishment for certain crimes, as was evident when Saudi Arabia abstained from ratifying the Universal Declaration on Human Rights in 1948 on the grounds that it was incompatible with the Sharia. Even though they proclaim that Islam is a merciful religion and that the death penalty is not *always* required to be enforced, they reject a concept of human rights that does not respect and reflect God's message as interpreted by their most influential religious leaders from their own religious sources.[48] This position has proved to be most problematic for the abolitionist cause where religious authorities have the political power not only to interpret the words of the Koran and Sunna as regards the punishment of death but also to enforce it through the legal institutions, in particular in Iran and Saudi Arabia, the countries in the region that have executed the most frequently. The criminal law in Iraq, Sudan and Yemen, all of which carry out executions regularly, is also, at least in part, based on the Sharia, and all are in the grip of civil disorder and acts of terrorism. It is likely therefore that the death penalty, while legitimated by religious authority, is mainly enforced in the hope that it will stifle opposition and act as an effective deterrent. The continuing recourse to public executions in Iran and Saudi Arabia is testimony to that.

While the death penalty seems entrenched in such countries, it is worth noting that five Muslim retentionist countries did not vote against the resolution for a moratorium in December 2016: Indonesia, Jordan, Nigeria (50 per cent Muslim) and the United Arab Emirates abstained and Somalia voted in favour.[49] In addition, amongst the Muslim countries that are abolitionist *de facto*, Algeria and Tunisia voted in favour of the resolution and Bahrain, Comoros, Djibouti and Morocco abstained. Most of those that are retentionist do not enforce the death penalty by executions on a regular basis each year. For example, both Indonesia (which neither voted for the resolution nor signed the *Note Verbale*) and Malaysia (which did both), countries where the criminal code is not based on the Sharia, have in recent years had spells when no executions have been carried out.[50] Both countries are in the process of reassessing their death penalty provisions; in 2016 an enquiry into the death penalty regime in Malaysia, carried out within the Attorney-General's department, was completed and is under consideration by the government, and the Attorney-General of Indonesia in 2015 issued a statement that the government was currently 'evaluating' its use of the death penalty, though making clear that this was not a signal for abolition.[51]

Of the two African countries that remain active retentionists, Ethiopia did not carry out any executions in the years 2010 to 2016, the last ones being in 2007; and Botswana is now the only country to carry out executions in Southern Africa: five in the seven years 2010–2016, the last one being carried out in May 2016. The recent support for total abolition by the Minister of Justice of Zimbabwe, which became abolitionist *de facto* in 2015, and the emergence of an Anti-Death Penalty Coalition suggest that it will soon be abolished there and it seems not unlikely that Botswana and Ethiopia will also soon join the majority of African nations that have abolished capital punishment completely, or at least ceased to execute.

The position taken by the United States, to be specific by the retentionist states and the United States Supreme Court, is discussed fully by David Garland in his contribution to this book (Chapter 25), so it is necessary here only to review briefly the prospects that the USA as a whole will abandon capital punishment. As in most of the rest of the world, the death penalty in the USA is in decline and distributed unevenly in frequency of use. Since 2007 the death penalty has been abolished in seven states: New Jersey, New York, New Mexico, Illinois,

Connecticut, Maryland, and most recently Delaware, bringing the total number of abolitionist states to 19. The number sentenced to death, according to the Death Penalty Information Center, fell from 315 in 1996 to only 31 in 2016. Just 16 of 3,143 counties or county equivalents throughout the United States imposed five or more death sentences between 2010 and 2015.[52] The number executed has fallen dramatically from 98 in 1999 to 20 in 2016. Just five of the 31 states that retain the death penalty—Georgia (nine), Texas (seven), Alabama (two), Florida (one) and Missouri (one)—executed anyone in 2016 compared with 20 states in 1999.

Despite the fact that the US Supreme Court has attempted to set 'super due process' standards for death penalty trials, wrongful convictions, error, arbitrariness and discrimination persist, as well as great disquiet at a number of seriously 'botched executions'. The influential American Law Institute decided in 2009 that it would withdraw its support for the death penalty 'in light of the current intractable institutional and structural obstacles to ensuring a minimally adequate system for administering capital punishment'.[53] According to the Gallup opinion poll, public support for capital punishment had fallen from 80 per cent in 1994 to 60 per cent in 2016. The remarkable dissenting opinion of Justice Breyer in the case of *Glossip v Gross* in 2015, which asserted that the attempts made since 1976 to heal 'the constitutional infirmities of the death penalty' had failed in respect of its serious unreliability, arbitrariness in application, and 'unconscionably long delays' that 'undermine its penological purpose', suggest that it may not be long before a majority of justices come to join him in agreeing that 'the death penalty, in and of itself, now likely constitutes a legally prohibited "cruel and unusual punishment"'.[54]

In Japan and Taiwan a return to executions (after short moratoria connected with the appointment of Justice Ministers in both countries who were opposed to the death penalty, but who were later replaced) has brought the subject more acutely into political debate. However, even though the case of the Japanese prisoner, Iwao Hakamada, who was released in 2014 after 45 years on death row for murders he had not committed, generated great concern internationally and within Japan, it did not halt executions. But in response, the Japan Federation of Bar Associations resolved for the first time in 2016 to work towards abolition of capital punishment by 2020.

Both countries have been criticised for failing to meet their obligations in relation to the ICCPR and for claiming that the strength of public support for the death penalty makes it impossible at present to abolish it (see above pages 406–407).[55] The President of Taiwan in April 2012, when introducing his country's first human rights report stated that he would 'seek public consensus on the issue to move towards the abolition of capital punishment'. The election to government of the Democratic People's Party in 2016 in Taiwan may herald a return to the moratorium that existed between 2006 and 2010, given that very few death sentences are now being imposed. The latest official pronouncement is that 'The Ministry of Justice currently adopts the approach to maintain death penalty but reduce the use of which, and gradually eliminate it in the future.'[56]

Neither China nor India is now *fundamentally* opposed to the prospect of abolishing the death penalty, despite their negative votes at the United Nations. The attitude of the Communist Party of China is changing. In 2007 the Chinese delegate at the UN Human Rights Council declared: 'The death penalty's scope of application was to be reviewed shortly … with the final aim of abolishment.'[57] Thus the debate in China is no longer stuck on the question of whether or not the death penalty should be abolished: it is about *how* abolition might be achieved and at what pace reforms should be introduced. That process began in

2007 with the return of the review of all death penalty sentences to immediate execution from the Provincial High Courts (to which it had been delegated during the 'strike hard' campaigns that began in the 1980s) to the Supreme People's Court (SPC). According to the then Chief Justice, Xiao Yang, in the year since this reform the death penalty had been meted out 'strictly, cautiously and fairly' to a tiny number of serious criminal offenders in China.[58] On 25 February 2011 the Chinese legislature adopted Amendment VIII to the Criminal Law which abolished the death penalty for 13 non-violent crimes, thus reducing the total number from 68 to 55 and abolished another nine offences in August 2015, reducing the total to 46 (including those under military law). Although regrettably China still refuses to publish data on its use of the death penalty, it is claimed that the number of executions has been reduced by at least a half since 2007. It cannot be doubted that the international movement has had a strong influence. As Professor Zhao Bingzhi of Beijing Normal University put it at an international meeting in 2009: 'Abolition is an *inevitable international tide and trend* as well as a signal showing the broad-mindedness of civilized countries ... *[abolition] is now an international obligation.*'[59]

In India where the normal punishment for murder is life imprisonment and special reasons are required to be given to impose the death penalty, which in principle is to be reserved only for a few of the 'rarest of the rare', the 'worst of the worst'[60] cases of murder, only one person has been executed for an 'ordinary murder' since 1995 and three men (Ajmal Kasab in 2012, Afzal Guru in 2013 and Yakub Memnon in 2015) for their part in terrorist outrages: a total of four executions in 20 years in a country of 1.2 billion people. Despite the introduction of the death penalty for aggravated rape and repeated gang rape in 2013 (which is almost certainly a violation of Article 6(2) of the ICCPR and the first UN Safeguard), the death penalty for 'ordinary murder' is in effect moribund. As a consequence, the Supreme Court issued a reference to the Law Commission of India in 2013 to study the death penalty to 'allow for an up-to-date and informed discussion and debate on the subject'.

In August 2015 the Commission issued its report. It stated decisively that 'The death penalty does not serve the penological goal of deterrence any more than life imprisonment'; that 'The administration of capital punishment ... remains fallible and vulnerable to misapplication'; that 'The exercise of mercy powers ... have failed in acting as the final safeguard against miscarriage of justice in the imposition of the death sentence'; and that the fact:

> That 140 countries are now abolitionist in law or in practice, demonstrates that evolving standards of human dignity and decency do not support the death penalty. The international trend towards successful and sustained abolition also confirms that retaining the death penalty is not a requirement for effectively responding to insurgency, terror or violent crime.

The Commission found 'no valid penological justification for treating terrorism differently from other crimes', but acknowledged the concern of law makers that abolition 'will affect national security'—the reason, it seems, for the government's opposition to the resolution for a moratorium at the United Nations. With this opposition in mind, the Commission decided not to wait any longer to take the first steps towards abolition. Thus it concluded and recommended:

> Informed ... by the expanded and deepened contents and horizons of the right to life and strengthened due process requirements in the interactions between the state

and the individual, prevailing standards of constitutional morality and human dignity, the Commission feels that the time has come for India to move towards abolition of the death penalty … The Commission accordingly recommends that the death penalty be abolished for all crimes other than terrorism related offences and waging war [but] sincerely hopes that the movement towards absolute abolition will be swift and irreversible.[61]

If this is put into effect it will have a very marked impact on the abolitionist movement throughout Asia. That said, its decision to retain capital punishment for persons convicted of terrorist offences is completely inconsistent with the human rights arguments against the death penalty accepted by the Commission, in line with world-wide practice to abolish the death penalty for all crimes in all circumstances (see above). It can only be explained as a matter of political expediency and as a tactic for reaching the eventual goal.[62]

Terrorism: a poor justification for retaining capital punishment

India is undeniably affected by terrorism and has suffered some terrible outrages due in most part to the instability caused by internal religious and political conflicts as well as with its neighbour Pakistan, which itself suffers from political instability. Indeed, Pakistan (where the criminal code is a mixture of English and Islamic law) recently joined the ranks of the five regularly executing countries. It had introduced a moratorium and not executed any civilians (and only one soldier under military law) since 2007. Then, in 2015 in the wake of the Taliban massacre of children at the army school in Peshawar in December 2014, it swiftly resumed executions as an act of revenge. It appeared originally only to be directed at members of the Pakistan Taliban who had been convicted of terrorist offences, but according to the Human Rights Commission of Pakistan 334 executions took place in 2015, at least 300 of which had been for murder not falling under the anti-terrorism legislation. Thus, while terrorism was used as a justification for resuming executions, once the gates were opened many more 'ordinary' cases flooded through.

Executions had declined greatly in Egypt since the 1990s.[63] However, with the Army back in political control since 2011 after the false dawn of the Arab Spring and the crushing of the Moslem Brotherhood following its electoral triumph, Egypt has increased its use of capital punishment. In 2014 at least 15 people were executed and more than 500 were sentenced to death. It seemed likely that the coming years will see a swathe of executions of the large number of political opponents and armed rebels, perhaps amounting to hundreds. Twenty-two executions were recorded by Amnesty International in 2015, and at least twice as many (44) were known to have been carried out in 2016.

Pakistan and to a much lesser extent Egypt so far, exemplify, as do Iran, Iraq, Saudi Arabia and Yemen, the age-old justification for employing capital punishment as an emphatic display of state power in the face of political opposition. Jordan, where no executions had taken place since 2006, also resumed executions of prisoners convicted of 'terrorism' in 2014. Similarly the swift enactment of capital punishment for terrorist offences and the subsequent execution of ten members of Boko Haram by Chad in August 2015, after 12 years with no executions, show how corrosive the upsurge of terrorism may become to the prospects of world-wide abolition.

It seems likely therefore that progress will have to await the establishment of peace and social tranquillity in the Islamic societies of the Middle East and troubled nations in Asia and for democracy to weaken the powers of autocratic theocracy so that the more merciful, harmonious and liberal interpretations of Islam within a modern context that respect the right to life can hold sway. Only then are the 'Islamic' countries likely to follow the lead of the more secular Muslim states that have abandoned the death penalty completely and of those that have shown restraint in their support for capital punishment. Similarly, Pakistan can take the lead from her neighbours to the east and consider how to once again reduce her reliance on capital punishment.

In fact, the experience of retaining the death penalty for resolving political conflict has shown that it suffers from all the faults inherent in its use for 'ordinary crimes', being equally prone to arbitrary, discriminatory, inappropriate and wrongful convictions; it often produces martyrs to the cause, thus fuelling further conflict; it fails as a general deterrent to those who are prepared to sacrifice their lives for that cause; and it denies them the right to be given the opportunity for redemption and negotiation of political differences with government while undergoing a period of punishment which respects, at least as far as imprisonment may allow, their humanity and human dignity, as required by Articles 7 and 10 of the ICCPR. Such was the celebrated case of Nelson Mandela.

Other countries in Asia and Africa have found peace following periods of considerable conflict and atrocious crimes while managing to abolish capital punishment: not least, Rwanda following the catastrophic genocide of 1993; Cambodia following the demise of the Pol Pot regime; and, as mentioned above, South Africa after the end of the brutal apartheid regime. When international law has responded to such events it has done so without recourse to this ultimate penalty. The UN Security Council excluded capital punishment from the International Criminal Tribunals to deal with atrocities in the former Yugoslavia in 1993 and Rwanda in 1994, and later in Sierra Leone and Lebanon. Nor is it available as a sanction for genocide, other grave crimes against humanity and war crimes in the Statute of the International Criminal Court established in 1998. If it is not available for these atrocious crimes, countries such as Egypt, Pakistan and India should accept that it is also not justified for acts of terrorism.

Conclusion

As shown above, there is now only a minority of countries that continue to oppose the attempt by abolitionist nations to bring about a universal end to capital punishment. They have employed two arguments. First they have by the wording of the *Notes Verbale* sent to the UN Secretary-General following the resolutions aimed to secure a universal moratorium, stigmatised the abolitionist movement as a form of cultural imperialism, as an attack on national sovereignty, an attempt to turn a 'domestic criminal justice issue' into a 'human rights issue', and 'to impose the values of one group of countries on others'. In our opinion this is to create a false antithesis. There are already international treaties that limit the powers of all governments in relation to how they treat their citizens and their prisoners. For instance, it is now agreed that no country should enforce or permit slavery or use torture. Although a choice of a system of punishments is a matter for sovereign nations to decide on, there is universal agreement to limit the power to punish convicted offenders in certain circumstances, such as those contained in the *Safeguards Guaranteeing the Rights of those Facing the Death Penalty* that protect those under the age of 18, pregnant women or persons who have become insane. The same case can be made as regards the weight and brutality of punishments inflicted on all *captive* convicted citizens. So although the choice of a system and implementation of punishments *is* a matter for national sovereignty and countries may legitimately reject interference from other nations, they should not impose punishments that are inflicted arbitrarily and inhumanely such that they breach the human rights of the convicted. In almost all the countries that retain and enforce capital punishment, the human rights dynamic has at least produced great restraint. It is in our opinion very significant that when the moratorium resolution came up for consideration at the UN in December 2016, countries that had been unhappy on the grounds of protecting national sovereignty, led by Singapore, put forward and got majority support for adding the following paragraph, which: 'Reaffirms the sovereign right of all countries to develop their own legal systems, including determining appropriate legal penalties, *in accordance with their international law obligations.*'[64] Many abolitionist countries opposed this formulation, but it nevertheless was a step forward towards accepting that international human rights obligations should not be regarded as irrelevant. Indeed, it clearly implied that the question of the death penalty was not 'essentially' a matter *solely* to be determined within the jurisdiction of any state without it being in conformity with universal human rights norms.

Second, there is the argument that there is 'no international consensus' that the death penalty should be abolished. This raises the question of how large the majority of nations which have completely abolished the death penalty, as opposed to those that retain it on grounds of national sovereignty, would have to be before it would become sufficiently universal to be regarded as a consensus that would determine the issue? In January 2004, Singapore turned to numbers to justify its argument that there was no such consensus by stating that, in 2003, 63 countries, or one-third of the UN's membership, had dissociated themselves from an attempt by the EU to persuade the UN General Assembly to adopt a resolution that called for a moratorium on the death penalty with a view to its abolition. However, by 2007 abolitionist countries were able to gain a majority for acceptance of such a moratorium resolution. As mentioned above, the number of countries supporting it increased from 104 in December 2007 to 117 in December 2016: from 54 per cent to 62 per cent, with only 21 per cent (40) voting against it.

Those countries that still favour capital punishment 'in principle' or believe that it is a necessary weapon in their penal armoury have been faced with convincing evidence of its lack of a unique deterrent effectiveness and the abuses, discrimination, arbitrariness, unfairness, error and inhumanity which *inevitably* accompany it in practice whatever attempts have been or may be made to reform the system. Abolition of capital punishment and its replacement by a humane and flexible system of imprisonment is becoming the litmus test for all countries that purport to respect international human rights norms that protect all persons from arbitrary deprivation of their right to life and from the imposition of cruel, inhuman or degrading treatment or punishment. It is now becoming increasingly clear that all those who are party to the ICCPR have an obligation under international human rights law to accept that Article 6(6) requires them to move forward beyond the minimum Safeguards to protect those facing the death penalty and not to 'invoke' their reforms in order 'to delay or to prevent the abolition of capital punishment'.

There is not yet an overwhelming consensus, but not withstanding set-backs and delays, and new challenges facing the human rights movement in relation to the growing tendency to replace capital punishment with life imprisonment without the prospect of parole, abolitionists have good reason to be optimistic that the final destination is near when all countries will have come to accept that the killing of captive criminals should be outlawed forever.

Notes

1 It draws on the Fifth Edition of Roger Hood and Carolyn Hoyle, *The Death Penalty: A Worldwide Perspective*, Oxford: Oxford University Press, 2015, which contains a full bibliography. Since being prepared for the Portuguese edition of this book in 2014, factual information in this article has been updated to 31 December 2016.

2 See Richard Bellamy (ed.), *Beccaria on Crimes and Punishments and OtherWritings*, Cambridge: Cambridge University Press, 1995, pp. 66–72, at pp. 66–67.

3 Venezuela (1863), San Marino (1865), Costa Rica (1877), Ecuador (1906), Uruguay (1907), Colombia (1910), Panama (1922), Iceland (1928).

4 Dates of abolition for ordinary crimes and dates of last execution: Denmark (1933/1950); Italy (1947/1947); Netherlands (1870/1952); Norway (1905/1948); Portugal (1867/1849); Sweden (1921/1910); Switzerland (1942/1944).

5 M. Ancel, *The Death Penalty in European Countries*, Strasbourg: Council of Europe, 1962, p. 3.

6 The Dominican Republic, Honduras and Monaco.

7 Hood and Hoyle (2015), p. 153 citing *Note Verbale Dated 16 April 2013 from the Permanent Mission of Egypt to the United Nations Addressed to the Secretary-General*, UN doc. A/67/841 (23 April 2013).

8 This had been recommended by Roger Hood in his third edition of *The Death Penalty*, Oxford: Oxford University Press, 2002, p. 77.

9 Resolutions 28/57, 1971 and 32/61, 1977.

10 F.E. Zimring and G. Hawkins, *Capital Punishment and the American Agenda*, Cambridge: Cambridge University Press, 1986, p. 20.

11 See Amnesty International, *The Death Penalty*, London, 1979, Preface by Thomas Hammarberg, and Appendix A 'Declaration of Stockholm', p. 199.

12 Zimring and Hawkins, at n. 10.

13 Quoted in Hood and Hoyle (2015), p. 15.

14 Hood, *The Death Penalty: A Worldwide Perspective*, Oxford: Oxford University Press, 1st edition, 1989, p. 159.

15 Two (Mongolia and Benin) had committed themselves to complete abolition and a cessation of executions by ratifying Protocol No. 2 to the ICCPR (see below) with the intention of expunging it from their domestic criminal codes. In December 2015 Mongolia excised the death penalty completely from its domestic criminal code, with effect from September 2016.

16 Four countries abolished the death penalty solely for ordinary crimes since 2001 (Chile in 2001, Kazakhstan in 2007, Guinea, and Chad, both in 2016), but ten of the 13 countries that had been abolitionist for ordinary crimes at the end of 1988 had, during this period, moved to abolish the death penalty completely.

17 According to the UN Secretary-General's Ninth Quinquennial Report, Russia can now be regarded as abolitionist for all crimes because the Supreme Court held the death penalty to be unconstitutional under the current laws of the Russian Federation. See UN doc. E/2015/49, para. 6, p. 7. However Amnesty International still counts the Russian Federation as 'abolitionist in practice'. See Amnesty International Global Report, *Death Sentences and Executions in 2015*, ACT 50/3487/2016, London: Amnesty International, p. 66.

18 For a list of the crimes subject to the death penalty in these countries see Hood and Hoyle (2015), Appendix 1, Tables A1, 5.1 and 5.2, pp. 509–513.

19 While the death penalty is a state secret in China, reliable sources estimate that they execute at least 2,000 a year; this represents a considerable decline from earlier years when it was at least double this.

20 See Saul Lehrfreund, 'The Impact and Importance of International Human Rights Standards: Asia in World Perspective', in Roger Hood and Surya Deva (eds), *Confronting Capital Punishment in Asia: Human Rights, Politics and Public Opinion*, Oxford: Oxford University Press, 2013, pp. 23–45; and Andrew Novak, *The Global Decline of the Mandatory Death Penalty: Constitutional Jurisprudence and Legislative Reform in Africa, Asia and the Caribbean*, Burlington, VT: Ashgate, 2014.

21 For a summary of the findings see https://maruahsg.files.wordpress.com/2016/12/nus-public-opinion-report.pdf.

22 Mai Sato, *The Death Penalty in Japan: Will the Public Tolerate Abolition?*, Weisbaden: Springer VS, 2014; Mai Sato and Paul Bacon, *The Public Opinion Myth: Why Japan Retains the Death Penalty*, London: The Death Penalty Project, 2015; Taiwan Alliance to End the Death Penalty (TAEDP), *Survey of Taiwanese Attitudes toward the Death Penalty and Related Social Values*, Taipei: TAEDP, 2015.

23 Dietrich Oberwittler and Shenghui Qi, *Public Opinion on the Death Penalty in China: Results from a General Population Survey Conducted in Three Provinces in 2007/08*. Forschung Aktuell/research in brief 41, Freiburg: Max Planck Institute for Foreign and International Criminal Law, 2009; Roger Hood and Florence Seemungal, *Public Opinion on the Mandatory Death Penalty in Trinidad*, London: The Death Penalty Project, 2012; Roger Hood, *The Death Penalty in Malaysia: Public Opinion on the Mandatory Death Penalty for Drug Trafficking, Murder and Firearms Offences*, London: The Death Penalty Project, 2013. For Singapore see n. 21 above. See also Carolyn Hoyle and Roger Hood, 'Deterrence and Public Opinion', in United Nations Human Rights Office of the High Commissioner, *Moving Away from the Death Penalty: Arguments, Trends and Perspectives*, New York: United Nations, 2014, pp. 67–84.

24 See Hood and Hoyle (2015), pp. 448–451.

25 *State v Makwanyane* [1995], (3) S.A. 931, para. 88.

26 See F.E. Zimring and G. Hawkins, 'The Path towards Abolition of Capital Punishment in the Industrial West', *Revue International de Droit Pénal*, vol. 58(3–4) (1988), pp. 669–687, at 680–681; and chapter 1 of *Capital Punishment and the American Agenda* (1986), n. 10 above. Also Hood and Hoyle (2015), pp. 464–467.

27 For a review of this evidence, see Hood and Hoyle (2015), pp. 389–417 and for a summary Hoyle and Hood, n. 23 above.

28 See www.unodc.org/documents/data-and-analysis/statistics/Homicide/Globa_study_on_homicide_2011_web.pdf.

29 Daniel S. Nagin and John V. Pepper (eds), *Deterrence and the Death Penalty*, Washington, DC: The National Academies Press, 2012, p. 3. See in general Hood and Hoyle (2015), chapter 9.

30 For a full account of the extent to which retentionist countries abide by the ICCPR and the UN Safeguards see Hood and Hoyle (2015), chapters 5, 6 and 7. Also, Saul Lehrfreund and Roger Hood, 'The Inevitability of Arbitrariness: Another Aspect of Victimisation in Capital Punishment Laws', in Ivan Šimonović (ed.), *Death Penalty and the Victims*, New York: United Nations Human Rights, 2016, pp. 140–153. Also Carolyn Hoyle, 'Victims of Wrongful Conviction in Retentionist Nations', in Šimonović (ed.), pp. 86–103.

31 Abolitionist *de facto* countries that have signed but not yet ratified the ICCPR: Comoros; Cuba; Nauru; and St Lucia. Neither signed nor ratified: Antigua and Barbuda; Myanmar; Qatar; and Tonga.

32 See Ninth Quinquennial Report of the Secretary-General, *Capital Punishment and the Implementation of the Safeguards Guaranteeing the Protection of the Rights of Those Facing the Death Penalty*, UN doc. E/2015/49, para. 61. 'That the Safeguards may be considered the general law applicable on the subject of capital punishment, even for those States that have not assumed any treaty obligations whatsoever with respect to the imposition of the death penalty, is borne out in the Universal Periodic Review mechanism of the Human Rights Council. Member states report on their compliance with international human rights norms, including those in the Safeguards, regardless of whether they are subject to any relevant treaty norms. Even States that are not subject to conventional obligations with respect to capital punishment have participated in the Universal Periodic Review process as if they were subject to international norms concerning the death penalty.'

33 Hood and Hoyle (2015), p. 33 citing *Al Saadoon and Mufti v United Kingdom* (Application No. 61498/08) Eur. Ct. HR 282 (2010), paras 118–120.

34 See William A. Schabas, 'International Law and the Death Penalty: Reflecting or Promoting Change?', in P. Hodgkinson and W.A. Schabas (eds), *Capital Punishment: Strategies for Abolition*, Cambridge: Cambridge University Press, 2004, pp. 36–63.

35 See Hood and Hoyle (2015), pp. 35–40.

36 See Bharat Malkani, 'The Obligation to Refrain from Assisting the Use of the Death Penalty', *International and Comparative Law Quarterly*, vol. 62 (2013), pp. 523–556.

37 However, it remains to be seen whether Chad, which abolished the death penalty for all ordinary crimes in 2016, but had executed persons for terrorist offences in 2015, will continue to do so.

38 In South and Central America only three small countries (Belize, Guyana and Guatemala) hang on to it, although none of them has carried out an execution for over 16 years. There have been no executions in Cuba since 2003.

39 Belarus abstained on the resolution to establish a moratorium on executions at the UN in December 2014 and again in 2016, and did not sign the *Note Verbale* in 2013 and 2015 following the votes in 2012 and 2014.

40 See n. 17 above for different interpretations of the significance of this.

41 Sri Lanka, Burma (Myanmar), Brunei, South Korea, Laos.

42 See www.refworld.org/docid/4b59adb73a.html.

43 In 2008, 2010, 2012, 2014 and 2016. It has become established as a biennial event.

44 Antigua and Barbuda, Bahamas, Barbados, Belize, Dominica, Grenada, Guyana, Jamaica, St Lucia, St Vincent and Grenadines, Trinidad and Tobago. In addition, Burundi (abolitionist), Qatar, Brunei, Maldives and Papua New Guinea (none of which had carried out an execution for more than ten years) all voted against.

45 They were: Bahrain, Belarus, Equatorial Guinea, Indonesia, Nigeria, Thailand, United Arab Emirates and Vietnam (all of which abstained), and Somalia which voted for the resolution.

46 Namely in the spring of 2008, 2009, 2011, 2013 and 2015.

47 For an analysis of the situation following the vote in December 2012, see Roger Hood, 'Staying Optimistic', in Lill Scherdin (ed.), *Capital Punishment: A Hazard to a Sustainable Criminal Justice System?*, Farnham: Ashgate, 2014, pp. 293–314, at pp. 303–311.

48 For a recent explanation and interpretation of Sharia law, prepared by Islamic scholars, see Penal Reform International, *Sharia Law and the Death Penalty: Would Abolition of the Death Penalty be Unfaithful to the Message of Islam?*, London: PRI, 2015.

49 Of these, only Nigeria and the United Arab Emirates had signed the *Note Verbale* in 2015.

50 No executions took place in Indonesia in the four years 2009 to 2012, but five persons were executed in 2013, 14 in 2015 and four in 2016, all for drug trafficking. There were no executions in Malaysia between 2003 and 2005, and the number of executions since then has been sporadic and relatively low. The Deputy Prime Minister of Malaysia announced at the end of March 2016 that 829 persons had been sentenced to death between 2010 and March 2016 but only 12 executions had taken place in this period.

51 This followed the international outcry at the 14 executions carried out in 2015. See Natashya Gutierrez, 9 September 2015, 'Indonesia: Death Penalty No Longer a Priority', www.rappler. com/world/regions/asia-pacific/indonesia/bahasa/englishedition/105250-death-penalty-indonesia. However, executions continued in 2016 when four drug traffickers were executed by firing squad.

52 Fair Punishment Project, *Too Broken to Fix: Part 1: An In-Depth Look at America's Outlier Death Penalty Counties*, August 2016, fairpunishment.org/wp-content/uploads/2016/08/FPP-TooBroken.pdf.

53 C.S. Steiker and J.M. Steiker, *Report to the ALI Concerning Capital Punishment*, Annex B to *Report of the Council to the Membership of the American Law Institute on the Matter of the Death Penalty*, New York: American Law Institute, 15 April 2009, p. 8.

54 *Glossip v Gross*, Breyer J dissenting, 576 U.S. _ (2015), p. 2.

55 See the Death Penalty Project, *The Death Penalty in Japan: A Report on Japan's Legal Obligations under the International Covenant on Civil and Political Rights and an Assessment of Public Attitudes to Capital Punishment*, London, 2013; and *The Death Penalty in Taiwan: A Report on Taiwan's Legal Obligations under the International Covenant on Civil and Political Rights*, London, 2014. Also: Mai Sato and Paul Bacon, *The Public Opinion Myth: Why Japan Retains the Death Penalty*, London: The Death Penalty Project, 2015.

56 *Republic of China (Taiwan), Implementation of the International Covenant on Civil and Political Rights. Second Report Issued under Article 40 of the Covenant*, April 2016, at para. 67.

57 UN Human Rights Committee, *Human Rights Council Opens Fourth Session*, UN doc. HRC/07/3, 12 March 2007, p. 9.

58 See http://news.xinhuanet.com/english/2008-03/10/content_7755664.htm.

59 Zhao Bingzhi and Wang Shuiming, 'Development Trend in Death Penalty in Contemporary Era and Its Inspiration for China', in *Proceedings of the Workshop on Trends of Death Penalty Reform and Applicable Standard: Experience of International Society andChinese Practice*, Guangzhou, China, 2009, pp. 37–39 (our emphases). See also, Roger Hood, 'Striving to Abolish the Death Penalty: Some Personal Reflections on Oxford's Criminological Contribution to Human Rights', in M. Bosworth, C. Hoyle and L. Zedner (eds), *Changing Contours of Criminal Justice*, Oxford: Oxford University Press, 2016, pp. 182–196.

60 This principle was established by the case of *Bachan Singh v State of Punjab* (1980) SCR (1) 145, *Macchi Singh v State of Punjab* AIR 1983 SC 957; and further elaborated on by *Santosh Kumar Satishbhushan v State of Maharashtra*, 2009 (6) SCC 498.

61 Law Commission of India, Report No. 262, *The Death Penalty*, New Delhi: Government of India, August 2015, paras 7.1.1 to 7.2.6.

62 See the insightful discussion of the case against the use of the death penalty in 'Capital Treason', in Gopalkrishna Gandhi, *Abolishing the Death Penalty*, New Delhi: Aleph Book Company, 2016, pp. 14–37.

63 See Hood and Hoyle (2015), p. 81.

64 *Moratorium on the Use of the Death Penalty*. Resolution 71/187 adopted by the General Assembly on 19 December 2016, UN doc. A/RES/71/187 (our emphasis).

25

PECULIAR INSTITUTION

America's death penalty today

David Garland

Introduction

This chapter discusses capital punishment as an issue in the sociology of social control. Using the facts of historical and geographical variation in the use of death penalties, it seeks to explain why capital punishment has largely disappeared in the West and why the USA remains an important exception to that pattern. Thereafter, it examines questions of institutional design and uses form as a guide to function. America's capital punishment complex – defined as the whole set of discursive and non-discursive practices through which capital punishment is enacted, evoked and experienced – exhibits a peculiar institutional form. This chapter argues that analysis of that distinctive form and the processes that produced it helps explain America's retention of capital punishment and provides clues regarding its institutional logic and contemporary social functions.

In coming to terms with America's system of capital punishment we need to answer three explanatory questions

First: Why did the death penalty disappeared throughout the West? A practice that was once universal has now all but disappeared. What happened? To answer this, we need a theory focused on state formation and development and its implications for the use of violence. Violence, especially lethal violence and the power to kill one's enemies, was once an elementary particle of state power. The projection of lethal violence was crucial in the early processes of state formation – to monopolize legitimate violence and to disarm and pacify the population. It became unnecessary and problematic as states developed into liberal democratic polities with a settled social order. Interests of state, as perceived by state officials – and as influenced by social forces and sentiments – explain the long-term course of capital punishment practice.

Second: Why does the death penalty persists in the USA, to the extent that it does, in the places that it does, in the specific forms it does? Here we need a theory of the American state, its history, its contemporary character and its impact on death penalty policy. In particular, we need to consider: (i) the failure of the American state fully to monopolize legitimate violence (cf. slavery, police powers in private hands, the frontier, etc.) or fully to pacify the population – generating high levels of interpersonal violence and persistently high homicide rates; (ii) the devolution of control over the power to punish to a radically local, populist democratic process; (iii) the tendency of the US Supreme Court to uphold the "will of the (local) people" in this respect, while simultaneously imposing multiple due process requirements.

Third: How does the death penalty function in the USA today? It seems evident that the standard criminal justice purposes do not adequately explain the structure and functioning of the death penalty today. Deterrence, retribution, incapacitation and victim satisfaction are stories we tell ourselves, not functional properties of the institution. We need a theory of the political and cultural uses of capital punishment; a theory about putting death into discourse for power, profit and pleasure. These "uses" of capital punishment are sectional, rather than social. They involve action by specific groups who make the death penalty work for them, or who seek to manipulate its possibilities and benefit from its existence.

My claim is not that the death penalty is functional for "society" – rather it is made to function for specific groups and specific sections of society. Nor is my claim that these functional uses explain the persistence of the death penalty. Rather, my claim is that given the (contingent) persistence of capital punishment – an outcome shaped by America's political institutions and the politics of the last 40 years – these actors have put the death penalty to a variety of uses, producing a variety of effects. Many of these effects are achieved by the discourse of death rather than by death itself – hence the disproportion between death penalty talk and death penalty deaths – though some actual executions are necessary to sustain the credibility of the system and its discourses.

What does it mean to refer to America's death penalty as a "peculiar institution"

First meaning: a comparative anomaly. Everywhere else in the liberal democratic western world, the death penalty has been decisively abolished. The Council of Europe and the European Union regard abolition as a condition of membership and as an important symbol of European identity. The International Criminal Court deals with genocide and crimes against humanity but has no power to impose the death penalty. Australia, New Zealand, Canada, South Africa and many other nations are also abolitionist.

America's death penalty is, in that comparative context, *a peculiar institution*, an anomaly. This is especially puzzling when one considers the long-term history. For most of the last 200 years, America (or at least certain of its regions) was in the forefront of death penalty reform. States such as Michigan, Wisconsin and Rhode Island abolished capital punishment in the 1840s and 1850s, long before most European nations. How did the USA go from being in the western mainstream to being an outlier; from vanguard to laggard?

Second meaning: an observation about institutional design. If we look at the *administration* of capital punishment in America, America's death penalty seems peculiar in a second sense – it seems oddly designed and poorly adapted to the ends it is supposed to serve.

Capital punishment exists in 31 states and the federal government (as of January 2017), but these death penalty states "have" the death penalty in very different ways. Some have the law on the books but never sentence anyone to death (e.g. New Hampshire until 2008). Some impose a few death sentences but never execute any of them (Kansas; the US military, New Jersey before it repealed the law in 2007). Some sentence many offenders to death but execute very few (California – 745 inmates on death row in 2016; only 13 executions since 1976). While others have the law, sentence offenders and regularly carry out executions (Texas – 542 executions since 1976; Oklahoma 112;Virginia 112; Florida 92). And of course 19 states, plus the District of Columbia, have abolished capital punishment altogether.

Death sentences are very rare, at least when compared to the number of murders committed. There were 30 death sentences in 2016 – while there were more than 14,000 homicides. (This is down from more than 300 sentences per year in the 1990s.) And once a death sentence is imposed, the case begins its long journey through the appellate and post-conviction review process.Typically nine stages, often more. In that process, a great number of death sentences are reversed. Between 1973 and 1995 fully 66% of death sentences were overturned (Liebman, Fagan & West 2000). Exonerations also occurred in 150 cases, 20 because of DNA evidence. Finally, the death penalty "exists" around the country but it is executed primarily in the South where more than 80% of the executions occurring since 1976 have taken place. Texas alone accounts for more than one-third of the 1,454 executions to the end of 2016.

Death row: The number of death sentenced prisoners awaiting execution is currently around 2,900.Today, the practical, lived reality of a sentence of "capital punishment" is actually lengthy, decades-long, incarceration on "death row" awaiting news of one's execution date or, more likely, of the reversal of one's sentence.The primary cause of death of murderers sentenced to death is, in fact, natural causes.The percentage of murders that results in executions is miniscule – less than 1%. In 2016 there were 20 executions – this, in a nation where there are now 14,000 homicides per year and where in the 1990s – from when many of today's execution cases date – there were more than 20,000 annually.

We should think too about the chosen method of execution – the lethal injection – which is designed to avoid pain, or at least the sight of pain, and to respect the body of the offender (or perhaps the sensibilities of the witnesses). This event takes place behind closed doors in front of witnesses who are prohibited from making notes or taking photographs.This is execution as an embarrassed form of euthanasia, not full-throated retribution.

All of this is, I would suggest, quite peculiar. Certainly it is quite different from the normal processes by which laws are enforced and punishments are carried out.

In the light of these arrangements, it is quite implausible to argue that the American death penalty operates as an effective deterrent, or as an effectively retributive punishment. If the death penalty is a functional social institution in America today – and its constant reproduction and re-investment of energies and resources strongly suggest that it is – these functions are not the conventional criminal justice or crime control ones. For an account of the system's functions, we will have to look elsewhere.

So, how did we come to have capital punishment in this peculiar form?Why does this form persist? And, why do we invest so much energy and so many resources in an institution that is seemingly so ineffective? (For a full account, see Garland 2010.)

Third meaning: an historical reference to slavery and racial violence. America's death penalty is peculiar in being anomalous, and peculiar in being oddly designed. But the primary reference of the chapter's title is, of course, to the "peculiar institution" of racialized chattel slavery, and to Kenneth Stampp's (1956) classic book of that name. It is a reference to slavery in the Antebellum South, and to the legacy of Jim Crow segregation, racial violence and lynching that slavery produced.

A striking feature of today's death penalty is the persistence of racism in its applica-tion, especially in the South. Not crude race-of-defendant discrimination so much as race-of-victim discrimination. This, together with the inadequate assistance of counsel for poor defendants, evokes memories of lynching and its more respectable cousin, legal lynching. As Stuart Banner (2006: 97) says: "When we think about the death penalty, we think … of black victims and white mobs, of black defendants and white juries, of slave codes and public hangings."

Of course, the *form* of today's death penalty does not resemble a lynching. An elaborate legal process, a lethal injection in a state prison, carried out by state officials, many years after a conviction in a court of law – these are antithetical to the spontaneous mob killing. But the *social dynamics* that produce these executions remain much the same as the social dynam-ics that produced lynchings 100 years ago: inter-racial crimes, enraged passions and powerful community sentiments in racially divided southern counties; compliant local officials; and the adoption of a hands-off approach by national government officials.

In conventional discussion and debate, the question that is posed is usually: why does the USA *retain* capital punishment? But sociologically, a prior and much more interesting question is, why did so many *other* nations *abandon* the death penalty – a practice that was once universal and which has lost none of its capacity for terror and effective elimination?

So, how are these phenomena to be explained? Let's take the first question: *Why does the death penalty persist in the USA today?* The *first* thing to notice here is that it barely persists. As we have seen, the American death penalty today is mostly a conflicted, ambivalent, attenuated version of the institution. It has been narrowed, reduced and restrained by 200 years of legisla-tive change and 40 years of Supreme Court jurisprudence. In fact – if one can risk a morally insensitive sociological observation – it is mostly a matter of discourse rather than death, of talk about execution rather than executed sentences. America may not have fully abolished the death penalty – in the way that all other western nations now have – but it has certainly diminished its use and surrounded it with legal and cultural restraints.

Second, the reason why the death penalty is able to persist in places like Texas or Virginia today is the same reason why the death penalty was able to be abolished in places like Michigan and Wisconsin 160 years ago. The State of Michigan abolished capital punishment in 1846, more than a century before most of the European nations. Michigan was able to do so, because in the USA, control of the power to punish is devolved to the states. In America – in contrast to the other western nations – the power to punish, to enact criminal law, and to decide penal sanctions is a local not a central or national power. Each of the 50 states possesses that power. They each decide whether and how to use it. Some states – usually homogenous, low-crime, Northern liberal-democratic states – have abolished it. Other states – often racially divided, high-crime, Southern, conservative-Republican – have retained it. It is a state choice, not a national one. Indeed, the decision to mount a capital prosecution is even more local, occurring at the county level.

Moreover, in another striking contrast with Europeans, the decision to indict is made *not* by neutral civil servants but by locally elected prosecutors who are, in effect, *politicians*. And the decision to sentence an offender to death is made not by a life-term judge but by local death-qualified juries in front of elected state judges. (You will look in vain for nations in Europe that have adopted such a radical, localist, populist form of democracy. The only example I could find is in Karl Marx's writings on the Paris Commune of 1870, where he proposes that the police, judiciary and other officials ought all to be "elective, responsible, and revocable" (Marx and Engels 1958: 519–20).)

These facts about the American system are important. They explain the marked variation that characterizes the nation's death penalty practices. Local group relations, local homicide rates, local legal professionals and local politicians are allowed, by the federal structure, to shape local outcomes. But they are significant in another respect too. Whenever the death penalty has been abolished in other countries, that abolition has occurred by means of a top–down, counter-majoritarian reform by national governing elites, undertaken despite the wishes of a majority of the population. The death penalty has never been abolished because it became unpopular with the mass of the people. It has been abolished because it has become inessential and problematic for state power and because governing elites have chosen to defy majority public opinion and abolish it. (When capital punishment was abolished in France in 1981, polls showed 73% support for retention; in Germany in 1949: 66% support for retention; in Britain in 1995, 30 years after abolition, 76% support for reintroduction. In Canada in the same year, 65% support Garland 2010.)

In America, the national government – the US Congress – lacks the legal power to impose a nation-wide abolition. To do so would require a Constitutional Amendment, which requires two-thirds of the votes in both Houses and ratification by three-quarters of the states. And because of America's populist, majoritarian politics, Congress has so far lacked the will to propose a radical change of this kind.

The structure of the American polity must play a prominent part in our explanation – as part of a comparative history of state formation and development in the western nations generally. But before asking why the USA retains capital punishment, we have to ask a prior question – why did the western world abandon this practice? We can then situate America's history in relation to this broader one.

Why did the death penalty slowly decline and then largely disappear throughout the western world? This is a profound question of real interest to sociologists. Recall that the death penalty was, as recently as 300 years ago, a cultural universal. Every organized society used the death penalty for a wide variety of offences. Today it is prohibited by all but one western government and widely regarded as a violation of human rights.

What happened? Death did not lose any of its efficacy or its terror. The threat of execution is as powerful today as ever, perhaps more so given our quality of life. But the conditions of its use by the state have changed markedly, making it less necessary and also less legitimate. Beginning about the late 18th century, the existence of alternative methods of punishment (especially the prison but also transportation to the colonies) and of stable, "enlightened" governments, made it possible to envision a reformed criminal justice that did not rely on punishments of torture and death.

What were the processes of transformation that drove these changes in the form and function of capital punishment? It could not have been modernization or economic development – or at least not these alone. There are many modern societies that continue to use capital punishment today – the USA, Japan, Singapore, are examples. In the recent past, the Soviet Union, Nazi Germany, Fascist Italy and the military junta in Spain and Portugal were clearly modern nations and also enthusiastic death penalty states. The key to understanding this process is not the development of the economy – or even the civilization of manners – but instead the character of the state.

The death penalty is always and everywhere an exercise of state power. And for much of modern history, it has been an elementary particle of state power, essential to the establishment and maintenance of the state's monopoly of violence. The primary determinant of the use of capital punishment is the character of the state that uses it.

Liberal-democratic states, especially liberal-democratic welfare states, tend to abolish. Other states – whether authoritarian, communist, socialist or theocratic – tend to retain. Beyond the *political character* of the state, which is the primary determinant, the following circumstances are also important: (a) the state's *context of operation* – that is, the extent to which the territory is pacified, the population disarmed, internal enemies defeated and social order established; (b) the state's capacities for control – the extent to which its powers are supported by an infrastructure, the existence of a police force, prisons, social policy and the consent of the population; (c) the nature of the political and cultural forces shaping state action. The most important of these forces in bringing about the reform and abolition of the death penalty have been liberalism and democracy and their cultural corollaries – civilized sensibilities and humanitarian ethics.

We might note, however, that although democrats have often opposed capital punishment, associating the power of the sword with tyranny, the death penalty is quite compatible with democratic government. Indeed, majority rule, by itself, would typically lead to capital punishment's retention and use. Liberalism, on the other hand, with its distrust of state power, its commitment to protecting individual life and liberty, its respect for the rule of law, and its anti-absolutist values of doubt and tolerance, has been the chief enemy of capital punishment.

And although much death penalty reform has been undertaken in the name of "civilized" values, the culture of civility and civilization is chiefly opposed to *displays* of suffering and cruelty and that culture may tolerate such behavior if it can be hidden or rendered less aesthetically repulsive. This is why civilized societies often abolish the public execution but permit executions to be conducted behind the scenes, in private; or are willing to permit the death penalty so long as it is carried out without the sights and sounds of human suffering. It is humanitarianism with its horror of violence and cruelty and its concern for the sanctity and dignity of the individual that is most effectively opposed to the death penalty.

The theory I would propose to explain these developments is therefore a *state-centric* one. I argue that the rise and fall of the death penalty in the West is to be explained by the changing capacities, institutions and interests of the nation-state.

All these processes were general social processes, affecting every western nation, including the USA. But each nation's history of state formation is a specific one, as is its history of capital punishment, and the specific history of the American state is what explains the trajectory of capital punishment in that country. Above all, I would point to the distinctive process of state formation that shaped the American polity and the distinctive characteristics that resulted, such as radical federalism, a weak central state, local autonomy, early democratization, politicization of state agencies including criminal justice, absence of intermediate institutions, incomplete disarmament and pacification of the population, high levels of interpersonal violence, racial and regional divisions and the Southern defiance of federal power.

Throughout its history, state power in America has been more divided, more contested and more subject to local popular control than is true elsewhere. The development of state capacity (especially police, prison, etc.); the imposition of social order and the pacification of everyday life; the coming of liberalism and full democracy, the emergence of a welfare state – all of these processes made the death penalty practically inessential and politically and culturally problematic in the USA, just as they did elsewhere. They transformed the American use of capital punishment and the form that American capital punishment takes.

But each nation's history of state formation is a specific one – and the distinctive history of American state formation is the context in which to understand the development of America's death penalty. In particular, America's radical local democracy made it difficult to complete the last stage of long-term reform process, i.e. national abolition. The mechanism that produced nation-wide abolition in other nations – top–down, counter-majoritarian reform carried through by governing elites – was absent there. America would require 50 separate state abolitions and federal abolition as well – and over the course of American history only about half the states have gone that route, with several of them subsequently reversing themselves.

There is, of course one national government agency in America that could impose nation-wide abolition – the United States Supreme Court. And the Court is at the center of three of my explanatory narratives: (i) why the death penalty persists; (ii) why it takes the peculiar form it does; (iii) why it is still marked by the shadow of lynching.

This takes us to my second question: *How did the American death penalty come to exist in such an attenuated, ambivalent form?* (And relatedly, how did it become so deeply imbricated in the culture wars and political discourse in the 1980s and 1990s?)

The fundamental explanation would point to the contradiction between state killing, which a majority of American voters support, and the norms of liberalism and humanism, which are embedded in America's modern institutions. But the detailed explanation of the forms in which this ambivalence is expressed must refer to the hundreds of Supreme Court decisions taken since the 1960s which – in an ongoing dance with state legislatures and state courts – have re-invented capital punishment and shaped its current, convoluted form.

How did the Supreme Court become involved? We need to trace this history because the events that drew the Supreme Court into the death penalty business – the civil rights struggle – would fundamentally change the meaning of the issue. What had once been a *penal* issue evoking moral and religious disagreement became, in the 1960s and 1970s, a *political* issue evoking racial, regional and cultural divisions.

Capital punishment was, before the 1960s, an issue determined by state legislatures, the state trial courts and state governors, with very little involvement of the appellate or federal courts. In the nearly 200 years before the 1960s, there are only a handful of Supreme Court death penalty decisions. In the 50 years since the 1960s there are literally hundreds of Supreme Court decisions on the issue, and every capital case is now transformed from a matter of state criminal law to a matter of federal constitutional rights.

What happened? The short answer is: the civil rights movement and the enlargement and rationalization of the American nation-state (i.e. the federal government) in the aftermath of the Great Depression and World War II. The Supreme Court was first drawn into the death penalty arena by complaints of "legal lynching" which is to say court proceedings that were so summary and grossly unfair as to make a mockery of justice. (A well-known example would be the Scottsboro Boys cases in the 1930s which revealed forced confessions, all-white juries and capital defendants who had no legal counsel.)

In the early 1960s, in a political context defined by the civil rights movement and the Great Society welfare state reforms and a legal context defined by a series of 8th Amendment cases and the Warren Court's due process revolution, Supreme Court Justice Arthur Goldberg issued a memo then published a dissent indicating that the death penalty might be open to constitutional challenge. Goldberg used the case of *Rudolf v Alabama* (1963) to make his point: Frank Lee Rudolf was a black man who claimed that his conviction and death sentence for the rape of a white woman were based on a forced confession. The civil rights community responded to Goldberg's invitation, mounting a litigation challenge that characterized the death penalty as a civil rights issue, the last trace of Jim Crow justice. Its claim was that the death penalty violated the 8th and 14th Amendments. To this end counsel developed a series of arguments about "evolving standards," rarefaction, arbitrariness, race discrimination and the absence of any rational state purpose in the use of death penalties.

After a series of cases, the litigants won a remarkable victory in *Furman v Georgia* (1972) but the victory was an ambivalent one. The decision ran to 200 pages of text, with each of the Justices in the majority – Stewart, Douglas, Brennan, Marshall and White – setting out separate opinions and arguments; and with the dissenting justices – Blackmun, Burger, Powell and Rehnquist – doing likewise. (Only Justice William Rehnquist indicated that he supported the practice – the other dissenters voiced criticisms and disquiet but regarded earlier law as binding.) The majority ruled that the death penalty, as then administered, was in violation of the 8th and the 14th Amendments and their decision had the immediate effect of rendering void each of the nation's capital statutes – affecting 40 states and effecting the release of 600 inmates from death row.

This civil rights challenge to capital punishment had begun in 1963 at the height of the civil rights movement, during President Johnson's administration – a period that was, in effect, the high point of American liberalism. But that challenge reached its apogee in 1972 with *Furman*, by which time the country had undergone a series of dramatic events and developments – urban riots, black militancy, anti-war demonstrations, political assassinations, the election of Richard Nixon, the second time in a landslide and so on – with the result that the center of political gravity had shifted markedly to the right.

The political backlash against *Furman* – which became part of a larger reaction against the civil rights movement and the gains made by African Americans – redefined what the death penalty meant. National and local politicians spoke out against the decision – notably President Nixon and Governor Reagan. Southern firebrands like Georgia Lt. Gov. Lester Madox called the *Furman* decision "a license for anarchy, rape and murder." And within two weeks, Philadelphia district attorney Arlen Spector had proposed a new law to reintroduce capital punishment in Pennsylvania. Over the course of a few years, popular support for the death penalty massively increased and came to be associated with three conservative political currents – the politics of "law and order," the backlash against civil rights and a revived "State's rights" movement.

Within two years, 35 states had passed new death penalty statutes and death row quickly became crowded once more as everyone awaited a ruling from the Supreme Court to decide on the constitutionality of the new statutes and the sentences passed under them. In 1976 the death penalty was re-instated by the Court's decision in *Gregg v Georgia*. "Thou Shalt Not Kill" became "Thou Shalt Not Kill Unless…" Henceforth this predominantly state institution would be regulated and supervised, more or less closely, by the federal courts.

Over the decades following the National Association for the Advancement of Colored People (NAACP) litigation, the Supreme Court effectively reinvented the death penalty in America. And it was the Supreme Court's decisions – and the response to them by state legislatures and the capital defense bar – that imparted to America's death penalty the peculiar form in which it is now enacted. But this fact prompts a further question – how was it possible for the death penalty to become an object of Supreme Court jurisprudence and yet remain so clearly and persistently racially discriminatory? To answer that question, we must look more closely at the pattern of Supreme Court decision making in respect of the death penalty.

The several hundred death penalty decisions handed down since 1976, and the labyrinthine jurisprudence to which they gave rise, can be reduced to a few simple propositions

First, the Supreme Court determined, in the 1970s cases, that if the death penalty is to exist, it must not be arbitrary, lawless or uncivilized – it must not resemble a lynching.

Second, to ensure this, the Court has developed a 14th Amendment doctrine of "super-due process" or what I call "juridification" and "rationalization." The Court's ongoing attempt to narrow the death penalty, and subject it to procedural limits, is what has had the effect of producing appeals and habeas petitions, together with the attendant delays, a massive death row, reversals, exonerations, etc. It explains the peculiar form that the death penalty now takes. In these decisions, the Court did for the US death penalty what state elites did in other nations, that is to say the Court civilized, liberalized and rationalized an increasingly problematic institution.

Third, throughout all of this, the majority of the Court has insisted, as a good American institution, that the ultimate decision about retaining or abolishing the death penalty must be left to the democratic process and more specifically to local political decision-makers: state legislatures, state governors, elected country prosecutors, elected state judges and community-based juries. The people must decide!

These same local processes – unrestrained by national government – produced lynchings in the South 100 years ago. Today they produce death sentences and executions, and now, with the imprimatur of the highest court in the land. The practical result of this democratization and localization strategy is that, in 31 states, local majorities elect representatives who support the death penalty. And in certain states, and certain counties, the old race and class divisions still shape the outcomes of capital cases.

As we have seen, many death penalty states "have" the death penalty and rarely execute it. But the death penalty has many uses, not all of which require bodies to be put to death. Included among these uses are the productive ways in which people put death into discourse for power, profit and pleasure. The credibility of these death penalty discourses – their force as threats and symbols, their worth as political commodities – rests on the work of the Southern executioner. Texas executions are the gold standard that sustains the credibility of the circulating currency of death penalty discourse.

Capital punishment in America today operates primarily on the plane of the imaginary and the great majority of its deaths are imagined ones. But the political and economic effects of these grim fantasies are no less real for being imagined. In American criminal sentencing, the availability of the death penalty permits very lengthy sentences of imprisonment, even life imprisonment without parole, to appear comparatively humane, thereby contributing to the nation's extraordinary rates of imprisonment.

In the American political system and in the entertainment zone of popular culture, talk about death permits symbolic acts, exchanges and representations that are used by groups and individuals in their pursuit of power, profit and pleasure. That the death penalty is increasingly declaratory and discursive makes it no less powerful in its political, legal and cultural effects. Nor any less lethal for the 1,454 men and women who have been put to their deaths since executions resumed three-and-a-half decades ago.

References

Banner, S. (2006) "Traces of Slavery: Race and the Death Penalty in Historical Perspective" in A. Sarat and C. Ogletree (eds) *Lynch Mobs and the Killing State*. New York: NYU Press

Garland, D. (2010) *Peculiar Institution: America's Death Penalty in an Age of Abolition*. Cambridge, MA: Harvard University Press

Liebman, S., Fagan, S. & West, V. (2000) *Broken System: Error Rates in Capital Cases, 1973–1995*. Columbia Law School, Public Law Research Paper No. 15. Available at SSRN: https://ssrn.com/abstract=232712 or http://dx.doi.org/10.2139/ssrn.232712

Marx, K. and Engels, F. (1958) *Selected Works*. London: Foreign Language Publishing House

Stampp, K. (1956) *The Peculiar Institution: Slavery in the Ante-Bellum South*. New York: Vintage Books

26

DESISTANCE

Envisioning futures

Hannah Graham and Fergus McNeill

Introduction

This chapter provides an overview of desistance scholarship, surveying some of the major theoretical and empirical explanations of how and why people stop offending, and exploring the implications of this body of work for criminal justice. Traditionally, criminology has been focused on the study of crime and in particular on the causes of crime, as well as criminal justice responses to it. By comparison, examining how and why people *stop and refrain from* offending, and considering which criminal justice responses might support or frustrate such processes has a much shorter history. We would argue that it is also an area of study which, despite being in some senses bound by its focus on crime and offending, nonetheless transcends more orthodox criminological concerns and ultimately compels those who study it to engage with more fundamental questions of political philosophy (as well as with other disciplinary perspectives). We want to argue therefore that desistance research is (or at least can be) a form of 'alternative criminology' both in the way it frames its objects of inquiry and in the ways it pushes towards disciplinary borders and intersections.

We want to stress at the outset that criminal justice – and indeed the contributions of criminologists – need not necessarily be oriented towards or supportive of desistance. It seems obvious to us (as it may be to many contributors to a volume concerned with 'alternatives') that some of what is done in the name of justice may be criminogenic rather than constructive. We know, for example, that in many jurisdictions incarceration in general tends to increase the risks of future crime and criminalisation (Gaes & Camp, 2009; Cullen, Jonson, & Nagin, 2011; Cochran, Mears, & Bales, 2014). The influence of some forms of probation supervision with regards to desistance may be more positive, but that influence appears to remain modest in most cases (see Farrall, 2002; King, 2014).

It is unsurprising therefore that desistance scholars have regularly called for the reconfiguration of criminal justice, arguing that systems-level change (and even structural and cultural social change) is needed to better support desistance and social re/integration (we use the form 're/integration' as a way of acknowledging that not all of those that criminal justice may seek to reintegrate have ever been meaningfully integrated in the first place (Carlen, 2012)).

This is not to say that desistance processes cannot begin and be supported in prison or during community supervision, but it is to recognise the need to unsettle any established assumptions, especially among criminal justice professionals and policymakers, that punishment can somehow produce positive change.

Nevertheless, in this chapter we take the opportunity to describe both a body of knowledge and a philosophical-methodological approach that is relevant to diverse forms of 'alternative criminologies' and their different visions of the future. Thus, in this chapter, we also support advances towards what might be termed 'epistemic emancipation' and shifts in the dynamics of penal power. Specifically, we illustrate how giving greater credence to the expertise and experiences of people with convictions, alongside the contributions of criminologists and criminal justice professionals, can reshape criminal justice debates.

The first section of this chapter establishes some of the key theories and landmark studies which underpin contemporary desistance scholarship. Following this, the potential implications of desistance research are explored in terms of penal power, professional power and people's lived experiences of punishment and re/integration. A more reflexive discussion follows this, engaging with a number of recent critiques levelled at desistance scholarship.

The final section of the chapter shifts to a more utopian, forward-looking vision, charting how and why this body of knowledge might inform 'alternative criminologies' as well as perhaps *alternatives to criminology* in pursuit of different, better futures. Throughout the chapter, we will strive to insist on the links between personal change, penal change and socio-cultural change. Within this exercise of examining the present and envisioning futures, compelling arguments for change in criminology also emerge. We suggest that criminology has found itself beleaguered by some unhelpful divisions. Diversity of alternatives is surely a good thing; and it need not preclude potential synergies or the development of a shared vision. In particular, we aim to explore perceived differences and potential alliances between 'critical criminology' and desistance scholarship.

Explaining desistance from crime

Defining desistance from crime

Despite an international body of knowledge developed over decades about how and why people desist from crime, defining what desistance is and figuring out how such a definition might be operationalised present enduring problems. Fundamentally, desistance refers to the permanent cessation of offending behaviour. It is probably fair to say that desistance research has tended to take a relatively un-critical approach to the terms 'crime' and 'offending behaviour'; and that its focus has been very much on the sorts of crime, offending and social harm that are commonly processed in the criminal justice system, rather than, for example, white-collar crime, corporate crime or state crime (for exceptions, see van Onna *et al.*, 2014; Hunter, 2015). However, there is no inherent reason why desistance research could not extend its conceptual and methodological reach into exploring how and why the powerful (sometimes) desist from their crimes; indeed, in the broader socio-legal literature on regulation and compliance, some such connections have begun to be made (see Crawford & Hucklesby, 2012; McNeill & Robinson, 2012).

Even leaving the question of the definition and scope of crime and offending aside – a difficulty emerges in accurately determining when someone has stopped offending, and how or from whom this information might be known. Most markedly in the 1990s, researchers sought to establish thresholds or timeframes for the absence of offending behaviour and the absence of criminal justice responses to it (whether re-arrest, reconviction or re-incarceration). For example, some defined desistance in terms of non-offending throughout a period of less than one year (Loeber *et al.*, 1991), or no arrests in three years following release from prison (Shover & Thompson, 1992; Uggen & Kruttschnitt, 1998), or the last conviction having occurred before age 31 years and having no reconviction or incarceration for at least ten years (Mischkowitz, 1994 in Kazemian, 2015: 4). These types of definitions characterise desistance as the absence of re-offending and/or the absence of processing within the criminal justice system (which, of course, are far from being the same thing), against somewhat arbitrary time and age thresholds (not one of which has attracted widespread consensus). In other words, they define what desistance is by seeking to clarify what it is not. On their own, these definitions risk becoming unhelpfully caught up with similar debates surrounding the definition and measurement of recidivism rates (e.g., some jurisdictions define recidivism against the threshold of reconviction in two years post-sentence).

Since the 2000s, desistance scholars have more commonly come to conceptualise and debate desistance as a process rather than an event or as the moment of crossing an arbitrary threshold. This shift does not mean that timeframes and ages/life stages become irrelevant, but rather that they are reframed as methodological concerns which are related to desistance, but do not suffice as an overarching definition in and of themselves. Kazemian (2015: 1) explains desistance as a gradual process which involves 'a series of cognitive, social, and behavioural changes leading up to the cessation of criminal behaviour'. This implies that the thoughts and actions of the individual are connected to or influenced by the social context and social dynamics of desistance processes. She uses the work of Le Blanc and Fréchette (1989) to show that reductions in the frequency and seriousness of re-offending, especially for those with a prolific criminal career, are often precursors to permanently stopping offending. The explanation used in this chapter complements Kazemian's definition. Here, we conceptualise desistance as a dynamic process of human development – one that is situated in and profoundly affected by its social contexts – in which persons move away from offending and towards social re/integration (McNeill, 2016).

Maruna and Farrall (2004) differentiate, on the one hand, the temporal and behavioural aspects of desistance from, on the other hand, its developmental and identity-related aspects. They explain these respectively in terms of *primary* and *secondary desistance*, mirroring Lemert's (1951) famous distinction between primary and secondary deviance. Primary desistance denotes the cessation of offending behaviour, including temporary absences or gaps in the commission of crime. This recognises the intermittency of offending behaviour, even for those with persistent criminal careers. It focuses on what a person is or is not *doing*. Secondary desistance explains the sustained cessation of offending behaviour over time. It involves the termination of a criminal career, and the adoption of new roles and identities which signify that a person or their situation has changed such that they now comply with the law and social norms (Maruna & Farrall, 2004). Extending beyond the behavioural realm of *doing* and related concerns about activities or events, secondary desistance shifts the focus towards *being* and *becoming* in a person's life. It recognises the existential and interactional nature of 'the looking glass self' in how people make sense of themselves and one another, in turn affecting how they act and relate in processes of change (see Maruna *et al.*, 2004). The negative impact of labelling prevalent in systems of punishment starts to be reversed when people identify themselves, and are identified by others, as parents, neighbours, colleagues, tax payers and other socially valorised 'master statuses' (see chapter 2 of Graham, 2016) which, in time, surpass those of 'offender' and 'ex-offender'.

More recently, McNeill (2016) has proposed the additional notion of *tertiary desistance*. This refers 'not just to shifts in behaviour or identity but to shifts in one's sense of belonging to a (moral and political) community', encompassing 'how one sees one's place in society' and how one is seen by others (McNeill, 2016: 201). An emphasis on *belonging* foregrounds the relational and structural contexts of desistance. Processes of secondary and tertiary desistance and of community re/integration entail more than instrumental compliance with the law and 'behaving well' (e.g., going straight, obeying rules, cooperating with authorities, demonstrating pro-social behaviours). They also sometimes involve processes of 'making good' (expressing the human need for generativity and for contributing to the well-being of others, for example, fulfilling obligations as a partner, a parent or citizen; see Maruna, 2001). But *belonging* also implies *being a recipient of social goods* (that is, someone enjoying fair access to all the resources, rights and opportunities routinely afforded to other citizens; see McNeill, 2012 on 'social rehabilitation').

If primary desistance signifies a superficial form of development or change, then perhaps tertiary desistance points towards the possibility of its fulfilment, where the status degradations of punishment become less pronounced or are reversed altogether (see Maruna, 2011) and where, for some, even the notion of desistance loses its explanatory power to make sense of a life-course in which neither offending nor desistance are defining features. In an era of penal states pursuing greater and greater post-punishment disqualification and discrimination, fuelled by populist punitiveness (Bottoms, 1995; Garland, 2013), the sobering reality is that significant numbers of people with convictions will never be allowed to realise tertiary desistance. These are the people who, to borrow Alessandro De Giorgi's (2014) phrase, experience 're-entry to nothing'. Nonetheless, their primary and secondary desistance can sometimes survive *in spite of* ongoing discrimination and social-structural exclusion, even decades later.

To summarise, event-driven and measurement-focused conceptualisations of desistance popular in the 1990s limit understanding to questions of 'what' offending has or has not occurred within a given timeframe. While useful at a practical level of explaining research design and findings, this paints a simplistic picture of desistance as measured by variables which fail to illuminate the meanings and circumstances influencing *how* and *why* some people desist while others do not. In contrast, process-oriented conceptualisations of desistance better reveal the influence of *both* agentic and socio-structural factors, situating human development and the struggle to desist in their relational and social contexts. Explaining desistance as a process does not mean that desistance scholars prescribe the route, nor expect 'going straight' to be a one-off rational choice and linear transition from A to B. Desistance, at least for people with significant histories of criminalisation, is typically much more complex than that. A significant body of empirical evidence identifies some of the key contributing factors and developments observed in many desistance journeys, as well as the structural impediments that frustrate them (see Farrall & Calverley, 2006; Farrall *et al.*, 2014). Yet the 'escape routes' and lived experiences of life after crime and punishment are diverse and varied (see Farrall *et al.*, 2011). There is no one cause of desistance, just as there is no one theory which can fully explain it.

Desistance theories and related concepts

Desistance theories are usually clustered into three or four theoretical perspectives, which are briefly summarised here.

Ontogenic desistance theories highlight the age–crime curve which demonstrates that both recorded and self-reported crime is disproportionately committed by young people under the age of 30, suggesting that most people, even those with prolific criminal careers, desist as part of the ageing and maturation processes (Uggen, 2000; Laub & Sampson, 2001; Sampson & Laub, 2005). Hirschi and Gottfredson's (1983; Gottfredson & Hirschi, 1986) age-invariance theory was a precursor to contemporary ontogenic theories. Their research established links between offending behaviour and issues of impulsivity, risk taking and low self-control, which they observed in the lives of some young people and which informed their view of ageing as the overarching influence on desistance from crime.

Sociogenic desistance theories emphasise the relationship between desistance as a human developmental process and associated shifts in social roles and social bonds, especially those commonly involved in the transition to adulthood. For example, in proposing an age-graded theory of informal social control, Sampson and Laub (2005) are critical of adopting too narrow a focus on ageing, suggesting that this presents a somewhat deterministic perspective which does little to explain how and why desistance occurs. Their theorisation instead locates human development and maturation in the context of the relationship between the individual and society, including the structural influences of social control. More recently, drawing on longitudinal data from the Pittsburgh Youth Study, Fabio and colleagues (2011) demonstrate how social-structural factors influence variations in the age–crime curve and mediate ontogenic theorisations of desistance. Their study of the age–crime curve for a sample cohort found that, 'compared with boys in advantaged neighbourhoods, rates of violence among boys in disadvantaged neighbourhoods rose to higher levels that were sustained significantly longer' (Fabio *et al.*, 2011: S325).

Sociogenic theories acknowledge the importance both of new social bonds (for example, intimate and/or co-habiting relationships) and of changing social bonds (for example, changing friendship groups or changes *within* friendship groups (see Weaver, 2015)). Both new and changing social bonds can have a positive influence on how a person sees and thinks about themselves, their identity and social standing, as well as their uses of their time (Giordano, Cernkovich, & Holland, 2003). Sociogenic theorisations share synergies with notions of secondary and tertiary desistance discussed earlier. They draw attention not just to the positive role played by certain social bonds in desistance, but also to the damage that is often done to such bonds by punishment. Thus a sociological account of the 'structuration' of desistance, attending to the interactions between human agency and structure, underscores how incarceration constrains or damages positive social bonds with family and significant others and frustrates maturation and desistance processes (Farrall & Bowling, 1999; Farrall & Calverley, 2006). Weaver's (2012, 2013, 2015) research builds on that of others in this area to offer one of the most cogent and integrated empirical accounts of the relational and social dynamics of offending and desistance.

The third theoretical perspective, loosely described as *identity theories*, highlights the subjective dimensions associated with ageing, human development and changing social bonds. Central to this theorisation is the need to understand changes in people's narratives and personal and social identities. People do not just become parents as a personal milestone or event;

they identify themselves and are identified by others as parents. Many people cite their children as the principal reason for their desistance. Others have children and yet persist in their criminal careers. It is for this reason that individual differences and diversity in the meanings and subjective value of life-course-related experiences are explored in identity theories which warn against over-generalisation or universal claims about new roles and social bonds, such as parenthood or employment (Farrall, 2002; Farrall & Calverley, 2006; Paternoster & Bushway, 2009). Maruna's (2001) phenomenology of desistance and Gadd's (2006; Gadd & Farrall, 2004) psychosocial theory of desistance and reform are prominent examples which emphasise issues of identity and narrative in their social context. Similarly, Soares da Silva and Rossetti-Ferreira (2002) conceptualise ending a criminal career as a developmental process located within a network of meanings, affecting personal and social identity. Identity theories draw attention to the de-labelling process of becoming known as someone or something else; that is, something other than the stigmatising labels of 'offender' and (even) 'ex-offender'.

Just as punishment can delay maturation and disrupt social bonds, it can also undermine positive shifts in identity or narrative, for example by reducing or removing opportunities to participate in personally and socially valued roles, and by creating structural impediments which negatively impact on people's identities, sense of *citizenship* and belonging. The concept of *generativity* is commonly used to explain positive transitions and features of human development, especially as people progress through adulthood, as well as the personal and moral dimensions of helping others in processes of desistance, irrespective of age and life stage (see McAdams, Hart, & Maruna, 1998). Taking on generative roles (e.g., peer mentor, volunteer, parent, animal foster carer, community activist) that involve altruistic helping and citizenship values can yield restorative benefits for individuals and their communities (for diverse examples, see Graham & White, 2015). Maruna's (2001: 117) Liverpool Desistance Study offers a cogent account of how 'the desisting self-narrative frequently involves reworking a delinquent history into a source of wisdom to be drawn from while acting as a drug counsellor, youth worker, community volunteer, or mutual-help group participant'. In this study, desisters described generative pursuits as fulfilling, exonerating, therapeutic and as a source of legitimacy or restitution (Maruna, 2001). To illustrate, one person who had desisted from offending, describes wanting to restore a sense of positive legacy for the benefit of his children, while another describes her desire to become a social worker so that she can use her lived experience to help others change their lives:

> I owe [my children] a lot, you see … I've been in [prison] twice since. I haven't actually paid them back to say I'm sorry. I want to do it in a nice way. I want to leave them something. I want to give them something back.
>
> *(Male, age 40, in Maruna, 2001: 122)*

> I want to show people the positive side of social work … I want to show people that I've been there, I've been through this stuff, so I can relate to what they're going through.
>
> *(Female, age 26, in Maruna, 2001: 120)*

However, people's efforts to change by 'making good', 'giving back' and taking on pro-social helping roles need to be recognised and reciprocated by communities, practitioners and civil society, and enabled by the law and the state (Weaver & McNeill, 2010). Generativity without reciprocity is likely to involve unequal social relations and conditions which may lead to some of the issues and critiques raised later in this chapter. Moreover, the deprivations of status and citizenship inherent in various forms of felon disenfranchisement and disqualification also inhibit and frustrate generativity (Uggen, Manza, & Thompson, 2006). Maruna highlights how people in Western societies seek to control or edit their narratives to conform to 'our' expectations of returning 'ex-offenders'. Instead, the hopeful optimism of desisters is contrasted with the expectations of 'sad' and sorry tales of guilt and shame expected by a punitive public suspicious of their reform and return (Maruna, 2001: 145).

In the Brazilian context, there are examples in some (but not all, see Macaulay, 2015) faith-based prisons and resocialisation centres where generativity and reciprocity appear to feature. Where this is realised, it is achieved through a combination of: (1) 'peer-facilitated rehabilitation', where former prisoners in desistance and recovery processes offer generative peer support to current prisoners embarking on such processes; (2) 'community-facilitated rehabilitation' and 'co-produced resocialisation', involving other citizens from faith groups, non-governmental organisations (NGOs) and other community groups and civil society; and (3) generative giving by prisoners as citizens through activities like helping with local community projects and donation of goods (e.g., food they have grown or produced) (Darke, 2015; Macaulay, 2015).

Recently, in addition to ontogenic, sociogenic and identity theories, Bottoms (2013, 2014) has suggested a fourth set of factors relevant to desistance that are situational in character (see also Farrall *et al.*, 2014). Drawing on his expertise in socio-spatial criminology, as well as on desistance research, Bottoms points out that various aspects of our social environments and of our situated 'routine activities' also provide importance influences on our behaviour, for better or worse. While our environments and activities are closely connected to our social bonds or ties (for example, bonds within intimate relationships and to families, work and faith communities), they deserve attention in their own right.

Applications and implications

Although desistance research has a considerable history, the development of debates about the policy and practice implications of the research is relatively recent; indeed, not much was written in this vein until this century. This may be accounted for partly by the emphasis in earlier studies on desistance as a 'natural' and normative process; if desistance is about 'growing out of crime' (Rutherford, 1986), and if scholars were primarily interested in observing and explaining this as a natural phenomenon, then the disjunction between the literatures on desistance and on rehabilitative interventions perhaps makes some sense. The two bodies of work are interested in similar outcomes (the ending of offending) but focused on quite different processes.

That said, as early as 1937, Sheldon and Eleanor Glueck (1937 [1966], see also 1950) did pose the question of whether criminal justice interventions could 'force the plant' in terms of accelerating 'natural' maturational processes. Even if desistance theories are now more complex and comprehensive, the question of whether a richer understanding of the process can support the design of better responses to offending remains an open one. We have already cited evidence that punishment in general (and imprisonment in particular) may often impede and frustrate desistance. But before we turn to the evolution of debates about desistance-based policies and practices, it might be helpful to offer at least one elaboration of the process that such policies and practices might seek to accelerate.

The most recent, and perhaps most complete, elucidation of this process has been provided by Bottoms and Shapland (2011). Their Sheffield-based study follows 113 men who had been involved in persistent offending and whose mean age at the time of first interview was 20. The men were followed up for three to four years, with an intended total of four research interviews during that period (see also Shapland & Bottoms, 2011). The model of the desistance process that they discerned involves seven stages in which (1) current offending is influenced by a triggering event; which leads to the formulation of (2) the wish to try to change. This leads the person (3) to think differently about himself or his surroundings; which leads him (4) to take action towards desistance. However, these fledgling attempts to desist may be (5) threatened by obstacles, barriers and temptations, so the desister must find (6) reinforcing factors (from within himself or more likely within his changing social relations) to maintain the change which, if successful, may ultimately enable (7) the establishment of a crime-free identity. The model also identifies the importance of two key drivers of change; these rest in the pre-programmed potential of the individual (that is, the personal assets or liabilities that they possess as a result of their life-course to date) and their social capital resources (in the form of networks of relationships that might support or impede their desistance efforts).

This articulation of the 'natural' process is a helpful starting point for debates about criminal justice interventions for several reasons. First and foremost, and in contrast with models of rehabilitative processes, it is *not* a model of intervention; it is a model of change. As one of us once put it, the process of desistance exists before, behind and beyond any intervention intended to support or accelerate it (McNeill, 2006), and the accomplishment of desistance is not in any simple sense a result of intervention, even if intervention could be shown to support the process (McNeill, *et al.*, 2012). In stark contrast with the implicit model of change in the voluminous literature on 'What Works?' to reduce re-offending (and even in contrast with the logic of that question), desistance is not an outcome that can be produced by applying well-engineered tools to unpromising raw materials; rather, it is an organic process; one that can be carefully cultivated or husbanded to enable flourishing – or neglected and trampled.

Thus while Bottoms and Shapland's (2011) account of the process of change neither mentions nor requires intervention at any stage, it is capacious enough to admit multiple points at which intervention might or might not be helpful in cultivating desistance. Intervention might be a trigger at step 1. It might develop or enhance motivation at step 2. It might encourage reflection at step 3. It might support action at step 4. It might remove obstacles, or help the person overcome them at step 5. It might provide the reinforcement required at step 6, and it might provide a means of recognising change at step 7. More generally, turning to the two drivers of change, intervention might work to enhance a person's potential and it might develop his or her social capital resources, so as to support change efforts.

The organic metaphor of cultivating a plant's flourishing (in the form of growth, flowering and fruitfulness) might however be extended further. Two common criticisms of 'What Works?' research on offender rehabilitation – or more accurately of its implementation through policies and practices influenced by new public management (McNeill, 2001) – are that it tends to neglect diversity (Kendall, 2004; Hannah-Moffat, 2005) and, more generally, to neglect the social and structural contexts of both offending and desistance. As such, 'What Works?' approaches (often reduced both in academic debates and in practice to the Risk-Needs-Responsivity model of offender rehabilitation (see Polaschek, 2012)) are sometimes accused of being too readily co-opted to the managerialising, commodifying and responsibilising tendencies associated with the late-modern 'culture of control' (Garland, 2001) or of the neo-liberal penal state (Wacquant, 2009). To extend our organic metaphor, they seem to pay insufficient attention to the soil, the weather and the wider climates that may affect growth (McNeill, 2012).

These criticisms can be and have been overstated. While it is true that approaches to rehabilitation that emerge from correctional psychology tend to predictably prioritise individual psychological 'targets of intervention' (often in the form of supposed 'cognitive deficits'), and usually commend cognitive-behavioural interventions, the underpinning theories are in fact *social*-psychological in character. Social and environmental factors do feature in their accounts of the aetiology of offending (see Bonta & Andrews, 2010), even if they tend to be written out of their prescriptions for 'treatment'. These sorts of interventions aim to feed and prune the plant perhaps, but they do not tend the soil, or build structures to protect it from the weather.

One of the key contributions of desistance theories has been to redress this imbalance. From the outset of their engagement with debates about policy and practice, desistance scholars have stressed the importance to desistance of both personal motivations *and* social contexts (e.g., Farrall, 2002), of both personal agency and social support or reaction (Maruna, 2001). Early forays into these debates also stressed the importance of personal and professional relationships in change processes, in an effort to de-centre correctional 'programmes' as the putative agents of change (see Rex, 1999; McNeill, 2003; Burnett & McNeill, 2005).

Desistance scholars also began to argue for a *less* offence-focused and more prospective outlook in practice. One oft-quoted participant in Farrall's (2002) landmark study summed up the problem with the then prevailing retrospective orientation of practice thus:

> Something to do with self-progression. Something to show people what they are capable of doing. I thought that was what [my Officer] should be about. It's finding people's abilities and nourishing and making them work for those things. Not very consistent with going back on what they have done wrong and trying to work out why – 'cause it's all going around on what's *happened* – what you've already been punished for – why not go forward into something … I know that you have to look back to a certain extent to make sure that you don't end up like that [again]. The whole order seems to be about going back and back and back. There doesn't seem to be much 'forward'.
>
> *(Farrall, 2002: 225)*

Aside from the content of this quote, it is also important that this insight and many others generated through studies of the lived experience of the struggle for desistance were taken seriously by desistance scholars, spawning a series of prescriptions for 'desistance-focused probation' (e.g., McNeill, 2003). Studies focused on the lived experience of desistance allowed people in these processes to emerge not as bundles of problems, needs or risks to be researched, classified, managed or treated but as people whose knowledge and experience could be a resource not only for their own development, but for the development of penal policy and practice. Arguments about the development of a desistance paradigm for rehabilitation (McNeill, 2006; Maruna & LeBel, 2010) took this approach further; recasting rehabilitation as a means of supporting individual *and* social change, partly by recasting its objects as human subjects. To borrow Rotman's (1990) distinction, the desistance paradigm argued both a normative and an empirical case for approaches to rehabilitation that were anthropocentric rather than authoritarian; rejecting a medical model of expert-led change.

By the end of the first decade of this century (also the first decade of research on how desistance might be better supported), it had become possible to discern eight practical principles that seemed to emerge from desistance research (McNeill *et al.*, 2012). First, the complex challenges of desistance (not least in unpromising social contexts) needed to be better understood in criminal justice contexts; practices had to better adapt to the realities of lapses and relapses, not treating all non-compliance as defiance. Second, given both the subjectivities involved in desistance and its differing cultural and structural contexts, practices needed to be more responsive to diversity in the process. Third, since research had begun to reveal the importance of hope in desistance, policy and practice needed to find ways to nurture hope. Likewise, if desistance involved the discovery of agency, then policy and practice needed to encourage self-determination, wherever possible. Fifth, since desistance could only be understood within the context of social relationships, policy and practice needed to engage with these relationships (and not just with individuals). In consequence, the sixth principle stressed the importance of working to develop social (and not just human) capital. Seventh, policy and practice needed to look beyond risk and need to identify and develop people's strengths and positive potential. Finally, policy and practice, both in its language and in its rituals (Maruna, 2011) needed to convey belief in and to recognise and celebrate change, rather than defining people by the behaviours they are asked to leave behind.

Although these principles were distilled from research that heard and heeded the voices of people with lived experience of the desistance process, the principles were nonetheless generated by academic researchers. By 2011, it had become apparent to some of us that a more sustained engagement with criminal justice reform required a different approach. In the UK, in consequence, the Desistance Knowledge Exchange Project was created to bring together people with convictions,[1] people currently under supervision or in prison, members of their families, practitioners, managers, policymakers and academics in order to share different forms of knowledge and experience and to develop proposals for reform.

McNeill *et al.* (2012) report the results of this project in more depth than we can here. But in sum, in addition to the sorts of principles outlined above, the participants called for greater involvement of people with convictions in the design, delivery and improvement of criminal justice processes; the development of more holistic and humanistic support services better connected to local communities and committed to challenging inequalities and promoting social justice; and public education about desistance and re/integration to break down the 'them and us' mentality. They also called for two more structural changes to criminal law and justice; first, they advocated less reliance on imprisonment as a sanction (especially for women, Black men, those with mental health problems and those serving short sentences) and suggested the money saved should be reinvested in communities. Finally, they argued the case for reforms to the UK Rehabilitation of Offenders Act 1974, which governs the disclosure of criminal convictions.

What is striking about these proposals is that they extend far beyond the reforms to probation practice that were the initial concern of the project. With the benefit of hindsight, it seems not too much of an exaggeration to suggest that they perhaps express the manifesto of a nascent social movement, at least in Scotland; one which has seen not just increasing influence of desistance research in criminal justice, but also (and arguably much more importantly) both the establishment of an organisation of people with convictions, Positive Prison? Positive Futures,[2] which now lobbies very effectively for progressive and practical penal reform and the establishment of a new creative practice organisation, Vox Liminis,[3] which exists in part to use the arts as a means of informing and challenging public discourses about punishment and re/integration (see McNeill, 2016).

Critiques

Despite the advances noted above, scholarship concentrated on how and why people stop offending, perhaps foreseeably, attracts concerns that it ignores or detracts from wider influences beyond the individual. Critics have begun to suggest that desistance scholars offer a reductionist account of crime and its cessation which simultaneously de-contextualises and responsibilises individuals for their own desistance and reintegration. In essence, desistance research is seen by some as being 'too agentic' and too heavily predicated on individualistic notions of rational actors exercising human agency (Baldry, 2010; Carlton & Baldry, 2013; Scraton, 2014). To de-contextualise and de-politicise crime is to belie its roots both as a social construct and as a social problem.

We agree that there are aspects of desistance research that, in similar vein with the critiques of 'What Works?' research noted above, if emphasised to the exclusion of other components, risk conflation or co-optation with responsibilising and reductionist approaches to punishment and rehabilitation. As desistance scholars we are painfully aware of the increasingly repetitive use of the catch-cry 'supporting desistance', often as though this is delimited to a set of prescriptions for how correctional workers can better support individuals to change, rather than looking beyond the individual both for the causes and the solutions of crime-related problems.

The 'too individualistic/too agentic' critique does usefully highlight a tendency within desistance research to focus on individuals as the primary 'unit of analysis' (see Weaver, 2015 for an important recent exception). There are some good reasons for focusing on the experiences of individuals. In our view, any body of research which decentred or discounted the lived experiences of people in desistance processes, while making claims about them, would lack legitimacy, both methodologically and politically. Instead, the question is *how* both individual and shared, collective experiences are best gathered, understood and explained, with critical emphasis on the reciprocal influences of context and structure.

However, despite the criticisms noted above, very few desistance scholars in fact advocate rational choice theorisations of desistance (for example, Paternoster & Bushway, 2009; Paternoster *et al.*, 2015). Indeed, most desistance scholars routinely reject and challenge reductionist and responsibilising approaches to rehabilitation (as should be obvious from the preceding section). Considerable intellectual work has already been done to develop sophisticated analyses of the relational, institutional and social contexts of desistance (see Farrall, 2002; Uggen, Manza, & Behrens, 2004; McCulloch, 2005; Farrall & Calverley, 2006; Halsey, 2008; LeBel et al., 2008; Farrall, Godfrey, & Cox, 2009; Farrall *et al.*, 2014; Weaver, 2015; Kay, 2016). Understandings of changes in life-courses are not divorced from but rather linked to changes in life chances and social conditions. Even those commonly identified as identity theorists and sometimes accused of offering accounts that are 'too agentic', like Maruna and Giordano, in fact tend to take a social interactionist approach; hence, for example, the importance for Maruna of *both* labelling and de-labelling processes.

Some feminist critical criminologists have challenged the utility of desistance scholarship on the grounds of its capacity to recognise and respond to diversity and discrimination.

Their criticisms centre on the argument that desistance scholarship has ignored gendered differences in processes of crime, criminalisation and desistance. Their research focuses on incarcerated women with experiences of victimisation and trauma and processes of re/integration (see Russell & Carlton, 2013; Carlton & Segrave, 2016). Carlton and Baldry (2013: 65) explain their abolitionist stance in rejecting liberal-reformist discourses of women's 'pathways' in terms of imprisonment and desistance as follows:

> Desistance, however, does not escape the criticism we bring to other criminal justice policies and programmes – that they are male centric. All the original desistance studies were conducted with men in the United States and the United Kingdom, so that the framework was built around men's experiences. At its heart, the desistance approach is male centric, individualistic and ignores the interlocking structural contexts of class, race and gender.

Pollack (2012: 107) sees liberal reformist gender-responsive 'pathways' approaches as complicit in the 'hegemonic logic' of correctionalism which imposes expert notions of 'who criminalised women are and what they need to stop offending'. Pollack (2012) argues this is a form of 'epistemic violence' which subjugates women's narratives and identities, and de-politicises the social-structural roots of crime as a social problem using the ideological tools of evidence-based practices to compel their reform, as if they cannot know themselves. Russell and Carlton (2013: 479) cite these various concerns, arguing that 'the resurgence of desistance and life-course approaches are not simply problematic, they are *limiting*' (italics in original), re-stating critiques of reductionism and of responsibilising vulnerable women for making 'better' choices in the future.

   While these are important warnings for desistance scholars, there are some inaccuracies in these critiques, which perhaps reflect a lack of familiarity with the wider desistance literature (and the debates within it). It is true – and it is both important and problematic – that most desistance research, like most criminology, started with and has privileged men's experiences. But, in contrast to the critics' claims, the international literature on desistance increasingly *highlights* issues of diversity, especially in relation to the gendered and racialised structural contexts of crime, criminalisation and desistance. If, historically, desistance scholarship was less sociologically well versed in the impact of macro-processes and generative structures, the same cannot be said of contemporary scholarship (for an overview, see Weaver & McNeill, 2010; Rodermond *et al.*, 2016). Indeed, even a cursory reading of some of the key desistance studies reveals the inclusion of girls and women as research participants (see Liebrich, 1993; Graham & Bowling, 1995; Maruna, 2001; Giordano, Cernkovich, & Rudolph, 2002; Blokland & Nieuwbeerta, 2005; Smith & McVie, 2003; McAra & McVie, 2009; Farrall, 2002; Farrall & Calverley, 2006; Farrall *et al.*, 2014). Furthermore, contrary to Baldry's (2010) and Carlton and Baldry's (2013) claims, there has been a proliferation of scholarship on gender in critically understanding desistance and re/integration (for example, Sommers, Baskin, & Fagan, 1994; Uggen & Kruttschnitt, 1998; McIvor, Murray, & Jamieson, 2004; Rumgay, 2004; Leverentz, 2006, 2014; King, Massoglia, & MacMillan, 2007; Søgaard *et al.*, 2016). Others have used intersectionality, critical race and post-colonial theories to explore relationships between ethnicity, racialisation and desistance (for example, Calverley, 2013; Glynn, 2013, 2015), including in relation to Indigenous people's experience of criminal justice in Canada (Deane, Bracken, & Morrissette, 2007) and Australia (Marchetti & Daly, 2016). Importantly, findings are also emerging to explain the criminal careers and desistance trajectories of white-collar offenders (see van Onna *et al.*, 2014; Hunter, 2015) and how these differ from others; although this area currently remains underdeveloped, as we alluded to earlier.

Just as feminist and critical researchers have used research on women's different pathways *into* crime and punishment to critique 'gender-blind' approaches to women in the criminal justice system, so they can and do use research on women's desistance to argue for more constructive approaches (whether abolitionist or not). More generally – and somewhat ironically – some critics write as if desistance *is* a criminal justice policy or programme. It is not. Policies and programmes can be *desistance-oriented* in that they can be (1) pointed to that purpose and/or (2) informed by desistance theories and research. However, like most desistance scholars, and as we have noted above, we conceive of desistance as a process that belongs to desisters themselves (McNeill, 2006), irrespective of which criminal justice professional(s) they interact with or which sanction is imposed upon them. It is important to stress that this is not to support individualisation and responsibilisation. Indeed, it is intended to hold states, civil societies, justice systems and practices to account for their roles in supporting or frustrating processes of change and development that (nonetheless) belong to individuals.

Similarly, for the reasons we have already examined above, it is simply erroneous to conflate desistance perspectives with correctionalist perspectives on 'What Works?' in reducing re-offending. While they are not entirely incompatible, there are considerable differences between these perspectives.

Utopia, alternatives and desistance

The critiques discussed in the last section represent a useful challenge to aspects of desistance research and of its criminal justice applications. However, desistance research itself has also begun to expose its own limitations and contradictions, principally by beginning to confront the question of what lies beyond desistance from crime? If desistance is a process of development – one that can be cultivated (to return to our earlier metaphor) – what does it lead to? What kind of human flourishing lies beyond desistance from crime?

The Sheffield Desistance Study suggests the importance of these questions in a particularly bleak and powerful way. Bottoms (2013) has argued some people desist through a form of extreme 'situational self-binding' which amounts effectively to the self-imposed incarceration of social isolation. Although Bottoms (2013) notes that this was a rare phenomenon in the Sheffield study, evidence from other studies suggests that it is not so unusual for those whose desistance processes lack personal and social support. Adam Calverley's (2009) exploration of ethnicity and desistance, for example, suggests that Black and Dual Heritage men in one London borough faced the greatest structural and cultural obstacles to desistance – and that they tended to desist through isolation. Two recent Scottish studies of very different populations (released long-term prisoners and young people exiting an intensive support service) also found common 'pains of desistance' linked to social isolation and the failure to secure work, connection and belonging (see Nugent & Schinkel, 2016).

These findings paint a dystopian picture of life after desistance, at least for some people. In a sense they expose the taken-for-grantedness of the assumption that ending offending is a 'good' outcome. Not offending may be a good outcome in the sense that it means less harm for society and for potential victims, but if it entails increases in the suffering of the person desisting (and perhaps of those closest to her or him) then, even on a cold utilitarian logic, the value of this outcome remains open to question. More importantly, for us at least, this sort of post-desistance existence cannot be a 'good enough' outcome for a justice process. We would argue that criminal justice must aim for more ambitious goals than crime reduction through self-incapacitation. Those in whose name punishment is delivered have an obligation to restore those whose debts are settled. And those whose offending flows from those social injustices and inequalities that the state permits, perpetuates and exacerbates, are owed additional duties of support.

Re/integration is inescapably a relational, a social and a political process. In contrast to much correctional intervention-focused research, desistance research has simultaneously made it clear *both* that improvements to criminal justice practices with individuals to support their change processes can be imagined and are required, *and* that these efforts can never be enough. Individual change, and work to support it, can be too easily trampled by failure to attend to the social and political dynamics at play in re/integration. As one of us has argued elsewhere (McNeill, 2012, 2014; Kirkwood & McNeill, 2015), any serious engagement with the meanings of desistance, rehabilitation and re/integration compels us to develop models, policies and practices that attend not just to 'correctional' processes aimed at individual transformation, but to moral reparation (or restoration), judicial rehabilitation and social re/integration too. In most cases – and particularly for people with serious and/or long histories of both offending and social *dis*integration – these four processes are almost always intertwined. It follows that if we want to support desistance, much of our work will need to be with communities, civil society and the state itself. We will need to work with people with convictions in that process – but not to 'correct' *them*. Rather, we need to learn from them and to work with them in a collective effort focused not so much on crime reduction as on building fairer societies.

Since this book is concerned with 'Alternatives', it seems fitting that we end in this somewhat utopian vein. Both in sociology (Dawson, 2016) and in criminology (Copson, 2013; Malloch & Munro, 2013; Scott & Gosling, 2016) of late there has been a resurgence of interest in utopia not just as critique but also as method. The work of Ruth Levitas has been one important inspiration in these debates. Levitas (2013: xii) defines utopia as 'the expression of the desire for a better way of being or of living'. She argues that visions of utopias can be developed as *compensation* for an unjust status quo (as in some religious utopias); as *critique* of how things are (by contrast with how they might be); and as more or less clearly articulated programmes of *change* (Levitas, 2000; see Dawson, 2016). Levitas' (2013) work on utopia also argues the need for an *archaeology* – one that excavates the vision of the good society implicit in any given utopia; for an *ontology* – one that explores the utopia's assumptions about human nature; and for an *architecture* of how the utopia is to be built in practice.

In our assessment, despite the variety of views it encompasses, desistance research has a common implicit ontology; it asserts and evidences the positive potential of human subjects and sees them as fundamentally social beings that are capable of growth and development, in the right circumstances. As such it undermines criminal justice responses (and social attitudes) that seek to define and to 'other' people with reference to their offending behaviour. To a certain extent, desistance research has begun to develop an architecture. Initially, that architecture aimed to design a programme of policy and practice reform. Latterly, it has expanded, as Levitas' work implies, to include a much more expansive but still nascent social movement in pursuit of wider structural changes.

What desistance theory and research perhaps lacks, however, is a well-developed archaeology. Perhaps because it begins with the assumed problems of offending and of ending offending rather than with what lies behind these problems and their construction, it lacks a well-articulated vision of the good society. But having said that, as our discussion above illustrates, by exploring how we can become better people, desistance research eventually forces us – through theoretical, empirical and normative work – to explore how to build better communities and better societies. Increasingly, it makes clear that these questions cannot, should not and must not be separated.

Notes

1 This is the preferred term of people with convictions in Scotland for those in their position. In other jurisdictions and contexts, more common terms might be 'formerly incarcerated people' or 'ex-offenders'.
2 See *Positive Prison? Positive Futures* www.positiveprison.org.
3 See *Vox Liminis* www.voxliminis.co.uk.

References

Baldry, E. (2010) 'Women in Transition from Prison to…' *Current Issues in Criminal Justice* 22(2): 253–267.
Blokland, A., & Nieuwbeerta, P. (2005) 'The Effects of Life Circumstances on Longitudinal Trajectories of Offending' *Criminology* 43(4): 1203–1240.
Bonta, J., & Andrews, D. (2010) *The Psychology of Criminal Conduct*. 5th edition. London and New York: Routledge.
Bottoms, A.E. (1995) 'The Philosophy and Politics of Punishment and Sentencing' in C. Clarkson & R. Morgan (eds.) *The Politics of Sentencing Reform*. Oxford: Clarendon Press.
Bottoms, A. (2013) 'Learning from Odysseus: Self Applied Situational Crime Prevention as an Aid to Compliance' in Ugwudike, P. & Raynor, P. (eds.) *What Works in Offender Compliance: International Perspectives and Evidence-Based Practice*. Basingstoke: Palgrave.
Bottoms, A. (2014) 'Desistance from Crime' in Ashmore, Z. & Shuker, R. (eds.) *Forensic Practice in the Community*. London: Routledge.
Bottoms, A., & Shapland, J. (2011) 'Steps towards Desistance among Male Young Adult Recidivists' in Farrall, S., Hough, M., Maruna, S., & Sparks, R. (eds.) *Escape Routes: Contemporary Perspectives on Life after Punishment*. London: Routledge.
Calverley, A. (2013) *Cultures of Desistance: Rehabilitation, Reintegration and Ethnic Minorities*. London: Routledge.
Carlen, P. (2012) *Against Rehabilitation: For Reparative Justice: 22nd Eve Saville Memorial Lecture* – available online at http://tinyurl.com/p8bcrtm (accessed 27 November 2015).
Carlton, B., & Baldry, E. (2013) 'Therapeutic Correctional Spaces, Transcarceral Interventions: Post-Release Support Structures and Realities Experienced by Women in Victoria, Australia' in Carlton, B. & Seagrave, M. (eds.) *Women Exiting Prison: Critical Essays on Gender, Post-Release Support and Survival*. London: Routledge.
Carlton, B., & Segrave, M. (2016) 'Re-Thinking Women's Post-Release Reintegration and "Success"' *Australian and New Zealand Journal of Criminology* 49(2): 281–299.
Cochran, J., Mears, D., & Bales, W. (2014) 'Assessing the Effectiveness of Correctional Sanctions' *Journal of Quantitative Criminology* 30: 317–347.
Copson, L. (2013) 'Towards a Utopian Criminology' in Malloch, M. & Munro, B. (eds.) *Crime, Critique and Utopia*. London: Palgrave.
Crawford, A., & Hucklesby, A. (eds.) (2012) *Legitimacy and Compliance in Criminal Justice*. Abingdon: Routledge.
Cullen, F., Jonson, L., & Nagin, D. (2011) 'Prisons Do Not Reduce Recidivism: The High Cost of Ignoring Science' *The Prison Journal* Supplement to 91(3): 48S–65S.

Darke, S. (2015) 'Recoverers Helping Recoverers: Discipline and Peer-Facilitated Rehabilitation in Brazilian Faith-Based Prisons' in Miller, V. & Campbell, J. (eds.) *Transnational Penal Cultures: New Perspectives on Discipline, Punishment and Desistance*. London: Routledge.

Dawson, M. (2016) *Social Theory for Alternative Societies*. London: Palgrave.

Deane, L., Bracken, D., & Morrissette, L. (2007) 'Desistance in an Urban Aboriginal Gang' *Probation Journal* 54(2): 125–141.

De Giorgi, A. (2014) 'Returning to Nothing: Urban Survival after Mass Incarceration' *Social Justice blog*, 28 May 2014. Available online at: www.socialjusticejournal.org/?p=2273 (accessed 23 April 2015).

Fabio, A., Tu, L., Loeber, R., & Cohen, J. (2011) 'Neighborhood Socioeconomic Disadvantage and the Shape of the Age-Crime Curve' *American Journal of Public Health* 101(S1): S325–S332.

Farrall, S. (2002) *Rethinking What Works with Offenders: Probation, Social Context and Desistance from Crime*. Portland: Willan Publishing.

Farrall, S., & Bowling, B. (1999) 'Structuration, Human Development and Desistance from Crime' *British Journal of Criminology* 17(2): 252–267.

Farrall, S., & Calverley, A. (2006) *Understanding Desistance from Crime: Theoretical Directions in Resettlement and Rehabilitation*. Berkshire: Open University Press.

Farrall, S., Godfrey, B., & Cox, D. (2009) 'The Role of Historically Embedded Structures in Processes of Criminal Reform: A Structural Criminology of Desistance' *Theoretical Criminology* 13(1): 79–104.

Farrall, S., Hough, M., Maruna, S., & Sparks, R. (eds) (2011) *Escape Routes: Contemporary Perspectives on Life after Punishment*. London: Routledge.

Farrall, S., Hunter, B., Sharpe, G., & Calverley, A. (2014) *Criminal Careers in Transition: The Social Context of Desistance from Crime*. Oxford: Oxford University Press.

Gadd, D. (2006) 'The Role of Recognition in the Desistance Process' *Theoretical Criminology* 10(2): 179–202.

Gadd, D., & Farrall, S. (2004) 'Criminal Careers, Desistance and Subjectivity' *Theoretical Criminology* 8(2): 123–155.

Gaes, G., & Camp, S. (2009) 'Unintended Consequences: Experimental Evidence for the Criminogenic Effect of Prison Security Level Placement on Post-Release Recidivism' *Journal of Experimental Criminology* 5(2): 139–162.

Garland, D. (2001) *The Culture of Control*. Oxford: Oxford University Press.

Garland, D. (2013) 'Penality and the Penal State' *Criminology* 51(3): 475–517.

Giordano, P., Cernkovich, S., & Holland, D. (2003) 'Changes in Friendship Relations Over the Life Course' *Criminology* 41(2): 293–327.

Giordano, P., Cernkovich, S., & Rudolph, J. (2002) 'Gender, Crime and Desistance' *American Journal of Sociology* 107: 990–1064.

Glueck, S., & Glueck, E. (1937 [1966]) *Later Criminal Careers*. New York: Kraus.

Glueck, S., & Glueck, E. (1950) *Unravelling Juvenile Delinquency*. New York: Commonwealth Fund.

Glynn, M. (2013) *Black Men, Invisibility and Crime: Towards a Critical Race Theory of Desistance*. London: Routledge.

Glynn, M. (2015) 'Towards an Intersectional Model of Desistance for Black Offenders' *Safer Communities* 15(1): [Online].

Gottfredson, M., & Hirschi, T. (1986) 'The True Value of Lambda Would Appear to be Zero: An Essay on Career Criminals, Criminal Careers, Selective Incapacitation, Cohort Studies, and Related Topics' *Criminology* 24(2): 213–234.

Graham, H. (2016) *Rehabilitation Work: Supporting Desistance and Recovery*. London: Routledge.

Graham, H., & White, R. (2015) *Innovative Justice*. London: Routledge.

Graham, J., & Bowling, B. (1995) *Young People and Crime*. London: HMSO.

Halsey, M. (2008) 'Risking Desistance: Respect and Responsibility in Custodial and Post-Release Contexts' in Carlen, P. (ed.) *Imaginary Penalities*. Cullompton: Willan Publishing.

Hannah-Moffat, K. (2005) 'Criminogenic Needs and the Transformative Risk Subject: Hybridizations of Risk/Need in Penality' *Punishment and Society* 7(1): 29–51.

Hirschi, T., & Gottfredson, M. (1983) 'Age and the Explanation of Crime' *American Journal of Sociology* 89: 552–584.

Hunter, B. (2015) *White Collar Offenders and Desistance from Crime*. London: Routledge.

Kay, C. (2016) *Desistance in Transition: Exploring the Desistance Narratives of Intensive Probationers within the Context of 'Transforming Rehabilitation'*. Unpublished Doctoral Thesis, Manchester: University of Manchester.

Kazemian, L. (2015) *Straight Lives: The Balance between Human Dignity, Public Safety and Desistance from Crime*. New York: John Jay College of Criminal Justice Research and Evaluation Centre.

Kendall, K. (2004) 'Dangerous Thinking: A Critical History of Correctional Cognitive Behaviouralism' in Mair, G. (ed.) *What Matters in Probation*. Cullompton: Willan.

King, R., Massoglia, M., & MacMillan, R. (2007) 'The Context of Marriage and Crime: Gender, the Propensity to Marry, and Offending in Early Adulthood' *Criminology* 45(1): 33–65.

King, S. (2014) *Desistance Transitions and the Impact of Probation*. London: Routledge.

Kirkwood, S., & McNeill, F. (2015) 'Integration and Reintegration: Comparing Pathways to Citizenship through Asylum and Criminal Justice' *Criminology & Criminal Justice* 15(5): 511–526.

Laub, J., & Sampson, R. (2001) 'Understanding Desistance from Crime' in Tonry, M. & Norris, N. (eds.) *Crime and Justice: An Annual Review of Research* 26. Chicago, IL: Chicago University Press.

Laub, J., & Sampson, R. (2003) *Shared Beginnings, Divergent Lives*. Boston, MA: Harvard University Press.

LeBel, T., Burnett, R., Maruna, S., & Bushway, S. (2008) 'The "Chicken and Egg" of Subjective and Social Factors in Desistance from Crime' *European Journal of Criminology* 5(2): 131–159.

Le Blanc, M., & Fréchette, M. (1989) *Male Criminal Activity from Childhood through Youth: Multi-Level and Developmental Perspectives*. New York: Springer-Verlag.

Lemert, E. (1951) *Social Pathology: A Systematic Approach to the Theory of Sociopathic Behaviour*. New York: McGraw-Hill.

Leverentz, A. (2006) 'The Love of a Good Man? Romantic Relationships as a Source of Support or Hindrance for Female Ex-Offenders' *Journal of Research in Crime and Delinquency* 43(4): 459–488.

Leverentz, A. (2014) *The Ex-Prisoners' Dilemma: How Women Negotiate Competing Narratives of Re-Entry and Desistance*. New York: Rutgers University Press.

Levitas, R. (2000) 'For Utopia: The (Limits of the) Utopian Function in Late Capitalist Society' *Critical Review of International Social and Political Philosophy* 3(2–3): 25–43.

Levitas, R. (2013) *Utopia as Method: The Imaginary Reconstruction of Society*. Hampshire: Palgrave Macmillan.

Liebrich, J. (1993) *Straight to the Point*. Dunedin: Otago University Press.

Loeber, R., Stouthamer-Loeber, M., Van Kammen, W., & Farrington, D. (1991) 'Initiation, Escalation and Desistance in Juvenile Offending and Their Correlates' *Journal of Criminal Law and Criminology* 82(1): 36–82.

Macaulay, F. (2015) '"Whose Prisoners Are These Anyway?": Church, State and Society Partnerships and Co-Production of Offender "Resocialisation" in Brazil' in Miller, V. & Campbell, J. (eds.) *Transnational Penal Cultures: New Perspectives on Discipline, Punishment and Desistance*. London: Routledge.

Malloch, M., & Munro, B. (eds.) (2013) *Crime, Critique and Utopia*. London: Palgrave.

Marchetti, E., & Daly, K. (2016) 'Indigenous Partner Violence, Indigenous Sentencing Courts, and Pathways to Desistance' *Violence Against Women*, first published 13 September 2016, Online First. DOI: 10.1177/1077801216662341.

Maruna, S. (2001) *Making Good: How Ex-Convicts Reform and Rebuild Their Lives*. Washington, DC: American Psychological Association.

Maruna, S. (2011) 'Reentry as a Rite of Passage' *Punishment and Society* 13(1): 3–28.

Maruna, S., & Farrall, S. (2004) 'Desistance from Crime: A Theoretical Reformulation' *Kölner Zeitschrift f ur Soziologie und Sozialpsychologie* 43: 171–194.

Maruna, S., & LeBel, T. (2010) 'The Desistance Paradigm in Correctional Practice: From Programmes to Lives' in McNeill, F., Raynor, P., & Trotter C. (eds.) *Offender Supervision: New Directions in Theory, Research and Practice*. Cullompton: Willan.

Maruna, M., LeBel, T., Mitchell, N., & Naples, M. (2004) 'Pygmalion in the Reintegration Process: Desistance from Crime through the Looking Glass' *Psychology, Crime & Law* 10(3): 271–281.

McAdams, D., Hart, H., & Maruna, S. (1998) 'The Anatomy of Generativity' in McAdams, D. & St Aubin, E. (eds.) *Generativity and Adult Development: How and Why We Care for the Next Generation*. Washington, DC: American Psychological Association.

McAra, L., & McVie, S. (2009) 'Youth Justice? The Impact of System Contact on Patterns of Desistance from Offending' in Goldson, B. & Muncie, J. (eds.) *Youth Crime and Juvenile Justice*. London: SAGE Publications.

McCulloch, T. (2005) 'Probation, Social Context and Desistance: Re-Tracing the Relationship' *Probation Journal* 52(1): 8–22.

McIvor, G., Murray, C., & Jamieson, J. (2004) 'Desistance from Crime: Is It Different for Women and Girls' in Maruna, S. & Immarigeon, R. (eds.) *After Crime and Punishment: Pathways to Offender Reintegration*. Cullompton: Willan Publishing.

McNeill, F. (2001) 'Developing Effectiveness: Frontline Perspectives' *Social Work Education* 20(6): 671–687.

McNeill, F. (2003) 'Desistance-Focused Probation Practice' in Chui, W.-H. & Nellis, M. (eds.) *Moving Probation Forward: Evidence, Arguments and Practice*. Harlow: Pearson Education.

McNeill, F. (2006) 'A Desistance Paradigm for Offender Management' *Criminology and Criminal Justice* 6(1): 39–62.

McNeill, F. (2012) 'Four Forms of "Offender" Rehabilitation: Towards an Interdisciplinary Perspective' *Legal and Criminological Psychology* 17(1): 18–36.

McNeill, F. (2014) 'Punishment as Rehabilitation' in Bruinsma, G. & Weisburd, D. (eds) *Encyclopedia of Criminology and Criminal Justice*. New York: Springer.

McNeill, F. (2016) 'Desistance and Criminal Justice in Scotland' in Croall, H., Mooney, G., & Munro, M. (eds.) *Crime, Justice and Society in Scotland*. London: Routledge.

McNeill, F., & Robinson, G. (2012) 'Liquid Legitimacy and Community Sanctions' in Crawford, A. & Hucklesby, A. (eds.) *Legitimacy and Compliance in Criminal Justice*. Abingdon: Routledge.

McNeill, F., Farrall, S., Lightowler, C., & Maruna, S. (2012) 'Reexamining "Evidence-Based Practice" in Community Corrections: Beyond "a Confined View" of What Works' *Justice Research and Policy* 14(1): 35–60.

Mischkowitz, R. (1994) 'Desistance from a Delinquent Way of Life?' in Weitekamp, E.G. & Kerner, H.J. (eds.) *Cross-National Longitudinal Research on Human Development and Criminal Behavior*. Dordrecht: Kluwer Academic, pp. 303–327.

Nugent, B., & Schinkel, M. (2016) 'The Pains of Desistance' *Criminology & Criminal Justice* 16(5): 568–584.

Paternoster, R., & Bushway, S. (2009) 'Desistance and the Feared Self: Toward an Identity Theory of Criminal Desistance' *Journal of Criminal Law and Criminology* 99(4): 1103–1156.

Paternoster, R., Bachman, R., Bushway, S., Kerrison, E., & O'Connell, D. (2015) 'Human Agency and Explanations of Criminal Desistance: Arguments for a Rational Choice Theory' *Journal of Developmental and Lifecourse Criminology* 1(3): 209–235.

Polaschek, D. (2012) 'An Appraisal of the Risk-Need-Responsivity (RNR) Model of Offender Rehabilitation and Its Application in Correctional Treatment' *Legal and Criminological Psychology* 17(1): 1–17.

Pollack, S. (2012) 'An Imprisoning Gaze: Practices of Gendered, Racialised and Epistemic Violence' *International Review of Victimology* 19(1): 103–114.

Rodermond, E., Kruttschnitt, C., Slotboom, A., & Bijleveld, C. (2016) 'Female Desistance: A Review of the Literature' *European Journal of Criminology* 13(1): 3–28.

Rumgay, J. (2004) 'Scripts for Safer Survival: Pathways Out of Female Crime' *The Howard Journal of Criminal Justice* 43(4): 405–419.

Russell, E., & Carlton, B. (2013) 'Pathways, Race and Gender Responsive Reform: Through an Abolitionist Lens' *Theoretical Criminology* 17(4): 474–492.

Rutherford, A. (1986) *Growing out of Crime: Society and Young People in Trouble*. Harmondsworth: Penguin.

Sampson, R., & Laub, J. (2005) 'A General Age-Graded Theory of Crime: Lessons Learned and the Future of Lifecourse Criminology' *Advances in Criminological Theory* 14: 1–28.

Scott, D., & Gosling, H. (2016) 'Before Prison, Instead of Prison, Better Than Prison: Therapeutic Communities as an Abolitionist Real Utopia' *International Journal for Crime, Justice and Social Democracy* 5(1): 52–66.

Scraton, P. (2014) 'Bearing Witness to the "Pain of Others": Researching Power, Violence and Resistance in a Women's Prison', Plenary Keynote at the 8th Annual Australian and New Zealand Critical Criminology Conference, 4–5 December 2014 at Monash University, Melbourne.

Shover, N., & Thompson, C. (1992) 'Age, Differential Expectations, and Crime Desistance' *Criminology* 30(1): 89–104.

Smith, D., & McVie, S. (2003) 'Theory and Method in the Edinburgh Study of Youth Transitions from Crime' *British Journal of Criminology* 43(1): 169–195.

Soares da Silva, A., & Rossetti-Ferreira, M. (2002) 'Continuidade/descontinuidade no envolvimento com o crime: uma discussão crítica da literatura na psicologia do desenvolvimento' *Psicologia: Reflexão e Crítica* 15(3): 573–585.

Søgaard, T., Kolind, T., Thylstrup, B., & Deuchar, R. (2016) 'Desistance and the Micro Narrative Construction of Reformed Masculinities in a Danish Rehabilitation Centre' *Criminology & Criminal Justice* 16(1): 99–118.

Sommers, I., Baskin, D., & Fagan, J. (1994) 'Getting Out of the Life: Crime Desistance by Female Street Offenders' *Deviant Behavior* 15(2): 125–149.

Uggen, C. (2000) 'Work as a Turning Point in the Lifecourse of Criminals: A Duration Model of Age, Employment and Recidivism' *American Sociological Review* 65(4): 529–546.

Uggen, C., & Kruttschnitt, C. (1998) 'Crime in the Breaking: Gender Differences in Desistance' *Law & Society* 32(2): 339–366.

Uggen, C., Manza, J., & Behrens, A. (2004) 'Less Than the Average Citizen: Stigma, Role Transition and the Civic Reintegration of Convicted Felons' in Maruna, S. & Immarigeon, R. (eds.) *After Crime and Punishment: Pathways to Offender Reintegration*. Cullompton: Willan Publishing.

Uggen, C., Manza, J., & Thompson, M. (2006) 'Citizenship, Democracy and the Civic Reintegration of Criminal Offenders' *Annals of the American Academy of Political and Social Science* 605(May): 281–310.

van Onna, J., van der Geest, V., Huisman, W., & Denkers, A. (2014) 'Criminal Trajectories of White Collar Offenders' *Journal of Research in Crime and Delinquency* 51(6): 759–784.

Wacquant, L. (2009) *Punishing the Poor: The Neoliberal Governance of Insecurity*. Durham, NC: Duke University Press.

Weaver, B. (2012) 'The Relational Context of Desistance: Some Implications and Opportunities for Social Policy' *Social Policy & Administration* 46(4): 395–412.

Weaver, B. (2013) 'Co-Producing Desistance: Who Works to Support Desistance?' in Durnescu, I. & McNeill, F. (eds.) *Understanding Penal Practice*. Basingstoke: Palgrave Macmillan.

Weaver, B. (2015) *Offending and Desistance: The Importance of Social Relations*. London: Routledge.

Weaver, B., & McNeill, F. (2010) 'Travelling Hopefully: Desistance Research and Probation Practice' in Brayford, J., Cowe, F., & Deering, F. (eds.) *What Else Works? Creative Work with Offenders*. Cullompton: Willan Publishing.

27

ALTERNATIVE CRIMINOLOGIES, ACADEMIC MARKETS AND CORPORATISM IN UNIVERSITIES

Pat Carlen and Jo Phoenix

> Researchers in the field of criminology should endeavour to: (i) advance knowledge about criminological issues; (ii) *identify and seek to ameliorate factors which restrict the development of their professional competence and integrity.*
>
> *(British Society of Criminology 2015, emphasis added)*

Chapter 1 of this book argued for a catholicity of theoretical and methodological approaches in criminology as a prelude to a collection which showcases a range of the newer theoretical and substantive issues in the anglophone criminologies of the late 20th and early 21st centuries. This final contribution now has the task of identifying and discussing a silent but growing threat to the academic ideal of open scientific inquiry: the combined marketisation of research dissemination by publishers and universities; and the resultant trend towards the corporatisation of criminological research within academia. The term 'corporatisation of research' as used in this chapter refers to the change from the traditional university where researchers were expected to be self-governing (under the auspices of the research principles of their discipline) to present-day arrangements where their research is governed by academic management according to the interests of the university as determined by government and markets.

The overall argument is as follows:

1. Conventional social science research is supposedly based upon professional principles that have ideally seen academic researchers as being autonomous and altruistic; and whose authority to define the procedures, parameters and problems of their chosen field is rooted in their competence as publicly certificated academics.
2. Though this ideal type of professionalism has seldom been realised, many of the ethical standards of criminology's professional associations still stem from an acceptance of the ideal-type professional.
3. Concern by governments about university costs has led to decreases in government funding and increased pressures on universities to adopt business models of financial management. Governments are increasingly developing National Research Assessment Exercises based on metrics as tools to aid the disbursement of government grants according to

universities' research quality ratings. As this chapter goes to press in early 2017 the UK government is presenting a bill to parliament which, if successful, will further increase the marketisation of UK university research.

4. While universities continue to claim a special competence in the production of new knowledge, they should feel obliged by this claim to ensure that their research continues to be conducted according to professional research criteria of openness and without regard either to researcher or university vested interest. However, by inducing senior academics to sit on subject assessment panels for the National Research Assessment Exercise, the UK government has attempted to clothe the Research Excellence Framework (REF) with a professional legitimacy.

5. Recent marketing cultures in universities, and especially the widespread international adoption of National Research Assessment Exercises, have led to the spectre of an incipient corporatisation of university research cultures whereby university managements increasingly make researchers understand that, in posing research questions, their main duty is to bring in large grants to the university rather than to engage in research which, even though it is innovative and scholarly, will neither bring in large grants nor be evaluated as having the required non-academic 'impact'.

6. Although corporatist research culture enhances market research culture, the threats posed by corporatist culture are more silent, hidden and insidious than those of market culture. Whereas market interests are, to a certain extent, declarable and explicit, corporate culture is taken for granted and operates without the 'noise' of the academic market-place.

7. Universities should not be tempted by National Research Assessment criteria to be more concerned with a university's image and government and private-sector goodwill than they are with safeguarding the freedom of academics to conduct research independently of the ideological interests of sponsors (including governments) or the corporate interests of universities.

8. The imperative for research independence (in the sense described at 1. above) is especially important in relation to research on crime and social justice where the research questions posed are often unpopular both with governments and all those with a vested interest in maintaining present structures of inequality via conservative ideologies, and where research impact is usually as much a result of prevailing political conditions as it is an indicator of research excellence. Indeed, in January 2017, Chris Patten, Chancellor of Oxford University, writing against the proposed UK higher education and research bill in the *Observer* newspaper, especially argued against universities being placed under closer government control, adding, 'There is much else that should be amended. The social sciences, for example, are absent from the list of research functions that should be supported' (Patten 2017).

9. Unchallenged, corporatist research culture is likely to lead to a decrease in critical alternative criminologies, qualitative criminologies and theoretical, library-based research.

Fundamental assumptions

Much has been written in the last two decades about the changing nature of universities, their funding and their functions. But while much has been written about the threats to academic freedom from university marketisation, there has also been a contrary concern – that the concept of 'academic freedom' implies that academics should be seen as an elite above democratic debate about the uses of knowledge and as a technocracy beyond legal constraint as to how research is conducted. That is not our position. When in this chapter we refer to 'academic freedom' we are only claiming that when academics are engaged in research they should be both obliged, and allowed, to conduct their inquiries according to the rules of their discipline (and the laws of society) and not according to the vested interests of either themselves or their sponsors (whether those sponsors be governments or campaigning groups). Furthermore, this chapter has not been written as another polemic against either marketisation *per se* or the (intelligent) use of metrics in research assessment. Neither of the authors has a desire to return universities to any imaginary golden age, nor to advocate that knowledge should be pursued as a good in itself.

Instead, the domain assumptions giving birth to this chapter are that:

1. It is essential to humankind that a public space be maintained where professionally approved research and critique in humanities, sciences and social sciences can proceed free of political interference.
2. Researchers are under an ethical obligation to follow, and make explicit, professional criteria for research practice.
3. Research should be conducted according to professional scientific criteria, free of external constraint and researcher or self-interest.
4. Once research findings have been made public, their social implications should be decided by struggles between interested parties in political debate.
5. At the stage of political and social debating of the findings, researchers should be free both to advocate their own political understanding of the research findings and their desirable policy implications.

Marketisation and the growth of National Research Assessment

There is an extensive literature about the marketisation of universities in the USA, UK and elsewhere (see for instance, Slaughter and Leslie 1997; Brown with Carasso 2013; Molesworth, Scullion and Nixon 2011; McGettigan 2013) though most of it has focused upon competition for students rather than on competition for research funds (an exception is Walters 2003). In this chapter we are concerned with only two aspects of marketing rhetoric and process. First, there is the rhetorical principle that under ideal market conditions the quality of the commodity is transparent, the buyer thereby being able to compare products and make an informed purchase at a competitive price. It is in celebration of this principle that there are regular evaluations of research quality. Second, there is the functional principle that it is the mark of a competent marketeer that she or he can either supply goods tailored to meet the needs of specific customers (i.e. in the case of criminological knowledge, governments, criminal justice agencies, campaigning groups); or can predict imminent and visible demand for new types of research knowledge, together with predictions about future costs and profits. It is in celebration of this second principle that the UK has recently added 'impact' assessment to its criteria for ranking universities on a research quality scale. Thus, in the UK, governments have set up regular research quality and 'impact' measuring exercises which can then be used by two different sets of potential customers: students searching for a university place for which they will have to pay fees and living costs that will result in the majority of them having considerable debt by the time they graduate; government, non-governmental organisations (NGO) and private research-funding bodies hoping to commission research in institutions where previous research has been ranked as being of high quality and with high impact.

In the search for an impossible transparency of quality evaluation and research impact, successive UK Research Assessment Exercises have set out more and more detailed criteria as to how quality and (most recently) 'impact' are to be assessed and measured (REF 2011a, 2012: 6, 68–74).[1] Although these evaluations have been presented as quality evaluation and enhancement measures, it has become apparent that such quality control and impact-measurement processes also have the potential to erode academics' traditional professional claims that, in the search for knowledge, research will be designed, conducted and interpreted according to the best methods accepted by the international research community and without vested considerations of personal or political gain by researchers, research institutions or research funders. It is therefore reassuring to note that the British Society of Criminology's (2015) revised Ethics Statement, is still based more upon academia's ideal professional ethic of academic freedom and altruism in research than upon its state-imposed market ethos. For in its revised Ethics Statement of 2015, the British Society of Criminology (BSC 2015) unequivocally states that: 'Researchers in the field of criminology should endeavour to … identify and seek to ameliorate factors which restrict the development of their professional competence and integrity' (cf. American Sociological Association 1999/2008). This statement reinforces the traditional and professionally endorsed obligations of researchers to ensure that academic research is designed and conducted according to professionally recognised protocols and not according to the vested interests of those who fund the research or the vested interests of the researcher and/or his/her employers. It is also the principle sometimes referred to as 'academic freedom'. This academic freedom is, as we have already stated, especially important where research is being funded by governments or others who may be vulnerable to criticism – or financial loss – as a result of the research findings. We assume that the same BSC statement of the academic freedom principle should also reinforce the reasonable and proper expectation of those who fund or commission university research – that the research product will be uncorrupted by research choices made primarily to further either the personal interests of the researcher or the corporate interests of the university.

The BSC reiteration of the ideal of academic freedom notwithstanding, however, it remains the main argument of this chapter that recent trends in university Research Assessment Exercises which have been presented and justified as enhancing the market competitiveness of universities at national and international levels, have also led to a corporatisation of university research which has the potential to have the following adverse effects on social science research in general and on alternative criminologies in particular: a diminution in any research not seen to have immediate policy impact; a diminution of theoretical, library-based and other small-scale investigations not seen to bring in large funds to universities; a diminution of theoretical research based on politically contentious questions not seen as being 'relevant' to the policy concerns of the government of the day; and a diminution of the cross-disciplinary research which has recently enhanced criminological inquiry with understandings gleaned from literature and the arts (see Ruggiero 2003; Rafter and Brown 2011).

In this chapter, most of the empirical examples of threats to knowledge production presently emanating from the ways in which governments worldwide have adopted National Research Assessments are taken from our observations of the operation of the UK Research Excellence Framework (REF). The threat from publishers' manipulation of academic journals via their gaming of the impact league tables is also worldwide and is exemplified in publishers' advice to editorial boards as to how best to improve their placing in the Journal Citation Reports, published annually as part of the Social Science Citation Index by the Institute of Scientific Information (ISI). However, although our empirical examples are taken from our experiences of working in the UK university system and involvement with the editorial boards of over a dozen academic journals, we think that our arguments about the UK universities' corporate response to the National Research Assessment are relevant to other societies which have undergone similar transformations of academic research culture (see, for instance the analytical commentaries of Mathiesen 2013: 52, Martin 2011, about Norway and Australia respectively). Already, National Research Assessments have been adopted in Australia, Brazil, Portugal, Italy, Norway, Denmark and the Netherlands while Sweden and Japan are said to be planning similar exercises (Schotten and el Aisati 2015). That, together with the report that the UK Higher Education and Funding Council for England (HEFCE 2014) has recently invited views on the 'benefits and challenges of expanding the UK's research assessment system, the Research Excellence Framework (REF), on an international basis ... to incorporate submissions from universities overseas' gives added urgency for debate of this issue at international level.

World literature and political history are replete with examples of how scientific inquiry and scientists as well as artists and social scientists have suffered repression under political dictatorships inimical to the concept of critique. There are also recurring reports of the repression of ideas and intellectual and artistic expression in countries calling their mode of government democratic. It would therefore be both fanciful and irresponsible either to argue or imply that contemporary social scientific and artistic production in the Western world currently faces the same degree of suppression as has, historically, and in some contemporary states, been instanced by brutal physical attack, book burnings, censorship, prosecution, imprisonment, banishment and other modes of oppression, including the torture, banishment and killing of intellectuals and authors. Nevertheless, in the cause of freedom of intellectual inquiry in general, it behoves academics committed to safeguarding the liberal traditions of diversity of investigation and impartiality and transparency of research method and interpretation, to be forever on guard against externally imposed constraints upon research diversity, project design and investigative strategies which, even when they do not violate human rights may be just as (or even more) effective in obstructing the freedom of academic inquiry. Yet, you may ask, is this a new threat? Has scientific and artistic endeavour ever been independent of researcher and sponsor self-interest? And what responsibilities do contemporary academics have to their communities and the publics which fund them? What are universities for?

John Henry Newman's tract *The Idea of a University Defined and Illustrated* first published in 1852 saw teaching as being the prime purpose of universities, with research being the concern of the specialist 'academies' of the time. But Newman also put emphasis on the importance of universities living up to their name – by being 'universal' or comprehensive – as exemplified by their teaching of all known branches of knowledge; and by not engaging in exclusion or censorship of any kind. The emphasis on inclusiveness was not merely a liberal stance; Newman also argued that the different disciplines could be used to enhance and strengthen each other's capacity for discovery. Even so, and Newman notwithstanding, as far as academia and the production of knowledge are concerned, it might still be claimed that the ideal that academics should conduct their research independently of self-interest and according to altruistic notions of the social good has always remained just that: an ideal.

Early philosophers and scientists were frequently dependent upon patrons. Modern academics have always had their professionalism ascribed to them by universities whose organisational structures have, in the UK at least, gradually grown into mega-managerialist bureaucracies organised nowadays to induct academics (and especially young academics) into a market ethos of high productivity tailored to an ever-changing, and sometimes imaginary, consumer demand. Nor (and despite Plato's/Socrates' sadly optimistic view of knowledge-mongers and Durkheim's rather rosy-eyed vision of professional ethics) would it be safe to assume that academics have consistently acted independently of the demands of their sponsors or their own self-interest (Plato 1996/380 AD; Durkheim 1957). As Talcott Parsons (1949/1954: 48) pointed out in 1949, professional interests are inevitably bound up with business, bureaucratic management and personal motivation; and even though how individuals act within these complex social structures is at least partly a matter of ethical choice, UK academics have recently had to make this choice within a rapidly changing occupational culture in British universities, an occupational culture which has been fashioned by government funding protocols to give priority to a market ethos rather than to a professional ethic of altruistic research unbiased by personal, institutional or political interest. None the less, we remain convinced that the ideal of academic freedom to ask questions and make investigations without consideration of personal or a university's corporate gain is one worth fighting for.

Meanwhile, questions about the institutional, professional, academic and ethical responsibilities of scientific inquiry in terms of the integrity of knowledge production, promotion and dissemination have perennially engaged criminologists as much as they do other social scientists. Most criticism of criminology's ideological conditions of existence at the end of the 20th century tended to centre on its embeddedness in state definitions of crime and justice and its concomitant neglect of alternative and more critical approaches to the study of crime, criminalisation and justice (e.g. Walters 2003; Young 1988, 2011). Then, just over a decade ago Hillyard, Sim, Tombs and Whyte (2004), at the beginning of the 21st century, raised issues about the impact of the UK national research exercise then known as the Research Assessment Exercise (RAE). In addition to noting that the RAE had increased and enhanced the advance of university marketisation, Hillyard *et al.* (2004: 380) noted that it had added to a 'culture of compliance' in universities. Citing Harvie (2000: 112) they argued that the RAE criteria for ranking departments had, furthermore, led to a hierarchisation of research grants and journals. Additionally, they claimed that a most radical attack had been made on traditional research values: the RAE ranking of research quality had moved away from assessing research *outputs* (in terms of the production and quality of new knowledge) to counting research *inputs* (in terms of the accumulation of grants). Hillyard *et al.* predicted that this change of research assessment – from positively assessing the social value of the research output to counting the grant income accruing to the university – was likely to have a deleterious effect on the quality of UK research output:

> Once a grant has been received, then there may be a tendency to become concerned less with the research activity at hand, and more with the need to secure *subsequent* funding – and this perceived (indeed for many researchers in universities, real) need may infect the nature and quality of the research being conducted, whether consciously or not.
>
> *(Hillyard et al. 2004: 381, emphasis in original)*

In more recent times, and in a different mode, criminologists themselves have debated their civic responsibilities; and in the debate about 'public criminology' (inspired by the similar concept of 'public sociology' – see Burawoy 2005; Clawson *et al.* 2007) have asked whether criminologists have been too preoccupied with talking to each other about rather abstruse issues, and too little concerned about communicating with the publics who fund research (Uggen and Inderbitzen 2006; Currie 2007; Loader and Sparks 2010). Yet, though this ethical issue of the public accountability of academic criminology has been taken up rather belatedly by criminologists working in the academy, the market accountability of academics has been of concern to cost-conscious governments for several decades.[2] One consequence has been that UK universities' 'mainstream quality research funding' (www.hefce.ac.uk/whatwedo/invest/) has become ever more increasingly tied to metrically assessed researcher quality and, most recently, to the contentious measurement of 'research impact' (both tools of the UK quality-assessment exercise currently known as the Research Excellence Framework (REF)). Concomitantly, the imposition of a strict managerialist and hierarchical organisation of university academic staff has closed off (or at least inhibited) the traditional lateral relationships between senior and less experienced staff which might possibly have resulted in a greater solidarity of opposition to the market logic being imposed. Thus, the trend which Hillyard *et al.* first identified in 2004 has, over the last ten years or so, become institutionalised. One particular instance of what they then called a 'stain upon the silence' – the attempted repressive socialisation of younger scholars into a conformist corporate culture – has, moreover, now become a most regrettable but established feature of UK universities: 'The RAE [Research Assessment Exercise] has encouraged the clone-like reproduction of an evaluative, safe, self-referential criminological culture into which younger scholars are brutally socialized to become self-disciplined subjects if they are to acquire permanent posts' (Hillyard *et al.* 2004: 382).

Corporatist criminologies defined and their problematic nature exemplified

The concept of corporatist criminologies is an ideal type and there is no intention of implying that the research practices of all criminologists are totally shaped by their university's corporatist interest. Nor, when reference is made to corporatist criminology is there any implied denigration of those who reply to calls to tender for research funding in named fields (e.g. victimology or policing). Corporatist criminologies – whether they present as 'pure' or 'applied' – is the term that this essay bestows on any criminologies where the criminological research-processes and decisions are made partly or solely to comply with the 'research excellence' or 'impact' indicators either formally defined by government quality control documents or second-guessed by impact gurus (ex-members of assessment panels hired by universities to sell them insider knowledge about how quality or impact assessments have been made in previous Research Assessment Exercises).

We do not use the term corporatist criminology to suggest that criminologists are nowadays failing to declare traditional and explicit 'conflicts of interest' in terms of funding or publishing. When we talk about 'corporatist criminology' we are referring, instead to a *culture* of university corporatism in which research and publication decisions are routinely and silently made more with an eye to 'research impact', 'a university's corporate image', 'brand consolidation' and 'customer satisfaction' than with a view to producing new knowledge, the impact of which may not be immediate or apparent – and which will almost certainly not be measurable. The threats posed by the profit requirements of publishers mesh with and reinforce those posed by universities' corporate culture insofar as they both risk over-promoting fashionable topics and methods (especially 'large data' and quantitative 'evidence') at the expense of library research, qualitative data and small-scale inquiry (Young 2011; Mathiesen 2013).

Although, of course, there is a relationship between research market culture and research corporatist culture – the latter certainly works in the interests of the former – the threats posed by corporatist research culture are, we think, greater than those posed by the vested interests of any individual funders operating in the research market – be they governments, charities, campaigning groups or commercial interests. Finance received from any of the 'funders' constitutive of the criminology market-place has to be declared – it having long been recognised that funders' vested interests might somehow shape the research design and, accordingly, the research findings. Second, although a market has always operated in criminology, non-funded research has also been allowed to co-exist with it. For in the UK from the 1970s onwards, alternative criminologies were allowed to flourish beside the administrative criminology and while the emphasis was on quality publishing, with the quality criteria still decided by peer review, criminologists were free to engage in theoretical work and to develop alternative criminologies, focusing on a range of issues not really amenable to large-scale investigation (e.g. corporate crime) nor attractive as providing the really sexy crime stories beloved by the media – and which certainly can expect to have immediate 'impact'. Thus, whereas market research culture allowed people to go to the market as individuals who could (and still can) negotiate with funders to have autonomy over the way they conduct research and interpret the findings, corporatist research culture, as embodied in universities' present responses to the 'impact' measurement tool, imposes one measuring rod on all research – however funded and whether funded or not. Moreover, everyone is involved in it. No-one can opt out, every member of a university department is made to be complicit. As a result, impact coercion operates in silent, taken-for-granted ways as researchers silently make project topic and project design choices on the basis of their likely contribution to the final research product's impact. We are not saying that any of these choices are necessarily corrupt or non-professional. What we are arguing is that they are 'impact-constrained' choices which will gradually squeeze out certain types of research from universities, especially theoretical critique, library-based research, qualitative research and work done *pro bono*. If you accept as a basic principle the notion that a university is a place where all knowledge claims can be debated (Newman 1852) then it seems that the effective suppression of certain criminological perspectives and methods is in complete contradiction of the concept of a university. In the meantime, it also seems that this process of impact coercion will have its greatest effect on the research choices of early career criminologists.

The remainder of this section on research corporatism is comprised of four subsections each of which exemplifies the dilemmas confronting university researchers in criminology as a result of corporatist university pressures to gain large grants and produce research and publications meeting the narrow and arcane measures of impact as defined by the UK National Research Assessment Exercise (in the case of universities) and as defined by the impact factor tables in the case of publishers.

Corporatism and research funding

In this opening example it is argued that university corporatisation poses a threat to academics' choice of criminological research topics and to the research methods to be used.

It is neither surprising nor unacceptable when NGO and single-issue funding bodies commissioning research define the topic that they wish to have researched and the type of investigation required – for example, a large-scale quantitative survey of the extent of crimes against the street homeless in a specific jurisdiction. Nor is it surprising or unacceptable that universities are pleased when their academics compete for such projects and win large grants. Such collaboration between universities and other organisations is certainly in line with the professional ethic of altruistic service. But the study of crime and society raises more fundamental questions about the causes and nature of crime than can be answered by quantitative research, important, expensive and pre-eminently marketable as it is. Consider the dilemma of the ethnographer in the corporatist university who wishes to do a small-scale ethnography about crimes against people living on the street – the type of research that requires a relatively small grant. Or consider the non-marketability of the critical criminology project which proposes to analyse and produce new theorisations of the causes of homelessness via library research into changing government policies and legislation on welfare and unemployment; and where the researcher could actually do the research without a massive grant – with the university only charging for research time and facilities, and maybe using the voluntary services of a campaigning group to do the interviewing of other project work. Where fewer grants are available for ethnography and library-based research (and when the funds that are available are quite small) issues arise both for academics as researchers and for those senior academics advising younger staff about their careers. Should researchers comply with university managers' insistence that university employees should always go for the largest grants in spite of professional reservations about the scientific probity (in terms of producing new knowledge) of either the questions being asked or the methods being used? Should senior academics advise early career university staff that in making their choice of research questions and methods of investigation they should always give primacy to the marketing and impact potentials of a topic rather than to an investigation's capacity for making new contributions to criminological knowledge? If their advice is always to go for the largest grant regardless of the probity of the questions being asked or methods to be used they violate the scientific ideal of conducting research impartially and without self-interest. If they advise the young researchers to stick to their principles and choose research which they think important in terms of knowledge innovation, they may be encouraging them to put their careers at risk.

Corporatism, 'research impact' and the integrity of research findings

In the second example of university corporatism it is argued that when funders require researchers to predict both the likely users of the research and its social impact, they are, in effect, creating the preconditions for policy-led evidence, rather than evidence-led policy; worse, the research design may be tailored to ensure that the prediction is a self-fulfilling prophecy (Beck 1992; Hope 2004). As Zedner, Hoyle and Bosworth (2016: xxii) have recently observed of UK research funding: 'The growing nexus between funding and the "impact" of academic research risks creating perverse incentives that may affect the issues that academics choose to address and how they go about doing so.'

For some time, government funding of university social research projects in the UK has been awarded by competition (RCUK 2014). Proposals for research are required to predict both the likely users of the research and its 'social impact'. Leaving aside for one moment the absurdity of implying that it is possible to identify, isolate and measure (or otherwise assess) the social, economic or cultural impact that an individual research project (one possible cultural influence amongst many in effecting social change) might have (or, in the mythology of the REF, *has* had) – formal requirements for researchers to make such predictions also imply that researchers always and already know either what they are going to 'find' or what they (or others) are going to 'make of' the research findings/products. Equally worrying, is the fact that not only are other academics excluded from being the sole predicted beneficiaries in the 'user' category of funding applications under 'impact' criteria, but that academic impact is also seen as being insufficient for the award of high 'impact' assessments in the Research Excellence Framework. In other words, research that is ground-breaking in terms of theory or methodology, but which might in the short term be useful to academics only, is seen as being unimportant. These two exclusions effectively have the potential to debar much ground-breaking social science research from being counted by the impact assessors in their extremely arcane measurements of a university's research contribution. Worse, such exclusions may have the result of side-lining critical research altogether. Market ethos aims at undercutting rivals; so why should a university support research which is either financially expensive because, being 'blue sky' it is unlikely to have impact *in the short term*, or is creating reputational risk for the university because, being *fundamentally* critical (as opposed to being *policy* critical and therefore likely to notch up the support of at least some policy-makers), it threatens the status quo – or at least the government of the day?

The extraordinary difficulties of assessing 'social impact' were highlighted in a study of programmes for women prisoners which was undertaken by one of the authors several years ago (Carlen 2002). A major concern of directors of all the programmes investigated was how best to present their work in such a way that their funding continued. There may be areas of social policy where it is easier to talk about 'what works' than it is in relation to crime and punishment. But in the area of penal policy, it is notoriously difficult to get agreement as to the nature of the problem to be addressed, let alone the best ways of addressing 'it' and then assessing 'what works'. The 'hard evidence' preferred by governments would demonstrate a positive relationship between intervention and a reduction in recidivism, and though (given the financial incentives to produce it) such 'hard evidence' might appear to be forthcoming in relation to participants in a particular project, without detailed knowledge of the selection and characteristics of project members, together with information about the other influences on them at a particular time, it is usually difficult (if not impossible) to isolate any one factor as being solely responsible for any individual's desistance from crime – even if such a complex phenomenon were likely to be amenable to sensible assessment in the short term (see Carter, Day and Klein 1992). Similarly, the favoured official modes for assessing research project impact often confuse matters still further, especially when demands for quantitative assessments of policy 'successes' or 'failures' are being made in situations where such quantitative measures are either impossible to produce in any meaningful form or where they are simply inappropriate. In their book *How Organisations Measure Success*, Carter *et al.* (1992: 14) point out that it is usually impossible to measure the impact on society of specific social policies for three main reasons: the problem of multiple objectives; the difficulties of specifying and understanding the relationships between intermediate outputs and output measures; and the inevitable time lag between input and impact, especially in programmes 'where the benefits only become fully apparent over decades'. All these strictures apply to the measurement of the social impact of criminological research. The limits to the quantification of qualitative measures become most apparent when criminological research projects are explicitly committed to developing theoretical work which will certainly not be amenable to measurement of impact in the short term and whose impact on society is likely to be both disputed and impossible to measure in the long term. Meanwhile, in the UK we have the unedifying spectacle of research project leaders begging putative research users to write letters testifying to a project's impact; of senior academics instructing junior researchers on how to make an 'impact case'; of theoretical criminologists having their research undervalued by their colleagues because 'it doesn't bring in much money' and has no 'impact' value according to the short timescale of National Research Assessments; and universities paying considerable fees to members of previous assessment panels to advise them about the 'ref-ability' of different members of staff, and the best way for departments to present their 'impact cases'. To make assurance doubly sure, young staff are reminded that being 'retweeted' 'counts as weak impact' – and advised to open and use their Twitter accounts!

Of course researchers should be able to list justifications for their proposed research being funded by public money. Upon completion of the project they should publish a full report detailing the results and how the money was spent. We are not advocating that university researchers should treat their research as a publicly funded hobby. But can positive predictions of benefits to named users and calculation of social impacts really be made without prejudice to research choice, research design and interpretation of the research results and without risk to the professional scientific ethic of altruistic inquiry (i.e. inquiry conducted without a view to self-interest or partial interests)? Certainly, in specifying the theoretical framework which will inform interpretation of the research results, research project leaders will indicate their theoretical and methodological preferences. Researchers in certain types of projects will also be able both to predict what they expect to find and to report honestly whether or not they find as expected. But in other types of research – especially those that depend on theorising the meanings and/or causes of certain social phenomena, the task of prediction may not be so easy; accurate prediction may well be impossible; and honest prediction may have the predictable impact of being prejudicial to the project's chances of winning government finance (see also Young 2016: 105). For, if researchers do predict findings honestly (according to the best knowledge available to themselves and endorsed as such by peer assessors in their discipline) will governments necessarily be altruistic in their assessment of which knowledge it is in the public interest (or their own) to fund? Similarly with definition of topic and methodology; 'problem families' may well be listed on a government's wish list of research priorities, but will the researcher be allowed to draw a sample which includes, for instance, the UK royal family, families whose children are sent to boarding schools from late infanthood to early adulthood; or families where the care of incapacitated adults is undertaken by children because of the lack of state provision? In short, should university social researchers, in the interests of their institutions and themselves, eschew the more politically contentious and hard-to-sell investigations and, instead, attempt to guess what knowledge governments want (or are prepared to hear), and then shape their proposals accordingly?

Finally, in relation to the creeping corporatisation of university research, might academics, by sitting on government grant awarding committees and/or by being party to national quality and impact assessments, themselves be contributing to a lessening of professional probity in the choice and conduct of research? The authors have discussed this last question informally with several UK academics implicated in the REF exercise as assessors. Although the issues involved were recognised, the general justification for academic participation in government Research Assessment Exercises was that, regardless of any intellectual reservations about the appropriateness of the funding criteria, academics would be irresponsible not to maintain some influence over the disbursement of public funds for university research. The people we spoke to hoped that by sitting on the assessment panels they would be well placed to defend the integrity (and funding!) of criminology as an academic discipline. Yet, perusal of articles and letters in *The Times Higher Education Supplement* suggests that UK academics are nowadays in a state of *anomie*. In Mertonian terminology, they experience a disjunction between explicit professional research rules and values and implicit (and operative) REF research rules and values but have dealt with the resultant sense of *anomie* by accepting positions where they feel that they can reduce the disjunction by being research assessors themselves. This type of response is typical of participants knowingly and unwillingly coerced into an imaginary structure of governance: they know the emperor has no clothes so attempt to kit him out with their own so as to keep the show on the road (in this case to avoid a breakdown of relations between university sector and government – see Carlen 2008). And there is the final irony! For by sitting on assessment panels, senior academics actually clothe the REF with the apparent 'ideal professional' legitimacy of professional *self*-evaluation! Meanwhile, it is not established academics who suffer under university corporatisation; many, indeed, thrive under its new managerialist structures both within universities and in the bourgeoning world of national research quality governance. The biggest threat of corporatist research culture is to the young researcher who may never have the chance to establish the relevance of alternative and original ways of thinking outside the constraints imposed by national and parochial definitions of 'research impact'.

Corporatism, publishing impact and academic journals

The third example of corporatism illustrates the argument that the twin emphases of publishers and funders on measurement of research quality and prediction of future findings and their social impact are also endangering the integrity of both research design and the interpretation of research findings.

That commercial publishers have usually assessed the market for any proposed academic book is not surprising. This is not to say that book publishers do not also require a book to conform to high academic standards; academic referees are usually required to comment on academic quality, as well as size and character of the potential readership. Publication of very specialised or very technical research reports, however, will usually be restricted to the peer-reviewed academic journals which have traditionally existed as outlets for articles chosen entirely for their academic excellence, and where the size of the article's likely readership is not one of the criteria for publication. In theory, this remains the case. Ethics statements by publishers of academic journals routinely claim that articles for refereed journals are reviewed anonymously by peer reviewers (other academics) and selected for publication on the basis of a variety of criteria, first among them usually being academic excellence and the originality of contribution to the journal's declared academic interests (for example in penality, probation, criminological theory or state crime). In practice, the annual publication of tables (known as 'impact factor' measurement) based on citation analysis is threatening the integrity of peer-reviewed journals.

Citation coercion (that is, persuading an author to refer to articles published in recent issues of the journal in order to raise the journal's impact factor) is only one of several violations of scientific ethics which publishers have recommended to journal editors as a ruse for raising their journal's impact ranking (see University of Alabama in Huntsville 2012; Carlen 2012: 25–26):

> Impact factor is a measure of a journal's 'impact' based on the number of citations to its articles during a specified period of time (usually two years). Because publishers argue that citation analysis is used by librarians in deciding which journals to take, by authors in deciding which journals to target, and by some [national] research assessment exercises to assess the quality of a university's research output, journal editors have been put under pressure from publishers … to abandon anonymous peer review and instead commission top academics to write for a journal and also, in the selection of articles, to focus on fashionable topics … [S]ome publishers employ statisticians solely for the purpose of analysing citation stats, so that the information can be available to editors who are invited to make use of it in deciding which authors and articles they should publish in future. … [T]his development violates scientific ideals … first, it is … dishonest for a journal to claim that all articles are anonymously reviewed and then to commission and publish articles from so-called 'top authors'; secondly, … focusing on high-impact authors is a threat to knowledge production as it [could] result in: no unknown theorists being published; no articles on new or unfashionable topics being published; and, given that well-known authors write as many dreadful articles as anyone else, an overall decline in standards of academic writing. (For views from the physical sciences see Hall 2007; Lawrence 2007.)
>
> *(Carlen 2012: 25–26)*

In conjunction with publishers' gaming of citation tables, new ironies and absurdities continually arise in relation to the effect that research output measurement has on the dissemination of knowledge. Take, for example, the academic tradition of book reviewing. It is rapidly becoming extinct for at least two related reasons: some journals have stopped publishing book reviews because they are not included in citation tables; and, on the other side of the coin, young academics are being advised not to write book reviews as they will not be 'counted' in their research impact profiles. Indeed, even some more senior academics approached to contribute to this book regretfully declined on the grounds that a chapter in a non-English language publication would not be 'REF-able'! UK REF gaming can also obstruct the speedy publication of research findings.

The UK universities' research quality assessment has recently run on a six year cycle. So, in order to conserve a university's research capital, senior academics and university bureaucrats have been known to advise staff who already have the requisite publications (usually four) for a current REF period to delay publication of further articles until commencement of the next REF cycle. But counting rules may have changed by the time of the next research quality assessment period. Bring on the impact guru. Confusingly, the impact guru explains that, even though publication in an academic journal is no longer seen as being evidence of a research project's impact (on non-academics) it may, nonetheless, be important because publication in an academic journal may be seen as a 'pathway to impact'! Let us hope so. Our point is that when, in the era of corporatist criminology both publishers and grant awarding bodies insist that the future marketability of the research product should be calculated and/or made explicit prior to its completion and/or publication as a new knowledge product, there is good reason to fear that the research design, the research findings and the final, published interpretation of the findings will be seriously flawed in that they will have been determined more by market criteria than by scientific procedures and professional ethics. In the meantime, young UK academics are being told to manage their publications and workloads solely with reference to their likely citation/impact 'value'.

It has always been assumed that one of the professional obligations of an academic is to disseminate research findings and new theories, via a peer review process, as soon as they are available. When publishers are either corrupting (or attempting to corrupt) the academic journal market by publishing substandard articles by well-known authors whose articles will sell, regardless of their merit, and when applicants for research funds are having to claim in advance of their project's completion both what they will 'find', and how they will ensure that it has 'impact' on non-academics, an academic committed to a search for knowledge that may currently have no predictable market value whatsoever, is posed with an ethical dilemma. Modify the proposal to suit the research market principles as currently laid down by the funders (and those principles change with each new assessment exercise)? Or be a responsible professional and describe all the 'unknowns' which may well make the research potential unmeasurable – and therefore unmarketable – *because the only market available is a rather dodgy futures* market? All futures markets are essentially risky markets insofar as they are subject to unknowable and incremental political, economic and cultural changes. But it is arguable that the market for social critique is both smaller and more at the mercy of political change and political expediency than are other markets. If, therefore, the academic publishing market-place becomes globalised without corporatist criminology being contested by criminologists worldwide, we fear that politically unpopular and qualitative criminologies may have no future at all.

Corporatism and ethics committees

In this final example of corporatist criminology, it is argued that since the rise of university/ departmental ethics committees, qualitative researchers in criminology have had superfluous research constraints placed upon them in the name of 'ethics', but that these obstacles to research have often had less to do with a researcher's moral obligations to research subjects and society, and more to do with the 'business' model employed by some university ethics committees.

A traditional task of a professional association has been to safeguard a profession's moral authority via the rules of ethical practice laid down in its Ethical Statement and by its authority to sanction members found guilty of breaking those rules. Enforcement of the professional code has never usurped the authority of the courts and therefore a professional person committing a criminal act might well be punished by the criminal justice system for breaking the law and further sanctioned by the professional association for engaging in professionally unethical practice and/or for bringing the profession into disrepute. A safeguard against the latter, as far as UK academic research is concerned, has traditionally been the requirement that applicants for research funds give a written undertaking that their research design has complied with the professional association's Ethical Statement and that they will knowingly do nothing to contravene either the letter or the spirit of the Statement while conducting the investigation. Where researchers have thought that there could possibly be doubt about the ethics of a proposed method of investigation they have been obliged to identify a potential ethically controversial issue, make a case for the proposed method and describe the safeguards built in to the research design to ensure that neither the letter nor the spirit of the ethical code will be violated. The ethical dimensions of research proposals in competition for research funds have traditionally been assessed by peer reviewers familiar with both the research discipline and the project context. Where research funds were not involved, the researcher (in the UK, at least) would often not be required to submit a research proposal and the research project's ethical dimensions would not come under close outsider scrutiny unless a formal complaint by a member of the public were to be made either to a researcher's university or professional association. Overall, the assumption was that while a professional association's Statement of Ethics outlines general principles of professional behaviour and practice, it is the duty of the researcher (and his and her peers) to interpret the general principles and their situational relevance and application to the research in question. With the increase in university marketisation, the situation has changed dramatically, and the last couple of decades have seen a new development in the governance of researcher ethics – the rise and rise of 'local' university/school/departmental ethics committees to whom university researchers are required to submit all proposals for empirical research – whether or not research funding is being applied for and, in some institutions, before project leaders can even approach an outside body for research support in terms of either access or finance. The abandonment of the 'light touch' in favour of the 'heavy hand' in relation to appraisal of the ethical dimensions of research projects has especially worked against the ability of qualitative researchers and, even more particularly, against criminologists, to design their projects ethically and primarily according to their contextual knowledge of a social phenomenon. (For an original critique of ethics committees and why criminologists especially should be wary of them, see Winlow and Hall 2012.)

Critics of ethics committees frequently make the point that the application of a medical model of ethics is not appropriate to social research. But the criteria being applied in the era of corporate criminology are less likely to be based on a medical model of ethics and more on a corporatist fear of insurance risk. Indeed, as universities move more and more towards competing solely as businesses, some of their personnel appear to embrace the business ethos at the same time as losing all sight of what type of business they are supposed to be in. One result of this is that we increasingly receive reports of PhD proposals in criminology being turned down by ethics committees which have translated the almost inevitable security, social and researcher risks inherent in studying lawbreakers into ethical grounds for prohibiting the research (see also Carlen 2016. For a more sympathetic view of the operation of university ethics committees, see Israel and Hay 2012).

Criminology, corporatism and critique

> For a privileged minority, Western democracy provides the leisure, the facilities, and the training to seek the truth lying hidden behind the veil of distortion and misrepresentation, ideology and class interest, through which the events of current history are presented to us.
>
> *(Chomsky 1967: 1)*

The so-called marketisation of higher education has, in many countries, resulted in a competitive business ethos which has adopted ethically dubious strategies to design out social research risk (in terms of unpopular research findings, theories or methods) and increase customer satisfaction, corporate research impact and university profits. Additionally, universities and publishers have united in their efforts to gain business prestige by gaming impact and citation tables and by encouraging publication with a view to maximising National Research Assessment advantage. We are not arguing against universities operating as businesses. We are, however, arguing that, in their drive to compete for funds and students, universities are not paying sufficient attention to a most important side of their business – the disinterested production and publication of new knowledge. Yet, whether or not criminologists in general are troubled by ethical issues in relation to corporatist criminology, we believe that qualitative and critical alternative criminologists in particular should be worried by the risks that marketisation and corporatism pose to their freedom – and even more to the freedom of their younger colleagues – to pursue their researches effectively and according to the methods appropriate to scientific, rather than market, research.

Universities have traditionally functioned as institutions for the pursuit of scientific enquiry. Their mission statements still routinely mention 'research excellence' and 'teaching and learning' as prime commitments. Yet nowadays university mission statements are also manifestos of business intent, often finalised (if not initially composed) by marketing managers. Even initial drafts of university mission statements are frequently developed by committees composed of academics who have chosen to stop doing research in order to climb the university administration ladder. Maybe that is why mention of 'research excellence' in university mission statements is so often mired in words more designed to highlight a university's attention to consumer demand – 'change', 'internationalism', 'globalism', 'impact', 'relevance' – than to emphasise the integrity and distinctiveness of its research products. This is not to argue that academic knowledge should be, or will ever be, accepted uncritically when it is related to social issues such as crime, law, politics and economics (nor when it is related to any other kind of scientific endeavour, in fact). But it is to argue that the only justification for academics to continue to work in the multiply privileged environment of a university is that when they engage in critical enquiry they also 'identify and seek to ameliorate factors which restrict the development of their professional competence and integrity' (British Society of Criminology 2015). This is why (and despite accepting that modern universities have several equally important functions) we are insisting that the one essential and distinctive job of universities is to provide a space where blue sky research and critical inquiry can proceed untrammelled by non-academic interventions from market- and corporate-oriented managements.

Meanwhile, some commentators have criticised the marketisation of universities from a slightly different angle. They have suggested that concerns about university marketisation should not be linked only to the diminution of academic control and the risk to research integrity. They argue that several adjuncts of university marketisation and corporatisation, such as mission statements (see Reisz 2010) and ethics committees (see Winlow and Hall 2012: 413) are also used by academic managers in more deliberately threatening ways – as disciplinary controls to stifle dissent and social critique:

> From a managerial perspective, says Brian Jones, senior lecturer in marketing at Leeds Metropolitan University, [mission statements] are "a force for good. They help grow brand value, communicate core university messages, build consent and serve as a totem around which stakeholders, often employees or customers, can rally." Yet a more critical analysis, suggests Jones, would raise questions about "why university management feel the need to have a mission statement. In part, they act as succour, a dummy, a form of reassurance, a message that spells out and justifies business and management

decisions. They serve to unify dissenting viewpoints around a managerial-driven theme or 'vision'."

(Reisz 2010)

Winlow and Hall (2012: 413) are very specific in their warning to criminologists as to why their research is especially at risk from the amateur socio-actuarialism of university department ethics committees:

> [T]he rise of institutional Ethics Committees is of special interest to criminology. The very substance of criminology seems to necessitate strict policing of research agendas and methodologies despite the fact that, in its relatively short history, it has not proven to be any more 'ethically problematic' than other branches of the social sciences ... Much of what empirical criminologists investigate seems to indicate some kind of rupture in the moral or ethical foundations of our world, or the inability of these foundations to regulate subjective or institutional corruption.
>
> *(Winlow and Hall 2012: 400–401)*

Moreover, if we are correct in our assumption that, though universities have many functions, their distinguishing characteristic is the production of new knowledge and theoretical critique, the only justification for any discipline's inclusion in the academy is that it is innovative and critical – not that it is extremely marketable and potentially profitable. Awkwardly, however, for critical alternative criminologies, social theory addresses political issues where authoritative answers have already been constructed by powerful ideologies emanating from religion, politics, law and common sense. So it is in an already-fraught cultural and political context that critical alternative criminologists are social theorists focusing on the politically sensitive meanings of crime and justice. As a result, when the conduct of academic research is policed by university managers over-concerned about pleasing their paymasters and their markets, critical alternative criminology projects are much more likely to be at risk of ideological attack and academic marginalisation than are those emanating from disciplines seen as being either less threatening or less immediately controversial (see Wacquant 2002 on the decline of prison ethnography). Yet several of today's officially recognised crime issues (e.g. victimology; gender, race and class biases in the administration of criminal justice) were first brought to prominence by university-based professional academic research directed by theoretical critique and supported by qualitative methods (see Young 2011).

Good criminological research is carried out in a range of agencies unconnected with universities (for example, government departments, non-governmental organisations, criminal justice organisations including charities and independent research centres). Criminologists working in such agencies rightly put their professional expertise at the service of the agency which pays them. Yet though the agency may be prepared to allow them to engage in theoretically informed qualitative investigation, it will be unlikely to pay for library-based theoretical critique. In contrast, we assume that the essential business of universities is to create, maintain and protect an intellectual space where, in the spirit of academic inquiry, all kinds of legally acceptable research methodologies and domain assumptions *from all round the globe* can be openly stated and debated (and maybe rejected) without fear of constraint or censure by university managers. (See Drake and Walters 2015 on the importance of criminologists – and societies in general – engaging in 'unbridled critique'.)

Our argument has not been about protecting academic privilege nor that academic knowledge should be the final arbiter in disputes about crime and justice. We merely insist that when academics come to the market-place or to the debating chamber they should at least be able to state honestly that their research goods have been designed according to the best academic research knowledge and practice available. Furthermore, they should feel free to engage in social critique without fear of putting their careers at risk. If, however, in the era of corporatist criminology, more and more early-career academics are obliged by their seniors to follow the corporate ethos rather than the professional ethic, it is likely that the amount of critical alternative and qualitative criminological research in universities will shrink.

Sceptical of the suggestion that the spectre of a corporatist criminology already beckons, some academics we have spoken to have argued that it definitely does not exist. Maybe they are correct. However, whether or not the spectre of a corporatist criminology already threatens, we have felt compelled to warn that the conditions favourable to its emergence are already in place. Meanwhile, the essays in this volume bear witness to the present strength, originality and power of critique of all the alternative criminologies. They also remind us that though always under attack, often inhibited and occasionally silenced, the human capacity for critique can never be destroyed.

Notes

1   Applicants for government social research funds in the UK must specify the likely 'impact' of proposed projects and are advised that 'beneficiaries must consist of a wider Group than that of the investigator's immediate professional circle carrying out similar research' (J-ES Helptext 2015). For the REF assessment, influencing the work of other academics cannot count as impact (REF 2011: 48). Instead, assessable impact is only in relation to non-academic constituencies, such as government bodies, campaigning groups or public awareness of a particular issue, and any claim to impact needs to be substantiated with 'relevant' evidence demonstrating the link between the research and the impact claimed, such as citations in official non-academic publications or old and new media (REF 2011b, 2012: 71–72).

2   For an early commentary on the marketisation of UK universities see Thompson (1970/2014). For a lively history of continuity and change in the functions of universities, see Collini (2012). For a stimulating discussion of public knowledge by a scientist, see Ziman (1968); for a treatise on the importance of the humanities see Nussbaum (2010). For a detailed account of government concerns about the financial accountability of UK universities throughout the 20th century, see Shattock (1994, 2012). For an early account of the corruption of professional academic values by marketisation see Walters (2003).

References

American Sociological Association (1999) *Code of Ethics and Policies and Procedures of the ASA Committee on Professional Ethics*. Reprinted 2008. www.asanet.org/images/asa/docs/pdf/CodeofEthics.pdf

Beck U (1992) *Risk Society: Towards a New Modernity*. London: Sage

British Society of Criminology (2015) *Code of Ethics for Researchers in the Field of Criminology*. http://britsoccrim.org/

Brown R with H Carasso (2013) *Everything for Sale? The Marketisation of UK Higher Education*. London: Routledge

Burawoy M (2005) 'For Public Sociology'. 2004 American Sociological Presidential Address. *American Sociological Review* 70: 4–28

Carlen P (2002) 'Women's Imprisonment: Cross-National Lessons' in P Carlen (ed.) *Women and Punishment: The Struggle for Justice*. Cullompton: Willan

Carlen P (2008) *Imaginary Penalities*. Cullompton: Willan

Carlen P (2012) 'Doing Critique, Doing Politics' in S Hall & S Winlow (eds.) *New Directions in Criminological Theory*. London: Routledge

Carlen P (2016) 'Ethics, Politics and the Limits to Knowledge' in M Adorjan & R Ricciardelli (eds.) *Engaging with Ethics in International Criminological Research*. London: Routledge

Carter N, P Day & R Klein (1992) *How Organisations Measure Success: The Use of Performance Indicators in Government*. London: Sage

Chomsky N (1967) 'The Responsibility of Intellectuals'. *The New York Review of Books*, 23 February. www.chomsky.info/articles/19670223.htm

Clawson D, R Zussman, J Misra *et al.* (eds.) (2007) *Public Sociology*. Berkeley: University of California Press

Collini S (2012) *What Are Universities For?* E-book. Penguin

Currie E (2007) 'Against Marginality: Arguments for a Public Criminology'. *Theoretical Criminology* 11(2): 175–190.

Drake D & R Walters (2015) '"Crossing the Line": Criminological Expertise, Policy Advice and the "Quarrelling Society"'. *Critical Social Policy* 35(3): 414–433

Durkheim E (1957) *Professional Ethics and Civic Morals*. London: Routledge and Kegan Paul

Hall P (2007) 'Measuring Research Performance in the Mathematical Sciences in Australian Universities'. *Australian Mathematical Society Gazette* 34: 26–30

Harvie D (2000) 'Alienation, Class and Enclosure in UK Universities'. *Capital and Class* 24(2): 103–132

HEFCE (2014) www.hefce.ac.uk/news/newsarchive/2014/news94764.html

Hillyard P, J Sim, S Tombs & D Whyte (2004) '"Leaving a Stain upon the Silence": Contemporary Criminology and the Politics of Dissent'. *British Journal of Criminology* 44(3): 369–390

Hope T (2004) 'Pretend It Works: Evidence and Governance in the Evaluation of the Burglary Initiative'. *Criminology and Criminal Justice* 4(3): 287–308

Israel M & I Hay (2012) 'Research Ethics in Criminology' in D Gadd, S Karstedt & S Messner (eds.) *Criminological Research Methods*. London: Sage

J-ES Helptext (2015) Impact Summary. https://je-s.rcuk.ac.uk/Handbook/Index.htm#pages/GuidanceonCompletingaStandardG/ImpactSummary.htm (accessed 8 January 2015).

Lawrence P (2007) 'The Mismeasurement of Science'. www.mrc-lmb.cam.ac.uk/PAL/pdf/mism_science.pdf

Loader I & R Sparks (2010) *Public Criminology?* London: Routledge

Martin B (2011) 'ERA: Adverse Consequences'. *Australian Universities Review* 53(2): 99–102

Mathiesen T (2013) *Towards a Surveillant Society: The Rise of Surveillant Systems in Europe*. Hook: Waterside Press

McGettigan A (2013) *Great University Gamble: Money, Markets and the Future of Higher Education*. London: Pluto

Molesworth M, R Scullion & E Nixon (eds.) (2011) *The Marketisation of Higher Education: The Student as Consumer*. London: Routledge

Newman J H (1852) *The Idea of a University Defined and Illustrated*. Alexandria: Library of Alexandria

Nussbaum M J (2010) *Not for Profit: Why Democracy Needs the Humanities*. Princeton: Princeton University Press

Parsons T (1949/1954) *Essays in Sociological Theory* (revised edn). New York: Macmillan Free Press

Patten C (2017) 'Leave State Control of Universities to China'. *Observer*, 1 January, p. 33

Plato (1996) *The Republic* (written around 380 AD). Oxford: Oxford Classics

Rafter N H & M Brown (2011) *Criminology Goes to the Movies: Crime Theory and Popular Culture*. New York: New York University Press

RCUK (2014) Peer Review. www.rcuk.ac.uk/funding/peerreview/

REF (2011a) *Decision on Assessing Impact*. Bristol: HEFCE

REF (2011b) *Assessment Framework and Guidance on Submissions.* Bristol: HEFCE. www.ref.ac.uk/media/ref/content/pub/assessmentframeworkandguidanceonsubmissions/GOS%20including%20addendum.pdf

REF (2012) *Panel Criteria and Working Methods.* Bristol: HEFCE

Reisz M (2010) 'Soul Searching, Not Soul Stirring'. *Times Higher Education,* www.timeshighereducation.co.uk/features/soul-searching-not-soul-stirring/411631.article

Ruggiero V (2003) *Crime in Literature: Sociology of Deviance and Fiction.* London: Verso

Schotten M & M el Aisati (2015) The Rise of National Research Assessments and the Tools and Data That Make Them Work. www.elsevier.com/connect/the-rise-of-national-research-assessments-and-the-tools-and-data-that-make-them-work

Shattock M (1994) *The University Grants Committee and the Management of British Universities.* Buckingham: Society for Research into Higher Education and the Open University Press

Shattock M (2012) *Making Policy in British Higher Education 1945–2011.* Maidenhead: McGraw Hill and Open University Press

Slaughter S & L Leslie (1997) *Academic Capitalism: Politics, Policies and the Entrepreneurial University.* Baltimore: Johns Hopkins University Press

Thompson E P (ed.) (1970/2014) *Warwick University Ltd: Industry, Management and Universities.* London: Penguin/Nottingham: Spokesman

Uggen C & M Inderbitzen (2006) 'Public Criminologies'. Paper presented at the 2006 Annual meetings of the American Sociological Association, Montreal. www.soc.umn.edu/~uggen/uggen_inderbitzin_TC2006.pdf

University of Alabama in Huntsville (2012) 'Research Ethics: Coercive Citation in Academic Publishing'. *Science Daily,* 2 February, www.sciencedaily.com/releases/2012/02/120202164817.htm

Wacquant L (2002) 'The Curious Eclipse of Prison Ethnography in the Age of Mass Incarceration'. *Ethnography* 3(4): 371–397

Walters R (2003) *Criminology, Politics and Policy.* Cullompton: Willan

Winlow S & S Hall (2012) 'What Is an Ethics Committee? Academic Governance in an Era of Belief and Incredulity'. *British Journal of Criminology* 52(2): 400–416

Young J (1988) 'Radical Criminology in Britain: The Emergence of a Competing Paradigm'. *British Journal of Criminology* 28(2): 159–183

Young J (2011) *The Criminological Imagination.* Cambridge: Polity

Young R (2016) 'Access to Criminal Justice' in M Bosworth, C Hoyle & L Zedner (eds.) *Changing Contours of Criminal Justice.* Oxford: Oxford University Press, pp. 87–108

Zedner L, C Hoyle & M Bosworth (2016) 'Mapping the Contours of Criminal Justice: An Introduction' in M Bosworth, C Hoyle & L Zedner (eds.) *Changing Contours of Criminal Justice.* Oxford: Oxford University Press, pp. xvii–xxix

Ziman J (1968) *Public Knowledge: The Social Dimension of Science.* Cambridge: Cambridge University Press

INDEX

Please note that page references to non-textual content such as Figures or Photographs will be in italics, followed by the letter 'f', whereas those for Tables will be in italics followed by the letter 't'. References to Notes will contain the letter 'n' followed by the Note number.